The Trial Presentation Companion

A Step-by-Step Guide to Presenting Electronic Evidence in the Courtroom

THE TRIAL PRESENTATION COMPANION

A Step-by-Step Guide to Presenting Electronic Evidence in the Courtroom

Shannon Lex Bales

FTI Consulting

Los Angeles

NITA®

NATIONAL INSTITUTE FOR TRIAL ADVOCACY

Address inquiries to:

Reprint Permission
National Institute for Trial Advocacy
1685 38th Street, Suite 200
Boulder, CO 80301-2735
Phone: (800) 225-6482
Fax: (720) 890-7069
Email: permissions@nita.org

ISBN 978-1-60156-733-8
eISBN 978-1-60156-734-5
FBA 1733

Library of Congress Cataloging-in-Publication Data

Names: Bales, Shannon Lex, author.
Title: The trial presentation companion: a step-by-step guide to presenting electronic evidence in the courtroom / Shannon Lex Bales, FTI Consulting, Los Angeles.
Description: Boulder, CO: National Institute for Trial Advocacy, [2018]
Identifiers: LCCN 2018013896 (print) | LCCN 2018014955 (ebook) | ISBN 9781601567345 (ebook) | ISBN 9781601567338
Subjects: LCSH: Electronic evidence—United States. | Evidence, Documentary—United States. | Electronic records—Law and legislation—United States. | Trial practice—United States.
Classification: LCC KF8947.5 (ebook) | LCC KF8947.5 .B35 2018 (print) | DDC 347.73/6—dc23
LC record available at https://lccn.loc.gov/2018013896

Printed in the United States.

Wolters Kluwer

Official co-publisher of NITA.
WKLegaledu.com/NITA

Dedication

I am a product of kindness and opportunity provided by people who believed in and trusted me. My sincere hope is that this book becomes someone else's opportunity to "do better" and that it raises the bar on standards for quality technical presentation at trial.

This book is dedicated to my grandmother Hazel Bales, whose unwavering support throughout her life made me (and so many others) who we are today. To my wife Olga and daughters Viata, Vikka, and Viviana—you are the best distraction to writing I could ever have. Every day I wrote, I only thought of making you proud. Also, my dad Larry was the definition of unwavering support—there for whatever was needed to help complete the book. (Dad, read this book and you might finally understand what I do for a living! Ha ha!)

I am thankful to have had the opportunity to work with some of the most amazing lawyers and legal teams in my career. One that stands out for me personally and professionally is the legal team of Bart Williams, Manuel Cachán, and Erin Cox. Leading by ethical example are values that these attorneys live and breathe, providing leadership, mentoring, and opportunity to attorneys and staff alike that makes every member of the team feel valued and like "somebody." The creation of the workflows, techniques, and skills covered in this book often came from working with them—and in the case of the "outline on steroids," that was completely Erin Cox. (I likely owe her half a beer for every book sold.)

Last but not least, there were mentors, managers, and people who were just plain good to me. Kim McKay, Glenn Shubb, and Trish Fettig were all amazing managers who taught me about Big Law and put their heart and soul into their work and instilled those same values in me. William G. Simon was a mentor who liked to say, "No problem can withstand the onslaught of sustained thinking," and he was right. I'm also forever appreciative to those at the United Nations who provided me with the opportunity to live and work in Africa and Asia.

Contents

Chapter Six: Courtroom Planning

Chapter Seven: Trial Software

Notes on Use

The National Institute for Trial Advocacy (NITA) is proud to publish *The Trial Presentation Companion: A Step-by-Step Guide to Presenting Electronic Evidence in the Courtroom*, our first-ever, comprehensive "how-to" manual on running electronic evidence in the courtroom. We hope this guide, written by award-winning trial technologist Shannon Lex Bales, will help you expand your comfort zone in working with all the bits and pieces—laptops, trial presentation software, document cameras, audio-visual components, . . . even the puzzling array of cords and cables—that are increasingly essential when presenting electronic evidence in court in the modern era.

Part One, Trial Presentation in Theory, is just that: a *theoretical* explanation, in plain (and often tongue-in-cheek) English, about why expert trial technologists do what they do during pretrial and in court—how to organize and name exhibit files, choose the best software for your needs, build a trial kit of equipment to take to court, comply with the Trial Management Order, develop an effective workflow, cultivate relationships that provide mutual support in court and out, and much more. Part One explains the method behind the apparent madness.

Part Two, Trial Presentation in Practice, shows you, step by illustrated step, how you, too, can bring that same game to your own legal team as you huddle for trial. Even if you don't know an HDMI port from a VGA and have never set up a folder system on your server before, *The Trial Presentation Companion* will show you how, and before you know it, you'll be running the show like you were born to it.

A crucial piece to your success is using forms and checklists to help you mind the details. Ready-to-use PDFs of the very forms that the author uses himself are available for you to download and save, print, and put into action. They are your free bonus, and can be accessed here:

Website http://bit.ly/1P20Jea

Password TriPreCom1

Finally, unless noted otherwise (especially in the case of Rachel Bennett's amusing original illustrations), all images in *The Trial Presentation Companion* appear courtesy of Shannon Bales.

Part One

Trial Presentation in Theory

Chapter One

Introduction to Trial Presentation

"If I had eight hours to chop down a tree, I'd spend six sharpening my axe."

—*attributed to Abraham Lincoln*

The purpose of *The Trial Presentation Companion* is to provide an understanding of the skills, workflows, and techniques necessary to plan and present exhibits at a trial, arbitration, or other presentation using trial presentation tools like TrialDirector, OnCue, or Sanction, or companion applications like PowerPoint. In this book, I will refer to the person presenting electronic and other forms of evidence as "you" or the "trial tech," but think of it as a role that anyone on the legal team—from attorney to paralegal to technical staff—might be asked to fill. This book covers basic skills, techniques, equipment needs, common issues, and planning considerations necessary to conduct a presentation. The skills and techniques covered will go beyond trial presentation software and discuss the use of document cameras, boards, and other techniques in order to create a broad presentation strategy. Where possible, guides and checklists are provided to help prepare and plan, which is the foundation of a good trial presentation. *The Trial Presentation Companion* will go a long way to helping many prospective techs know what skills and techniques are critical to competently present electronic evidence in a courtroom.

Experienced trial technicians will tell you that the easiest part of trial presentation—albeit under tremendous stress—is calling up an exhibit on screen. It is relatively easy to teach someone how to enter the digits to call up an exhibit. The "hard part" of trial presentation is the preparation, experience, and long hours that go into creating a system that lowers risk and is efficient, high quality, and complies with the rules and preferences of the judge, the clerk, the courthouse, and the legal teams. For example, the process of editing video clips or creating an exhibit creation workflow that complies with courtroom technical requirements can be more difficult than putting an exhibit onscreen because it is a technical process that potentially involves converting files from one format to another. Each one of these groups will have its own rules and preferences with which the trial technician must comply. With their personal preferences and past experiences in mind, the judge and clerk control how technology will be set up in their courtroom, while the courthouse security team may have rules about how and when equipment is brought into the courthouse. Meanwhile, the Trial Management Order (TMO) will dictate many extra layers of responsibility on how exhibits will be created, branded, and named—and last but not least, the trial tech will also need to negotiate a mutually beneficial presentation environment (i.e., presentation equipment, shared costs, presentation responsibility) with the other side and make their own legal team content with the courtroom setup to provide them with the confidence necessary so they can present their case without incident.

Teams generally make the mistake of not understanding the courtroom presentation environment. For example, are the displays square or rectangular?[1] What is their resolution? When a team understands these two key parameters, it greatly increases the quality, legibility, and comprehensibility of the presentations without much effort at all. It is very embarrassing to show up the first day of trial and find out that your presentations look bad because they were

1. This question refers to shapes, i.e., aspect ratios of either 16:9 or 4:3, respectively.

created in the wrong aspect ratio and resolution. Sadly, many teams do not understand that they have a problem at all and plod along with illegible presentations because they think there is nothing they can do to "fix" it.

Did the legal team test the equipment beforehand? Displaying your lack of technical competence in front of jurors is not a very good idea when you could have—indeed, should have—resolved it ahead of time via testing and configuration in advance. Perhaps, for example, the courtroom projector makes red appear green or yellow highlights look brown. Wouldn't you want to adjust the projector beforehand, if possible? This book teaches you how to evaluate a courtroom so you can determine the best technology choices to ensure your presentation makes the "best use of available technology." What about so-called simple pieces of equipment, like a document camera or an easel to display your exhibit boards—did the team members take the time to ensure they knew how to use this "simple" equipment so they look competent and self-assured in front of the jury? "How many lawyers does it take to put together an easel?" sounds like a joke, but is a serious question I can answer: three, plus a paralegal. At a recent trial, I watched (with complete glee, I must admit) as one lawyer after another went up to the witness stand to put together an easel so they could rest their exhibit board. Three in a row, and finally they called up their paralegal, who got it done. The point is, this maneuver should have been practiced and rehearsed just like everything else going into the trial. Your competence, in every sense, is on display when you stand before decision-makers. This book will teach you how to evaluate a courtroom so you can ten determine the best technology choice to ensure your presentation makes the "best use of available technology."

The phrase "best use of available technology" has real meaning here. You have to be able to do the best you can with what you have available in the courtroom. A few courtrooms are amazing technical environments with everything you need already built in. However, most courtrooms have no technology whatsoever, or they offer a few basic pieces of equipment and allow you to bring in equipment to supplement, replace, or make use of the equipment already present. Then, there are the courts that view technology as a hassle and want nothing to do with it. But technology will aid decision-makers with cognition and greatly aid efficiency in the courtroom; the proceedings will move more quickly, and jurors will understand better. *Always* ask the court's permission before bringing in equipment, regardless of whether you wish to build a presentation environment from the ground up or to supplement existing equipment. You may need a special order from the court to bring in equipment through security.

You are likely working in a much higher resolution in your office than what most courtrooms are using. Moreover, you are likely using a rectangular, 16:9 monitor, whereas many of the courtroom monitors are still square 4:3. I'm fairly confident that nobody reading this book is using the lower resolution of 1024x768. (To check, right-click anywhere on your desktop, then select either Screen Resolution or Display Settings > Advanced display settings.) Contrast what you are using with what the court is using. Courtrooms are often low-resolution environments (i.e., 1024x768) and simply cannot display graphics created in a high-resolution environment correctly.

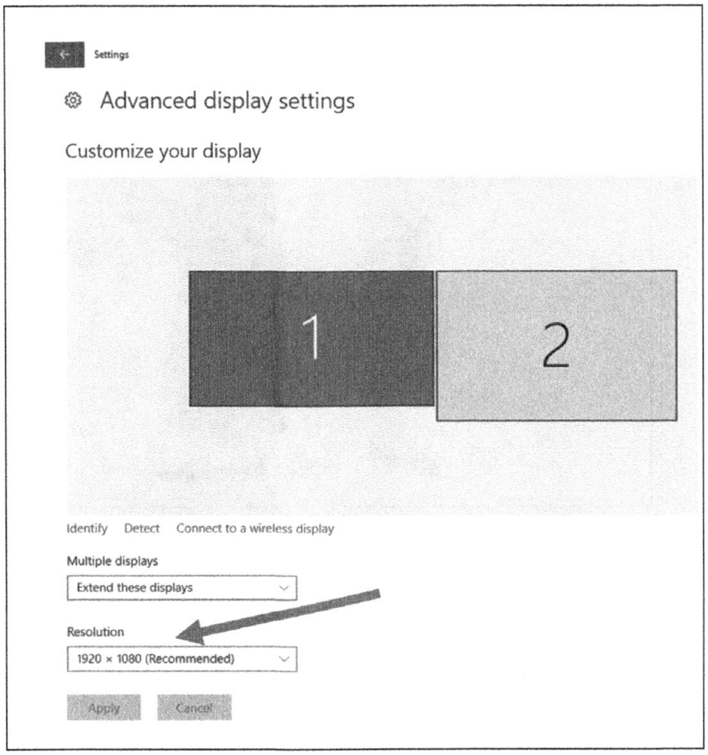

Figure 1. ***To check your display resolution, right-click anywhere on your desktop and select either Screen Resolution or Display Settings > Advanced display settings.***

It is incredibly embarrassing for teams to spend hours of time and potentially thousands of dollars on presentations and graphics that can't be displayed correctly on the screens in the courtroom for which they were intended. The text doesn't display correctly, or the aspect ratio is off, cutting off or making the presentation too small. In this book, I can't stress enough the importance of advance testing of your equipment, exhibits, video clips, and presentation prior to going live in court. Most courts will allow advance testing in conjunction with their IT group if necessary—indeed, many courts mandate it. The lesson here is to know your technical environment so you can avoid crashes and tailor your presentation to the courtroom you will be presenting in. In this book, I'll discuss in detail how to evaluate courtrooms. Be sure to review the forms in the back of the book that will assist you in your technology evaluations.

1.1 Perspectives

There are a couple perspectives to consider when it comes to the introduction of technology into the courtroom. Understanding the court's goals on technology will help you get the technology plan you want. The judge's perspective is that technology will bring great efficiency and improved comprehension of complex issues to the courtroom, while lawyers believe technology will help them be more persuasive. Both perspectives are good—technology helps trials move along more quickly, which potentially saves days' worth of trial time. While slick graphics and presentation style can help legal teams be more persuasive, good planning and implementation of a trial technology plan helps both judges and lawyers reach their respective goals.

Figure 2. ***Points of view. (Image by Rachel Bennett.)***

When done incorrectly, technology brings anger, delay, and frustration, and can cause decision-makers—the judge, the jurors, your clients—to question the credibility of your legal team. The courtroom is no place to demonstrate poor technical skills, inadequate equipment, or a lack of planning. It shows disrespect for the time of all decision-makers if you do not pretest equipment and demonstrate basic technical competence.[2] In my discussions with judges, clerks, court staff, court IT workers, and jurors, they have shared how overwhelmingly they *hate* avoidable technical issues. They are usually savvy enough to discern that you failed to take the basic step of equipment testing or rate the experience as being so poor that it was a drain on court time rather than bringing efficiency to the proceedings. Courthouse IT staff typically attribute most technical problems to a lack of testing and configuration before trial, and to legal teams not having basic skills, like being able to configure their laptop's resolution or to connect to an external monitor. Once they have been burned, judges and legal staff can become reluctant to allow technology back in the courtroom, thus making the job that much harder for any legal technologists who follow. In other words, the message of technology efficiency is lost because of problems that were entirely avoidable in the first place. *Note*: if you have an IT problem with your equipment, own up to it.[3]

1.2 Take Your Technology Obligations Seriously

Not all courtrooms are behind the times. Many are refurbished or newly constructed with high-resolution displays and audio technology built right into the courtrooms themselves. For example, the newly constructed Los Angeles Federal Courthouse is state of the art, with high-resolution displays and many options for connecting to the courtroom audio/visual system (VGA, HDMI, and audio inputs, just to name a few). Moreover, its IT group is among the most technically savvy and customer-facing groups of *any* IT group. The people and equipment are the gold standard for audio/visual presentation—reflecting one instance where private industry needs to catch up to government innovation. However, even high-tech courtrooms potentially require modification or need to be supplemented to accommodate backup equipment, additional or larger displays, or to remove the burden of switching off the video source from the clerk or attorney at the podium,[4] as they both have other immediate priorities.

2. Technical competence can be demonstrated by having either the requisite technical skills yourself or in a legal team member who responsible for technical items at trial.

3. Exclaiming that the courtroom equipment, rather than your own equipment, is not working correctly endears you to no one at the courthouse. The message of who was actually at fault eventually does work its way back to the judge. Be humble and take responsibility for your technical problems.

4. New courthouses are substantially it right with their technology offerings, but switching at the podium or via the clerk remains a pain point.

For many, the first use of trial presentation technology is trial by fire: they are thrown into a less-than-ideal situation. After all, everybody gets their start somewhere. It is my hope that *The Trial Presentation Companion* will put you well on your way to knowing all the things not typically taught in trial presentation software training. It is with this thought in mind that I believe a great trial tech can be the equalizer in the courtroom, such that even solo practitioners can match the professionalism and high-quality presentations of a mega firm in their ability to create and present electronic evidence at trial.

Figure 3. ***Trial by fire: the approach many lawyers seem to have to using technology at trial. (Artwork by Jan Luyken (1685), in the public domain and courtesy of Wikimedia Commons.)***

Law firms sometimes seem to forget that going to trial is the most visible and high-stakes aspect of the work they do—and if the media are involved, their audience will go far beyond their clients and colleagues. Many law firms simply do not have the commitment to trial technology that they should have, which can create an advantage in the courtroom for the team that does. How can a team that doesn't understand its own data, doesn't take basic QC steps for its own technology, or doesn't know how to comply with simple exchange standards be working efficiently itself?

Teams are increasingly being held accountable for avoidable technology issues and attempts at burden shifting. If your system fails too many times in court and causes delay (thereby voiding the "efficiency" perspective discussed earlier), you might be called on it in court and asked to shut down and not use your technology again for the duration of the trial. Later in the book, I'll discuss burden shifting, where parties either purposely or incompetently don't do their part at trial, thereby pushing their technology responsibilities onto the other party. By not doing their part, they risk creating a technology implosion for both parties, as both sides rely on quality work product being provided in the exhibit exchange to present at trial. Many times, non-compliance is just an attempt to slow down or hide information from the other party. Other times, a party did not take its technology obligations seriously and hope to get by without doing it right. Burden shifting forces the opposing party to double its work, which takes away valuable resources from this demonstrably more technically competent and compliant team.

Legal teams that "do it right" have more confidence in, and mastery of, their case facts because they have created a support system that gives them every reason to believe that they should. There is a measurable (and highly visible) difference between a team in a mad scramble to find an exhibit with no idea how to locate it and a team simply looking where in its system it should be. Watching teams that do not have it together is comical theater when you are on the other side and doing it right. Technical efficiency helps us present our case better because we are organized and have the data at our fingertips, it lowers the cost to clients, and, by being faster, eases the burden on courts due the backlog of cases. Unfortunately, for many legal teams the use of technology at trial is an afterthought. Teams that don't fully work out and understand the technical requirements for exhibit exchange or test their equipment prior to trial (or worse, ignore agreed-to specifications during trial) create barriers to efficient exchange of information at trial, slow down the administration of justice, and risk technical failure at trial. Skimping on the equipment budget,[5] not performing quality control, or poorly staffing a case only serves to make presentations slower and less reliable. It is bad planning at its worst.

Quality, stability, and risk reduction come from taking the appropriate steps in building a solid foundation for a presentation—and not merely learning how to push a few buttons to put a trial exhibit image onscreen. No matter which trial presentation tool you use, they all share a common need for planning, preparation, quality control, and a multitude of companion skills that are not taught in the training for your tool of choice. While trial presentation can be simple, it can also be deceptively difficult if you paint yourself into a corner by choosing the wrong image format, using an overly difficult exhibit branding scheme, don't test the equipment in advance, or lack the skills necessary to do the job.

Your credibility, technical competence, and conduct make the difference between being viewed as capable or incompetent when a legitimate technical issue occurs in trial. You may get more latitude if you have repeatedly demonstrated to the court that you take your commitment to technology seriously if you have tested your equipment and the courtroom system, have backups in place, and displayed technical competence over someone who has not. When difficulties occur, it is often an all-or-nothing proposition: either you did it right and the exhibits are all loaded and displaying correctly, or you didn't and they won't. This is why quality control (QC) is so important. *Everything must be checked (repeatedly) because there is no second chance.* The court is not going to reschedule the opening or the closing, or have a witness come back, on account of missing data or your constant computer crashes. Openings that were prepared weeks in advance sometimes go unused because the team's trial technology does not work the first time—and this means the team has to wing it. Wing it for opening? Time spent prepping and testing equipment, exhibits, and presentations is well spent, not wasted.

There are great working benefits to legal teams of having your technical house in order (e.g., organization, technical compliance, war room performance). Simply being able to quickly create, share, and print an exhibit is a tremendous benefit (and possibly a competitive edge) to a legal team in terms of being able to prepare and present. Going into trial, teams should have a very solid understanding of what their technical responsibilities and burdens will be when they agree to the technical specifications for an exhibit exchange. Lawyers should consult with team members who are familiar with the data as it currently stands and those who will be working with it at trial (typically a database/lit support person and a trial tech) so the best decisions can be made in working with the teams' data. You would be surprised at how often the plaintiff and defendant make combined decisions that are counter to their own self-interest and create tremendous burdens on their respective support staff to comply with that are completely unnecessary. A final point: there is a vibrant in-house and consultant community that can assist and should be consulted when preparing for and being at trial.

The book covers the companion skills, workflows, and techniques necessary to present electronic evidence at trial. It is a "trial companion" because it will work in conjunction with almost any trial presentation tool on the market. For example, you likely already know how to connect your laptop to a projector—but what do you do when you connect to the projector and the aspect ratio is wrong and your presentation doesn't look right (or it fails to display at all)? This book contemplates a courtroom site visit in advance that evaluates the aspect ratio, resolution, and other presentation parameters so your presentation looks right the first time. Likewise, what is important in crafting the technical aspects of the TMO, and what are the basic IT skills necessary to present competently at trial? *The Trial Presentation Companion* will also cover tasks, from the mundane to the complex, that are typically learned through experience, such as the correct way to tape down cables in the courtroom or how to create an organizational system for your exhibits and video. It may seem silly to learn how to tape cables to the carpet, but if you use the wrong kind of tape and rip up the carpet, you will soon understand why it is important to know.[6]

5. How does having outdated equipment and software help your team at trial? Hint: it doesn't. Yet legal departments that don't involve themselves in technology decisions hobble themselves with their lack of involvement.
6. I'm not saying that I learned this from experience—but I'm not saying I didn't either.

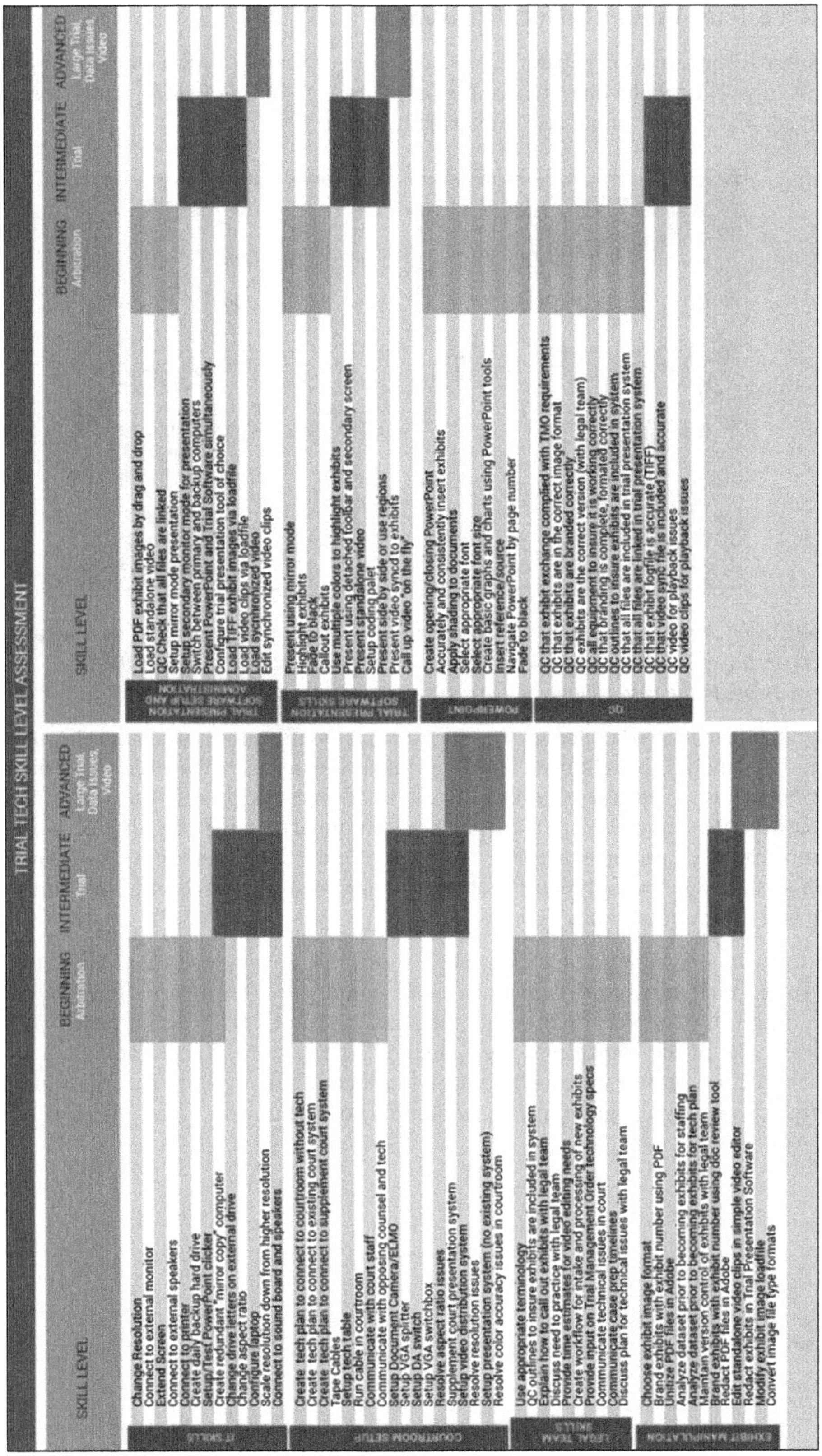

Figure 4. ***Skills evaluation: do you have the minimum skills necessary for a basic presentation?***

1.3 Why to Use Trial Presentation Software

The goal of using trial presentation software is to help bring efficiency to the courtroom by placing all of the exhibits, video, and video clips at the fingertips of the presenter. Exhibits and video can be displayed in any order, on any page, enlarged, highlighted, enhanced, and explained on the fly.

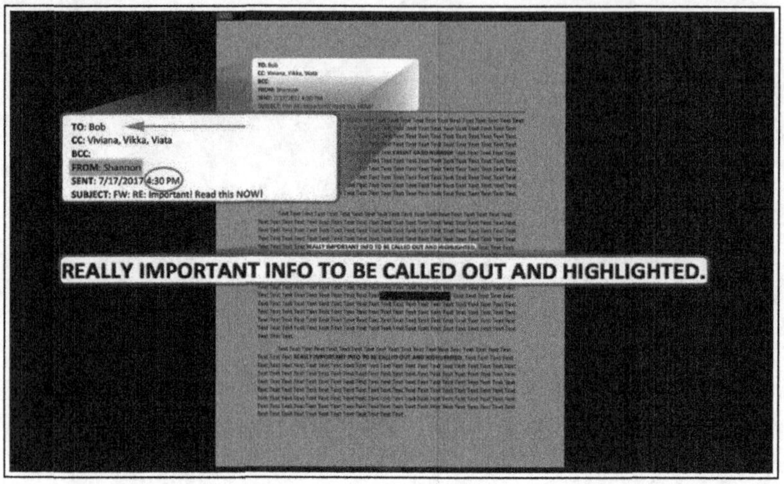

Figure 5. ***An example of an annotated exhibit in TrialDirector. Exhibits can be annotated with a variety of tools such as highlighting, arrows, circles, etc. and in a number of colors. Annotation can be done on the fly in seconds, allowing the presenter flexibility as issues in the case change.***

PowerPoint is typically used to great effect in opening statements and closing arguments because both are planned in advance and can (and should) be rehearsed and fine-tuned. But for use in witness examination, PowerPoint is far too static for practical use. It requires significant work in advance each page of the exhibit, as each slide must be manually created by inserting the exhibit, graphics, and annotations (i.e., highlights, arrows, circles, etc.) to make it presentation-ready. For example, creating the work product shown in Figure 5 in PowerPoint (instead of TrialDirector, as in this example) would require you to crop (or edit) the image (multiple times) and individually apply highlighting and other annotations.

PowerPoint necessitates a custom graphic every time and for every page: 1,000 pages of exhibits equal 1,000 pages of slides in PowerPoint. It is simply not practical. In contrast, trial software allows for a consistent presentation of files with drastically less preparation time: the preparation of 1,000 exhibit pages would be a *single* data load and QC process, and in the courtroom, they all could be called up and annotated *at any time* and *in any order*, with minimal time to annotate with highlights and callouts.[7] The prep-time comparison for the 1,000-page example would produce a savings not in terms of minutes or hours, but *days*.

7. Callouts are excerpts of text that have been enlarged for easy viewing.

PowerPoint vs. Trial Presentation Software		
Generalizations	PowerPoint	Trial Software
Must be created in Advance?	X	
Static	X	
Flexible		X
More Prep	X	
Less Prep		X
Better for Opening	X	
Better for Witness Examination		X
Better for Closing	X	
Better with video		X
Video "On the Fly"		X
Annotate Exhibits "On the Fly"		X

Figure 6. ***Comparison of PowerPoint and trial presentation software.***

In the past, key exhibits were traditionally displayed on a board, which forced legal teams to make difficult decisions, days or weeks in advance, as to which exhibits they would use in court, with additional exhibits being passed around to jurors or viewed from a distance after they were pulled out of a box or a three-ring binder. In the modern courtroom, your technology team can be ready to pivot along with case issues and questions as they arise, giving you the ability to present evidence and/or impeach testimony with video, deposition text, or exhibits. The result is that you have increased flexibility to change your trial strategy, or at least respond to inaccurate testimony, on the fly.

Using trial software can reduce the length of a trial by hours and days. The savings and efficiency can be substantial; beyond attorney time, trial software saves on expenses like staff time, hotels, and meals, just to name a few. Trial times are significantly reduced by the efficiency of your team's entire set of case exhibits being available to you at a moment's notice. Think back to our pre-technology days, when we'd remove a document from an exhibit binder and pass it around to jurors for individual inspection. Think about all the steps that were involved: 1) pulling the binder; 2) finding the correct page; 3) removing the exhibit from the binder; and 4) showing it to the judge, the witness, and then the jury (from a distance, using a standard-sized sheet of paper). Note that while trial time is significantly reduced and results in time and cost savings, there remain expenses associated with using trial presentation software (such as equipment/software costs and labor, whether through in-house talent or a vendor)—but on balance, the savings far outweigh these costs.

Trial software is also effective at aiding in tasks like impeachment, creating highlights for jurors to follow along with difficult text, and enlarging text that may be difficult to read. For example, there is no more effective means of impeachment than being able to show a witness's contradictory testimony, in their own words, from a videotaped deposition that has been loaded into a presentation system. Text can be highlighted and clarified through the use of magnification and highlights, to aid in jurors' comprehension. Simply put, trial presentation software is fast, efficient, and effective.

The quality and persuasiveness of your legal team's case will be directly impacted by the quality of the presentation and the smoothness of the communication between trial technician and lawyers. This will also reduce the frequency of technical errors and the legal team's ability to respond to them.[8] Successful teams will adapt to new methodologies and workflows that will help leverage the efficiency of trial presentation software. Teams may not have worked with a technician or technology in the past, so integrating them into the team successfully should be a top priority. It is not enough to simply have a trial technician on the team: the tech must be involved at the highest levels and given authority so that decisions can be prioritized and the team can spend time practicing and perfecting its interactions.

8. Teams would be wise to recognize the "master-servant" relationship between technician and lawyer and devising a communication style that is not discomfiting for decision-makers to observe.

Efficiency comes in many "flavors," so at the earliest stages of the litigation lifecycle, the best teams will begin identifying exhibits, issue-coding deposition testimony and video, and using related litigation support software to do fact analysis. One best practice is storing documents in a document review application, such as Relativity e-Discovery Software, LexisNexis Concordance, or Summation, so documents can be identified for use in trial. Potential exhibits and synced video testimony are issue-coded and evaluated in deposition programs like LiveNote Stream or LexisNexis TextMap. Using these tools will save you time and effort on the majority of work when you can leverage work product, existing searches, and reports into exhibits and outlines for use at trial. One benefit is that many of these litigation support software packages have built-in compatibility with trial presentation software, which makes you even more efficient.

That said, using boards or a document camera is still a relevant form of presentation—though subjecting jurors to hundreds of slides or images, end to end, on a screen is likely not a very good plan for presentation. Teams would be wise to incorporate a variety of presentation methods so that they can keep the attention and focus of the decision-makers (i.e., the judge and jurors) via engaging technologies and interactions.

1.4 Risk Management and Law Firms that Get It

Lawyers and firms that "get it" understand that what is presented at trial reflects upon them and is thus the most public and high-stakes mission of what they do. Therefore, firms and lawyers that get it are highly involved in the decisions about trial technology and workflows used at trial. Success is typically dependent on a few things.

1) **Legal team involvement.** Have the lawyers set an expectation among the firm's decision-makers (e.g., managing partner, IT director, trial technician staff, and others) as to equipment and personnel performance?[9] In other words, have decision-makers provided those at trial with the people, equipment, software, and support necessary to win?

2) **Technician involvement.** Have the lawyers integrated the trial technician into the team? In other words, have they created a contributing member of the team, or merely designated a "button pusher" who does what they are told? Did the tech visit the trial site in advance and meet court staff? Did they help create the trial plan? Did they free to share issues or concerns about software and equipment? Has the tech been given enough time to do the job?

3) **Team empowerment.** Is your team empowered to help you? Has everyone been trained on specific trial procedures and workflows? Has the teen been provided sufficient time to prepare for trial?[10] Are there workflows in place for exhibit creation and redaction, binder creation, and attorney support? Is there a clear message across the firm (and especially within IT support) as to the priority and urgent need of trial support, should something go wrong?[11]

4) **Equipment and software.** Does the legal team have the tools it needs? Does the team have the correct IT support in place? Does the equipment comply with the minimum standards recommended by the trial software vendor? Have you kept current with the tools and software available in the industry?

Tending to these details in advance, creating a technology plan, and making a backup plan are all important components of your trial planning and preparation. When you take shortcuts in preparing your trial technology plan—shortchanging the budget on equipment, not doing an advance site visit, overburdening the tech with diverse and unrelated tasks, or pressing someone into service who is not ready—your legal team runs the risk of disaster. It is clear to observers in the courtroom when a team is unprepared to present its legal arguments at trial. But what about the team that is prepared to argue, but has underestimated its presentation strategy? How will the

9. Namely, do they want the best? If not the best, then what is the expectation?

10. Teams often wait for settlement negotiations to completely run their course before preparing for trial. This strategy puts teams at a deficit from the beginning.

11. Firm IT groups often don't get the message that a team is in trial. Nor do they understand the priority and urgency that trial teams should have. Should a trial team wait in line behind someone's routine and non-urgent computer issue with a help desk ticket?

team look when timing is off, exhibits are missing, team members are unable to keep up with exhibit exchanges, and confusion and miscommunication reign in open court? It is an absolute disaster.

Figure 7. ***The many hats one wears in court. (Image by Rachel Bennett.)***

Firms and vendors that get it have a commitment to reducing their risk and increasing their efficiency through:

- Involving the trial tech at early stages of the case
- Evoking firm partner buy-in in trial workflow, firm procedures, and budget
- Planning an effective workflow that contemplates how the team will receive, process, and place exhibits into trial exhibit and trial presentation databases
- Owning or renting high-quality equipment
- Planning for redundancy (backups) in equipment and software in case of failure
- Controlling the "versions" of exhibits
- Committing to training, practice, and specialization
- Alleviating trial techs of unrelated duties and burdens
- Fostering harmonious teamwork
- Assigning appropriate staff in support roles

Another fundamental idea that is frequently discussed in the context of trial preparation is managing risk. The point of understanding "trial site risk" is so that the appropriate planning and quality control go into the planning for trial. Trial site risk is defined as the exposure to negative action at the trial site that can be avoided through preemptive action. It is the *intentional interaction with uncertainty*. The key concept of redundancy and quality control are infrequently given the attention they need by legal teams. We understand that cases "might not" go to trial, but if we wait until the last moment to prepare for one that does, it adds a layer of risk that is entirely avoidable. Trial teams that understand what is at stake create time in the schedule for planning, testing equipment, and creating exhibits.[12] In a legal setting, "redundancy" may include spare laptops and computer equipment, backup external drives, extra peripheral equipment like cables and power plugs, and alternative means of presentation, like boards or a document camera. Teams can be their own worst enemy when they make bad decisions in this area. They won't have saved money on the IT budget—rather, they will have hampered their ability to present electronic exhibits and look good at trial.

1.5 How Courtroom Issues Occur

If you think that trial presentation is just "button-pushing," you should stop here. Preparation is *key*, and if you assume that button-pushing is all it takes, you are vastly underestimating the amount of work that actually goes into preparing technology at trial.

Courtroom issues occur when:

- **The breadth of skills necessary to present at trial is underestimated**. Showing up in court without knowing how to hook up and configure a laptop to the video source.
- **When vendors or in-house techs lack the correct equipment**. Coming to court with a single laptop and no backup, then having it fail, causing embarrassing and unreasonable delays in court.
- **No one does a site visit or equipment test in the courtroom before the trial**. Expecting that the courtroom and your equipment will interface and work perfectly the first time, without first knowing how to configure the intricacies of that particular site.
- **Communication about technical standards, like branding and naming requirements, is done without input of the trial tech**. Using file- and exhibit-naming standards that are not easily created or take multiple passes by software vendors to create.
- **The technical requirements and timelines for the TMO are done without input of the trial tech**. Creating standards that are not narrow enough, so parties that are either incompetent or unethical can shift the burden of their exhibit exchange upon you.
- **Communication with the trial tech begins on the eve of trial**. Leaving it to the last minute to realize that your team does not know how to communicate (i.e., what to call particular documents through naming conventions) about displaying or enhancing a document for the jurors to see.

If crashes and technical issues occur frequently enough, you will shake the confidence of everyone involved in the trial—everyone from your legal team to the judge and jury. Getting "shut down" by the judge is horrible; getting shut down by your own legal team is a fiasco. Getting shut down is the worst penalty that the judge (and perhaps your own legal team) can impose on a technician in court. However, even worse is the damage to personal and law firm reputations, embarrassment, and possibly even losing the case, after plodding through a day (or days) of mistakes, crashes, and problems—which are largely avoidable—that make your team look unprepared and unprofessional.

12. Including video prep.

Even so, fiascos and horror stories happen *all the time.* Take, for example, these stories I've heard (or witnessed) in my years as a trial tech.

- The time when the law firm sent a new associate to use a popular trial presentation tool in court. He was told how to put a few exhibits up on screen . . . but not how to connect his computer to an external monitor. Observers in the courtroom could literally see the confidence depart his corporal body and the nervousness and fear takeover as he had to choose between asking for help in open court or admitting he wasn't ready. Do you think he wanted to be flustered about his equipment rather than focused on his legal argument?

  Moral: Have a good idea of your capabilities before going to trial.

- The time the judge told a legal team to turn off their computers and not to turn them back on. The judge then pointed across the room and said, "You need to ask the opposing tech very nicely to put up some of your exhibits. I'm tired of your crashes and unpreparedness that are slowing us down." The lawyer turned (well, he turned beet red, to be honest) to face his opponent and asked, "May we please use your trial tech?" Would *you* want to be in that position in open court in front of your client, the judge, the jurors, your colleagues, the public?

  Moral: Computer glitches and failures harm the reputation of the entire legal team, but mostly harm the lawyers and the law firm themselves. Listen to your trial technician about the needs of your case.

- The time a partner said he had previously worked with technology "lots of times" so there was no need to practice communication ahead of time or to develop a common reference for documents. Then, in the courtroom, when he called out, "Please display the memo," the tech could only answer, "Which memo? What is the exhibit number?" The partner did not know the exhibit numbers, and his cross outline referenced the documents by the names only *he* knew them by . . . and nobody else.

  Moral: Always agree to use the exhibit number when referring to documents both in outline and in court.

- The time the team members requested and wrote in the TMO the format they wanted—then tried to change their minds when they discovered the format would create lots of extra work and expense. This team learned an expensive lesson on cutting corners for the sake of budget.

  Moral: Always perform quality control in advance and test your data plan to ensure it works.

- The time the legal team did not create a shared location where they could put redacted documents and new exhibits. Perhaps they thought the new exhibits would magically appear in the trial presentation system? In any event, they didn't, and the trial team looked *bad* when unredacted exhibits appeared onscreen and the trial tech was missing new exhibits.

  Moral: Have a system in place for version control of exhibits, and notify the trial tech about the electronic files the legal team intends to use.

- The time the trial laptop was destroyed when someone dropped it and there was no backup laptop immediately available for use.

  Moral: Have redundant equipment ready to go.

- The time the VGA cables used were substandard and untested, and inaccurately highlighted parts of an exhibit because the cables couldn't handle the computer's resolution. (Some cables have their limits.)

  Moral: Always test *all* of your equipment.

- The time the legal team went out to dinner, exercised, and came back to work at 10 p.m., only to give an all-nighter's worth of work to the trial tech (again) at the last minute—then wondered why the next day in court the tech was asleep and the presentation lacking.

Moral: Get your tech started on tasks as soon as possible. The tasks you request may seem easy or quick, but often they are not.

- The time a law firm decided to cut costs on trial equipment on "bet the company" litigation, then suffered endless technical problems throughout the trial.

  Moral: Do not cut costs on the most visible of a firm's work product.

- The time(s) the lone copy of an opening presentation was corrupt and there was no time to replace it . . . yet, the show must go on.

  Moral: Backup planning and redundancy must be at the forefront of your trial technology plan.

Knowledge of your trial presentation application of choice is just one of many skills necessary to get the job done. Throughout *The Trial Presentation Companion*, we will examine how problems and issues occur and how to prevent them by learning what technical skills are absolutely necessary, planning, devising version control schemes, effectively managing exhibits, creating courtroom communication conventions so that everyone on the trial team understands what is being talked about or asked for, and brainstorming other ideas on how to prepare and present at trial.

1.6 Evidence Presentation Obligations of Lawyers "On Trial"

Many times, law firms going to trial have not taken steps to have the correct support in place—period. Big picture: there is an expectation from judges, jurors, and clients that trial support[13] is a "core competency" for law firms. In other words, at a minimum, if you are going to trial, you should be able to connect your laptop to a screen and present exhibits—or bring someone along who can. Technical responsibilities are scalable to the complexity and volume of technical need. Therefore, for a limited court appearance (such as a hearing), you should be capable of handling the minor technical tasks necessary to show a few exhibits on screen,[14] whereas for "bet the company" litigation, the presentation should make maximum use of the technology available in the courtroom and have instituted a comprehensive process that, through planning and redundancy, minimizes risk. Whether big or small, all uses of technology should have a backup plan in place just in case things go wrong, so teams can minimize downtime and wasted time in court.

We are heading toward a new expectation for firms and lawyers in that they have made at least the minimal commitment of having the technical skills and ability required for trial presentation. Firms should decide on the minimal level of service and support they will offer at every trial, and whether they will absorb or pass through some of those costs. Lawyers who are an "army of one" must understand that possessing the minimum of technical competencies is on their shoulders and they must take steps to ensure they comply. For those worried about "plugging in" to a court system, much of the worry and doubt can be removed simply by *testing in advance*. By making an appointment with the court to test the equipment in the courtroom in advance, you will have the undivided attention of a court IT person, who wants to see you succeed (in connecting your computer, at least). Contrast this with a rushed, angry call from the judge or clerk requesting help for some incompetent soul who can't connect and never tested his equipment. The choice is clear: the opportunity and the tools are available, but too few trial teams take the *minimum* of steps necessary, let alone the reasonable ones, to ensure a smooth courtroom presentation.

Courts are now issuing rules establishing minimum technical standards for legal teams when they use high-tech equipment at trial. The required skill level is referred to as "Evidence Presentation Obligations," and these obligations are *mandated* by many courts, along with the *mandated* use of technology. Legal teams are in a real bind if they don't know how to use their own and/or the court's equipment. Below are a few excerpts from a list of evidence presentation obligations that some federal courts now use:

---

13. Or the ability to hire the right vendor for trial support.

14. Perhaps using Adobe Acrobat (as the key issue in so-called "minimal" cases is having basic technical skills).

- "No court time will be provided during court proceedings to allow the parties to troubleshoot issues."
- "The Court will not tolerate any delays during any proceedings caused by a party's unfamiliarity with the Court's system or by the failure of a party's equipment."
- "In addition to familiarizing themselves with the Court's electronic evidence presentation system in advance of the hearing/trial, *the parties must familiarize themselves with their own equipment and how to connect their own equipment with the Court's system prior to the hearing/trial.*"

I italicized the important takeaway in the last bullet point: "the parties must familiarize themselves with their own equipment and how to connect their own equipment with the Court's system prior to the hearing/trial." How many people came to court without knowing how to use their own equipment? Apparently enough to where courts had to make a rule.

Again, it's kind of silly that one of the highest profile and profitable undertakings that a firm might perform—namely, going to trial—is often done without the basic level of support necessary to alleviate risk and allow for efficient operations. The legal team can become "tech poor" from bad planning and decisions when it lacks the proper software, equipment, or experience that will further its trial presentation goals, or if they don't have redundant equipment that minimizes disruption and delay in the courtroom if problems do occur. Firms often lack the most basic commitment to courtroom technology.

Most lawyers who read this would never think that their firm is shortchanging their trial responsibilities, or that trial is not #1 in their firm—until, of course, they get their butts handed to them by a firm doing it right. It is easy to lose sight of the type of equipment a firm needs, the value of experience in trial tech, and the return on investment when you properly train, prep, and do quality control testing. Firms that are otherwise able to afford equipment but skimp on it anyway (because they "only" use trial equipment twice a year) will be in a technology deficit and potentially incompetent twice a year. Lawyers are often aghast (far too late) at the purchasing decisions their firm made on equipment and expertise; for example, they may wonder, in the middle of trial, why exhibits are slow to come up or why there are multiple crashes. Typically, the answer is simple: their equipment was just not good enough[15] and no one at the firm understood that quality equipment and support are the minimum standard necessary.

Collectively, partners often, and wrongly, think:

- The best equipment is already being used by the firm.
- Courtrooms have a support system in place to cover emergency IT needs.
- Trial needs will be prioritized and expedited internally at the firm.
- Workflows and processes have been established and standardized in advance.

15. Did not meet trial software minimum standards or were not maintained correctly.

Figure 8. ***Lawyers drown themselves by not taking technical needs seriously. (Image by Rachel Bennett.)***

The thinking seems to be that if the need occurs only a few times a year, then they can scoot by with a subpar system (or trial tech). But the partners and legal team fail to realize that this thinking results in an unnecessarily risky presentation environment with a dramatically higher risk of crashes and performance issues. This poor logic seems to apply in other areas as well by limiting preparation: performing quality control, testing court equipment prior to trial, or being able to distinguish that one vendor might be a better option for the firm than another. The reality is that there is no trial small enough that it does not require planning, support, or testing—yet time and again, these tasks are just ignored. (Believe it or not, they are ignored in the big trials, too.)

Lawyers should also be *personally* involved, along with other professional staff, in creating the minimum technical standards and workflows for trial support for both themselves and their firm. They need to ensure that the tools, training, and knowledge (and associated budgetary flexibility) is a top priority at their firm—or else they will simply be second best (and that is not so great at trial, right?). I must reiterate: trial is the culmination of potentially years of work that both the firm and the lawyers have their reputation staked on. Firms that skimp on planning, equipment, and personnel seriously undermine their own efforts. Partners set the expectation with management and budgeting over the levels of service offered—they should make sure that trials, well-trained staffers, equipment for trial, and well-vetted vendors are at the top of the list of priorities, *always*. Otherwise, the firm runs the risk of being outmaneuvered by outdated technology, which not something you want to work out a week or two before trial. Be sure to bring your technical experts into these conversations so that everyone understands the issues. A firm's commitment to trial can also be shown by hiring outside vendors with the skills and equipment to do the job.

Consider these short narratives:[16]

16. These are not, for the most part, "David and Goliath" examples. They are "*Goliath* and Goliath" examples.

- Two large firms of roughly equal size battle it out in trial. Firm 1 sends its tech team to the trial site one month before trial to discuss setup and test equipment with the court clerk and security. Firm 2 shows up first day of court, laptop in hand, and is lost, stumbling, bumbling . . . and they lost the case. This illustrates why your firm must demonstrate its commitment to trial by allowing your tech team to visit the trial site in advance to test and create a tech plan.
- Firm 1 has acquired several additional rooms at the hotel to turn into workrooms that are networked and have high-speed printers, office equipment, individual workstations, and dedicated internet and telephone lines. Firm 2 has a single conference room in which fifteen people worked around a table, with a single shared printer. Cell phone and hotel internet connections were intermittent. Which team do you think got the job done? Which team could make the binders, materials, and presentations that mattered? Which firm made the better impression on the judge and client? Who took its obligation to trial seriously?
- Firm 1 brings its full IT capacity and support, described above, to the trial site. Firm 2's legal team arrives at the trial site with laptops and their personal phones. Team members try to use public Wi-Fi for high-speed printing and encountered lots of downtime due to technical issues—and there is no IT support onsite to assist. Every legal task is difficult, and communication slow.
- Now we have a big firm and a small firm.[17] The big firm had poor, outdated equipment; its version of PowerPoint was several generations out of date; and it cut costs by having an associate (in addition to his legal duties in trial) run the presentation. The small firm hired a vendor and created a more persuasive presentation that ran more smoothly than that of the big firm. Technology is the great equalizer—never forget it.

At the end of the day, if you're the lawyer and your technology fails at trial, the judge and jurors are *not* going to think negatively about your trial tech, and it wouldn't matter if they did. When things go wrong, jurors often look straight past the trial tech and stare right at the lawyer—that's who they want to see sweat and dance off the stage like Mariah Carey on New Year's Eve 2017.[18] They don't know if you brought the trial tech onto the team at the eve of trial or forced some poor associate without any training to do it. They don't know that you didn't rehearse, or learn basic terminology to communicate well with your trial tech, or that you don't have the appropriate equipment. The only thing these decision-makers know is that *you* screwed up. What makes matters even worse in their eyes is if you throw your tech under the bus when the equipment fails, rather than apologizing or finding an artful way to be kind and take responsibility for what just happened. At the end of the day, the buck stops with the lead attorney on the case.

1.6.1 Toward Standards?

In the last ten years, we've seen a complete change in the way that e-discovery is handled by law firms. We've gone from "cowboy culture" to an accepted and routine business process. Collection, processing, review, and production have all changed and become more efficient and standardized. Firms have made tremendous investments in people and technology in these areas to improve the process and make it better. What hasn't changed much in ten-plus years is the presentation of digital evidence, due to three primary barriers to technology adoption, which I'll discuss in a moment. Regardless of whether actual standards take hold, firms and lawyers should hold themselves accountable for either having the minimal skill set to do the job themselves or bringing a competent staff member or vendor to court to assist. In Chapter Six, Courtroom Planning, I propose basic court standards for testing and redundancy planning.

The first barrier to technology adoption is the lack of standards governing the presentation phase of the litigation lifecycle. The exchange of electronic files process works very well in the production phase of the litigation

17. A small firm can equal a big firm by having a commitment to technology.
18. Google it.

lifecycle. There is no doubt when produced records are exchanged in an image format that they need to be named correctly, in a consistent technical format, and be branded. The process begins with a collaborative discussion and is very flexible, routine, and efficient, with multiple production formats to choose from. The process should be no different at trial; a discussion followed by clear and concise technical specifications that should be documented in the TMO and used to guide the exhibit creation and exchange process.

Another collaborative process occurs regarding the technical setup that must be negotiated between the parties and the court staff. There are tremendous benefits for all parties to facilitate a generous amount of time to setup, test, and remedy any issues that occur throughout the trial. Anecdotally, courtroom IT staff report that more than 50 percent of courtroom technical issues would never occur if people simply tested their equipment in advance.

Testing and access cuts two ways because if the court does not provide access and time to test equipment, the risk of technical errors increases. Similarly, teams that don't test their equipment raise the risk of technical issues and potentially the ire of decision-makers. The inverse is also true: teams that test and QC rigorously will dramatically lower the risk of technical issues in court. Legal teams should use an independent third-party vendor to avoid disputes about equipment.

The second barrier is enforcement. The lack of enforcement of any technical standard has kept the efficiencies seen in other phases of the litigation process from occurring at trial. "Garbage in, garbage out" is the saying, but it also has another name: ***burden shifting***. Courts are reluctant to get involved in what is often viewed as a petty dispute between parties. The disputes however are far from petty, as the burden for compliance with agreed-upon technical formats is shifted from one party to the other—or worse, not complied with at all. Teams that do it right are essentially penalized by doing the work of two teams. The lack of standards and enforcement governing the trial exhibit process has inhibited the efficient exchange of exhibits and, as a result, slows down the trial process.

Furthermore, when a file is not named correctly, other inefficiencies occur as a result. For example, when a party does not use the exhibit number to call out exhibits in court or they are not branded with the exhibit number, there will be significant courtroom confusion over what exhibit is being referred to. (Often an old Bates or production number is used instead.) Judges simply expressing a concern that documents are not properly branded will often remedy the issue overnight. Likewise, it is often clear that parties who don't know what exhibit number they are using typically don't have their technical house in order either. A court inquiry would likely find that files were not named or branded correctly, and parties with such problems should be directed by the court to comply with technical requirements and proper exhibit references, which will aid courtroom efficiency and compliance by legal teams.

The last barrier is technology adoption by law firms and lawyers, which encompasses people, software, and commitment to workflow and a process that is efficient. When it comes to trial technology, nearly every barrier to entry for lawyers has been drastically reduced over the last few years: 1) equipment costs are lower; 2) there are many software options available for presentation; and 3) there is a very capable trial technology consultant community.

Firms are often their own worst enemy when it comes to trial presentation. The actual costs of trial technology investments in software, expertise, and equipment pale in comparison to those made in document processing and review. It is incredibly puzzling that the highest stakes and most visible portion of legal work is often done by firms trying to spend as little as possible, and without the level of support necessary to do the job.

Testing and QC by legal teams have become so bad that some courts have created "Evidence Presentation Obligations" that describe the technical responsibilities of legal teams. The rules and sample language below might be the best support of all that courts recognize problems with technical compliance and adoption:

1) **Parties should know how to use their own equipment**. "[P]arties must familiarize themselves with their own equipment and how to connect their own equipment with the Court's systems . . . ."

2) **The court does not like delays due to technology issues.** "The Court will not tolerate any delays during any proceedings caused by a party's unfamiliarity with the Court's systems or by the failure of a party's equipment."

3) **You should take advantage of the opportunity the court provides for you to test and QC in advance.** "Any party wishing to familiarize themselves with the Court's electronic evidence presentation systems are strongly encouraged to set up an orientation session with the Court's IT staff. . . at least three (3) weeks before your trial or hearing."

In conclusion, if we want to support the adoption and use of trial technology, we need to 1) develop better standards that mirror the document production process; 2) increase enforcement of standards by sweating the details of exhibit exchanges; 3) encourage technology use and adoption by law firms and attorneys via outreach, standards, and enforcement.

1.6.2 The Importance of a Trial Tech Plan

Like a car, your trial tech plan is the sum of all its parts. A car doesn't merely show up one day on a dealer's lot; it is built by a team that has invested time engineering and creating the different parts that make up the car. If a car is not built upon a solid foundation of sound choices and rigorous testing, it will be junk from the beginning.

Likewise, planning, preparing, and presenting evidence at trial require a solid foundation of foresight, good decision-making, rigorous testing, ingenuity, and just plain hard work—long days and late nights—to prepare for the presentation. As we will discuss in the coming chapters, the components of a good trial tech plan include:

- Analyzing the courtroom and its presentation capabilities.
- Assessing your equipment needs[19] (not to be confused with war room needs).
- Developing a workflow for exhibit creation.
- Setting up presentation, exhibit, and deposition databases for use at trial.
- Discussing exhibit version control.
- Orchestrating the exhibit exchange with opposing counsel (TMO input).
- Organizing files.
- Ensuring "right size" staffing.

1.6.3 Evaluate Support and Technical Needs Separately from Legal Needs

When analyzed, the paradigm of what is a "big" or "small" case can be debated. The size of the case based on the amount at issue or case budget is important to know so that a plan can be created that is consistent with those needs. However, what is often thought of as a big or small case from a legal perspective may not be so from a technical perspective. What is the state of the data or how much video is in the case will often dictate how much time will need to be spent on the case to prepare it. Legal teams would be wise to consider a number of other factors when considering the size and scope of the case that might not be in their traditional decision-making wheelhouse.

There are several factors that must be analyzed in their entirety when considering the use of trial presentation tools so that the case team can make appropriate decisions about their case. Legal teams should ensure that the case is properly staffed and the trial tech is qualified. Non-technical factors to consider include:

- **Budget.** Is the client billable for expenses, or will costs pass through? Will the firm rent or buy equipment?

19. This is strictly what is necessary for the technician to carry out their trial presentation goals.

- **Number of attorneys supported.** Will the tech have enough time to do a "run through" of each attorneys outline to ensure that 1) every exhibit is accounted for; 2) the location of any callouts or highlights are known (and potentially created in advance); 3) the files come up smoothly; and 4) the presentation equipment is running correctly?
- **Number of legal staff supported.** Will the tech also be fulfilling blowback requests for binder creation or have other support duties in addition to the trial presentation database and courtroom presentation?
- **Monetary amount at issue.** Do the budget and staffing reflect the seriousness of the matter?
- **Length of trial or presentation need.** Will the demands on the trial tech be such that additional staffing will be necessary? There is only so long a single member of the team can work all-nighters before the quality and level of support dwindle and the risk of serious mistake increases.
- **Trial team culture.** How are tasks communicated by the trial team? Are needs communicated in a timely manner? Is the team cooperative in assisting the trial tech in obtaining exhibits, communicating goals, timing, etc.?
- **David versus Goliath.** How will your legal team appear if your technical systems appear to be unbalanced as compared to the other side?
- **Trial Management Order (TMO).** How does the TMO dictate the exchange of exhibits, and in what format? What are the branding requirements?
- **Courtroom Rules.** Does the courtroom facilitate or impede the use of technology? Does the court allow prior testing of the courtroom and early access on a daily basis to set up equipment? Will equipment need to be set up daily, or can it remain in the courtroom?

There are also technical factors to consider:

- **Type of data.** Is the electronically stored information (ESI) a native document (i.e., a document that hasn't been processed into an image) or an image? Will the files require processing to PDF or TIFF to make them easily exchangeable and presentable?
- **Volume of data.** How much data is at issue in the case? What steps will be necessary to get the data "presentation ready"? Are there exhibits with unusually high page counts?
- **Condition of data.** Are the exhibits properly unitized? Are the files corrupt? Are they password protected? Are there large, single-file exhibits that might be troublesome to call up on the presentation laptop?
- **Video and number of edits to be used.** Has the video been synchronized to a transcript or standalone? What is the volume of the video? How many edits will be needed? One rule of thumb is that editing video takes at least three times the clip length to create. A ten-minute clip could take thirty minutes or more to properly edit. A "small case" with six hours of video and hundreds of clips could take weeks to prepare.
- **Access to appropriate equipment in firm inventory or through a rental vendor.** Is the tech setup redundant? Does the computer have enough RAM? Fast enough CPU?
- **Trial tech's qualifications.** Is the trial tech for the case qualified to present when the technical and non-technical factors are considered?

In the end, deciding what a small or large case is might be dictated by what your technical needs are rather than the legal factors. If a small case has become a large one due to the scope of data involved, it may force legal teams to make better decisions about the choices they make regarding video clips, exhibit processing, and other data decisions in order to bring technical needs up to expectations. One consideration might be that using a trial presentation program is not the right choice for your case.

1.6.4 Review Your Internal Policies and Procedures

Firms should review their workflows and procedures for trial. There is no greater disconnect with lawyers (especially at big law firms) than the level of support they *believe* (wrongly) is available to them. Small firms are more nimble and can quickly make decisions that at a large firm would need to go through many layers of review. Nevertheless, the reality of what the "real world" support picture is and what lawyers think are often different.

For example, if a cable broke at trial, is your IT staff able to quickly bring a cable to you at a trial site? Think about how this works. Is someone designated to support the trial? Do they have equipment available to them for emergencies? Is it clear they would be reimbursed if they needed to buy something? Would they be able to leave the office? Is trial support prioritized over other types of support? Does everybody in the firm get the message that trial is stressful, visible to the public and clients, and hard on equipment and people? Have you prepped non-legal personnel how to act when in court?[20]

Below are some things to consider as you create policies and procedures for hardware, software, planning, and people, as they relate to trial presentation. It is helpful if these items are settled prior to being in the rush of trial planning so there are no surprises or missteps. Again, decision-makers need to send a clear message as to the level of support expected, and then provide the support needed to reach that level.

Policies and procedures regarding trial hardware and software:

- **Frequency of replacing equipment**. There is a two- to three-year lifecycle for trial-used laptops.
- **Review software at major updates and version changes**. Early adoption is not always the best idea. Give software a chance to be debugged by other more experienced users before updating. Call the software company to obtain their advice.
- **Applying updates and new software to a trial laptop**. What is the testing procedure after it has been installed?
- **Other programs that should, and should not, be on the trial laptop**. *No* to iTunes, games, untested codecs. *Yes* to the companion software recommended in Chapter Five.
- **Imaging and reimaging of laptops**. What is your firm's policy on reimaging of laptops after trial? Also, remember that laptops take a beating during trial. Reimage to refresh the computer and purge old trial data (after it has been appropriately backed up or destroyed). What is your software creator's guide on reimaging?
- **Competitive analysis**. What are the other software packages out there, and what are their pluses and minuses? Is it time for a change? Stay abreast of industry changes. Don't be a dinosaur.
- **Laptop compliance with the minimum software standards** specified by the manufacturer.
- **Equipment to rent versus equipment to buy**.

Procedures, as they relate to people:

- **Stakeholders who make planning decisions**—an attorney, the legal department, the IT department, admin departments? Are the stakeholders included in trial planning?
- **Trial tech training and practice time**. Does the trial tech have the experience required to do the job?[21]
- **Designating who is responsible** for hardware, software, and updates.
- **Designating who is responsible** for responding to emergency needs.

Procedures as they relate to trial:

20. Don't take this for granted. It might be your runner's first day in court!
21. A beginner at a hearing is appropriate; a beginner at "bet the company" litigation is not.

- **Deciding how trial tasks are prioritized.**
- **Authorizing who can help** (for example, in the "cable" issue described above).
- **Designating who is authorized** to help with IT tasks and emergencies.
- **Designating a runner** to take things to and from court.
- **Discussing the service expectation** for replacing equipment with the rental vendor.
- **Including the trial tech in planning**: six months before the trial, three months before the trial, one month before the trial.
- **Ensuring the trial tech is not overburdened**. Do you need more than one tech?
- **Choosing vendors** for equipment rental and setup, ESI processing, document branding, trial presentation, and a courier for taking items to and from court.

1.7 Trial and People

Perhaps the most important resource at trial is the *human* resource: your people. First, law firms need to instill "ownership" of the case in their team members, from staffers to partners. People can't own what they aren't a part of, and too often, when one moves down the chain of command, the message of what the case is about, the goals of the trial team, and how the case is progressing does not reach the people supporting the trial (including associates and paralegals). I recommend you have a designated contact (if not the partner) who provides information and regular updates about the case to the entire team. It can also be helpful to post a whiteboard in a common area in the office that is updated daily with news about upcoming witnesses, team members on break, and other useful information.

Second, law firms need to develop policies and procedures to ensure their people are taken care of and properly incentivized to work at trials. Many firms actually *disincentivize* people to work trials by adhering to rigid policies meant for 9-to-5 office workers, not people killing themselves at trial. For example, if your support staff works around the clock, will you make them use benefit time if they go home at 6 a.m.? For long trials, will they have opportunities to catch up with family and/or to communicate with them? How will you feed them?[22] Do your reimbursement policies make sense for large metropolitan areas? Properly incentivizing trial work is not a license for runaway costs, of course, but rather it is an important consideration for firms, to ensure its policies are sensible and encourage your people to want to go to trial and be part of a team—and that they want their team to *win*.

Third, teams often wrongly overburden their trial tech—in particular, by thinking the trial tech's job is merely to push buttons instead of prepare and troubleshoot data. While everyone at trial is prepared to pitch in, be careful about overburdening your tech with too many unrelated tasks. Smart teams get their support moving as soon as possible. For example, some lawyers come back from court, go eat a nice meal, work out, catch up with family, and don't get their support team moving until late at night. Not only does this devalue the support team's time, but it puts them in a position to where they may have to work around the clock or rush and take shortcuts—all because the team lead wanted to get in a workout first. When that occurs, only the most important tasks get handled—the fine details get lost.

Last, trial is not in everybody's blood: watch out for stress, substance abuse, and mental health issues related to being away from home.

22. There is nothing more horrible than sandwiches and pizza for breakfast, lunch, and dinner for weeks on end. Try to incorporate healthy options and variety into the mix, and seek feedback from team members on the meals.

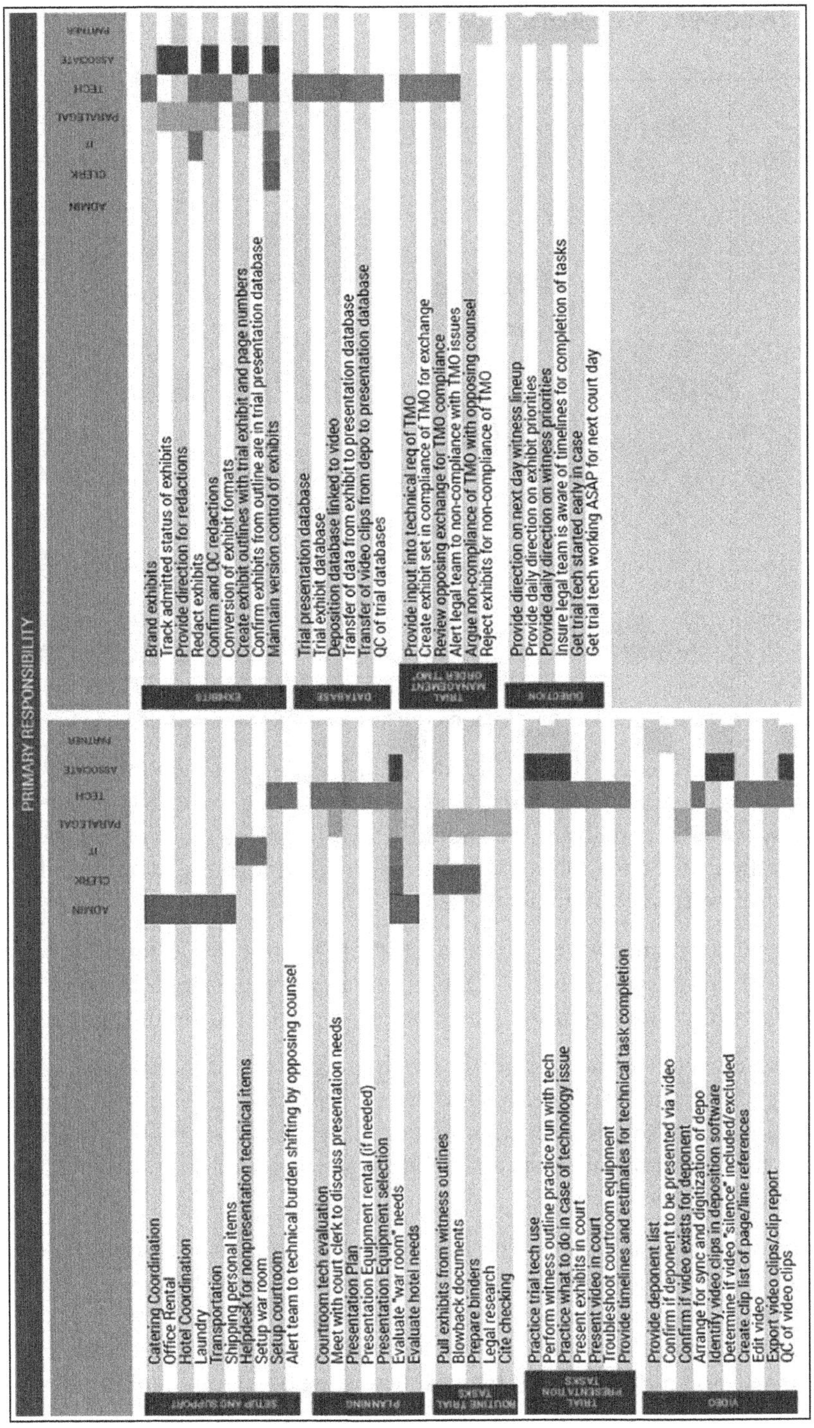

Figure 9. ***Suggested division of labor.***

1.8 Electronic Discovery Reference Model

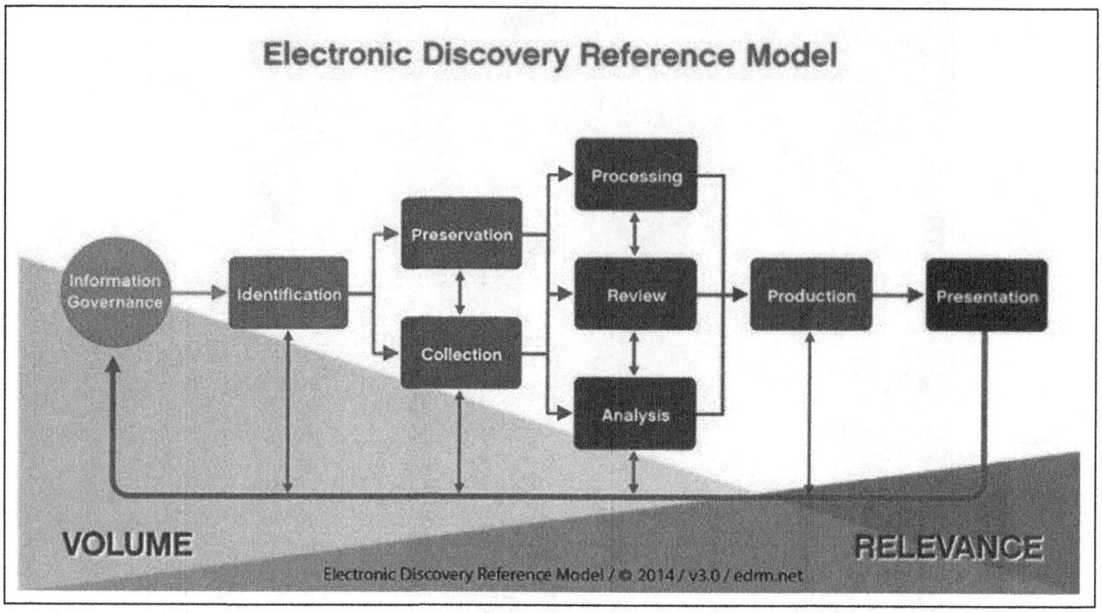

Figure 10. ***Electronic Discovery Reference Model. (Image courtesy of EDRM, edrm.net.)***

The Electronic Discovery Reference Model (EDRM) is a "conceptual view of the e-discovery process"[23] and is often called "the litigation lifecycle." The EDRM explains each stage within the model, with a goal of being utilized as a basis for "discussion and analysis" and not a "prescription for the one and only right way to approach e-discovery."[24] Moreover, the EDRM describes the "iterative process" that the litigation lifecycle is with repetition, refinement, and interplay between the different phases.

> The diagram also portrays an *iterative* process. One might repeat the same step numerous times, honing in on a more precise set of results. One might also cycle back to earlier steps, refining one's approach as a better understanding of the data emerges or as the nature of the matter changes.[25]

The Presentation phase, depicted at the far right in the figure above, is dependent upon the phases that precede it to have a quality source of ESI and/or images for use in a presentation. The previous stages form the foundation of files to be used in a presentation, so it is important that great care is taken at each stage. Also important to note is that each stage represents a different technical specialty within the litigation support field[26] that may not necessarily be suited for a trial presentation role.

In a typical case, after identifying and preserving potentially relevant custodians and sources of ESI, the data are collected from a custodian's electronic devices using forensic software that preserves the metadata of the files. The ESI is then "processed" using a program that converts an individual electronic file into a database record by fielding its metadata and building a link to the native file or converting it to an image format like PDF or TIFF.[27] Once placed in a review database,[28] the file is reviewed by legal teams, who will evaluate the ESI for relevance and privi-

23. ERDM, 2015.
24. *Id.*
25. *Id.*
26. This is an important distinction for legal teams to understand. The personality traits and skills that make a good trial tech are unique and not necessarily found in technicians working in other areas of the EDRM (and vice versa).
27. This gives the legal team the ability to *efficiently* search through fielded metadata (for example, search by date, author, recipient, or keyword) and then view a linked image of the file or the file itself with a native link.
28. Concordance, Relativity, and Summation are common document review databases.

lege from which it is produced, exchanged, and may ultimately become an exhibit. In theory, movement through the stages of the EDRM should reduce data volume as the data are analyzed, reviewed, and culled. In practice, however, the movement of data through the process is not as smooth as it may seem due to factors like changes in strategy, or technical or new legal issues, so it can take years to go from collection to presentation.

Because the EDRM is an iterative process, many decisions about processing that were made in the early stages may need to be revisited so that better quality exhibits can be created for use at trial. For example, files may have been reviewed or exchanged natively or processed into a grayscale image for production, but may need to be reprocessed into a color image for trial. Alternatively, maybe the formulas used in a spreadsheet are at issue and the native file (i.e., the Excel spreadsheet) will need to be presented rather than a static image that may have only captured the result of the formulas.

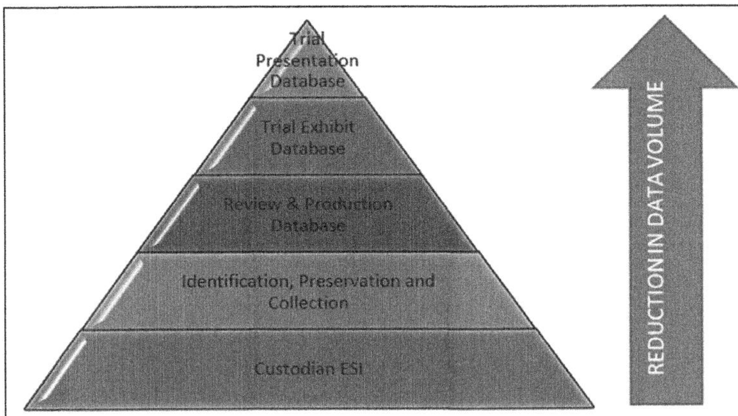

Figure 3: Quality starts at the beginning. Each level is dependent upon the one below it for quality source material. Each level is also a different technical skill or specialty within the litigation support field. As volume is reduced the level of work increases to prepare exhibits for trial thus illustrating the need for early involvement of the trial tech.

Figure 11. ***Quality starts at the beginning. Each level is dependent upon the one below it for quality source material.***

Just because data have been reduced along the EDRM does not mean the work is reduced. The exhibit identification process is time consuming and difficult. Many of the processes and workflows, like page unitization[29] of exhibits, are manual and not automated. Because of the potential for new document unitizations (changing the document boundary of a document), branding, grayscale to color changes, and all of the other related tasks, workload increases exponentially. In sum, as trial approaches, the iterative processes of the EDRM are a valuable lesson in understanding that there will be much work to do as new exhibit exchange standards are agreed upon via the TMO and other agreements between parties.

29. Unitization is when you change, add, reorder, or delete pages from a document. Multiple documents can often make up a single exhibit and are part of the unitization process. It's sometimes also called reunitization.

Chapter Two

Getting Started

"Do you want to win—or do you want to sleep?"

—*David Boies*

2.1 The Basics

Using courtroom technology is full of potential *gotcha* moments. If, as a new trial tech, you can get a small trial or arbitration—with a limited set of documents to unitize, redact, and brand in Adobe Acrobat PDF format; load into your trial presentation tool of choice; and present in court—you will have the perfect opportunity get started. Be careful not to go too far outside of your skillset and comfort zone, as you might be asking for trouble. (That is why the companion chapter to Chapter One includes the basic skills necessary to get started.

Most trial techs would consider the actual presentation of evidence the easiest part of their job (albeit under tremendous pressure). The true test for trial techs lay in their ability to devise a system that creates a stable foundation for the presentation of exhibits at trial. The "plan" relies upon quality work performed in the earlier stages of the EDRM so it can be easily converted into exhibits that, in turn, will be imported into the trial presentation software. In this chapter, we focus on technical skills and related issues. Issues about exhibit creation are discussed in Chapter Three, Exhibit Creation and Workflow.

Trial presentation is neither impossible nor overly technically difficult, but there are bars to entry—namely, a minimum technical skillset, the right equipment, and the basic knowledge necessary to create electronic exhibits (in PDF or TIFF format) in PowerPoint or trial presentation software like TrialDirector, Sanction, or OnCue. Too often, people wanting to use courtroom technology are thrown into situations that are beyond their ability. Casual tech users often over simplify or lack the basic IT skills they need to perform a relatively simple "plug and play"[1] courtroom setup. Embarrassing problems and technical glitches occur when people are in over their head. Let's start by calling it what it is: a competency and experience issue.

The requisite skills and experience need to be correctly applied to the case at hand, a concept that should be entirely familiar to lawyers in the partner system. The most senior heavy-hitters are brought in for the biggest and most difficult cases, while new associates cut their teeth on smaller or less difficult legal matters. Staffing for the technical aspects of your case is really no different. For larger and technically difficult cases, experience matters and you'll want to use the services of an experienced trial technician, while smaller cases might be the right opportunity to develop someone on the legal team into a trial technician.[2]

1. "Plug and play" means you simply plug your computer into a video and sound connection that already exists in the courtroom.
2. Sorry if it seems as if I'm beating a dead horse here, but I see people out of their league so often—and when I do, the theme to *Jaws* starts playing in my head.

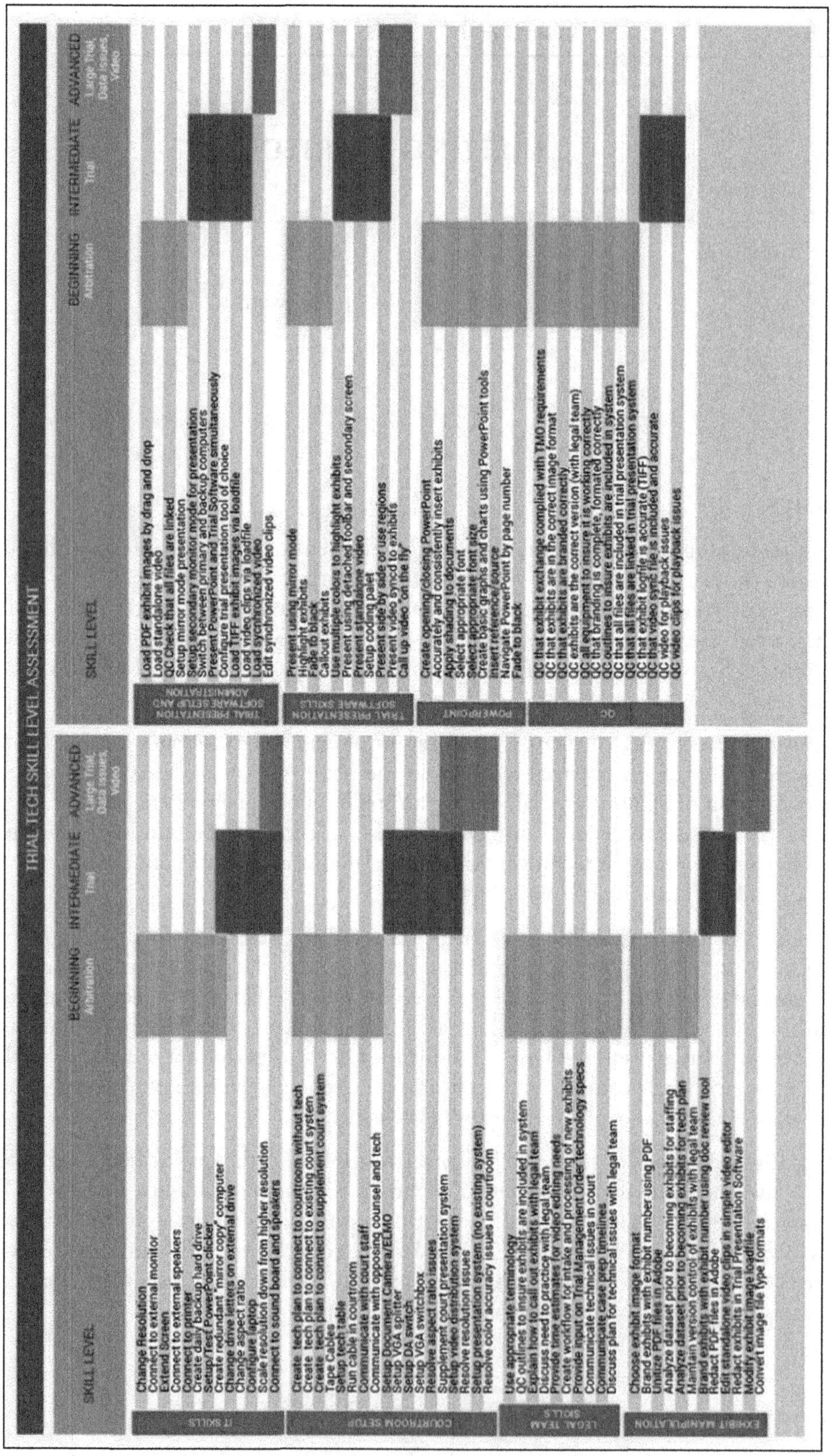

Figure 1. ***Technical assessment: do you have the skills necessary to present at trial?***

Most issues that occur in a presentation are not due to a sudden technical calamity. They *can* be anticipated. Why? Because most issues are usually due to a lack of planning, noncompliance with team workflows, and poor preparation by the legal and tech teams. Poor choices made in planning and the late involvement of a trial tech almost always result in an embarrassing courtroom failure. It's mortifying to explain yourself to decision-makers (especially when they are a client) for a failure that could have been avoided with an advance visit to the courtroom or extra money for appropriate equipment. Even worse is explaining why an exhibit didn't make it into the presentation system.

Most often, issues can be avoided if the trial tech has performed basic QC steps or has the minimum set of IT skills necessary to connect to a courtroom system. Such failures slow the adoption of courtroom technology through bad prior experiences of users (i.e., the judge and lawyers). For a professional trial tech, it is completely disheartening to come to a courtroom and be told by the clerk that the judge does not like technology due to the multiple bad experiences in trials. Too often, the average trial tech's first visit to the courtroom is on the first day of trial because they couldn't get permission to leave the office and review the trial site, were hired too late in the process, or the legal team thought it silly (or did not want to pay) to send them out there "just to look at the courtroom." This lapse alone causes irreparable harm. How will the legal team know what resolution to create their presentation in? Or what size and scale? Will the aspect ratio of the courtroom change the presentation to make it unreadable to viewers? The graphic below shows the effect of aspect ratio when it is done incorrectly (for example, a PowerPoint created on your 16:9 work computer being displayed on a 4:3 court monitor).

Remember: technology is allowed into the courtroom to help speed things along and make the trial process more efficient.[3] Courtroom technical problems have a profoundly negative effect on decision-makers like the judge and jury. It's a bit like baseball—three strikes and you're *out*, because from the court's perspective, you're messing with the number-one goal of courtroom technology: the swift and efficient administration of justice.[4] Maybe MMA fighting is the better analogy: you may get pummeled and embarrassed and lose in seconds if you're incompetent right out of the gate.

The judge (nor anyone else) doesn't want to watch you bumble and stumble through technical problems because you don't have the skills necessary to run your computer or software, didn't bother to prepare, or can't connect your laptop to the presentation system. I'll say it again: *much of this drama can be avoided if you test and prepare your equipment in advance.* Testing not only helps you lower the risk of technical glitches, but also gives you an idea as to what resolutions will work in the courtroom and to which shape (i.e., 4:3 or 16:9) you should tailor your presentations.[5] We'll talk more about resolution and setup issues in a moment, but *the takeaway here is that you want to test your equipment (and self-assess your ability) in advance* (and the person doing the presentation and setup should be the one to do it).

A trial presentation setup that allows that crashes sometimes *will* occur and reduces risk by taking steps to deal with failure in advance is often the difference between catastrophe and *perception* of perfection. Teams that are in denial over the risk and frequency of issues and don't prepare will, unfortunately, have the most public and embarrassing of problems—they will panic and flail when they don't know what to do. The perception of perfection is often *wrong*, as every team experiences computer crashes, technical glitches, and problems. It's *how* problems are dealt with at the time of crisis that shapes how the presentation will ultimately be perceived: as a success, or a failure. One time, I had an external drive literally go up in a puff of smoke (that inexplicably nobody noticed and did not set off fire alarms in the courtroom), but I was able to just switch to the backup system so presentation was seamless. I've only had a hard drive go up in flames that one time, but I've dealt with numerous other technical errors or problems—thanks to my redundant equipment setup, no one ever knew.

3. As stated before, the legal team's perspective is different; it is looking for persuasiveness, credibility, and presentation "showmanship." But the judge isn't. The judge just wants to help things move faster and be efficient.

4. When problems occur, decision-makers can't be blamed for thinking that implementing technology in the courtroom is difficult and problematic—which then delays technology's adoption and use.

5. For example, PowerPoint has templates for 4:3 and 16:9.

Most experienced trial techs use a redundant setup with two laptops connected into a video switchbox,[6] along with a document camera to provide a diversity of presentation choices and to plan for computer crashes. A dual setup allows the tech to seamlessly switch to a backup computer if the primary one crashes and needs to be restarted. It also allows the tech to prep exhibits and video on a backup laptop while presenting on the primary one. When the new data is needed, the tech simply switches to the second laptop and is ready to go.[7]

In the unlikely event that both laptops fail or the electronic version of the exhibit is missing (it happens), the document camera is a reasonable alternative. Everyone on the team needs to keep a calm demeanor while they get the paper copy of the exhibit for use on the document camera. Nobody should display panic or act as if anything is wrong. For any equipment failure to become visible to the judge and jurors, it needs to have gone through the high bar of two laptop failures and the lack of a paper copy of the missing exhibit. When you calmly move to the document camera, the judge and jurors will have no idea whether it is a presentation preference or a problem. (The document camera is a great tool for breaking up the monotony of presenting slides and should be part of a diverse and interesting presentation strategy.)

The risk is on the presenting party to ensure that their presentation is going to work correctly right out of the gate. There are no do-overs in court and rarely a second chance to present information when there is a glitch or technical issue. Court IT staffers are not a safety net for resolving technical issues (and are often expressly barred from fixing your equipment). If your case is absolutely dependent on technology for your presentation (such as for opening statement), then this should be well rehearsed and tested in advance, with a backup plan and redundant equipment, *period.*

Trial teams must practice what to do in case of failure. Glitches are not completely unavoidable, but they can be minimized by having the minimum technical skills necessary to run your presentation and having a backup plan and the right equipment. Recognizing early on that you're having some technical difficulties in the courtroom and pivoting to a different plan while you work to resolve the problem keeps the team in positive territory with the judge and jurors (who may never even know, if you can smoothly pull it off), and that comes with practice. For example, the trial tech and the lawyer should both understand in advance:

- That if a document does not come up on screen, you will either switch to the document camera or have a set of paper copies available to distribute.
- You must practice how a technical issue will be communicated to the judge and the legal team. The tech and legal team needs to be calm, cool and collected. Watching a legal team panic, yell, shake their heads, and twist their bodies around to see what's going on does not portray the image they want to decision-makers.
    - How will the message be relayed from a tech table in the back of the courtroom to the front?
    - What is the alternative plan?
    - Note: The legal team must remember where they are (i.e., in court), so berating the tech is not a good idea.

Quite simply, law firms need to do a better job of preparing for trials where they will use electronic presentation systems. Teams need equipment that complies with the standards issued by the manufacturers of the software they are using. The trial tech's role[8] needs to be taken seriously and discussed at the earliest stages of trial preparation (and perhaps as early as collection, if you are thinking about your endgame strategy) and should include planning

6. I'll explain later what each one of these pieces of equipment is.
7. Think of exhibits being provided to you during a break in court or you need to quickly edit video.
8. The trial tech should also be compensated fairly for the numerous late hours they put in, the high-pressure environment in which they must work, and the value their know-how brings to the case. Firms would be wise to devise not only a unique compensation system, but also flexible time off that is not counted toward vacation or sick time. Keeping people connected with their families during long trials is important as well, and policies and procedures should be in place to incentive people to work their hardest and give it their all.

for trial, site visits, the budget, obtaining appropriate equipment, and rigorous testing procedures of data and the presentation site before the presentation. IT support should be treated as a separate skillset than trial support; your trial tech should be working on exhibits and presentation, not fixing printers and connecting people to the internet.[9] There is a tendency to oversimplify and underestimate the amount of work that goes into creating a risk-adverse, quality work product with trial presentation systems. If the trial tech wasn't involved early enough in the trial planning stages or lacks the correct equipment, budget, or authority to test the data or the trial site, then he has his hands tied before the trial presentation even starts.

2.1.1 More on Evidence Presentation Obligations

"Evidence Presentation Obligations" is the title of the courtroom rules circulated within several federal courtrooms that lists the "obligations" of parties using trial technology and the *minimum* skill set needed to present evidence in court. Here are a few such "obligations," according to the FAQ from the Electronic Evidence Presentation System for the Western District of Kentucky, as well as a similar list from California. The consequence of noncompliance is clear:

> Parties will be required to present their cases without the aid of the electronic evidence presentation systems in the event that the systems are unavailable due to the party's unfamiliarity, due to equipment failure or due to any other "technology" delays.

When you read the list of obligations below from the Western District of Kentucky and the Eastern District of California (and duplicated at courts elsewhere), you get the sense that it developed after an untold number of judges across the country sat in frustration as they watched one lawyer after another bumble through their presentations.

- "No court time will be provided during court proceedings to allow the parties to troubleshoot issues"
  - If a party is unfamiliar with the Court's system, they are strongly encouraged to attend an orientation prior to the hearing/trial (see procedures below).
  - The Court will not tolerate any delays during any proceedings caused by a party's unfamiliarity with the Court's system or by the failure of a party's equipment.
  - The parties will be required to present their cases without the aid of the electronic evidence presentation system in the event that the system is unavailable due to the party's unfamiliarity, due to equipment failure or due to any other "technology" delays.
  - Please note that the Court's staff cannot work on and/or provide support for any non-court equipment.
- In addition to familiarizing themselves with the Court's electronic evidence presentation system in advance of the hearing/trial, the parties must familiarize themselves with their own equipment and how to connect their own equipment with the Court's system prior to the hearing/trial. Specifically, the parties should be familiar with:
  - Adjusting the screen resolution (1024x768)
  - Switching the display
- The Court strongly encourages parties to bring a backup laptop with power supply, flash drive and or CD that contains all documents if technical issues were to arise.
- Any party wishing to familiarize themselves with the Court's electronic evidence presentation system is strongly encouraged to set up an orientation session.

9. Depending, of course, on the complexity and size of the case and team. On a team, we all chip in as needed.

- Parties who attend an electronic evidence presentation system orientation should bring the equipment they will use to connect to the system as well as samples of the content they intend to present at the hearing/trial through the system.

Evidence Presentation Obligations:

- ***Parties presenting evidence electronically via the Court's electronic evidence presentation system must be familiar with the system prior to the hearing/trial. No court time will be provided during court proceedings to allow the parties to troubleshoot issues with the parties' equipment or the equipment in the courtroom.*** If a party is unfamiliar with the Court's system, they are strongly encouraged to attend an orientation ***prior*** to the hearing/trial (see procedures below). The Court will not tolerate any delays during any proceedings caused by a party's unfamiliarity with the Court's system or by the failure of a party's equipment. The parties will be required to present their cases without the aid of the electronic evidence presentation system in the event that the system is unavailable due to the party's unfamiliarity, due to equipment failure or due to any other "technology" delays. ***Please note that the Court's staff cannot work on and/or provide support for any non-court equipment.***

- In addition to familiarizing themselves with the Court's electronic evidence presentation system in advance of the hearing/trial, the parties must familiarize themselves with their own equipment and how to connect their own equipment with the Court's system prior to the hearing/trial. Specifically, the parties should be familiar with:

- Adjusting the screen resolution on their computer (e.g., 1024x768 or 1680x1050).

- Switching the display on their computer to send video to the Court's A/V system (e.g., Fn + F5, F7, F8 or F9 key).

- Adobe zoom feature.

- The Court strongly encourages parties to bring a backup laptop with power supply, flash drive and or CD that contains all documents if technical issues were to arise.

Electronic Evidence Presentation System Orientation:

- Any party wishing to familiarize themselves with the Court's electronic evidence presentation system ***<u>is strongly encouraged</u>*** to set up an orientation session.

- To do so, please contact Courtroom Services, (502) 627-5600, at least **14 days prior to the scheduled hearing/trial.**

- Orientation will be held in Courtroom 1, 5th Floor (7th St. Elevators), 601 West Broadway, Louisville, Kentucky 40202

- Parties who attend an electronic evidence presentation system orientation should bring the equipment they will use to connect to the system as well as samples of the content they intend to present at the hearing/trial through the system.

Equipment:

- **Electronic Evidence Presentation Inputs.** Video inputs are located at the lectern, counsel tables and courtroom deputy desk. The available input types include VGA and HDMI. ***Parties must provide their own equipment to utilize these inputs.***

- **Evidence Monitors.** Evidence monitors for viewing evidence presented through the courtroom's electronic evidence presentation system are located at the witness stand, lectern, counsel tables, Judge's bench, courtroom deputy desk and law clerk's desk.

- **Document Camera.** A document camera is located at the lectern. The document camera provides zoom capabilities which is controlled by the courtroom deputy.

Figure 2. ***Evidence Presentation Obligations from the Western District of Kentucky.***

Evidence Presentation Obligations

- ***Parties who intend to present evidence electronically via the Court's electronic evidence presentation systems must be familiar with the systems prior to the hearing/trial. No court/jury time will be provided during court proceedings to allow the parties to troubleshoot issues with the parties' equipment or the equipment in the courtroom.*** If a party is unfamiliar with the Court's systems, they are strongly encouraged to attend an orientation with the Court's IT representative ***prior*** to the hearing/trial (see procedures below). The Court will not tolerate any delays during any proceedings caused by a party's unfamiliarity with the Court's systems or by the failure of a party's equipment. The parties will be required to present their cases without the aid of the electronic evidence presentation systems in the event that the systems are unavailable due to the party's unfamiliarity, due to equipment failure or due to any other "technology" delays.

- In addition to familiarizing themselves with the Court's electronic evidence presentation systems in advance of the hearing/trial, the parties must familiarize themselves with their own equipment and how to connect their own equipment with the Court's systems prior to the hearing/trial. Specifically, the parties should be familiar with:

    - Adjusting the refresh rate on their computer (to 60 Hz)
    - Adjusting the resolution on their computer (to 1024x768)
    - Switching the display on their computer to send video to the Court's A/V system (the Court uses the Extron DSC 301 HD compliant scaler and XTP R (& T) HDMI systems at the attorney tables and the Extron DVS 605 compliant scaler and XTP R (&T) HDMI systems at the lectern).

Making the physical connections between the electronic evidence presentation systems and their equipment. The parties are responsible for providing any cable adapters required to connect to their equipment to the Court's systems. For example, to display content from an iPad to the Court's systems, the parties must provide their own iPad-to-VGA or iPad-to-HDMI adapter. ***Please note that the Court's staff cannot work on and/or provide support for any non-court equipment.***

Electronic Evidence Presentation Systems Orientation

Any party wishing to familiarize themselves with the Court's electronic evidence presentation systems ***<u>are strongly encouraged</u>*** to set up an orientation session with the Court's IT staff.

Figure 3. ***Evidence Presentation Obligations from the Eastern District of California.***

There is no excuse. Every court offers training on their evidence presentation system and time in advance of trial to test and QC equipment, from California:

> **Electronic Evidence Presentation Systems Orientation**
>
> Any party wishing to familiarize themselves with the Court's electronic evidence presentation systems ***are strongly encouraged*** to set up an orientation session with the Court's IT staff.
>
> To do so, please contact the courtroom deputy ***at least three (3) weeks before your trial or hearing***. The courtroom deputy will coordinate with the Court's IT representative to schedule a convenient time to conduct the orientation.
>
> Parties who attend an electronic evidence presentation systems orientation should bring the equipment they will use to connect to the systems as well as samples of the content they intend to present at the trial/hearing through the systems.

. . . to Oklahoma:

> **Connecting a computer in the courtroom:**
>
> 
>
> The court will provide the necessary computer cables to get you connected. Your laptop can be connected at counsel table, or at the podium. Please ask the courtroom deputy for assistance regarding your specific needs. Please contact the deputy at least a week prior to your trial or hearing.

. . . to Virginia (which further stipulates that trial teams must present written authorization from chambers to bring in a laptop to orientation—which proves it always pays to read the fine print):

> 2. Orientation prior to any use of the equipment is encouraged. Once you have received approval to use the evidence presentation system, please email the Court Technology Administrator at courtroom_tech@vaed.uscourts.gov to schedule an orientation. Attorneys must attain written authorization from chambers to bring a laptop computer to the scheduled orientation. Orientations are for learning how to use the court's evidence presentation system and testing the attorneys' laptop computer connections. Practicing presentations and preparing witnesses is not authorized.

. . . and every point in between.

2.1.2 What Are the Basic Technical Skills Anyway?

The Evidence Presentation Obligations are as close to a list of basic technical skills that you are going to get from the court. With these obligations in mind, I have expanded the list of "*basic* technical skills" by supplementing them with *companion* skills that are important to know. Mandatory skills are in **bold**; the rest, in plain text, are highly recommended.

1) **Organization**
    a) **Data structure**—where to put data and how to find it
    b) Project plan—how to document exhibits
    c) Time management—how to estimate how long tasks will take
    d) **Establish a routine**—effective habits
2) **The ability to make basic configuration changes to your laptop thru the settings for**
    a) **Power**—for best performance

    b) **Sleep**—turn off "sleep" mode to avoid your computer shutting off in the middle of trial
    c) **Background image**—turn the background to black to create a consistent presentation environment[10]
    d) **Sound**—turn off startup and default sounds
3) **The ability to connect to a video source VGA/HDMI and speakers**
    a) **Troubleshooting cables**
    b) **Changing resolution**
    c) **Extend or duplicate desktop**
    d) Identify monitors
    e) QC the display and courtroom monitors
    f) **Plug in speakers**
4) **Understanding technology choices for**
    a) Exhibit workflow and planning
    b) Aspect ratio of 4:3 or 16:9

2.1.3 Early Planning Considerations

As you move forward with your trial planning, compile lists of your data sources used throughout the case—databases, folders of information, deponent lists, and video. The information should be placed into a project plan, which we will discuss shortly. Many teams make the mistake of only providing partial information to their technology team, thinking, "We don't need to prep 'that guy.'" Undoubtedly, "that guy" always needs to be prepped and it's an expensive, risky, and stressful proposition to prepare last minute.

Start your plan with:

1) A list of data sources
    a) Databases
    b) Folders of information
    c) Production records
    d) Collection information (who, what, and how collected)
2) Transcripts
    a) Who was deposed?
    b) Was the deposition videoed, digitized, and synced to the transcript?
3) Attorney Work Product
    a) What attorney work product will you need at trial?[11]
4) Project documentation
    a) How were files collected, processed and produced?

10. As cute as your kids or pet are, their photos are a poor choice for your desktop background for court.
11. In other words, if offsite what will you need to bring?

2.1.4 Know Your Case Data History

It is helpful to know background info for the exhibits and video being used. Often a trial tech is given the exhibits and video to be displayed and nothing more. Furthermore, teams often limit themselves by *only* using an exhibit database at trial. In other words, teams should have all of the case data available used throughout the preparation of the case so they can provide context and background to exhibits and depositions. For example, what good is a standalone attachment to an email if you don't know who received it, when it was sent, and by whom? The trial tech should know basic info about the exhibits and depositions to understand where the exhibits came from and the data set in case questions come up in court.

For example, in a last-minute substitution of counsel trial, many files were missing that would provide context to exhibits and potentially make new exhibits. Upon review, we found out that raw data collected from custodians was processed using key terms and that family groups of documents (that is, the main document and attachments) were not included unless they had the key terms themselves. Most of the time, if a key term hits one document, the entire family is included in processing—but that's not what happened here. Understanding potential processing issues was therefore helpful in finding a new source of exhibits for use at trial (i.e., the entire family group of an exhibit) and provided further context for the legal team to question witnesses.

1) Collection: How was the electronically stored information (ESI) originally collected from custodians? Was it a forensic collection? Did custodians self-collect? Were key words, dates, or other culling methods used?
2) Processing/Database: How were files processed? Image or native? Where key words, dates or other culling methods used? How were family groups identified and processed?
3) Production
4) Deponent/Video

Collection	Processing/Database
• Targeted forensic collection of all custodians • Culled by date and file type	• Relativity database for early case assessment • Relativity document review database • Culled by date • Family group duplicates identified in database • Native review
Production	**Deponent/Video**
• Documents produced as TIF images • Family groups produced	• 23 depositions • 15 depositions video tapes • 10 depositions synchronized

Figure 4. ***Knowing background information about the data in your case is essential.***

2.1.5 Exhibit Planning

When your case is "of size," contains thousands[12] of pages of exhibits, or has more than a handful videos to synchronize and clip/edit, you must start on a plan well in advance of trial, potentially weeks and months ahead. This gives you time to iron out potential technical difficulties and makes the process cost less because you won't need to pay expedite fees or throw extra bodies at the problem as you approach trial. If you don't have a good idea of the history and kind of data you will be working with, it will be difficult for you to make plans for the exhibits.

This sample timeline shows case milestones at six months, three months, one month, and two weeks prior to trial. It shows the minimum planning necessary to have an idea as to your data population, so it may not be aggressive enough for a particular case you are working on. There is much to consider beyond the minimum, as is discussed throughout this book—but this is a good start.

12. Low, not high, thousands.

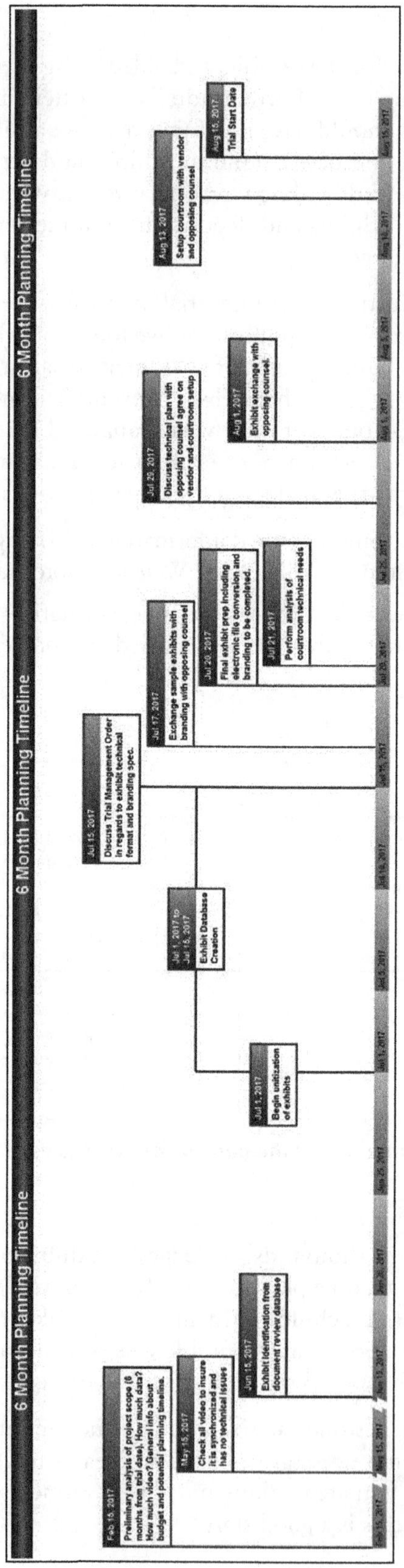

Figure 5. *Planning timeline.*

Six Months	Three Months	One Month	Two Weeks
• Understand the data population—how much data are there? • Get a rough understanding of the size of the potential exhibit population • Estimate the number of videos (and video clipping/editing you must do)	• Create a workflow for identifying video clips and exhibits with legal team • Send video for conversion and synchronization • Identify records that will be exhibits and discuss whether they will be provided in their entirety or unitized into new exhibits	• Start unitizing the exhibits • Start video clipping high-priority witnesses • Discuss potential branding and exhibit naming schemes • Craft narrow Trial Management Order on technology with the court • Exchange sample exhibits with opposing counsel	• Upoad data to the trial presentation system • Begin opening statement creation • Test and QC exhibits • Provide exhibit numbers to legal team for inclusion in outlines

Figure 6. ***Suggested planning milestones.***

One argument quite often made against preparing the technology for trial is that a case might settle before it goes to trial. Perhaps it's a good idea for the legal team to stand down somewhat, but the technical team still needs to have a plan in place. Most teams wait far too long,[13] and then it's a mad rush at twice the price and three times the risk. At that point, you can't even be sure your vendor will be available to come through for you at the last minute. There is a point when tasks just can't get done, regardless of the money and resources being thrown at them. Moreover, last-minute time pressures lower the quality of work output and increase the risk of failure. Advance planning helps you avoid these calamities. Regardless of settlement discussions, there should be an analysis of the potential exhibit population (including videos and video clips) so you can create a timeline and prepare for trial. In the end, you want your support team focused on QC'ing witness outlines and presentation, rehearsing, and reviewing exhibits—not scrambling to find a vendor that can synchronize videos on a Saturday or dealing with unitization and exhibit creation issues.

What other obligations are you creating for yourself and team by not fully understanding the technical ramifications of your choices? How might you make the process more efficient by bringing in your technical people at an early stage of planning? Below are some of the basic items you will want to understand as you plan ahead for trial. These considerations are important because you need to know what it will cost and how much it will take to go to trial, as well as your obligations and responsibilities to the court and opposing parties. For example, obligating yourself to OCR 100,000 pages of exhibits at .02 cents per page is $2,000. Branding, conversion, and other prep work can lead to even higher costs. Unitizing records, video editing, and file conversion can add significant time commitment and cost. Legal teams often obligate themselves (at significant cost) to converting exhibits from one format to another when, in fact, their existing format would have been just fine. (Teams make this mistake *all the time.*)

- **The court's technical requirements, per the Trial Management Order (TMO)**
  - Are the tech requirements specific? If not, have you considered making them specific to avoid burden shifting with opposing counsel?
  - Is there a required image format?
  - Are there branding specifications?
- **Opening statement and closing argument**
  - How many slides are there?

13. Literally, an order is given to do "nothing," so of course nothing happens.

- Are custom animations or graphics needed?
- Are there video clips?
- Do exhibits need callouts or highlighting?

- **Size of the case**
  - Is this a big case or a small one?[14]
  - Volume of exhibits?
  - Number of videos?
  - Estimated number of edits to each video?
- **Branding, redaction, and unitization**
  - What are the court and legal team preferences for branding?
  - What steps are necessary to brand the documents?
  - How complicated are the branding requirements?
  - How much redaction?
  - How much unitization?
- **Technical difficulty**
  - Are there issues with file size or corruption?
  - Are image formats compatible with trial presentation software?
- **Format**
  - Converting from native or an image format?
  - What format are exhibits currently in?
  - Does the tech have the tools or a vendor to convert and conform files to the TMO?
- **Tracking**
  - How will the team maintain version control of exhibits?
  - How will exhibits be tracked via a project plan?
- **Pace of the case**
  - Are there many requests, or a few?
  - Will there be a long time to prepare, or is it last minute?
- **Support**
  - Is the case staffed appropriately?
  - Will there be support needs late at night or on the weekends?
  - How will emergencies and high-priority items be communicated?
  - Do you have the right equipment to do the job?
  - What about vendor support?

---

14. Many small cases have big-case needs, so every case's *technical* needs should be analyzed separately from their *legal* ones.

2.1.6 Time Management

Understanding the amount of time it takes to undertake certain tasks is the first step. Being able to provide a time "rule of thumb" to legal teams so that you can manage their expectations and assist with planning is an important one. Legal team members will often ask you to undertake tasks without knowing the full impact of their request. They may have the impression that their trial tech can just punch up some issue codes and the task will be automated and easy—which is simply not accurate. In the case of video, for example, it can take three or four times the clip length to edit it. That means editing a ten-minute video could take forty minutes—or more. Think about it: you have to identify the page and line range, remove the sections that were requested, then review for objections and other colloquy for removal—and don't forget you still need to QC the finished video clip by actually watching it. You *can* create video clips without reviewing internal content fairly quickly—but do you really *want* to? (Not reviewing the clip doesn't sound like good QC, does it?) Therefore, communication needs to flow two ways so that everyone is on the same page as to what needs to go on screen and when. As a trial tech, you are wise to push back at times and ask for clarification and prioritization of tasks so the legal team can make informed decisions. In turn, legal team members need to prioritize and use discretion when assigning tasks so you, as their trial tech, can easily manage the workflow.

Time Rule of Thumb Guide for Trial Tech Tasks (Includes Time Spent for QC and Revision)	
Task	**Time**
Video Edit with objections and colloquy removed	3-4 times clip length
Video Edit without review of internal content	10 minutes per cut
Powerpoint slide with image and callout	20 minutes per slide
Load, Copy, Export Data	volume dependent
Reunitize individual records	5-10 minutes per record
Stage callouts for an exhibit	5 - 10 minutes per stage

Figure 7. ***Time estimates for tasks when QC and revisions are included.***

Another example would be how teams manage the time for their opening statement and closing argument. Opening is usually well planned and thought out ahead. Closing takes into account the issues and points made at trial and counters opposing counsel's points. Thinking from the beginning about the time it will take to create your closing presentation is an important time management step. Start by noting your slide ideas for closing from the very beginning of trial. If possible, create rough versions or placeholders for slides throughout the trial 1) to get things started and 2) so you don't lose potentially good slides or run out of time to create them. How is it possible that a single slide take twenty minutes to create? Think once again about the creation and editing process: you must place the image on the page, resize it, and apply the appropriate graphics and highlights. The slide is then reviewed by the legal team, which might request changes to the heading, image placement, and highlighting choices. By the time the entire process is complete, it can take quite a bit of time to create a slide.

Last, the time that it takes to create exhibits and presentations for trial is often dependent upon teams doing it right from the start of the case. For example, how are the exhibits organized and named on the network? It can take forever to find data if it isn't organized. Video designations are dependent on the issue codes used being accurate in deposition management software—otherwise, someone is QC'ing designations. It's important that teams get their technical house in order from the beginning so that the entire litigation process runs smoothly.

2.2 Create a Project Plan

Much of this book is focused on obtaining the appropriate technical equipment and planning. However, it is in the preparation of electronic exhibits that often lacks planning and is the crucial difference between success and failure. It is important to understand, months or weeks ahead of time, the details for the case data that will be used for exhibits. Understanding the volume of exhibits, the number of exhibits the team anticipates, and the unitization[15] needs for exhibits, as well as the video volume and number of clips, will shape decisions about the staffing, equipment, and skills necessary to support the trial. For example, if the team plans to unitize exhibits (that is, to take pages from one or more documents to create a new exhibit or change the page boundaries of an existing document), this could place a tremendous burden on the team. Knowing it in advance is very important.

A project plan is essential to a successful trial. No two trials are alike, so having a plan in place to deal with project milestones and tracking is important. Many teams blow it by waiting until they are 100 percent certain the trial is a go and do *no preparation* until that time—inevitably resulting in a mad rush at twice the price and half the sanity.

Because trials come in all shapes and sizes, the sample project plan below is merely a starting point. The particulars of your case needs should be analyzed, with tasks added to the list. A project plan should assess the five key technical areas of your case (though by no means should planning be limited to the *technical* portion of the case).

1) **Trial timelines**
   a) When will the trial begin?
   b) What is at stake?
   c) Budget?
   d) What are the milestones for preparation?
   e) How long will it take to get exhibits prepped and ready? How many?
   f) How much video and clipping will need to take place?
2) **Exhibit and data analysis**—what workflow needs to be in place to prepare the exhibits for trial? Just as no two trials are the same, neither are any two data sets.
   a) Processing decisions (e.g., black and white versus color) made early in plan may need to be revisited.
   b) What are the branding requirements for court, and how will we comply? (More on this topic in Chapter Three, Exhibit Creation and Workflow.)
   c) Is document unitization necessary?
   d) How should the TMO be crafted for technical needs?
3) **Exhibits**
   a) Include a list of all exhibits and their page ranges. (This information should also be in an exhibit database, but it is handy to have it as a hard copy or in a spreadsheet on your local computer.)
   b) Date exhibit was added?
   c) Was the exhibit admitted?

15. Unitization is when you change, add, reorder, or delete pages from a document. Multiple documents can often make up a single exhibit and are part of the unitization process. Also called reunitization.

4) **Depositions and Video**

   a) Deponent names and dates.

   b) Was the depo video-recorded? Digitized and synced to the transcript? QC'd?

   c) Include a list of all video and their deposition page ranges.

   d) Designation plan—how will clips be identified? What issue codes were used?

   e) How many clips will need to be created?

   f) Each clip should get a name or code as it is prepped so it can be included in the legal team outline (e.g., Alan Smith Depo page 4 line 10 to page 5 line 20 is clip "AS01"[16]).

5) **Presentation Options**

   a) Trial tech in-house or consultant?

   b) Will you need custom graphics?

   c) Opening/closing slide needs?

2.3 What to Track in a Project Plan

What a trial tech needs to track is different from what a lawyer or paralegal needs to track. Some of the data points mentioned below— the date added, its admission status, deponent, etc.—might be helpful to be tracked in the team trial exhibit database, but typically Excel works just fine for creating the lists and reports that make up a project plan. I've always found it helpful to create a daily report from the database and keep it in a three-ring binder in the courtroom for team use, and which I also keep with me at all times.

Exhibits

- Admitted status
- Redacted status
- Date added during trial
- Page range

Deposition/Video

- Deponent
- Volume
- Video sync status (*example*: Is the John Smith video synced and ready to go?)
- Deposition page range
  - Also helpful if page range goes over two different transcripts (Volume 1 and Volume 2)
  - Sometimes subsequent volumes page numbering may start over at 1 rather than continue from previous deposition
  - Page range matches the paper deposition

16. This code should be inserted into the correct legal team outline.

- Clip name and page/line range
- Date of deposition (Legal teams get confused sometimes on page number, volume, and date. Dates often help clear up that issue.)

The information in a project plan helps you 1) know your data population (*example*: when someone mentions Exhibit 252 and your tracking only goes to Exhibit 211, that means there is a problem); 2) ensure accurate data entry (I like to create cheat sheets containing this information—particularly the video clips so that I can easily call them up without looking to the computer); and 3) do valuable QC because it allows you to compare what is in the trial presentation database against what is in the shared-team trial exhibit database or in paper binders. *Note*: We often compare page by page what is in the trial exhibit database and what is in paper binders or other data sources to ensure we have an accurate page count. Moreover, knowing the date of depositions taken often helps avoid the embarrassing error of the legal team using the wrong reference. In the end, these are all potential QC points to check and compare against the attorney outline and your various sources of data.

This list above is the minimal information necessary that a trial tech should track; there are far more data points that may need to be tracked, depending on size of the case or team. For example, trial techs may need to know *if* and *when* exhibits were admitted or whether it has been redacted (and if the redacted or unredacted version should be used). An exhibit that has not been admitted should *never* be put on screen without first alerting the legal team and giving members an opportunity to properly admit it.

Exhibit Tracking (When Added)

Exhibit Page Range			
Exhibit Number	**Exhibit Begin**	**Exhibit End**	**Admitted?**
TX0001	TX0001-0001	TX0001-0052	No
TX0002	TX0002-0001	TX0002-0777	No
TX0003	TX0001-0001	TX0001-0052	Yes

Date Added	Exhibit Begin	Exhibit End
1/5/2018	TX0001	TX0250
1/10/2018	TX0251	TX0276
1/11/2018	TX0277	TX0278
1/12/2018	TX0279	TX0366
1/13/2018	TX0367	TX0401
1/14/2018	TX0402	TX0407
1/15/2018	TX0408	TX0556
1/16/2018	TX0557	TX0888

Figure 8. ***Tracking exhibits' page range, admitted status, and date of admission.***

Deposition Ranges and Clip Prefix Information					
Deponent Name	**Beg Depo Range**	**End Dep Range**	**Prefix Used**	**Date**	**Video Synced?**
John Smith	1	153	JS	12/10/2018	No
Hazel Bales	1	99	HB	5/10/2018	Yes
Olivia Underwood Volume 1	1	156	OU1	6/10/2018	Yes
Olivia Underwood Volume 2	157	335	OU2	7/15/2018	Yes
Bob Stoops	1	125	BS	8/1/2018	No

Figure 9. ***Track the page range of transcripts, the prefix used, date of transcript, and whether video has been synced.***

Video Clip Identification		
Deponent	**Clip ID**	**Page Range**
Hazel Bales		
Hazel Bales	HB1	3:05 – 8:02
Hazel Bales	HB2	15:09 – 15:17
Hazel Bales	HB3	23:22 – 24:07
Hazel Bales	HB4	86:09 – 93:01
Olivia Underwood Vol 1		
Olivia Underwood Vol 1	OU1_1	2:01 – 3:15
Olivia Underwood Vol 1	OU1_2	101:08 – 108:12
Olivia Underwood Vol 1	OU1_3	124:05 – 125:11
Olivia Underwood Vol 2		
Olivia Underwood Vol 2	OU2_1	159:18 – 160:02
Olivia Underwood Vol 2	OU2_2	167:24 – 168:03
Olivia Underwood Vol 2	OU2_3	171:01 – 171:11
Olivia Underwood Vol 2	OU2_4	180:22 – 180:24
Olivia Underwood Vol 2	OU2_5	201:09 – 201:24

Figure 10. ***Track individual clips by deponent.***

2.4 Data Organization

Typically, firms have a "matter-centric" way of organizing data that uses the client name (perhaps in number form) and a numerical matter. This is often called the "client-matter" number for billing. It is usually a five-digit client number and five-digit matter number. (So, for example, Shannon Bales, Inc., may have the client matter number of 12345-00001.) This is a great starting point for case organization on the network and is easily transferred to local computers for use at trial. For example, X:\12345-00001 would be the name of the network location where data related to that matter is stored. Then, within that network location there is further organization by application. There could be folders for Databases, Transcripts, Video, Trial Data, or Misc. You can keep the descriptions generic or organize them by application name. Try to limit the number of files in any single folder to 1,500 or less. When a folder contains too many files, it can cause issues when you navigate through them. Finally, try not to use punctuation or other symbols—such as *(^@(*.,*^&%$@—in file names, as symbols can cause problems with pathing to exhibits and videos.

Note that in the image below, you are seeing items organized by application for the client "12345" and the matter "00001" on the C drive.

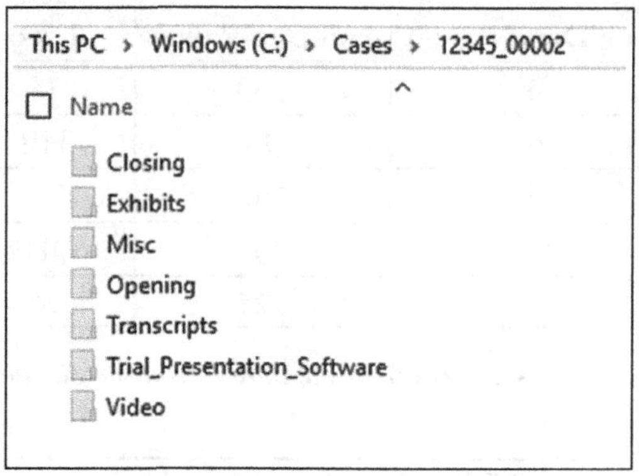

Figure 11. ***Case organization structure.***

Trial data are slightly different and should be organized on the network within the appropriate folder, but it should mirror the organization on the local hard drive of the trial presentation laptop(s) and backup media that will go to court. Anything to be shown in court must be on the trial laptop; thus, taking steps to make it easy to locate should be a high priority. You must keep the same organizational structure among your network storage location, backup materials, and mirrored laptops so that if you have a computer problem, you can simply change the paths in your trial presentation tool of choice and continue moving forward.

The folders shown in Figure 11, above, are:

- **Closing**—for closing materials and presentations.
- **Exhibits**—for documents that have been processed for trial and that comply with the TMO branding and naming requirements. This is the "loading zone" for exhibits to be placed into trial software; they can be in a variety of image formats (e.g., PDF, TIFF, JPG, PNG, etc.).

  Note: You should have a backup copy of the exhibits before processing and branding in case you must make changes or there is a mistake.
- **Opening**—for opening materials and presentations.
- **Trial_Presentation_Software**—for the trial presentation software you are using (e.g., TrialDirector, Sanction, OnCue, etc.). This is where I place the "case file" for my chosen software. This folder is optional, and you can keep the default locations if you are uncomfortable storing the software here.
- **Transcripts**—for transcripts and depositions, with or without video. Video files should remain within the deponent folder they are associated with rather than being saved in a large, unorganized folder that contains all of the case videos.
- **Video**—for standalone videos. This is typically non-deposition video.

Note: when I add exhibits, I place them in dated subfolders (YYYYMMDD) in the Exhibits folder, as demonstrated in the graphic below.

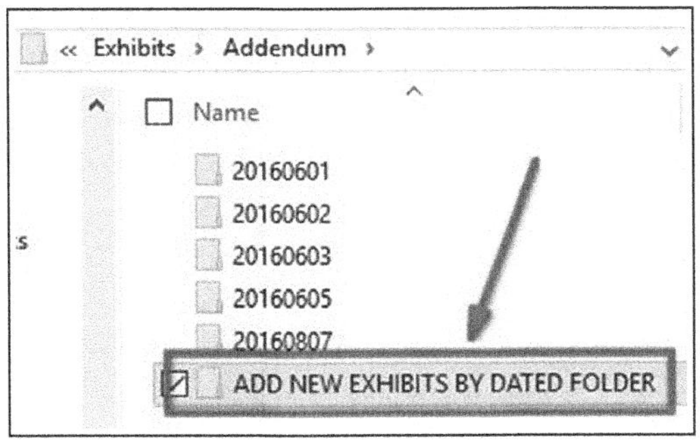

Figure 12. ***Addendum folder.***

Remember to maintain pristine files of your source documents in case there is a technical issue with the work product, the exhibits are renumbered, or you encounter one of the many other problems that can pop up and send you back to the drawing board.

As a final note, keep in mind that teammates will need to be familiar with how (and where) you organize your data, so your project plan must relay this information.

2.5 Staffing

Just as with legal services, there are many options for staffing trial presentation staff. Legal teams can have someone whose job is to take preprocessed data (i.e., exhibits), place them in a presentation system, and project them onscreen. Indeed, this may be all that some legal team members think a trial tech's duties are—but that would be just scratching the surface of what a trial tech can do for them.

The relationship between lawyer and trial tech should be close—such that the trial tech understands the team's goals, knows how to complement the lawyer's unique style, and has practiced using the technology with the lawyer. The trial tech must understand 1) what the document contains so he knows what to emphasize with callouts, zooms, or highlights; and 2) what the lawyer prefers for annotations and emphasis. For example, is it acceptable to highlight information by using arrows, underlines, or another annotation, or must yellow highlighting be used exclusively?

A good trial tech will make recommendations based on the viewing environment in the courtroom, use techniques of displaying evidence that differentiate them from the other side, be aware of burden shifting and how to respond to it, and have input into the TMO to provide efficiency to the legal team. They will also understand how to support the entire team with efficient processes to keep them working throughout the trial. This level of consultation only occurs though if the tech has been brought in early enough and empowered to help, *or* for particularly large teams that they have brought in additional techs to provide the appropriate case coverage. Including coverage after the trial tech goes back to get some rest for the day.[17]

If your tech is overburdened with tasks, the attention to detail will drop and only the most urgent items will receive attention. The technical team needs to be given enough time—*and people*—to do a quality job.

2.6 Exhibit Exchange

Exhibits exchanged with the other side are the subject of the TMO, which sets out the rules for the management of the case. It is a mutually beneficial document that should discuss the technical format of the exhibit exchange and any branding (more on branding in Chapter Three, Exhibit Creation and Workflow). If there is no TMO (such as in an arbitration), parties must establish rules for exchanging data throughout the case.

17. It's important that the trial tech is well rested enough to be responsive and alert in the courtroom.

Typically, there is a large exchange of exhibits with opposing counsel a few weeks before trial and then new exhibits are added throughout the entire process. New data should be stored first in a network location and kept in a pristine, untouched state, while a copy is sent for processing by a vendor or the tech team. As the new data is received back, it should be organized by dated folder and added to a project plan so that you can easily tell when exhibits were received.

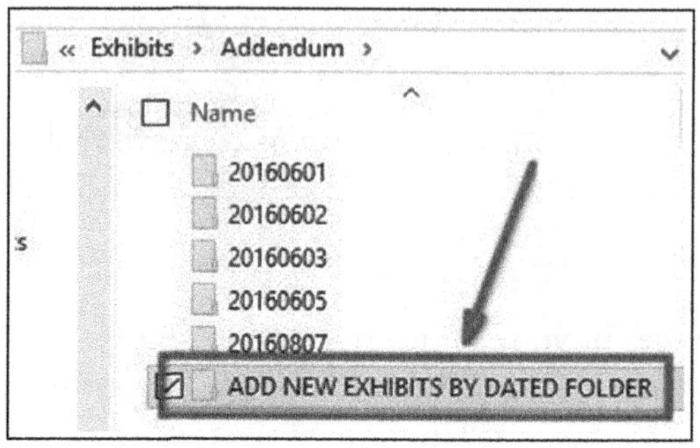

Figure 13. ***Add new exhibits by dated folder.***

2.7 Effective Courtroom Habits

As you move into trial, it's very important to establish routines not only for your sleeping and eating,[18] but also for your technical responsibilities. You need to be fresh and alert in court, so know your limitations as both a trial tech and a human being. When trial techs arrive in court at the same time as the trial team, the day is already getting off on the wrong foot. Trial techs should be at the courtroom when it opens so they can set up and test their equipment for the day's proceedings. (This recommendation is also true for right after lunch, when you might have to take your laptop with you.) Make no mistake—it is a pretty great feeling to walk in with your large team, but it may not be the best idea. Also, try not to bunch up into a herd or communicate wildly or loudly with the team.[19]

Effective Trial Habits				
Establish a routine	Arrive early (before the legal team or at court open in the AM)	Test equipment and presentation after breaks and lunch	Have a backup plan	Practice

Below are my recommendations for creating an effective court routine:

- Do the same thing *every day* and in the same order. Think *Groundhog Day*.[20]
- Arrive early.
- Set up and configure laptops as soon as you enter the courtroom. It is your top priority to get the trial laptops up and running.[21]

18. Eat healthy foods, and avoid repetitive meals of nothing but sandwiches and pizza.
19. The same goes in court as well. Keep it professional and the drama out of it. The same goes if you win—no wild celebration (in court).
20. Including setting up redundant wakeup calls and alarms to ensure you wake up.
21. It is almost impossible to troubleshoot equipment once court is in session.

- Plug in peripherals in the same order.
- Start your computer the same way every day, usually from complete shutdown ("powered off").
- Test your trial database the same way every day.
- Have test images that are appropriate for your aspect ratio.
- Have a sound you can play in open court to test audio speakers.
- Walk on top of your tape and cables daily to ensure there are no loose edges or damage.
- Check with clerk regularly and ask if is everything OK.
- Be a good guest: clean up your area.

Figure 14. ***Rest your trial techs, or they will be a zombie in the courtroom. (Image by Rachel Bennett.)***

As we move forward in this book, there are highly detailed chapters about exhibits, equipment, and courtroom planning that will cover items and tasks that people often miss when they are learning and doing trial presentation. In the end, you need to do your due diligence and find the equipment and software that are right for you.

Chapter Three

Exhibit Creation and Workflow

"Success depends upon previous preparation,
and without such preparation there is sure to be failure."

—*Confucius*

The use and/or exchange of electronic exhibits entail a variety of technical tasks to prepare files for use in trial presentation systems, but also to comply with court rules, agreements with opposing counsel, and personal preferences. The process is not unidirectional, but rather an iterative one, in which earlier decisions may be revisited to improve clarity and accuracy. For example, production records processed in black and white might be processed again in color to create a better, more accurate exhibit.

Treat your trial like a business project. The creation of opening statements and closing arguments, exhibits, video clips, and other trial-related work product are all distinct and separate projects that must be managed. For example, teams often wait until too late to begin working on their closing statement presentation. It is often rushed and important points lost because the project wasn't organized until the end of the trial. Instead, have a gatekeeper responsible for those important points and pass them along throughout the trial. Use placeholder slides (i.e., a slide with just a title and perhaps some notes) for ideas and concepts you may want to flesh out toward the end of trial.

We discussed in the previous chapter the importance of project management. Legal teams need to carefully consider and analyze their technical options because decisions are often made without considering the time, expense, or labor it will take to achieve them. A plan for your exhibit needs is essential because there are many diverse goals, such as exchanging exhibits with opposing counsel and complying with court-mandated specifications negotiated in the Trial Management Order (TMO). Often, using a database to help the legal team manage and track exhibits and maintain version control, in conjunction with workflow and project planning, is a good idea. Legal teams can be their own worst enemy if they didn't consider the burden they have unknowingly placed on themselves by agreeing to certain image formats, naming conventions, or branding schemes. For example, there might be one format agreed upon to exchange with opposing, another necessary for the legal team's document database, and yet another for the trial presentation system. Negotiating an exhibit exchange format that lets you be efficient is an easy win for your team before the trial even starts. Consult with your technical team throughout the trial planning process.

Evaluating the data in your case is an absolutely critical component to trial planning. Since the files have likely already been processed by a vendor and reviewed by a legal team in previous stages of the EDRM, the options can be very limiting, technically difficult, and often have to be revisited. The typical problem areas are electronic file processing, redaction, unitization, branding, and video editing because they can be complex tasks that take time, expertise, and expense—tasks vastly underestimated by legal teams.[1] For example, there may be native productions where files have not been processed to an image format or an Excel spreadsheet (or other file) might contain color,

1. Think back a moment to my discussion on time management in the previous chapter. How long will it take for you to undertake all these tasks?

formulas, or hidden columns that are not visible because of how the document was processed. These decisions often must be revisited and a plan devised on how to get the exhibits into your presentation system.

For the most part, firms should work with a vendor[2] that specializes in legal work, such as e-discovery and legal printing.[3] As the legal industry transitions away from paper docs and toward electronic files, your vendor must have experience processing electronically stored information (ESI), branding, optical character recognition (OCR), and coding. They should be able to deliver data in a variety of formats that will satisfy your exchange obligations and software needs. Your vendor must have the capacity and the expertise to manage high-volume printing and binder jobs to supplement and support your legal team's requirements.[4] They should be adept at a variety of technical deliverables used in trial presentation and document hosting software ranging from Concordance and Relativity to your trial presentation software of choice. Treat your vendor as a member of your team because you may have to call them late at night and after hours—but that said, you should also always be ready to go it alone in case of emergencies or last-minute needs.

Your legal team may need help understanding the impact of their requests on you, their trial tech, and how the requests might monopolize your time. The additional time and work might be better spent on preparation and other support tasks, so having a conversation about the difference between a simple trial exhibit naming convention and a potentially difficult one is important. In other words, ask, "How long will this take?" because there is often a disconnect between an idea and the reality of its execution. Look again at our time estimate table, below. Clearly, it is not a good idea to send hundreds of video clips to the trial tech if there is a low probability they'll be used and it will take days to clip them—but requests like this happen all the time.[5] After all, most trial teams would likely prefer their trial tech to be working on improving presentations or practicing presentation timing rather than clipping video that has a low probability of being played and can be approached in a more efficient way such as being played "on the fly."[6]

Time Rule of Thumb Guide for Trial Tech Tasks (Includes Time Spent for QC and Revision)	
Task	**Time**
Video Edit with objections and colloquy removed	3-4 times clip length
Video Edit without review of internal content	10 minutes per cut
Powerpoint slide with image and callout	20 minutes per slide
Load, Copy, Export Data	volume dependent
Reunitize individual records	5-10 minutes per record
Stage callouts for an exhibit	5 - 10 minutes per stage

Figure 1. ***Time estimates for tasks when QC and revisions are included.***

2. Copy shops are now "imaging" vendors.
3. The average Kinko's would be lost as to the in's and out's of legal printing. Choose a vendor who specializes in legal work.
4. War rooms often resemble a copy shop and are busy 24/7.
5. This is the number one area that partners change their mind in once they have a comfort level with the technology. Having some items cut in advance is a good idea, as spending days editing hundreds of items is a waste of time.
6. I'll talk more about video options later. "On the fly" is playing a video that has not been precut.

To the extent that a team can help itself, it should try to take a "one size fits all" approach, in which it uses the same files for the team's internal use, the exchange with opposing counsel, and the trial presentation. Firms often agree to one format with opposing counsel, while needing another format for their document database, and yet another format for their trial presentation system, which creates great deal of redundant work. But "one size fits all" is entirely possible if, to your own benefit and efficiency, you can negotiate your preferred technical specification into the TMO. This maneuver would leave just a little fine-tuning for you to get the files presentation-ready.

3.1 Initial Considerations

The old adage of KISS—"Keep It Simple, Stupid"—definitely applies here. Some of the initial considerations when contemplating exhibits are outlined below, and should help your legal team gauge how much work the case will need so you can create time and cost estimates for planning, preparation, budgeting, and staffing. Many teams underestimate the amount of time it takes to comply with their own preferences, let alone the burdens added by the court. For example: overly complex branding or naming schemes, or taking on all redaction, unitization, or exhibit creation tasks for *both sides* without considering the added work, cost, or staffing burden. These tasks should not be contemplated without including the appropriate technical resources in the conversation.

Trial is very much a team effort, but if legal teams overburden their tech, they will potentially suffer with quality control and technical issues in court. Trial techs expect to put in many late nights, but we all have our limits. Trial techs are often a "single point of failure" in the courtroom, and upon return from court, teams should get their trial tech started ASAP on the next day's tasks, rather than waiting until after dinner or a workout to get them started. Legal team members need to prioritize and use discretion when assigning tasks so the tech can manage the workflow in conjunction with team priorities. Communication needs to flow *two ways* so that everyone is on the same page as to what needs to get done (and what *can* get done).

The tech should analyze exhibits that go into the trial presentation system.[7] PDFs of exhibits that have been OCR'd (that is, scanned with optical character recognition software and rendered as "image only," rather than text) are great for general legal team use and for beginning trial techs, but they are not a good idea for your trial presentation system. Each time you call up an exhibit for display, your trial software has to open the file, and if the file is enormous, it may take too long to open. This is true of any large-size electronic exhibit, and it can also occur with multipage TIFF, AutoCAD, and video files. Hence, you must test what you have and how it works so there will be no surprises in the courtroom. Look at the file sizes of documents by going to the folder in which they are saved and view the "size" column. If there are some large outliers, then test opening them to ensure they can come up quickly and under stress. Moreover, I recommend you test exhibits at the resolution the presentation will be *played in*. Don't just call up a single exhibit and confirm that it works; use your witness outline and call up both your big files and all of your file *types*. How do both the computer and exhibit react when you call up and take down several types of files, multiple times, with enlargements and highlighting? Typically, if you're using PDF, you might consider not having OCRs (i.e., "image only" PDFs) in the trial presentation system; if they are still large in file size or the number of pages, break them up into manageable pieces. Some techs prefer using a single-page TIFF file, as it ensures that you won't have extremely large or difficult-to-open files lurking in your system. I discuss PDF versus TIFF files in detail later in this chapter, but the takeaway now is that you must stress-test your exhibits and witness outlines so that you can adjust and modify any problem files and thus avoid surprises in court.

7. This is the "fine tuning" I previously mentioned.

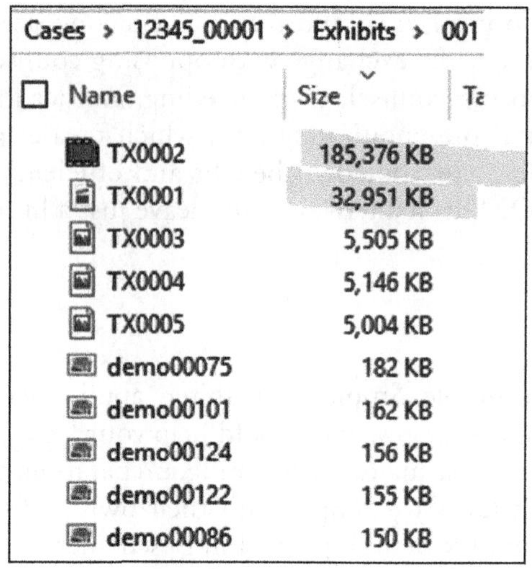

Figure 2. ***Beware of large file size exhibits that might slow down or crash your presentation system. Sort by file size in Windows Explorer to find large files.***

3.2 Document Authenticity

Document Authenticity is a strategy whereby exhibits are presented in as original a state as possible, along with providing a description (e.g., email, attachment, contract, memo, manual, etc.) of the document, when and by whom it was created, and other relevant information that aids in building the credibility of both the document *and* the legal teams, by virtue of being open and honest about the exhibit. Being open, honest, and "authentic" means providing context (rather than just bits and pieces) of a document to establish credibility with decision-makers.

Revealing a document's imperfections demonstrates to decision-makers (i.e., jurors, judge) that your side is credible and honest and that you haven't manipulated the exhibits. Imagine for a moment a situation in court where one side puts up an exhibit and it is perfect, straight, and without imperfection. (You might think that is what we trial techs should be doing, right?) Now imagine the other team puts up the same exhibit that shows imperfections—it might be less clear, for example, but it is still clearly authentic. Might some jurors think the documents have been tampered with? Thus, teams should consider how much they want to "improve" documents—if at all. *Note*: Trial techs should not decide on their own whether an exhibit should be changed or "modified." Rather, they should present this strategy as an option and consult with the legal team.

3.3 Exhibit Format Choices: PDF or TIFF?

One of the most basic decisions a trial tech must make is what image format to use in their trial presentation database. A smart plan is to use the same image format for 1) your team's trial exhibit central repository (which could be a database[8] or perhaps a shared folder); 2) your trial presentation database;[9] and 3) exhibit exchange with opposing counsel. It makes incredible sense, doesn't it? But many teams don't even know what technology their firm uses (or that they have options), so they just agree to whatever they are asked.[10]

8. Meaning, a database used by the entire legal team to create work product.
9. Meaning, a database used solely by the trial tech to present exhibits at trial.
10. During such negotiations, bring your nerd with you!

For a novice trial tech, PDF is the clear winner to use in trial presentation tools, but it becomes more of a toss-up as a case or exhibit size becomes bigger and more complex. PDFs are portable and shareable, and can be unitized and redacted with built-in tools featured in the professional (paid) version of Adobe Acrobat. (*Note*: You can find free online versions that offer the same tools.) The ease of use and portability of a PDF is a great benefit to teams that do not have litigation or e-discovery software (or expertise) and can be easily transferred to any computer, along with Adobe Reader, Adobe's free PDF-viewing software. In a pinch, you may not need trial presentation software and can simply open PDF files and view them on a shared screen.[11]

When they are OCR'd, PDFs can be searched using key words. Key word searching has limited usefulness with any kind of volume of exhibits. However, you can "turbocharge" the usefulness and searchability of your exhibits by linking them into a fielded database where bibliographic information like author, recipient, and date can be coded; objective coding like the deponent the exhibit was used with and admitted status; and subjective coding, like legal issue and digests of info the exhibit may contain. This info is coded, meaning a legal team member or vendor (typically, a vendor) will either manually or programmatically type the information into individual fields for searching, thus leveraging a team's ability to search for information. (Otherwise, you would be reading each individual exhibit looking for the desired information, which is not ideal.) The primary issue with a PDF is that it's a single file that contains every page of a document; thus, the size of the file can be quite large and cause a lag time in presentation. TIFF files, in contrast, tend to be small and consistent in file size, so they offer better performance. In some instances, the PDF file size becomes so big that you are spending all day either splitting PDFs into a manageable size or overwhelming and crashing your laptop due to large file size—in which case, you should consider using TIFF images instead.

Regardless of the image format you choose, performance lag time could be an equipment- and software-related issue. You should regularly test your laptops by cycling through numerous exhibits—perhaps every exhibit—to ensure they come up and don't crash or create technical issues. Needless to say, if your computer does not meet or exceed the specifications for the software tools you are using, you are simply asking for trouble. The earlier you can work with the exhibits, the better, as you may need to adjust (and/or acquire) the hardware or software, if you find your particular dataset is just not working. You could also discuss your issues with an imaging vendor to see if there are any techniques to reduce the file size of the documents. For example, you may want to remove OCR from PDF files used in the trial presentation system to reduce their file size. If you have a computer with a higher performance spec, you'll likely be able to open files faster, more smoothly, and with less of risk of technical failure—but in the end, if you have a 500mb or 1gb PDF and you're hoping to open it in ten to thirty seconds, you will likely be disappointed.

The next considerations as to whether to use TIFF or PDF are 1) whether you are using an exhibit database for version control of exhibits; and 2) your comfort level with unitization of database log files. If you have no trial exhibit database, then PDFs can be managed by keeping them all in a central location for team use (e.g., a file folder on the network), so long as the team maintains version control. PDF unitization is easier than TIFF image log file manipulation, so your technical skillset should guide your decision. If these decisions are overwhelming, it's a good sign that perhaps more training is needed or hiring an outside vendor would be a good idea.

11. Using the extended desktop in Windows in this case is very helpful.

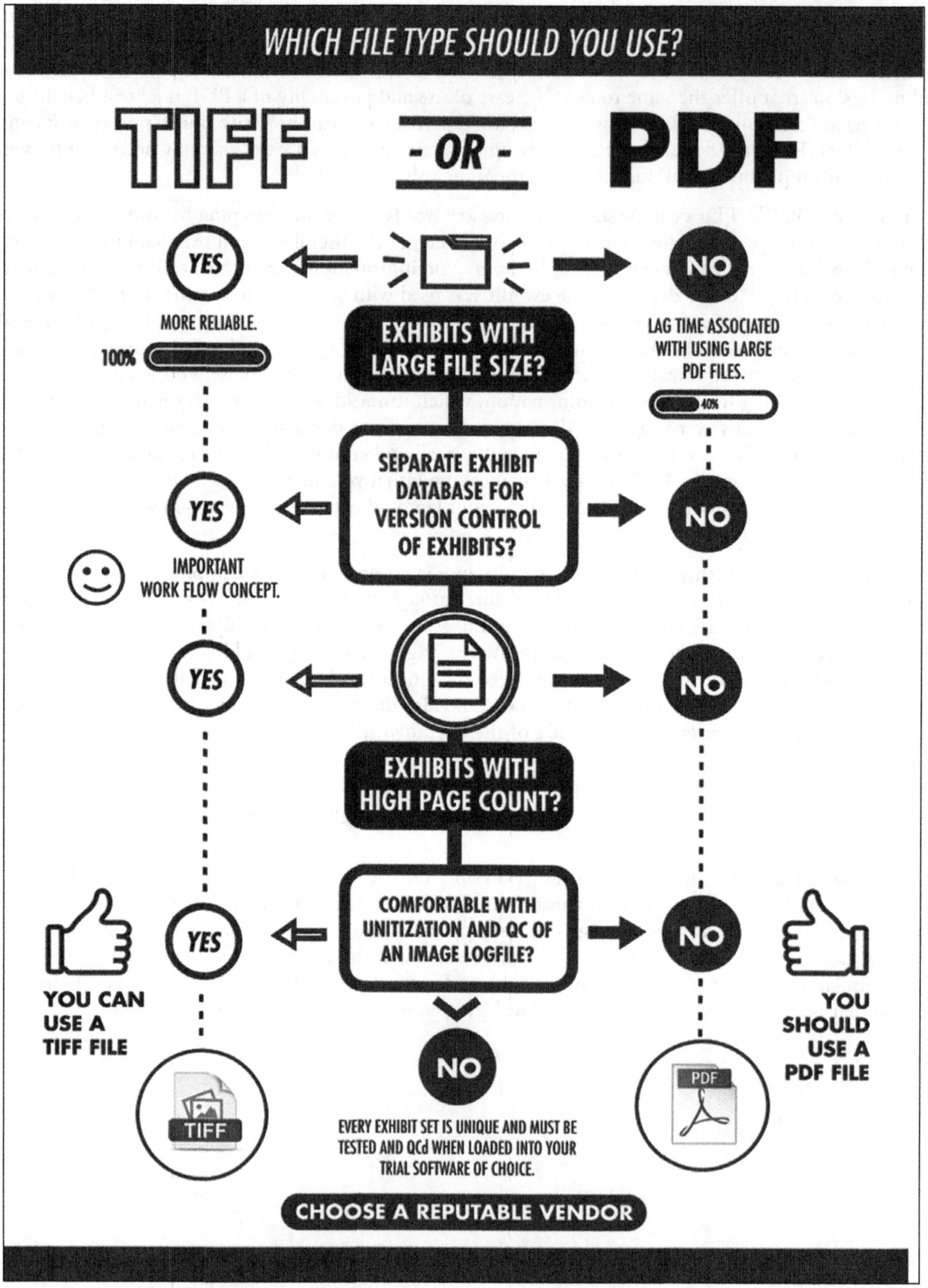

Figure 3. ***TIFF versus PDF decision tree.***

3.4 Exhibit Naming Guidelines

Always orient your legal team to a standardized page-numbering scheme for exhibits—and the earlier, the better, as this creates a consistent record and reduces confusion for jurors and the judge as to which page they need to look at. It also creates a common reference point the entire legal team understands so that they can communicate efficiently amongst themselves.[12] For example, if one team member references a document by its production number, and another member by an old page number, and yet another by its exhibit number, there are bound to be problems.

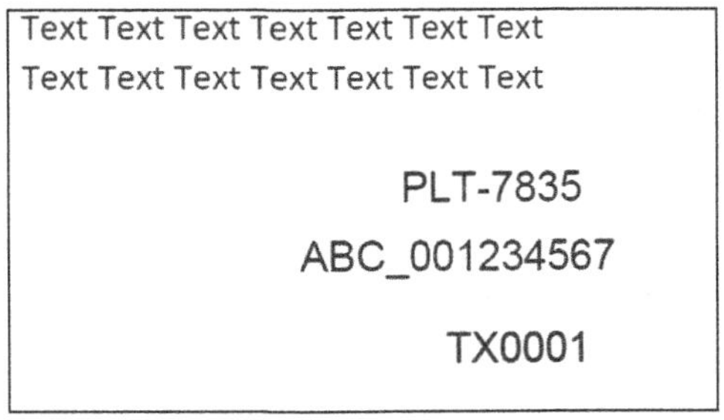

Figure 4. ***Use only the exhibit number when referring to documents within your team and in court (not old numbers).***

There are slightly different guidelines for naming PDF or TIFF format exhibits. Why? Because PDF files are on a document level, and TIFF files on a page level. This means that if you're using TIFF files, every page must be "named," whereas with PDF files, it's typically the entire document—which is usually serialized into individual pages by your presentation system of choice. PDF files should simply be named after the exhibit—"TX0001," for example—with no distinction for pages because it will be assigned by the software. The suggestions below apply mainly to TIFF files, but there is important information to be learned about both formats.

The first rule is KISS—"Keep It Simple, Stupid"—followed by the file name. Such a naming convention gives you your exhibit number, so that you get a consistent log file without alias issues. Some people make the mistake of not naming their exhibits after their exhibit number. Maybe they use, for example, the original file name (The Smith Memo, 12345xyz.doc) or the original production number, rather than the exhibit number. However, using anything but the exhibit number leads to confusion. When the exhibit number equals the file name, it also makes it easier to find a file for QC, troubleshooting, or exchange with opposing counsel.

Here is my list of best practices for devising your exhibit file-naming convention:

- Keep it simple, stupid—no complicated naming conventions. If you can't explain it in ten seconds, your decision-makers won't understand it.
- Exhibits should be named as follows: "TX0001-0001," where "TX0001" refers to the exhibit number and "-0001" refers to the page number of the exhibit. When you use PDF files, the software typically adds the page number. Maintain consistency when you name exhibits.
- Every page of the exhibit should be branded in the lower right corner with the exhibit and page number in the specified format.
- File name = exhibit number. Exhibit number = file name.
- For branding, use 12 or 14 point type (nothing smaller than 10 point), in the lower right corner or center of the page. Format consistently

12. It significantly aids in internal communication as to which records to pull or print, rather than having to correlate between an older naming scheme (like a production number and the exhibit number).

- No spaces. Spaces cause uncertainty and data-entry problems.
- Avoid using the underscore (_) and em dash (–) symbols. Use a hyphen (-) instead. The underscore and em dash each require an extra keystroke (the Shift key), which only slow you down, and potentially introduces confusion when people try to figure out where these keys are on the keyboard as they work on exhibits. In contrast, the hyphen is a single keystroke and is on the numeric pad of keyboards, which makes it even easier to find.
- If you must use the underscore and em dash, then use them in a consistent way. But again, use the hyphen for data input if you must.
  - TX_0001-0001 = no (inconsistent _ and – are hard to input)
  - TX0001-0001 = better (no space or - between TX and 0001 for faster data entry)
  - An advanced method is to remove the TX from exhibit prefixes in your presentation system to avoid typing the additional characters. Speed matters.
- For padding, use the largest number of exhibits and page number to determine how many digits to pad (for example, if your largest document has 11,989 pages, then use five digits for page number padding; if there are 1,000 exhibits, use four digits). Whatever you use, be consistent so you'll always type the same number of digits into your trial presentation system.
- Be aware of this common issue: a legal team member creates the witness outline before exhibit numbers are applied, and maintains the old identification numbers. The solution here to swap out the old exhibit numbers for the new in the outline so that the documents are correctly referenced in court.

In sum, you must make the case to the legal team for adhering to these best practices, as they are clear and easy. Teach them to strive for consistency. Consistency is their friend and yours; keep that in mind, and when you are stressed or in a panic, the information you need will come back to you.

As your technical skills increase, you may want to streamline the naming of exhibits used in your trial presentation system so that they are quick to load. For example, consider naming schemes that take away prefixes, as they are just more keystrokes to perform.

You may encounter a court that mandates that exhibit stickers be placed on the face of a document. In many cases, demonstrating to the court how electronic exhibit branding can produce a substantially similar result is sufficient. Your vendor might be able to electronically brand the sticker onto documents or scan them onto the face of the document, which, in terms of workflow and quality, is less desirable. There are also a number of exhibit sticker utilities[13] for Acrobat that can help get the job done if they must be in the same visual style as traditional stickers.

Figure 5. ***An exhibit sticker. They come in all shapes and sizes.***

13. Visit www.exhibitsticker.com.

3.5 Processing Basics

What is processing? Processing is the workflow used by e-discovery software to separate the metadata from a native (meaning, original) file and/or create a static image of the file as it existed when it was collected.[14] The metadata is typically placed into a database for review and linked to either the native file or an image, or both. Oftentimes, for the sake of efficiency, prior decisions about process were made "in bulk" rather than on a customized, document-by-document basis (i.e., "Here are the rules for processing *all* spreadsheets, documents, and presentations."), or perhaps they were just bad decisions or came through a bad vendor. In any event, at the time, it was simply not considered efficient at the beginning of the case to make individual processing decisions when dealing with thousands, or perhaps millions, of electronic files that resulted in a massive page count. These bulk choices are often revisited immediately prior to trial, as the process may not have produced the best result for display.

Any file can be displayed natively by using either a trial presentation tool or the native application itself, but for true efficiency, the image—PDF or TIFF—is still king. It simply can take too long in court to bring up native versions of a document and get to the right page. Images, however, can also be branded and numbered so that both sides are working with a common reference point; they are also easier to annotate, redact, and work with in general. Nevertheless, sometimes native documents are chosen for particular exhibits. For example, spreadsheets and/or databases are typically displayed in their native version, as they don't usually process well because of how they were created. Or, sometimes the team's goal is to display formulas versus the results or, in the case of databases, a special interface is required to view them correctly. In any event, the team must decide how exhibits will be displayed and what the best options are. I typically will image any native files that are used in court (no matter what the page count[15]) so that there is a common reference point—the exhibit page number—that we all can use. It's important that your opposing side cooperate in this effort because different processing results can be reached by different vendors, choices, and processes, resulting in mismatched results and page counts.

Examples of processing decisions you may want to revisit:

- **Color**. Were documents processed in color or black and white? Does the color carry any meaning in the document?
- **Date/time/time zone**. Were dates processed correctly on the face of the document? This is important to consider, as dates may be set by default to update automatically, such that the date of *processing* is captured rather than the actual date the document was sent or created. Also, what time zone was used for processing? The time zone used for processing could result in a time differential that needs to be explained (for example, an email made in California but processed in New York would result in an incorrect, three-hour differential due to time zones).
- **Formulas versus results**. Were formulas captured at time of processing or results?
- **Formatting**. Was the document formatting used by the electronic discovery processing software accurate?
- **Notes**. Were the notes pages of documents processed or not? Is there valuable information missing?
- **Linked images**. Were the linked images in a document included in the processed version?
- **Comments/markup**. Are there comments or other editing information that provide insight into the document?

14. This is dependent on how the file was collected as well. Was the file collected in a forensically sound manner that preserved the metadata? These are often legal questions decided throughout the life of the case, but our concern here is how it could affect the processing of the native file.

15. The page count used to be a bigger concern when vendors charged per page. If you are still paying per page, you may want to look into paying by the gigabyte or the hour.

- **Native files.** Files that were processed natively may need to be revisited and processed to TIFF so that there is a common exhibit and page number to reference. You may still use the native file in court, but having a TIFF available provides options for display and viewing.
- **Error log.** Are there documents that were corrupt, password protected, or unprocessed that should now be revisited?

3.6 Common Processing Options

The first questions to ask are, 1) what did you choose to see when the data was processed; and 2) what do you need to see? You may want to revisit some of those decisions because of what might be important in your case. Is it the formula in Excel that is a problem, or is it the result? What time zone was the document processed in? If processed in GMT, potentially it will be off several hours from where you are. Does the correct date show up in the email or document? If it wasn't collected or processed correctly, it may not turn into an accurate image. In court, your legal team must explain any mismatches in metadata and/or processing issues. More than once, such mismatches have been used to embarrass someone as they gave testimony, like this:

"Witness, you sent the email to the plaintiff on 1/1/2017, correct?"

"Objection. The document clearly shows it was sent on 1/15/2017."

Perhaps the win in understanding processing is being able to anticipate and explain the issue in court rather than getting caught off-guard. By identifying and understanding the issue, perhaps the document can be recollected and/or reprocessed in a forensically sound manner so the date shows up correctly, or it is in color, or the notes, formulas, or revisions are visible. Ultimately, you must understand why your data looks the way it does so that you now can make informed decisions and, if necessary, revisit prior processing decisions.

Excel	Word	PowerPoint	Time Zone	Use Placeholder Image
Final copy	Final Copy (no revisions)	Slides Only	Pacific PST	Excel – use placeholder for all records
Use print zones	Show comments	Slides and Notes	GMT	PowerPoint – use placeholder for all records.
Show hidden?	Show revisions	Color	Other (user zone choice)	Password protected
Embedded objects	Embedded objects	Embedded objects		Error
Gridlines, graphics, scaling				

Figure 6. ***Common processing options that you may need to revisit for exhibit creation.***

3.7 Branding, Electronic Bates Stamping, and Endorsements

Branding (also called EBS, Electronic Bates Stamping, or Endorsements) is the process of permanently adding text and numbers to every page of an electronic exhibit. Trial exhibit numbers might be branded, along with a statement of confidentiality or other legal language, on a document. Problems occur when naming or branding schemes become overly difficult or require multiple passes in software.

In a document, brands are typically placed on the lower portion on the page, at the left, right, or center (or some combination thereof). When documents are branded there are two techniques: 1) an overlay, which does not change the size of the document but could potentially be on top of existing text; or 2) a footer, whereby the document is slightly reduced in size (typically 2 percent) before the footer is placed, which, because no text is covered by the branding, ensures the document remains legible.

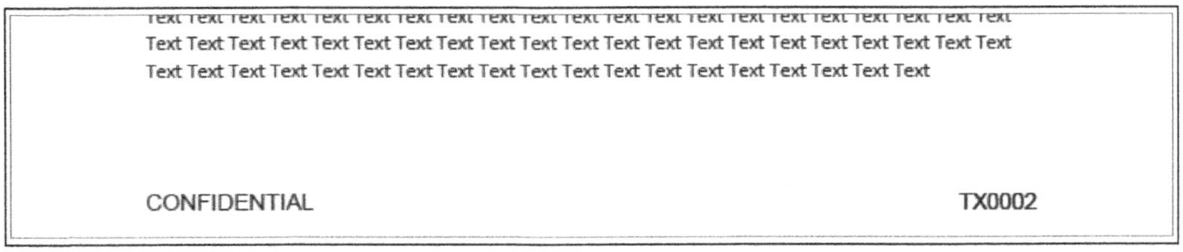

Figure 7. ***Branding in 12-point type, with the exhibit brand on the right and "CONFIDENTIAL" branded on left.***

3.7.1 Redaction

Redaction safeguards sensitive information by removing or blocking it from a document, typically by placing a large black box over the sensitive text (e.g., Social Security numbers, credit card numbers, information blocked by court order or motion, etc.). Redaction markings should be accurate, consistent, and, to the extent possible, not cover any unredacted text. Note that using a white box instead of a black box may look like you are hiding something. If you use a white box, I recommend identifying it with the word "REDACTION."

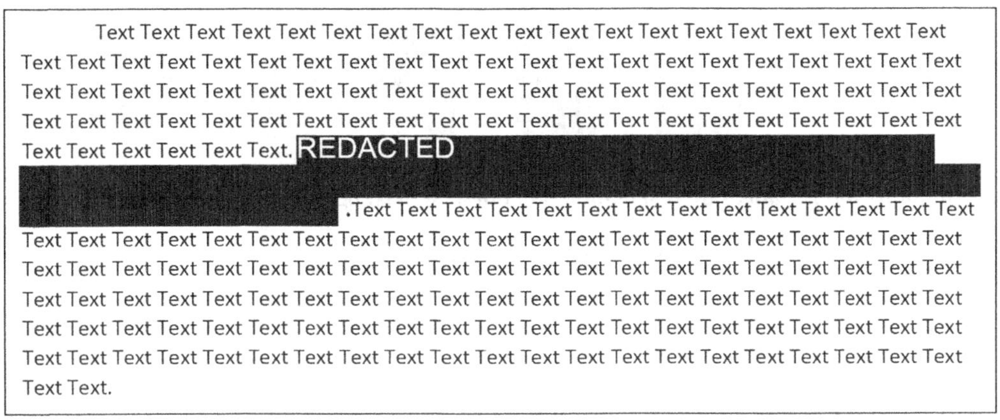

Figure 8. ***Redactions should be neat and "square" with the surrounding text.***

Redactions are one more task that can be added to your workflow. Often, each team member will pitch in to redact documents in a shared exhibit database or the PDF versions. As a trial tech, you should also know how to redact documents in your trial presentation tool of choice, but it may be easier to simply redact in Adobe or some other tool, and import the file into your trial presentation software. I strongly urge you establish as a naming convention that redacted documents need an "R" in their file name (TX0001R-0001, for example) so that you are absolutely sure that a redacted version is being displayed on screen.

You also must keep a pristine, unredacted copy of all exhibits available, just in case the redaction issue is reopened in court and the exhibit must be redone, removed, changed, or supplemented. Some trial tools allow you to "burn in" redactions (i.e., make them permanent) or to toggle them on and off. Again, however, redacting in Adobe and importing the redacted version into your trial presentation database may be easiest. Take great care with redacted documents to ensure the correct one is on display. Practice makes perfect, and this is a crucial area for increased communication between a legal team and its trial tech.

Lastly, accuracy and symmetry with redactions is a skill. Be sure to create consistent and clean redactions.

3.7.2 Unitization

Unitization is when you change, add, reorder, or delete pages from a document. Multiple documents can often make up a single exhibit and are part of the unitization process (which can also be called reunitization). Teams should consider the amount of unitization necessary at trial, as it can be a substantial burden on the trial tech. Due to the capacities of modern computer equipment, it may be more practical to include the entire document.

Always consider the *volume* of document unitization for your case, as it can take a substantial amount of time to take documents apart and put them back together: five to twenty minutes per document (or more, with complexity and QC). PDF has a substantial advantage in its ease of unitization and redaction.

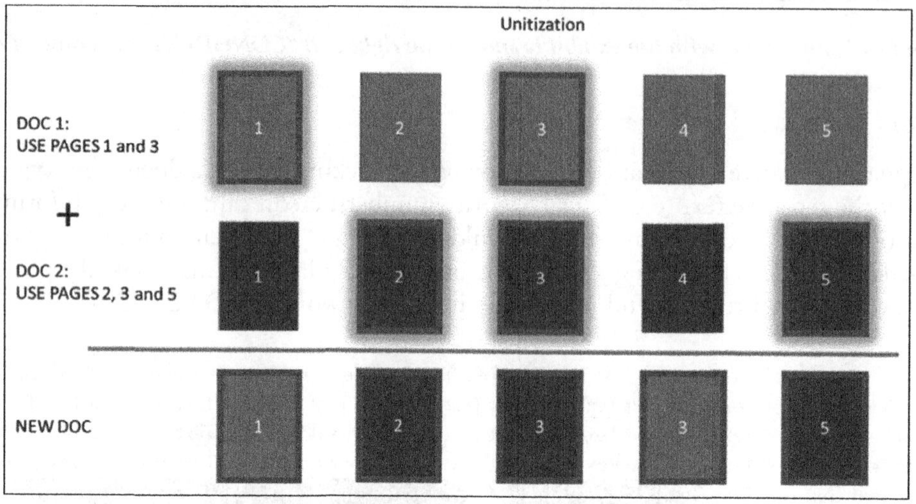

Figure 9. ***Document unitization changes the pagination and physical makeup of a document.***

3.8 Optimizing Files for Use at Trial—Advanced Topic

Once received, exhibits should be placed in a common workspace like a trial exhibit database, shared network folder, or passed around on thumb/external drives. This set of exhibits forms the basis of what will then be loaded into the trial presentation system. Simply copying the files "as is" might be a bad idea, however, because the files could be oversized or suboptimally named for document call-up.

Some techs like to "optimize" their files by running them through Adobe or another image-processing tool to reduce file size or straighten, darken, or lighten the contents of the file. I don't like to do that for the following reasons:

1) It modifies the exhibit as received.[16]

2) It affects document authenticity, a strategy where exhibits are presented in as original state as possible.

3) It reduces image quality.

By running the document through a process that reduces file size, you run the risk of degrading its quality, so always run a test first, load the new file into your presentation system, and see the difference for yourself. And remember, you will be blowing up, enlarging, and highlighting the exhibits at some point, so you will need to test this for quality as well.

Some images must, of course, be improved because they're in terrible shape. For those documents, I suggest an individualized approach that might incorporate the "bad" version, and improved version, and an explanation of the improvements made between the two.

16. There are exceptions to this. Some documents just need to be improved, but it shouldn't be done without consulting the legal team and carefully considering potential negative effects.

You'll want to make sure the legal team is aware of any improvements to a document so if there is an accusation that they were modified it can be rebutted. You may even want to mention to the jury that the document was "improved for legibility" just to be authentic and honest.

If you are using PDF files and some are large or slow to load, you may try removing the OCR from them to see if that helps with performance. If not, break down larger files into smaller ones to ensure that they load quickly.

Modifying the file names in bulk (usually by using a rename utility, like Total Commander[17] or UltraEdit,[18] and potentially by modifying an image log file) to remove prefixes from exhibits can speed up loading the individual exhibit. I keep the numbering scheme uniform so that I always know the number of digits needed to call up exhibits. When exhibits are padded with different length page numbers, exhibit call-up issues can occur if you don't know the number of pages for each record.

Think "fewer digits = faster data entry."

Before: TX0001-0001

After: 0001-0001

3.9 Workflow

Every law firm has a different technical tool kit[19] and every trial has a unique data set, so there is no one-size-fits-all solution. The important takeaway is that you prove your workflow by practice, setting expectations, and testing. If you are working with a vendor, this means you will send several tests to the vendor to "prove" their work. If you are converting and branding the files yourself, this means you should test both on-site and in your war room or working location to ensure everything is working and going according to plan.

Just like a widget factory, legal teams need to create a workflow that churns out exhibits the same way every time—only your widgets are exhibits. Your legal team will be able to create the outlines, binders, and other work product that is necessary throughout the trial because the team knows it can rely on your workflow to handle anything they (or opposing counsel) toss your way.[20] Many teams are thrown into disarray and are unable to create work product (or else create low-quality work product) because they simply did not contemplate the issues in advance and are tested "under fire" during trial to produce the work product. You, in contrast, will have planned for these issues in advance. As I said earlier, every trial is unique, so testing and validating your workflow process before the trial starts is absolutely critical—and by testing, I mean providing sample files and issues to the vendor, and leading a team discussion to ensure everybody is on the same page.

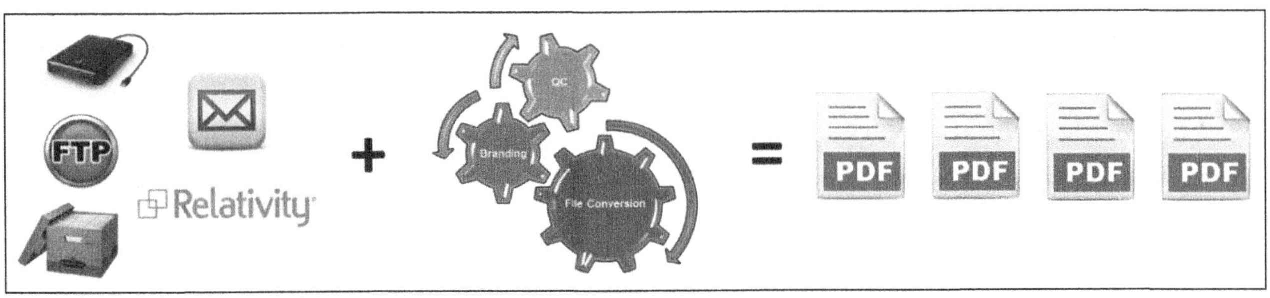

Figure 10. ***A proven workflow efficiently results consistent exhibits from multiple types of data.***

17. Total Commander is available at https://www.ghisler.com/. It should be part of every trial tech's standard tool kit.
18. UltraEdit is available at http://www.ultraedit.com/.
19. That is comprised of hardware, software, budget, and technical expertise.
20. Many legal teams don't comply with the technical requirements of their trial, as set forth by the judge, in the TMO.

You may find yourself having documents dumped onto your team[21] late at night that will require an inordinate amount of work to prepare for the next day's trial. It is your exhibit prep workflow and the team's ability to understand the steps necessary to prepare exhibits (along with exceptions that may require an alternative workflow) that will allow you to stay ahead of the competition and create a quality work product for trial. Specialization is your friend—make sure everybody knows how to do their job and what the expectation is.

Having an *efficient* and *proven* workflow is key: the finished exhibit work product not only goes into the trial presentation system, but is also the basis for all other work product for the legal team. Workflow becomes efficient by *exhaustive* testing and refinement prior to implementation, and proven by continuous analysis of the results obtained. I'll take a proven workflow over an untested one anytime. Once a team's workflow is proven, they shouldn't change it in the middle of trial. Always go with what works, not with what is experimental. Trial is much different than the day-to-day office work at a law firm, and only the best lawyers, staffers, and vendors can keep up with demands.

Speaking of vendors, be sure to talk to them in advance about:

- **Service expectations**. Availability (including nights and weekends), project turnaround time, how high-priority projects should be handled.
- **Workflow**. What is the process for sending and receiving work product?
- **Testing**. Have you tested the workflow and service expectations?
- **Dedicated point of contact**. Who is your dedicated point of contact? Are they available 24/7 to resolve issues?
- **Additional services**. Can the vendor do *more* to help you? Can they deliver in a variety of load files and formats? Can they produce an OCR'd PDF set and a non-OCR'd set, along with TIFF (image) files in a variety of deliverable formats? Can they load data into a database template for you, thus freeing you to keep your focus on trial prep and quick and efficient service for the team? Usually, the cost for these services is minimal.

Trial Tip: Post a whiteboard that you update daily with the next day's witnesses and tasks so everyone is on the same page as to priorities. The whiteboard should also list the upcoming witnesses for the weeks ahead, thus giving advance notice to the team.

Successful workflows have the following traits:

- A documented workflow (i.e., procedures that are written down).
- Are a repeatable process—everything is done the same way *every* time, like an exhibit factory.
- Specialization in tasks like branding, conversion, QC, log file creation, and data organization through a gatekeeper.
- Team education on version control issues, communication, etc.
- Will acknowledge exceptions, with strict rules.
- QC steps that are part of the workflow.
- Are planned in advance.

3.9.1 Version Control

Version control is about ensuring that the right version of the exhibit ends up on screen. The worst-case scenario is when an unredacted exhibit is mistakenly presented in court. It is one of the most prevalent problems that come up in court and really can only occur in a handful of ways. In most cases, either the message never made it to the tech or gatekeeper to redact an exhibit or there was a version control issue. This means that someone likely worked

21. Perhaps by your own team!

outside of the established workflow or the exhibit never made it to the tech—again, violations of the workflow that should be setup on every team. If you don't have a document database like Relativity or Concordance, you might consider using a tool like CaseMap to manage exhibits; also, there is always the option of a shared folder on the server or an external drive.

What is most important is that any changes are quickly relayed to the trial tech, as there is no way for a tech to monitor changes to a folder or database unless it is expressly messaged to them or identified in the database with a tag or issue code. Likewise, a trial tech cannot guess if someone has taken files outside of the system to perform a task and the changes never come back. The message should not be in the middle of a giant email sent to multiple team members sent in the middle of the night, but instead a direct message that if not replied to, should be followed up on. That might sound unfair, but what we're really doing is confirming that exhibit changes have made it to the presentation. There is too much at stake not to. Personally, I tend to work larger cases that are staffed 24/7 with a nightshift so that I can get some rest. The nightshift prepares exhibits that are added after I leave, and places them in a dated folder (the Addendum folder, as discussed in section 2.4, Data Organization) that I check at the courthouse when I arrive in the morning.

- Central location to keep and modify exhibits, with communication to advise the tech of changes. Best practices include:
    - Exhibit database
        - Keep and modify exhibits using an exhibit database as the version control system (alternatively, a single folder location that contains the most recent and correct version of exhibits).
        - Keep a pristine, unmodified set of images the tech can go back to if further changes become necessary to the exhibit.
        - Pristine and branded set of exhibits should be placed into a named and dated subfolder for intake of exhibits (i.e., Branded Exhibits, PRISTINE_SET).
    - If no exhibit database, then a central/shared network folder (or external drive, if a small firm)
        - Same considerations as to gatekeeper, communication, one-off tasks, etc.
- Gatekeeper
    - Authorize only a limited number of people (or a single person) to redact exhibits.
    - A plan to handle exhibits when the gatekeeper is unavailable.
- Communication
    - The trial tech *must* be made aware of any changes to exhibits. This *must* be a top understanding and priority for the team.
    - Put rigid communication standards in place, along with reminders, to ensure the trial tech finds out changes have been made outside of the workflow.
    - Need to be contemplated and understood how to fit back into the system for legal team use and integration into the trial presentation system.
    - An email sent in the middle of the night, in a sea of hundreds of others, may not be noticed. Legal teams must confirm with their trial tech that emails have been received (especially after hours).
- A naming scheme for redacted records.
    - Adding "R" to an exhibit name to show redacted—e.g., TX0001R-0001
- One-off tasks for the trial tech must be kept to a minimum.

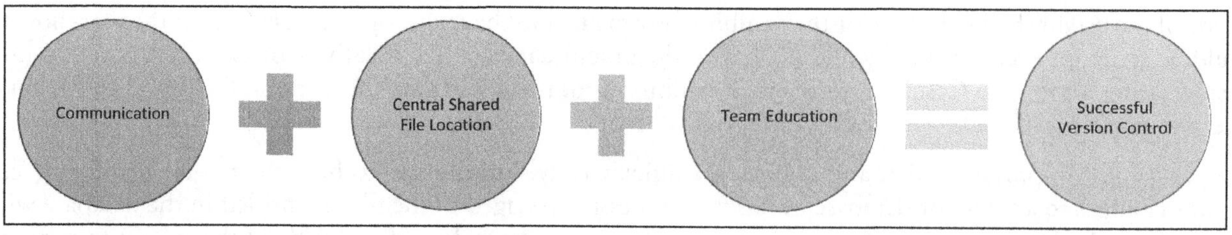

Figure 11. ***Educating the entire team on version control is essential to avoiding embarrassing mistakes.***

3.9.2 Gatekeeper

Whether big or small, every team should have a gatekeeper—even if that means someone is wearing multiple hats. The gatekeeper manages the intake and processing of data so that it is handled consistently, from processing to branding. In the workflow example below, Viviana is responsible for the intake and documentation of the exhibits, performing an initial assessment of the data (e.g., does it comply with the TMO, what format is it in, what do we need to do with it?), QC of the vendor work product and deliverable to the trial technician.

Teams that handle data in ad hoc or unorganized way are in for trouble when exhibits aren't provided to the trial tech on time or are forgotten (or, even worse, when the wrong version of an exhibit is provided, which is typically a last-minute redaction that somebody one-offs outside of the established workflow and results in problems in court).

Workflow documentation doesn't have to be a burdensome process. As a matter of fact, the simpler it is, the better. It is important that the *entire team* is educated on the workflow process, the expectations on how long tasks will take, and what steps are needed to expedite or make an exception. Below is a sample memo detailing an effective exhibit workflow.

> Viviana will be our gatekeeper. All files upon receipt either internally or from opposing counsel go to Viviana, who will log them as received and copy them to a dated network location here: X:\1234_Case\Exhibits\Received\#received_date. [*Files in this location will not be modified.*]
>
> Viviana will perform an initial assessment of the received files and determine if further work is necessary to comply with the TMO. A copy of files that require further processing will be sent to the designated vendor [*mail to ProjectManagement@abc123.com with CC to team members*] to be processed into a single-page TIFF file for black and white and JPG for color. They will be branded with the exhibit number provided by the legal team and loaded into a trial exhibit database by Viviana that she maintains. Viviana will also create an export for the trial presentation technician into a dated folder that complies with any TMO format and branding requirements (which is a QC of the vendor work product that should also comply with the TMO requirements):
>
> X:\1234_Case\Exhibits\Processed_Branded\#loaded_date.
>
> *Exceptions*: This process should take two to three hours for most deliverables. When Viviana or the trial tech are unavailable[22] and there is a RUSH, the trial team will create a PDF file and email it to Viviana and the trial tech, then look for a "confirmation" of receipt.
>
> *Note*: The vendor is ABC123 E-Discovery Reprographics and can be reached at 1-800-555-1212; the rep is Susan Bird [Susan.Bird@ABC123.com cell: 949-555-1212]. The after-hours email is 911@abc123.com.
>
> *Summary*:
>
> - Viviana will receive all files for assessment and send to the vendor if necessary.

22. They need to sleep sometime!

- ABC123 is our vendor, and Susan Bird is our point of contact [Susan.Bird@ABC123.com cell: 949-555-1212].
- Exceptions will be PDF'd and sent to Viviana and the trial tech—please look for confirmation that it has been received.

This example was for a fairly large trial team, in which Viviana was handling the trial exhibit database and litigation support for the entire team, while the trial tech was focused on trial presentation support. I've been in teams where there were ten to twenty people just on the trial tech and graphics team. For example, the tech might be practicing witness exams or opening/closing statements with the legal team or loading data to the trial presentation system. The tech can focus on presentation-related tasks rather than support-related tasks, which is a very good idea. In many cases, the gatekeeper will also be the trial tech and litigation support.

Note: Workflows must be discussed in a meeting with the entire legal team. Also, as cases get bigger, consider your staffing options wisely so people can specialize in specific trial-related tasks. A single trial tech cannot work 24/7, so coverage for teams that are working around the clock need to be supplemented with litigation support or specialized trial resources.

3.10 Trial Exhibit versus Trial Presentation Database

The trial exhibit database is the working database used by the legal team to prepare documents for trial and research. It is also the working location where electronic files are modified by branding and unitization prior to being imported into the tech's trial presentation database, if this task is not performed by a vendor. Software that you might use to maintain trial exhibits for the *team's use* are Relativity, Concordance, CaseMap, and Summation.

The tech will use a trial *presentation* database to present exhibits in court. It is a mirror copy of the trial *exhibit* database, but is used solely by the tech as a source for exhibit presentation. The trial presentation database is where exhibits might be staged in advance, along with callouts and highlighting. Software that you might use to maintain trial exhibits for presentation in court and used by the *trial tech* are TrialDirector, Sanction, and OnCue.

To maintain version control, I recommend designating a single gatekeeper to perform data intake and redactions and modifications to exhibits and to have a plan in place for any emergency or last-minute needs while the tech is away (usually late at night, sleeping). The legal team simply must take version control and notification of the tech as a top priority because this is a primary area where trial mishaps happen. Even an email at 2:00 a.m. may not be a sufficient method of notifying a tech about an exhibit modification done while the gatekeeper is away. Rather, the exhibit should put in the tech's hand.

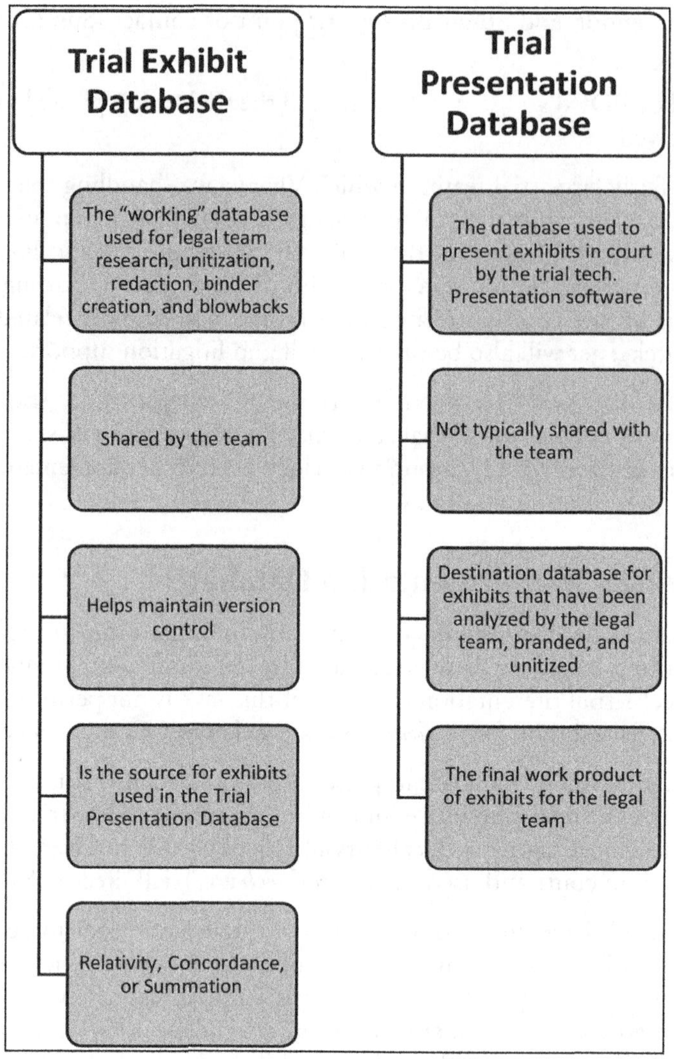

Figure 12. ***Understand the difference between exhibit and presentation databases.***

3.11 Trial Management Order

The Trial Management Order (TMO) is an order by the court that provides the framework and rules of how the trial will be run. The TMO lays out the court's routine administration of cases, like the number of trial days, the trial start date, conferences, and the courtroom rules, to name a few. However, the TMO also enumerates the rules for the technical details of the case, as agreed upon by both parties. As for technology, it is often overlooked by trial teams, but this is an area in which the trial tech can provide considerable value by reviewing and consulting the TMO. The technical portions of the TMO are often abused by parties so they can take shortcuts in preparation or shift the burden of preparation to their opposition.

The boilerplate TMO language most courts use is fairly generic and provides for a multitude of different formats and technologies to be used in the exhibit transfer. Legal teams often dismiss as unimportant discussions regarding exhibit exchange, but it is an area that can cause significant issue via burden shifting. Teams may not grasp until too late that by undertaking the other party's obligations, they have actually harmed their own support structure. Legal teams should first have a good understanding internally of what technical formats, branding, and file-naming conventions would benefit the swift administration of justice, lower risk in the courtroom, and simultaneously benefit their team by using file specifications that are most compatible with their legal software and processes. Second, legal teams would be wise to memorialize in the TMO the *exact* exhibit specifications agreed upon in the case—such as format, naming convention, branding requirements, and data file formats—so that any subsequent data dump of unbranded or unprocessed exhibits can be rejected until they're fixed and the parties' noncooperation potentially discussed with the judge.

Below is recommended TMO text for electronic exhibits and video.

> **Electronic Exhibits**
>
> Electronic exhibits for black and white (binary) documents shall be provided in single-page TIFF format. Color exhibits shall be scanned in color and provided in JPEG (24-bit) format. All images shall be scanned at a resolution of 300dpi. A load file for the images containing document structure and path shall be provided for a popular viewing program (i.e., TrialDirector, Iro, Concordance, Opticon, DocuLex, etc.). There shall not be any duplicates in the load files, even across multiple CDs or DVDs.
>
> Exhibits shall be named as follows: "TX00001-0001," where the first number, "TX00001," refers to the exhibit number and the second number, "-0001," refers to the page number of the exhibit. Every page of the exhibit should be branded in the lower right corner with the exhibit and page number in the specified format. A corresponding load file shall be included with the images. Each party reserves the right to introduce any previously produced exhibit in native format, but need not provide such exhibits in native format prior to trial and in accordance with the court's order. All such exhibits shall be exchanged solely in TIFF or JPEG format prior to trial. Any exhibit in native format that has not been previously provided to the other side shall be exchanged in such native format prior to trial in accordance with the court's order.
>
> **Video**
>
> The offering party is responsible for editing the videotaped deposition testimony to reflect the offering party and opposing party's designations and providing a correctly edited videotape for use at trial. The opposing party shall have the right to view the edited video for accuracy twenty-four hours before the deposition is to be used at trial.

Some of the key sentences to watch out for (and that are abused):

- **Electronic exhibits for black and white (binary) documents shall be provided in single-page TIFF format. Color exhibits shall be scanned in color and provided in JPEG (24-bit) format.**

  Parties often deliver in a format other than the one specified. Providing a consistent deliverable between parties makes them efficient, which, in turn, helps aid court efficiency.

- **A load file for the images containing document structure and path shall be provided for a popular viewing program (i.e., TrialDirector, Ipro, Concordance, Opticon, DocuLex etc.).**

  Parties have taken this as a license to change the deliverable format midstream or to use any format they wish. Parties should specify the *exact format*, along with trading sample work product, prior to trial used for exhibit exchange.

- **Exhibits shall be named as follows: "TX00001-0001," where the first number, "TX00001," refers to the exhibit number and the second number, "-0001," refers to the page number of the exhibit.**

  Files are often misnamed or not named at all with an exhibit number, causing quality control issues and burden shifting. The offending team did not take the time to correctly name their electronic files. Sometimes they will provide a list that correlates the exhibit number with a file name—that's not good enough.

- **Every page of the exhibit should be branded in the lower right corner with the exhibit and page number in the specified format.**

  When exhibits are not branded or not referenced by the exhibit number, decision-makers (especially jurors) become confused and the court record is imperfect. Files are often misbranded or not branded at all, causing quality control issues and burden shifting. The offending legal team did not take the time or expense to brand their electronic files.

- **The offering party is responsible for editing the videotaped deposition testimony to reflect the offering party and opposing party's designations and providing a correctly edited videotape for use at trial.**

  Video is especially burdensome at trial. Because of the amount of work it takes to edit video, there is much gamesmanship with the creation and exchange of video. First, parties should agree on a naming scheme for individual clips so that opposing counsel doesn't simply make a copy of the entire video and drop it in your lap with a list of clips to be cut. Clips should come precut, with a key that coordinates the clip name and page/line reference.

Prior to memorializing the TMO, parties should rigorously test the file formats created by opposing counsel. It greatly benefits legal teams and the court to discuss and agree upon the exhibit exchange details in the early planning stages of the trial, with the appropriate technical people involved, and to facilitate an early "test" exchange of exhibits to ensure that everything is working correctly and any issues are ironed out. If there is any variance from any of the technical specs, parties can go back to the sample exchange to show where the variance occurred. Variances or "non-compliance" should be remedied quickly and repeat issues dealt with appropriately in the courtroom, if necessary.

The TMO is also helpful in discussing and analyzing the workflow that will be needed by the case, as duties and responsibilities are specified in it. Sometimes the TMO can be very tricky, like how the deposition testimony section discusses who is responsible for designations, along with rules of exchange. The TMO has saved me on several occasions when opposing counsel has tried to avoid their responsibilities by delivering in formats other than what was agreed to or were unbranded and misnamed—as if they could just change their mind mid-case and we would have to figure out how to fix it, or that we should cover their own support obligations via burden shifting.

Courts are often reluctant to dive into these issues. Counsel takes advantage of this by simply not complying with the TMO technical requirements. Parties should be held to the technical standards they agree upon (and which are court ordered), and non-complying parties should be taken to task. It is patently unfair to have one party going through the effort and expense to comply and the other is not.

Noncompliance with technical specifications creates efficiency and quality control issues in court due to confusion and technical error. The tech spec is most often abused by parties not complying with the branding requirements and appropriate video clipping, which, in turn, creates a substantial burden on the party that wants to comply by having to fix the other's work. This is burden shifting. Again, the cost of noncompliance to the court is efficiency. It creates considerable confusion if one party does not use the exhibit number to identify records both on the face of the documents and in references to court (often using old Bates and production numbers).

At the beginning of the trial, the court should include the legal teams' tech staffers in its conversations[23] about the parties' responsibilities, expectations, and technical obligations, and question why exhibits are not in compliance with the TMO when shown in court. This discussion goes a long way to ensuring that parties take their evidence presentation obligations seriously with the court, which, in turn, leads to courtroom efficiency, higher quality presentations, and a clear record.

3.11.1 Cooperation with Opposing Counsel

In general, trial techs from opposing trial teams should assist one another for shared needs (equipment, courtroom troubleshooting, replacement of corrupt files, creating exchange standards, cooperation, etc.), but you should always keep an eye out for burden shifting. The offending party often claims it's no big deal for you to brand their exhibits, or process their files, or identify their video clips. It's a bluff—always. In reality, these tasks are a lot of

23. This should be beyond a "Ready!" shout-out in open court.

work and a substantial burden. In most cases, the offending legal team is unwilling to engage a vendor or bring the appropriate technical resources to court, or it is purposefully creating a burden. For example, it's not unusual for one party to offer to do all of the video clipping, engage a vendor for the benefit of both parties, or split costs—this is cooperation, not burden shifting. But if opposing counsel does something that is unethical, not compliant with the TMO, or shifts the burden onto you, you must discuss with your legal team any corrective action first.

If opposing counsel violates the TMO, then call them on it—set the expectation of quality and compliance with the TMO early. Educate your team and let everyone know that the cost of burden shifting will be less time for you to work on their case and that the additional responsibilities are not inconsequential. After all, you wouldn't send another paralegal, attorney, or clerk to their office to help out with their responsibilities, so why do it with technical responsibilities?

Always consult your legal team prior to any nonstandard/unfriendly communication with opposing counsel as well. The legal team chooses when and where to wear a white hat and whether a given action is OK. The tech's additional burden might be the legal team's strategic decision.[24] Remain cool, friendly, and ethical at all times—never let them see you sweat or be stressed (but don't be a pushover either).

I'm always wary when opposing counsel offers to provide equipment or split equipment through their own trial presentation vendor unless I have a preexisting relationship with the vendor. It's better to use an independent, third-party vendor, where the expectation of service and support will be equal. Otherwise, you can be on the short end of the stick in setup and customer service issues, and you'll always be in second place to their team's needs.

3.11.2 Burden Shifting

Burden shifting is when opposing counsel moves the responsibility of conforming with the TMO onto the other party. Exhibit exchanges should generally occur with exhibits that are completely processed in a "trial ready" format, in that they are named correctly, already branded, and comply with the technical specifications that the parties and court agreed on. It is a mutually beneficial process and helps ensure that proceedings in the courtroom move smoothly. If you don't agree on a standard, along with test exchanges to QC and test your protocols, one side will always try to wiggle out of doing its part.

Examples of burden shifting include:

- Not complying with the TMO spec
- Delivering unprocessed native files where processed files are required
- Not branding or naming exhibits correctly
- Delivering files in unusable formats
- Delivering a DVD with unclipped video and using a single exhibit number to cover "all video clips"
- Delivering multiple clips with a single exhibit number (or none at all)

Teams may make themselves vulnerable to burden shifting by the opposing party by not providing enough specificity as to the details of the exhibit exchange specifications in the TMO, or when they have an unscrupulous or incompetent opponent who will try to take advantage of a loophole. Sometimes teams don't recognize burden shifting for what it is, or they think that it's not worth their time to draw a line in the sand. What many teams don't realize is that when burden shifting is not confronted, they harm themselves by putting their own people to work for the other team. Smart legal teams put a stop to burden shifting or attempts to "share" staff.

Here are some examples of burden-shifting language I've encountered:

- "Attached are files we intend to use tomorrow and are exhibits 21, 22, and 23."

24. For example, branding all of their exhibits or clipping video.

The shifted burden here is that the receiving party will need to process, brand, and prepare these files for use in court between 2:00 a.m. and court start time.

- "We have decided to change the format for exhibits from single-page TIFF to multipage TIFF [and likely will not be branded] because the TMO states we can deliver in any one of these formats."

  The burden shifted here is that the files will need to be processed and converted from an unproven format to the one your team has chosen.[25]

- "Attached is a CD containing the video clips we intend to use tomorrow. They will be exhibits 101 thru 157."

  The files do not comply with the naming requirements in the TMO. The burden here is figuring out which exhibit is which and what the page/line references are for each clip.

- "We noticed that you are using the equipment much more than we are. As such, we will not be paying for the shared cost of the equipment."

  The burden here is financial.

3.12 Understanding Load Files and Log Files

Typically, exhibits are exchanged in an image format compatible with a variety of document review software, with native files supplementing some file types (e.g., spreadsheet, PowerPoint, database). The image format is typically a standalone PDF or a single page tiff with an associated file called a "log file"[26] that describes the document unitization of each document and where it is located. Novice users will likely want to use PDF to start, but there are a few areas where PDF doesn't work well, such as with files large in size and number of pages. There are many different image and data formats, so it is critical for the legal team to work with the court and opposing counsel in the TMO or some other agreement to create a mutually beneficial agreement that reduces the amount of work for both parties during the exhibit exchange. Modifying a log file is complicated. If the case is becoming too technically difficult or your eyes are glazing over because of your dataset complexity, it might be time to bring in an experienced consultant to assist.

A log file tells the database where the image resides and the unitization of the record. Every legal database and trial presentation tool has its own proprietary log file format. However, the most common format used (and one of the Department of Justice production choices) is using an "Opticon" load file This term is a bit out of date because Opticon is no longer the primary viewer used by Concordance (it is now Concordance Image), but the standard remains and it is the primary production format in use in the industry. This standard is also used by Relativity, which is now one of the most widely used legal database tools by firms and vendors. A log file should not be confused with a *load file*, which is the file that contains the metadata and coding to be loaded into the database.

An Opticon log file is one of the more straightforward formats for loading image files and for that reason, it is usually found as an option for data loading in trial software. This also makes it extremely convenient if you have Relativity or Concordance because you can use the same data load in both your trial exhibit database and trial presentation software. In addition, it can be quickly and easily converted into a variety of other formats, though your mileage may vary in using different file utilities found in iPro and the trial software itself.

The log file contains three parts.

- **Alias** = Plain meaning. It is the database reference to the image. Image name and alias should usually be the same, just like the exhibit number and exhibit image file name should be the same.
- **Path** = The file path from the alias to the image. The "map" from the database to the image.

25. Trial presentation programs can display a wide range of image formats, but consistency is your friend and switching formats mid-trial is just a cheesy tactic.
26. It is often called a load file, which is the filetype used to load the metadata into a database, but it has become somewhat synonymous.

- **Image Name/Key** = The user-defined field in the database that links the database field, "the key," and the image.

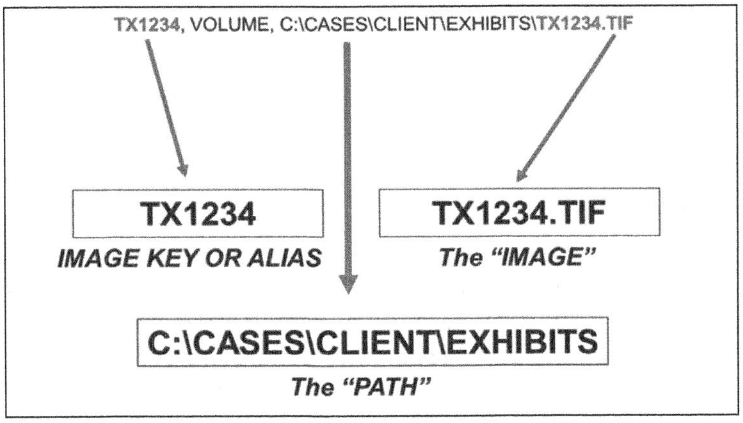

Figure 13. ***The image key is on the left, and the image is on the right.***

The log file, shown above and below, actually contains one line like you see above for *every image/page in the database*. Also, note the C:\ in the file path. It is only there so that you can replace the C:\ with your own path because you will receive a data deliverable from opposing counsel or a vendor. Some vendors use other letters or symbols. A final point: when you deliver a log file, make it generic, with no path information other than X:\images. You wouldn't want to give away information to the other side by using folder names that describe the exhibits' important (or lack thereof)—like this, for example, C:\RED_FLAG_DOCS\IMAGES\.

TX0001-00001,SAMPLE,C:\IMAGES\TX0001-00001.tif,Y,,,1

TX0002-00001,SAMPLE,C:\IMAGES\TX0002-00001.tif,Y,,,3

TX0002-00002,SAMPLE,C:\IMAGES\TX0002-00002.tif,,,,

TX0002-00003,SAMPLE,C:\IMAGES\TX0002-00003.tif,,,,

TX0003-00001,SAMPLE,C:\IMAGES\TX0003-00001.tif,Y,,,1

TX0004-00001,SAMPLE,C:\IMAGES\TX0004-00001.tif,Y,,,1

The lines above are part of a sample log file containing the path and image location for exhibits TX00001 through TX00004.

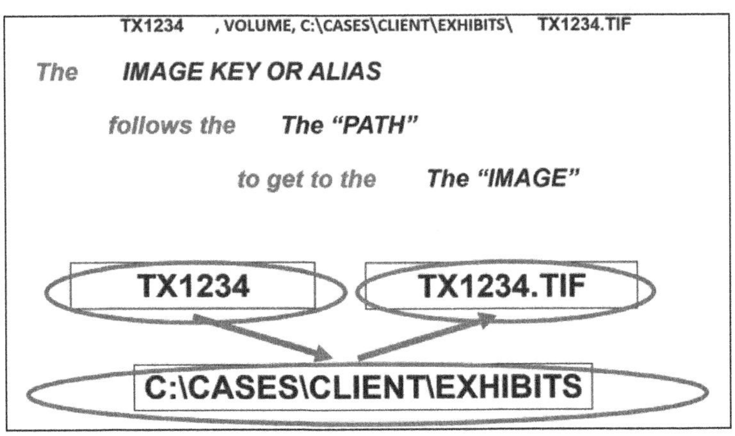

Figure 14. ***The image key/alias (TX1234) follows the path (C:\cases\client\exhibits) to the image (TX1234.tif).***

The log file is the alias or "image key" follows the path to the "image." The log file can be tricky and is much more technical than using a PDF. But a log file can also setup a more rigorous method for QC, as you can more easily account for every page and image in the database by ensuring there is a matching image for each line in the log file. Most trial software has a built-in utility to verify that all images are in the system. Now, you would think every tech would run the utility without fail, huh? *They don't.* Images, PDFs, and exhibits are always missing in the database, so it is important that you use every technique and tool available to QC and check that the files are there.

3.13 Companion Applications

As you develop your technical skills, you'll want to have the ability to manipulate data more efficiently than the standard tools provided by Windows. Using Notepad, which is included in Windows, is great for editing log files . . . until they start to become really big. Instead, you may want to look into tools like Notepad++ or UltraEdit. You may also need to bulk rename files past the capabilities within the program, but that can be done in a program like Total Commander, which can replace and rename files. If I'm clipping video other than transcripts with synced video, I tend to use Windows Movie Maker. Many of these companion apps are free or low cost.

Much of this can be done within the trial software application itself, but at that point it may not be usable for the entire team. Typically, it is a more efficient workflow for teams to create work product outside of the trial software so the entire team can share in its creation and end work product—which is subsequently imported into the trial software. This is also consistent with how exhibits are typically created, with documents being processed by a vendor into a document review database, or standalone PDF files, which are subsequently reviewed and redacted by a legal team and then placed into a trial presentation database. Clearly, there are solo practioners and small offices doing it all, and the workflows and training tend to be scalable.

3.14 Case Conclusion

Trial presentation materials and work product are often forgotten in the mad dash to close out the trial site. At the conclusion of the case, firms should maintain and archive cases materials. This is true of both work product created and used by the team and work product created by the trial tech. Having an effective strategy for keeping case materials accessible is important so that if the case comes to life again, it can be started quickly and efficiently. Some suggestions:

1) Try to use the same image format in your document review database, TMO, and trial presentation software to minimize conversion of image formats.
2) Single-page image files should be named the same as their exhibit *and* page number. Single-page image files should have a log file that has an image alias that matches the file and exhibit number.
3) Native and multipage files should be named after their exhibit number.
4) Do not have empty spaces in your exhibit file names.

CHAPTER FOUR

EQUIPMENT

"Better. Faster. Tougher. Scarier."

—description of a Los Angeles law firm that knows its way around a courtroom

4.1 Getting Started: What Equipment and Software Do You Need?

In this chapter, I discuss specific pieces of trial equipment. Depending on your needs, presentation equipment can be as simple as a laptop, a projector, and a screen; or it can be extremely complex, with multiple inputs for each party, distributed video, and sound systems. As I review the different pieces of equipment, think about whether it is better for your firm to buy or rent. Most firms will do fine with a combination of purchased and rental equipment. After all, nobody wants to buy a 70-inch monitor[1] to store, service, and deliver to each trial site (especially if you only go to trial sporadically). In this regard, rental companies and trial presentation vendors are a clear winner for many firms.[2]

Careful attention to detail and ongoing support need to be devoted to the "trial laptop" to ensure it is powerful enough for team needs, is actively maintained,[3] and is built to ensure maximum performance. Any update and maintenance, no matter how big or small, should trigger a round of testing to ensure it remains in perfect working order. Partner involvement is often key in obtaining the right equipment. I've said it before, but it's worth repeating: legal teams are only shortchanging themselves when they skimp on trial equipment. Legal teams (and firm partners in particular) should send a clear message to those who make purchasing decisions that trial equipment is different and requires *special attention*. Too often, law firms will attempt to use the same generic cookie-cutter computer that they give to every laptop user in the firm or to shoehorn in other equipment that doesn't fit the needs of the trial team.[4]

Making good choices about the equipment used at trial seems like a no-brainer, but too often firms just install trial presentation software on an untested or spare computer ("It's easy, plug this in, input the exhibit number, ...") and hope for the best. It is actually pretty easy to make good choices for trial technology; 1) choose equipment that complies with the trial software requirements; 2) have basic tech skills; 3) practice using the software; and 4) write the check. There are many reasons why computers crash and perform poorly during trial; some are human and others technical. Below is a list of the biggest causes of slow response[5] and crashes during trial. The items that are equipment related are in **bold**.

1) **Slow or old equipment.** Does your trial laptop comply with the minimum standards required by your trial presentation software of choice?

2) **Electronic file issues.** Are you trying to open files larger than a few megabytes? Have the files been optimized for trial use? Have they been tested?[6]

1. Along with some kind of shipping box that would likely be more expensive than the monitor.
2. If you have a large enough volume of trials, it might make sense to purchase more equipment.
3. Once purchased, trial laptops require ongoing maintenance and support.
4. Often to the dismay and embarrassment of attorneys who experience problems in court that could have been easily avoidable.
5. Slow response means it takes the trial software too long to load an exhibit or video clip.
6. This can be a hardware, software, or electronic file issue.

3) *Poor communication/disorganization.* Have the lawyer and tech worked out how exhibits will be referred to? Does the tech have an outline (in advance) of the legal teams opening, closing, and witness examination?

4) **Maintenance.** Has the laptop been maintained, updates applied carefully, and *been tested*? Has the firm exerted too little discipline in adding and testing software? Have you been keeping software overhead[7] low, by, for example, not loading iTunes, games, and other unnecessary applications to your trial laptop?

5) **Poor equipment setup.** Have the wrong settings, such as those for resolution and video, been enabled on the computer?

6) *Lack of practice.* Have the attorney and tech practiced and rehearsed their respective parts?

7) *Poor technical skills.* The person responsible for the trial presentation does not have the skills necessary to effectively do the job.

As you can see, many of the reasons for poor performance are equipment related. Not having the appropriate equipment and software is one of the leading areas where lawyers and firms shortchange *themselves*. In Chapter Two, I discuss in-depth the folly of going to court without the required technical skills; going to trial "tech poor," without the right equipment, is just as bad. This is an absolute travesty when it occurs, and especially so when it's a big firm. Any firm with an IT department should have the resources to analyze equipment options and make informed decisions. A solo practitioner, on the other hand, who wants to do trial presentation work and has the budget for just a single laptop should be obtain one[8] that complies with the standards of their trial software choice. This will not be the smallest, most portable, or coolest laptop (and definitely not an Apple . . . yet), but it will still be a big, beefy brute capable of handling everything thrown at it.

Firms should concentrate on obtaining the best presentation laptop[9] they can afford,[10] along with some quality switches, speakers, and a high lumens (i.e., bright) projector as their presentation capability expands. As far as advice on models, rather than provide specific advice on a model or brand that will be outdated the moment the book is in print, I'll point you toward online resources and a podcast: the LinkedIn Trial Technology group,[11] the Court Technology Blog by Ted Brooks,[12] and Robb Helt's Trial Technology and Litigation Support Podcast on iTunes.[13] These are a great source of information and guidance within the trial technology sphere. When it comes to making mistakes, it's much better to be taken to task in the LinkedIn group than taken to the woodshed in open court. Moreover, if you are in over your head, these sources are a great place to find a reputable consultant. My final piece of advice on this point is to have a discussion with your trial presentation software provider about what laptops and equipment they use and recommend. Too many firms try to marry their existing equipment to the software, rather than look at their technical needs and build around them.

Three Great Online Resources for Court Technology		
LinkedIn: Trial Technology Group	**Court Technology Blog by Ted Brooks:** http://trial-technology.blogspot.com/	**iTunes:** *Trial Technology and Litigation Support Podcast* by Robb Helt

Figure 1. ***Online resources for court/legal technology.***

7. This just means don't overload your computer with a bunch of software unrelated to trial presentation. Each installation injects risk into the equation by potentially breaking file associations or replacing software drivers with incompatible ones.
8. Keeping in mind a tremendously strong need for redundancy in the courtroom.
9. Keeping in mind that they should have two for redundancy!
10. So long as what you can afford meets the minimum technical standards of the software you want to use.
11. https://www.linkedin.com/groups/2276605/profile.
12. http://trial-technology.blogspot.com/.
13. https://itunes.apple.com/us/podcast/trial-technology-litigation-support-podcast/id1278015295.

4.1.1 Redundancy

A redundant setup is recommended by all trial presentation software vendors and is a minimum standard in use by trial technicians. Having a redundant setup with duplicative equipment is your primary method of avoiding the risk of failure. In practicality, if your laptop freezes, crashes, or becomes problematic, you merely switch over to a duplicative laptop that you've already booted up. Redundancy is a key concept that should be built into every courtroom presentation and starts with two trial laptops with complete copies of the trial presentation database. The video switch I describe in this chapter is a key piece of equipment that allows you to switch easily amongst primary and backup laptops and a document camera.

> Two For One.
>
> Each subscription offers two activations because if you aren't running a backup laptop in court, you probably should be.
> When you can't leave things to chance, redundancy is the best insurance.

Figure 2. ***Advice from the OnCue trial presentation software website. Enough said.***

As you think about redundancy, remember some key points from federal court about technology use in the courtroom, per the Evidence Presentation Obligations discussed in Chapter Two:

- "No court time will be provided during court proceedings to allow the parties to troubleshoot issues"
  - The Court will not tolerate any delays during any proceedings caused by a party's unfamiliarity with the Court's system or by the failure of a party's equipment.
  - The parties will be required to present their cases without the aid of the electronic evidence presentation system . . . due to equipment failure or due to any other "technology" delays.
- In addition to familiarizing themselves with the Court's electronic evidence presentation system in advance of the hearing/trial, the parties must familiarize themselves with their own equipment and how to connect their own equipment with the Court's system prior to the hearing/trial.
- The Court strongly encourages parties to bring a backup laptop with power supply, flash drive and or CD that contains all documents if technical issues were to arise.

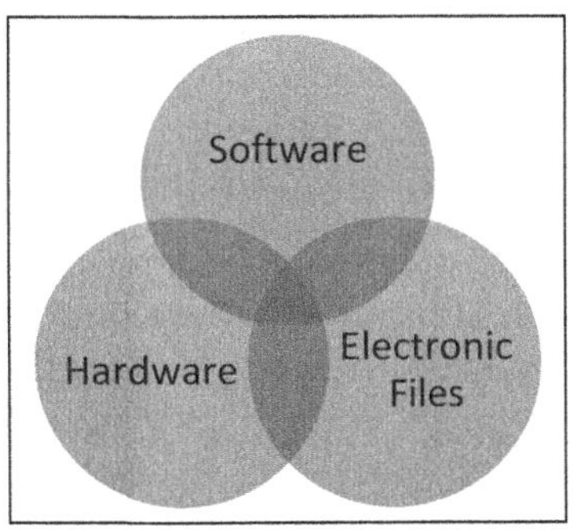

Figure 3. ***QC and testing should cover hardware, software, and electronic exhibits. Missing QC in one area puts the rest at risk.***

Having dual mirrored laptops and a document camera connected to a switch provides a reasonable safety net in case of courtroom presentation technical problems. However, keep in mind that hardware problems are only half the equation; the other half is the software and the electronic exhibits themselves. The same rigorous testing needs to be applied to each piece of your presentation, whether it is testing equipment like laptops and switches, opening electronic exhibit files to ensure they are not corrupt, or running exhibits through your trial software to test its limits.

4.1.2 Rent versus Buy

Equipment is expensive to buy, maintain, and modernize over time. By renting equipment instead of buying, the upkeep, storage, and maintenance costs are pushed to the vendor and rental costs pass through to clients. Most techs rent courtroom equipment and purchase their laptop and software, or they use a professional trial presentation vendor to handle the entire process. Experience matters in this regard, so be sure to stick with a vendor that specializes in the legal market because they know their way around a courtroom and courthouse security.[14] Depending on your situation, it might be a better decision to focus on purchasing a good trial laptop and paying for the related equipment and setup via a vendor.

Vendors fill an important need in the industry because high-tech courtrooms may need to be supplemented with additional equipment for specific trial needs. For example, the court clerk and trial tech might agree that moving the video switch from the clerk to the tech is a good idea so that the tech can control the screens and the clerk can focus on other tasks during trial. Or maybe the existing courtroom setup is inadequate and the team can bring in bigger and better presentation equipment or more monitors for the judge, jury, witness, and counsel. However, most courtrooms simply have no presentation technology built in whatsoever, which, in terms of potential, gives you a blank slate. Don't be intimidated by the setup task; it is often as simple using as a projector, screen, and a video connection to show a few exhibits, slides, or video clips. It does not need to be overly complicated.

One benefit I've experienced in using an equipment rental vendor is that I can ask for a variety of equipment, different projectors or a large monitor, to see what works best in a given courtroom. It is important that you have some experience with the equipment beforehand, so consider renting it a few days ahead of the trial or have a duplicate video switch in your office or war room so you can practice and become familiar with its functions. While the equipment itself is not overly difficult to use, you should be familiar enough to troubleshoot basic problems like a loose connection or broken cable.[15] In the end, your legal team should be focused on their arguments rather than technical setup, so being able to simply make a phone call and have the setup taken care of is a great option. Be sure to talk to the vendor about the level of service you can expect, such as whether it's time to replace faulty or broken equipment, the availability of spare bulbs or extra cables, etc. For example, does the vendor have a spare projector available, and how long would it take to replace the existing one?

4.1.3 Trial Equipment Potluck and the Projector Scam[16]

There are so many difficult technical decisions as you approach trial, and one of them is equipment selection. It is often thought of as a distraction to legal teams, but just a few minutes of their attention on this issue (which might mean discussing it with the judge) can potentially prevent disaster. Let's get out of the way that there are cases where parties might cobble together a few pieces of equipment they own and work together using what they have due to budget, case size, and technical ability. However, in cases where two equally yoked parties have agreed to split costs, there can only be one solution and that is to use a neutral third-party equipment vendor.

While on its face it might be reasonable, these kind of bring-your-own-equipment arrangements (equipment potluck!) are potentially problematic. A legal team runs the risk of having a less professional-appearing presentation—or worse, one with technical issues that can't be resolved because you don't have a responsive vendor with an obligation to assist you. Undoubtedly, "potluck" equipment tends to be much lower quality than the cutting-edge equipment you can get from a vendor. Remember that no good deed goes unpunished, so if you use your own equipment to share and reduce costs, you may open yourself up to criticism if it fails during the other side's case.

14. This is important because there might be specific rules for bringing equipment into the courthouse. Moreover, having vendors that are familiar with basic courtroom protocols is essential to having a happy courtroom clerk and judge.

15. Please review Chapter Two, Getting Started, in which I discuss inspecting the VGA cable before plugging it in and starting computer from OFF.

16. Section 4.1.3 originally appeared as a post on *The Legal Advocate*, the National Institute for Trial Advocacy's blog, at http://blog.nita.org/2017/10/avoid-trial-equipment-potluck/. It was one post in a four-part series I wrote about trial technology. The piece has been edited lightly for use in this book.

Using a third-party vendor provides equal access to quick replacement equipment and technical know-how. Separate invoices can be created and each party will be responsible for its portion, thus giving both parties equal access and expectation to a vendor to service and support their trial needs. A reputable, third-party vendor will have replacements available and technical expertise, and be on call for any issues that occur, as well as likely having a large selection of equipment (and expertise) that can be used to equip your particular need. How likely is the court to delay proceedings for a team if the equipment malfunctions and there is no plan for immediate replacement? Last, if things get contentious (and don't they all at trial?), can you rely on the other side to troubleshoot and configure your equipment as you could a third-party vendor?

Regardless of where the equipment comes from, you must have a plan on how malfunctioning equipment will be replaced and how long will it take to replace it. An independent vendor is much better situated to address the needs of both parties and replace problematic equipment. The court might grant a long lunch to get a replacement together, but is it going to wait a day for equipment to be shipped from afar or purchased locally? What is the responsibility of the team providing equipment to replace, configure, and troubleshoot the equipment for the other side? If it comes down to servicing their own team or troubleshooting technical issues for the other side, where do you think they will come down? Your problem will quickly become unimportant to them and you will be left holding the bag, with a potentially error-prone presentation or one that simply does not look right on screen because you didn't get the attention a third-party vendor brings. Parties should be able to clearly answer these questions, or else they are simply injecting unnecessary risk into the equation or, worse, are trying to pull a fast one.

A common ploy being used by less reputable teams is to offer to substitute a key piece of equipment (usually the projector) for their own projector. While not always unscrupulous, the risk of not having a replacement or equal access to technical expertise far outweigh the benefit of using a single, lower-priced piece of equipment. Most often, this is done so the offering team can either obtain the rental fee for its equipment ("XYZ Company is charging $500 per week for a projector—I'll only charge my client $250!") or avoid its half of the shared, setup bill. Worst-case scenario is when one party holds the setup "hostage" (i.e., will not proceed with setup) so it can get what it wants. On the other side of the coin, if you are providing equipment and it breaks during the other side's presentation, are you ready to take the heat, and the ugly accusations that come with it? It's great if you have a projector at your firm that you can lug around for client meetings, but do you have a second one in case the bulb burns out or you drop it on the courthouse steps? Do you want to be in the business of supporting your rival? It's just not worth it.

Another tactic to look out for in equipment provided by opposing counsel is equipment that could provide them with an unfair advantage. For example, what if they bring a large, touch-screen monitor that you have no experience with? Do you want to fumble through your presentation and put your technical incompetence on display by using equipment they have likely practiced on for months? Again, in such cases, it's important to agree on the equipment to be used, to take time to familiarize yourself with it, and if it is something that could potentially provide an unfair advantage, to insist that access and training are provided or else it's excluded from use.

First, get an agreement with the court to committing to using a third-party vendor so gamesmanship doesn't occur and the setup is a formality rather than a hostage negotiation. Second, use a third-party vendor to handle equipment needs, which provides stability and lowers risk of technical malfunction. Both parties are able to have an equal expectation of service and support, as well as being able to split the bill on separate invoices, thus avoiding headaches and unnecessary drama.

4.1.4 Evaluating Trial Software

Before purchasing a trial laptop or other equipment, first select the best trial presentation software for your firm. The capability of trial software is bifurcating into two primary areas. First, trial software is becoming easier to use. The skills barrier to entry is falling for presentation. However, it's the preparation and planning of electronic files to become exhibits that is getting more difficult, due to the volume of data and issues related to increasing complexity (e.g., how to find exhibits in massive collections, choosing the correct processing option), as well as navigating the technical challenges of trial setups that each unique courtroom brings.

Second, trial software is becoming more collaborative. Traditionally, the tech was a single point of both failure and bottleneck because they were the only ones (absent some difficult workflows) that could work on a case. The process is becoming more efficient as software packages like TrialDirector integrate a collaborative workflow, such that an entire team can now work on a case online, as opposed to the single trial tech who worked on it locally. Teams that will be able to leverage the growing collaborative nature of trial software will be more cost efficient and responsive, thus allowing entirely new support options to the team[17] and reducing the risks inherent to trial because of better preparation.

Trial Software Due Diligence Checklist

- Review and perform due diligence on the top trial software packages available.
    - □ What tools work best for your firm? What tools will be the easiest to convert from your review databases to your trial presentation database?
- Call software companies and talk — who is most helpful?
    - □ Ask for equipment recommendations and real-world hardware requirements.
    - □ Download demo versions of software and evaluate — consider TrialDirector, Sanction, Visionary, and OnCue to start.
- Find out what the minimum hardware spec is for the trial presentation software and exceed it in every way possible. Again, run your short list of equipment and its spec by the trial software vendor. Look to them for specific laptop recommendations.
    - □ Budget for the most you can afford, but never buy equipment that does not meet the software spec.
- Understand the basics of how your software works:
    - □ Does the software import images and convert them into some internal location or build links to existing images?
    - □ How long does the import and conversion take?
    - □ If converting to another format, how does it work with oversized images, odd-sized images, skewed images?
    - □ Does the conversion make any kind of corrections to the image?
    - □ What kinds of tools installed create conflicts for your software?
        - □ Subsequent installation of video players and codecs can cause substantial problems with trial presentation software.
    - □ What is the effect of installing encryption software on your laptop?
        - □ Does it affect performance or reliability?
- Choose the suite of tools that works best with your firm environment. There are other tools that you may want to consider, but this is a fairly common and generic list to get you started.
    - □ Trial Software: TrialDirector, OnCue, Sanction
    - □ Document Review: Concordance, Relativity
    - □ Transcripts: Case Notebook, TextMap
    - □ Text Editor: UltraEdit, Notepad++
    - □ Screen Capture: Snagit
    - □ Video editing: Windows Movie Maker (free), Adobe Premier Lite
    - □ Total Commander is a file manager that helps with synchronization, file renaming, etc.
    - □ Adobe Acrobat Professional
    - □ Microsoft Office
- Join the "Trial Support" LinkedIn group. It is a great group, with some popcorn-worthy drama from time to time.
    - □ Ask questions. Experienced people are more than willing to help, and you might find a good vendor resource if trial technology is not for you.
- Listen to the Trial Technology and Litigation Support Podcast, by Robb Helt, which has interviews with software vendors, techs, product comparisons, roundtables, and a variety of other industry professionals.
- Read Ted Brooks's Court Technology Blog, http://trial-technology.blogspot.com/.

Figure 4. ***Trial Software Due Diligence Checklist (available for free download; see the Notes on Use for access).***

17. For example, collaboration will allow team members to work from the home office rather than go onsite to trial, thus avoiding the expense of travel, food, and lodging, as well as being able to modulate their downtime.

The trial laptop should have its own "build" that allows your firm to set up trial laptops quickly and recycle those that have been utilized (i.e., beaten to death) in court so they can work like new. Once all of your software is loaded, create a disk image of your trial laptop in case it needs to be rapidly rebuilt due to software error or another problem. Standardize the image and it can be easily deployed to additional equipment or to a backup in case the computer hardware fails.

The trial laptop should not be thought of as a "cookie cutter" device onto which trial presentation software is added to a standard firm "build."[18] Firms need to choose the companion software packages that best complement their trial software and should be included on their trial laptop build. It is akin to building a race car in that you are building for performance and must make tradeoffs as to what software to include or not to include. Too much software and it will affect performance—too little and you won't be able to get the job done. Trial laptops typically include a video and image conversion tools like Adobe Photoshop and Premiere (the "lite" and consumer versions of these software packages is typically good enough), renaming and text editing utilities,[19] and let's not forget about security and virus checking. It's vitally important that when you install software and updates you then rigorously QC everything to ensure everything still works correctly.

4.1.4.1 Trial Laptop

Your choice of trial laptop goes hand in hand with your choice of trial software. Start by first finding the software that best works for your needs, then build your equipment around that. If you are building around existing equipment, you'll need to significantly test it to determine the right software fit and whether the equipment complies with the minimum standards. Never go below the minimum standards of the trial presentation software you intend to use; always buy the best computer you can. We're lucky nowadays, as the price for high-performance equipment like laptops has rapidly fallen.

Items to consider as you choose a trial laptop:

- **Build your laptop for speed and performance**. Only install applications for use and preparation for presentation in court. Keep iTunes, bloatware, games, and other non-essential tools off of your laptop.
- **Video/Resolution**. This is a primary area to review. How high of a resolution is there, and can it display in the lower resolutions (1024x768)?
- **Hard drive**. There are two areas to review when considering hard drives:
  - Performance—how fast is the hard drive's performance?
    - Look to computers with SSD (solid state) hard drives for best performance.
  - Size—how much storage do you need? Don't skimp on hard drive space.
    - You may need room for multiple video depositions or big cases—both are a space hog. Many faster computers have smaller hard drive storage.
  - Have at least 1tb available.
  - While often necessary, using external drives is just one more thing to troubleshoot and its performance is lower than if you place the data on a local drive of your trial laptop.
- **Testing**. Every time you add new software your laptop triggers you to conduct extensive performance testing, with a variety of file types, images, and video thrown at the laptop. Software that installs video or other codecs can be especially problematic.
- **Install trial software last**. This helps to ensure your trial software will not be overwritten by another software's codecs or files.

18. A "build" refers to a standard and repeatable process a firm uses to add software to a computer usually via a disk image.
19. We previously spoke about UltraEdit and Total Commander.

- **Create an image** of your trial laptop for ease of installation and emergencies. Trial laptops should be reimaged often, as they take a beating in terms of use and performance.
- **Trial laptops have a shorter lifespan** than most other computer equipment because of their heavy use/abuse and increasing horsepower needs. Consider a two-year rotation for moderately used hardware.
- **Buy extra power bricks and adaptors** for the laptop that can get lost or be left overnight in court without causing a crisis. For example, I leave an extra set of power bricks (one for each laptops) in court so I don't have to plug and unplug every time the day in trial is done. Again, if it can be accidentally lost without causing a crisis and is required for your laptop to work (perhaps a VGA/HDMI adaptor or other display adaptor) anyway, you'll want more than one.

Hardware requirements by trial presentation software vendors as of January 2017:

TrialDirector®

System Specifications

May 10, 2016

inData revised the system requirements for desktop and laptop systems running TrialDirector. Using these specifications allows customers to have the best experience possible with TrialDirector in the courtroom.

HIGH END PERFORMANCE

- **Processor:** Intel® Quad-Core i7 Processor (2.60GHz, 6MB Cache)
- **Operating System:** Windows 10 Pro
- **Display:** Full HD (1920 x 1080) or Ultra HD (3840 x 2160)
- **Discrete Graphic Card:** NVIDIA GeForce GTX 960M 4GB
- **Total Memory:** 16.0GB DDR4 2133 MHz
- **Hard Drive:** 1 TB SSD
- **Optical Device:** 8x DVD Recordable Drive
- **WLAN:** LAN 1000 M, Up to WiFi 2 x 2 a/c + Bluetooth® 4.0
- **Supported Operating Systems:** Windows 7, Windows 8, and Windows 10

RECOMMENDED

- **Processor:** Intel® Core™ i7 Processor (2.60GHz, 6MB Cache)
- **Operating System:** Windows 10 Pro
- **Display:** 15.6" FHD IPS LED (1920x1080)
- **Discrete Graphic Card:** NVIDIA GeForce GTX 960M 4GB
- **Total Memory:** 16.0GB DDR4 2133 MHz
- **Hard Drive:** 1TB 5400 RPM Hard Disk Drive or 512 MB SSD
- **Optical Device:** 8x DVD Recordable Drive
- **WLAN:** LAN 1000 M, Up to WiFi 2 x 2 a/c + Bluetooth® 4.0
- **Supported Operating Systems:** Windows 7, Windows 8, and Windows 10

LOW END

- **Processor:** Intel Core i5 Processor (6MB Cache, up to 3.20GHz)
- **Operating System:** Windows 10 Pro
- **Display:** 15.6" FHD IPS LED (1920x1080)
- **Discrete Graphic Card:** NVIDIA GeForce GTX 960M 4GB
- **Total Memory:** 8GB DDR4 2133 MHz
- **Hard Drive:** 500GB Hard Disk Drive, 5400rpm, 2.5", SATA3
- **Optical Device:** 8x DVD Recordable Drive
- **WLAN:** LAN 1000 M, Up to WiFi 2 x 2 a/c + Bluetooth® 4.0
- **Supported Operating Systems:** Windows 7, Windows 8, and Windows 10

Figure 5. ***TrialDirector computer specifications. Hint: always go with high performance options.***

If you want to OnCue on your PC, here's what it takes:

- Windows 7 or 8 or 10 or Windows XP or Vista. 32 or 64 bit
- 1 gigahertz (GHz) or faster 32-bit (x86) or 64-bit (x64) processor
- 2 gigabyte (GB) RAM (32-bit) or 4 GB RAM (64-bit)
- 1 GB available hard disk space (32-bit) or 2 GB (64-bit)

But in general, just try to have a snappy machine, the job you're using OnCue for is important, so try and upgrade from the machines that should be polluting a landfill by now.

Figure 6. ***OnCue computer specs.***

1. Installing Sanction®

Minimum System Requirements

- 2 GHz or faster 32-bit(x86) or 64-bit(x64) processor.
- 2 GB RAM
- Approximately 1 GB of free disk space on the system drive.
- XGA (1024 x 768) or higher-resolution monitor with 256 colors.
- Microsoft Windows 7® or higher - 32-bit(x86) or 64-bit(x64).
- The Microsoft® Framework version 4.5.1 is required.
- Windows Media Player 12 is highly recommended to support media file playback.
- Microsoft Expression® Encoder 4, Service Pack 2 is required for Media Clip export feature.

Figure 7. ***Sanction computer specs.***

The trial laptop must be optimized for performance and reliability to ensure smooth operation in court. Optimization and performance are achieved through vigorous testing and software configuration. Do not merely load your exhibit database and view a few images for testing. Instead, put your exhibits, software, and equipment to the test by "extreme" testing. Run through 100 or 200 exhibits in presentation mode;[20] cycle through every image; go through documents forwards, backwards, and by page number; put an exhibit up, then take it down and put it back up again. What happens? The goal is to see if you can force an error and whether it is repeatable so you know your laptop's limitations.

4.1.4.2 Laptop Speed

You should be able to input the number of an exhibit you want to present and have it display within a second or two. If it takes longer, it's too long to wait. Try counting, "one-one-thousand, two one-thousand, three-one thousand" after inputting the exhibit number. If you are at "two one-thousand," you are borderline; if you hit three "one-thousand," you are *slow* and will not have good timing for the presentation of your exhibits. Test your exhibits and video for loading performance.

4.2 Build a Trial Kit

After you've obtained the best trial laptop you can afford, you should next consider building a trial kit that contains supplemental hardware to aid in trial presentation. Even with a moderate trial schedule, renting is a great option,

20. Or better yet, every exhibit.

but you'll still want to create a trial kit for emergencies, to fill in gaps, and to practice with.[21] The trial kit contains equipment that works with your laptop to connect to, repair, or supplement a court or war room presentation system, and contains items like your own video switch, cables and accessories, adaptors, and speakers. For example, cables are often eaten up at night by vacuum cleaners or run over by chairs until they don't work. How will you fix it? As your skills increase, you'll add additional items to your kit, but let's start off with some of the basics. Much of what you will need is decided by how often your firm is in trial, your budget, and the equipment you are comfortable with using. Include a few extra VGA adaptors, gender changers, and a variety of VGA/HDMI cables in different lengths so you'll be ready to go. Having a good power strip in the kit, for example, can save the day for both sides when there's only a single power outlet for the entire courtroom. Lastly, remember that most courts still use VGA connections, while modern laptops don't come with VGA connections anymore. You'll want an adaptor or two (think redundancy) to ensure you can connect your HDMI laptop in VGA courtrooms.

Basic Kit - For Emergency Repairs	Advanced Kit: For Full Presentation Needs
VGA Cables: Variety (3 x 3ft, 1 x 15ft, extension)	Projector
A single speaker TBD	A single speaker TBD
4 port or 6 port video switch: Extron or Kramer	4 port or 6 port video switch: Extron or Kramer
VGA Adaptors: Various Various	D/A switch: Extron or Kramer
Mini Stereo Audio Extension Cable M/F 10ft	VGA Cables: Variety (3 x 3ft, 1 x 15ft, extension)
Heavy Duty Power Strip	VGA Adaptors: Various
10 ft. Power Extension Cord	Mini Stereo Audio Extension Cable M/F 10ft
VGA Y splitter	25 ft. Power Extension Cord
Gaffers tape	Heavy Duty Power Strip
	VGA Y splitter
	Gaffers tape

Figure 8. ***Trial kit checklist.***

4.2.1 Projector

Projector technology is an area in which the features are rapidly improving and the price dropping, with big enhancements to resolution, brightness, and features. There is a lot of variety in this space, so while my firm does own a few projectors, I tend to rent them and ask the vendor to bring more than one so I can test them in the proper environment. The projector has a tremendous advantage in viewing area onscreen versus a big-screen monitor, as a project can display in a 4:3 square aspect ratio (in addition to other aspect ratios). The viewing area is a very important feature to consider and is often overlooked; lawyers often never connect the dots between their presentation and whether it appears legibly on the projector or monitor.

Below are the most important features to review when you choose a projector.

- **Projector brightness**. A lumen is the unit of measurement for projector brightness. In general, the brighter the projector, the better. *As a general guideline, your projector should be 5000 lumens or brighter.* This level of lumens allows for projecting in bright light—thus, you won't have to dim the lights in the courtroom to see what is being projected. Think of the extra time and effort it takes just to dim the lights in the courtroom,[22] especially if you are going back and forth between presenting an image and witness examination.
- **Resolution options**. Does the projector have the ability to HD 1080p? Can it display in lower resolutions, like the outdated 1024x768, if necessary?
- **Aspect ratio**. The older 4:3 aspect ratio is best in the legal environment, as it allows you to get more of the document on screen. Try to use only a single aspect ratio in court. For example, if there are existing 16:9 monitors on the counsel table, then you should use a 16:9 projector and screen.

21. For practice and war room use, you can find some quality used equipment on eBay.
22. The light controls are usually at a door panel, meaning someone would need to stand by the lights to turn them off and on.

- **Throw distance.** Throw distance refers to how close and how far the projector can place an image that fills a screen. Typically, the issue is one of cramped quarters: how close to the screen must the projector be to legibly show an image. Some projectors specialize in a "short throw," which means it can be closer to the projector screen. This is an especially good option in cramped environments (but potentially, a flat-screen monitor would also work).
- **DLP.** This is a feature meant to bring color balance to movies, but it can significantly affect yellow highlighting. It is increasingly difficult to find projectors without DLP, so be sure to test your yellow highlights before your trial starts.[23] Sometimes orange, pink, or green work better for highlighting.
- **Fan noise.** How noisy is the projector's fan? (Keep in mind that the brighter the projector, the hotter it gets, which means the louder the fan.) Fan noise might not seem like a big deal, but judges will shut down the projector in the middle of cross-examination if the projector is too noisy.
- **Keystone.** This refers to the projector's ability to adjust to the screen at odd angles.

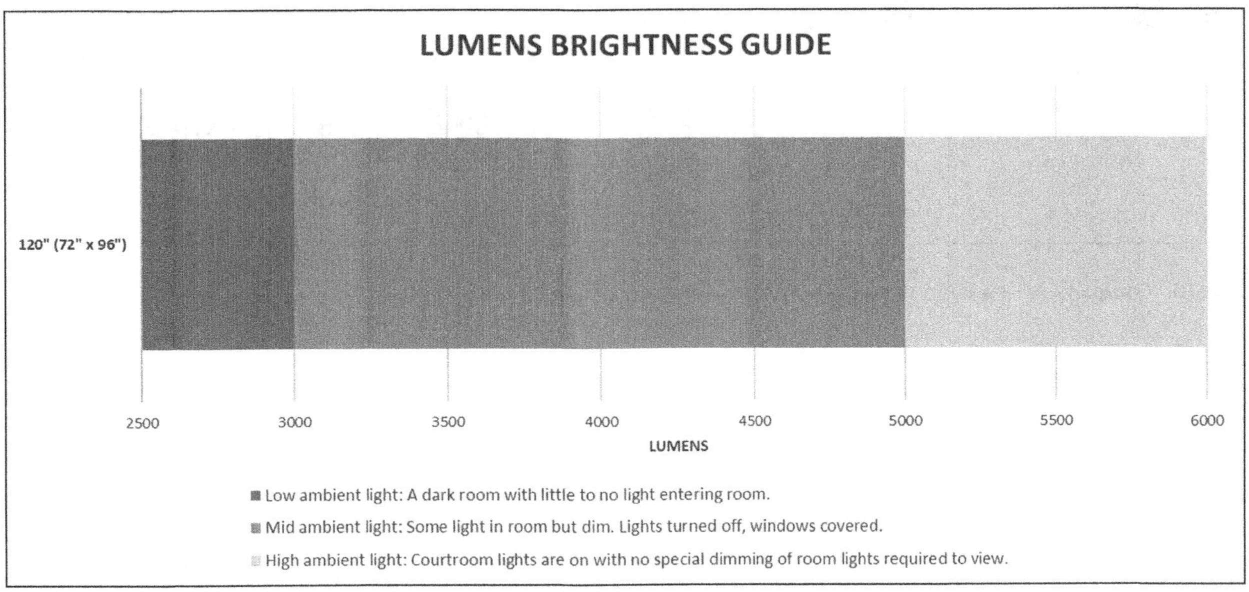

Figure 9. ***How bright a projector should be for the room it's in. Always use the brightest, highest resolution projector you can.***

4.2.2 Projector Screen

The screen choice may seem like a no-brainer, but the challenges of a courtroom never fail to cause an issue. Issues typically involve mixed aspect ratios or placement. Here are some features to consider with a screen:

- **Mounting options.** How will the projector stand? How it will be mounted and placed in the courtroom? Your screen may need to fit between chairs in the audience or on top of a cabinet. This is why it's important to evaluate the courtroom in advance and know your placement options and mounting hardware.[24]
- **Viewing area/size.** Go bigger than what your instinct tells you. Size goes hand in hand with placement. A projector typically has a much bigger (by multiples) viewing area than a monitor, which is an important feature to consider.

23. Maybe you'll use orange or green highlights if yellow doesn't show. Provide options to the legal team.
24. If you are renting, ask the vendor to bring a few options and use what works best.

- **Screen surface.** This should be white or matte white (not gray) and one that will provide true color representation.
- **Aspect ratio.** The ratio between the width and the height of a picture, expressed in units 16:9 or 4:3.

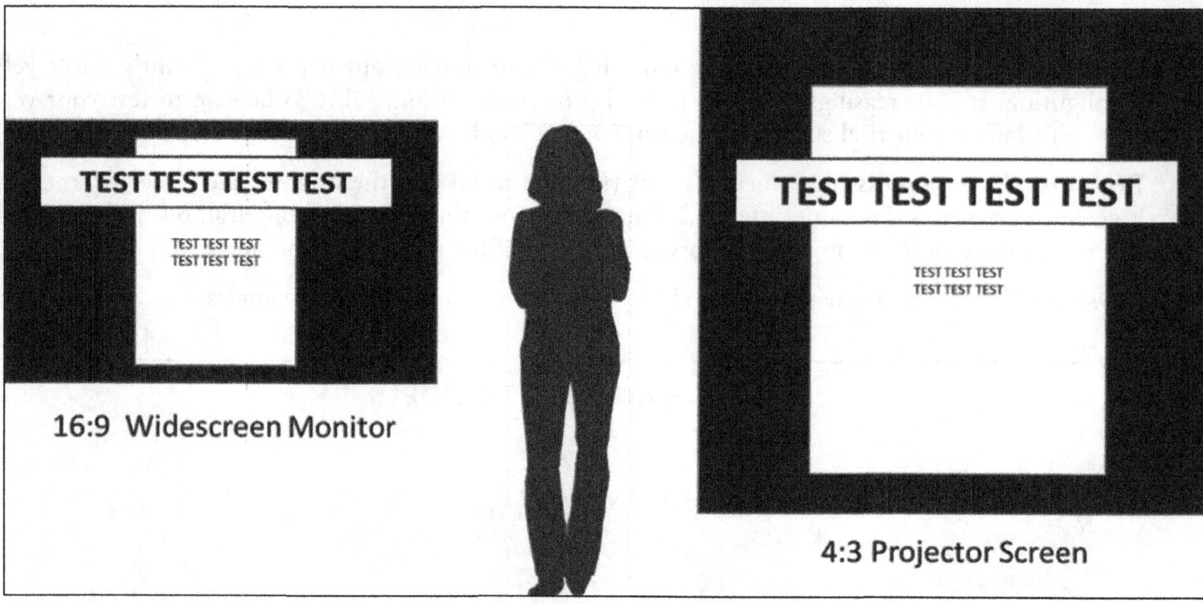

Figure 10. ***Comparison of a wide-screen monitor to a projector screen.***

4.2.3 Primary Monitor

An alternative to using a projector is using a big-screen monitor.[25] Obtain the largest screen possible for your courtroom (sixty-five or more inches) to get the best result—go bigger than you think you need. On a 16:9 "rectangle" screen, the usable portion for viewing document exhibits is relatively small (the sides are not usable), so you might think about using a monitor larger than what you first considered, or you might use a projector. Remember you are trying to view text and fine detail, not a football game. Don't consider anything smaller than sixty-five inches (and even then, only if it is positioned close to the decision-makers). Pay particular attention to the distance between your audience (the judge and jury) and the monitor. If there is too much distance between them, you may want the size and viewing area that a large projector can bring.

Monitors are much brighter and crisper than projectors due to their higher resolution. They also don't cast a shadow when you gesture or stand in front of them. Incidentally, the smaller monitors placed on counsel and judge's tables should be the same aspect ratio as the primary viewing screen. Big-screen monitors are a slam dunk in smaller courtrooms, but in a larger courtroom, you should take advantage of the greater viewing area that a projector and screen can bring.

Features to consider:

- **Brightness.** Monitors are typically brighter, but there are exceptions. Look to how "white" the whites are and how "black" the black is. Is it color accurate?
- **Viewable area.** One negative with monitors is their viewable area. Moreover, their *usable* viewable area is much smaller than most because the sides of a 16:9 screen aren't used.

25. Think big-screen TV.

- **Resolution.** Modern big-screen monitors have extremely high resolutions, and it's possible that your laptop won't be able to reach the resolution or the monitor can "dumb down" to a lower one. Always test in advance.
- **Placement.** The monitor is a great choice for smaller courtrooms or in spots where a projector can't be easily placed.

	PROJECTOR	MONITOR
Viewable Area	✓	
Placement flexibility		✓
Brightness	✓[26]	✓
Ease of installation		✓
Resolution		✓
Aspect Ratio	4:3 or 16:9	16:9

Figure 11. ***Pros and cons between a projector and a big-screen monitor.***

4.2.3.1 Working with Multiple Monitors: Duplicate Screen or Extended Desktop

Whenever possible, work in "extended desktop" mode; it should be one of your basic skills. Extended desktop allows you to work on the computer on one screen while presenting on the other, thus allowing for presentation and prep at the same time. Even if you are not using trial presentation software, you could open files on one screen (as depicted in Figure 12, below) and drag them across to the other screen. Both screens can present independently, meaning you can work on the first screen and send everything showing on the second screen to the projector and other connected monitors in the courtroom. This method can be pulled off easily and might be a good option for those who will present only a few documents and are not comfortable with trial presentation software.

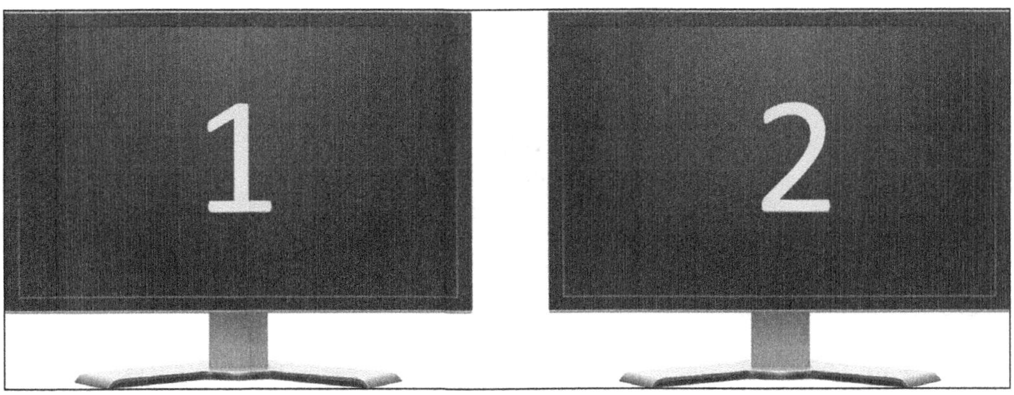

Figure 12. ***Extended desktop.***

Duplicate screen, or "mirror mode," means that whatever appears on one screen is duplicated on the other. It is a simpler way to set things up. Just keep in mind that people will see *everything* you do—if you have to navigate to a location on your hard drive or you have your witness outline open, for example, the audience will see it. I recommend working in extended desktop whenever possible.

26. 5000 lumens or brighter.

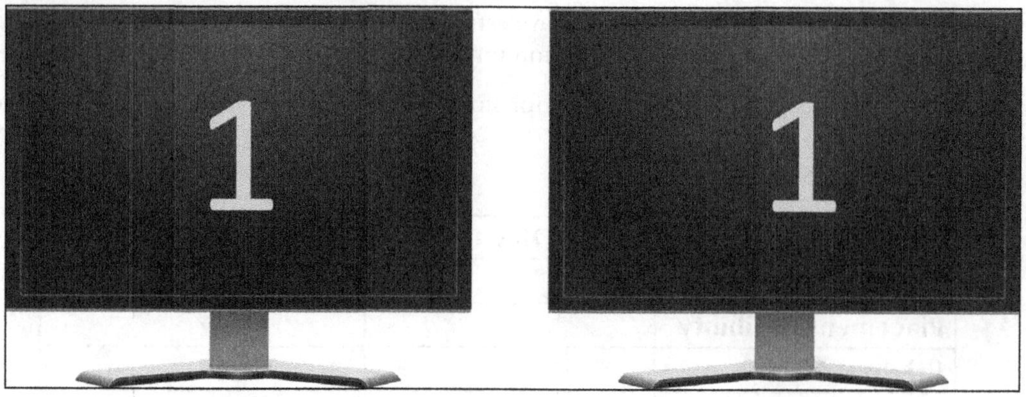

Figure 13. ***Mirror mode.***

A final note: keep in mind that when you connect to a court system, the second screen will show up on every monitor in the courtroom regardless of whether you are in mirror or extended screen mode.

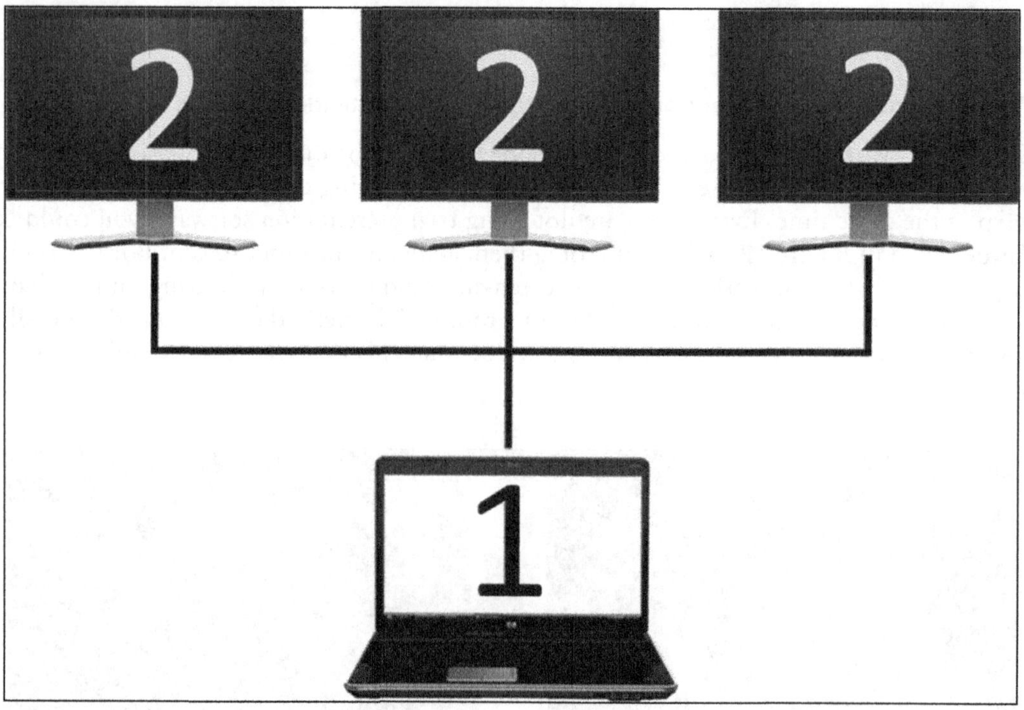

Figure 14. ***Extended desktop on multiple screens.***

4.2.3.2 Understanding Aspect Ratios

A monitor's aspect ratio is the ratio between the width and the height of a picture expressed in units. For our purposes, 4:3 is "square" and 16:9 is a "rectangle" and is considered "widescreen." This is discussed in detail in Chapter Six, Courtroom Setup, but it is worth a brief mention here to underscore how important it is. Think about how you'll deal with any mismatch in aspect ratio between yourself and the court system but also between legal team members and vendors. By deal with, I mean either configuring the courtroom or your own equipment so that your images are optimally displayed and are neither stretched nor squished. Anyone creating or displaying graphics for you, including your vendors, must be told about the courtroom aspect ratio so they can create the best graphics possible. Be sure to read about aspect ratios in Chapter Six, as it goes into great detail.

4.2.3.3 Understanding Resolution

Resolution is the number of pixels that can be displayed in a dimension. Dimension refers to the width x height ratio in pixels.

Understanding resolution is important for two reasons. First, you will likely be downgrading from the resolution you use on your office computer to a significantly lower resolution in the courtroom (provided there exists equipment). This can have a negative effect on your presentation, as it can change how graphics appear on screen.

Second, the resolution is the shape of the screen (usually square 4:3 or rectangle 16:9), as I mentioned above. Always customize your presentation to the aspect ratio and resolution of the displays used in the courtroom.

The most common aspect rations and resolutions are below.

4:3	16:9	Aspect Ratio
640x480	1280x720	**Resolution**
1024x768	1365x768	**Resolution**
1400x1050	1920x1080	**Resolution**
1600x1200		**Resolution**

Figure 15. ***Screen resolution by aspect ratio.***

4.2.4 Other Common Presentation Equipment Used in the Courtroom

Now I will introduce you to equipment typically used in trial presentation that may be unfamiliar to you. Some of this equipment may be built into an existing court system, or you may need to rent it from a vendor or include it in your trial kit. Sometimes, there is nothing in the courtroom and you must build from scratch—which, in many cases, might be preferable. Most often, however, you will simply supplement an existing courtroom system.

4.2.4.1 Video Switch (VGA or HDMI)

The video switch allows you to connect multiple devices (e.g., laptops, computers, document cameras, or anything with a VGA or HDMI connection) to a switch that allows multiple inputs to share a single video source, which, in turn, might be distributed to multiple monitors or projectors in the courtroom. Each input is assigned a number, and you select the number of the piece of equipment you want to use. Each input is called a port, so typically you ask for a four- or six-port switch. (Switches come in two to twelve, or more, port inputs.) The switch is easy to use and allows teams to move between laptops, backup laptops (when needed), a document camera, and over to opposing counsel. Always create a cheat sheet that lists the port number and the piece of equipment it corresponds to and post it where it can be seen.

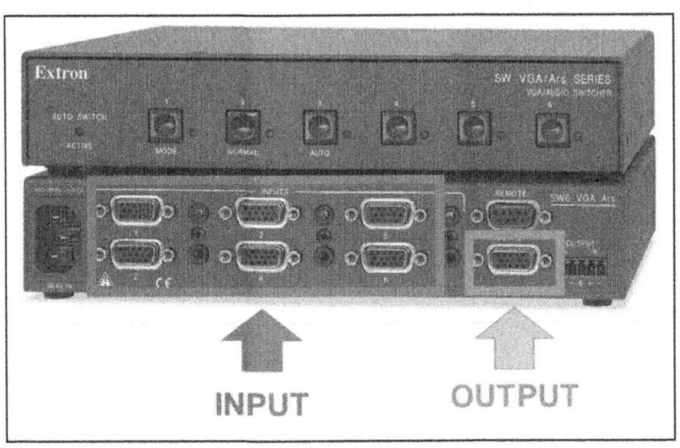

Figure 16. ***The front and back of a switch. Six inputs with one output.***

In most cases, I get a six-port switch and plug my laptop and backup into the first two ports (#1 and #2, respectively), leave a port unused (#3), the document camera (#4) and another unused port (#5), and then opposing counsel (#6). The unused ports (#3 and #5) are important because you might want to quickly turn off the signal to all monitors, and all screens will turn black when you simply switch to an unused port. Fading to black or switching off the video signal to the courtroom monitors occurs frequently due to sidebar and exhibit admittance disagreements. Typically, you must take down the exhibit on display while an issue is being resolved, then quickly resume where you were in the presentation once the sidebar or issue is over. Say, for example, you called up an exhibit, called out a section and highlighted it, and then there was a sidebar and you were asked to take down the exhibit from courtroom display. While you could use the trial software to do this, you won't be able to continue working on the exhibit image (say, to adjust a highlight) if you use the switch to remove the image from all courtroom screens.

Switch Number Cheat Sheet

1. Primary laptop
2. Backup laptop
3. Not used
4. Document camera
5. Not used
6. Opposing counsel

Figure 17. ***Tape this cheat sheet where it is readily viewable.***

As your skills increase, simultaneously using two laptops will have you feeling like a DJ, as you run a presentation on one side and cue up the next video on the other. As with any piece of equipment, you should practice using the switch with your court outlines to see how each movement (i.e., physically pushing the buttons to the various pieces of equipment) works. For example, does it take ten seconds for the document camera to wake up when you switch to it? If so, perhaps it's not a good idea to switch between the document camera and your trial software multiple times if you must keep a fast pace. Practicing with the switch is important, so I typically get one[27] for the war room to practice with and to determine if an outline is overly technically ambitious (i.e., impractical), or to practice merely to ensure everything runs smoothly.

Typically, both the plaintiff and defense connect their equipment to a single switch that, by agreement of both parties, is run by one side. Sometimes, both parties want to run the switch. In that case, I suggest playing Rock Paper Scissors to decide who gets the switch. The side not running the primary switch may want yet another switch on their own side so they can select amongst their trial laptops and backup equipment. Obviously, it can all get very complicated and there can be compatibility issues to consider, so testing and cooperation between parties is imperative.

27. eBay is your friend here.

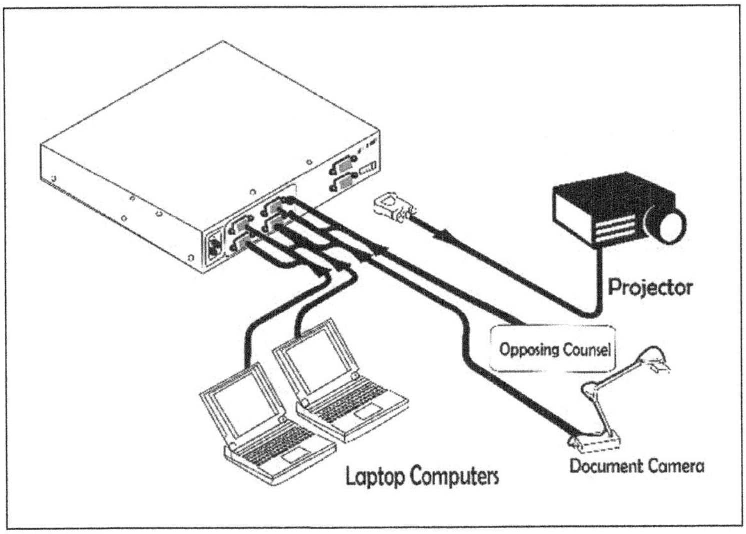

Figure 18. ***A switch with two laptops, a document camera, and the opposing counsel feed connected to a projector.***

Quality equipment matters here; most in the industry use Extron and Kramer for video switches and distribution. Firms need not maintain a stock of expensive and seldom-used equipment if they have a reputable vendor[28] for rental equipment in their area. However, a switch might be one of your first major trial kit purchases after your laptop and projector. I mention these brands because they are likely not known by consumers and their reliability and quality are worthy of special mention. (Also worth noting is that most of the federal courthouses use Extron switching equipment behind the scenes.) Remember, always test equipment you will use in the courtroom in advance to see if the switch produces an accurate image on screen or affects the resolution or aspect ratio. You don't want nasty surprises in the courtroom.

4.2.4.2 Video Distribution

Video distribution is the opposite of the input switch. Whereas the video switch allows multiple inputs, the video distribution allows you to split the signal from your video source (laptop, document camera, etc.) into multiple outputs.[29] Video distribution takes a single signal from a laptop or switch and splits it to be displayed on multiple monitors, thus allowing the team to place monitors for the judge, witness, and counsel, and a main screen for shared viewing.

28. Unless you live in a location that does not have good local vendors and you need to revisit purchasing or travel costs for a vendor in a big city.
29. The splitter also amplifies the video signal, which might be an issue when using long cables throughout the courtroom.

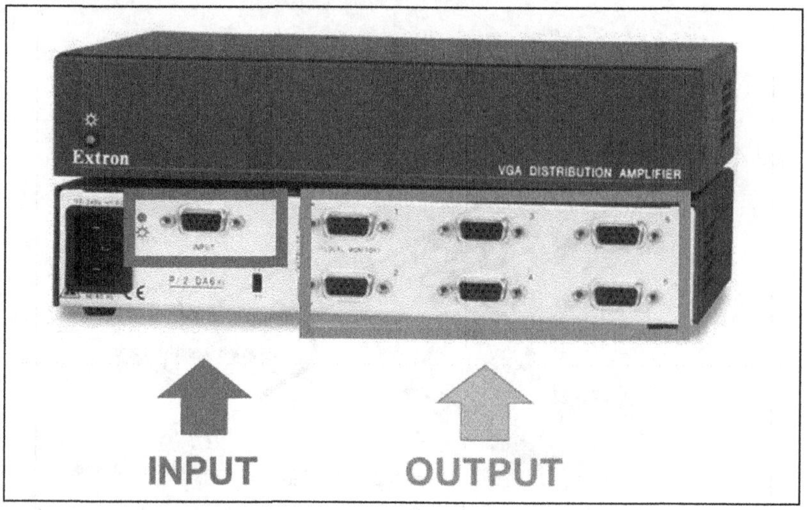

Figure 19. ***A splitter splits the signal from a single input to multiple outputs.***

4.2.4.3 Distribution Amplifier Switch

The distribution amplifier (DA)[30] switch allows you to keep a local monitor for working and prep while the other side is presenting. The switch connects to the video output of the laptop and splits the video signal, so that one signal can be sent to a local monitor and the other to the court system. Keep in mind if you are extending your computer screen to a shared courtroom system, it is only yours while you are presenting. It allows you to continue to work on the second screen while the other side is presenting. The DA switch is typically for more advanced courtroom setups.

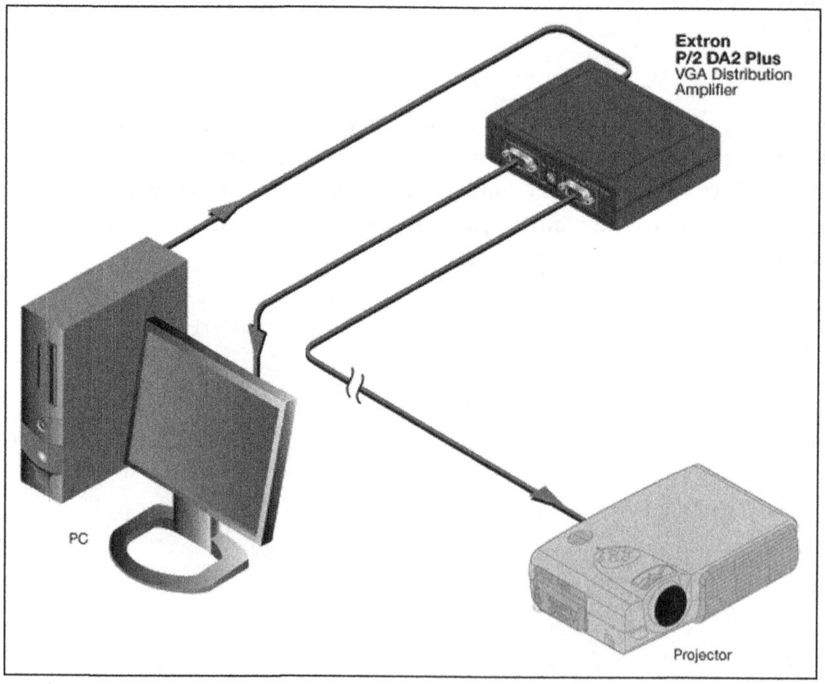

Figure 20. ***Split signal to local monitor and projector.***

30. The distribution amplifier distributes the video signal and provides increased power so the signal can make it down long video cable runs (i.e., longer than twenty-five feet).

Figure 21. ***Splits signal from a single input.***

4.2.4.4 Sound Mixers and Speakers

The primary ability that a soundboard brings is to raise or lower the sound level on the speakers beyond what you can do with the volume control on your laptop. I use a soundboard to modulate the volume of poor quality audio. All the dials that you see on the soundboard below are rarely used, so don't be intimidated if you need to use one. For example, on a video with very low sound quality or low volume, the soundboard boosts the volume level higher than your computer volume level can do. Often, the use of a soundboard can be negated by quality control of the audio and video you are using by resending the video to have the sound levels adjusted. *Warning*: Be careful that any adjustments made to the video don't alter the timing or format of synced video; test it again once returned.

Figure 22. ***Soundboard.***

As far as speakers, you'll want to balance something practical and portable that is a little beyond the small desktop speakers you are using now. In particularly large courtrooms, you might consider renting a larger speaker that provides sufficient coverage for the room. Lastly, as many courtroom speaker systems are problematic, we often bypass courtroom audio systems in favor of a speaker attached to the presentation system.

Figure 23. ***Speaker.***

4.2.4.5 Lapel Microphone

A lapel microphone is a wearable mic that attaches to a lapel or necktie. They can be a frustrating piece of equipment, in that people make preventable errors when they use them. The placement and testing of the lapel mic is everything; try to place it mid-chest, with the mic pointing up. Ensure that it is not touching any clothing. A few minutes of practice and testing will help you avoid a lot of problems.

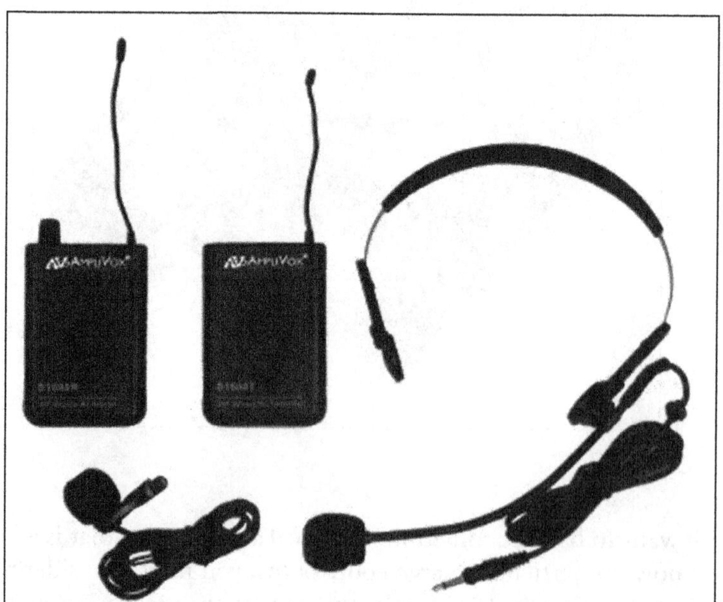

Figure 24. ***Lapel mic set. (Image courtesy of By Terodaktil (own work) CC BY-SA 4.0 (via Wikimedia Commons).***

First, test the mic by having the presenter speak as they will to decision-makers—*not* by holding the mic up to their lips and having them say, "Testing, 1-2-3." Position the mic to where it works best. With some models, it will be low on the body; others, high. Second, even if you rent other equipment, I recommend purchasing the microphone portion of the lapel mic. Some mics are unwieldy and ridiculously big. Third, make sure you use the "windmuffs" that cover the mic (and have extras on hand), so that every bump, scratch, and body sound doesn't end up amplified to the entire courtroom. Last, know how to mute it (typically, there's a button somewhere on the mic) so that when you go to sidebar or whisper a confidential aside to your co-counsel, it isn't broadcast in court.

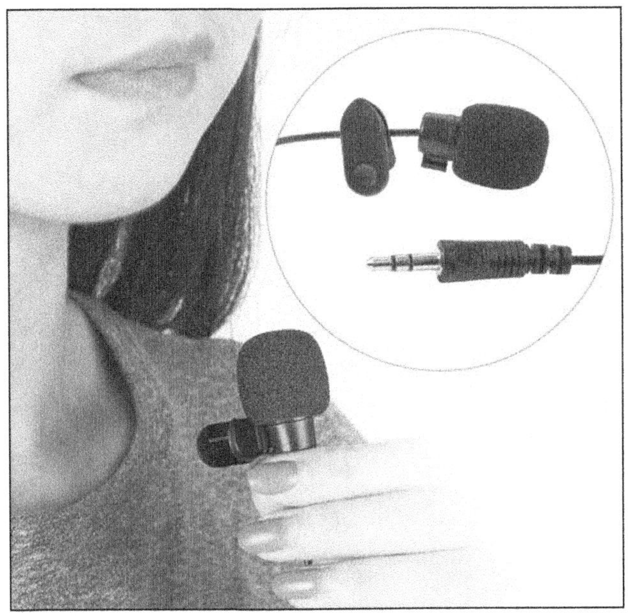

Figure 25. ***Don't test a lapel mic like this. Test it clipped to your lapel.***

Here are a few tips to help you avoid feedback and other sound issues:

- Remove your cell phone from your front pocket.
- Place the microphone (and yourself) behind the main speakers.
- Point the speakers away from the microphone.

4.2.4.6 Document Camera

One of my favorite pieces of equipment to use in conjunction with trial presentation software is a document camera.[31] The document camera can typically plug into your video switch, just like your laptop(s). The document camera can supplement and enhance the presentation by legal teams by changing the pace, breaking up the monotony, or adding an air of drama and urgency that may not be conveyed by trial presentation software. For example, a lawyer can pull a paper copy of an exhibit used in the opposing party's opening statement to immediately address an issue in your side's opening, then highlight, circle, and emphasize your argument.

31. The document camera is also a great piece of equipment to consider if you have a very small set of documents and aren't comfortable with trial presentation software.

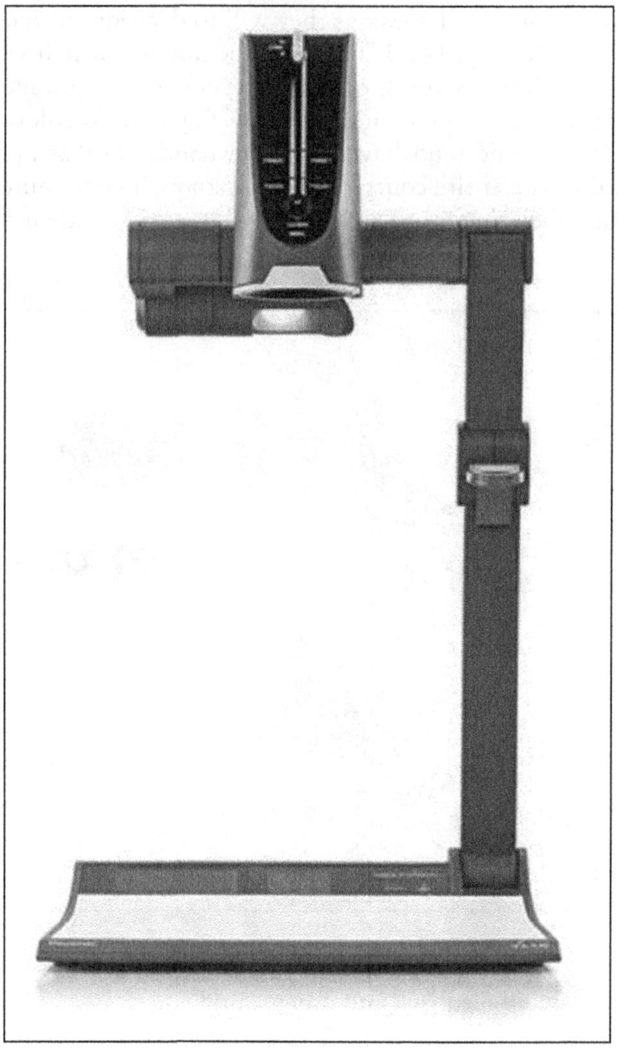

Figure 26. ***Document camera.***

Most courts and rental vendors use WolfVision document cameras. Get to know the basic controls (e.g., zoom in, zoom out) and which direction the document will need to be placed so it's not upside down on screen (*do this before court, not during!*). Typically, the document camera has an autofocus and a dial for speedy zoom in and zoom out. You'll be in pretty good shape if you leave it on autofocus and just use the dial to zoom. Practice makes perfect—don't underestimate how silly you will look fumbling at the controls.

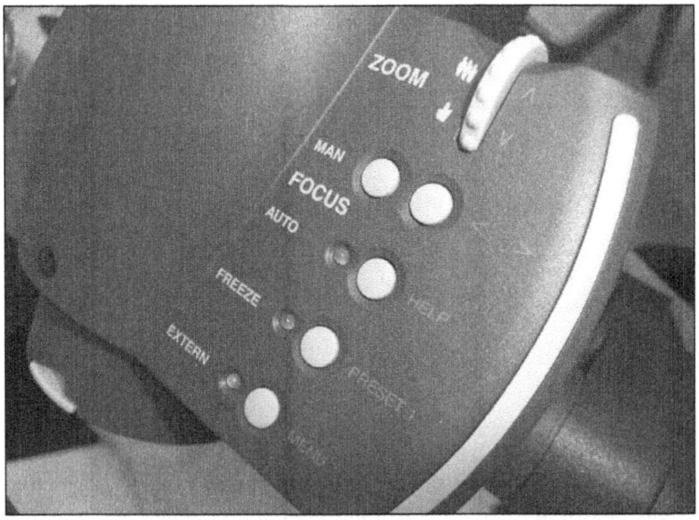

Figure 27. ***Familiarize yourself with the control panel of a document camera before you need to use it.***

There are many things to like about the document camera, and I highly recommend adding one to your standard trial setup. They are:

- **Easy to use**. Just put place your document under the camera.
- **Interesting**. A limited set of documents placed on the document camera breaks up the monotony of slide after slide and trial presentation software.
- **Redundancy/backup**. If your trial laptop breaks down or you're missing an exhibit, you can quickly and smoothly transition onto the document camera—as long as it is integrated into your setup.

There is a surprising amount of showmanship that can be used in conjunction with the document camera. The document camera gives the legal team the opportunity to be more than a talking head behind a podium or keyboard, with some interesting movement and interactivity options. A few tips:

- Look at your fingers and fingernails. Are they clean?
- Point using the correct finger—and of course, never use the middle finger.
- Bring a variety of colored pens and highlighters to use on the paper document. Circle items, scribble, highlight, zoom in or out, and use your hands to point and emphasize.

4.2.4.7 Equipment Stands and Tables

Don't forget you'll need to place all of this equipment on something in the courtroom. Never assume there will be a place for your equipment or that you can bring your own in; always check with the court first. Vendors usually have a plethora of equipment options here—so ask them to bring several to see what works. For example, they might have a very thin table that fits in the rows of the gallery or a tech table that is long and a little narrower than usual that is perfect for laptops and switches.

If allowed, the trial tech and/or their equipment can be placed anywhere from counsel table to a "tech" table wherever there is space or in the gallery with the audience. Each of these locations presents their own unique challenges, with counsel table being the best and the gallery the worst (because nothing fits!). A few tips:

- Be sure to have a tablecloth to help hide the cables and equipment.
- If you get stuck presenting on a wooden bench, bring a chair pad to sit on. Your back will thank you.

- Remember, you should always have a clear view of the main screen and what the legal team is gesturing toward onscreen.

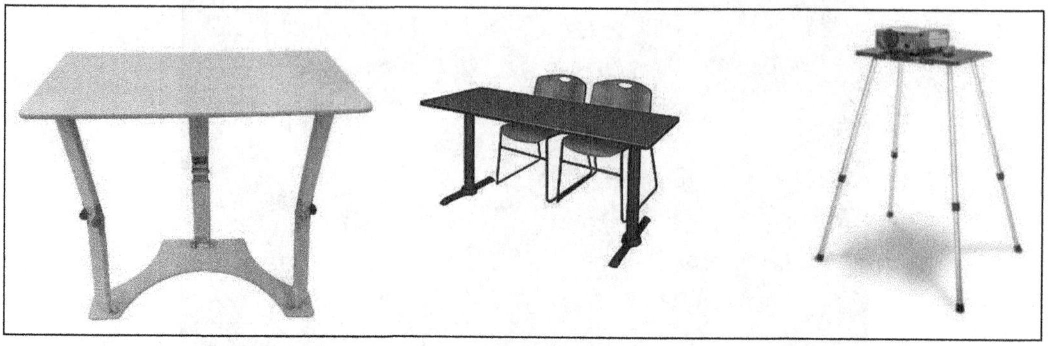

Figure 28. ***Left to right: Project-O-Stand; very versatile and can hold more than just projectors. Tech table; don't forget the draping to hide your cables. Spider-legs table; good for fitting in between gallery seats.***

4.2.5 Gaffing Tape

I'm going there! Yes, I'm going to talk about the most rookie mistake made. The one that causes the most damage to the courtroom, as well as creates an unsafe environment: *not using the right tape!*

You must use gaffing tape if you are taping down cables in the courtroom—*and you should always tape down cables in the courtroom.* Gaffing tape does not leave residue or rip up the carpet when you remove it. There is nothing worse (if your side does it) than to hear *rrrrrrripppppppppp* and see a huge section of carpet come up or a big chunk of stained wood come off a table. Do not use masking tape, do not use packing tape—there is only *gaffing tape!* Also, there is a right way and wrong way to tape down cables, and I cover that in Chapter Six, Courtroom Planning.

Figure 29. ***The all-important gaffing tape.***

4.2.6 Cables, Adaptors, Power Strips, and Extension Cords

Always ensure that the trial site (and your trial kit) has a good mix of extra cables, power strips, extension cords, and adaptors. It's common for cables to get destroyed in court, from everything like the night janitor's vacuum to being pinched under a chair in the courtroom. Being able to quickly bypass a problem cable is critical to keeping things moving forward. For example, I once had a presentation that would intermittently go black. What was the cause? A lawyer had moved his chair over a video cable, and every time he leaned back it pinched the cable. I rerouted and replaced the pinched cable on a break. VGA adaptors in a variety of genders are helpful in extending short cords or quick fixes. Lastly, keep in mind that many of our courtrooms are fairly old and may not have a lot of power options, so always keep an extension cord and power strip in your kit. Courts typically don't have adaptors or a variety of connections options for your laptop, so again, bring everything you need to connect to VGA and HDMI video inputs.

Figure 30. ***VGA Y cable.***

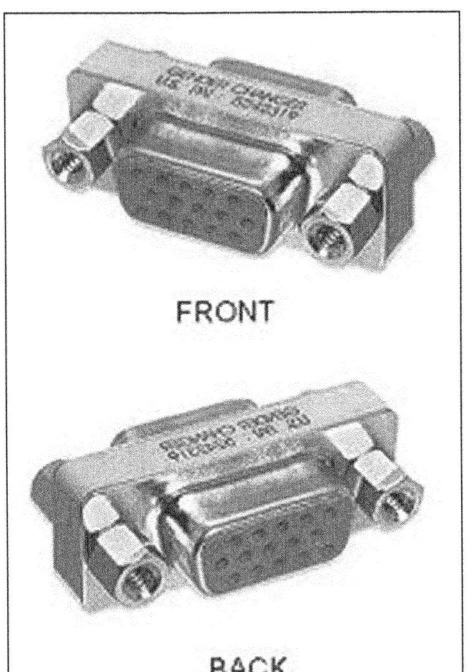

Figure 31. ***VGA adaptor, female to female.***

Figure 32. ***Audio cable extender.***

Figure 33. ***VGA extension cable.***

Figure 34. ***Power strip.***

4.2.7 *Trial Server*

While technically not a piece of courtroom or trial presentation equipment, the trial server is worthy of consideration for your offsite war room setup. The trial server allows users to create a high-performance environment in their war room via the server's local computing power. Many offsite trials have unreliable or slow internet service, so bringing the data local brings reliability and performance. It can be used to host video, exhibit databases, print documents, and fulfill other support needs.

4.2.8 *iPad*

The iPad and other tablets will have their day in court. However, they may not be ready for primetime just yet. While there have been early adopters who have done really well with tablets, tablets are still somewhat underpowered for all but the smallest cases. The other issue is redundancy. I have yet to see dual tablets being used at trial. When I have seen tablets used successfully, they are usually attached to a reliable VGA cable—so at that point, the presenter should probably be using a laptop for its increased horsepower. Lastly, the infrastructure of an Apple TV or consistent wireless isn't in enough courtrooms—but we are getting there.

4.3 Technology Used in Courtrooms

Courtrooms come in all shapes and sizes, from cutting edge to no technology whatsoever. A courtroom may have data inputs at counsel table or the podium, but the switch remains with the judge or clerk or at the podium. To assist the court, we will sometimes move the switch to another location and set up a tech table. Below are some generalizations about levels of court technology.

- **Cutting edge**. Wired courtrooms with many connection options (HDMI, VGA, Apple TV) that can take multiple inputs, high resolution of 1920x1080, single aspect ratio for all displays, large displays and sound coverage, individual displays for counsel table, witness, judge, and jury. Document camera.
- **High tech**. A built-in video presentation system, resolution under 1920x1080 (typically 1024x768), shared large display, mixed aspect ratio, shared or limited individual monitors, limited sound options, document camera.
- **Limited**. Single shared display (typically a projector and screen), no sound, perhaps a mobile presentation cart with a document camera
- **None**. No technology, a blank canvas. These courts might be enthusiastically receptive to technology or completely reject it.

Courts are reluctant to allow legal teams to supplement or change their courtroom, and for good reason. Legal teams often do a poor job of putting everything back together—so be a good guest and take care of any equipment that you use.

4.3.1 *Electronic Podium*

The high-tech podium in use in most federal courtroom today has a monitor, a document camera, and video and audio input. The podium is not conducive to a redundant setup because lawyers are quickly going back and forth between counsel table and the podium, and it would be silly to bring an entire redundant setup with them. It's also silly to do troubleshooting while at the podium, so it is not the best location to use as an input for trial software unless, of course, you are an army of one. Otherwise, plug in at the counsel table and use a clicker for PowerPoint and/or a person familiar (i.e., a trial tech) with trial software to follow along and present exhibits.

The input panel for the podium or a VGA/HDMI cable is how parties connect to the system. (Often the input is available at counsel table also). When adding a video switch to the courtroom to bring redundancy and efficiency, the technician chooses an input from the court and "wires" the courtroom. As stated just above, a system with a built-in switch at the counsel table would greatly aid in courtroom efficiency and dramatically lower technical issues via redundancy.

Soapbox Moment: Courts need to encourage the legal teams' ability to be "redundant" via a primary and backup presentation laptop—should I say it twice?

Figure 35. ***A federal courthouse's electronic podium, featuring inputs and a document camera.***

Inputs used at podium and counsel table. In some jurisdictions, you need to bring your own cables.

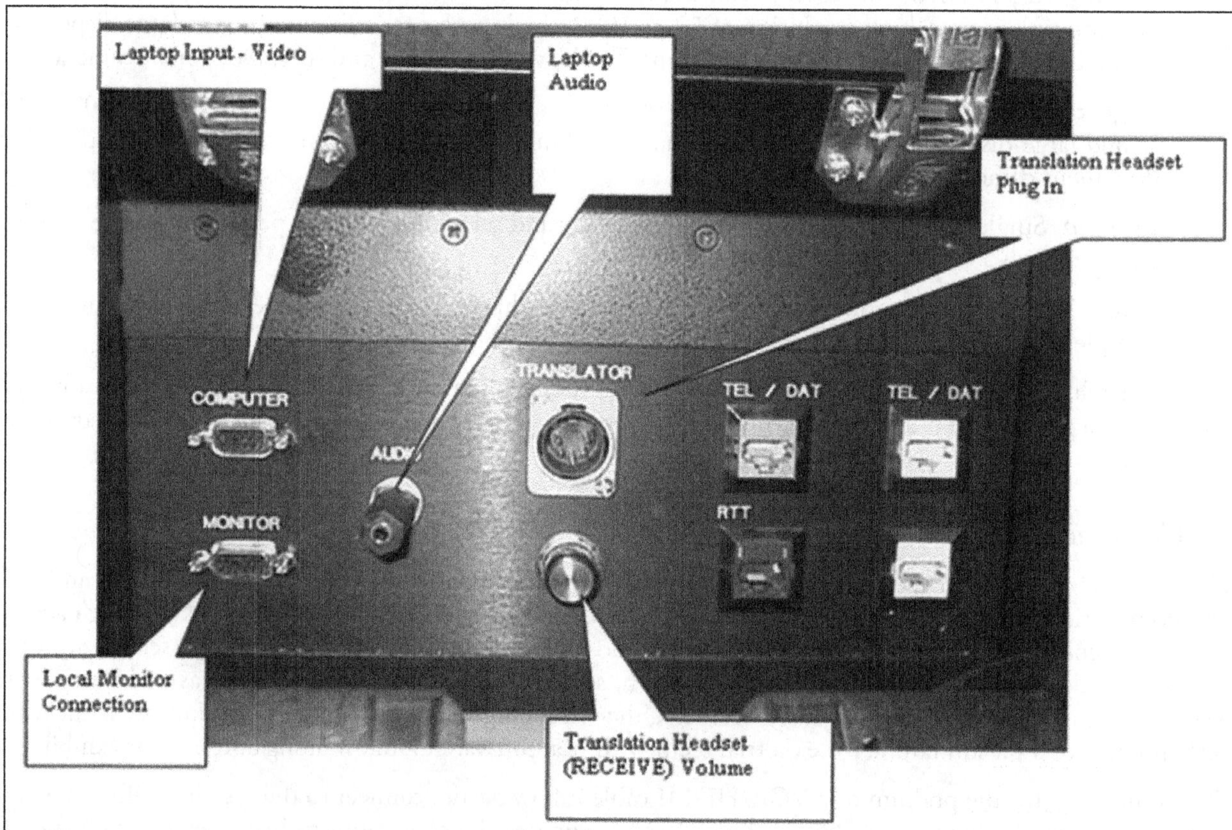

Figure 36. ***Input for presentation system in federal court. (Bring your own cables!)***

4.3.2 Annotation Touchscreen Monitors

Most high-tech courtrooms have touchscreen annotation monitors. The monitors have hotspots that allow the user to change the pen color, undo the last annotation, or clear the screen of all entries. The worst issue is the unintended marking that become visible when people are pointing and gesturing to the screen and accidentally touch the screen—which is distracting to everyone in the courtroom. It's important that you are familiar with the basic function of the annotation monitor so that you can 1) clear the screen after it's been inadvertently touched and 2) annotate documents.

Figure 37. ***A witness box with a touchscreen monitor.***

4.4 Putting It All Together

In Chapter Six, Courtroom Planning, I'll review specific courtroom setups, from basic to advanced. However, to get an idea of how the equipment I've just discussed works together, please review the below schematic. As you can see, the video switch controls everything—it is the nerve center. Also, note how your video signal (i.e., your presentation) is going through a number of different pieces of equipment (and there might be more in a courtroom video cabinet), so testing and quality control are essential. It's not like plugging into a single monitor at home or your office. The courtroom environment is easy to navigate—*if* you know your equipment and test it in advance. Alas, so many fall into the trap of thinking it "too easy." Take your technical obligations to the court seriously.

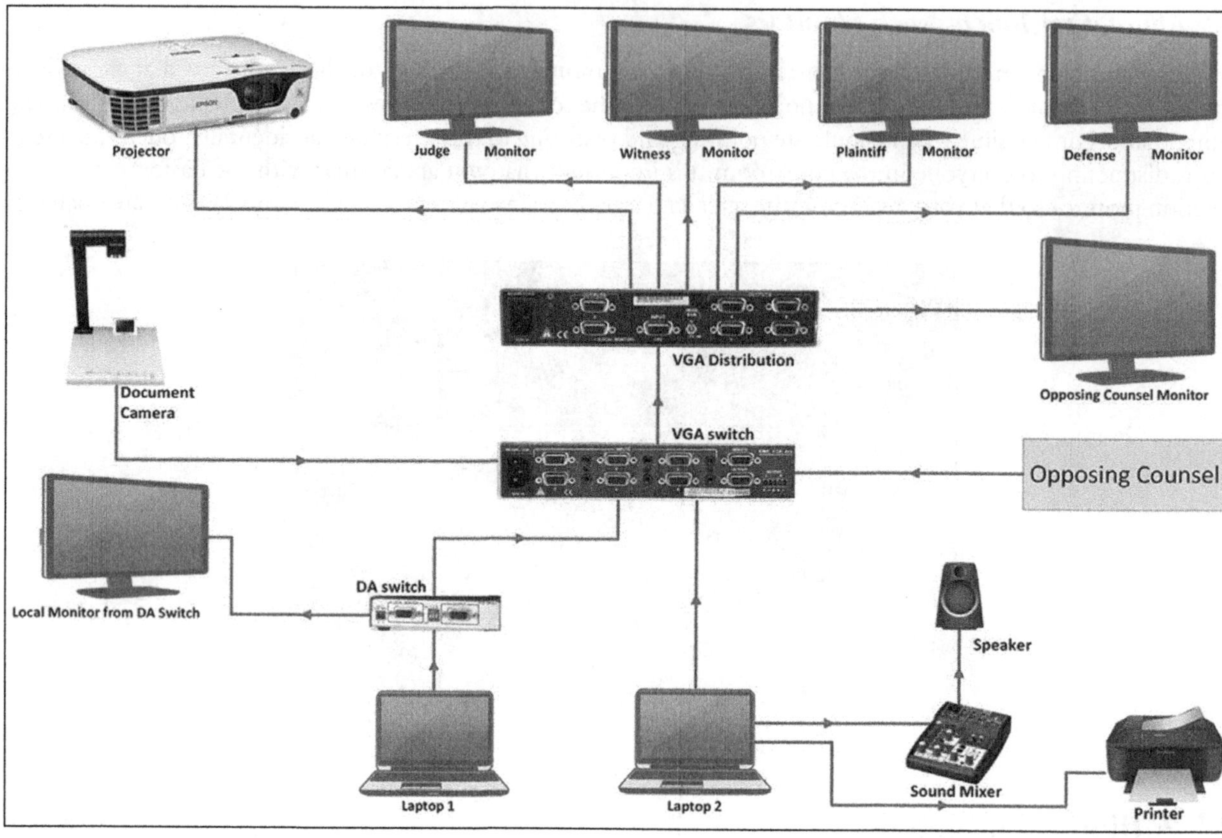

Figure 38. ***Intermediate setup.***

4.4.1 Testing

You must test and maintain all of your equipment to ensure proper working order. The equipment should be tested by putting your "system" together for a test run prior to going to court—with enough time to replace equipment, if necessary.

A few of the benefits of using a vendor is that the service, testing, and maintenance burdens are on them and they can be paid to set up the equipment for you. Moreover, the vendor will have multiple offerings for equipment redundancy.

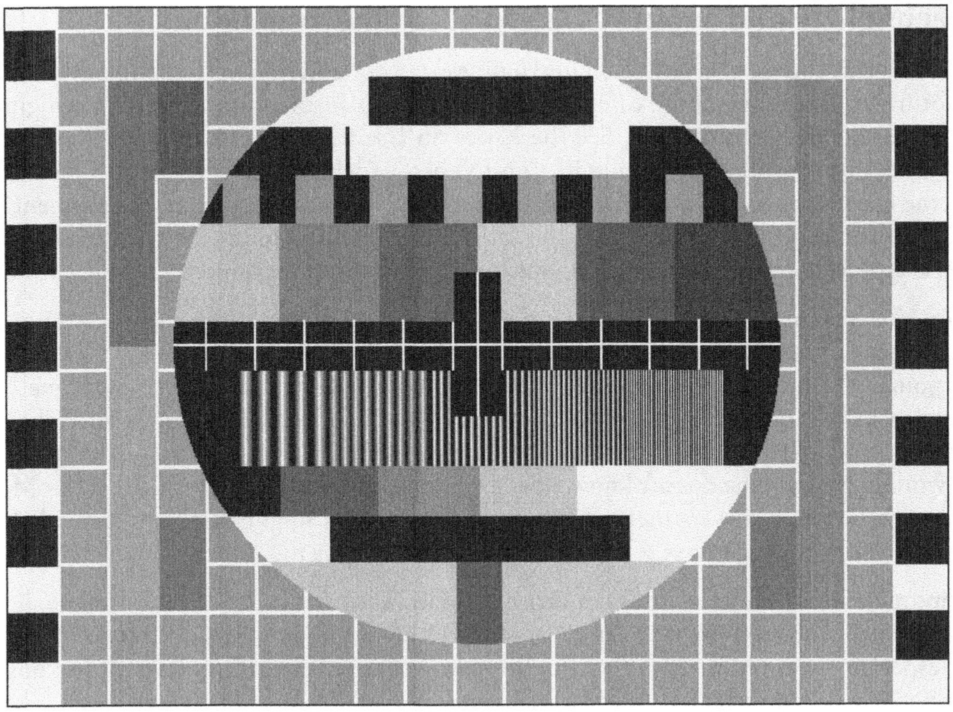

Figure 39. ***Test image for 4:3 monitor. (A full-color version of this test image is available for free download; see the Notes on Use for access.)***

Below are some critical times for you to test your equipment. Perform tests by viewing a test image on every monitor and playing a snippet of audio/video so you can calibrate the sound levels and ensure video playback is working.

- **Prior to court setup**—test your equipment to ensure it works (rather than finding out in court).
- **At initial court setup**—heavy testing with multiple images, audio, and video. Use your PowerPoint template to ensure the text is viewable and a test image with the correct aspect ratio to ensure the image is properly centered, the color is accurate, and all four corners are visible.
- **Court start and before return from lunch**—with a test image and short audio/video.

You should be hands-on in the setup for a few important reasons:

1) **To demonstrate to the court your commitment to a quality setup**. This will help address any concerns about equipment reliability or damage to the courtroom. The tech should be the point of contact for issues and maintain a "the buck stops here" attitude.
2) **To gain hands-on experience with the equipment**. Again, it is important that you have access to equipment prior to it being used live in court. A duplicative setup in the war room or obtaining the equipment a few days ahead of time is advisable.
3) **To test your cables**. Test all cables you intend to use before they are taped down to ensure they work. Don't use cables that are damaged, have a pinch or kink in them, or whose pins appear to be crooked or damaged.

4.5 Trial Technology and Support Checklist for the War Room

In Chapter Ten, Forms and Checklists, you'll find a nine-page document, Trial Technology and Support Checklist, which is a form that lists many of the case needs for trial. (This form is also available for digital download, so that you may use this in your own practice. See the Notes on Use for access.) Completing a form like this helps define responsibilities and provides the team with "go-to" people when they need help. This is a much broader document than the courtroom evaluation and instead goes over supplies, people, and equipment needs, and gets down to the nitty-gritty of documentation, like the serial numbers for equipment so a proper inventory can be performed. This is especially critical when offsite, but is useful for internal planning as well.

The legal team *should know* who is in charge (namely, the lead attorney and the chain of command) and whom to see for direction and information (usually someone deputized by the lead attorney). Legal team leadership should make a point of communicating regularly (via the deputy) with the team so everyone knows what the goals are for the case and for the moment. It's also important that the team understands what the issues are in the case and who the players are. (After all, you wouldn't want your delivery man telling the other side in the elevator what jerks they work for because he doesn't know who the attorney or witnesses are in the case.) More importantly though, remember that as non-lawyers themselves, courtroom staffers might be able to provide legal teams with valuable insight into the thought process of fellow non-lawyers (such as the jurors).[32]

Especially important is to have everyone's contact information, such as cell phone numbers, hotel room numbers, etc., so they can be contacted in case of an emergency. Don't overlook needs like access to telephones and the ability to print (especially to print *in volume*). Also, no matter the trial size, it's important to know what to bring and who will bring it—so plan early.

Finally, as trial techs, you will likely need an area that allows sufficient room for multiple computers, monitors, and sound (for video editing), so an office is often appropriate. Moreover, you should strive to have an area that approximates the size of the courtroom environment. This is especially important for the aspect ratio and resolution of monitors. Also, try to approximate a display that is about the same size as the large central display in the courtroom. These steps will provide an accurate assessment of how your graphics will be viewed and a good practice area for your entire legal team.

32. A great idea is to do your opening, closing, and witness practice with a few staff members involved.

CHAPTER FIVE

COMPANION SOFTWARE

"You have a grand gift for silence, Watson. It makes you quite invaluable as a companion."

—*Sir Arthur Conan Doyle*

Along with your trial software of choice, you need a number of companion tools to prepare electronic files for use at trial. These are software tools that that help in either preparing or presenting electronic files in court or for team use. While many of these tools have features that are duplicated in trial software, it is often more practical to use a specialized application and/or one that more team members are familiar with. Here are the software applications trial techs often find the most useful:

- **Relativity,**[1] **Concordance, Ringtail**—document review software, typically the source database for exhibits. This could be a standalone database or a plug-in utility for your internet browser.
- **Microsoft Office**—to view and create commonly used files like PowerPoint for opening statement, witness presentations, and closing argument. Use Word for outlines of all kinds and Excel for project management.
- **Snagit**—screen captures and annotations (highlights, arrows, circles, etc.). Very useful in creating graphics for PowerPoint.
- **Adobe Acrobat Professional**—for PDF exhibit creation and editing. Typically, you don't want to use the free version (Adobe Reader) because it doesn't have tools you need, like OCR, Redact, Brand, etc.
- **Case Notebook (formerly LiveNote), TextMap**—transcript organization, issue coding, and video review.
- **Windows Movie Maker (free), Adobe Premiere Lite**—video editing for basic video cuts of video not synced to a transcript.
- **Total Commander**—file manager that helps with synchronization, file renaming, comparisons, etc.
- **UltraEdit, Notepad++**—text editors used to rename and manipulate lines of text in a text file. Used for advanced log file/load file tasks and data manipulation.
- **VeraCrypt**—to encrypt and decrypt files sent to you.
- **Anti-virus software**—to keep your computer safe from viruses. Be very careful with anti-virus software, as it can slow down or corrupt your trial presentation software. Test often.

1. It is important that you have access to source databases so you can perform further research on exhibits if necessary. Often unanticipated issues at trial come up, and it's extremely limiting to have only the exhibits to review.

5.1 Trial Laptop Setup

The trial laptop should be built for performance and be loaded with software strictly related to trial presentation and preparation. There are a variety of tools and apps that people routinely use in their digital lives and profession that might not be a good idea to install on a trial laptop, things like iTunes, games, video players, software codecs, etc. Some might be crucial to your own practice and thus necessary, but if not, then don't install it. What's important is to rigorously test your trial presentation laptop with your new software installed. Furthermore, you should also document what software is installed on your trial laptop, how it's configured, who "built" it, and a list that verifies that you've tested each application.

Below is a Trial Presentation Laptop Build and QC Sheet. The build sheet lists the applications listed above, plus a few more that are optional. The "verified" column is for the initials of the builder, as it's important that each application is opened and tested to ensure it works. You may want to place licensing codes and information into the "notes" column so that if you need to rebuild the laptop, you'll have everything at your fingertips. I've included columns for the install order and software version. The install order is important because you want to install your trial software last so that its program files aren't overwritten by anything else that is installed afterward. If you work for a large firm, you may want to use the "check in" and "check out" spaces included here, too. Always have a process in place for removing data and backing it up, if necessary, after a trial ends.

Trial Presentation Laptop Build and QC Sheet

Laptop Name: ______________________________

QC'd by: ________________________ **Assigned to:** ______________________

Date Released : ___/___/___ **Expected Returned Date to IT:** ___/___/___

Verified	Software	Optional	Install Order	Version	Notes
	Trial Software	NO	LAST		
	Adobe Acrobat	NO			
	CD Burner XP Pro	NO			CD/DVD Burner
	eDrawings Viewer	Yes			For viewing AutoCAD files
	Adobe Flash Player	Yes			
	Deposition Software	Yes			
	Microsoft Office	NO			
	Snagit	Yes			Highly recommend
	Total Commander	Yes			
	UltraEdit	Yes			
	WinRAR or Winzip	NO			
	E-Transcript Viewer	Yes			
	InforMatik Image driver	Yes			Image
	Windows Essentials	Yes			**(Movie Maker)**
	VeraCrypt	Yes			Encryption software
	QuickTime	Yes			

Configuration

Verified	Hardware Check	Instructions	Notes
	Sound	Connect an audio device, and verify the audio	
	Sound	Turn Windows default to "No sounds"	
	Video Driver	Verify 1024x768 and 1920x1080 resolutions	
	Power Profile	Edit Power Options to **Never** for all Categories	
	Background	Change background to "black"	
	Sleep	Turn Sleep option to **Never**	
	Additional Power Settings	Change power plan to "high performance"	

Builder Signature: ______________________________

Trial Tech Signature: ______________________________

Figure 1. ***Trial Software Due Diligence Checklist (available for free download; see the Notes on Use for access).***

While presenting, use only the software necessary to get the job done so you don't overburden your laptop with too many unrelated applications. Think about what you are running and why you are running it, because you need to save all the performance you can for your laptop and ensure the software doesn't crash mid-trial.[2] On your primary laptop, don't have multiple applications and files open, browse the internet, or download files while running (or waiting to run) your presentation. If you need to, use your backup laptop to prep exhibits,[3] edit videos, browse the internet, and download files and devote your primary laptop to running the presentation.

Rebooting (restarting) your laptop regularly is also a good idea, as it ensures that it's running properly and you've flushed the system of potential problems. Say, for example, you're heavily using video and it's pushing the video card to its limits. A reboot flushes the memory and restarts from scratch. Or perhaps you've loaded a lengthy series of huge PDF files. Again, a restart flushes the memory and starts from scratch. Of course, you need to find the right time to restart the computer—and it's yet another reason why having a backup laptop is so great. I always start my computer in the courtroom from OFF and restart it at lunch time. If I encountered issues in the beginning startup—the mouse driver was slow, for example, or a program was slow to load—I restart it again. If the day has been particularly heavy on presentations, I'll restart my laptop on breaks as well. The great thing about having a mirrored backup in the courtroom is that you can restart one in open court if you need to—just switch over to your backup laptop.

Recall that in Chapter Two, Getting Started, I recommended a few configurations to your system, such as turning off the default sounds and changing your laptop background to black. These, too, aid in readying your laptop for trial.

Tip: Always start with your laptop powered OFF and restart it at lunch and, if in heavy use, during breaks.

5.2 The Bare Minimum

It's difficult to make a recommendation as to what the "bare minimum" software should be on a trial laptop. For many, simply having Adobe Acrobat Professional and Microsoft Office, in addition to your trial software, is sufficient. With these three tools, you should be able to intake files, brand them, and create and/or present a number of different native files. In some cases, you don't even need trial software to present a limited number of exhibits; you can simply use Adobe for your exhibits and a media player for video.

On the other hand, it really is the data and your support needs that dictate if you'll need any additional tools. As you gain experience and the complexity of data you encounter grows, you'll need more specialized tools to do the job. Perhaps you have a team to support and need to modify files for their use and import into other databases like Relativity, Concordance, or CaseMap. It's when there is a mismatch between the technical needs of a case and the trial tech's skillset there is a problem. The mismatch could be anything from basic technical skills, like connecting your computer to a display, to difficult ones, like video editing or electronic file manipulation.

5.3 Document Review Software

Think of your document review software as the library and your electronic exhibits as the reference desk. Often teams make the mistake of not bringing or preparing their library for trial. Recall that I've previously described the trial exhibit database as the working database used by the legal team to prepare documents for trial and research. It's also the working location where electronic files are modified by branding and unitization prior to being imported into the tech's trial presentation database if not performed by a vendor. Software that you might keep trial exhibits in for *team use* are Relativity, Concordance, CaseMap, and Summation.

- **Trial presentation**—the database used by the trial tech to present information using trial presentation software

2. Especially because you were internet shopping or playing a game.
3. There is a significant amount of exhibit prep done in court as issues twist and change.

- **Trial exhibit**—the database used by the legal team to search, track, and prepare exhibits
- **Document review database**—the database used by the legal team to review electronic files, respond to request for production, and create privilege logs

I am adding the document review database to the support picture because it brings additional capability to the legal team. While it's true that only the exhibits can be used at trial, the document review database provides additional context and information about the documents that are related to exhibits and is a source for additional exhibits to be added during the trial. Teams often limit themselves to only bringing exhibits with them, which handicaps them while at trial by not mastering their own data.

It is a good idea for legal teams to keep these three databases separate and distinct from one another, but some smaller teams, solo practitioners, and those with lessor data volumes may place all this data in a trial presentation tool for ease of use. Keeping them separate, however, allows for more direct and easy searching and fewer unrelated results. There are likely searching and data organization methods where parties might combine the trial exhibit and document review databases into a single database, but it is probably too complex and difficult for the average user. Separate and simple are best.

I've found that adding these fields to be helpful when converting a document review database to an exhibit database.

- Trial Exhibit Number
- Trial Exhibit Number Beg/End
- Pages (If newly unitized be sure to update the page count)
- Admitted? Yes/No
- Date Admitted: Date
- Witness Used: Which witness was the exhibit used with

It's also important that you transfer or retain as much of the coding as possible from one to the other. However, the most important data to bring over are the previously used numbering systems, whether it is the initial control numbering from the vendor, the production numbers, or any other historical numbering placed on the document. The legal team may have prepared the outlines, etc. using identifying numbers *other* than the exhibit number, and if you have this data on hand, you can avoid a crisis. (Reminder: get your team using the exhibit number to reference documents early and in their outlines).

Last, as I discuss in Chapter Six, Courtroom Planning, you must keep your data (or a copy of it) on a local drive during trial so you can continue preparing and working in case of a loss of connectivity to your home office (assuming, of course, you are in a war room). Always go in with the assumption you won't be online or that it will break at the worst possible moment, and proceed from there. If you are technically capable, bring local copies of your Relativity[4] or Concordance database with you to the trial site, as the performance gains in printing alone are worth the extra time and effort (not to mention the reduction in risk to a trial site by faulty and unreliable Wi-Fi or internet connections).

5.4 Adobe Acrobat Professional

Adobe Acrobat Professional's crucial functions enable you to:

- Extract pages
- Insert pages

4. This is a little more difficult and expensive with Relativity.

- Change page order
- Delete pages
- Redact PDF documents
- Apply Bates number and brand files
- Reunitize files
- OCR files

No doubt you are familiar with PDF (Portable Document Format) documents. PDF is a common method of creating files for viewing, not editing. There are free PDF viewers, such as Adobe Acrobat Reader, available online for free download, and many web browsers allow you to view PDF files. The format of a PDF is fixed and flat, which means that graphics and text will appear consistently from file to file and computer to computer (hence the "portable" in their name), which is not true for Word or other commonly office documents. This trait makes PDF files desirable in the legal community, as the format is easy to use and share. All major trial software is compatible with the PDF format and, in many cases, is the preferred format to other image options like TIFF and JPG.

In order to do more than simply view files, you will need the "professional" (i.e., paid) version of Adobe Acrobat. The professional version brings a plethora of useful features, but the companion skills for the trial tech are branding and unitization. If you can extract, insert, delete, and change page order, you can unitize documents into exhibits if you are putting them together from different files.

5.5 Microsoft Office: Focus on PowerPoint

PowerPoint's crucial functions enable you to:

- Create a template to display documents/exhibits
- Insert an image
- Create a callout (along with using shadow and line options to aid visibility) and highlights

Microsoft Office is the software package used overwhelming by law practitioners; therefore, you must have it installed on your trial laptop. Depending on the case, you could use PowerPoint as your trial presentation software, but it is inefficient in the courtroom if the case calls for more than a handful of documents. Each page from an exhibit must be prepared in advance (taking a minimum of five to ten minutes apiece). Typically, an advanced strategy at trial is to use a mix of PowerPoint and your trial presentation software for opening statement and closing argument, then strictly using the trial presentation software for the rest of the case.

There are books available on creating effective PowerPoint slide shows and presentations,[5] but in the companion part of this book, I briefly describe how to create a basic exhibit with a callout in PowerPoint. The companion piece instructs you on how to insert an image (usually a document) into a presentation, along how to use shadowing and lines to make it more visible onscreen. *Note*: You'll get more screen "real estate" and better legibility using trial software, so you may want to consider either using a mix of PowerPoint slides and trial software or simply loading everything into your trial software. The advantage with PowerPoint is that you get to use the clicker, so the control is slicker if you are a lawyer who isn't working with a trial tech in the courtroom.

Be sure to keep legibility in mind as you create your presentation—this deals with fonts you might choose to use in your presentation, as well as their point size. Typically, I use sans serif fonts, which are typefaces that don't have "curly" extensions on the letters. They give your presentation a neat, uncluttered look. Sans serif fonts include Helvetica, Arial, Calibri, Gil Sans MT, Lucida Sans, and Tahoma, among others. (In contrast, serif fonts do have the small lines embellishing the end of letter strokes; serif fonts include Times New Roman, Garamond,

5. Including John Cleaves, *Demonstratives: Making Effective Graphics for Trial* (National Institute for Trial Advocacy 2016).

Baskerville Old Face, and Courier.) Don't go crazy using too many different fonts. Keep your presentation neat and choose a single font, perhaps two at the most. Lastly, there has been much said in recent years about font "personalities," which refers to the emotional impact of font choices. The graphic below does a good job of showing the potential impact of various fonts on readers.

Figure 2. ***Common sans serif fonts: Helvetica, Arial, and Lucida Sans. (Images courtesy of Wikimedia Commons.)***

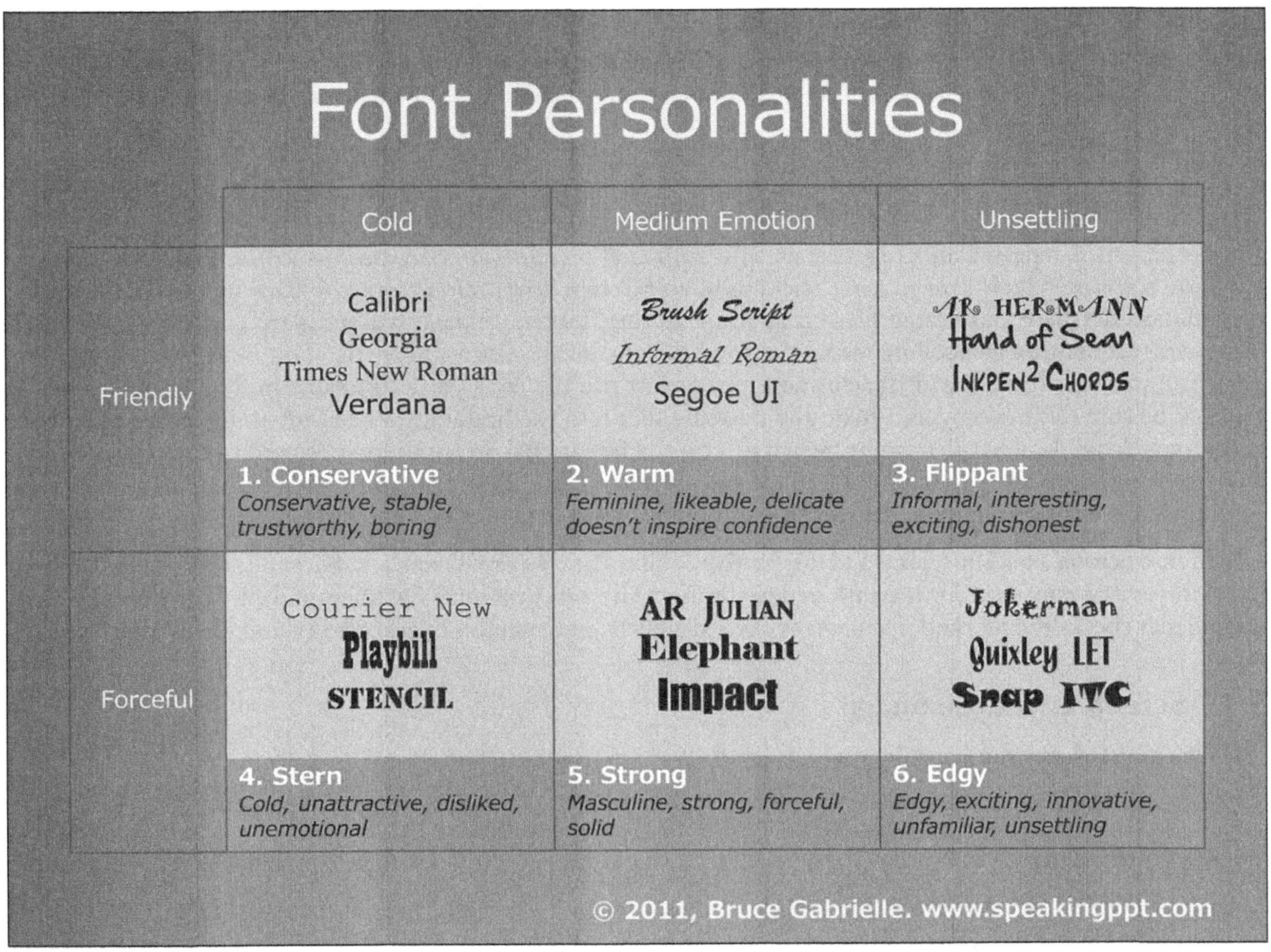

Figure 3. ***Font personalities from Speaking PowerPoint, by Bruce Gabrielle. (Image courtesy of Bruce Gabrielle.)***

As for creating highlights, PowerPoint is not the cleanest, most efficient process (lawyers like to highlight a lot). Using a tool like Snagit to do screenshots and highlights for use in PowerPoint is much quicker and more efficient and produces a superior result. Use balance when you create highlights: if everything is highlighted, nothing is.

5.6 Running with USB: A Word on File Corruption

There is a lot riding on a presentation or the display of exhibits, so take the time to ensure your goals are met by first lowering your risk of failure. One of the biggest issues is corrupt presentations and files. This can happen when a user puts finishing touches on the presentation and exhibit files right up to the very last possible moment, then does a final "save" of the presentation to a thumb drive (or other media), which is then incomplete because the user removed the thumb drive from the computer before the save was complete. This is an extremely common occurrence.

Here are a few tips on how to create a backup and test it. The following is a redundant process and is perfect for anything you have that you want to present in court, whether it's exhibits, video clips, or your trial presentation database.

1) Be sure the copy is complete and do a test-open of the file(s) on the laptop it will be presented on in the courtroom. This not only QCs that the presentation is working, but also that the presentation software and laptop are working.

2) Click on the thumb drive copy of the presentation or file(s) and make sure it opens up—this is your backup. You may also want to email or place the file(s) in a secure cloud-based storage service—this is your "backup to the backup."

3) If you make any changes to the presentation, be sure to give it a new name (or version number) so that you can update your various backups.

This process is repeated on a bigger scale with your trial presentation database. As you update your trial presentation software, you'll want to make backups to an external drive.[6] Don't forget to back up the complete trial presentation database and related files, in addition to the files and folders that you have created on your local computer (yet another compelling reason for good file organization) for use at trial. You can use a program like Total Commander to help with synchronization, or just use the copy/paste functions in Windows. A word of caution: be sure to *fully* copy and paste any database files into the backup; it's been my unfortunate experience that some related database files can be missed in a sync. The external drive can then be used to copy the files back down to your backup laptop (laptop #2 in redundant setups). The folder organization should remain intact and be duplicative from computer to computer to aid in QC and comparing file numbers.

Redundancy via a backup laptop and duplicative equipment is key to having a stable and less risky presentation. Don't forget that once the copy is transferred to additional devices, you must QC them as well—typically a random sample that checks the files and opening any backed-up trial presentation database to ensure the files are linked.

5.7 Screen Captures: Snagit

Snagit's crucial functions enable you to:

- Capture an image
- Highlight an image
- Create a torn-edge effect

Screen-capture software allows you to "capture" an image onscreen and then annotate it with highlights and other effects that you may want to import into PowerPoint or your trial presentation software. Screen-capture software is essential to your toolkit if you are creating presentations. PowerPoint's highlighting features are fairly limited or require multiple steps to undertake, so Snagit really makes the job easy. It allows you to work quickly and professionally to build presentations and other annotated work. It's also flexible—I can send a quick capture of a slide rather than an entire deck to get feedback, or conveniently do a quick screen capture of where data resides in a set of directories or instructions for steps I need to follow to accomplish an unfamiliar task.

6. As well as possibly a network location.

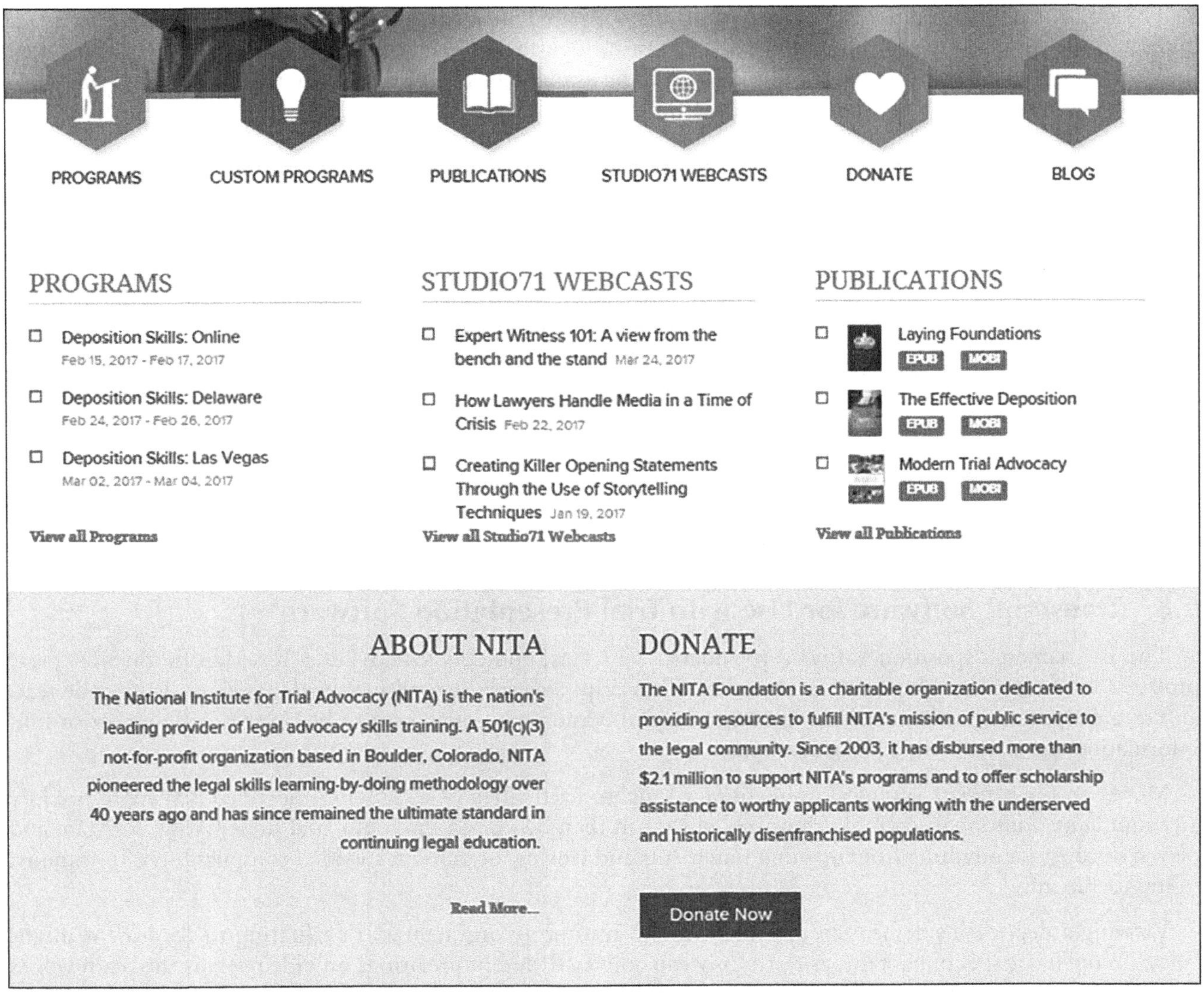

Figure 4. ***Original image before capture and annotation of "About NITA." (Image courtesy of the National Institute for Trial Advocacy.)***

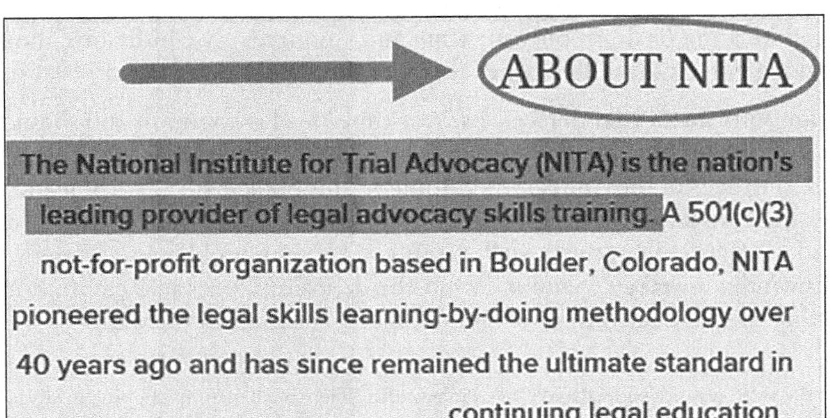

Figure 5. ***Example of screen-capture work product. (Image courtesy of the National Institute for Trial Advocacy.)***

The tradeoff in using screen-capture software versus a native image is that you *may* see degradation in image quality in the captured image. Thus, you must QC it to look for pixelization that will lower the quality of your presentation. If you are getting pixelized output as in the example below, try capturing the image at a higher resolution or zooming into the source image before capturing, for a higher quality capture.

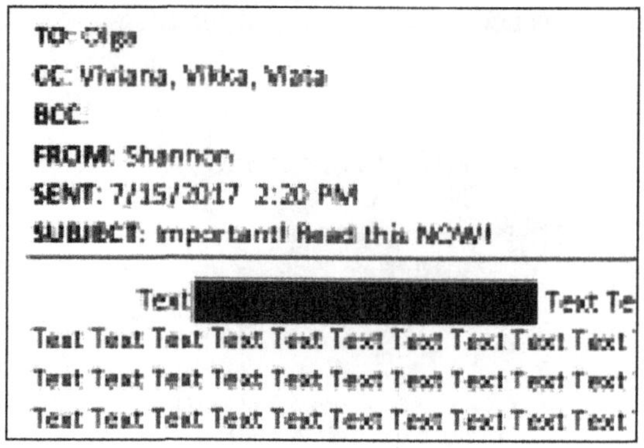

Figure 6. ***Example of pixelization.***

5.8 Transcript Software for Use with Trial Presentation Software

The two largest deposition software providers, West Case Notebook and Lexis TextMap, both offer great products for deposition taking and issue coding. Transcript software is used to take depositions, issue code text, and create reports of testimony. Issue coding is helpful because you may want to be able to easily report or find information associated with a particular issue.

Moreover, the software is typically able to play synchronized video of testimony (the video is synchronized by a vendor at an additional cost). Synchronized video can then be loaded into your trial presentation software and played in court for anything from opening statements and closing arguments, to video compilations of testimony, to impeachment.

Viewing a deponent's demeanor, appearance, and testimony onscreen and evaluating to see how it might "play" in open court is important, as testimony can convey different meanings on video versus the plain words that appear in a transcript. It is imperative that legal team members review video clips so that the appropriate meaning is conveyed by their use. A good workflow is to link video to the transcripts themselves, whereby team members view the video as they are issue coding and then send final requests to the trial tech for clipping. Otherwise, there is a lot of back and forth with QC'ing and reviewing the clips. Always keep in mind that video clipping can be a major drain on your time and resources—be judicious about what you want to clip, and consider playing video on the fly[7] rather than endlessly producing clips.

The use of deposition software in trial to receive a "real-time" feed is common and should be set up on a separate laptop[8] from the trial presentation laptop.[9] While there is built-in compatibility between deposition and trial presentation softwares, the focus of the companion tutorial in this book is on exporting and converting page/line reports from the depositions to a format that is easily importable into most trial presentation tools. The built-in compatibility or "Send to" feature works very well, but it can become problematic as the volume of depositions increases. Trying to unwind a mistaken "Send to" from the deposition packages can be tricky, so I like the QC opportunity of exporting the page/line numbers and reimporting into trial software.

7. "On the fly" means that the video was not clipped and QC'ed in advance. There is a benefit in clipping in advance in terms of clip quality and speed, but it comes at the detriment of spending significant time on those tasks.

8. Another alternative is to receive a rough copy at the end of the day, but then you lose the benefit of in-courtroom review and searching that the live feed brings. If you can afford it, *always* get the live feed.

9. To be clear: run only the *minimal* software necessary on your trial laptop and do not have multiple programs open while presenting.

Each of the major trial presentation programs can create both individual and "clip lists" that are exported from deposition software. A clip list refers to multiple clips that are joined together to create a single video, such as a "day in the life" video. Other times, a clip list can be a string of separate clips that is being imported in bulk so that they don't have to be created individually. It is important to understand the technical format for your software program—they all do it slightly differently. Often, the trial tech is simply taking a report from an issue code and stripping everything out except the page/line numbers, which are then conformed into the clip formats below.

TrialDirector clip format for import:

Pages/lines are separated by a "." or ":" and a "-" between starting and ending page/line reference, with no spaces. For example:

- 6:5-11
- 6.5-11
- 6:5-6:11
- 6.5-6.11

Sanction clip format for import:

Page/line are separated by a "." and a "+" between starting and ending page/line reference, with no spaces. For example:

- 4.14+4.22
- 6.12+6.16
- 7.2+7.7
- 8.13+8.17

OnCue Clip format for import:[10]

Page/line are separated by a variety of delimiters (some are not visible, like "tab"). For example:

- 6:5-7:11
- Page 6, line 5, page 7, line 11
- 6, 5, 7, 11

There have been recent improvements in software to distinguish between an issue and a designation. While they are both similar, a designation is used to identify video or textual testimony to be played or read in court, while an issue is related to identifying legal and other interesting testimony to analyze for legal arguments and prepare for impeachment purposes. These improvements allow teams to create both designations and issue codes in a single database and to toggle back and forth between the two. Previously, everything was done with an issue code, so the database could become quite confusing with multiple issue codes and deposition testimony overlapping one another. Legal teams may want to consider having separate designation and issue code databases if the system of "designation and issue" is overly complicated or if you have older software.

5.9 Text Editor: UltraEdit

A text editor enables you to:

- Change a file path in a log file

10. OnCue requires additional header information to be placed into the import file. TrialDirector also has options where header info is needed (or not), depending on the feature used.

A text editor is software used to manipulate and change text files. The software is versatile and can do a number of different things, so be advised that I'm only scratching the surface here. The typical uses of a text editor are to change file paths in log files or change the technical format of load files and log files (ANSI or DOS); there are a number of other advanced skillsets as well. Text files are simple files with a large variety of uses in legal software—for example, they can be the dataload for database coding, a transcript, or a log file that contains pathing information for images. In other words, it is used to load and import information into databases and typically has a file extension of .txt; it can also have any number of different file extensions (such as the three-letter extension at the end of the file, such as .doc for Word files and .xls for Excel files) to show the application it is associated with. The extension can be changed to any format and opened in virtually any text editor. The advantage to using something like UltraEdit or Notepad++ over the version of Notepad that comes preloaded with Windows is improved performance and capability. Notepad crashes on larger files while UltraEdit and Notepad++ are just getting warmed up. Below are some common text file extensions you can edit using a text editor.

- .DII text file format associated with Summation
- .OPT, .LOG text file formats for loading images associated with Concordance Image/ Opticon/Relativity
- .LFP text file format associated with IPRO
- .OLL text file format associated with TrialDirector
- .SDT text file format associated with Sanction
- .DAT generic format used by a variety of database tools using "tab" as a delimiter
- .CSV generic format used by a variety of database tools using ","(comma) as a delimiter
- .TXT text file format—widely used for data delivery, OCR, and transcripts

5.10 Total Commander: File Synchronization and Renaming Utility

Total Commander's crucial functions enable you to:

- Synchronize files
- Compare directories
- Rename files (and in bulk)
- Create a file list

Total Commander and other similar utilities allow you to easily synchronize files and folders, as well as perform a bulk renaming of files. For example, you might need to move files from your network to your laptop, or to backup media or to your backup laptop—this software helps you do that. *A bold proviso*: Be careful when synchronizing any database software, as it can cause major issues due to how they are structured—use this software to sync large volumes of images and video but *not for the database files* themselves which should be completely overwritten or replaced (if moving or syncing from one to the other). More importantly, Total Commander will tell you what is missing from a file location, which is an important QC step to ensure you have all of your exhibits in a single location.

Another commonly used feature in Total Commander is its renaming utility, which is much more robust than what UltraEdit can do. Total Commander can easily and quickly rename, renumber, and *replace* text repeated in file names. Say, for example, you want to use TX instead of EX as an exhibit prefix, or pad file names with more or fewer digits, or remove text in a file name as it was delivered. Total Commander is extremely flexible in this capacity, and once you learn the basics, the more advanced options become fairly easy to use.

In the companion section of the book, I'll show how to create a quick file list of files in a directory. (We're always creating our lists in the legal field, aren't we?) Some examples:

- TX0001 to EX_0001
- TX0001 to TX0000001
- TX0001-0001 to TX0001
- TX0001_Confidential.pdf to TX0001
- TX1230, TX1231, TX1237 to TX0001, TX0002, TX0003

5.11 Windows Movie Maker

Total Commander's crucial functions enable you to:

- Create and export a clip

Windows Movie Maker is a free and easy-to-use video clip editor to create clips to use in PowerPoint or trial presentation software. While both software apps have their own clipping functionality built in, it can be easier and quicker to clip without them. There are likely some videos that you *only* want to clip in your trial presentation software—for example, deposition testimony with synchronized text. But there are many times where you need a simple and quick clip, and want the ability to create the clip outside of trial software because you need to play it standalone or to insert it into PowerPoint. (*Note*: Movie Maker gives you the option of editing in 16:9 or 4:3.) Movie Maker was discontinued in early 2017, but as of this writing can still be found online for download. There will likely be a replacement, so keep your eye out for it.

In the alternative, I would look at Adobe Premiere Elements which is a consumer, or "lite," version of their professional video editing software package, Adobe Premiere.[11] There are also alternatives like VSDC Editor[12] and Shotcut[13] that are free. Again, as with any program be sure to test your trial presentation software after installing new applications.

5.12 Other Applications

5.12.1 AVS4you[14]

Media encoding software allows techs to convert files from one video/audio standard to another. This is potentially important if files have been provided in an incompatible format or need to be changed in some way for smoother or better presentation. This is more of an advanced skill, so if you find yourself with media playback issues and aren't sure what to do, it might be best to use a vendor.

5.12.2 CD BurnerXP[15]

A CD burner is a necessity if your computer or laptop has a CD-ROM/DVD drive. CD BurnerXP is a free CD burner program that works well.

11. Visit http://www.adobe.com/products/premiere-elements.html.
12. Visit http://www.videosoftdev.com/free-video-editor.
13. Visit https://www.shotcut.org/.
14. Visit http://www.avs4you.com/.
15. Visit https://cdburnerxp.se/en/home.

5.12.3 *Informatik*[16]

Informatik is an image driver that allows you to convert any printable document to a graphics file. In other words, you can convert files like Word, PowerPoint, and Excel into an image format that can be imported into your trial presentation software.

5.12.4 *eDrawings Viewer*[17]

eDrawings Viewer is a basic (and free) AutoCAD viewer software allows you to view multiple CAD files in a single viewer. This is important for cases that require this type of software. There are times where you might need the entire software package—for one-off uses, you should test extensively.

5.12.5 *Exhibit Sticker Utility*[18]

This software allows you to place exhibit stickers on the first page of every document (including PDFs) and exhibit, with a variety of placement and automated options.

16. Visit http://ftp.informatik.com/imagistik.html.
17. Visit http://www.edrawingsviewer.com/.
18. Visit https://doneby5.com/ and http://exhibitsticker.com/.

Chapter Six

Courtroom Planning

Thirty-six seconds. That's the amount of time it took Ashlee Simpson to walk off stage
on *Saturday Night Live* (Google it) when a technical glitch occurred
during her musical performance and caused her performance to completely implode on stage.
Ashlee's performance never recovered (she walked off stage)
and her career was tarnished forever from that glitch.
Would you be able to recover?

Nowadays, we are seeing an extreme range of technology options in courtrooms throughout the country and the world. Technology has taken hold in the most unexpected places. For example, the United Nations (UN) has created and left an amazing legacy of high-tech courtrooms in a number of developing countries and they get the benefit of starting with technology from the ground up, and often in modern buildings. The UN builds the courtroom (often in partnership with the host country) and brings in technology and experts to help with efficiency and to leave a lasting impact of trained people and efficient processes and procedures on the home country. Technology is part of the equation for tribunals because they want an open and accessible justice system that everyone can participate in. Technology has helped shorten war crimes tribunals by months or years and make them more efficient. A high-tech courtroom also provides significant aid to the numerous judges, translators, legal teams, and investigators involved at a tribunal.

Figure 1. ***Cambodian tribunal. Note the monitors everywhere.***

In the United States, we have a long history of justice and court systems on the state and federal levels. Courts are often in historic buildings with long and revered histories. Unfortunately, most courtrooms weren't designed with technology in mind and have significant technological hurdles because they have nothing, or worse they have an outdated system that needs to be supplemented. However, courtrooms are becoming better technical environments all the time. New courtrooms are being built and old ones refurbished. That said, the courtrooms you encounter will not be uniform in their capabilities, and that's why it's important to evaluate the courtroom's technical capacity, test your equipment on site and to check with the court in advance to find out what the boundaries and rules are.

Some courts are enthusiastically receptive to technology and others completely reject it (with many in between), so acceptance of or resistance to technology is something we will have to deal with, making it crucial that technical issues be approached in the right way. Trying to explain what might be "wrong" with a courtroom is delicate work. Always be gentle, as the courtroom setup may well be someone's "baby" that was put together on a limited budget. The two ends of the spectrum—resistance and acceptance—are actually the easiest for you to work with: a new courtroom with true "plug and play" features reduce your need for planning and certain equipment, while a courtroom with no technology is a blank canvas. It's the many courtrooms in the middle, then, with aging equipment or a partial setup, that can be more problematic. First, you face the need to explain what is wrong and what is needed, which might get shot down by the court or IT staff. You also may encounter problems connecting to older display equipment, with their lower resolution and associated issues.

Recall the generalizations about the levels of court technology that I explained in Chapter Four:

- Cutting edge
- High tech
- Limited
- None

The United States Courthouse in downtown Los Angeles is a great example of a "cutting edge" courthouse and a model for future courthouse construction and renovation. The courthouse IT and management are of incredibly high caliber and customer service. More than being "cutting edge" it is the gold standard for trial technology in terms of capability and support. This courthouse, which opened in late 2016, is a major step forward in terms of technology, in part because it offers plug-and-play capability; high-resolution video; an amazing sound system including microphones; and individual screens for jurors, counsel, and the court. High resolution means better courtroom visibility and a sharper view of detail on exhibits displayed in court, which helps decision-makers understand the case better. High-quality, built-in, plug-and-play equipment lowers the bar to technology use for all and substantially lowers costs for equipment rental.

Below are the tech specs for the federal courthouse in Los Angeles, which you will likely see duplicated throughout the country.

Display

- Aspect ratio: All monitors are 16:9
- Resolution: 1920x1080

Video Input

- HDMI and VGA inputs
- Two input points on each counsel table and one at the podium
- Access points can be opened in the back corner(s) of courtroom, which could be used for a tech table
- Switching occurs at the podium and with the clerk—educate your legal team in advance.

Audio

- Wired courtroom audio via HDMI or audio cable

Guidelines

- Switch at counsel or tech table is OK. This will allow a redundant setup.
- No tape/no wiring—courtroom is sufficiently wired for presentation.
- Court IT is your friend—an amazing and responsive staff.
- Best time to test and contact court IT staff is Wednesday through Friday.

Looking at these specs, there are a few takeaways:

- Any presentation, graphic, or video should be created or configured for 16:9.
- Your computer should be able to display in 1920x1080. Presentations should be created in that resolution as well.
- War room monitors and working screens in your office should be 16:9 and 1920x1080 so that you can accurately assess graphics and exhibits that will be put on screen.
- For redundancy, you'll need to connect your switch to one of the courtroom inputs at counsel table or request a tech table for the back of the room.
- Test all equipment (laptops/switch) on a Wednesday, Thursday, or Friday several days or weeks before the trial starts.

Note that even though the Los Angeles federal and other high-tech courtrooms are "plug and play," it is still important that you test your equipment in advance. Start by testing your laptop and any switches you might use for backup purposes. (Remember, switches can have compatibility issues, too.) The testing should occur as far in advance as possible, just in case you need to replace or rent equipment—and definitely not the day before. The court IT department is your friend here—even more so if you test in advance. Earn their respect by showing them that you will do things the right ways.

As you approach the plan, consider the different perspectives of the judge, clerk, and legal team, as well as considering how you are going to reach agreement with opposing counsel for the setup. Rule number one is to be a good *guest* in the courtroom. You should put a lot of thought into your setup and how it will best support your team's style of presentation,[1] but it is equally important to leave the courtroom in the same or better condition as you found it. In addition to technical issues, I have mentioned that legal teams are often disrespectful to courtrooms and leave them dirty and disorganized; sometimes ripping the carpet, damaging furniture, or breaking technical equipment—all due to irresponsible and inept setup practices (not using gaffing tape to tape down cables, for example).

Recall the federal court instructions in the Evidence Presentation Obligations that stated:

> In addition to familiarizing themselves with the Court's electronic evidence presentation system in advance of the hearing/trial, the parties must familiarize themselves with their own equipment and how to connect their own equipment with the Court's system . . . .

It doesn't appear that legal teams are taking their technical obligations seriously if the court has had to make rules that parties should know how to use their *own equipment*. In other words, it wasn't a single clown attorney that made a mistake, but an entire circus. The mistakes clearly are often substantial and time consuming, and cause significant delay and damage. Don't be a clown—take your technical obligations to the court as seriously as your legal ones.

1. Individual monitors for jurors are great unless you have an attorney who wants all eyes on him (or her), so be sure to discuss which presentation setup will best strengthen their style of argument.

It might be helpful if you print the Courtroom Technology Evaluation discussed this chapter and included as a free download to this book, as it lists many of the common planning considerations for courtroom setup. In the next several sections, I will discuss the planning considerations point by point. Regardless of whether you use the checklist, it's a good starting point for evaluating the courtroom for your technology needs. The first page is an evaluation of the courtroom, the second page covers equipment and each party's responsibilities, and the third page is a rough courtroom floorplan for analysis and planning.

Figure 2. ***Don't be a clown. Take your technical obligations seriously. (Image by Rachel Bennett.)***

6.1 Sweat the Details

Every detail of your courtroom plan will need to be vetted and tested to make it disaster proof. For example, can you bring in equipment without a court order? Is there a separate procedure for security? When can the courtroom be set up, and where will equipment be placed? Answers to these questions are not always obvious, so collaborate with the clerk of court and your opposing counsel as to what is best for the trial. For example, if it's a small courtroom, where will you place an easel? It seems simple, right? But will the easel block someone's view? Are they going to be OK with that? Consider these issues in advance.

Don't assume:

- That you can bring in equipment. Obtain permission from the court *and* court security. If you need to bring a lot of equipment (or boxes), what time may you bring them in? Is there a special loading dock you should use?
- You know where the equipment can be placed.
- Where you can sit. It can be a "big deal" for the tech to sit at counsel table, but is fairly common.

- That the other side will agree on equipment, shared costs, etc.
- What the legal team will want, even for a short trial or hearing.[2]
- That courtroom equipment will work properly. Advance testing and QC is important. Know who the courthouse IT contact is.
- That there are backups and replacements for courtroom and rented equipment. Have a plan with your equipment rental vendor or key items in your inventory.
- That Wi-Fi will work reliably. Keep your data local on your hard drive!

6.2 How Courts Can Greatly Increase Efficiency and Minimize Technical Problems

With only modest involvement, courts could dramatically raise efficiency and minimize technical downtime with the following rules (or guidelines, or obligations). The key here is judicial involvement in setting the expectation for technical competency and compliance. As long as teams are not being held accountable for the technical standards of the courtroom and burden shifting is seen as no big deal, they will continue to flaunt the rules and the implementation of court technology will suffer.

Over half of courtroom service calls by court IT staff are for people who never bothered to test their equipment in advance. This results in a rushed call for courthouse IT to try to troubleshoot a visitor's equipment[3]—which easily could have been resolved in advance. Not testing in advance is the leading cause of technical issues and delays in the courtroom. The takeaway is that courts should mandate testing in advance.

The next biggest source of issues is when parties do not comply with the technical standards they agreed upon for courtroom presentation and exhibit exchange. Courts simply noticing whether parties have complied with the branding requirements (i.e., placed the exhibit numbers on the face of the exhibit) and enforcing the rules would aid courtroom efficiency. Courts have been reluctant to get involved in this area, but it would help with technological efficiency if the court stressed the need for compliance. Exhibits should be correctly named, branded, and exchanged. It is incredibly frustrating to spend weeks getting exhibits into compliance with the TMO, only to have the other team not comply with the rules, leading to technical issues and delay. Often, the rules are violated simply for gamesmanship and sabotage; we need the court's help to put an end to it. The potential result is that courts will be more efficient and have more "up" time by enforcing compliance.

Redundancy is an area that the trial tech professional community and software manufacturers have fully embraced. Note the motto of OnCue, which sells their software in pairs for the sake of redundancy:

> If you aren't running a backup laptop in court, you probably should be. When you can't leave things to chance, redundancy is the best insurance.

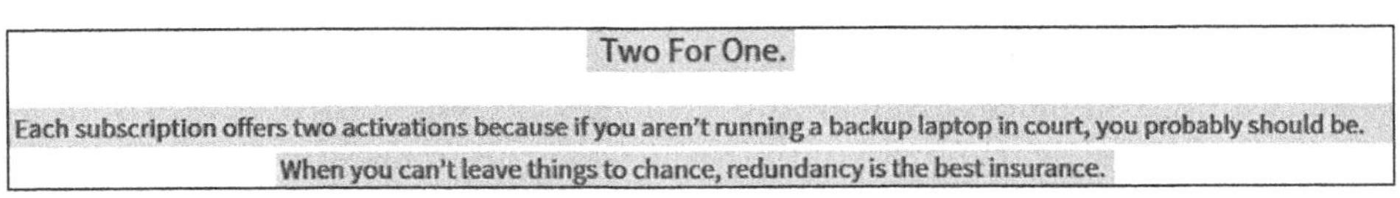
Two For One.

Each subscription offers two activations because if you aren't running a backup laptop in court, you probably should be. When you can't leave things to chance, redundancy is the best insurance.

Figure 3. ***A stern warning from OnCue. Take heed!***

Judges need to question why firms aren't practicing redundancy.[4] Setting the expectation that law firms must have a backup plan in place (so that if a single piece of technical equipment breaks, the trial can still proceed) should be standard for courts.

2. The legal team may want a complete setup for a small hearing. *Ask*!
3. It is also simply unfair to court IT to press them into service on a moment's notice for something that could have been resolved in advance.
4. Maybe they should ask twice? Kidding!

Without redundant setups, courts are creating a technologically risky situation because the presenter may rely on a single "hot" (already turned on) computer to be connected to a court system. Using a hot computer to connect to a presentation system invites trouble. The better plan therefore is to have a switch (the switch is key) for a laptop *and a backup laptop* in case the main laptop crashes.

Below are standards I propose that should supplement and build upon the Evidence Presentation Obligations discussed in Chapter Two, Getting Started.

1. Mandatory testing of equipment in advance—by the user of the equipment and for *all* equipment planned for courtroom use.
2. For longer trials, a mandatory courtroom technology walk-through at the beginning *and* end of a trial.
    a. Court IT staff signs off at the beginning and end of trial that equipment was tested, trained on, and left in working order
3. Meet and confer for trial techs, including the legal team and court staff.
    a. Courtroom setup
    b. Exhibit exchange
    c. Ongoing compliance
4. Create and submit a technology plan to the court.
    a. What is the redundancy plan to minimize downtime?
        i. *Example*: The team will have a backup laptop connected to a switch that will be available without delay. Also, the team has been trained in use of the document camera in case an exhibit has not been digitized.
5. Judicial involvement to encourage and facilitate technology use.
    a. Encourage redundancy (two laptops on a switch, mandatory!)
    b. Recognition and punishment of noncompliance with technology standards
    1. Have branding and naming requirements been met? If judges see an exhibit out of compliance, they must ask *why*.
6. Minimum technical standards for lawyers to meet either themselves or through a qualified consultant.

6.3 Build from Scratch or Supplement?

Why should you supplement equipment? First, bringing additional capability for a long or technically difficult trial can be vital—the existing equipment just may not be enough. Second, if there is an existing system, the court clerk might appreciate moving the switch to one of the trial technicians so that the tech can control the courtroom monitors and viewing. This is a good idea because it frees up the clerk, who often needs to focus attention on other tasks. Having redundant equipment on hand in case of failure, bringing a document camera, and actively working the switch brings a great deal of efficiency to the courtroom because downtime and problems are minimized. These are also great selling points to the court clerk or judge who might be resistant to technology in the courtroom.

Most courtroom technology supplements revolve around moving the switch from the clerk to a tech, who can then actively monitor the courtroom and switch to the appropriate party, individual piece of equipment, or backup equipment. The clerk has a variety of duties in the courtroom and switching video inputs is not a top priority. Most clerks welcome having the switch become someone else's responsibility. *Note*: if you can't move the switch from the podium, be sure to train any attorneys (in advance) how to use the switch—and while you're at it, be magnanimous and teach the other side, too.

If there is an existing system, you'll either want to use it completely or find a way to supplement it. This could be difficult depending on the level of technology already in the courtroom. Typically, supplementing a courtroom becomes more important for longer trials or those with particular case needs or in courtrooms with inadequate equipment. For example, your courtroom may have a large central screen but no monitors on the witness, counsel, or judge's bench, or maybe the courtroom monitor is too small, old, or isn't bright enough. Perhaps it's a bench trial, and it would be helpful to provide large monitors for the judge, clerk, witness, and counsel table. There are a wide range of possible situations, with some courtrooms needing you to simply "plug in," others needing everything, with most somewhere in between.

Keeping in mind that we want to listen first, it doesn't hurt to explain and discuss the issues with the clerk and to delicately push for your setup of choice. The most important rule for me in setup is to be in a location where I can see where the legal team is gesturing toward. Sometimes, that is at counsel table; other times, it's a row or two in with the spectators.

6.4 Equipment and Trial Tech Placement

Here are three rules for placing the equipment and trial tech in the courtroom:

1) Techs should *always* have a clear view of the main screen and podium so that they can see where the attorney is pointing and gesturing.
    a) When possible, the tech should be sitting at counsel table to communicate easily with the rest of the legal team.[5]
    b) If the tech cannot be seated at the counsel table, choose a location directly behind the counsel table (with a clear view of the main screen and podium, as described above).
2) Cables may need to take an indirect route to the input source (laptop/switch) so that they are not in high-traffic or problem areas.
    a) All cables should be taped down with gaffing tape.
    b) Factor the indirect route into your cabling lengths.
    c) Hide cables that are not taped down (e.g., at the tech table) with a table cloth/draping.
3) Audio speakers should be placed so decision-makers can hear them.
    a) Consider using a stand to raise speakers so audio can be heard from wherever speakers are placed.
    b) Speakers may need their own lengthy cabling setup and soundboard.
    c) Your laptops computer speakers and small desktop speakers are inadequate for playing audio to the courtroom.

6.5 Addressing Courtroom Concerns

Many times, the first barrier to technology is simply whether the clerk and judge have had positive experiences in the past. Unfortunately, the answer is far too often "no," thanks to terrible experiences dealing with frustration, delays, and "bad guests." Teams often walk into a courtroom like a bull in a china shop, disregarding the court's rules and preferences. Bad guests usually start by telling the clerk where everything will go instead of listening to what has worked in the past and the staff's concerns about equipment placement, security, and potential damage to the courtroom. Bad guests don't take care of the courtroom or take their technical obligations seriously, making it more difficult for future teams to do it right.

5. The tech often does so much more than just put up exhibits—for example, showing the team additional pages or providing context for an exhibit that is being displayed. Having the trial tech at the counsel table is very useful.

Courts *really* don't want to modify their courtrooms, but do allow it because it creates a more efficient system through fewer technical errors, raises the quality of presentation, and relieves the burden on busy clerks at trial. A few points on efficiency:

1) When a tech is running a switch with backup equipment, it lowers the risk of technical and hardware errors in the courtroom; if the software crashes or the equipment fail, the tech simply switches to the backup.

2) The tech brings efficiency by managing equipment that lawyers typically fumble with.

3) A tech is a full-time helpdesk *in the courtroom*, monitoring for maximum uptime by constantly monitoring the technical aspects of the trial—thus freeing up the clerk, who has bigger and better things to do.

Start your plan by discussing with the clerk (and possibly the judge and court IT staff) what *their preferences are*. This initial discussion with the court should start with you being a good listener, whereby you *hear* the concerns of the court and address them, one by one, with your plan. This is especially true if you want to bring in equipment, tape down cables, or supplement an existing court system. In other words, you need to have a good reason to modify the existing system.

It is important to work closely with the court and opposing counsel in a team effort to create a courtroom setup that benefits the court, your team, and the opposing team. Unfortunately, there is often a mismatch in the dynamic, so it behooves the savvier party to lead by example. First, make a site visit to the court without opposing counsel to evaluate the existing technical layout and get a feel for the court's thoughts on trial technology. This will demonstrate (especially if there is travel involved) to the court that you are serious about addressing their concerns, respecting their courtroom, and creating a high-quality presentation system that yields an efficient and smooth-running trial. Address the following during your discussion with the court:

- You will take steps to preserve and protect their courtroom.
- You are the responsible party and the buck stops with you.
- You will work with opposing counsel to create a plan and fix issues.
- You will be available both during the trial and afterward to address any concerns the court has.
- You will share your email and phone number with the clerk so you can immediately address any concerns the court may have.

New courthouses like the new federal courthouse in downtown Los Angeles are the gold standard. There is little a visiting legal team would need to do to in order to use technology at trial. The federal court system information technology group has a real culture of customer support and excellence, so with very few exceptions they do a great job and are there to help. Other courts that have not been upgraded or have limited technology available will, in many locations, bend over backwards to accommodate your technical needs—but you can't always count on this, so remember that every courtroom needs its own unique plan and consultation.

6.6 "David and Goliath" Syndrome

Is the presumption of David and Goliath behind us yet? Many attorneys are reluctant to use technology in the courtroom because they believe it will look like a David-and-Goliath situation—in other words, that they will appear to have unlimited resources and are a juggernaut, while the other does not. The David-and-Goliath concern was much more valid in the recent past and still remains something to be evaluated by legal teams. However, judges and juries are much more sophisticated about the use of technology now. Decision-makers have come to expect that the technology they have in their personal and work lives, as well as what they see on television, will be used in court to make the case easier to understand and to move proceedings along more quickly.

Figure 4. ***David and Goliath perception. (Image courtesy of Rachel Bennett.)***

Indeed, there is anecdotal evidence that *not* using technology can produce a negative reaction in the minds of judges and jurors. If the court has a tech system, there is no reason for either side not to use it.[6] How might judges feel if they see sophisticated legal teams come to court but not use the technology that is available?[7] Besides, if one side decides to bring in technology and the other side doesn't, the latter risks looking uncooperative, unsophisticated, and like they don't value the time and intelligence of decision-makers—which is hardly the optics of David and Goliath.

There is some thought that technology can create an unfair advantage in the courtroom between the haves and the have-nots, which is a bit misguided because trial presentation software might be the most equalizing factor available to teams in the courtroom. Care should be taken to ensure the technology setup gives the appearance of balance and that the teams don't stack laptops, tablets, or other gear at or near the tech table. Technology gives the "little fish" the ability to present in equal quality to the "big fish." It is the great equalizer in the courtroom and can bring parity with very little effort (after you read this book!). Lastly, courts should also note if one side is simply not taking its responsibilities seriously. There is no excuse for two large firms to have a technology imbalance in the courtroom.

6. Jurors will likely see you carrying your briefcase with your laptop and cellphone, so if you can master those skills, why not make their lives easier with courtroom technology as well?

7. It's like going to a buffet—put a little of everything on your plate.

Figure 5. ***Technology is an equalizer in the courtroom. (Image by Rachel Bennett.)***

6.7 Keep Data Local

It is important for trial teams to keep a copy of their data local (that is, saved to a local drive on their trial laptops) in case the trial site goes down. This is especially true for both war rooms and offsite trials that may not have the reliable connectivity of their home office. *Never* rely upon an online connection for presentation of evidence. Sometimes teams assume that the level of Wi-Fi or internet service in a courtroom (or hotel/war room) is constant and always "up," and they may have even tested the connection—but that is not the same as testing or using connectivity during peak hours (i.e., everyone showing up to court at the same time and watching ESPN on court Wi-Fi).

Keep a complete dataset onsite and at the war room – you may want to consider taking a copy of "everything" on an external drive to have at your fingertips in the courtroom. If you have the technical capability, bring local copies of your Relativity[8] or Concordance database with you to trial, as the performance gains alone in printing are worth the extra time and effort (not to mention the reduction in risk to a trial site caused by faulty Wi-Fi or internet connections). Lastly, have a backup and a backup for your backup.

Note: Many firms have developed specialized servers (a "trial server") used to host data locally at trial. There are many performance benefits to bringing your data with you, such as printing, access, and reliability. Moreover, the server can be networked to enhance team collaboration. Consider the use of a trial server if you have voluminous data, a large team, or a wonky technical environment.

6.8 Old Tech: Still Relevant!

Although this is a book about courtroom technology, older or classic methods like using exhibit boards and a document camera are still relevant. Presenting slide after slide and image in PowerPoint or exhibit after exhibit using a trial presentation tool doesn't provide enough variety to engage decision-makers. It is, in a word, *boring*. Storyboards, dry-erase boards, and document cameras remain relevant and useful pieces of equipment in the courtroom and provide a significant opportunity to create variety and interest for your decision-makers. (Also, an endless stream of slides simply turns the attorney into a "talking head" and does not increase cognition in decision-makers.)

As I discussed in Chapter Four, Equipment, one of the most underrated, underutilized pieces of trial equipment is the document camera. The document camera provides a more personal, and potentially dramatic, opportunity for the legal team with movement and spontaneity. I always recommend using big, thick pens of various colors—and for attorneys to use their hands, fingers, and pens to point, scribble, circle, and gesture. The movement, color, and "authenticity" the document camera can bring make it interesting in limited use.

8. A little more difficult and expensive with Relativity.

Also, the document camera is both a great companion and backup for trial presentation software. First, it mixes up the presentation to keep the judge and jury interested, but it is also a great backup in case of equipment failure. Two important rules to follow when using a document camera: 1) don't point with your middle finger; and 2) make sure your fingernails are clean. Finally, remember that the document camera will be hooked into your video switch, so look at the video resolution it outputs because you can encounter switching issues due to low resolution output.

6.9 Evaluating the Courtroom

Page 1 of the Courtroom Technology Evaluation that evaluates courtroom technology needs asks you to document the courtroom environment (e.g., distances, resolutions, aspect ratios) and detail what features are currently in the courtroom so that you can create a technology plan. Knowing the details allows you to discuss intelligently with the court, legal team, and opposing counsel the needs of the courtroom and allows you to fine-tune your graphics and presentations for optimal display. Exercise great care when tapping into an existing courtroom system to add monitors, speakers, and other equipment.

Be sure to review this chapter and Chapter Four, Equipment, because together, these chapters provide in detail the function of each piece of equipment and why it is necessary. Keep in mind that courtrooms with existing systems may have considerable equipment stored in a technical cabinet somewhere that helps distribute and conform video and audio throughout the courtroom. In general, such systems are beneficial, but they must be tested with your own equipment to check for compatibility issues or whether additional configurations are necessary.

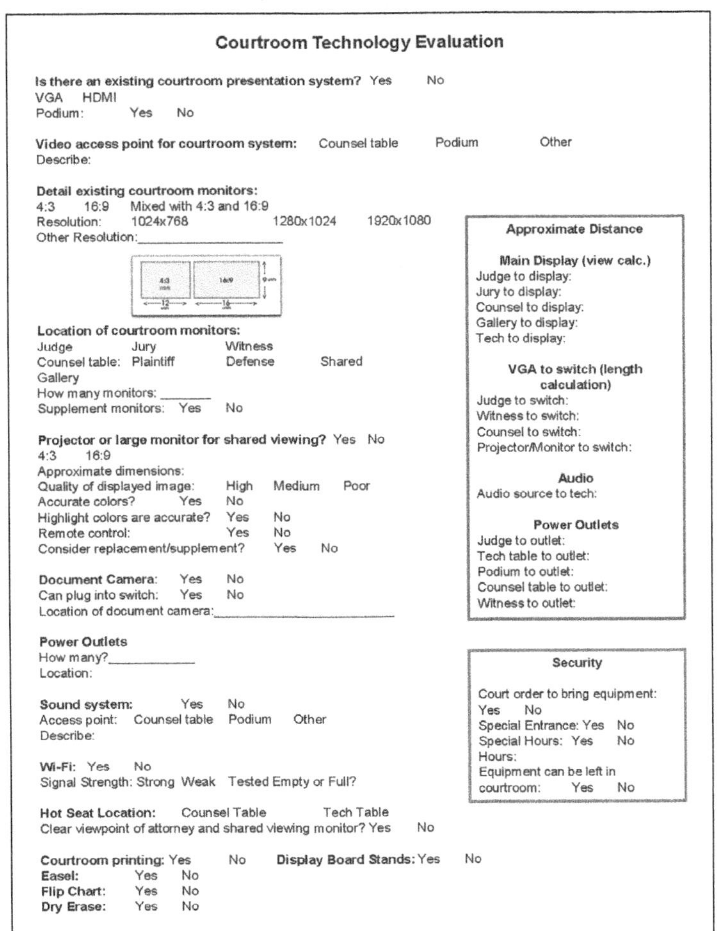

Courtroom Technology Evaluation

Is there an existing courtroom presentation system? Yes No
VGA HDMI
Podium: Yes No

Video access point for courtroom system: Counsel table Podium Other
Describe:

Detail existing courtroom monitors:
4:3 16:9 Mixed with 4:3 and 16:9
Resolution: 1024x768 1280x1024 1920x1080
Other Resolution:____________

Location of courtroom monitors:
Judge Jury Witness
Counsel table: Plaintiff Defense Shared
Gallery
How many monitors: ______
Supplement monitors: Yes No

Projector or large monitor for shared viewing? Yes No
4:3 16:9
Approximate dimensions:
Quality of displayed image: High Medium Poor
Accurate colors? Yes No
Highlight colors are accurate? Yes No
Remote control: Yes No
Consider replacement/supplement? Yes No

Document Camera: Yes No
Can plug into switch: Yes No
Location of document camera:____________

Power Outlets
How many?________
Location:

Sound system: Yes No
Access point: Counsel table Podium Other
Describe:

Wi-Fi: Yes No
Signal Strength: Strong Weak Tested Empty or Full?

Hot Seat Location: Counsel Table Tech Table
Clear viewpoint of attorney and shared viewing monitor? Yes No

Courtroom printing: Yes No **Display Board Stands:** Yes No
Easel: Yes No
Flip Chart: Yes No
Dry Erase: Yes No

Approximate Distance

Main Display (view calc.)
Judge to display:
Jury to display:
Counsel to display:
Gallery to display:
Tech to display:

VGA to switch (length calculation)
Judge to switch:
Witness to switch:
Counsel to switch:
Projector/Monitor to switch:

Audio
Audio source to tech:

Power Outlets
Judge to outlet:
Tech table to outlet:
Podium to outlet:
Counsel table to outlet:
Witness to outlet:

Security
Court order to bring equipment:
Yes No
Special Entrance: Yes No
Special Hours: Yes No
Hours:
Equipment can be left in courtroom: Yes No

Figure 6. ***Completing a Courtroom Technology Evaluation is essential. This form is available for free download; see the Notes on Use for access).***

6.9.1 Step 1: Consider the Existing System and Access Points

Is there an existing courtroom presentation system? You need to know if there is existing system and how to connect to it. Whether there is an existing system will guide your entire planning process: Are you stuck with what is there? Can you supplement or build a system from scratch?

Is there an existing courtroom presentation system? Yes No
VGA HDMI

Video access point for courtroom system: Counsel table Podium Other
Describe:

Figure 7. ***From Page 1 of the Trial Technology Checklist.***

Where are the video input access points? You must know where they are so you can build a plan that includes a schematic of the courtroom. Knowing where the video input access points are is important so that you know what your alternatives are in case one fails.

6.9.2 Step 2: Note the Aspect Ratio and Location of All Courtroom Monitors

Is the aspect ratio of displays in the courtroom 4:3 or 16:9? Tailor your presentations to the aspect ratio of the displays in the courtroom, or else you will experience the mismatches discussed in sections 4.2.3.2 and 6.11.5.

Detail existing courtroom monitors:
4:3 16:9 Mixed with 4:3 and 16:9
Resolution: 1024x768 1280x1024 1920x1080
Other Resolution:____________________

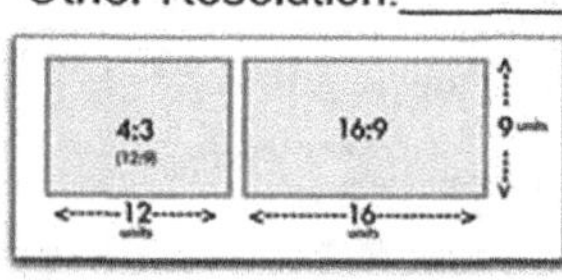

Location of courtroom monitors:
Judge Jury Witness
Counsel table: Plaintiff Defense Shared
Gallery
How many monitors: _______
Supplement monitors: Yes No

Figure 8. ***From Page 1 of the Trial Technology Checklist.***

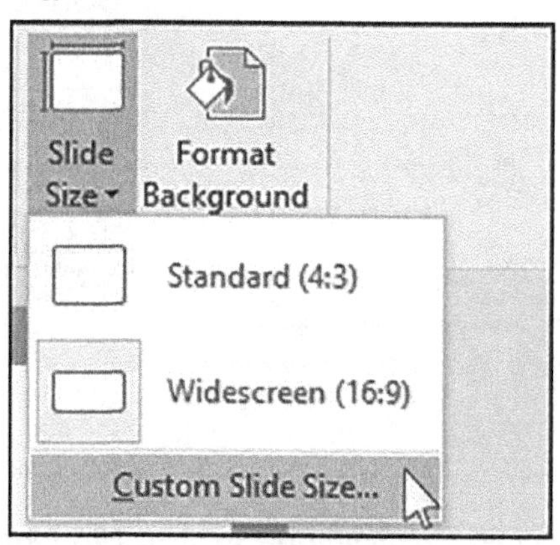

Figure 9. ***PowerPoint config shown from "Design" tab and "Slide Size" option.***

Is there a combination of mixed aspect ratio (4:3 and 16:9) monitors and projectors in the courtroom? A mismatch produces a distorted result onscreen and needs to be configured out by changing the aspect ratio using the display settings on each individual display.

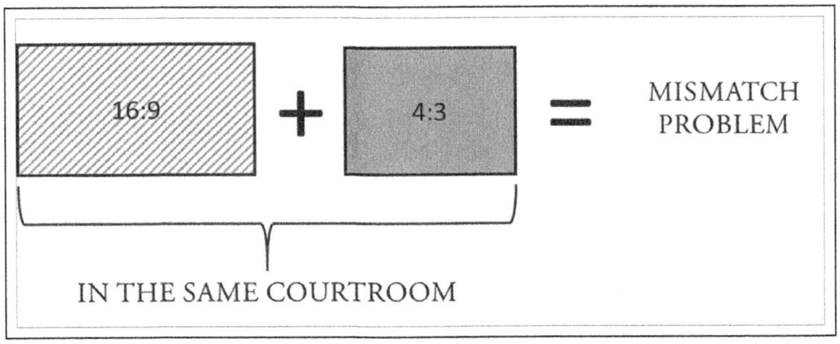

Figure 10. ***What happens when you mix aspect ratios in the courtroom.***

- Configure everything to the same aspect ratio in a mixed environment.
- Opt for 4:3, as the sides of the screen on a 16:9 display are not typically used and you will fill more of the screen vertically.

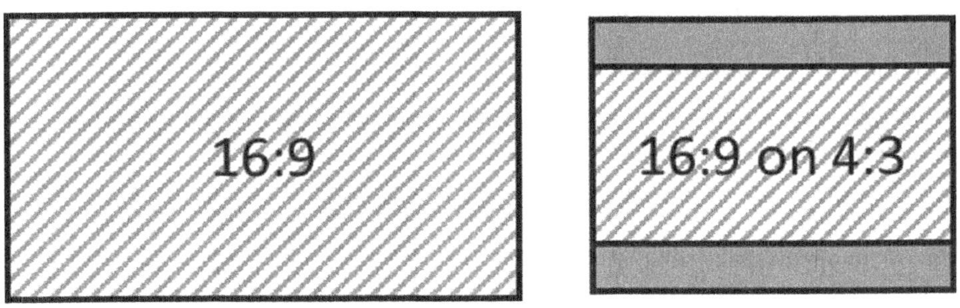

Figure 11. ***16:9 on 4:3.***

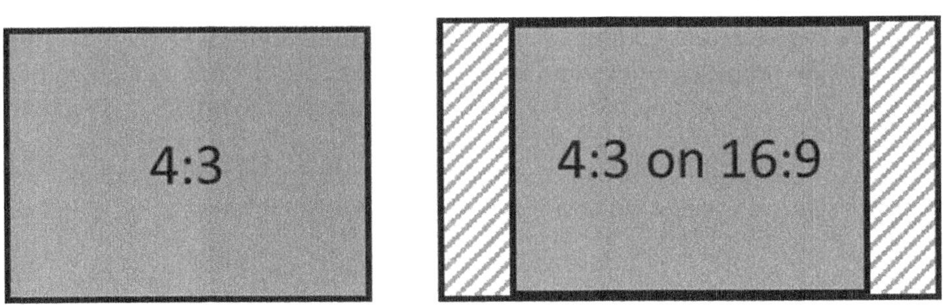

Figure12. ***The reverse: 4:3 on 16:9.***

Where are the courtroom monitors? To ensure that everyone has a clear view, you may need to supplement with additional equipment. It's typical to supplement the judge, clerk, witness, and counsel table with monitors.

6.9.3 Step 3: Look for a Shared Courtroom Display

Projector or large monitor for shared viewing? Yes No			
4:3 16:9			
Approximate dimensions:			
Quality of displayed image:	High	Medium	Poor
Accurate colors? Yes	No		
Highlight colors are accurate?	Yes	No	
Remote control:	Yes	No	
Consider replacement/supplement?		Yes	No

Figure 13. ***From Page 1 of the Trial Technology Checklist.***

Is there a shared view central monitor (i.e., projector and screen or big-screen monitor)?

- What is its aspect ratio? Does it match the other monitors in the courtroom?
- How big is it?
- How far from decision-makers and lawyers is it?
- Are the colors accurate? If not, what colors work?[9]
- Is there a remote with the main screen?
  - You may want the remote next to you (rather than in a drawer) in case you need to make changes to the screen or it loses its configuration.
  - Familiarize yourself with the remote and display controls.
- If you are bringing a shared display or supplementing courtroom equipment, what will work in the space available in the courtroom?

6.9.4 Step 4: Calculate Approximate Distances

What is the distance between the viewers of your presentation and their displays in the courtroom? This helps guide the font and point size of text and how much to enlarge the images that will be used in the trial presentation, PowerPoint, and any display boards. Presentations are often planned in a vacuum, without regard to legibility from a distance. Try it out in your war room or office using the same distance calculation before presenting in court to see if the presentation can be seen and read. The graphic and explanations below will help you make important decisions as your team plans its presentations.

9. For example, many DLP projectors have a problem with yellow highlights and they come out brown. In this case, I use green, pink, or orange to highlight.

Approximate Distance

Main Display (view calc.)
Judge to display:
Jury to display:
Counsel to display:
Gallery to display:
Tech to display:

VGA to switch (length calculation)
Judge to switch:
Witness to switch:
Counsel to switch:
Projector/Monitor to switch:

Audio
Audio source to tech:

Power Outlets
Judge to outlet:
Tech table to outlet:
Podium to outlet:
Counsel table to outlet:
Witness to outlet:

Figure 14. ***From page 1 of the Trial Technology Checklist, a handy chart for recording distances between "objects" in the courtroom.***

Measure the distance between the following people in court and make good decisions about display placement and presentation creation:

- Judge
- Jury
- Counsel
- Trial tech—the tech should be able to see the main display and follow along with the lawyers' presentation gestures and instructions (i.e., what they are pointing at)
- Gallery

As to the distance from the VGA to the switch, you should generally know the length of cables between the switches and splitters. When cables have too lengthy a run, there isn't enough power for the signal to travel the length of the cable. Each splitter or switch typically boosts the video signal. As long as there is a powered device between each cable longer than fifty feet, you should be OK. But do try to keep cable length at a minimum. I recommend cable runs no longer than twenty-five to fifty feet per segment.

From the audio source to the speakers: measure the distance between the speakers and listeners.

From your equipment to the power outlets: power sources and number of outlets can be a *significant issue.* Understand and plan for the energy needs of both your equipment and opposing counsel's.

A quick note on security: It's important to find out if there are any special requirements from security *in addition* to what the court requires. Sometimes, you need to show an order from the judge, use special loading zones, or bring in equipment only during certain hours. Ask whether you can leave equipment in the courtroom overnight or will need to setup daily.

Security

Court order to bring equipment:
Yes No
Special Entrance: Yes No
Special Hours: Yes No
Hours:
Equipment can be left in
courtroom: Yes No

Figure 15. ***From Page 1 of the Trial Technology Checklist.***

6.9.5 Step 5: Take Stock of Additional Equipment Needs

Never assume anything. Ascertain whether a particular piece of equipment is in the courtroom and is always available (as opposed to being shared among other courtrooms), or else bring it in.

- **Document camera**—the best piece of equipment at breaking up a long series of slides and a rock-solid backup in case of equipment failure or a surprise paper exhibit
- **Sound system**—court sound systems are often problematic, so bring your own speakers
- **Wi-Fi**—don't rely on court Wi-Fi to fulfill your most critical needs
  - Keep your data local
  - Consider bringing in your own Wi-Fi (in a pinch, your phone may do as a hotspot)
- **Printing**—a quiet printer nearby can be very helpful
- **Easel**—it would be embarrassing to have a giant board and nothing to display it on
- **Flip chart**
- **Dry-erase board**

Document Camera: Yes No
Can plug into switch: Yes No
Location of document camera:____________________

Power Outlets
How many?__________
Location:

Sound system: Yes No
Access point: Counsel table Podium Other
Describe:

Wi-Fi: Yes No
Signal Strength: Strong Weak Tested Empty or Full?

Hot Seat Location: Counsel Table Tech Table
Clear viewpoint of attorney and shared viewing monitor? Yes No

Courtroom printing: Yes No **Display Board Stands:** Yes No
Easel: Yes No
Flip Chart: Yes No
Dry Erase: Yes No

Podium to outlet:
Counsel table to outlet:
Witness to outlet:

Security

Court order to bring equipment:
Yes No
Special Entrance: Yes No
Special Hours: Yes No
Hours:
Equipment can be left in
courtroom: Yes No

Figure 16. ***From Page 1 of the Trial Technology Checklist.***

6.10 Supplementing Courtroom Equipment

Page 2 of the Courtroom Technology Evaluation specifies the equipment you plan to bring to court, who is responsible for bringing it, who will run the switch, where supplemental equipment will be placed in the courtroom, and how it will be configured. This page will help you flag potential technical issues.

Courtroom Technology Supplement

Equipment Rental Responsibility

The [Plaintiff Defendant] will be the party responsible for contracting with the vendor.
Costs will be paid by: Plaintiff Defendant Shared
Vendor:__________________ **Switch Control:** Plaintiff Defendant
Court order necessary to bring in equipment: Yes No

DISPLAY

Shared viewing screen: **Projector** **Large Monitor Screen**
Size:
Main screen aspect ratio: 4:3 16:9
Counsel table monitors: Yes No
Monitor aspect ratio: 4:3 16:9
How many:________
Projector stand: Yes No

Warning: Avoid mixed aspect ratio and signal degradation on long cable runs.

Location of courtroom monitors:
Judge Jury Witness
Counsel table: Plaintiff Defense Shared
Gallery **Hot Seat**
Will supplemental equipment create a mixed aspect ratio environment?: Yes No
Can displays be configured to avoid aspect ratio mismatch? Yes No
Amount of VGA cable needed +30%____________
Is VGA length >30ft: Yes No
VGA Switch: Yes No [4 port 6 port 8 port]
VGA splitter: 4 6 8
D/A Switch: Yes No How many:_________

AUDIO SYSTEM

Audio Mixer: Yes No
Audio cable length: _________
Speaker Rental: __________
Speaker stand: Yes No

Warning: Consider standalone system if court system is inaccessible or locked down.

Document Camera

Video resolution of document camera:
Brand: ________________
Remote: Yes No
Location of document camera:_______________________

Warning: video resolution mismatch can cause reset

Printing

In courtroom printing needed: Yes No
Quiet color printer: Yes No
Connection: Wireless Bluetooth Cable

Print drivers provided Yes No

Power Outlets

How many?___________
Location: _____________
Extension cords: Yes No How long:_________ How many:_______
Power Strip: Yes No How many:_________ Heavy duty: Yes No

Misc.

WiFi: Yes No Service provider:____________
Easel: Yes No iPhone power: Yes No
Flip Chart: Yes No USB power: Yes No
Dry Erase: Yes No

Figure 17. ***Courtroom Technology Supplement (available for free download; see the Notes on Use for access).***

6.10.1 *Step One: Determine Responsibility for the Courtroom*

Courtroom Technology Supplement

Equipment Rental Responsibility

The [Plaintiff Defendant] will be the party responsible for contracting with the vendor.
Costs will be paid by: Plaintiff Defendant Shared
Vendor:________________ **Switch Control:** Plaintiff Defendant
Court order necessary to bring in equipment: Yes No

DISPLAY

Shared viewing screen: **Projector** **Large Monitor Screen**
Size:
Main screen aspect ratio: 4:3 16:9
Counsel table monitors: Yes No
Monitor aspect ratio: 4:3 16:9
How many:________
Projector stand: Yes No

Warning: Avoid mixed aspect ratio and signal degradation on long cable runs.

Location of courtroom monitors:
Judge Jury Witness
Counsel table: Plaintiff Defense Shared
Gallery Hot Seat
Will supplemental equipment create a mixed aspect ratio environment?: Yes No
Can displays be configured to avoid aspect ratio mismatch? Yes No
Amount of VGA cable needed +30%__________
Is VGA length >30ft: Yes No
VGA Switch: Yes No [4 port 6 port 8 port]
VGA splitter: 4 6 8
D/A Switch: Yes No How many:________

AUDIO SYSTEM

Audio Mixer: Yes No
Audio cable length: ________
Speaker Rental: __________
Speaker stand: Yes No

Warning: Consider standalone system if court system is inaccessible or locked down.

Figure 18. ***Who is the responsible party?***

Who will take the lead with vendor selection, equipment choices, and setup?

- Parties should agree on an independent third-party vendor. The clerk will often express a preference on who will lead setup based upon who has shown the strongest commitment to the setup of the courtroom and how the court's concerns have been addressed.
- Parties should be *invoiced separately and responsible for their own share of equipment rental costs.*
- Using a third-party vendor mitigates many potential conflicting issues, such as claims of sabotage, setup issues, etc. Both sides are on the hook for shared costs, like cables, switches, displays, delivery, and setup. There are legal teams that try to pay for "just the monitor" and nothing else, or they try to back out of the agreement, often mid-trial, by claiming they did not use the equipment enough. (It's as if they think the monitor operates on its own without the aid of cables, switches, and setup.) Another issue that arises often is that one party may not want a certain piece of equipment, such as a document camera, and the other party does. As long as that equipment is "stand-alone" and not critical to display, it should be OK to request an adjustment on the rental bill. Avoid these issues by arranging for separate invoicing from the vendor.

  Then there is when one party wants its trial technology presentation vendor to supply all equipment for the courtroom. Decide this on a case-by-case basis. Will their technician be responsive to your side's equipment needs and questions? Will you be forced to use equipment that you are unfamiliar with or don't want to use? Quite simply, both sides are better off with an independent vendor about which you both have an equal expectation of performance.[10]

10. Think about a situation where multiple parties are involved and one settles out of the case. What if that party is the one that brought equipment? It gets awkward as they leave and want to take everything with them. Use an independent, third-party vendor.

Who will run the switch?

- Typically, the person responsible for taking the lead on courtroom planning runs the switch.
- The person needs to be attentive to both side's needs. Work out a communication system for things like switching to the document camera, cutting the signal to all monitors, and coming to an understanding on both parties' preferences on the back-and-forth of the switch.
- In case of disagreement on who will run the switch, I recommend Rock Paper Scissors (best two out of three). Seriously.

6.10.2 Step Two: Decide on the Main Display, Number of Desktop Displays, Screen Ratio, and Location of Video and Audio Equipment

Courtroom Technology Supplement

Equipment Rental Responsibility

The [Plaintiff Defendant] will be the party responsible for contracting with the vendor.
Costs will be paid by: Plaintiff Defendant Shared
Vendor:____________________ **Switch Control:** Plaintiff Defendant
Court order necessary to bring in equipment: Yes No

DISPLAY

Shared viewing screen: **Projector** **Large Monitor Screen**
Size:
Main screen aspect ratio: 4:3 16:9
Counsel table monitors: Yes No
Monitor aspect ratio: 4:3 16:9
How many:________
Projector stand: Yes No

Warning: Avoid mixed aspect ratio and signal degradation on long cable runs.

Location of courtroom monitors:
Judge Jury Witness
Counsel table: Plaintiff Defense Shared
Gallery Hot Seat
Will supplemental equipment create a mixed aspect ratio environment?: Yes No
Can displays be configured to avoid aspect ratio mismatch? Yes No
Amount of VGA cable needed +30%__________
Is VGA length >30ft: Yes No
VGA Switch: Yes No [4 port 6 port 8 port]
VGA splitter: 4 6 8
D/A Switch: Yes No How many:________

AUDIO SYSTEM

Audio Mixer: Yes No
Audio cable length: ________
Speaker Rental: ________
Speaker stand: Yes No

Warning: Consider standalone system if court system is inaccessible or locked down.

Figure 19. ***Display and audio.***

- Use a large main screen (projector or big-screen monitor) for shared viewing. Review Chapter Four, Equipment, to get a better idea of what will work in your courtroom.
- Consider placing or supplementing desktop monitors for the judge, jury, witness, clerk, and counsel table. It is difficult to place a desktop monitor in the jury box. Ensure the shared viewing monitor is visible and readable from a distance.
- Using the same aspect ratio of all monitors in the courtroom is key to a quality presentation.
  - Both projectors and big-screen monitors can typically be configured for 4:3 or 16:9.
  - If there are existing courtroom monitors, use their aspect ratio to configure your main screen.
  - If there are no monitors in the courtroom and you must set up from scratch, consider using 16:9 because that is likely what you are using in your office.

- *Note*: The aspect ratio your legal team selects should also be used for presentations and graphics created by vendors and legal team members. This small tie-in is *key* to good and compatible graphics.

- Regardless of whether there is wired courtroom audio, always bring your own speakers, as built-in audio in the courtroom is often problematic. Bring speakers that transmit sufficient coverage for the courtroom. Your desktop speakers are not powerful enough.

6.10.3 Step Three: Note Miscellaneous Equipment and Considerations

AUDIO SYSTEM

Audio Mixer: Yes No
Audio cable length: ________
Speaker Rental: ________
Speaker stand: Yes No

Warning: Consider standalone system if court system is inaccessible or locked down.

Document Camera

Video resolution of document camera:
Brand: ____________
Remote: Yes No
Location of document camera: ____________________

Warning: video resolution mismatch can cause reset

Printing

In courtroom printing needed: Yes No
Quiet color printer: Yes No
Connection: Wireless Bluetooth Cable

Print drivers provided Yes No

Power Outlets

How many? ________
Location: ________
Extension cords: Yes No How long: ________ How many: ______
Power Strip: Yes No How many: ________ Heavy duty: Yes No

Misc.

WiFi: Yes No Service provider: __________
Easel: Yes No iPhone power: Yes No
Flip Chart: Yes No USB power: Yes No
Dry Erase: Yes No

Figure 20. ***Miscellaneous technical needs.***

- **Document camera**
  - Review the detailed discussion of document cameras in Chapter Four, Equipment.
  - Ensure your document camera can project at the same resolutions as the rest of your equipment. Otherwise, it may go through a setup process every time you switch to it.
  - A document camera remote allows you to "lend a hand" from a distance if someone is fumbling with the controls.
- **Printer**
  - Bring a small, quiet, color printer to the courtroom. It can save the day.
  - A printer is necessity for longer trials and when there are no printing options nearby.
- **Power outlets**
  - Understand the power limitations of the courtroom. In many older courtrooms, there may be just one power outlet for both parties' equipment needs.
- **Miscellaneous**
  - Does the courtroom have easels, dry-erase boards, or flip charts available for your use, or should you bring your own?

6.11 Create a Courtroom Floorplan

Page 3 of the Courtroom Technology Evaluation form is a blank courtroom floorplan for you to complete. It is important to memorialize the courtroom layout on paper and propose where to place your equipment. Circulate your plan among team members and firm decision-makers to ensure it meets their expectations and to help with creating an equipment budget. Note that you may have a limited amount of time to prepare the courtroom (often the day before or during lunch), so you must get your plan right the *first time.* The earlier you can get into the courtroom to set up, the better—but often what you get is the early morning, lunchtime, or the period right after jury selection. If you have a particularly large trial, you must try to get in to perform setup and testing a few days before it starts so that you can work out any issues or problems you may encounter.

Courtroom Plan

Rough sketch of courtroom

Has each location been accounted for?				
Video	**Audio**	**Switch**	**Cabling**	**Presentation Aids**
Projector or Large Monitor	Speaker	VGA switch	Video	Podium
Screen	Mixer	VGA splitter	Audio	Easel
Judge monitor		DA switch	Power	Flip chart
Plaintiff monitor		Judge kill switch		Dry erase
Defendant monitor		Power strip		
Tech(s) monitor				
Tech table (can view atty direction?)				

Courthouse address:

Courtroom number:

Figure 21. ***Page 2 of the checklist: schematic and checklist.***

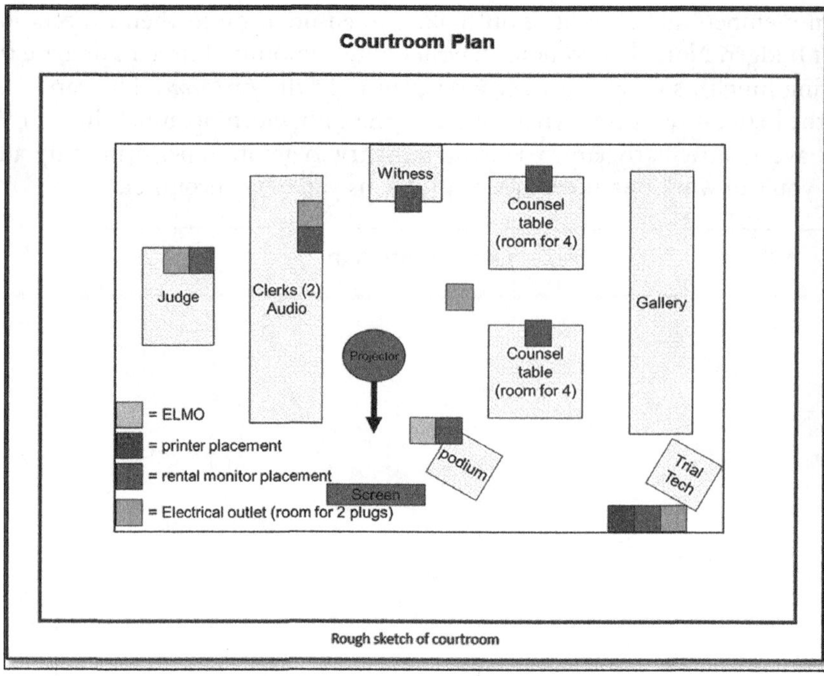

Figure 22. ***Courtroom plan filled in with a plan created in PowerPoint.***

Below is a checklist of all the items that have been discussed in this chapter so you can review it and ensure you've considered everything in the courtroom. As a final note, the address of the courthouse and your courtroom number may seem like a no-brainer, but they are *very important.* Double-check and write it down.

Has each location been accounted for?				
Video	**Audio**	**Switch**	**Cabling**	**Presentation Aids**
Projector or Large Monitor	Speaker	VGA switch	Video	Podium
Screen	Mixer	VGA splitter	Audio	Easel
Judge monitor		DA switch	Power	Flip chart
Plaintiff monitor		Judge kill switch		Dry erase
Defendant monitor		Power strip		
Tech(s) monitor				
Tech table (can view atty direction?)				

Courthouse address:

Courtroom number:

Figure 23. ***Check off each item as it is accounted for.***

6.11.1 Setting Up Your Courtroom

When setting up your courtroom, first make sure everyone is on the same page with the setup plan. Again, legal equipment rental vendors excel in this area, so find a good one to work with if you have anything more than a basic setup need. (And even then, it is helpful to have someone else take care of these details like carrying large pieces of equipment like monitors, tables, and screens.[11])

11. Although no excuses for not knowing how to troubleshoot or replace problem cables and equipment.

Check, then double-check, to make sure you don't need special permission[12] or an order from the judge to bring in equipment either through the front door with security or through a loading dock. Your vendor should arrive early for the inevitable delays of using a loading dock or bringing a lot of equipment through security. Security is generally tighter in federal courthouses than all others. It is often helpful to bag together in a Ziploc bag the items you take with you daily in your briefcase, like your mouse, cables, headphones, etc., so you can get them through security more quickly.

One last point of decorum: I don't walk in the "well" of the court without permission. The well is the area between the counsel table and the judge's bench, and it is usually off-limits. As a showing of respect, always ask the judge for permission to enter. Also, be mindful that during the trial you might be going through security with the jurors on your case, so being organized, polite, and helpful is a good thing.

After I get all of the necessary approvals and permissions, I typically set up the courtroom using the Advanced Courtroom Setup Sheet below.

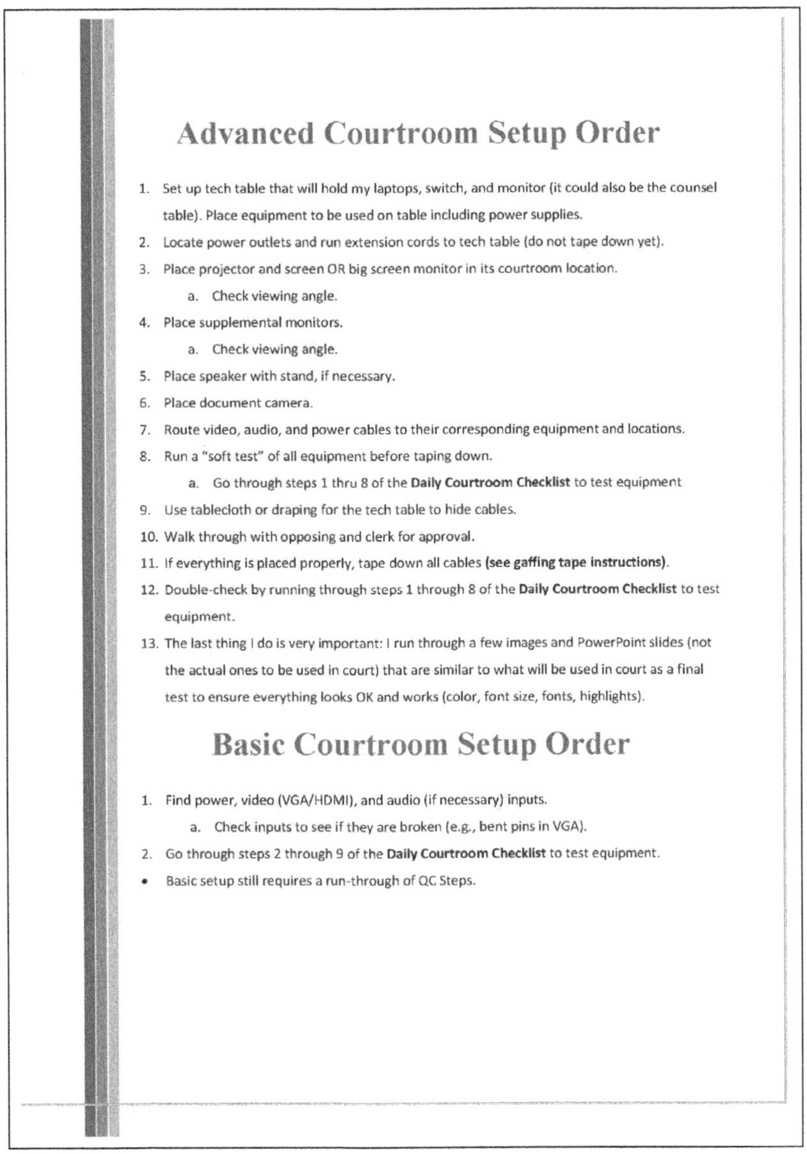

Advanced Courtroom Setup Order

1. Set up tech table that will hold my laptops, switch, and monitor (it could also be the counsel table). Place equipment to be used on table including power supplies.
2. Locate power outlets and run extension cords to tech table (do not tape down yet).
3. Place projector and screen OR big screen monitor in its courtroom location.
   a. Check viewing angle.
4. Place supplemental monitors.
   a. Check viewing angle.
5. Place speaker with stand, if necessary.
6. Place document camera.
7. Route video, audio, and power cables to their corresponding equipment and locations.
8. Run a "soft test" of all equipment before taping down.
   a. Go through steps 1 thru 8 of the **Daily Courtroom Checklist** to test equipment
9. Use tablecloth or draping for the tech table to hide cables.
10. Walk through with opposing and clerk for approval.
11. If everything is placed properly, tape down all cables **(see gaffing tape instructions)**.
12. Double-check by running through steps 1 through 8 of the **Daily Courtroom Checklist** to test equipment.
13. The last thing I do is very important: I run through a few images and PowerPoint slides (not the actual ones to be used in court) that are similar to what will be used in court as a final test to ensure everything looks OK and works (color, font size, fonts, highlights).

Basic Courtroom Setup Order

1. Find power, video (VGA/HDMI), and audio (if necessary) inputs.
   a. Check inputs to see if they are broken (e.g., bent pins in VGA).
2. Go through steps 2 through 9 of the **Daily Courtroom Checklist** to test equipment.

- Basic setup still requires a run-through of QC Steps.

Figure 24. ***Initial order for setting up.***

12. A judicial order is the norm not the exception.

6.11.2 Courtroom Plans

Each courtroom is unique and thus requires its own plan. In this section, I review some of the most common courtroom setups. (Keep in mind that the projector used in these examples might just as easily be a big-screen monitor.) Courtrooms of different shapes have different needs as well, so you'll need to evaluate them carefully to design a presentation strategy that works best for your team. I'll say it again: many legal teams present exhibits, graphics, or slides in court without regard to their legibility in court. The images probably looked great when they were making them, but then they never followed through to see how they worked in the room they would be presented in. Always test your presentations by displaying your images in court, as well as in your war room or office in spaces that approximate the specs of the courtroom.

Basic. Below is the most basic court setup, featuring two parties that are providing input. It is a simple setup, with each party's laptop connected to a projector through a VGA switchbox.

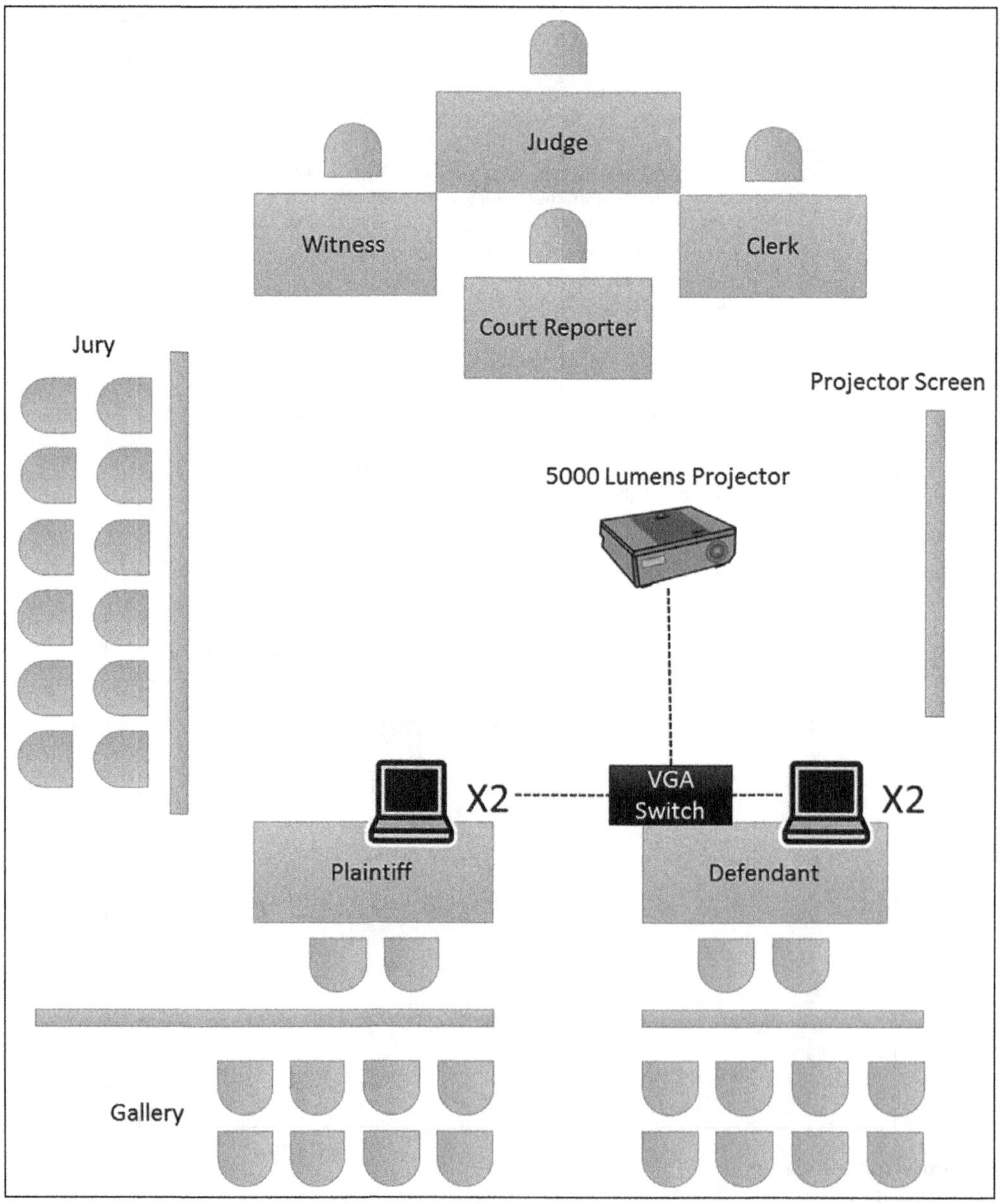

Figure 25. ***A basic setup.***

Intermediate. This is the setup you'll most often see. Each party's laptop and a document camera are connected through a video switchbox, which is then connected to a "1 in, 6 out" video distribution box that splits the single signal into multiple displays and the projector. The distribution box allows for additional monitors for the judge, clerk, witness, court reporter, and counsel table. Note that audio has been added and is usually an amplified speaker that can be shared (but each team usually brings their own speakers). Trial techs may consider using a DA switch so they can use the monitor on their table independently of what is being viewed on the other monitors in the courtroom.

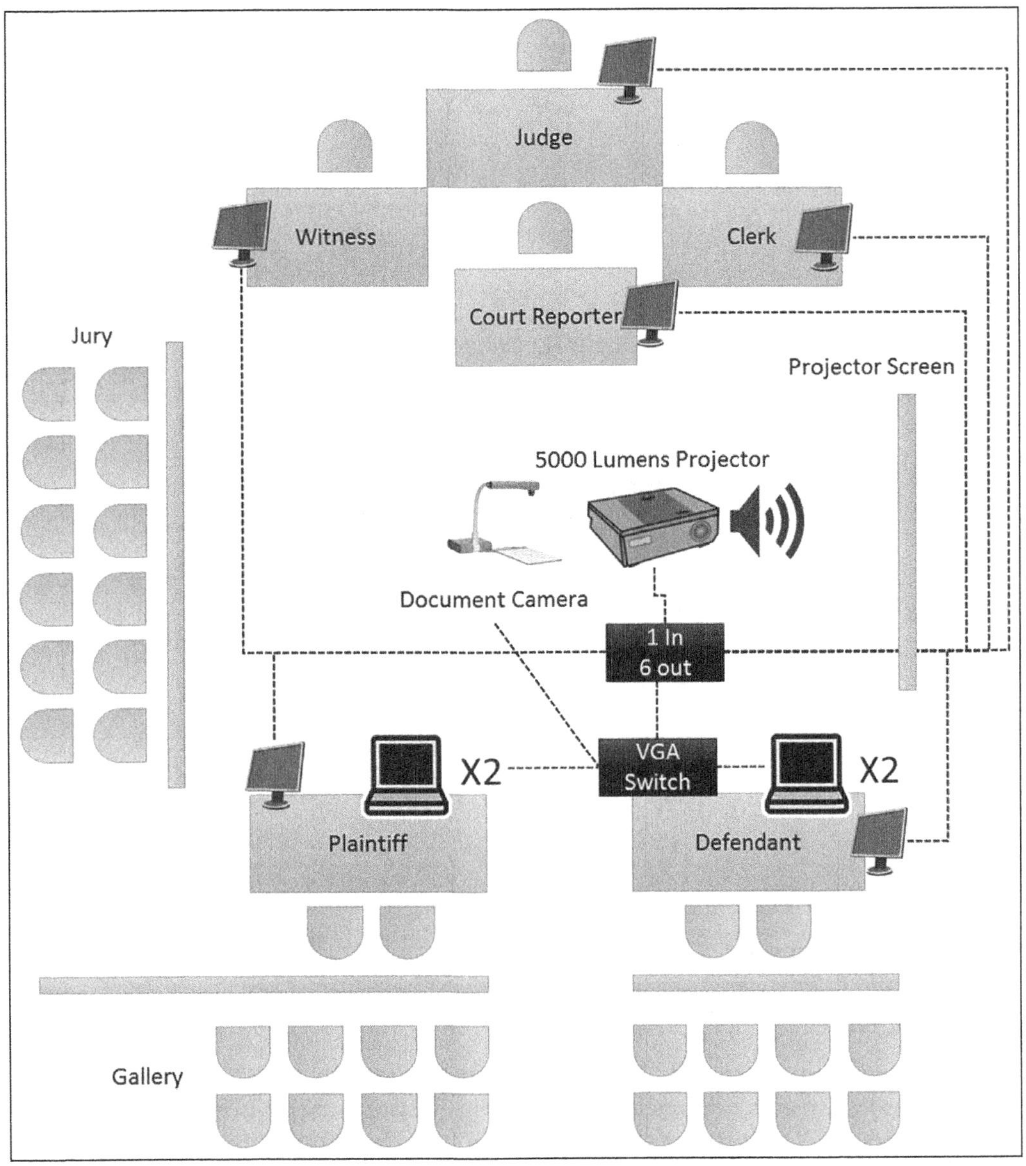

Figure 26. ***An intermediate setup.***

Advanced. Each party's laptop and a document camera are connected through a video switchbox, which is then connected to two "1 in, 6 out" video distribution boxes that split the single signal into multiple displays and the projector. The distribution box allows for additional monitors for the judge, clerk, witness, court reporter, jury, and counsel table. Note that audio has been added and is usually an amplified speaker that can be shared (but each team usually brings their own speakers). Trial techs may consider using a DA switch so they can use the monitor on their table independently of what is being viewed on the other monitors in the courtroom.

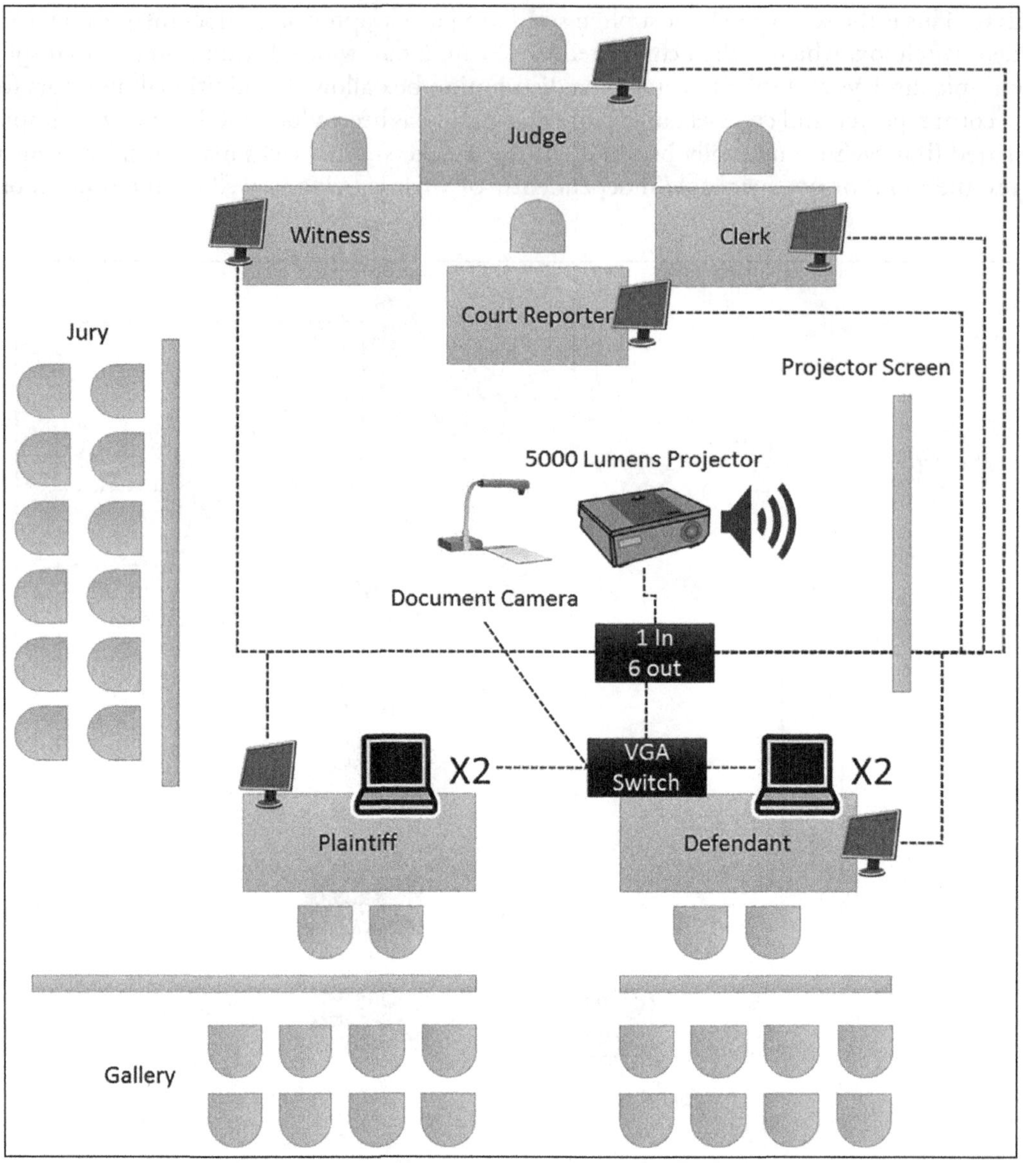

Figure 27. ***An advanced courtroom setup.***

6.11.3 Graphics Legibility

Testing your presentation and setup for legibility is important to ensure that decision-makers can *see* the important message your legal team's exhibits are transmitting. Testing benefits both the setup (i.e., screens, projector, measured distances from viewers) of the presentation and the presentation itself (i.e., the quality of the PowerPoints, timelines, exhibits). Incredibly, many firms spend tens of thousands of dollars on presentations that simply cannot be seen from the jury box. What is going wrong?

Clearly, there is a disconnect between the setup and tech team and whoever is creating the graphics if the appropriate aspect ratios and physical measurements between courtroom monitors and viewers are never communicated. Keep in mind that presentations are created and shared on computer monitors that rest about twenty-four inches from someone's face—it's disastrous when people assume that just because an exhibit looks good two feet in front of their faces that it will also look good when twenty or thirty feet away. Hence, always test the presentation in an environment that approximates the courtroom. If you are particularly worried and want to fine-tune a presentation, I recommend creating a slide that uses the same approximate point size, fonts, and colors and displaying it as a test during court downtime (typically at testing, setup, or court start) to gauge whether it will work.

Comfortable Viewing Distance for Text on Presentation Visuals
4:3 screens (projectors, older monitors)

Assumptions:
- Visual acuity of 20/40 (about the same that is used for highway road signs)
- Projected image fills the screen
- Screen and image have a 4:3 width to height ratio (the standard ratio for most projectors and screens)

How to use the table:
- Locate the row that corresponds to the width of the screen you are using
- Locate the column corresponding to the smallest font used for text on your slides
- The intersection of the row and column is the maximum distance from the screen that an audience member should be seated in order to be able to easily read the text
- For example, if you are using a 60 inch screen and have 32 point text on your slides, the farthest that someone should be is 57 feet from the screen

Screen Width (inches)	Font size (in points) 18	24	28	32	36	40	44
36	19	27	31	34	38	42	46
48	25	36	41	46	51	56	61
60	32	44	51	57	64	70	76
72	38	53	61	69	76	84	92
84	44	62	71	80	89	98	107
96	51	71	81	92	102	112	122
120	64	89	102	114	127	140	153

Comfortable Viewing Distance for Text on Presentation Visuals
16:9 screens (widescreen TVs, monitors & projectors)

Assumptions:
- Visual acuity of 20/40 (about the same that is used for highway road signs)
- Projected image fills the screen
- Screen and image have a 16:9 width to height ratio (the standard ratio for most widescreen TVs, monitors & projectors)

How to use the table:
- Locate the row that corresponds to the diagonal measurement of the screen you are using (the typical way to measure these screens)
- Locate the column corresponding to the smallest font used for text on your slides
- The intersection of the row and column is the maximum distance from the screen that an audience member should be seated in order to be able to easily read the text
- For example, if you are using a 32 inch TV and have 28 point text on your slides, the farthest that someone should be is 18 feet from the screen

Diagonal screen size (in inches)	Font size (in points) 18	24	28	32	36	40	44
15	5	7	8	9	10	11	12
19	7	9	11	12	13	14	16
22	8	11	12	14	15	17	18
27	9	13	15	17	19	21	22
32	11	15	18	20	22	24	27
36	12	17	20	22	25	27	30
42	15	20	23	26	29	32	35
47	16	23	26	29	32	36	39
52	18	25	29	32	36	40	43
60	21	29	33	37	41	46	50
72	25	35	40	45	50	55	60
80	28	39	44	50	55	61	66

Figure 28. ***Font size guidance for distance. (Source: David Paradi, ThinkOutsideTheSlide.com.)***

Test the projector and display setup with a screen test image. A screen test image is one of those funny images (Figure 15) with color bars and lines that ensure images are displaying properly in the courtroom; they also help fine-tune projectors and monitors so that images are centered. (I describe how to use this image properly in the Chapter One, Getting Started.) Be sure to use the correct image for the type of monitor you are using— whether 4:3 or 16:9—and ensure that all four corners appear on each monitor in the courtroom.

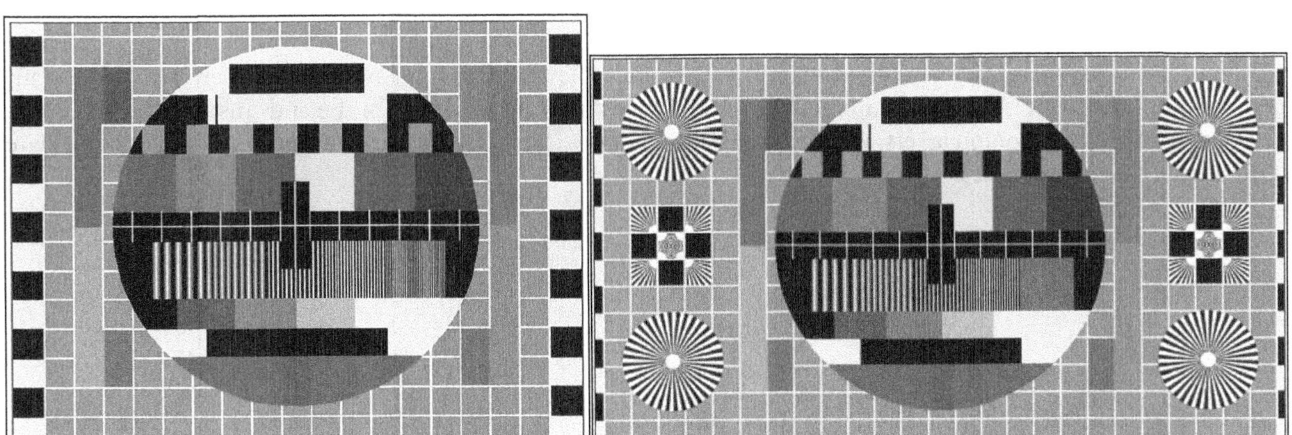

Figure 29. ***A 4:3 and 16:9 test image. Check colors, corners, and legibility.***

Remember, where you place the screen and how you angle it matter. Courtrooms are not one-size-fits-all, so each must be considered individually. I suggest that in smaller courtrooms a big-screen, flat-panel monitor is often a better choice than a projector—but as your courtroom size increases, a bright (and quiet) projector may be your better option.

6.11.4 *Cabling the Courtroom*

Correctly cabling the courtroom goes a long way to avoiding problems, creating a safe courtroom, and putting your professionalism on display. First and foremost, you must use gaffing tape, and nothing but, to tape down cables in the courtroom. Anything else and you will rip up the carpet and ruin the furniture.

The direct route for cables is not always the best one and rarely the safest. Avoid high-traffic areas and spots where the cables will be run over by furniture and people. People can't trip over walls, so run your cables around the perimeter of the room whenever possible. Remember, when running longer cables, be sure your cable lengths are not too long, which can result in a weaker video signal (typically thirty to fifty feet or longer). Cabling is one area where a good vendor is very helpful.

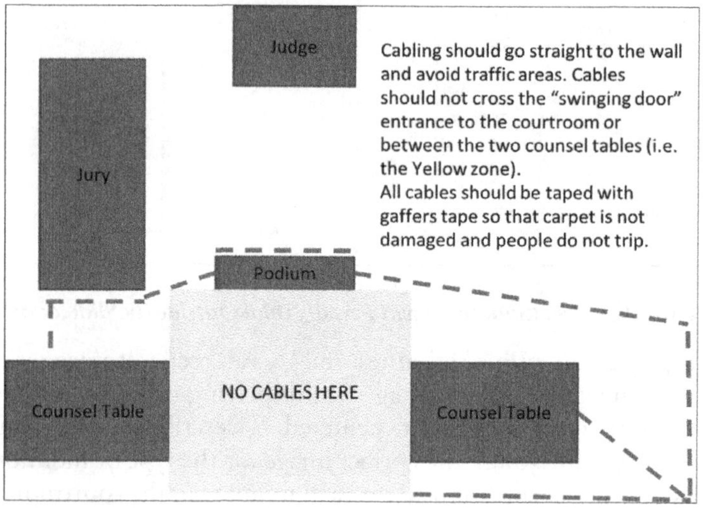

Figure 30. ***An example of indirect cabling.***

Believe it or not, there is a technique to taping down the cables, as shown below. Perhaps even more important than taping them down is how you pull them up. Never just rip up the cables from the end. Instead, peel the horizontal layers off, as with onion layers, while firmly holding down the end, and you won't go through the nightmare of unpeeling tape from cables.

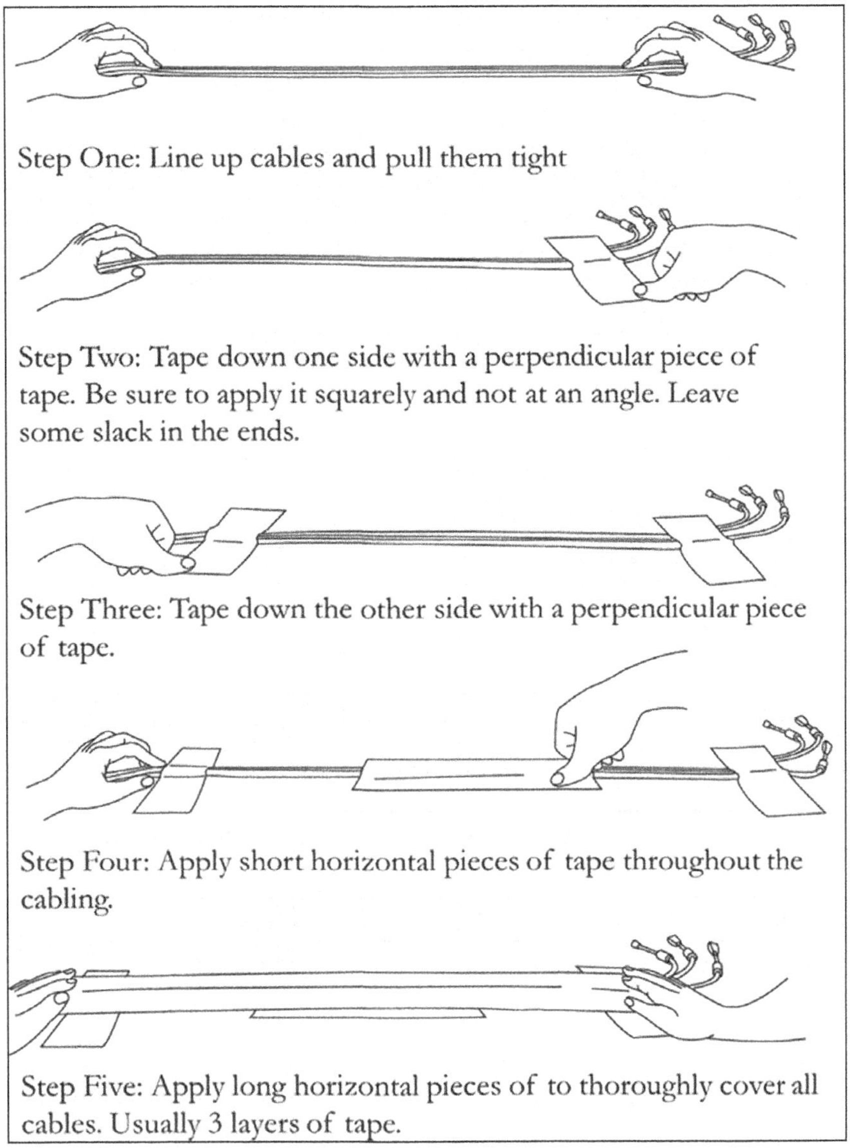

Figure 31. ***How to tape cables.***

6.11.5 Understanding Aspect Ratios and Resolution

Some of this material about aspect ratios and resolution appeared in Chapter Four, but it's crucial and merits more discussion. A monitor's aspect ratio is the proportion between the width and the height of a picture expressed in units. For our purposes, 4:3 is "square" (kind of) and 16:9 is a "rectangle." Imagine spending hours, if not days (and thousands of dollars), on the "perfect presentation," only to have it ruined when displayed in the courtroom because of issues that were completely avoidable. Onscreen distortion is a common occurrence when the aspect ratio used to create exhibits, video, and presentations doesn't match the aspect ratio of the display in the courtroom. With mismatch issues, it's like trying to force a square peg through a round hole. If you are trying to move from a square 4:3 to a rectangle 16:9 (or vice versa), you are going to have technical problems, legibility issues, or lose valuable real estate (via letter or pillar boxing) that reduces legibility. This issue of mismatching commonly occurs in two situations.

First, a mismatch occurs because a presentation is created at a different aspect ratio and/or resolution than what is used in court. The same issue happens if you create a presentation in a high resolution and then try to show it on a much lower resolution monitor. Some common effects are the text is truncated or the graphics go askew. Why? Because you are trying to force something from a very large pallet (1920x1080) to a smaller one (1024x768 or 1280x720). Look at the PowerPoint screen capture below and notice that you have a choice between 16:9 and 4:3 in the "Slide Size" setup of your presentation. Are you creating a mismatch before you ever enter the courtroom by not matching your aspect ratio to what is used in the courtroom? For example, say you create your presentation on your laptop or desktop computer and when you try to present it in court, it turns out squished or stretched. (I call it getting "egged.") The solution is to always test your graphics at the aspect ratio and resolution they will be displayed in court.

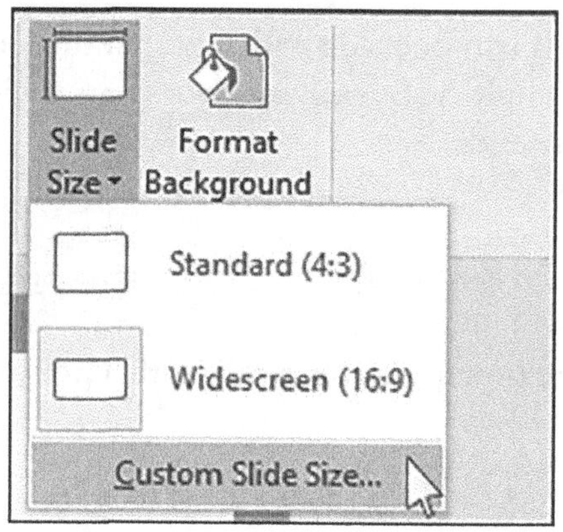

Figure 32. ***Are you creating a mismatch in how you are creating presentations?***

4:3	16:9	Aspect Ratio
640x480	1280x720	**Resolution**
1024x768	1365x768	**Resolution**
1400x1050	1920x1080	**Resolution**
1600x1200		**Resolution**

Figure 33. ***Image resolution table for 4:3 and 16:9.***

Second, note the effects in Figures 34 and 35, below, when a 16:9 or 4:3 image is displayed on a mismatched monitor (i.e., a square on a rectangle, or a rectangle on a square). When the monitors in the courtroom are mismatched with both 4:3 and 16:9 aspect ratios (i.e., both square and rectangle monitors), it causes one of the egg-shaped issues you see below[13] on the displays that don't match. The image becomes distorted and looks like an egg.

Sometimes you can compensate for the egg effect by configuring the display to a different aspect ratio—but note that it will be at the expense of the screen's "real estate," because it creates a pillar box or letterbox where either the sides or the top and bottom are not usable.[14] (See discussion below about 16:9 being a bad ratio for legal display of exhibits). It is vitally important to take the time to learn how to configure the courtroom equipment *and* tailor your presentation to the capabilities of the courtroom. Simply knowing in advance what the aspect ratio and resolution allows you to create a presentation that works in the courtroom you will be presenting in. Far too often, presentations just come out wrong or are hard to read because of these issues in planning, creation, and mismatch.

13. And potentially *egg* on your face.
14. This is one of the reasons we configure our screen background to black; it will blend into any pillar or letterbox displays in the courtroom.

For example, if you create a presentation in 16:9 (rectangle) and display in a letterbox 4:3 (square) monitor, it will shrink. Did you compensate for the shrinkage? Will decision-makers be able to see your presentation? Another example: if there are square monitors on every desktop but a large rectangular display in the middle of the courtroom, you may want to configure the rectangle to display in 4:3 (square).[15] In the end, you likely should configure the mismatch in favor of a 4:3 aspect ratio, but always test both settings to determine what works best for you.

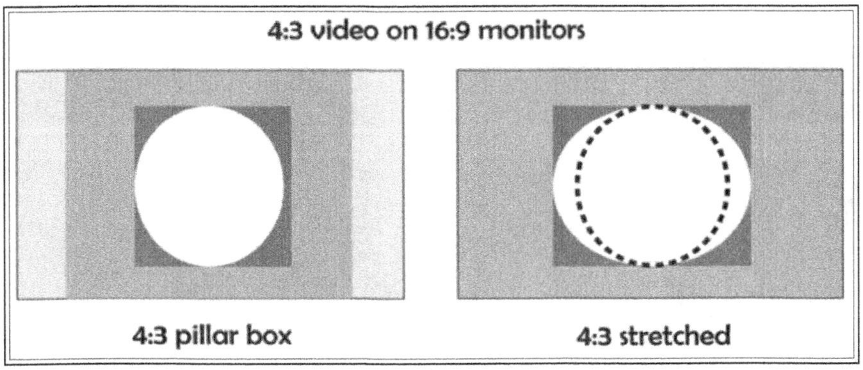

Figure 34. ***The effects on an image when a 4:3 aspect ratio is applied to 16:9 monitors.***

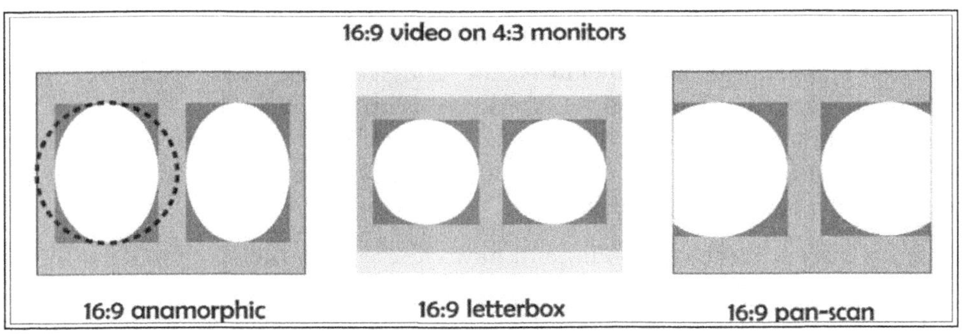

Figure 35. ***The effects on an image when a 16:9 aspect ratio is applied to 4:3 monitors.***

Truthfully, *16:9 can be wasted in the legal environment.* Depo videos are narrow and focused on the individual in the center of the screen. The same is true for most document exhibits (with exceptions for PowerPoints and Excel spreadsheets), where the image will be focused on the center of the screen. However, 16:9 screens do allow you to make good use of callouts and other annotations. Note how in the image below the two callouts can go edge to edge and the document is still largely visible.

15. Which is usually as simple as finding the remote and cycling through the options.

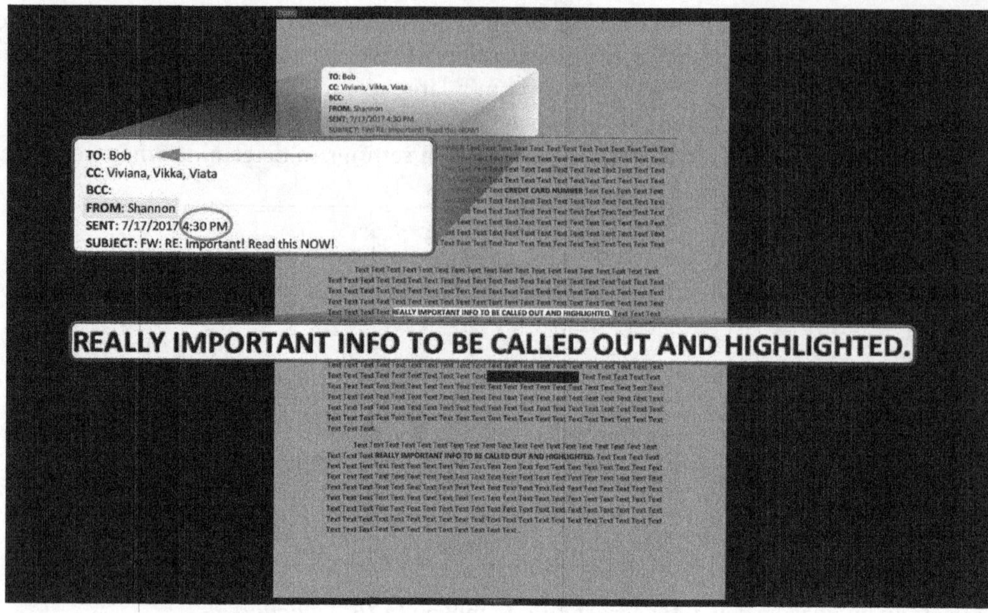

Figure 36. ***Sample of 16:9 screen use of screen "real estate" (unused area).***

You should also be thinking about how you'll deal with any mismatch in aspect ratio not only between yourself and the court, but also between legal team members and vendors. I once had a vendor tell me, "It's our job to make the presentation and graphics. How you get it onscreen is up to you." Whoa! (*Quick side note*: be sure your attorneys know you need to have input with the vendors, or they will simply bypass you, despite what you might need for trial.) In the end, your vendors and anyone creating graphics should be keyed in to the courtroom aspect ratio so they can present the best graphics possible.

Where the screen is placed in the courtroom and how close it is to the jury (along with considering what works best with the legal team presentation style) are very important. After all, you could have an extremely large point size, but if the font makes it illegible at a distance, it just won't work. This issue occurs with surprisingly regularity—teams make a presentation without regard as to whether it's legible, and then they put it onscreen. Try to put some distance between the projector and people in the courtroom, but especially the judge, court reporter, and jury, so when you test it sit right next to it and imagine the noisy projector fan spinning up and disturbing their concentration (especially if you are in a hot courtroom!).

6.12 How to Supplement the Typical High-Tech Courtroom

Make sure you have permission from the clerk to make any of the changes I'm about to discuss. Changing the switch takes a great burden off of the clerk, but you need to make sure you can "go back" if you make a mistake—so don't take apart the courtroom without knowing how to put it back together. If you bypass the system already in place, you may cut off features that are important to the clerk and judge—things like the ability to only show the image on a sidebar monitor and not the entire courtroom—so again, tread carefully. That being said, supplementing technology in the courtroom is fairly common and brings *great* efficiency to the proceedings.

First, find a video access point in the courtroom that you will use as the sole video source for the duration of the trial. The clerk will only enable this "one" access point for the entire trial. You can use any access point in the courtroom, from podium to counsel table, but I typically use the podium connection due to its central location and proximity to other pieces of equipment. Using either an adaptor or a female receptacle VGA cable, you connect to the input at the podium and run the video cable to your tech table switch. All equipment is then plugged into the switch, including your own backup equipment, a video feed for opposing counsel, and the document camera. Keep in mind that because it is a high-traffic area, you may not use a direct route with the cables.

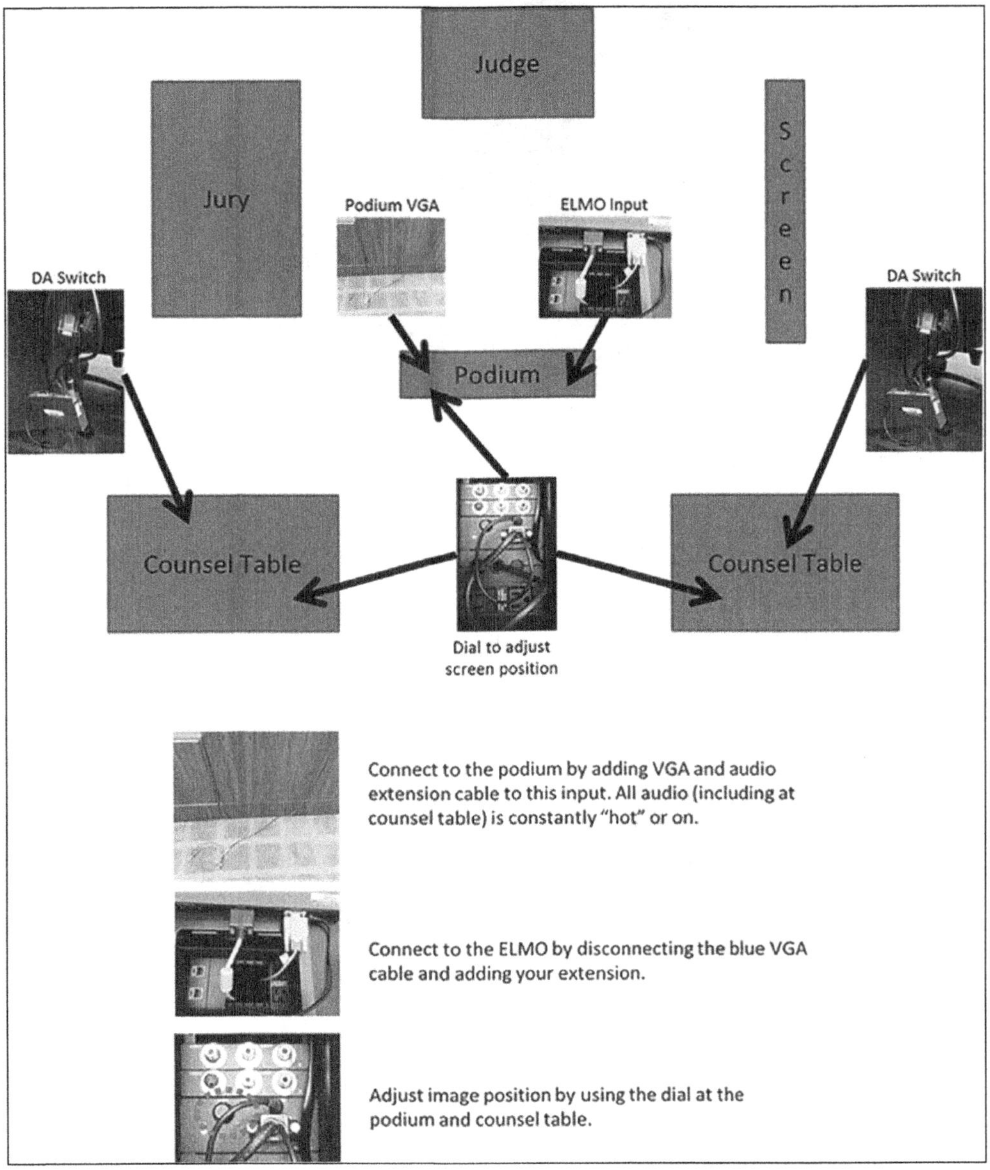

Figure 37. ***Understand where video input can be accessed.***

6.12.1 Adding Monitors

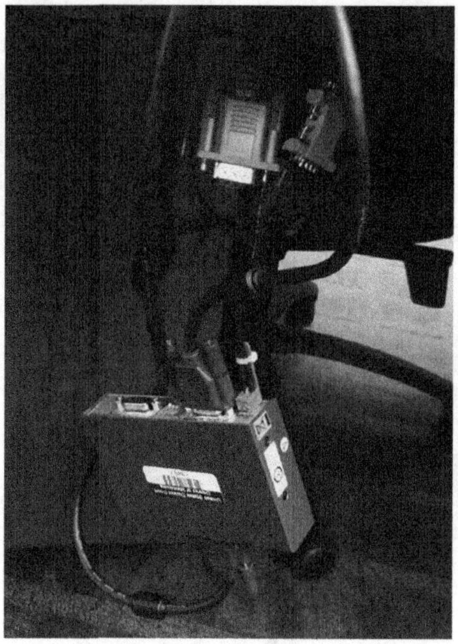

Figure 38. ***The DA switch under a table.***

The underside of each counsel table typically has a DA switch mounted to it that can be split to add monitors, projectors, etc. to the courtroom. They often split the signal to the monitors placed on the counsel table. Be sure to check that each connection is working. They can become unhooked, which is a primary reason why a signal might not be coming to every monitor on the table. If there is an empty port, you can supplement with additional monitors or try a VGA Y connector to tap into the switch and add monitors.

Figure 39. ***VGA Y cable that splits the video signal to two displays.***

6.12.2 Adjusting Image Position on Courtroom Monitors

Each table (including the center podium) has a dial that allows you to adjust the position of the image on the display, shifting the image left or right. The podium dial only adjusts the large projection screen, while the plaintiff and defense each control the monitors on the tables. The dial only makes some adjustments to the position of the video on the screen; additional adjustment on *each individual monitor* is often necessary to adjust the vertical and horizontal image. *The dial is fragile, so please be careful.*

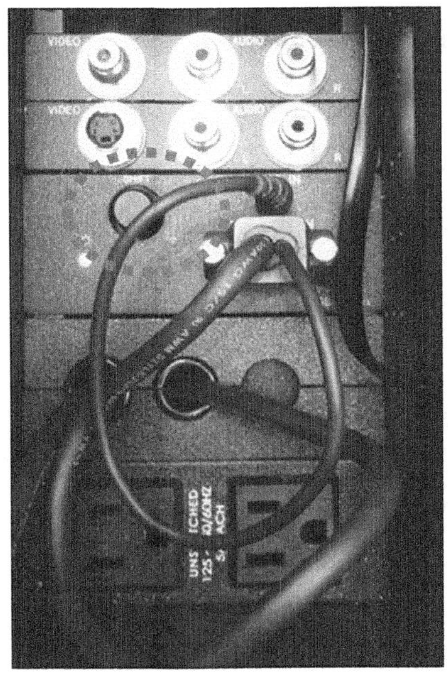

Figure 40. ***Dial that adjusts horizontal image position.***

6.13 Daily Testing

Once setup, the courtroom is still never really complete. Every day, when you first arrive at the courtroom, you should perform a basic QC check of your cables and equipment to ensure proper operation. This QC check should be a top priority because you certainly don't want to find out the main video cable is broken after the jury is seated in the morning—so test daily. The Daily Courtroom Checklist below shows the steps you should take each day to QC test both your own and shared equipment.

Daily Courtroom Checklist

1. CHECK COURTROOM
- ☐ Check gaffing tape/cables.
- ☐ Is there any damage? Missing tape, cables pulled up and moved, cables pinched under chairs or around furniture?
  - ☐ Replace and/or retape any problem areas.
- ☐ Check equipment.
  - ☐ Is equipment present and placed in the correct location?
- ☐ Check in with the clerk.
  - ☐ Is the clerk OK with setup?
  - ☐ Does the clerk want any changes?

2. SET UP LAPTOP
- ☐ Plug in everything *before* starting (mouse, sound, video, printer, power)

3. START AND CONFIGURE LAPTOP
- ☐ After computer is *fully* booted up.
- ☐ Place computer in extended desktop or mirror mode viewing.
- ☐ Are all drive letters accounted for and assigned the correct drive letter?

4. START TRIAL PRESENTATION AND OTHER SOFTWARE
- ☐ After computer is *fully* booted up.
- ☐ Start trail software.
  - ☐ Verify all images present using built in QC tool for trial presentation software.

5. START ANY ADDITIONAL PROGRAM INDIVIDUALLY AND WAIT UNTIL IT IS FULLY OPEN AND READY BEFORE OPENING THE NEXT PROGRAM.
- ☐ Do not start multiple programs at the same time.
- ☐ Is the software being started necessary for today's presentation?
- ☐ Open PowerPoint.
  - ☐ Check that PowerPoint is on the correct screen (displaying on the extended screen in presentation mode).

6. TEST SWITCH
- ☐ Cycle through each connected video source twice to ensure they appear.
- ☐ Looking for smooth transition free of setup and delay each time you switch.

7. TEST VIDEO
- ☐ Check that video is on *all* screens.
  - ☐ If projector, is it in focus and the image accurate on the screen.
  - ☐ Keystone?
- ☐ Use screen test image for correct aspect ratio and ensure video is accurately placed on monitor(s).
  - ☐ Check *all four corners* of the display for accuracy.
  - ☐ Consistent configuration for 4:3 or 16:9 on all monitors?
- ☐ Check document camera.
  - ☐ Place object on document camera to test.
- ☐ Play quick test video clip.

8. TEST SOUND
- ☐ Play test sound.

9. NOTIFY LEGAL TEAM YOU ARE READY!

10. AT THE END OF THE DAY
- ☐ Check cables.
- ☐ Check with clerk and legal team to ensure everything is OK — be humble and helpful.
- ☐ Keep the courtroom clean.
- ☐ Get ready for tomorrow!

Figure 41. ***The Daily Courtroom Checklist (available as a free download; see the Notes on Use for access).***

6.14 Uncooperative Parties

In Chapter Three, Exhibits, I discussed burden shifting in regards to parties trying to shift their responsibility for creating exhibits onto the other party. Courtroom setup is no different. Parties should strive for technical cooperation and mutual assistance, but be aware that *somewhere* there is a *line in the sand* where the other party is simply not doing its part. Often, an unprepared or unscrupulous party will try to burden shift by not delivering according to the technical agreements made, or they have a strange interpretation of the technical specifications, or they try to back out of their part of equipment rental agreement. Then the panic starts to set in with opposing counsel when they realize they came to the fight unprepared and did not take their technical obligations seriously. (This happens *a lot*). Teams that did not plan appropriately or take their technical obligations seriously *should not be supported by their opponent*—namely, *you*.

When burden shifting occurs, it's the documentation that will save your bacon. If you have a plan that has been circulated and agreed upon in an email or is embodied in the TMO, you have a rock-solid footing if the other party decides to unfairly cry foul. Just like the TMO, setup decisions should be memorialized in a summary email or other documentation that is cc'd to all attorneys.

Regardless of the issue, trial techs are *not free* to argue on their own or make claims unless done under the direction of the legal team. Legal teams *should take a stand* against abuse early on to knock out monkey business from the beginning and place the burden back on the proper party. Teams that don't take a stand reduce their support by half—because their own tech will be supporting two teams. Teams that take a stand will push the burden back onto a team that is likely unprepared (and will cause even more panic as it tries to keep up). By *not* taking on the other team's burden, you, as trial tech, will be able to focus on supporting your own team.

Taking a stand usually involves creating a list of the technical violations of the agreement or TMO. The violations should be substantial and cause significant work to remedy so that if it reaches the judge, it will be readily understood as a violation. The violations are especially egregious if the files were given late at night for the next day's court, leaving no time to prepare.

Substantial violations include situations where a vendor needs to be involved to get the exhibits in compliance or there is substantial work on behalf of the trial tech that takes them away from their own duties. You can only enforce compliance if you've agreed upon the format for exchange. Otherwise, you open yourself up to the Wild West. These issues, of course, get more serious as data volumes get larger:

- **Delivering exhibits in a technical format contrary to the agreement**. *Example*: files are delivered in their native format without processing or naming. The burden on the receiving party is having to analyze the fileWs and going through the expense and time of processing the files to bring the exhibits into compliance.
- **Incorrect naming or branding of exhibits**. Providing a spreadsheet that correlates file names to exhibit numbers is not sufficient for most TMOs. By not naming or branding documents, courtroom efficiency and cognition will be significantly reduced and calling up an exhibit will be a confusing process. This issue will require considerable vendor or tech intervention to bring the files into compliance.
- **Not providing video clipped or in a format that is readily usable**. The burden is shifted to the receiving party to clip video simply so it can be analyzed in advance and then placed into standard tools for viewing.
- **During video deposition, playing playback exhibits *over* the deponent's reactions so the decision -makers don't see the look of surprise, shock, or horror when a question is asked, and they instead see a document**. When dealing with this unscrupulous technique or less-than-honest parties, ask for a video capture of the entire playback instead of merely a script (called a run sheet).[16]

Parties should use a third-party vendor for equipment rental and setup rather than one side using their own equipment and charging the other side for it. A third-party vendor can issue separate invoices, as each party will be separately responsible for their portion of the fee. Disagreements and complaints over responsiveness, sabotage,

16. Also, if you see multiple cameras in a video deposition, ask if the videographer is keeping the entire feed of each camera or making editing decisions as they go. You'll want a single uninterrupted face shot of your depositions.

and shoddy equipment are decreased when each party has their own relationship with a vendor. For example, if the projector fails, it is better for a vendor to be the responsible party (who will quickly replace the equipment) than one of the trial techs. Alternatively, if the opposing team's trial tech provides the equipment, what will they do if they are split between servicing their own client and you as a rental client—we know who will lose that battle. Lastly, if an opposing party tries to back out of equipment rental, their argument will be with the vendor, and not with you as a go-between—that alone is worth every penny.

Chapter Seven

Trial Software

"Put it before them briefly so they will read it, clearly so they will appreciate it, picturesquely so they will remember it, and, above all, accurately so they will be guided by its light."

—*Joseph Pulitzer*

In Part Two of this book, which is hands-on instruction, I show the basics of how to start a new case, import and QC exhibits, and perform a basic presentation using callouts and highlights in TrialDirector, Sanction, and OnCue. These basic presentation skills, along with having basic technical know-how (and the right case), provide a solid starting point in knowing how to present electronic evidence in court.

You must perform your own due diligence to find out what software is best for your needs. Each trial presentation software package offers the same basic features, such as yellow highlighting, callouts, and basic annotation tools. They all have free trials where you can test-drive the software. The checklist below and the forms Chapter Ten, Forms and Checklists, will help you determine your best software fit.

7.1 Presentation Basics

When you present exhibits, keep it simple. Put the exhibit up on screen and move to callout and highlight the sections the legal team has directed you to show. All trial presentation tools offer features that allow you to place exhibits and video (annotated, clipped or not) in a folder so they can be clicked through, PowerPoint style. Foldering and advance prep is especially important when dealing with time issues; otherwise, you can afford to consider the appropriate balance and risks between advance prep and presenting on the fly.

As you present, remember that consistency is your friend. Train yourself to call out text on exhibits in a consistent way from exhibit to exhibit, so it becomes a habit. For example, on an email exhibit, start with the header, then, in a separate callout, move to the body of the email. Always allow a quarter- to a half-inch of space from the top corner of where you start your callouts. Use color consistently. I've seen enough yellow highlights on white paper to know that after a while they all blend together, so consider using a variety of colors for highlighting and annotating as you increase your skills.

Recognize that jurors may think the tech is the most interesting thing in the room. Therefore, trial techs should dress like a lawyer and hold themselves to very high standards of conduct. Trying to figure out what your duty is to the court versus your client can be a balancing act. In times like these, I defer to simply doing the right thing—whatever that might be. Thankfully, most of the time the trial tech is simply in a back corner somewhere, putting up exhibits and making sure everything is running OK. It is stressful, exciting, and immensely satisfying job.

7.2 Develop a Consistent Style in Calling Up Exhibits

Once you understand the lingo of how to call out and annotate an exhibit, develop a consistent stylized approach to develop consistency with decision-makers. There are many creative approaches to calling up an exhibit, so you'll have to find what works for you from case to case. Below is an example of an approach I use to show exhibits.

(1) Show the first page in its entirety to explain what it is: "Trial exhibit 5 is an email . . . ."

(2) Enlarge the header of the email so that the top half of the document is visible as it is being explained.

(3) Call out the sender, recipient, date, and subject line: ". . . sent from Shannon to Bob, with a CC to Vikka, Viviana, and Viata on July 17, 2017 at 4:30 p.m., the subject is . . . ."

(4) Call out the sentence to be read: "Please call out and highlight in the second paragraph from the top, the second sentence beginning with the words 'really important . . . .'"

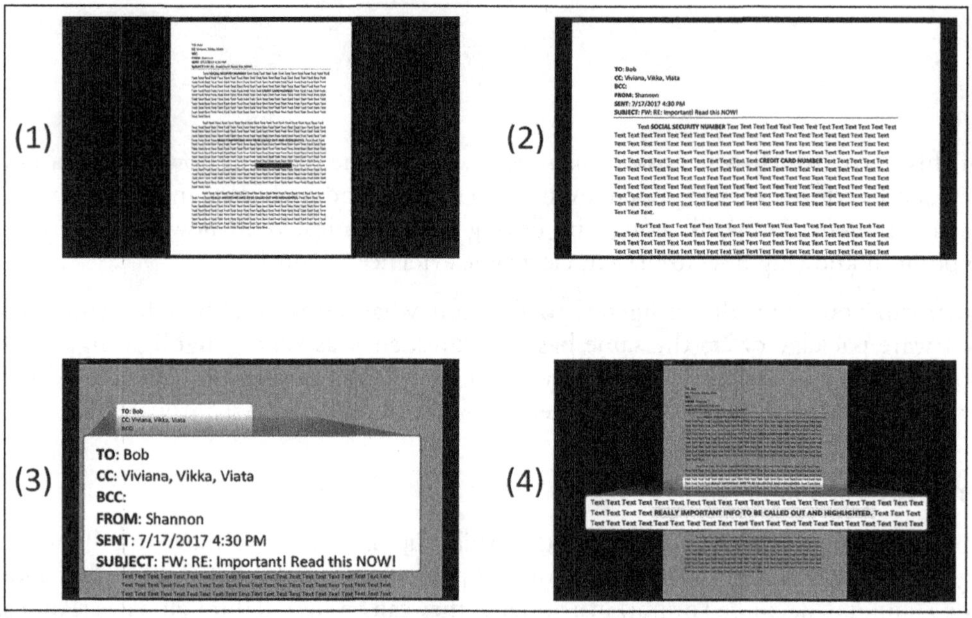

Figure 1. ***Exhibits (1) through (4) that correspond with the appropriate language for "calling up," as shown in the numbered list appearing before the graphic.***

Below are more examples of how to describe exhibits when they are being called out. Keep in mind this should be practiced, rehearsed, and refined until perfect.

- "Exhibit 101 is the employee manual from XYZ Industries [*show first page of manual and enlarge title*]. Let's turn to page 35 of exhibit 101 and go to the paragraph with the Harassment Policy heading . . . ."
- "Exhibit 201 is page one of the memo dated 1/1/2010 from Larry to Justin [*show header, to and from, date, subject*]. Let's go to the section on page 10 about XYZ . . . ."
- "Exhibit 301, page 3, is an email from Smith to Jones sent on 1/1/2010 at 11 a.m. [*Note: the trial tech first shows the to/from/date/time of the originating email on the last page because it is the first in a chain of emails.*] The email on the last page is the first in time, so let's go the third page of the email to show where it started. Now let's turn to the first page where the relevant email section is that we want to discuss . . . that was forwarded to Nguyen on 1/5/2010 at 3 p.m."

In some cases, I might omit a step from the illustrated example to save time. Keep in mind our discussion on document authenticity in section 3.2, where we show as much of the document as we can to be open and up front about our exhibits.

7.3 Be Different

In trial technology, we encounter a nearly complete lack of differentiation in presentation. The exhibits placed on screen are uniformly presented in the same manner, using the same techniques, and the same yellow highlighting and provide little chance for the judge and jury to visually differentiate between the plaintiff and the defendant.

At risk is creating confusion in your decision-makers. If the judge and jury view many documents that are visually similar to previous, subsequent, and opposing counsel's exhibits, it's difficult for them to distinguish one from the other. Exhibits that are a wall of yellow highlights carry no weight or impact. Legal teams that don't create interesting visuals of their exhibits miss a valuable opportunity to show some creativity, visually impress the decision-makers, keep the proceedings interesting, and provide unique visual ques that decision-makers can remember and use as a common reference point. You often hear, "If you highlight everything, you highlight nothing." A good example of this concept is in Figure 2, below, and it's quite typical of what you see in most trial presentations. The lawyer starts by showing the To and From, then the Date and Subject, then reads the body of the message. Line this document up with all of the other exhibits being presented in the exact same way by both parties and you really have something that is not memorable at all—just a continuous wall of yellow-highlighted documents.

From: Bales, Shannon
To: Bales, Shannon
Subject: Same, Same but Different!
Date: Thursday, July 06, 2017 12:14:34 PM

Yellow highlights are boring and don't provide differentiation between parties or provide visual ques for decision makers to remember the point you are trying make.

Shannon Lex Bales
Managing Director, FLC – TS Technology

FTI Consulting
714.478.7426 M
Shannon.Bales@fticonsulting.com

633 West 5th Street | Suite 1600
Los Angeles, CA 90071-2027
www.fticonsulting.com

Figure 2. ***All-yellow highlighting makes for an utterly forgettable exhibit.***

There are many great trial presentation software tools available, but there is a lack of variety in the tools and presentation options they make available. Nearly all of the software tools have highlighters, a circle, square, and arrows, and even with these limited annotation options, one still can create a unique, memorable display of each exhibit. Using just about anything but a wall of yellow highlighting already sets your exhibits apart.

More often than not, though, it's the *legal team* that decides to not venture beyond the yellow wall. This is often due to the lawyer's lack of comfort with the technology and uneasiness with handing over some potentially on-the-fly decisions about document annotation to a trial tech. This keeps many teams from releasing the complete creative range of visual options at trial. If you are working with a trial tech don't be afraid to let them be a bit creative in working with exhibits. Lawyers with some level of discomfort with the technology or releasing a trial tech's creative side could practice the night before and even pre-annotate documents so they know exactly what they are getting.

Contrast the previously shown yellow wall of highlighting with the sample below. To be sure, I'm not saying you should use all the colors of the rainbow, but there are options to make your exhibit presentation more memorable. The use of color and colored shapes in the below example gives lawyers with a way to focus the decision-maker's attention where they want it. "The text in the blue box," "the recipient is in the green highlight," and "the sender is circled in purple at the bottom of the page," for example, all help the lawyer focus a judge's and jury's attention where they want it to be.

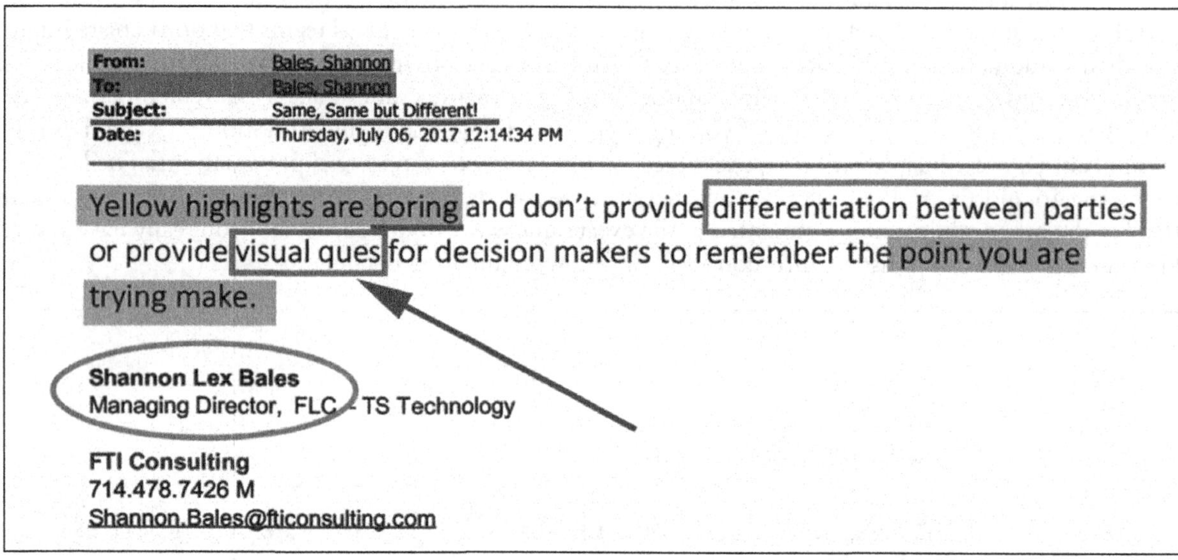

Figure 3. ***Different colors and shapes make your exhibit more memorable to decision-makers.***

Legal teams should also consider how they can vary their presentation from time to time to keep viewers interested. Stacking endless slides or electronic exhibits in a row is boring. Perhaps switching to a display board, using document camera, or presenting through another method could be incorporated into your strategy, just to break up the monotony and keep the presentation engaging. A document camera, for example, can result in a significant impact when hand movements and gestures, colored markers, and scribbles and underlines are used to draw attention to parts of the exhibit.

Be different. Use a variety of colors and annotations to help keep your viewers interested and to provide a reference point for their focus and recall. Familiarize yourself with the visual capabilities of your trial presentation software to add impact to every exhibit viewed in the courtroom. Get over your discomfort in working with trial presentation tools by pretreating the annotations (in advance) or practicing the night before.

7.4 Recognize When You Need Help

Recognizing you are in over your head is a good thing. If you truly are in over your head, consider using a vendor to provide support or creating a less ambitious technology plan. Trial presentation encompasses many skills, so knowing how the various pieces fit together is mostly gained through experience and it is hard to find the right entry-level case to start with. The trial of the century is not the best place to begin, but the arbitration of the week or the hearing of the day is. Don't worry; everyone gets their start somewhere and mistakes do happen. It's *how* you deal with the errors that is important, as well as showing that you took reasonable steps to avoid the error. However, if errors become a pattern, then it's probably time to consider, once again, whether you are in over your head.

Often, it can be difficult to manage your time and find the right balance of images and video that should be pre-annotated and saved as either a stage or static image. Saving a stage or layer (same thing, different word) in the same place where you save annotations for an exhibit for later recall creates a much higher quality image and allows for the annotations to be changed, deleted, or created on the fly. But this comes at a cost during moments when the trial tech's time is at a premium. Remember our time rule of thumb for preparation: pre-annotating and staging everything in advance is often a poor use of your time because you can easily annotate documents in court. Perhaps you'll annotate and save some documents in advance and do others on the fly. Striking the right balance here can be difficult.[1]

It's also important to know your priorities for exhibit preparation. Getting documents to comply with the TMO and exhibit exchange agreement is your first priority; this means proper technical format for exchange and fulfilling branding and naming requirements so it can be added to the trial exhibit database and exchanged with counsel in a timely manner. Once the exhibits are branded, your next step is to comply with redaction requirements and get them out the door to opposing counsel. You simply cannot display information that should be redacted, so the entire team needs to be aware of this reality, which then gives the support team a heads up on documents that may require redaction.[2] Finally, when you realize that tasks may take an unusually long time to complete, it's wise to circle back to the legal team for input on their priorities and expectations. (They may have thought, for instance, that video clipping would only take an hour, rather than a day.)

There will likely be files handed over last minute or emailed while you are in court that won't have time to be put through your workflow to turn them into TMO-compliant exhibits. I give those exhibits a quick read and ask the legal team if there are any redaction issues with the document.[3] I copy those exhibits to my dated, exhibit addendum folder, then add them to my trial software. (I'm probably only concerned about the file format if it is something that my trial software can't display.) Sometimes an exhibit may not comply with your naming convention—for example, it might be named "Export report of John Smith in the Case of Texas vs. Oklahoma." If it is awkwardly named, I might give it a short, temporary name like "20180110A," add it to a folder in my trial software with the day's date and other descriptive information so I can easily find it (something like "20180110 expert," for example). Then, at the end of the day, when I catch up back at the office, I'll put it through a previously created work flow (if, that is, it hasn't been emailed or taken care of while I was in court).

This is where understanding and having an effective naming convention for redacted records, version control system for exhibits, and outlines for the legal team come into play. It's everyone's job to check and recheck that documents needing redaction have been redacted and they've been correctly cited in the attorney outline. If you are a paralegal or attorney reading this book, please do your own due diligence as well, to ensure the record you intend to call complies with court orders in force. Redactions are often a team effort, so enlist the entire team to handle particularly large redaction jobs. Finally, a practice run of the lawyer outline done with the trial tech is an opportunity to practice and improve presentation and perform a valuable QC.

Remember, your trial presentation software is a great tool that can help you prepare presentations in PowerPoint or place an image in Microsoft Word or other software. As you annotate documents, you can typically save them as static images to be used in other software to prepare files. The highlighting, callout, and annotation features in trial presentation software are relatively easy to use and offer "one-stop shopping" for image annotation. For example, you can use the more robust annotation features of trial presentation software to create an annotated image, save it, and then use it in PowerPoint.

1. Personally, about 10 percent or fewer of the exhibits I use at trial are annotated in advance.
2. It's important that you know how to take down documents as quickly as possible. Practice with your software (Escape or Exit) and hardware (Switch) techniques to remove documents from the screen.
3. The burden should be on the legal team as to whether the exhibit is OK to display.

Figure 4. ***Trial techs should focus on trial technology. (Image by Rachel Bennett.)***

As a trial tech, you are in a key position to realize when you need additional support. Perhaps you realize you need help with redactions, QC'ing video, verifying exhibit numbers, assisting with outlines, or, in huge cases, one or more additional trial techs to get the job done and provide a fresh set of eyes in the courtroom. Be careful you don't allow yourself to become overburdened with unnecessary tasks; ask for assistance when you need it.

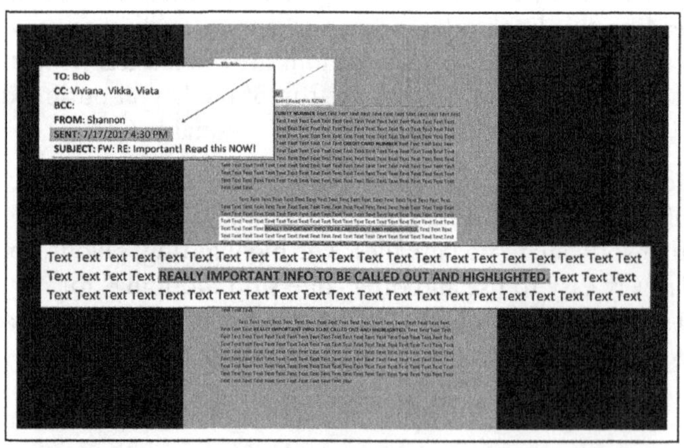

Figure 5. ***Great tip: use the annotation tools in trial presentation software, then transfer the annotated file to PowerPoint.***

Throughout this book, I've discussed the companion skills and knowledge necessary to present exhibits electronically. It is companion skills—ranging from having the budget to obtain the right equipment, to having the technical skills to be able to connect your laptop to a court presentation system— that often come up short in trial presentation. The presentation part is relatively easy, but only if you have the companion skills you need. Many of the companion skills discussed can be done with the trial presentation software, but that comes at the expense of being able to use and share the files in a team environment. For example, a document that was redacted in trial software using stages won't be available for team members to use in applications they use on a daily basis like a redacted PDF will. Here, the redacted PDF is more easily shared via email, printed for binders, and can be changed by anyone on the team, thereby reducing the workload on the trial tech.

7.5 Five Basic Skills

There are five basic functions you must be able to perform in your trial presentation program before you should attempt to them in court.

1) **Configure your laptop for the courtroom**
   a) Connect to a video source (HDMI/VGA).
   b) Connect sound input or add speakers.
   c) Choose between mirror mode and extended desktop.
   d) Change the background to black.
2) **Understand the basics of aspect ratio and resolution**
   a) Choose between 4:3 and 16:9 aspect ratios.
   b) Predict how a high-resolution presentation will look in a lower resolution environment and plan accordingly.
3) **Load and QC your exhibits**
   a) Drag and drop files into exhibit folders of the trial software. This is a good method for cases where you are using PDF files.
   b) Use a log file. When you use single page image files, you should load them via a log file where the path has been modified for the location of files on your laptop. *This is a more advanced method and you should only use it once you have reached the appropriate skill level.*
4) **Annotate exhibits with callouts, highlights, redactions, and enlargements**
5) **Present exhibits**

   The slicker method of presenting exhibits is by using the extended desktop mode in your trial presentation software. This is when you have a working screen where you input exhibit numbers and a presentation screen where you show exhibits. If you are uncomfortable with extended desktop, you can simply duplicate displays by using mirror mode.

7.6 What You Need to Know About Trial Software

Most presentation tools operate in a similar way for loading data where you either drag and drop exhibits or use a log file to load exhibit images. The software either creates a shortcut from the program to the image or goes through a conversion process for exhibits that are imported into the software. Each method has their positives and negatives.

Programs that ingest images and undergo a conversion process take longer to prepare and can have conversion issues. Files are often handed over in court and need to be ready right away; smaller files shouldn't present an issue, but larges ones could. On the other hand, software that links to images is susceptible to corrupt images or a broken links. The broken link occurs when exhibit files are moved or renamed, or the folder names were changed without updating in the presentation system. For example, if you rename the "Exhibit" folder to "Trial_Exhibits," this action breaks the link to all the files and subfolders in the directory.

Files can become corrupt simply by copying and moving them, and sometimes they are corrupt from the start. When you are dealing with thousands of pages of files to be used as exhibits, it may be impractical to check each one—although time willing, you might want to. File corruption often occurs when people literally pull the plug and disconnect equipment before a copy job is complete. Some applications have built-in tools to ensure that all your files are present and accounted for; you should run these tools every day, just to be safe. Absent such tools, it's important for you to check images and ensure they are where you expect them to be by sampling files and clicking around your folders. Be vigilant, QC often, and repeat. Again, have a backup and a backup for your backup.

CHAPTER EIGHT

VIDEO

"You can impeach the smell of pasta."

—*overheard at trial*

Video is often one of the most difficult and time-consuming pieces of trial preparation. Teams vastly underestimate the amount of time it takes to prepare video and often flippantly (yes, flippantly) *over*-issue code and designate video for use in trial. For every case, somewhere there is a balance between what is pre-clipped and what is done on the fly.

Below is a rule-of-thumb guide for how much time you should allot to complete tasks. While there are always shortcuts, it may not necessarily be a good idea to take them. With video exhibits, it's important to ask a team member to view the clips to ensure they are what the team intended.

Time Rule of Thumb Guide for Trial Tech Tasks (Includes Time Spent for QC and Revision)	
Task	**Time**
Video Edit with objections and colloquy removed	3-4 times clip length
Video Edit without review of internal content	10 minutes per cut
Powerpoint slide with image and callout	20 minutes per slide
Load, Copy, Export Data	volume dependent
Reunitize individual records	5-10 minutes per record
Stage callouts for an exhibit	5 - 10 minutes per stage

Figure 1. ***Yep, here it is again: my rule of thumb for task time allotment.***

The advantage of clipping in advance is that you have QC'd the clip in advance and you know exactly what will be played on screen. When playing video on the fly, you never know if, for example, a bathroom break will occur between the start and the end of a clip, or whether there is something that shouldn't be included, such as objections, technical errors, or a long period of silence that is not the result of a question. Some long periods of silence that are not the result of a question can go on for minutes, but they are not reflected in the page/line numbering of the transcript.

This is why it's important that the legal team QC's the videos they intend to show in court and, likewise, have a good understanding of video that might be played on the fly. If a video contains many long pauses in the deposition (for whatever reason), it may be a good candidate for pre-clipping. Alternatively, if the team receives a case at the last moment and the trial tech is being pulled in every direction, it might be better (to hire a second tech?) to limit video clipping so that team needs can be met.

There are a few ways to be more effective with video clipping. First, if you are recording the deposition, pay the extra fees for digitization and synchronization of the video at the time of creation, not on the eve of trial. This is a process through which video is matched to the text of the transcript so that it can be played in sync when you use compatible transcript software.

Second, as early in the case as possible, link video to software like TextMap and Case Notebook (formerly LiveNote). Depositions can be viewed at the time of issue coding so that those evaluating video testimony can determine if a deponent's actions, words, silence, or demeanor are what they thought they were on paper. It's also an early opportunity to QC the video sync because syncs can be inaccurate. Video and the text of the transcript can often portray two different pictures. For example:

Question: Did you rob the bank in Tustin, California?

Answer: No.

Now imagine on video:

Question: Did you rob the bank in Tustin, California?

[*Long pause . . . nervous demeanor, subject looks away from the camera . . . more silence.*]

Answer: No.

Video can be very effective—but it doesn't come easy.

Third, it's a good idea to jot a quick note of sections of the video that might be problematic or have long periods of silence. This gives a heads-up to the trial tech as to what to look for and possibly remove.

8.1 A Few Things to Watch For

A rookie mistake often made with video is that lawyers will view the video and use the time stamps that appear on the face of the video. Instead, they must use the time stamp of the media player, which shows at the bottom of the video, as shown below. Correlating a time stamp from the face of the video that is off is a burdensome and difficult task for a trial tech.

Figure 2. ***Use the time stamp on the video player, not the time stamp on the face of the video.***

I've noticed a deposition technique that lawyers should watch out for. In depositions, a videographer will set up multiple cameras within the room. One of the cameras catches over-the-shoulder document video footage. The footage is edited to show the deponent's face, then cut to the over-the-shoulder shot of the document, thus rendering a recording that misses the deponent's key reactions to questions and documents. Be aware of this technique. Sometimes this editing occurs at the site of the deposition, with the result that there is no master tape of "just" the face shot. When you see multiple cameras at a deposition, request that each feed is fully captured.

QC your video by playing it all the way through to ensure it rendered correctly. This action is part of why my time estimate for producing a video clip is three to four times the clip length: the video must be viewed, edited, adjusted, and viewed again. Clipping videos in bulk can take a lot of time.

8.2 Editing Tips

As you begin editing a video in your trial presentation software, always insert a couple of seconds of silence before the video starts so that it doesn't awkwardly begin as soon as your legal team cues you to play it in the courtroom. Also, be sure to review the "run report" or "run sheet" that is generated by your trial presentation software. This report includes the text and run times for each clip, as well as the total running time. When you review the run report, look for unusually long running times in the segments. It's important to review how long the video is to make sure you didn't capture twenty minutes of silence in the middle and that it renders correctly after it's been exported. Share the video times with the legal team so it can make adjustments, if necessary.

Many teams also synchronize exhibits to the video onscreen along with annotations. It's important to make sure all of the exhibits have been admitted and that opposing parties have discussed whether they need to *disclose the existence of synced exhibits*. There can be some *gamesmanship* here were exhibits are used to mask deponent reactions, aren't disclosed or are displayed in a less than ethical manner (too long, too short, etc.). If you feel that you are working with a party who may play these games then instead of a "run sheet" ask for a video screen capture of the entire video with sync'd exhibits. This way you'll know exactly what will be played onscreen in court and hold their feet to the fire to not play any games.

For practical reasons, one party often designates a single edited video for both parties. It's important that you review the video, along with any synchronized exhibits rather than a run sheet. While the run sheet is very useful it is not the same as seeing the complete video. Note, there is a lot more work involved in exporting a complete video with sync'd exhibits – so only use this option if you believe the other party isn't completely trustworthy.

MR. Bond: Would you hand the witness ...

SK-01803 3 SEGMENTS (RUNNING 00:00:59.100)

1. PAGE 18:03 TO 18:04 (RUNNING 00:00:02.667)

MR. Bond: Would you hand the witness
Exhibit 417, please.

2. PAGE 18:13 TO 18:21 (RUNNING 00:00:21.400)

Q. BY MR. Bond: 417 is the document
that's been produced to us by Greerborne as the Greerborne
phone log with respect to the Cave-Corp transaction.
Reviewing that document, does it refresh
your recollection as to whether you had seen it prior to
filing the First Amended Complaint in this case?
A. I don't really know. I mean, I might
have seen it, and if so, exactly when, I'm just not
sure.

3. PAGE 20:07 TO 20:21 (RUNNING 00:00:35.033)

Q. And looking at Exhibit 417 doesn't
refresh your recollection as to whether you had seen the
phone log prior to the time that you filed the First
Amended Complaint; is that correct?
A. Well, it's a pretty big document. So,
it's not like I've looked at it. I've glanced at the
first page or two and kind of skimmed through it here.
Doesn't really refresh my recollection.
You know, like I say, if it was in that batch of
documents that came over, then we would have looked at
it. We were told we got op. man.'s entire file.
Whether that's accurate, I don't know. But we were told
we had the entire file of op. man., which was the unit
that was running the loan at that point. So, we went
through what we thought was their entire file.

Figure 3. ***A run sheet with three clips. Note the run time of each clip (Clip 1, 2.667 seconds; Clip 2, 21.400 seconds; Clip 3, 35.033 seconds) and the total running time of 59.100 seconds. Look for unusually long clip run times to QC. For example, if one of the clips was five minutes long but the transcript contains only two lines of text, you might have a problem.***

Chapter Nine

Trial Communication

"I think it's very important to have a feedback loop, where you're constantly thinking about what you've done and how you could be doing better. I think that's the single best piece of advice: constantly think about how you could be doing things better and question yourself."

—*Elon Musk*

There is a wide range of styles used in calling up exhibits in the courtroom. Some presenters, for example, use a laser pointer to show what should be called out in an exhibit. Not all presentation styles are good at building an accurate record or aid in juror comprehension. By not walking decision-makers (i.e., judge and jurors) through exhibits in a clear and concise manner, attorneys are hurting their own case via a lack of understanding. Moreover, the court record can be wrong if lawyers use old production/Bates/page numbers[1] or use generic references without context like "the memo" without connecting it to an exhibit number or issue.[2] Last, if you are working with a trial tech, you must discuss and practice your communication style so that exhibits and annotation requests are quick and accurate. Below are a few suggestions on how to communicate about exhibits.

There are three companion skills that relate to trial technology use in the courtroom:

1) Use exhibit and page numbers to call up exhibits
2) Use "stage direction" in exhibit narration (i.e., navigation through the document)
3) Create witness exam outlines that use "stage direction" and leverage the use of different forms of electronic media, like exhibit images and video, by having all the relevant information at your fingertips

9.1 Use Exhibit Numbers to Communicate

Using exhibit and page numbers to communicate to decision-makers and within the legal team is a medium that is clear, concise, and effective. Everyone instantly understands if you've followed my suggestions in this book for keeping naming conventions simple. There is zero confusion if someone is asked to create a witness binder and is provided with a list like what appears below (and if you have a database, you can easily search for exhibits by number, or they can be sorted and plucked out of a network location—remember version control?):

TX0001

TX0007

1. Often, by the time documents make it to trial, they might have multiple numbers that have been branded on them at one time or another. Decluttering and being consistent is key—perhaps put the exhibit in the center or on the left if the right side has existing branding.
2. "The memo" or other nickname might seem like a good way of describing a particularly important exhibit. But often attorneys just don't know what the exhibit number is, so *every* document gets a nickname—and that is terrible.

TX0123

TX1123

On the other hand, requesting an exhibit binder with a list like the one below is less than clear. When communication is not specific, there is time wasted in database searching, back-and-forth communication, and additional QC necessary to gather the documents.

The email from Blake to Adam sent around 7/7/2017

The memo that we showed on Tuesday

The contract signed by Shane in December

While exhibit, production, and Bates numbers are common concepts and vernacular in the legal community, they are less so with the average citizen. In opening statement or very early in the trial, the lead attorney should explain to decision-makers (i.e., judge and jurors) how your exhibit-naming convention works so they can follow along and take notes. Don't assume that they know what a Bates number, exhibit number, or other file-naming scheme is. For instance, in the sample below, you should explain that the exhibit is branded in the lower right corner of the document and starts with a "TX." Later, if the other side hasn't branded their exhibits in violation of the TMO, you can make a point of clarification on their exhibit numbering for *each document*. If appropriate, you can ask decision-makers to write down exhibit numbers that support your case or even create a slide that lists them in closing—ask them to take out their notepad and *write the exhibit numbers down*.

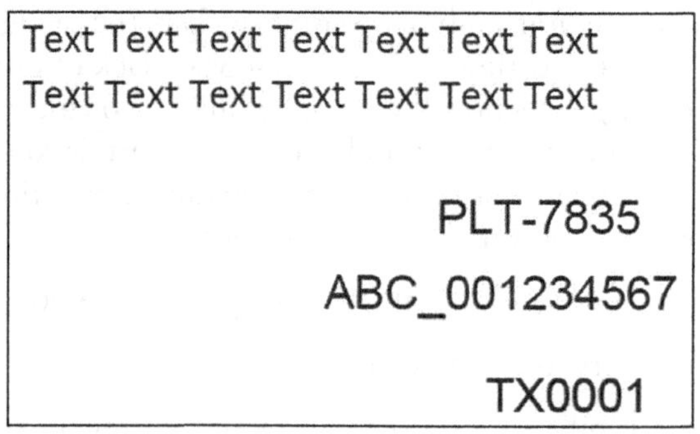

Figure 1. ***Explain what an exhibit number is and how documents are branded for this case.***

9.2 The Language of Trial Presentation: Annotation, Callout, and Highlight

Document annotations help explain an exhibit. Annotations, such as enlargements, highlights, and callouts, aid in viewer comprehension and emphasis the point you want to make. Interesting annotations that keep viewer interest by the use of color highlighting, underlining, circles, arrows, and boxes can help counsel appear slicker than they actually are. There is no standardization in the language of trial presentation, but understanding some of the lingo will go a long way to ensuring you are either requesting or doing the right action. Each application has its own way of referring to document annotations. It is important to note that multiple annotations are often applied to a document, so a paragraph might have a callout, with a sentence highlighted and keywords underlined or circled.

It is an uncomfortable experience watching attorneys who haven't practiced with their trial tech or don't know how to describe what they want to appear on screen. Sometimes they don't even know their tech's name. (So much for seeming like a regular person!)

Attorney: Errrr . . . can you show . . . exhibit 12?

Tech: I don't believe that's been admitted into evidence.

Attorney: Put it up!

Tech: OK. [*calls up exhibit onscreen*]

Judge: Take that down.

Many attorneys say they don't need to practice; you can imagine how it turns out with an attitude like that. One of my best (or worst) examples was when an attorney that said they didn't need to practice, then had referenced old production numbers rather than exhibit numbers, and only knew the docs by nickname:

Attorney: Can you put up the memo?

Tech: Ummmm, which memo? [*never a good sign*]

Attorney: Oh, its exhibit XYZ1234.

Tech: I believe that is a production ID. Do you have an exhibit number? It begins with TX?

Attorney: No.

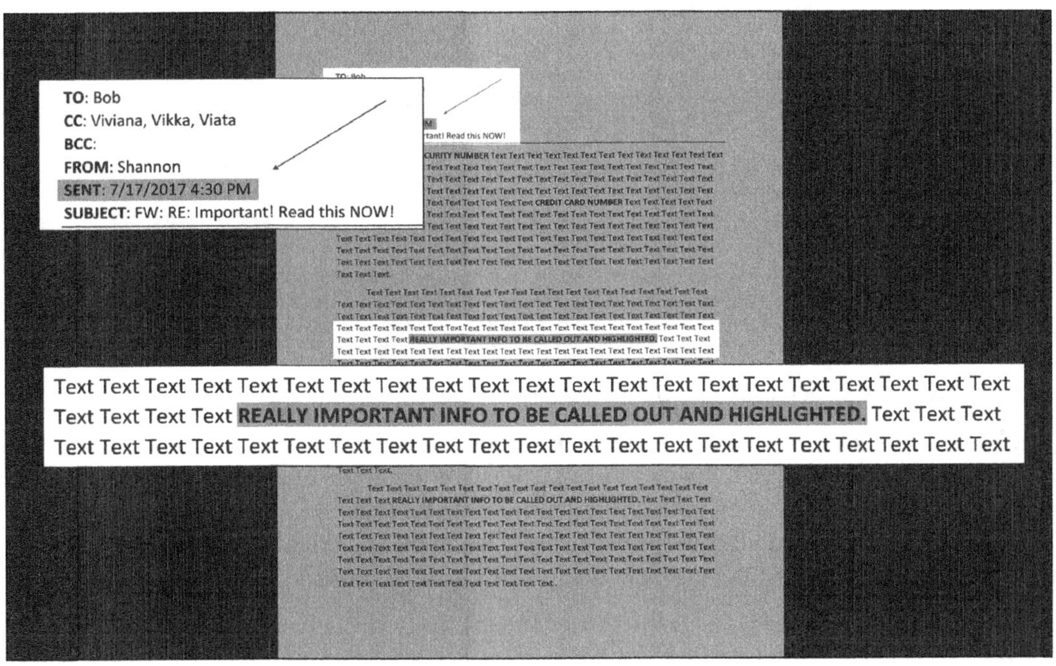

Figure 2. ***Exhibit with many annotations. Two callouts, highlights, and arrow.***

9.3 Terminology to Know

Below is some terminology for the entire trial team to understand and use. (*Note*: these terms are listed in a sequence of increasing familiarity rather than in alphabetical order, as some definitions build on the definition before them.)

Annotation. In trial presentation, an annotation is using highlighting, magnification, and other visual tools to aid a viewer's comprehension and understanding of a document.

Example: The arrow, highlight, and enlarged sections of document are annotations.

Call up. The process of presenting an exhibit on screen.

Example: "**Call up** Exhibit 123 and put it onscreen for all to see."

Callout. An enlargement of a section of text in a document that is displayed above the document. By keeping the document in the background, it aids in navigation and understanding of the document.

Example: "**Callout** the first paragraph of Exhibit 123."

Example: The two enlargements of the email header and body text are callouts (also **zoom**, **projection zoom**, and **tear out**).

Enlargement/enlarge/zoom in. Magnifying a specific section of a document to fill the screen.

Example: "**Zoom in** to the map of the City of Norman," or "Show the top half of the email." (You sometimes may need to interpret the true meaning of a command.)

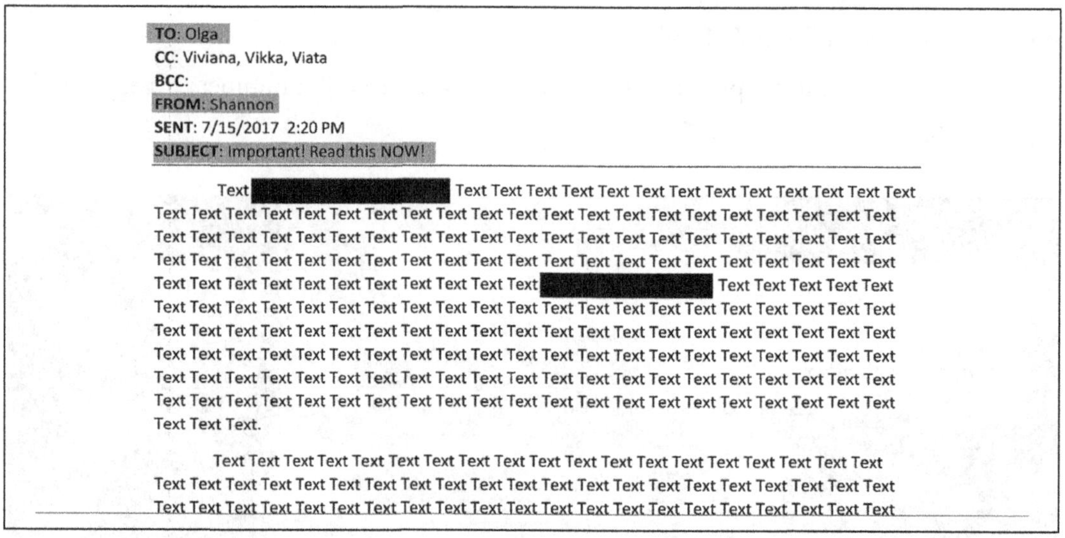
TO: Olga
CC: Viviana, Vikka, Viata
BCC:
FROM: Shannon
SENT: 7/15/2017 2:20 PM
SUBJECT: Important! Read this NOW!

Text ██████ Text Text Text Text Text Text Text Text Text Text Text Text Text Text Text Text Text Text Text Text Text Text Text Text Text Text Text Text Text Text Text Text Text Text Text Text Text Text Text Text Text Text Text Text Text Text Text Text Text Text Text Text Text Text Text Text Text Text Text Text Text Text Text Text Text Text Text Text Text Text Text Text Text Text Text Text Text Text Text Text Text Text Text Text Text Text Text Text Text ██████ Text.

Text Text Text Text Text Text Text Text Text Text Text Text Text Text Text Text Text Text Text Text Text Text Text Text Text Text Text Text Text Text Text Text Text Text Text Text Text Text Text Text Text Text Text Text Text Text Text Text Text Text Text Text Text Text Text Text Text Text Text Text Text

Figure 3. ***Zoom fills the entire screen with a portion of the exhibit.***

Highlight. Using a color to annotate text to emphasize and aid in viewing. Don't be afraid to use a color other than yellow to differentiate yourself from the other side and to make your presentation more interesting. Be consistent if you use multiple colors—for example, every "From" is orange, every "To" is yellow, and every "Subject" is green. (*Note*: This book is printed in black and white, so you can't see the different colors in the example below unless you are reading the eBook.)

Example: "Please **highlight** *the sentence in paragraph two starting with "Oklahoma football is the best . . . ."*

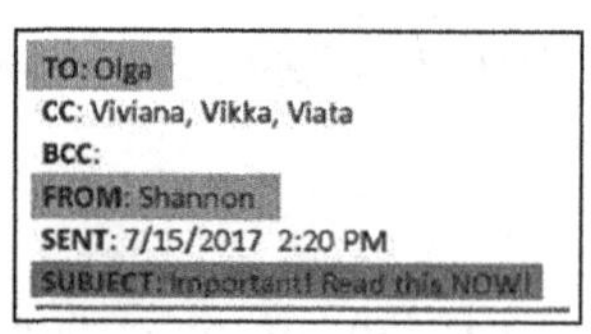
TO: Olga
CC: Viviana, Vikka, Viata
BCC:
FROM: Shannon
SENT: 7/15/2017 2:20 PM
SUBJECT: Important! Read this NOW!

Figure 4. ***Use color consistently to differentiate your presentation and aid clarity.***

Redaction. Obscuring a portion of text or an image so that it cannot be viewed. Redactions are often the subject of pretrial motions, so be careful what obligation you are taking on. If not created in advance, redactions often occur on the fly on a backup laptop or on the "working" screen of an extended desktop. I highly recommend using a naming convention that signifies a redacted document with an "R" suffix at the end of the exhibit name. For example, if the unredacted exhibit number is TX0123, the redacted version would be TX0123R.

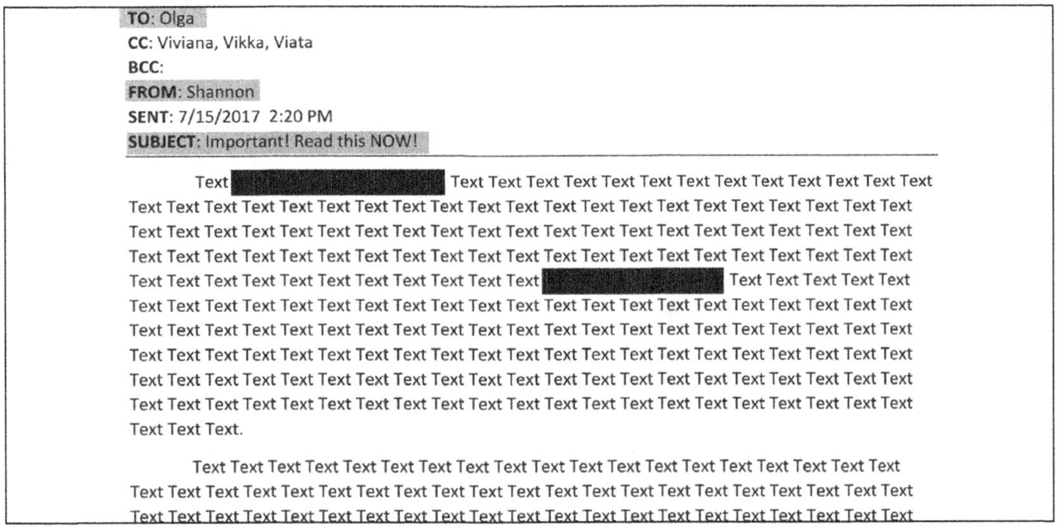
TO: Olga
CC: Viviana, Vikka, Viata
BCC:
FROM: Shannon
SENT: 7/15/2017 2:20 PM
SUBJECT: Important! Read this NOW!

Text [redacted] Text Text Text Text Text Text Text Text Text Text Text Text Text
Text Text Text Text Text Text Text Text Text Text Text Text Text Text Text Text Text Text Text Text Text
Text Text Text Text Text Text Text Text Text Text Text Text Text Text Text Text Text Text Text Text Text
Text Text Text Text Text Text Text Text Text Text Text Text Text Text Text Text Text Text Text Text Text
Text Text Text Text Text Text Text Text Text Text Text [redacted] Text Text Text Text Text
Text Text Text Text Text Text Text Text Text Text Text Text Text Text Text Text Text Text Text Text Text
Text Text Text Text Text Text Text Text Text Text Text Text Text Text Text Text Text Text Text Text Text
Text Text Text Text Text Text Text Text Text Text Text Text Text Text Text Text Text Text Text Text Text
Text Text Text Text Text Text Text Text Text Text Text Text Text Text Text Text Text Text Text Text Text
Text Text Text Text Text Text Text Text Text Text Text Text Text Text Text Text Text Text Text Text Text
Text Text Text.

Text Text Text Text Text Text Text Text Text Text Text Text Text Text Text Text Text Text Text
Text Text Text Text Text Text Text Text Text Text Text Text Text Text Text Text Text Text Text Text Text
Text Text Text Text Text Text Text Text Text Text Text Text Text Text Text Text Text Text Text Text Text

Figure 5. ***Redactions should be neat and accurate.***

Miscellaneous annotations. Arrow, underlining, rectangles, circles, etc. These annotations are often underutilized and are a great way to personalize, differentiate, and build interest in your team's exhibits.

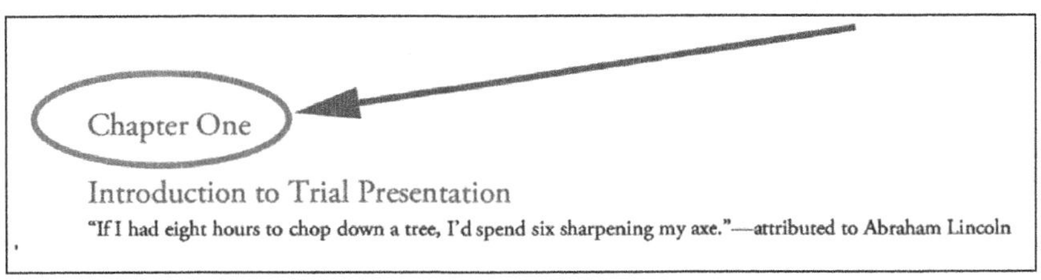

Figure 6. ***Don't be afraid to use underline, circle, and create arrows (to name a few) to highlight important information and make your exhibit memorable.***

On the fly. This phrase typically refers to video clips presented without preplanning. Video clips are often created in advance, but some are done "on the fly," meaning they're created live or in the moment. You don't normally differentiate between a preplanned or an on-the-fly video clip. Video clips either have a code—"Please play page 10 lines 15-20 of John Smith's transcript, which is clip 23"—or if there is no precut clip, state the page/line reference. Teams need to decide how many clips should be done in advance and how many on the fly because clip production is very time consuming. (Recall our rule of thumb for estimating how much time it takes to work with video.) Clips with a low likelihood of being played probably should not be clipped in advance, whereas clips that you know you will play should be cut in advance, if possible.

Static image. An image that has already been annotated. Note that annotations cannot be modified on a static image where they have already been "burned" in, but new ones can always be added.

Layer. Each individual annotation is called a layer. Exhibits can have multiple layers as they are divided into callouts, highlights, and underlines. As an example, you may have an exhibit with multiple callouts and annotations, as in Figure 2. Steadily build the layers in order: callouts first, then highlights, then arrow annotations.

Stage. A stage is when you save multiple annotations to an exhibit so that they can be quickly presented and still be manipulated. Stages are in contrast with a static image, in that each layer of annotation can still be manipulated once presented. For example, you could change the highlighting area on a staged document once the stage is presented, but you could not change highlighting on a static image that is highlighted. (Also called a presentation.)

It is important to practice annotating exhibits so that you can master the features and best navigate individual exhibits. A good practice is to take the attorney's witness outline and practice which type of annotation works best to emphasize their point. Reviewing the witness outlines is also a great way to QC both the outline for correct references and to ensure that all of the exhibits, video, and clips mentioned in it are in the trial presentation system. Consider adding individual steps to your copy of the witness outline (or, if working with a tech, to their outline) so you know what to do to each exhibit. I'll discuss this in more detail below.

Performing a run-through of each witness outline (*with the attorney*[3]) is a key to success. Practice it until it is seamless—many never practice at all, and it shows. The run-through will also build up the lawyer's comfort level and familiarity with the presentation, which helps them appear confident and capable, so you may want to do several run-throughs. As you do the run-through, you may want to note on the witness outline any special annotations, notes, timing, or other instructions so you'll know what to do when you get there. In addition, if working with a large team where witness outlines have been divided up amongst many lawyers, it is a good idea to do a run-through with them as well or have them sit with you during trial. Having new associates sit with the trial tech is a great way for them to gain experience in the courtroom and deepen their involvement in the case, as well as having a person more familiar with the exhibits available to provide direction to the tech. Other methods are for the attorney to use a laser pointer[4] or to stage their exhibits in advance and provide an exhibit code for each one. Staging exhibits in advance is a good idea when you are pressed for time, as it takes a few seconds to annotate each document on the fly and those seconds really add up.

Understanding the legal team's comfort with technology is another key to success. After, all it's not helpful to create an amazingly annotated document if a lawyer is thrown off by annotations the trial tech has created without express direction. Some individuals have a high comfort level, shooting from the hip with annotations, and will say, "Follow along," and go for it. This is an area that is imperfect and improves greatly over time.

This next suggestion may sound silly, but it's true. Remember, the trial tech is your nerd buddy. I know that sounds strange, but the lawyers present should want to "humanize" themselves before others in the courtroom, so not treating their trial tech like they're just another "tool" in the room is important. When working with a trial technician, be sure to know his or her name. At the beginning of the case, you should introduce them by name to the jury. Often, to avoid the appearance of a "master and servant" relationship, it can be beneficial to address them as "Mr." or "Ms.," while they address you by your first name. This tactic often helps you seem accessible and open to everyone on your legal team, not just your fellow lawyers. Also, be mindful that your tech isn't doing all the heavy lifting (literally) in front of the jury. If he is carrying big heavy loads back and forth to court while you walk in with nothing in your hands, it may lend the wrong impression of you to jurors. The optics are bad. Always make a "visible offer" to the tech to lend a hand. Most techs won't need your help and you'll look like a team player.

Last, a quick warning about communication. Often other members of the legal team have an epiphany as to what should be on screen and relay instructions to the tech to put up a document *immediately*. My experience has shown me that 9.9 times out of 10, this is a horrible idea. It is extremely distracting to both the presenter and the trial tech to try to put an exhibit onscreen without them knowing it is coming. It throws off whatever great point the presenter was making because there is now a random exhibit placed on screen. It's important to make clear beforehand that this be done sparingly and only with the permission of the presenter. The legal team member should send the presenting attorney a quick note to see if they want the exhibit up as well first, or calmly ask or whisper whether the exhibit should be displayed or the requestor just needs to own the request.

3. Or yourself, if you are a single force to be reckoned with.
4. I try to use a green laser pointer rather than red when we do use one (green means "go," red means "stop").

9.4 Use Stage Direction in Exhibit Narration

The smartest associate (now a partner) I ever met was at her first big trial and had a revelation, of sorts. It was a real "*aha*" moment for me as well. Instead of merely listing exhibit numbers in witness and other outlines, she treated exhibits and navigation through them like stage direction. *It was a game changer.* Partners whose outlines she prepared valued her work greatly, as her outlines and directions brought clarity to the ideas that needed to be expressed onscreen.

Guiding decision-makers through an exhibit by explaining and describing the document, page, paragraph, and sentence aids in their understanding and gives context to the document and credibility for the lawyer.[5] *This is stage direction for exhibits.* It's the difference between having a map to find the courthouse in a city you've never been to and trying to find it with a flashlight in the dark—sure, *you* might know where it is, but can you give good directions so that *everyone else* can find it?

Helping decision-makers navigate exhibits makes you a partner[6] in finding an answer at trial, as well as helping you to appear upfront and honest through your genuine interest in showing the exhibit. Most legal teams simply call up an exhibit by number and presume everyone is following along, or *can* follow along. This is simply not true—sometimes it's impossible to follow along, especially if an exhibit is wordy, hard to see, or inadequately annotated.

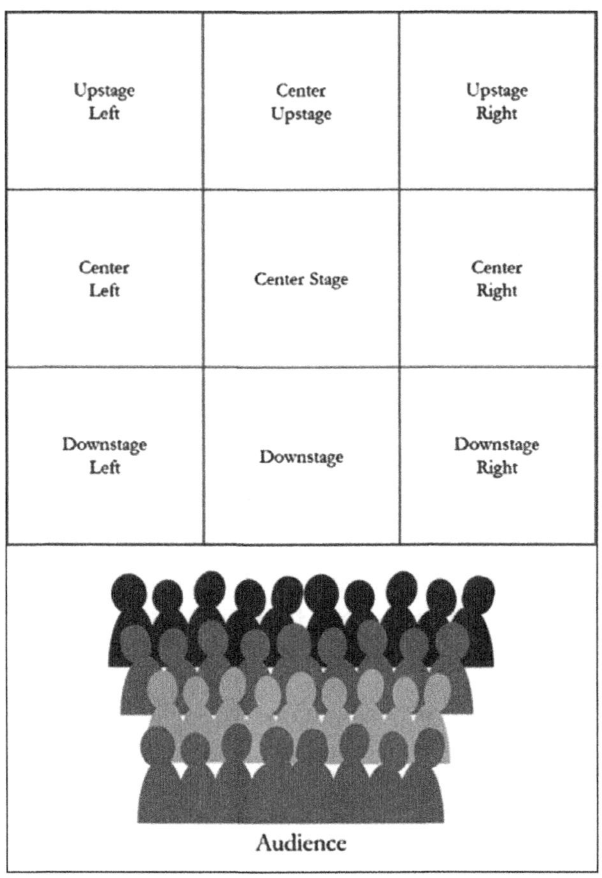

Figure 7. ***Stage direction for theater tells the actor where to go and how to navigate the stage. Use stage direction in trial presentation to help your viewers navigate the exhibits.***

5. You can also use a laser pointer to show the section to be called out—but it's a bit inelegant compared to using stage direction. Perhaps a combination of the two works best for you.
6. Or it will help you *make* partner!

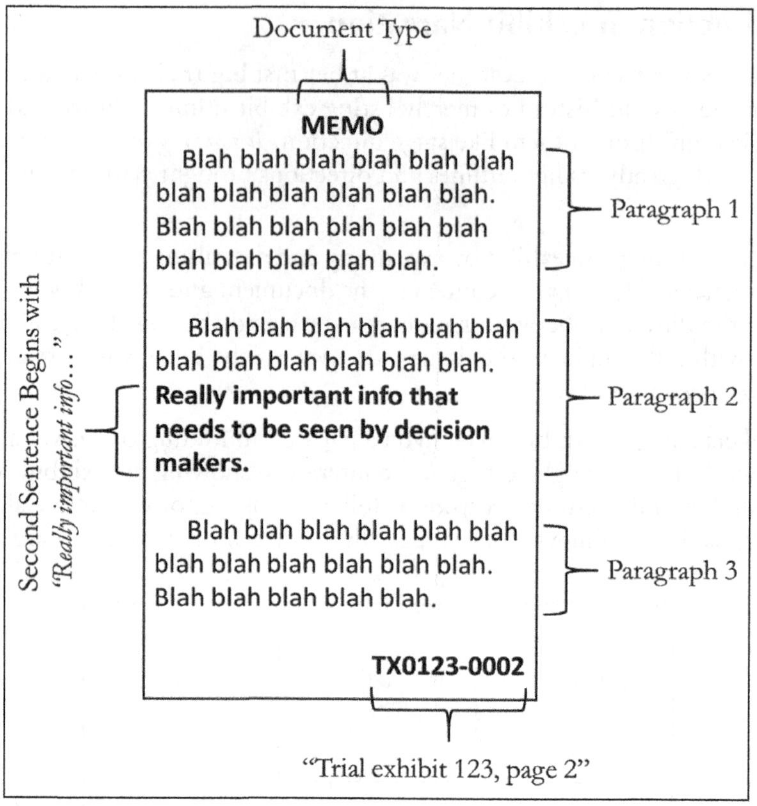

Figure 8. ***Use stage direction for exhibits.***

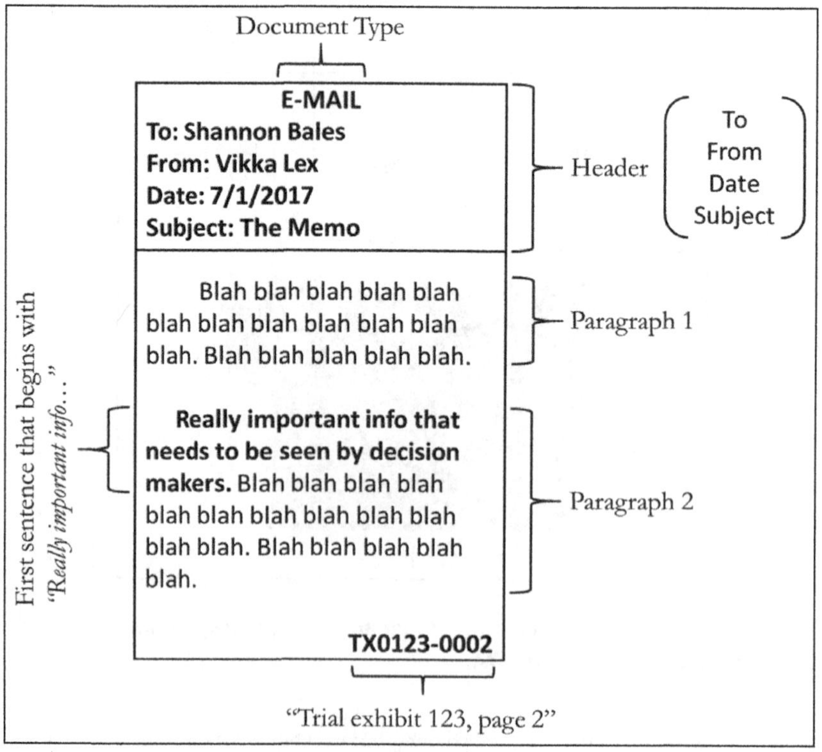

Figure 9. ***Stage direction for email.***

Examples:

- Start by showing and explaining email header information that contains the date, author, recipient, and title when showing an email. Move to the body of the email, directing the viewer to the correct paragraph by number (such as "the third paragraph from the top") and the first words in the sentence you are directing their attention to (e.g., "Go to the sentence starting with 'The contract is invalid . . . .'").

RECEIVED:	2/11/2017 @ 5:30 PM PST
FROM:	Shannon Bales
TO:	Larry Lee
SUBJECT:	FW: Did you get the contract?

Figure 10. ***Taking the time to show the header info provides context as to the content.***

- Show and explain the title and author for a publication which is usually the first page. Instead of turning directly to a page in the book, start by showing the title and author page. Then navigate to the relevant page, providing direction as to the paragraph that the sentence to be called out is located in and using the first couple of words of the sentence. "On page 110, in the second paragraph in the column on the right, callout the sentence that begins with 'The best of the best . . . .'"

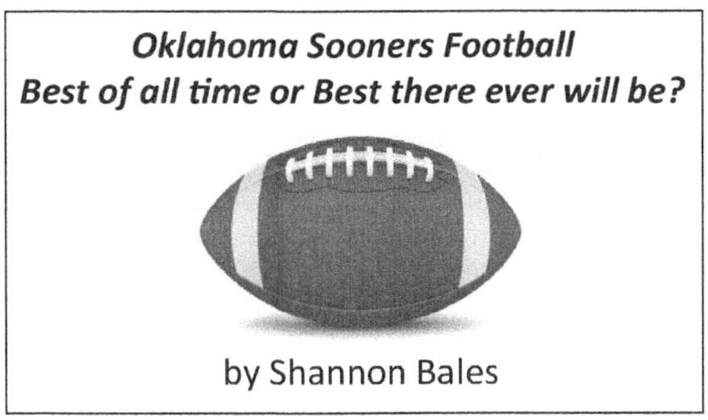

Figure 11. *My follow-up book . . . .*

As a final suggestion, consider introducing your trial tech to the judge and jury at the beginning of the trial. It's important that legal teams humanize the people in the courtroom and show that they respect non-lawyers. Legal team members should be patient, kind, and humble, especially if there is an error. Decision-makers might not think very well of them if they look impatient, ignore "the little guy," are rude, or throw their trial tech under the bus at the first sign of trouble.

9.5 Witness Outlines on Steroids

That smart associate I mentioned earlier who is now a partner (*partner!*) wasn't finished with just using stage direction to help navigate documents. She also created an outline that made her indispensable to the trial team. This meant she was included in every strategic decision and was always in the courtroom—usually at counsel table (or at least next to me in the geek seat!). Her outline was a modern update of the classic outline that nearly every attorney uses and is express recognition of the diverse multimedia and complex data that is being used at trial today. Most lawyers cannot remember where every sentence in a document is to be called out, the page/line reference for impeachment or the references

There is often a mismatch between presentation and precentor. Litigators need to connect with decision-makers in the courtroom. Having "stage direction" and a more robust outline gives the attorney all the information at their fingertips. You aren't just helping your own team find the relevant text—you are helping the entire courtroom find the text. Lawyers become over-familiar with the exhibits and quickly rush through what is often the first viewing for the judge and jury.

The subsections below contain best practices for presenters as they walk decision-makers through documents as they're shown in court. When appropriate, I've included graphics to illustrate (literally) the principles behind them.

9.5.1 Typeface

Set the outline in 16-point, sans serif type so the presenter can read it with ease. See the difference?

16 POINT TYPE — 12 POINT TYPE — 10 POINT TYPE

9.5.2 Table of Contents

A table of contents can be used as easily as an outline—whatever organizational layout that ties to your legal issues will work just fine.

9.5.3 Screenshots

Place screenshots and highlighted portions of exhibits into your outline. This allows you to have an easy visual reference to the document and what should be highlighted. If you're working with a trial tech, screenshots and highlights make it a snap for them to follow along. Windows features a snipping tool in its software that's straight-forward to use, or you can opt for a more robust tool like Snagit to capture screenshots.

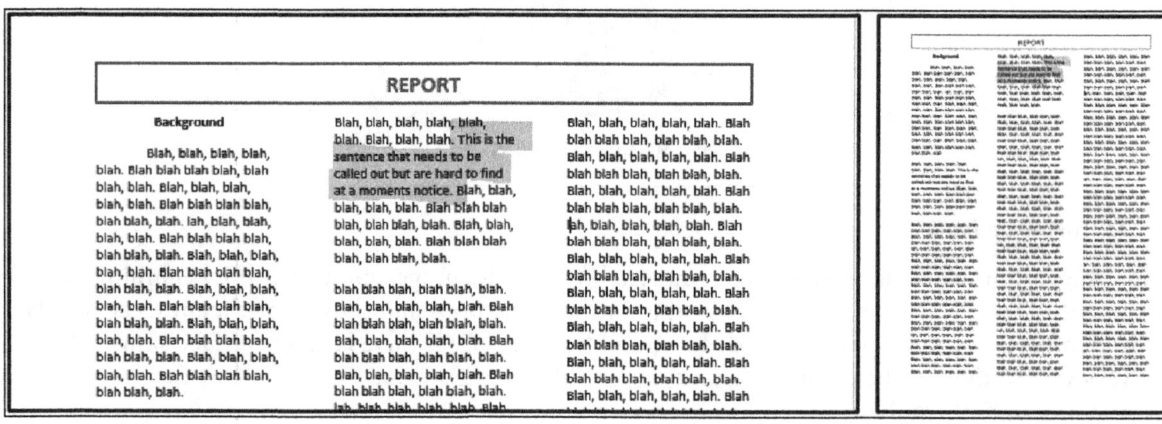

Figure 12. ***A screenshot in your outline provides a visual reference where to direct your audience.***

9.5.4 Color Coding

Color coding is a simple way to distinguish exhibits that have been admitted (green) from those that have not (yellow). See section 7.3 for a refresher on how and why using color in exhibits is so important.

Q. Are the test results cited in your report?

Exhibit X500 Report at page 25. "The test results were positive"

Figure 13. ***Color coding whether exhibits have been admitted provides a quick visual reference as to their admitted status and helps you avoid embarrassing errors. Note that Exhibit X500, above, is highlighted yellow and thus has not been admitted.***

9.5.5 Prepared Answers

To the degree possible, try to anticipate what questions or issues will be brought up by opposing counsel and write the response, along with noting the exhibit number and/or transcript page and numbers that support it. This tactic ensures that the legal team is ready with as many responses as possible, and no one has to scramble through exhibits or transcripts for support.

Q. You initially found that there was no connection between the plaintiffs pain and the injury?

TAB 1, Page 122:3-4
Transcript of Dr. Bill Nguyen, VOL 1 12/11/2017

3 Q. Is there any connection between the accident and her back pain?
4 A. I don't that kind of injury can cause that type of pain.

Figure 14. ***Note that the reference also contains a tab number that directs the witness to the appropriate location in the witness binder.***

9.5.6 Stage Direction

Think about how the decision-makers in the room are going to follow you through your opening statement, closing argument, and witness examinations. You are likely very familiar with your documents, while they aren't at all. Incorporating stage direction in the outline itself allows for presenting attorneys to have, right at their fingertips, all the information they need. In so doing, you aren't just helping your own team find the relevant text; you are helping the entire courtroom find the text. Attorneys sometimes become over-familiar with the exhibits and quickly rush through what is often the first viewing for the judge and jury.

Help them help you by taking the time to navigate documents using stage direction whenever you can. It greatly aids comprehension to be descriptive in explaining where callouts are coming from and provides context and openness about the exhibit. Below is an outline, starting with the exhibit number, showing how one might consider describing an exhibit leading to the callout and annotation of specific information.

- **What is the exhibit number?**
- **What kind of document is it?**
  - Describe the exhibit: what kind of document is it?
    - Memo
    - Email
    - Author
    - Contract
    - Spreadsheet
    - Report
    - Fax
    - Expert Report
    - Policy Manual

- **What are the details that give the exhibit context?**
  - Title of the document
  - Subject line of email or memo
  - Provide any author, authority, or company identifying information:
    - Author
    - Recipient, CC
    - Company
    - Date sent/received/created
  - Examples:
    - Email
    - Sent by Bob on 5/4/2017, with the subject line XYZ
    - A memo written by Bob titled ABC Rules for XYZ company on 5/4/2017
    - A spreadsheet created by Bob on 5/4/2017 to track mortgage rates
    - Employee manual given to Bob on 5/4/2017 that details the time entry policy
    - Expert report on damages written by Bob on 5/4/2017
- **What page is the information on?**
  - Where on the page can the information to be called out be found?
  - If a document organized by paragraphs, which paragraph?
  - How many paragraphs from the top or the bottom?
  - Sentence location
  - Left or right side?
  - Top or bottom?
  - Handwritten information in the margin or not?
- **Callout and annotate**
  - "Callout the second paragraph in the center column . . . ."
  - "Highlight the portion starting with . . . ."
  - "Underline the word . . . ."
    - "Highlight the first sentence in paragraph one . . . ."
    - "Callout the second sentence starting with '*The Trial Presentation Companion* . . . .'"

9.6 Team Building

Related to trial communication, and often ignored, is *team building*. Throwing a diverse group of people together who may be away from their significant others for long periods of time, while working extreme hours for days at a time without consideration of the team dynamic, can be a recipe for disaster. Here are a few tips to create team unity:

- Recognize at an early stage that trial is not for everybody. Tuning in early so personnel corrections can be made at the onset might be the best non-legal decision you make at trial. Get negative influences (substance abuse, emotional issues, dramas, etc.) out of the trial site as quickly as possible.
- The lead attorney should regularly communicate goals and feedback. If the lead can't, then designate someone who can. Not knowing what is occurring at trial and what the priorities are is a sure-fire way to lose ownership by your team.
- Consider a "kickoff" meal or get-together for the *entire team*. For long trials, try to get together regularly—a regular Friday night meal, for example.
- If you want ownership from those around you, seek their opinions and integrate into the team.
- Offer the team a variety of healthy food and meals. (Napoléon was right: "An army marches on its stomach.")
- Put up a wall of photos—family, pets, funny shots—in the war room.
- Work out a time-off schedule for each team member.
- Immediately after court business each day, team leadership must relay to the trial tech any instructions for exhibit creation or trial presentation needs for the next day. Understand that if team leaders first go to the gym to work out or grab dinner with the client, and don't get the tech team started on tomorrow's task until the leaders are on their way to bed, there will be problems.
- The need for sleep is *not* a flaw.
- The entire legal team must support those who are *in court* as a priority. In addition to the lawyers themselves, this includes supporting the team's paralegals and trial technologists, all of whom need to be fully functional, alert, and awake.
- Engage in some team exercises. One great paralegal I have worked with (named Jeff) regularly leads his teammates in a few fun exercises. It is always a great morale booster, and his efforts help keep everyone engaged.
- Don't change proven workflows mid-trial.

Chapter Ten

Forms and Checklists

Ready-to-use PDFs of these forms and checklists are available for you to download and save, print, and use. They are your free bonus, and can be accessed here:

Website http://bit.ly/1P20Jea

Password TriPreCom1

Form 1

Trial Software Due Diligence Checklist

Trial Software Due Diligence Checklist

- Review and perform due diligence on the top trial software packages available.
  - What tools work best for your firm? What tools will be the easiest to convert from your review databases to your trial presentation database?
- Call software companies and talk — who is most helpful?
  - Ask for equipment recommendations and real-world hardware requirements.
  - Download demo versions of software and evaluate — consider TrialDirector, Sanction, Visionary, and OnCue to start.
- Find out what the minimum hardware spec is for the trial presentation software and exceed it in every way possible. Again, run your short list of equipment and its spec by the trial software vendor. Look to them for specific laptop recommendations.
  - Budget for the most you can afford, but never buy equipment that does not meet the software spec.
- Understand the basics of how your software works:
  - Does the software import images and convert them into some internal location or build links to existing images?
  - How long does the import and conversion take?
  - If converting to another format, how does it work with oversized images, odd-sized images, skewed images?
  - Does the conversion make any kind of corrections to the image?
  - What kinds of tools installed create conflicts for your software?
    - Subsequent installation of video players and codecs can cause substantial problems with trial presentation software.
  - What is the effect of installing encryption software on your laptop?
    - Does it affect performance or reliability?
- Choose the suite of tools that works best with your firm environment. There are other tools that you may want to consider, but this is a fairly common and generic list to get you started.
  - Trial Software: TrialDirector, OnCue, Sanction
  - Document Review: Concordance, Relativity
  - Transcripts: Case Notebook, TextMap
  - Text Editor: UltraEdit, Notepad++
  - Screen Capture: Snagit
  - Video editing: Windows Movie Maker (free), Adobe Premier Lite
  - Total Commander is a file manager that helps with synchronization, file renaming, etc.
  - Adobe Acrobat Professional
  - Microsoft Office
- Join the "Trial Support" LinkedIn group. It is a great group, with some popcorn-worthy drama from time to time.
  - Ask questions. Experienced people are more than willing to help, and you might find a good vendor resource if trial technology is not for you.
- Listen to the Trial Technology and Litigation Support Podcast, by Robb Helt, which has interviews with software vendors, techs, product comparisons, roundtables, and a variety of other industry professionals.
- Read Ted Brooks's Court Technology Blog, http://trial-technology.blogspot.com/.

Form 2

Trial Presentation Laptop Build and QC Sheet

Trial Presentation Laptop Build and QC Sheet

Laptop Name: ______________________________

QC'd by: ______________________ **Assigned to:** ______________________

Date Released : ___/___/___ **Expected Returned Date to IT:** ___/___/___

Verified	Software	Optional	Install Order	Version	Notes
	Trial Software	NO	LAST		
	Adobe Acrobat	NO			
	CD Burner XP Pro	NO			CD/DVD Burner
	eDrawings Viewer	Yes			For viewing AutoCAD files
	Adobe Flash Player	Yes			
	Deposition Software	Yes			
	Microsoft Office	NO			
	Snagit	Yes			Highly recommend
	Total Commander	Yes			
	UltraEdit	Yes			
	WinRAR or Winzip	NO			
	E-Transcript Viewer	Yes			
	InforMatik Image driver	Yes			Image
	Windows Essentials	Yes			**(Movie Maker)**
	VeraCrypt	Yes			Encryption software
	QuickTime	Yes			

Configuration

Verified	Hardware Check	Instructions	Notes
	Sound	Connect an audio device, and verify the audio	
	Sound	Turn Windows default to "No sounds"	
	Video Driver	Verify 1024x768 and 1920x1080 resolutions	
	Power Profile	Edit Power Options to **Never** for all Categories	
	Background	Change background to "black"	
	Sleep	Turn Sleep option to **Never**	
	Additional Power Settings	Change power plan to "high performance"	

Builder Signature: ______________________________

Trial Tech Signature: ______________________________

Form 3

Courtroom Technology Evaluation

Courtroom Technology Evaluation

Is there an existing courtroom presentation system? Yes No
VGA HDMI
Podium: Yes No
Judge/clerk kill switch: Yes No

Video access point for courtroom system: Counsel table Podium Other
Describe:

Detail existing courtroom monitors:
4:3 16:9 Mixed with 4:3 and 16:9
Resolution: 1024x768 1280x1024 1920x1080
Other Resolution:__________________

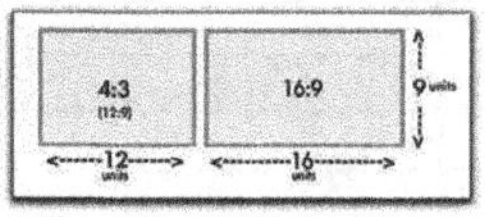

Location of courtroom monitors:
Judge Jury Witness
Counsel table: Plaintiff Defense Shared
Gallery
How many monitors: ______
Supplement monitors: Yes No

Projector or large monitor for shared viewing? Yes No
4:3 16:9
Approximate dimensions:
Quality of displayed image: High Medium Poor
Accurate colors? Yes No
Highlight colors are accurate? Yes No
Remote control: Yes No
Consider replacement/supplement? Yes No

Document Camera: Yes No
Can plug into switch: Yes No
Location of document camera:______________________

Power Outlets
How many?__________
Location:

Sound system: Yes No
Access point: Counsel table Podium Other
Describe:

Wi-Fi: Yes No
Signal Strength: Strong Weak Tested Empty or Full?

Hot Seat Location: Counsel Table Tech Table
Clear viewpoint of attorney and shared viewing monitor? Yes No

Courtroom printing: Yes No **Display Board Stands:** Yes No
Easel: Yes No
Flip Chart: Yes No
Dry Erase: Yes No

Approximate Distance

Main Display (view calc.)
Judge to display:
Jury to display:
Counsel to display:
Gallery to display:
Tech to display:

VGA to switch (length calculation)
Judge to switch:
Witness to switch:
Counsel to switch:
Projector/Monitor to switch:

Audio
Audio source to tech:

Power Outlets
Judge to outlet:
Tech table to outlet:
Podium to outlet:
Counsel table to outlet:
Witness to outlet:

Security

Court order to bring equipment:
Yes No
Special Entrance: Yes No
Special Hours: Yes No
Hours:
Equipment can be left in courtroom: Yes No

Courtroom Technology Supplement

Equipment Rental Responsibility

The [Plaintiff Defendant] will be the party responsible for contracting with the vendor.
Costs will be paid by: Plaintiff Defendant Shared
Vendor:_________________ **Switch Control:** Plaintiff Defendant
Court order necessary to bring in equipment: Yes No

DISPLAY

Shared viewing screen: **Projector** **Large Monitor Screen**
Size:
Main screen aspect ratio: 4:3 16:9
Counsel table monitors: Yes No
Monitor aspect ratio: 4:3 16:9
How many:________
Projector stand: Yes No

> **Warning**: Avoid mixed aspect ratio and signal degradation on long cable runs.

Location of courtroom monitors:
Judge Jury Witness
Counsel table: Plaintiff Defense Shared
Gallery **Hot Seat**
Will supplemental equipment create a mixed aspect ratio environment?: Yes No
Can displays be configured to avoid aspect ratio mismatch? Yes No
Amount of VGA cable needed +30%____________
Is VGA length >30ft: Yes No
VGA Switch: Yes No [4 port 6 port 8 port]
VGA splitter: 4 6 8
D/A Switch: Yes No How many:_________

AUDIO SYSTEM

Audio Mixer: Yes No
Audio cable length: _________
Speaker Rental: ___________
Speaker stand: Yes No

> **Warning**: Consider standalone system if court system is inaccessible or locked down.

Document Camera

Video resolution of document camera:
Brand: _______________
Remote: Yes No
Location of document camera:______________________

> **Warning**: video resolution mismatch can cause reset

Printing

In courtroom printing needed: Yes No
Quiet color printer: Yes No
Connection: Wireless Bluetooth Cable

> Print drivers provided
> Yes No

Power Outlets

How many?___________
Location: ______________
Extension cords: Yes No How long:_________ How many:_______
Power Strip: Yes No How many:_________ Heavy duty: Yes No

Misc.

WiFi: Yes No Service provider:_____________
Easel: Yes No iPhone power: Yes No
Flip Chart: Yes No USB power: Yes No
Dry Erase: Yes No

Courtroom Plan

Rough sketch of courtroom

Has each location been accounted for?				
Video	**Audio**	**Switch**	**Cabling**	**Presentation Aids**
Projector or Large Monitor	Speaker	VGA switch	Video	Podium
Screen	Mixer	VGA splitter	Audio	Easel
Judge monitor		DA switch	Power	Flip chart
Plaintiff monitor		Judge kill switch		Dry erase
Defendant monitor		Power strip		
Tech(s) monitor				
Tech table (can view atty direction?)				

Courthouse address:

Courtroom number:

Display Cheat Sheet

Generally, text height of 1" for every 15' of distance. Source: Extron Electronics

Comfortable Viewing Distance for Text on Presentation Visuals
4:3 screens (projectors, older monitors)

Assumptions:

- Visual acuity of 20/40 (about the same that is used for highway road signs)
- Projected image fills the screen
- Screen and image have a 4:3 width to height ratio (the standard ratio for most projectors and screens)

How to use the table:

- Locate the row that corresponds to the width of the screen you are using
- Locate the column corresponding to the smallest font used for text on your slides
- The intersection of the row and column is the maximum distance from the screen that an audience member should be seated in order to be able to easily read the text
- For example, if you are using a 60 inch screen and have 32 point text on your slides, the farthest that someone should be is 57 feet from the screen

Screen Width (Inches)	Font size (in points) 18	24	28	32	36	40	44
36	19	27	31	34	38	42	46
48	25	36	41	46	51	56	61
60	32	44	51	57	64	70	76
72	38	53	61	69	76	84	92
84	44	62	71	80	89	98	107
96	51	71	81	92	102	112	122
120	64	89	102	114	127	140	153

Comfortable Viewing Distance for Text on Presentation Visuals
16:9 screens (widescreen TVs, monitors & projectors)

Assumptions:

- Visual acuity of 20/40 (about the same that is used for highway road signs)
- Projected image fills the screen
- Screen and image have a 16:9 width to height ratio (the standard ratio for most widescreen TVs, monitors & projectors)

How to use the table:

- Locate the row that corresponds to the diagonal measurement of the screen you are using (the typical way to measure those screens)
- Locate the column corresponding to the smallest font used for text on your slides
- The intersection of the row and column is the maximum distance from the screen that an audience member should be seated in order to be able to easily read the text
- For example, if you are using a 32 inch TV and have 28 point text on your slides, the farthest that someone should be is 18 feet from the screen

Diagonal screen size (in inches)	Font size (in points) 18	24	28	32	36	40	44
15	5	7	8	9	10	11	12
19	7	8	11	12	13	14	15
22	8	11	12	14	15	17	19
27	9	13	15	17	19	21	22
32	11	15	18	20	22	24	27
36	12	17	20	22	25	27	30
42	15	20	23	26	29	32	35
47	16	23	26	29	32	36	39
52	18	25	29	32	35	40	43
60	21	29	35	37	41	48	50
72	25	35	40	45	50	55	60
80	28	39	44	50	55	61	65

Source: David Paradi ,"ThinkOutsideTheSlide.com"

16:9 source video in a 4:3 profile

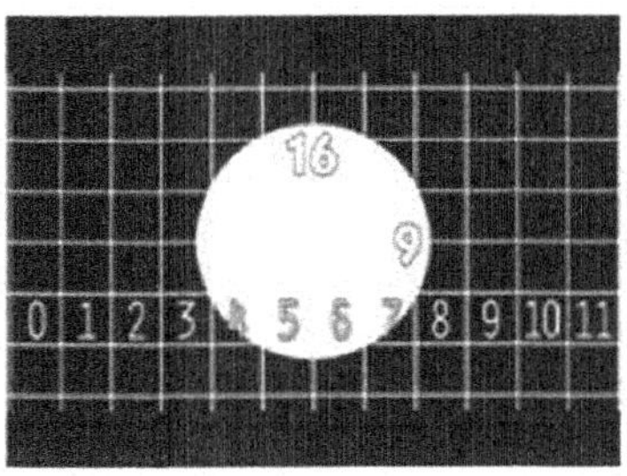

Letter-boxed

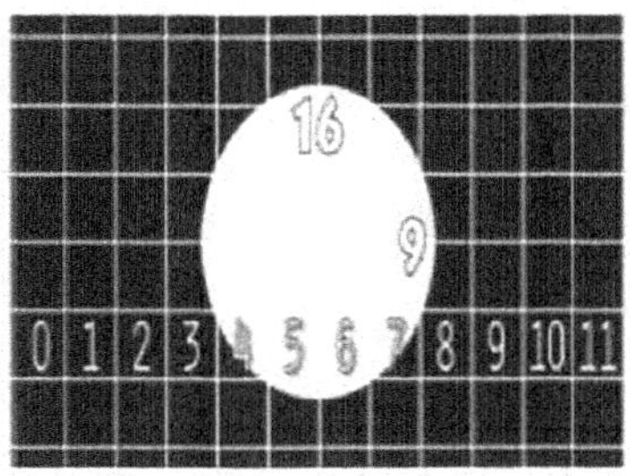

Interpreted as 4:3 (squashed)

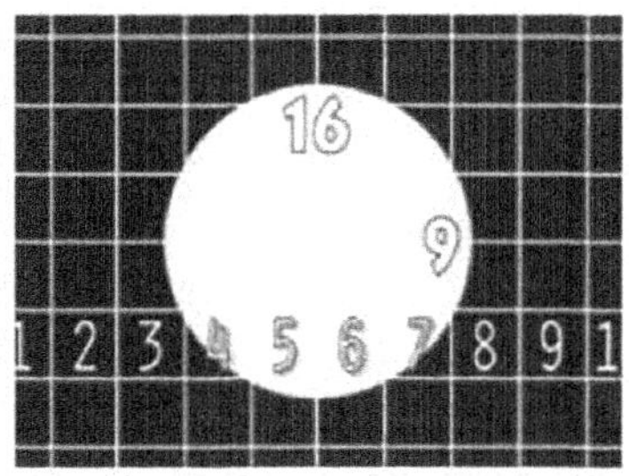

Expanded & cropped to 4:3

4:3 source video in a 16:9 profile

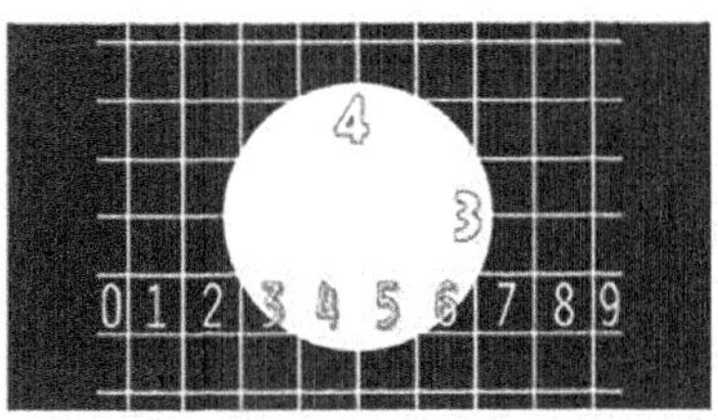

Pillar-boxed

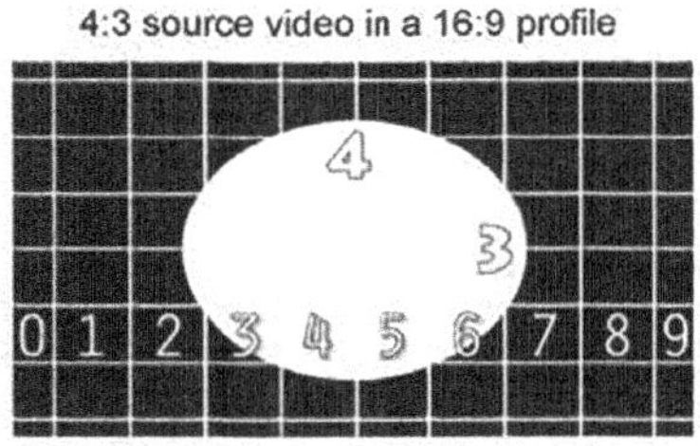

Interpreted as 16:9 (stretched)

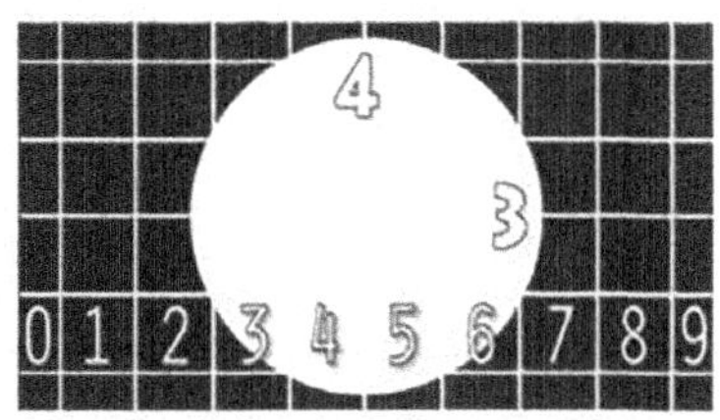

Expanded & cropped to 16:9

4:3	16:9
640x480	1280x720
1024x768	1365x768
1280x960	1600x900
1400x1050	1920x1080
1600x1200	

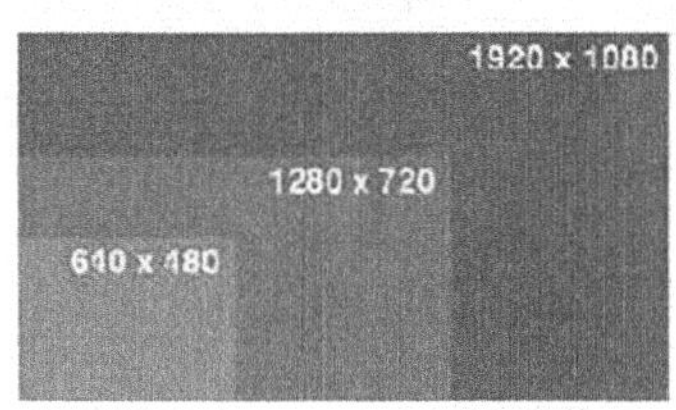

Form 4

Advanced and Basic Courtroom Setup Orders

Advanced Courtroom Setup Order

1. Set up tech table that will hold my laptops, switch, and monitor (it could also be the counsel table). Place equipment to be used on table including power supplies.
2. Locate power outlets and run extension cords to tech table (do not tape down yet).
3. Place projector and screen OR big screen monitor in its courtroom location.
   a. Check viewing angle.
4. Place supplemental monitors.
   a. Check viewing angle.
5. Place speaker with stand, if necessary.
6. Place document camera.
7. Route video, audio, and power cables to their corresponding equipment and locations.
8. Run a "soft test" of all equipment before taping down.
   a. Go through steps 1 thru 8 of the **Daily Courtroom Checklist** to test equipment
9. Use tablecloth or draping for the tech table to hide cables.
10. Walk through with opposing and clerk for approval.
11. If everything is placed properly, tape down all cables **(see gaffing tape instructions)**.
12. Double-check by running through steps 1 through 8 of the **Daily Courtroom Checklist** to test equipment.
13. The last thing I do is very important: I run through a few images and PowerPoint slides (not the actual ones to be used in court) that are similar to what will be used in court as a final test to ensure everything looks OK and works (color, font size, fonts, highlights).

Basic Courtroom Setup Order

1. Find power, video (VGA/HDMI), and audio (if necessary) inputs.
   a. Check inputs to see if they are broken (e.g., bent pins in VGA).
2. Go through steps 2 through 9 of the **Daily Courtroom Checklist** to test equipment.

- Basic setup still requires a run-through of QC Steps.

Form 5

Daily Courtroom Checklist

Daily Courtroom Checklist

1. CHECK COURTROOM
- ☐ Check gaffing tape/cables.
- ☐ Is there any damage? Missing tape, cables pulled up and moved, cables pinched under chairs or around furniture?
  - ☐ Replace and/or retape any problem areas.
- ☐ Check equipment.
  - ☐ Is equipment present and placed in the correct location?
- ☐ Check in with the clerk.
  - ☐ Is the clerk OK with setup?
  - ☐ Does the clerk want any changes?

2. SET UP LAPTOP
- ☐ Plug in everything *before* starting (mouse, sound, video, printer, power)

3. START AND CONFIGURE LAPTOP
- ☐ After computer is *fully* booted up.
- ☐ Place computer in extended desktop or mirror mode viewing.
- ☐ Are all drive letters accounted for and assigned the correct drive letter?

4. START TRIAL PRESENTATION AND OTHER SOFTWARE
- ☐ After computer is *fully* booted up.
- ☐ Start trail software.
  - ☐ Verify all images present using built in QC tool for trial presentation software.

5. START ANY ADDITIONAL PROGRAM INDIVIDUALLY AND WAIT UNTIL IT IS FULLY OPEN AND READY BEFORE OPENING THE NEXT PROGRAM.
- ☐ Do not start multiple programs at the same time.
- ☐ Is the software being started necessary for today's presentation?
- ☐ Open PowerPoint.
  - ☐ Check that PowerPoint is on the correct screen (displaying on the extended screen in presentation mode).

6. TEST SWITCH
- ☐ Cycle through each connected video source twice to ensure they appear.
- ☐ Looking for smooth transition free of setup and delay each time you switch.

7. TEST VIDEO
- ☐ Check that video is on *all* screens.
  - ☐ If projector, is it in focus and the image accurate on the screen.
  - ☐ Keystone?
- ☐ Use screen test image for correct aspect ratio and ensure video is accurately placed on monitor(s).
  - ☐ Check *all four corners* of the display for accuracy.
  - ☐ Consistent configuration for 4:3 or 16:9 on all monitors?
- ☐ Check document camera.
  - ☐ Place object on document camera to test.
- ☐ Play quick test video clip.

8. TEST SOUND
- ☐ Play test sound.

9. NOTIFY LEGAL TEAM YOU ARE READY!

10. AT THE END OF THE DAY
- ☐ Check cables.
- ☐ Check with clerk and legal team to ensure everything is OK — be humble and helpful.
- ☐ Keep the courtroom clean.
- ☐ Get ready for tomorrow!

Form 6

Trial Technology and Support Checklist

Trial Technology and Support Checklist

Name of case:	Client/matter number:
Trial location:	Estimated length of trial:
Coordinating attorney:	Coordinating paralegal or admin:
Trial tech:	IT contact: Litigation support contact:
Trial team members:	
War room offsite or in office:	
War room location:	
Date war room should be operational:	Date war room available for setup:
Number/type of workstations required:	
• Attorney:	
• Paralegal:	
• Secretarial:	
• Other:	
Network access requirements:	Special application needs:
Printing requirements:	Local area network required:
Local copy of database (i.e., Relativity, Concordance, LiveNote, Access, etc.) required?	Please name database(s) required:

1

Resources for Assistance	
Technology contact:	
Graphics contact:	
Trial tech contact:	
Rental company contact:	
Imaging contact:	
Internet/telephony contact:	
Records storage contact:	
Supplies:	
Trial presentation services:	
LiveNote/Case Notebook/Realtime assistance:	
Database assistance:	

Trial Team Contact List

Name	Phone	Email

2

Realtime Transcription Needs
Coordinator with court reporter:
Arrange time to test in advance of need:
Assign daily transcript loading procedures/responsibility:
Trial Presentation Equipment
• Projection/Display Equipment
• Firm or vendor?
• If consultant, contact info:
• If firm, arrangements to visit courtroom and design layout:
• Projector? Large Screen? Multiple Monitors? (see Courtroom Evaluation)
Display Needs
• Documents:
• Depo video:
• Demonstrative graphics/PowerPoint:
• Who will do graphics: firm or consultant? Consultant contact info:
• Easel for foam boards:
Special Courtroom Needs
• Laptops:
• Printing:
• External hard drives/thumb drives:
• Displays/monitors: •

3

Telephony Requirements	
Coordinator:	
Coordinator hotel:	
Conference phones:	
Fax requirements:	Photocopier requirement:
External media requirements (thumb drive, external drive, CD/DVD):	Onsite tech support requirements (all client billable at usual rates):
Furniture Requirements	
Coordinator/provider (hotel/firm):	
Tables:	
Chairs:	
Shelving:	
Electrical:	
Office Supply Requirements	
Coordinator:	
Telephone directory:	
Fax sheets:	
Stacking trays:	
Paper cutter:	
Stapler:	
Hole punch:	
Extension cords:	
Power strips:	
Tape:	Gaffing tape:
Boxes:	
Envelopes:	
Misc. supplies:	
Pens, pencils, highlighters:	
Post-It Notes:	
8.5 x 11 paper:	
8.5 x 14 paper:	
Floorplan layout of equipment:	Copier requirements:
Vendor (hotel/firm):	Coordinator (hotel/firm):
	Protective covering for floor: Yes No

4

Laptop Computers	
Source (firm/rental):	Quantity:
Contact info:	
Configuration:	Locations:
Configuration contact:	
Testing?	
Op system:	
Applications:	
Modem?	
Spares/repairs/contingency needs	Power cables and cords:
Contact info:	

Printers	
Source (firm/rental):	Quantity:
Contact info:	
Configuration:	Locations:
Contact:	
Driver install setup/testing:	
Paper trays:	
Local/network:	
Special needs:	
Spares/repairs/contingency needs	Power cables and cords (check lengths)"
Contact info:	

Internet/Telephony	
Source (firm/rental):	Quantity:
Contact info:	
Line splitters:	Locations:
ISDN:	
Spares/repairs/contingency needs Contact Info:	Telephone cords (check lengths):

5

Database Needs (detailing any local [versus cloud or Citrix] needs.)	
Concordance/Relativity:	Opticon? Other?
Contact info:	
CaseMap:	Local or WAN access to database?
Excel:	*Software* loaded onto client PCs?
Access:	*Database* loaded onto client PCs?
Spares/repairs/contingency needs Contact info:	Contact info:

Real-Time Deposition Needs (Case Notebook – LiveNote – TextMap)	
Deposition courtroom laptop:	Court reporter setup:
	Locations:
Spares/repairs/contingency needs Contact info:	Adaptor needed for deposition laptop?

6

MFD/Printers	
Source (firm/rental):	Quantity:
Contact info:	
Configuration:	Locations:
Contact:	
Driver install setup/testing:	
Paper trays:	
Local/network:	
Special needs:	
Spares/repairs/contingency needs	Power cables and cords (check lengths):
Contact info:	

Miscellaneous Equipment	
Source (firm/rental): Contact info:	Quantity:
Fax:	Locations:
Copier:	
Imaging:	
Projectors:	
Screens:	
Miscellaneous:	
Spares/repairs/contingency needs Contact info:	

Rental Company Information	
Company:	Address:
Phone number:	Contact: Backup contact:
Spares/repairs/contingency needs Contact info:	Delivery date/time: Pickup date/time:

7

Rental Company Information	
Company:	Address:
Spares/repairs/contingency needs Contact info:	Delivery date/time: Pickup date/time:

Rental equipment (including serial numbers): Delivery dates:

Make	Model	Serial Number	Comments	Returned?

Firm-supplied equipment (including serial numbers): Delivery dates:

Make	Model	Serial Number	Comments	Returned?

8

Part Two

Trial Presentation in Practice

Note: These instructions were accurate when this book went to print.

However, manufacturers frequently update their operating systems and software applications, such that what you see on your computer may differ from what appears in this book.

In case you have questions, be sure to check the documentation or online help for the version or release of the system and/or software you're using.

Chapter Eleven

A Primer on Getting Started

11.1 Computer Configuration for Trial

The first step is organizing the directories of files related to the case on your laptop. These are the exhibits, videos, depositions, presentations, and other documents that you will use throughout the trial. With organization, you'll know where to jump to make a quick fix if there is a problem. Files can also be exchanged fast and furious in the courtroom, so again, being well organized will save you in the long run. In conjunction with your file organization, keep a project plan of the files you've created and received and record details like page range, date received and whether they are redacted, and any other data that is pertinent to your case. For example, you might want to track the status of depo synchronization via a vendor if it hasn't already been done—you'll certainly want to know if a video is synced or not.

We will then configure the laptop by optimizing settings for trial. The dings, power-saving features, and background image of your kids are great for the office but not so good at trial. We will optimize the power settings for the laptop and turn off the default settings for the laptop going to "sleep" and its default background image and sounds. These settings help prepare your laptop to be a good guest in the courtroom. The power and sleep settings keep your laptop from turning off in the middle of trial. The sound configuration changes keep unnecessary "dings" and other sounds from playing when you click on something (which is amplified when connected to a court sound system). Finally, you'll set the display background to black to keep the presentation screen clean and distraction free.

11.1.1 Organize Your File Data

Task 1. Create a folder to store and organize your cases.

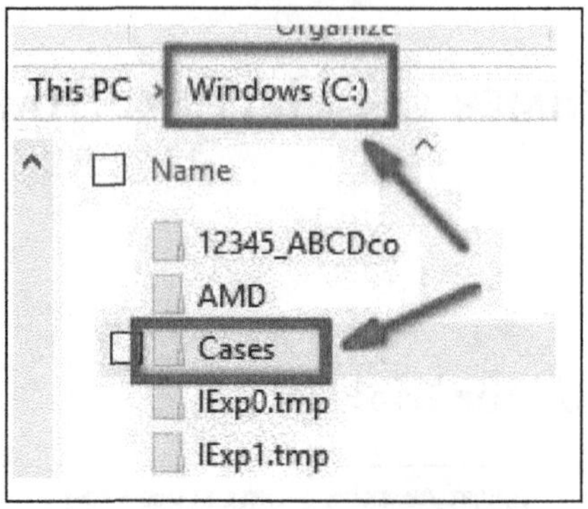

Create a **Cases** folder at the root of your C drive by right-clicking anywhere directory window. Then select **New** > **Folder**. Name the new folder **Cases.** This folder keeps all of your trial data in one place so that it can be easily backed up and shared with your second laptop and backed up to an external drive.

Task 2. Create folders for the data you plan to store.

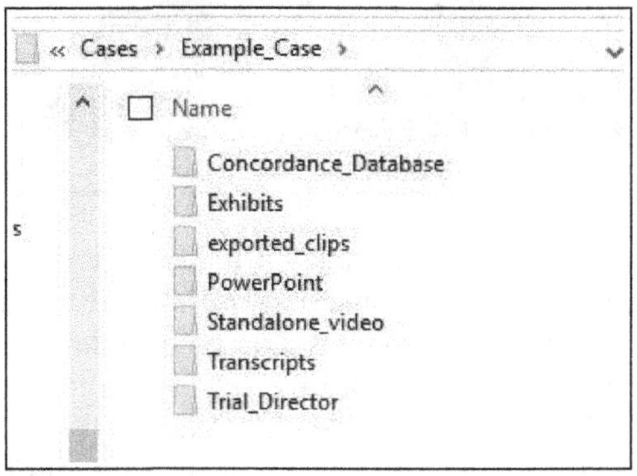

Organize your case data by creating folders named by data type (e.g., **Exhibits**, **Transcripts**, etc.) and application type (e.g., **PowerPoint**, **TrialDirector**, etc.). Some trial presentation programs have their own organizational structures that you may want to use. However, I find incorporating an application-related organizational method into a larger organizational structure is better and makes it easier to back up all of your case data in one action rather than multiple locations. You can't go wrong with organization—at the end of the day, go with the organizational method that works for you.

Task 3. Create an Addendum folder for exhibits added after the initial exchange.

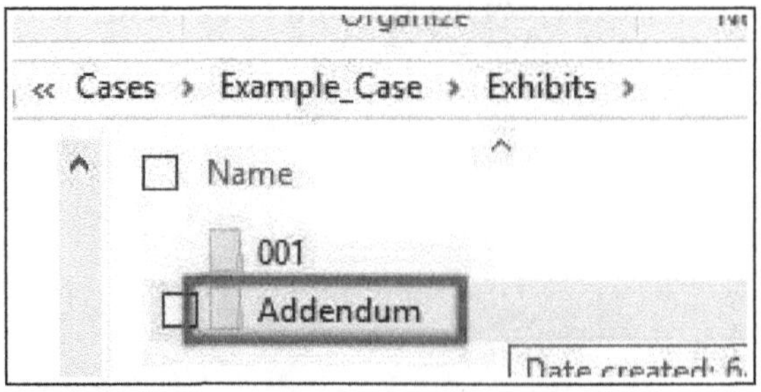

Within the **Exhibits** folder, create an initial folder that contains the first exchange of exhibits (in this case, it is folder **001**). You'll perform your initial load of data from this folder.

Create a subfolder called **Addendum** in the **Exhibits** folder. Exhibits that you add *after* the initial set (**001**) will go into a new folder that is named according to date the exhibits were added using the format YYYYMMDD. I use a dated folder to help keep me organized and transfer the information to my project plan. Moreover, this arrangement makes it fairly easy to go "back in time" to earlier versions of exhibits if you need to.

Task 4. Add new items daily.

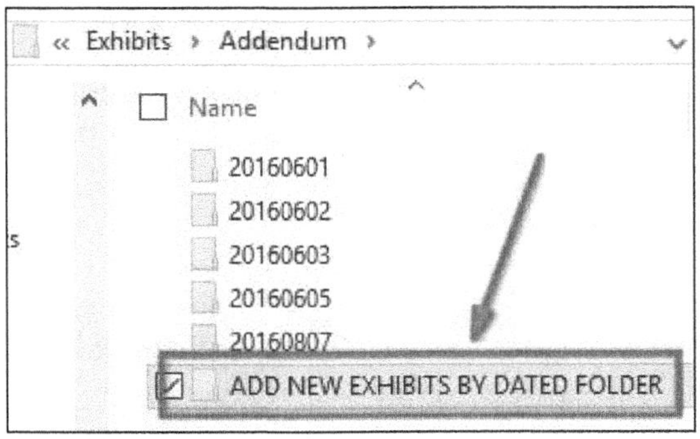

To your **Addendum** file, add new items received and processed daily to a dated folder (named YYYYMMDD, e.g., **20160601**, **20160602**, etc.) to your main trial laptop and synchronize to your backup trial laptop, network, and any backup media.

Be sure to keep a pristine copy of the exhibit (i.e., a copy of the exhibit before it is redacted, branded, or altered) in case it must be rebranded. If I have disk space on my laptop, I might add it to my organizational structure, but it is often on my backup hard drive due to space limitations. The pristine copy is pretty handy to have available in case redactions need to be redone in court or someone from the legal team needs to read what's under the redactions.

Task 5. Track exhibits in a Project Plan for your case.

	A	B	C
1	Exhibit Tracking		
2	Date Added	Exhibit Begin	Exhibit End
3	1/5/2017	TX0001	TX0250
4	1/10/2017	TX0251	TX0276
5	1/11/2017	TX0277	TX0278
6	1/12/2017	TX0279	TX0366
7	1/13/2017	TX0367	TX0401
8	1/14/2017	TX0402	TX0407
9	1/15/2017	TX0408	TX0556
10	1/16/2017	TX0557	TX0888
11			

As exhibits are added to folders, track them in a project plan that lists the date exhibits were added. You may also want to know if the exhibits are redacted, which party submitted them and a variety of other data that might be unique to your case. Microsoft Excel is a good software application for tracking exhibits.

Again, organization always helps, I like to send the project plan to the entire legal team so its members know exactly what I have and there are no misunderstandings. The project plan has saved me on a number of occasions, such as when the wrong exhibit was sent and it was discovered by comparing page counts between the project plan and the exhibit.

Task 6. Track individual exhibit page ranges.

Exhibit Page Range

Exhibit Number	Exhibit Begin	Exhibit End
TX0001	TX0001-0001	TX0001-0052
TX0002	TX0002-0001	TX0002-0777
TX0003	TX0001-0001	TX0001-0052

Track individual page ranges for quick reference. This information may already be tracked by your presentation system, but you should also have it readily available for legal teams and as part of your plan.

Task 7. Retain deposition information.

Deposition Ranges

Deponent Name	Beg Depo Range	End Dep Range	Prefix Used	Date	Video Sync'd?
John Smith	1	153	JS	12/10/2017	No
Hazel Bales	1	99	HB	5/10/2017	Yes
Olivia Underwood Volume 1	1	156	OU1	6/10/2017	Yes
Olivia Underwood Volume 2	157	335	OU2	7/15/2017	Yes
Bob Stoops	1	125	BS	8/1/2017	No

Capture deposition information—deponent name, page ranges, the prefix used for clipping video (see the video section), date, and whether the video has been synced. Manage video by denoting whether it has been synced and whether there are multiple volumes. This log comes in handy if someone calls a page that is outside of the page range, gives the wrong date or volume, etc.

Task 8. Track video designations.

Video Clip Identification

Deponent	Clip ID	Page Range
Hazel Bales		
Hazel Bales	HB1	3:05 - 8:02
Hazel Bales	HB2	15:09 - 15:17
Hazel Bales	HB3	23:22 - 24:07
Hazel Bales	HB4	86:09 - 93:01
Olivia Underwood Vol 1		
Olivia Underwood Vol 1	OU1_1	2:01 - 3:15
Olivia Underwood Vol 1	OU1_2	101:08 - 108:12
Olivia Underwood Vol 1	OU1_3	124:05 - 125:11
Olivia Underwood Vol 2		
Olivia Underwood Vol 2	OU2_1	159:18 - 160:02
Olivia Underwood Vol 2	OU2_2	167:24 - 168:03
Olivia Underwood Vol 2	OU2_3	171:01 - 171:11

Individual video designations (clips) should be tracked so that you know which code to use to call them in your trial presentation software and what their page range is. It's very helpful to provide a project plan with clip identification references to the legal team so they can add the correct clip ID to their outline.

Moreover, you begin to create a potentially useful witness outline creation and QC workflow where team members (e.g., partner, associate, paralegal, trial tech, clerk) can review the witness outline and replace bad exhibit references, add clip IDs, and compare the deposition page ranges for accuracy.

11.1.2 Configure Your Laptop Screen to Remain On

Task 1. Navigate to the Windows Settings.

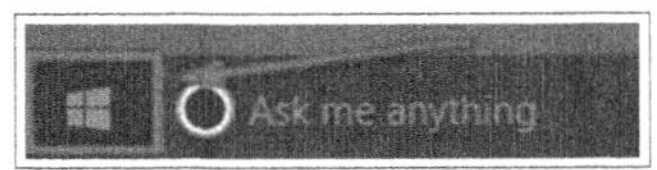

Click on the **Start** button for Windows. (In earlier versions of Windows, navigate to the **Control Panel**, select **System and Security**, then **Power Options**.)

Task 2. Locate the Settings button.

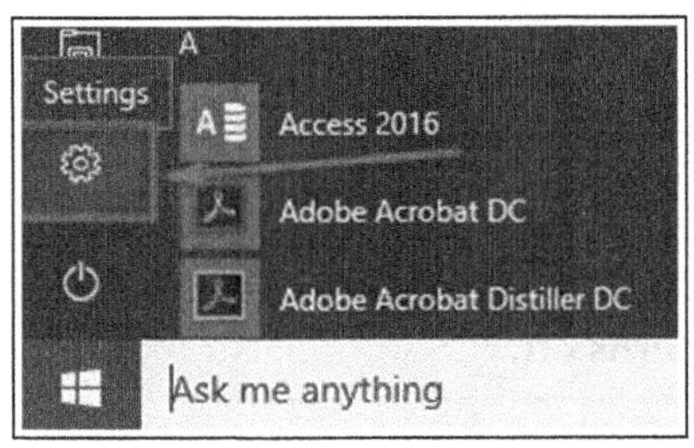

Select **Settings**. Its icon resembles a spoked wheel.

Task 3. Change your system settings.

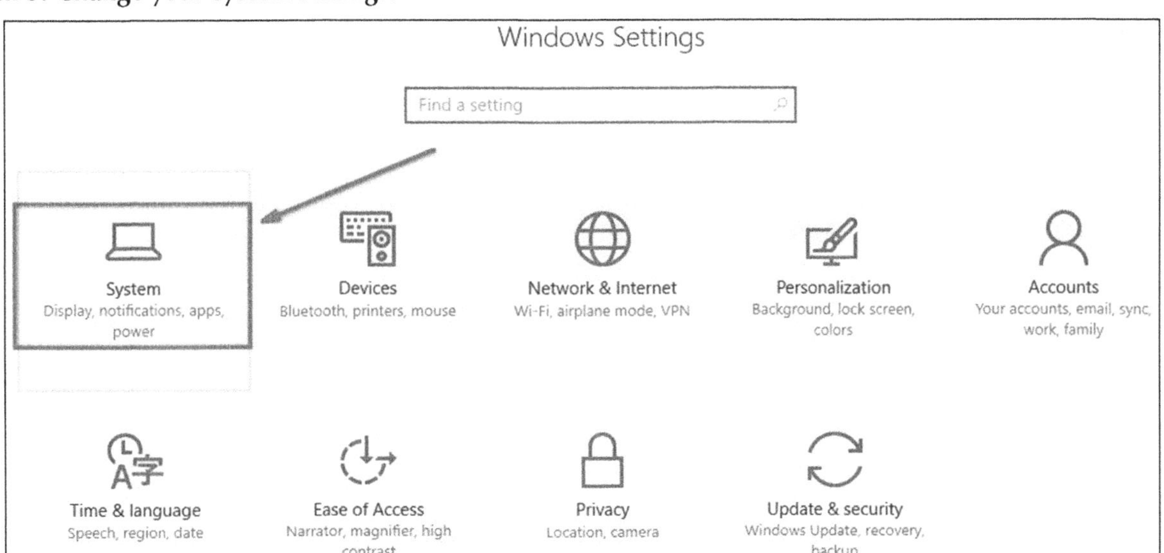

Select **System** in **Settings**.

Task 4. Change the Power and Sleep settings.

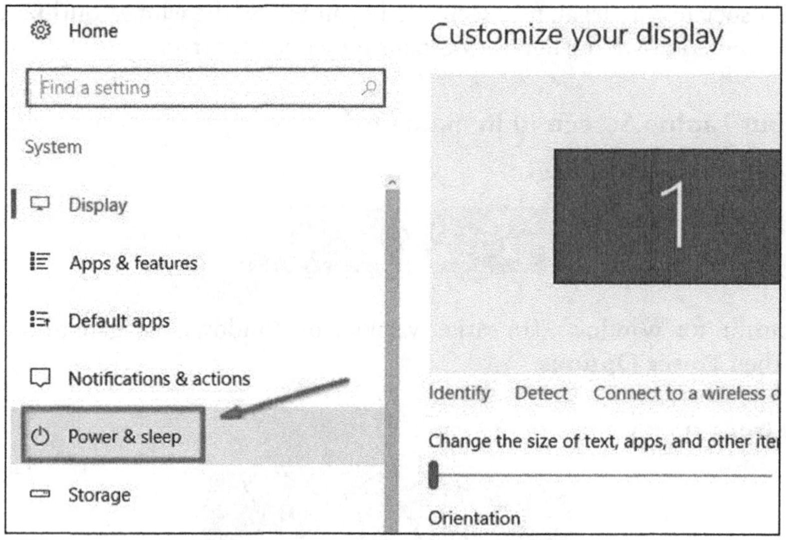

Select **Power & sleep**.

Task 5. Make sure the screen never turns off.

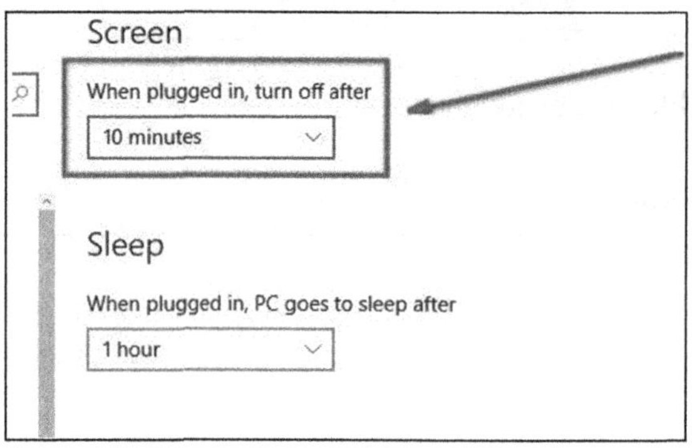

Click on **When plugged in, turn off after** in the dropdown menu, then select **Never**.

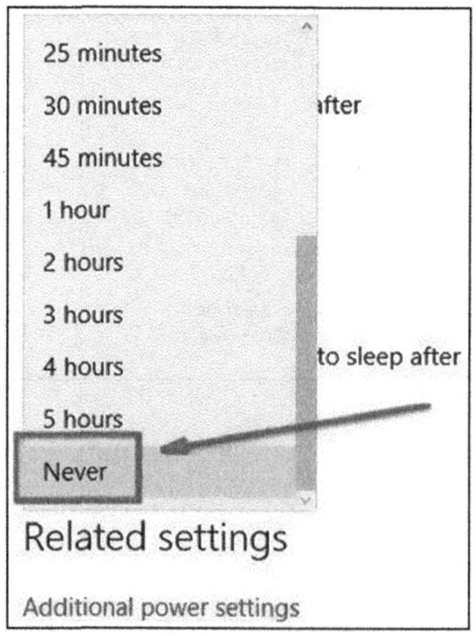

11.1.3 Configure Your Laptop Not to "Sleep"

Task 1. Navigate to the Windows Settings.

Click on the **Start** button for Windows. (In earlier versions of Windows, navigate to the **Control Panel**, select **System and Security**, then **Power Options**.)

Task 2. Locate the Settings button.

Select **Settings**. Its icon resembles a spoked wheel.

Task 3. Change your system settings.

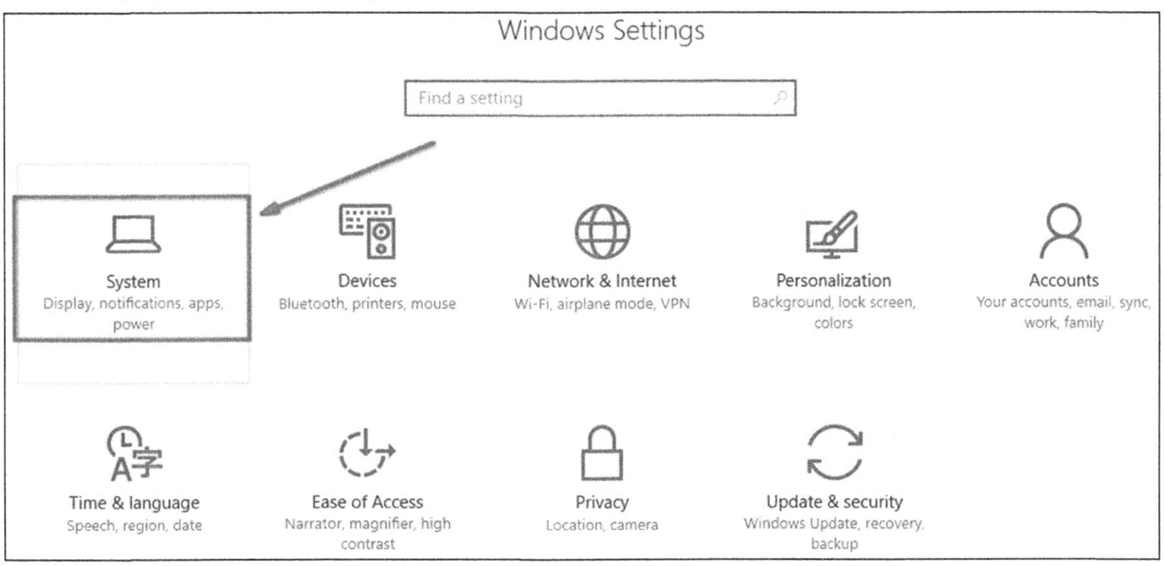

Select **System** in **Settings**.

Task 4. Change Power and Sleep settings.

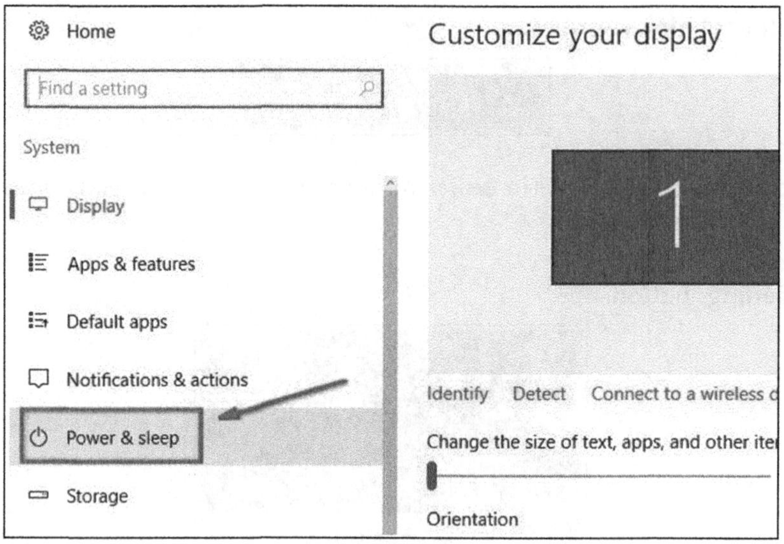

Select **Power & sleep**.

Task 5. Make sure the laptop never "goes to sleep."

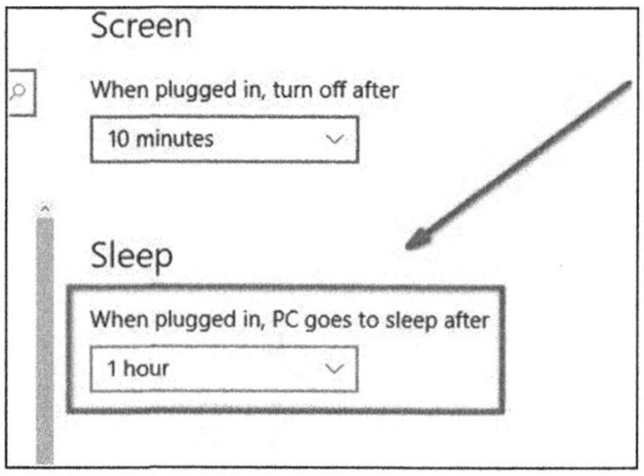

Click on **When plugged in, PC goes to sleep after** in the dropdown menu, then, select **Never**. When your laptop goes to sleep, it can cause many problems upon "waking up."

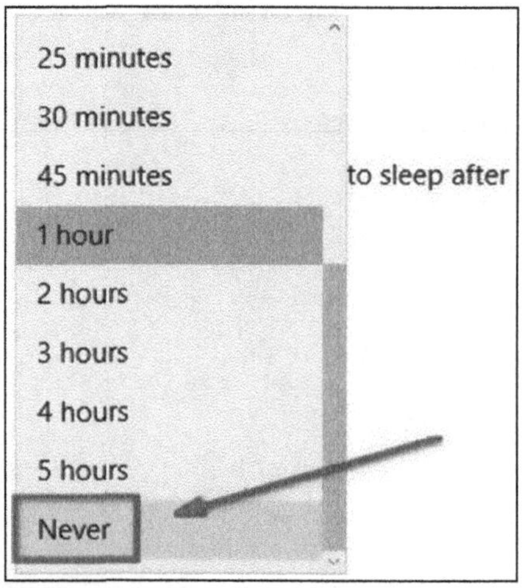

11.1.4 Configure "Additional Power Settings" for Increased Performance

Task 1. Navigate to the Windows Settings.

Click on the **Start** button for Windows. (In earlier versions of Windows, navigate to the **Control Panel**, select **System and Security**, then **Power Options**.)

Task 2. Locate the Settings button.

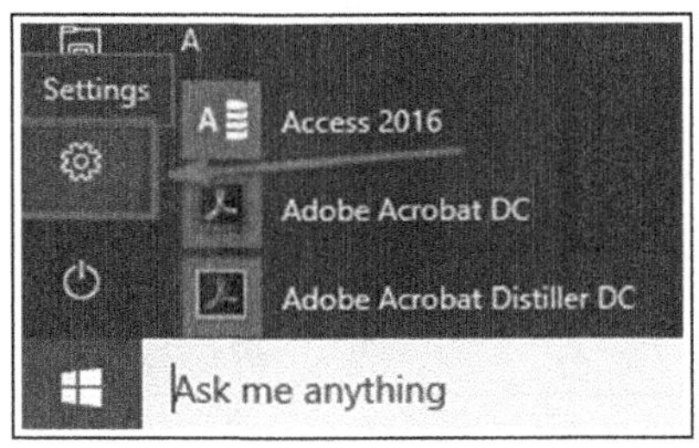

Select **Settings**. Its icon resembles a spoked wheel.

Task 3. Change your system settings.

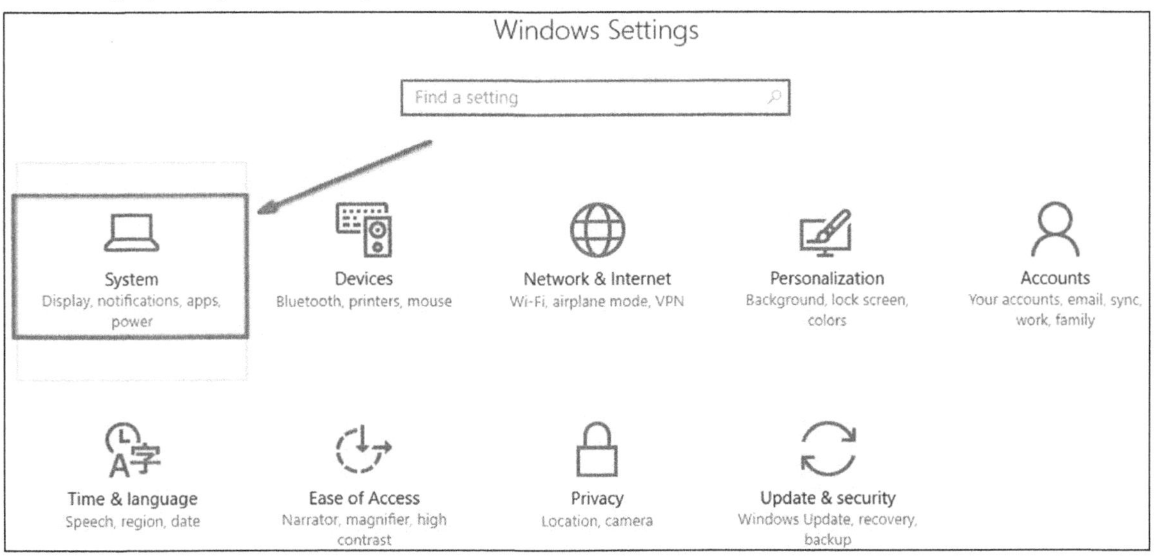

Select **System** in **Settings**.

Task 4. Change Power and Sleep settings.

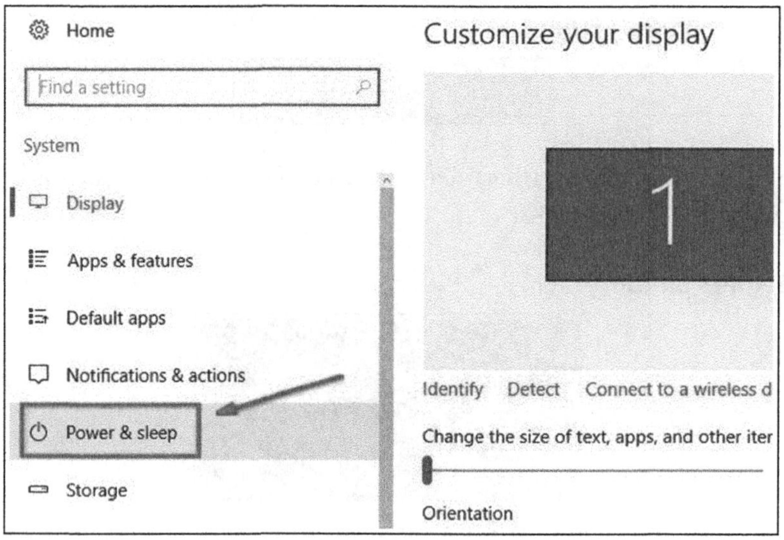

Select **Power & sleep**.

Task 5. Configure "Additional Power Settings" for increased courtroom performance.

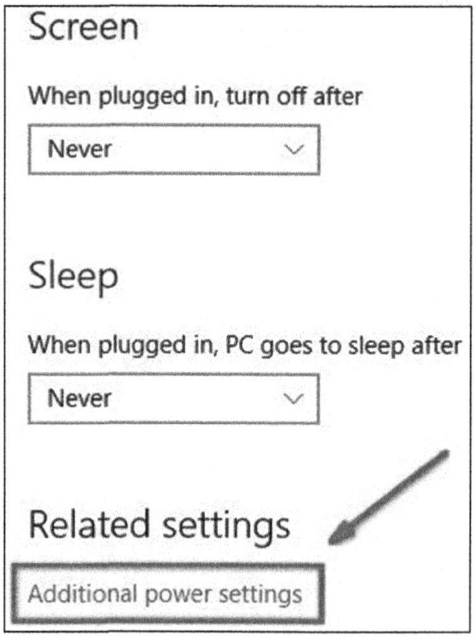

Select **Additional power settings**.

Task 6. Check for additional Power Plans to use the "High Performance" plan.

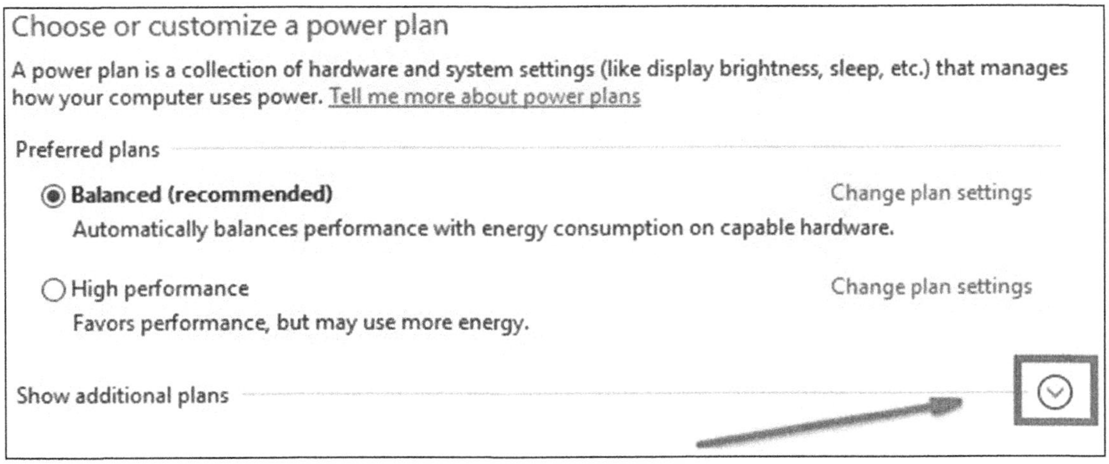

Select **Show additional plans** to customize a power plan.

Task 7. Make Your Laptop's Power Plan "High performance."

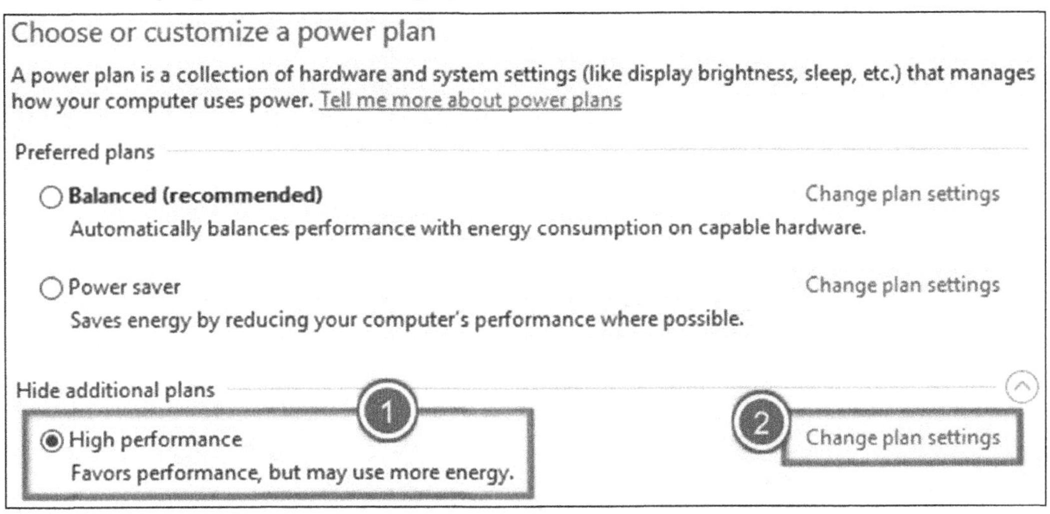

Select **High performance** > **Change plan settings**.

Task 8. Double-check that "High performance" is correctly configured.

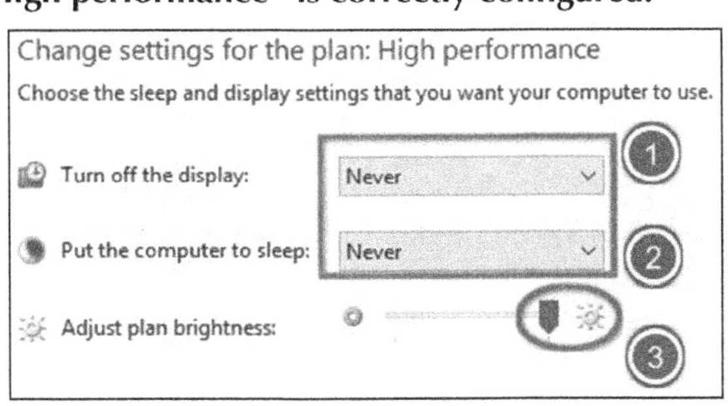

Ensure that **Turn off the display** and **Put the computer to sleep** are both set to **Never**. Slide **Adjust plan brightness** to the brightest setting.

11.1.5 Change the Background to Black

Task 1. Select Personalize to change your background color.

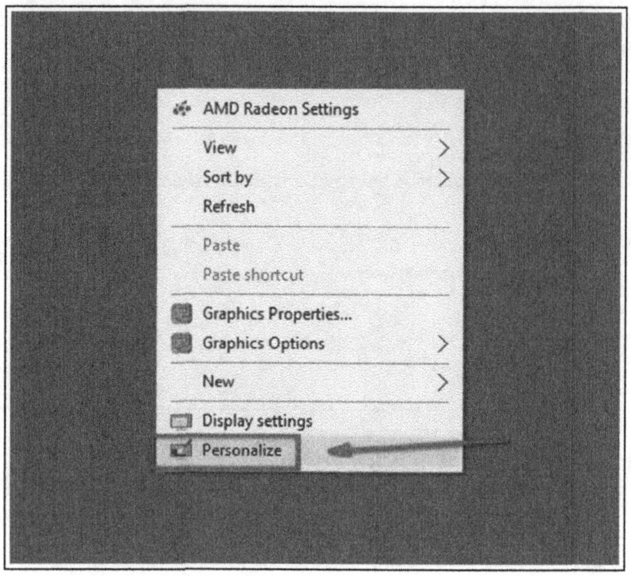

Right-click on the desktop and select **Personalize**.

Task 2. Change background color to black.

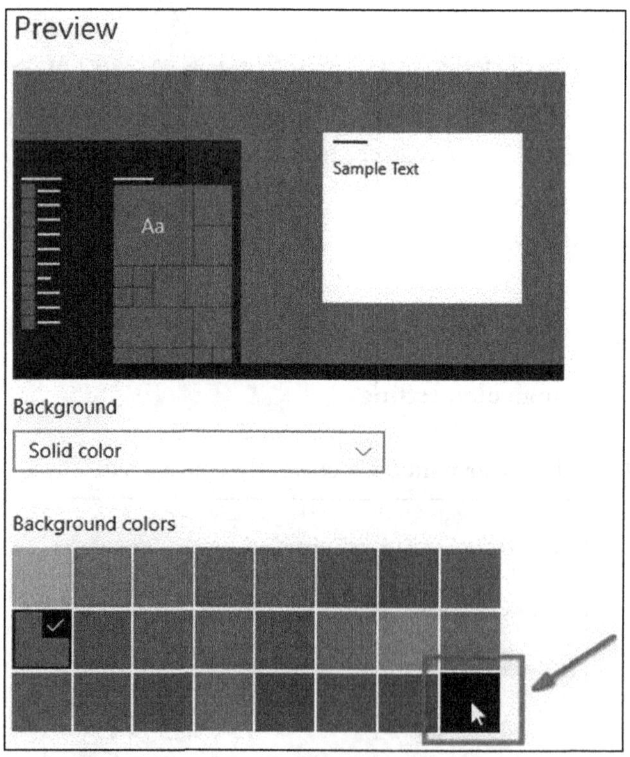

Select the black square in **Settings**. (Above, I'm changing from green to black.)

Changing the background to **black** ensures it blends in with your presentation options. This is a good color selection because black matches the default background color in presentation software.

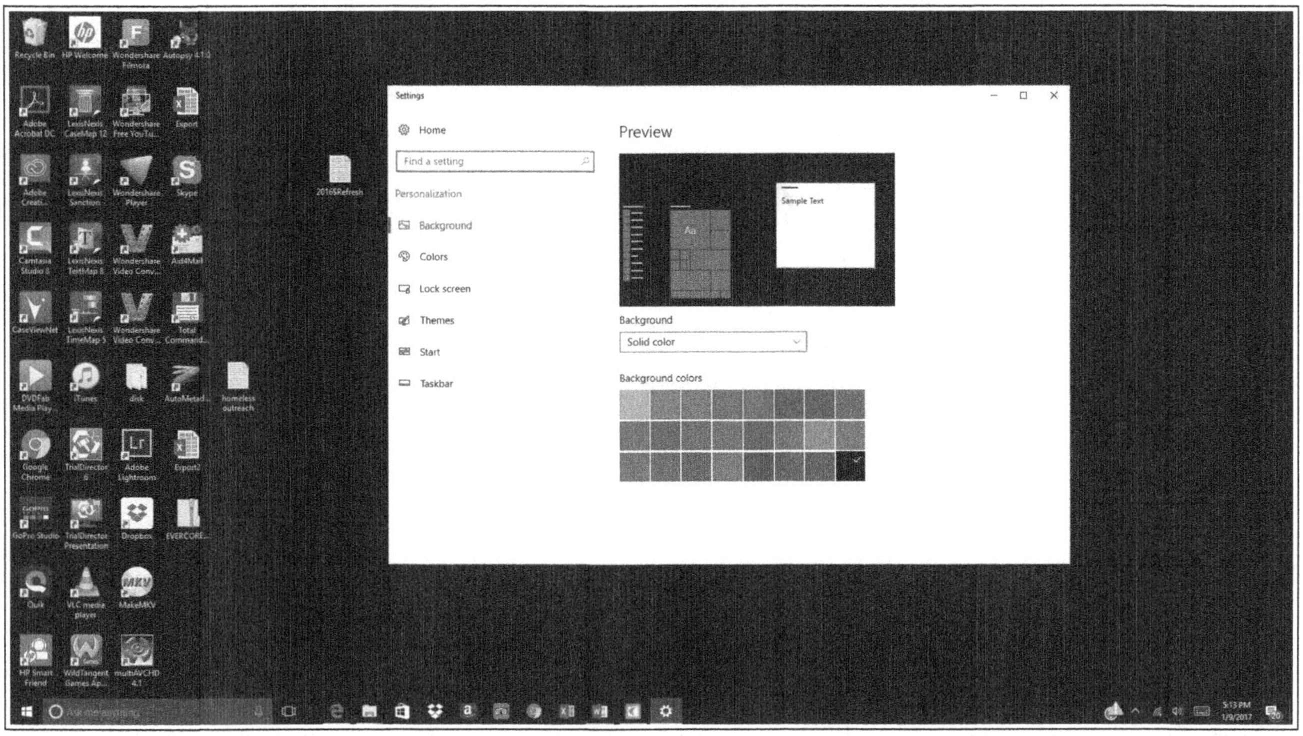

11.1.6 Configure Sound Settings

For trial, you don't want the beeps and boops of every click and action making a sound. (You'll be working on an exhibit, for example, while the other side is up, and having your sounds broadcast while doing so is unprofessional.) Imagine a very loud Windows startup sound being played through the court sound system when opposing counsel is up. (*Hint*: you don't look good if that happens.)

Task 1. Open your speaker/audio settings.

Right-click on the **Speaker** button in the bottom right of your screen. (This is the default location; it could be elsewhere on your desktop.) Choose **Sounds** from the dropdown menu.

Task 2. Deselect the Windows Default.

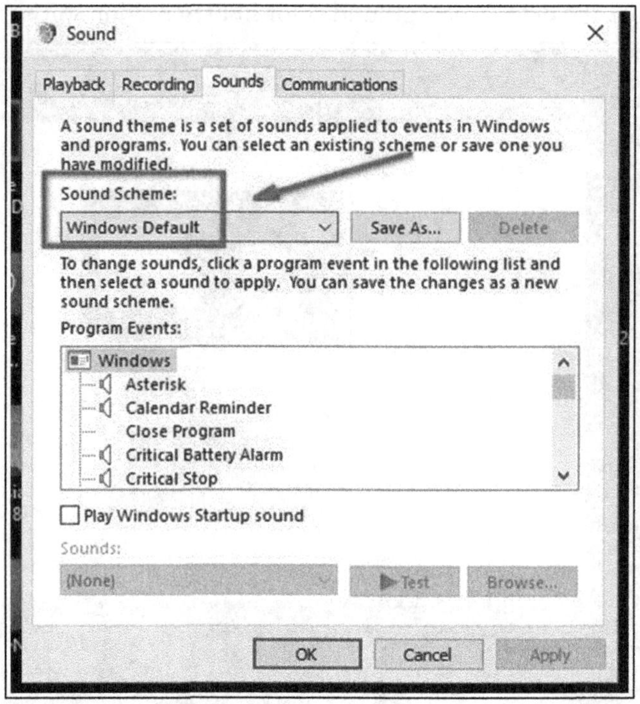

In the **Sounds** window, select **Sound Scheme** > **No Sounds** in the dropdown menu. This action deselects the factory preset called **Windows Default**.

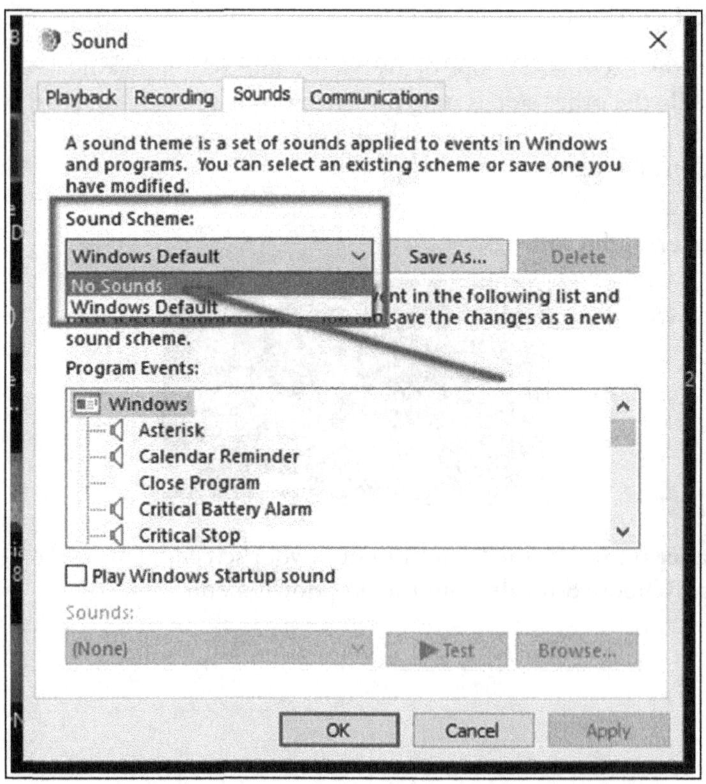

Task 3. Click OK.

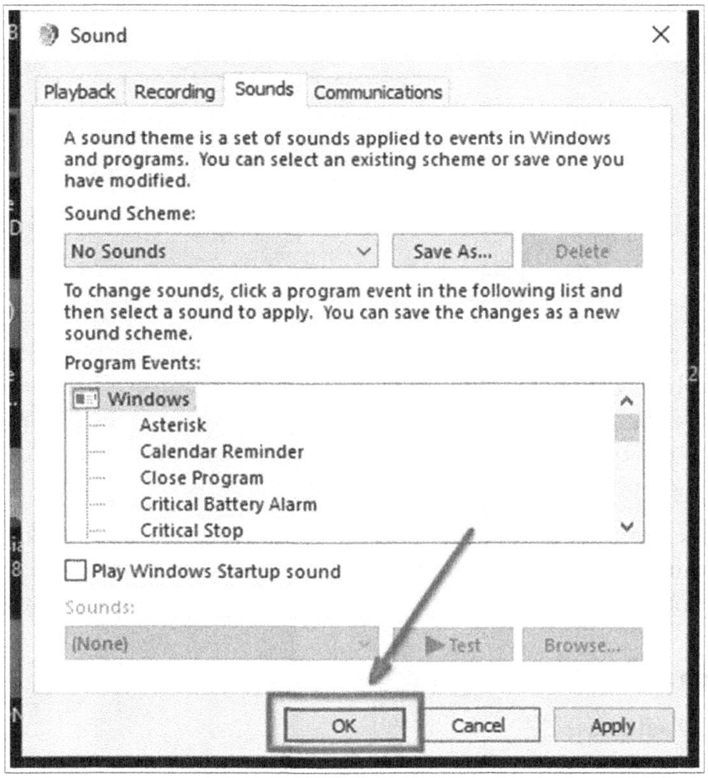

Click **OK** to apply your new settings.

11.2 Video Connection and Configuration

11.2.1 Connect to VGA or HDMI.

Task 1. Ensure your laptop is off.

Start with your laptop shut off. Trying to connect to VGA or HDMI while the laptop is "hot" (i.e., turned on) is a bad idea.

Task 2. Inspect the cable you need to connect to.

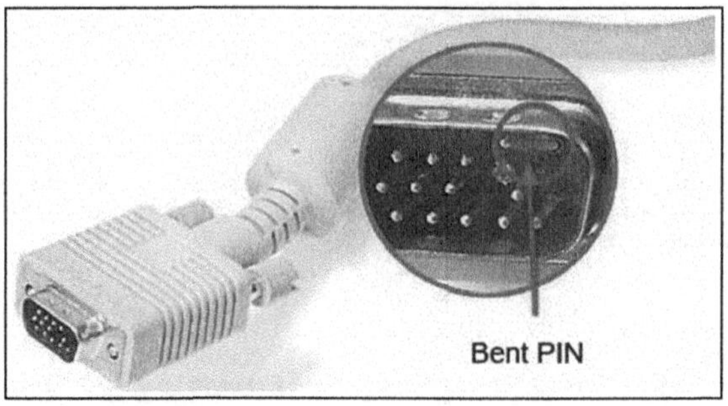

Inspect the video cable that will connect your laptop to the video source in the courtroom. If it is a VGA cable, ensure that its pins are not bent before you plug the cable into your laptop. If the pins are bent or broken, you need to replace the VGA cable because you can damage your laptop or smash the pins even more if you try to force the cable to connect. If it is an HDMI cable, as there are not pins that can break off but it can be broken as well. Always inspect what you plug into your computer before plugging it in.

If you get interference or colors that are off, there is likely a connection issue or the cable is being pinched somewhere. Maybe it's getting run over by a chair or a mobile device or other electronic equipment is interfering with it. Try not to lay cables on top of each other or across other electronic pieces of equipment.

11.2.2 Change the Laptop Resolution

Task 1. Open the Display settings.

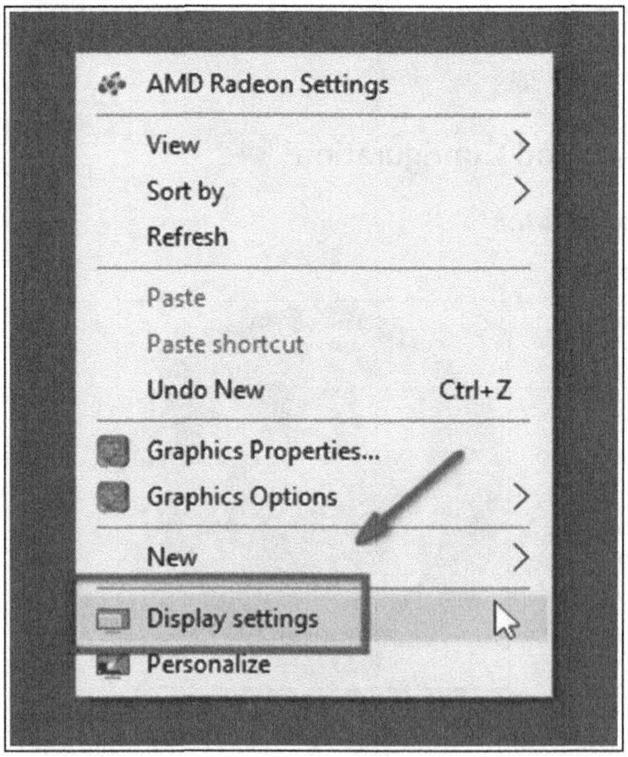

Right-click anywhere on your desktop and select **Display settings** > **Advanced display settings**.

Many computers have additional or proprietary software to change the resolution and graphics properties that circumvents Windows settings. This is often made by graphic card and computer manufacturers as an easy way to change settings. If you have such software, check the manufacturer's instructions to ensure that you know how to use it and whether the software circumvents Windows.

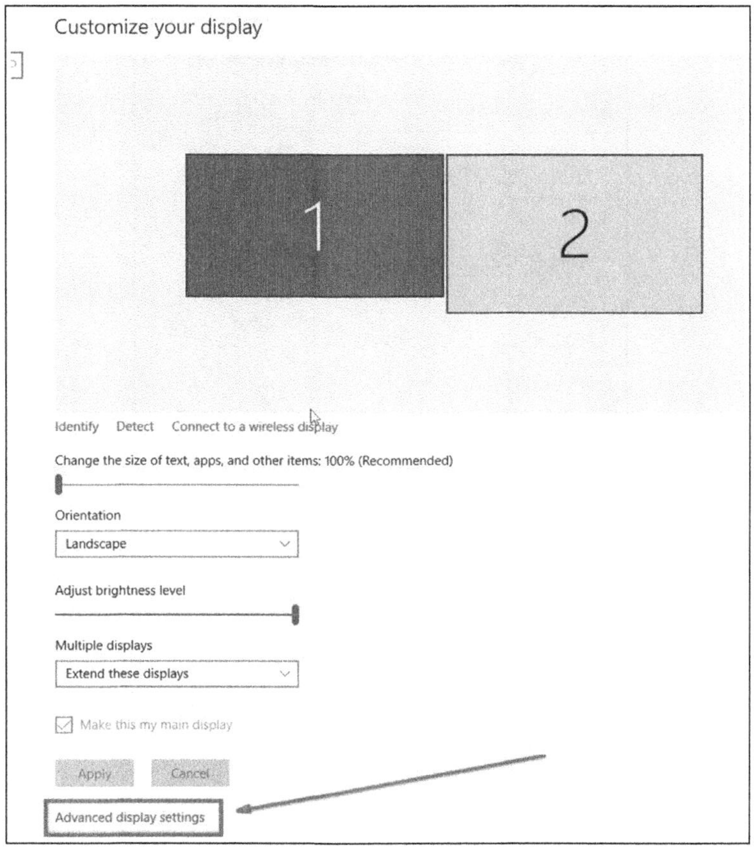

Task 2. Adjust the resolution of your display.

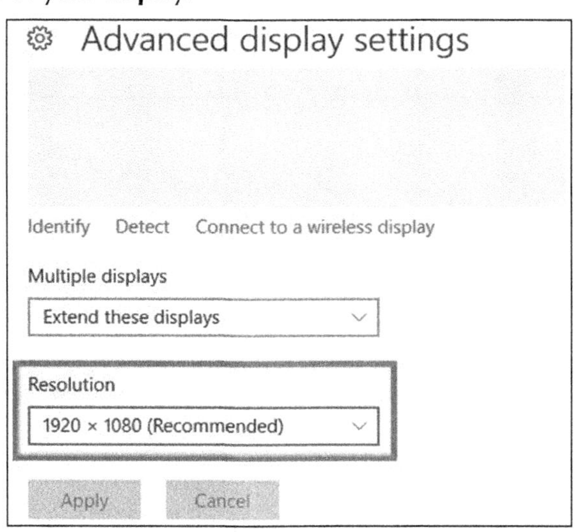

Click on the **Resolution** dropdown menu.

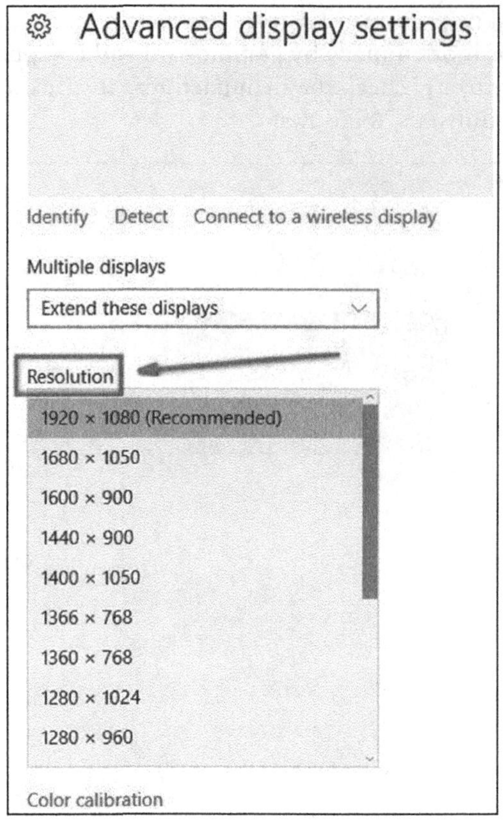

You will see there are many different display settings. Search for the setting that matches the resolution of the monitors in your courtroom. If your laptop does not have the resolution that matches that of the courtroom equipment, choose a resolution that is in the same "shape" (either 4:3 "square" or 16:9 "rectangle") as the screens in the courtroom. Test until you find one that works. Sometimes you can "bump" up the resolution, but you'll only know if you test in advance.

Task 3. Consider 4:3 and 16:9 aspect ratios.

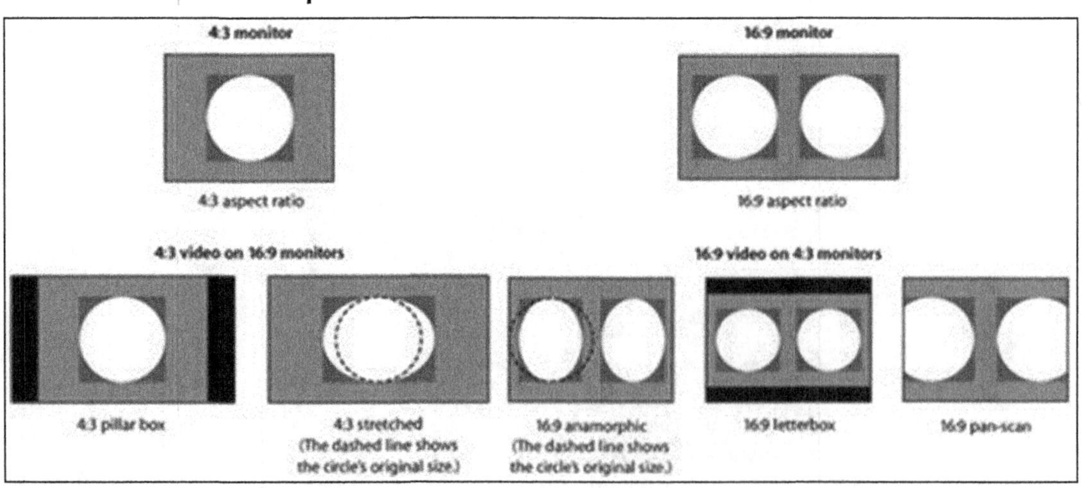

Consider the many issues that can occur if you choose the wrong aspect ratio and resolution. Your exhibit images and video could be stretched, shrunk, or distorted—and sometimes the mismatch can cause problems with your equipment as well. You could also spend a lot of time making a presentation that simply won't look good in the courtroom. None of this is good for consistent and quality display of exhibits.

Below are common resolutions and their associated aspect ratio. Use the information below to select the right resolution for your presentation needs.

4:3 aspect ratio resolutions: 640×480, 800×600, 960×720, 1024×768, 1280×960, 1400×1050, 1440×1080 , 1600×1200, 1856×1392, 1920×1440, and 2048×1536.

16:9 aspect ratio resolutions: 1024×576, 1152×648, 1280×720, 1366×768, 1600×900, 1920×1080, 2560×1440 and 3840×2160.

Task 4. Change your resolution, if necessary.

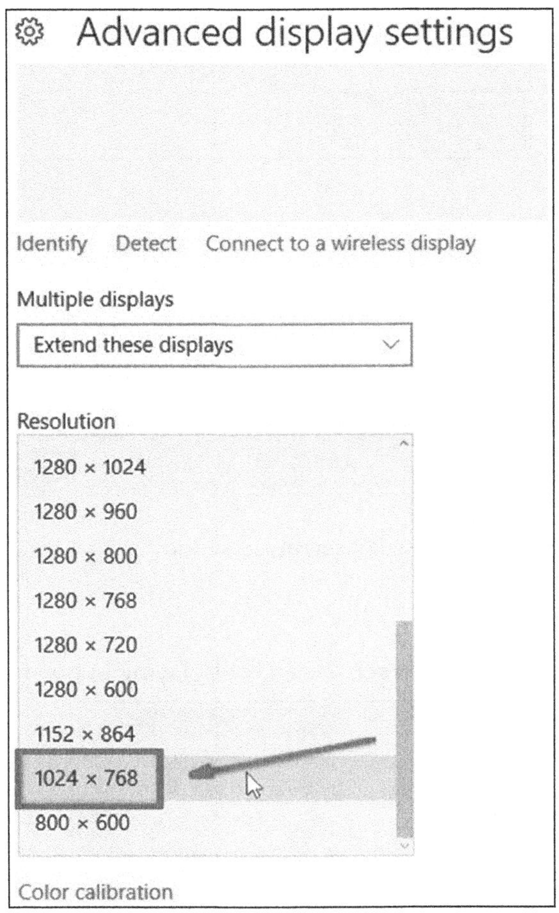

Click on **1024 × 768**. This is the resolution that most courtrooms use, but the concept would be the same no matter what resolution you need to work in. You should know in advance the resolution and shape of screens so you can optimize your presentation.

Task 5. Apply the resolution you have chosen.

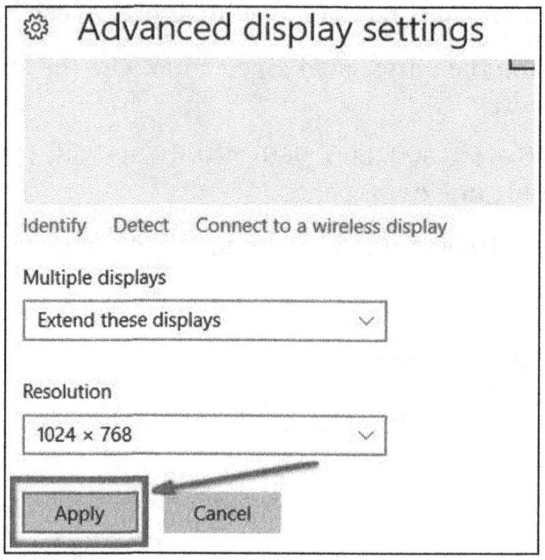

Click **Apply** to save your settings.

Task 6. Confirm your changes.

Select **Keep changes** in the **Keep these display settings?** window.

11.2.3 Identify Monitors

Task 1. Identify monitors to ensure the correct screen is displaying in open court.

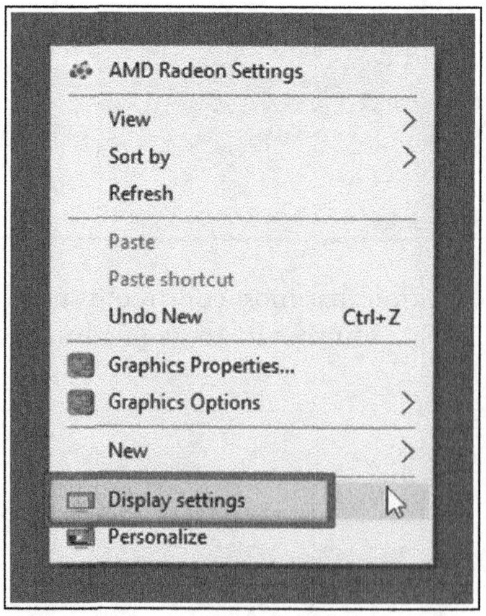

Right-click anywhere on your desktop and select **Display settings**.

Task 2. Identifying the correct screens.

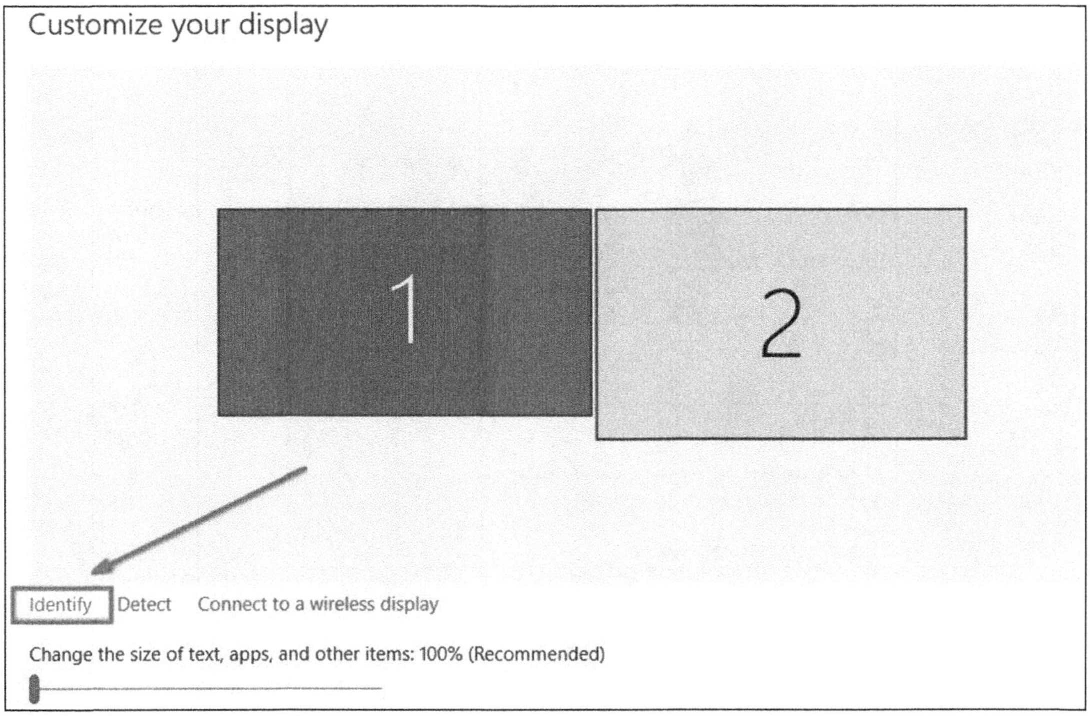

Click **Settings** > **Identify**. The number associated with your screen will flash on all the screens connected. First, ensure that the right screen is showing in court (did you intend screen 1 or 2 to show in open court?) and second, ensure that your duplicate or second screen is displaying correctly on all available monitors.

11.2.4 Extend the Desktop

Task 1. Open Display settings.

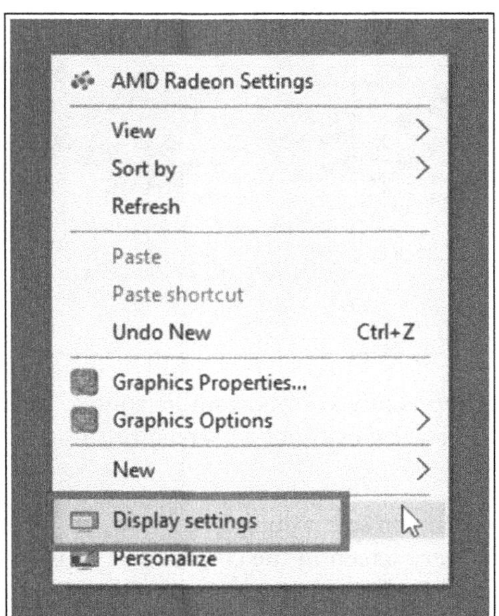

Right-click anywhere on your desktop and select **Display settings**.

Task 2. Select multiple displays to Choose To Duplicate or Extend Your Screen.

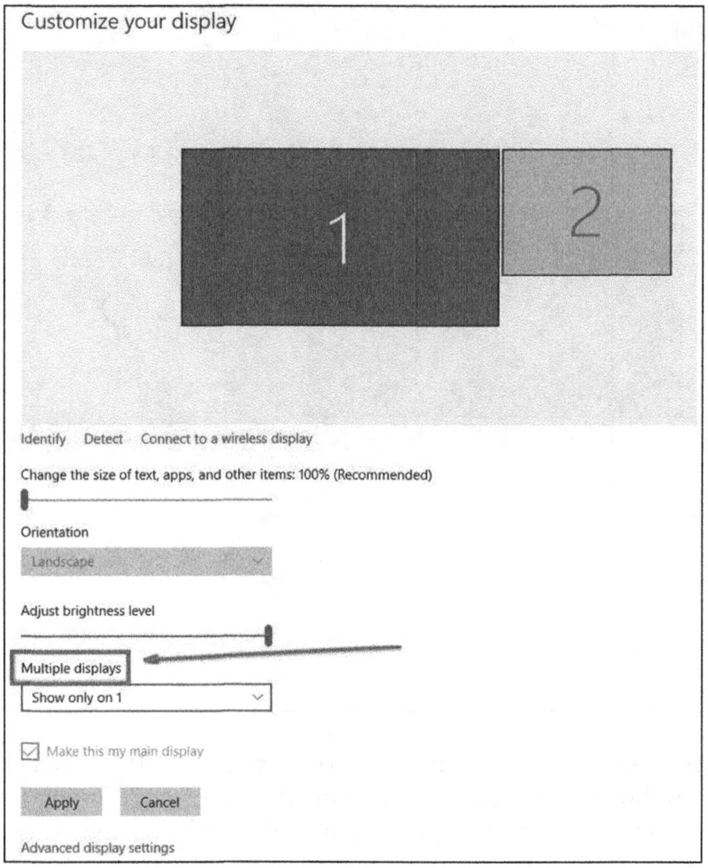

Open the **Multiple displays** dropdown menu.

Task 3. Choose duplicate displays or extended displays.

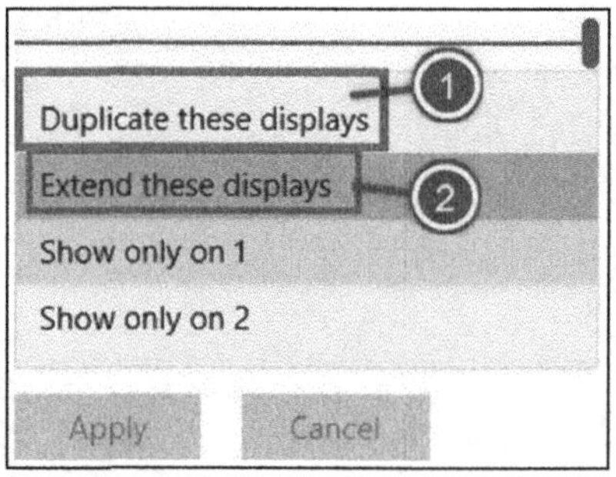

Your technical ability with your laptop is just as important as your software knowledge. Time and again, legal teams go into court knowing how to put a few exhibits on screen but not knowing how to extend the desktop or adjust their resolution—and they blow it.

If you are a beginner, I recommend that you select duplicate displays (Choice 1) so that everything on the screen in front of you is what is displayed on every screen in the courtroom. This works well when you have a limited set of exhibits and video. As your technical needs become more complex, so do the skills necessary to present. The courtroom is not the place to experiment with your technical ability (or lack thereof). It is extremely important that presenters stay within their technical ability with both equipment and software. Recognizing that you may need more training or a consultant might be the best thing you ever did for your trial.

If you are comfortable working on multiple monitors, you can choose **Extend these displays** (Choice 2). Extending the desktop allows you to only show one of your screens in the courtroom (the "extended" screen) so that you can concurrently work and create content on the other. The extended desktop is the optimal way to present in the courtroom, so it's worth your time and effort to learn how to properly configure your laptop.

Note: When you extend the screen in Windows, you may also need to configure your trial presentation software or PowerPoint to take advantage of the extended desktop. This, of course, should always be tested daily when you enter the courtroom to ensure the right screen is showing up in the right place.

11.2.5 QC the Display

Task 1. Download a screen test.

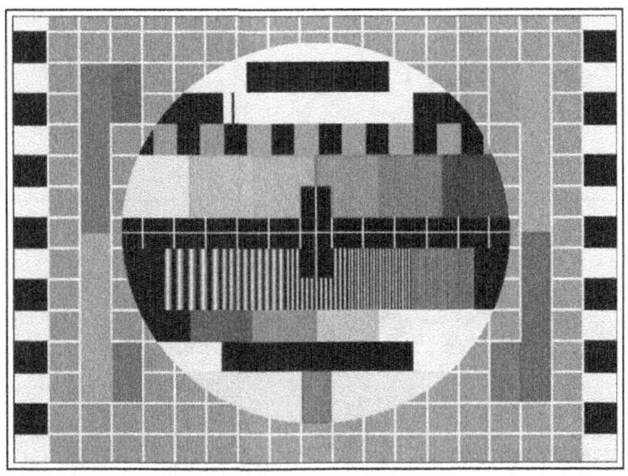

Above is an image of a screen test image that can be found in a quick online search (search term "television test pattern," or see the Notes on Use to access images available as a free download). This one is for a 4:3 monitor. There are similar screen tests for 16:9.

It is a good idea to download and save the image to your laptop so you can test whether your laptop image is displaying correctly and that it is centered on the monitors and screens in the courtroom. (For example, projectors often get out of alignment with the screen. People bump into them, the cleaning crew moves them . . . the daily startup and takedown affect courtroom equipment.) I typically add an image such as this to my trial presentation database to test daily in the courtroom. But you can also just have a stand-alone test image that you click to open and drag to the appropriate display.

Task 2. Perform the screen check.

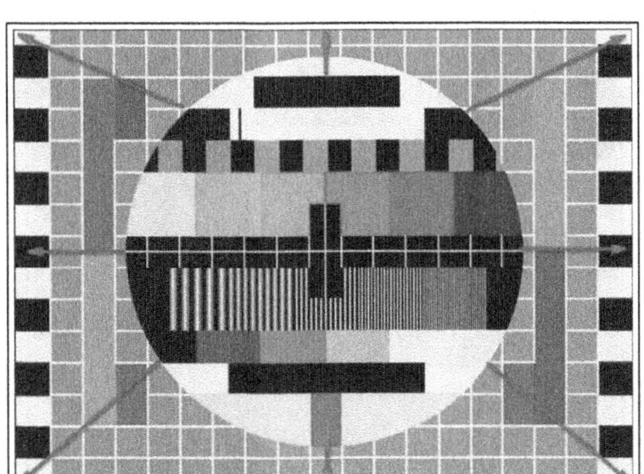

First thing is to check to see *on every monitor and screen* in the courtroom that the four corners, top, bottom, and sides fit on the screen. This is testing the alignment of the screen to ensure that external monitors match your monitor. It is not unusual for them to be off. If they are off-center, you must individually configure each monitor and screen in the courtroom. Remember, the image can be off top to bottom or left to right.

You'll want to determine if there is any question that the fonts you are using in your presentations are too small or the equipment rented not big enough. Put up an image that has the same fonts, point size, and colors as your opening PowerPoint to determine if your presentation or equipment selection ought to be adjusted.

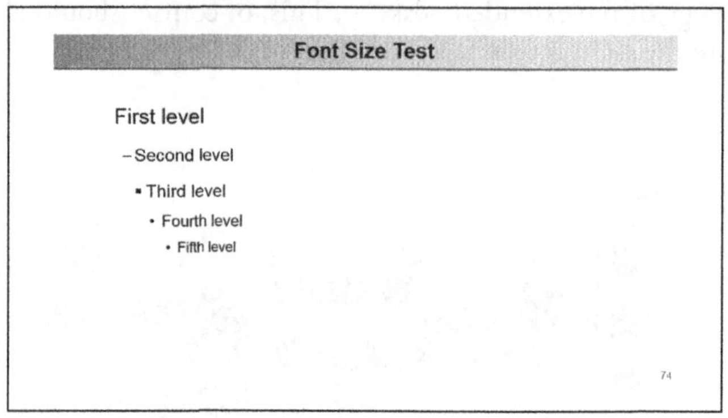

Task 3. Check the colors.

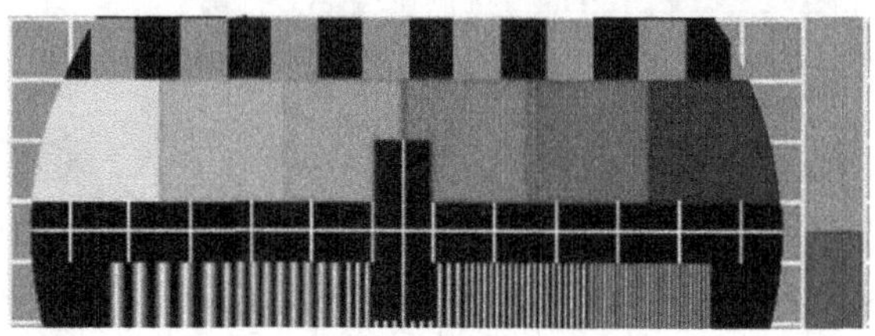

The next step is to check to ensure *on every monitor and screen* in the courtroom that the color is accurate. Some kinds of DLP (digital light processing) projectors do not project the color yellow well, and it looks brown on screen. Unless the court is willing to let you replace the projector, you should consider using colors other than yellow to do your highlighting, colors such as green or orange. (This touch will also differentiate your team from opposing counsel.)

Note: Consider using a large screen monitor (60+ inches) instead of a projector to display exhibits in the courtroom. The color, resolution, brightness, and legibility are often much better than that of a projector.

11.2.6 Configure Aspect Ratio

Task 1. Configure aspect ratio for 16:9 or 4:3.

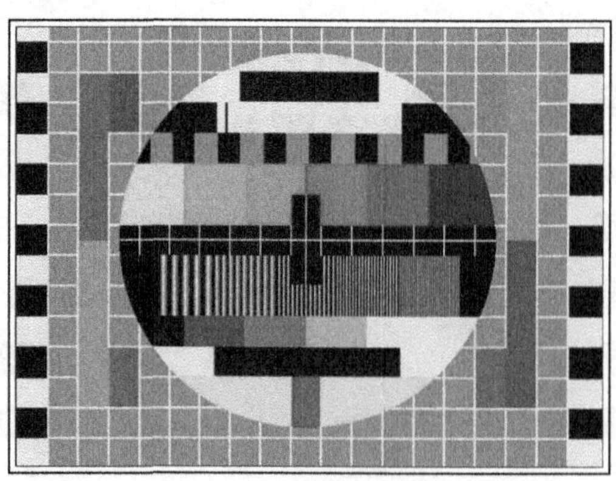

There are two widely used aspect ratios for computer screens, monitors, and projectors—16:9 and 4:3. Problems occur when there is a mixed environment of monitors, so you'll want to configure them all to be the same aspect ratio (unless it can be independently configured within Windows or on the monitor itself—and that is often too much trouble). For our purposes, 4:3 is "square" and 16:9 is a "rectangle."

Usually, these problems occur when the courtroom has 4:3 monitors for the judge, witness, and counsel tables, but a large 16:9 monitor for the jurors or courtroom audience. You should try to set up the large 16:9 monitor to 4:3 rather than configuring multiple monitors in the courtroom. Also, 16:9 is largely lost in the legal context, in that the extra real estate isn't typically used in deposition video (we are usually focused center-screen on the deponent). However, it does provide a bit more real estate for callouts. It is sometimes helpful if you retain all the remote controls for courtroom equipment so if it reverts to the wrong aspect ratio, you can fix it without having to approach the monitor.

Task 2. Note the effect of mixed aspect ratios.

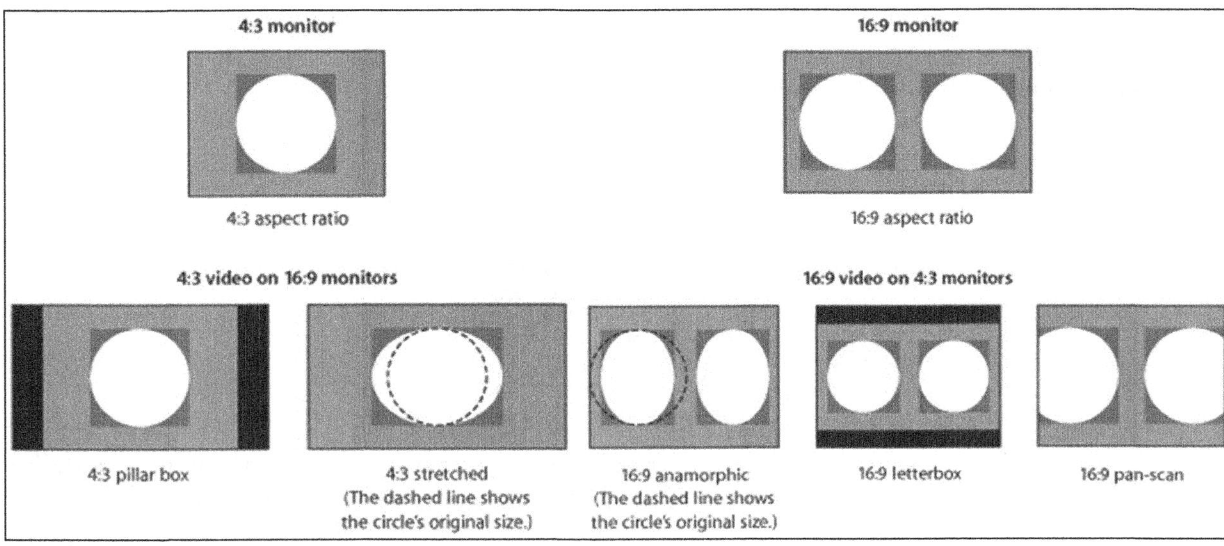

Mixed aspect ratios will stretch, squeeze, and otherwise distort your pages on screen. Proper display configuration is necessary and be time consuming. Plan ahead in mixed environments with two aspect ratios.

11.3 Establish a Routine

Task 1. Make sure your laptop is off.

Start with your laptop switched off. Trying to connect while the laptop is hot (i.e., turned on) is a bad idea. Try to run through the following steps simultaneously on both laptops (primary and backup).

Task 2. Plug in peripherals while your laptop is off.

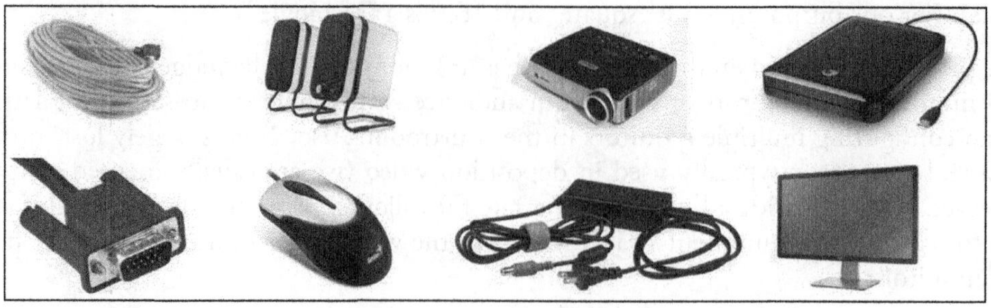

Before you start your laptop, plug in all peripherals in the same order and into the same port—*every time.* Trying to diagnose a drive letter that inadvertently gets reassigned five minutes before court starts is no fun.

Task 3. Inspect the cables to which you are connecting your laptop.

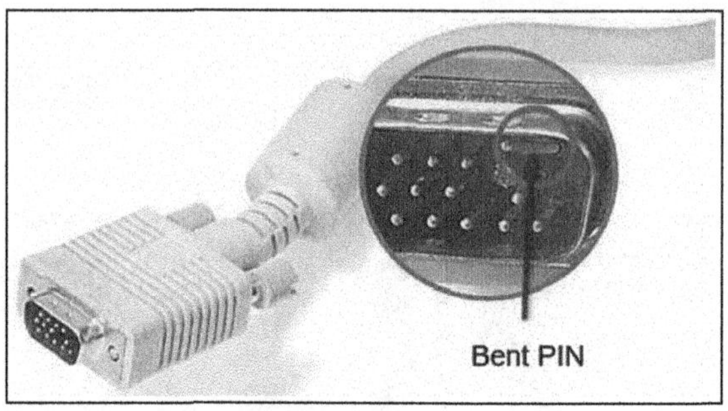

Inspect the VGA cable to ensure the pins are not bent before you insert it into your laptop or other device. If it is an HDMI cable, there are not pins that can break off but you should inspect it to ensure it works correctly. If the pins are bent or broken, replace the VGA cable; you can damage your own laptop or smash the pins even more if you are trying to force the connection. If you get interference or colors that are off, there is likely a connection issue or pinch in your cabling. Plug in the cable firmly (and if it has screws, tighten them) for a good connection. Inspect video cables to make sure they have not been run over by a chair, vacuum, etc.

I once had a problem with interference on all of the courtroom monitors. I inspected the cables, VGA pins, and connections, but nothing seemed to help in this randomly occurring issue. Then one day in court, I saw an attorney lean back in his chair and the screens displayed the interference. I realized that every time the attorney would lean back in the chair, the chair would slightly roll backwards and run over a video cable, pinching it and causing the interference. We replaced the damaged cables and rerouted the new ones, and slightly repositioned the chair a bit. Yet another reason to have extra video cables on hand whenever you present.

Task 4. Turn your laptop on.

When all peripherals are connected, turn on your laptop.

Task 5. Start applications to be used in court *one at a time*.

1, 2, 3, 4....

Wait until the laptop is completely booted up and logged in and then start any applications one at a time (typically, your trial software and PowerPoint). By starting applications one at a time and letting them *fully open*, you ensure that they start correctly and will not crash. *Be calm and patient—there's no shortcut to starting your equipment correctly*. At trial, people often get in too big a hurry and it can lead to application and system crashes. Last, open only the bare minimum of applications necessary for your presentation needs. You want your presentation laptop to be a high-performance, lean, mean fighting machine. All applications utilize computer resources, like memory and CPU, and there is no way to ensure that the memory or resources are released—even if you close them.

Task 6. Perform QC on the trial software and database.

In your trial presentation software, are files present and linked? Are your files coming up in the preview/working screen when you click files? Does a test image in presentation mode present correctly? What about a test video clip? How are the volume levels? Does everything look correct? The goal is to see that the trial presentation software started correctly and that files appear to be linked.

Task 7. Select your resolution.

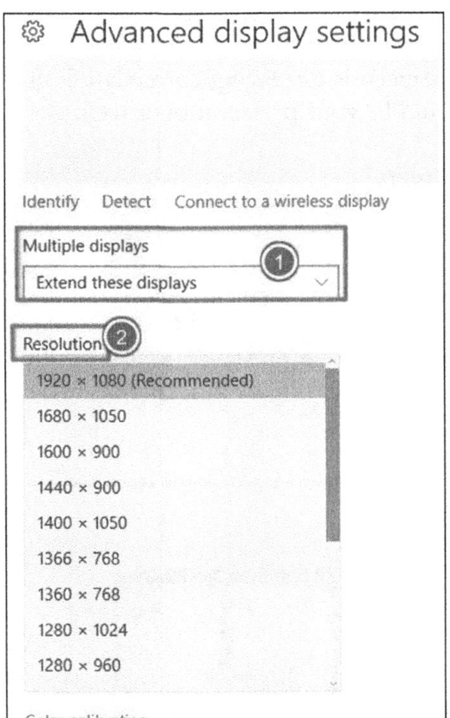

(1) Choose to extend the desktop or use mirror mode, then (2) select the correct resolution.

Task 8. Identify your screens.

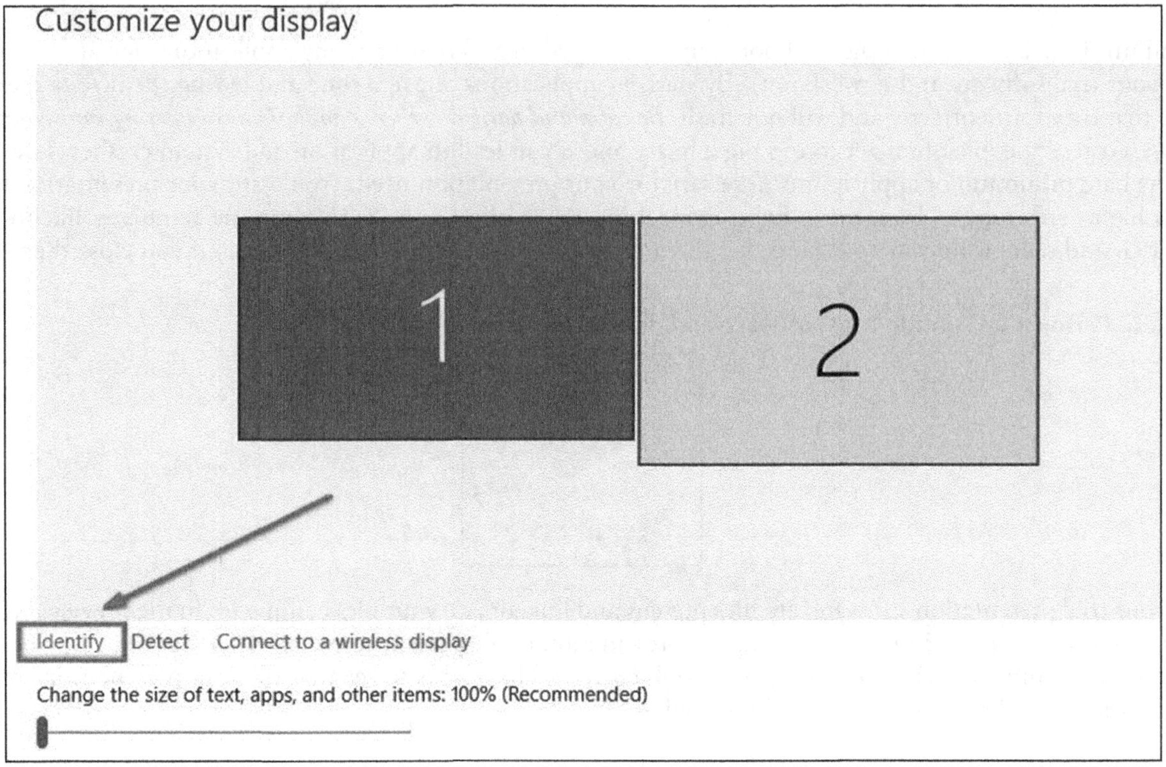

Click **Identify** in **Settings**. The number associated with your screen will flash on all the screens connected. First, ensure that the right screen is showing in court (did you intend screen 1 or 2 to show in open court?) and second, ensure that your duplicated or second screen is displaying correctly on all available monitors. Screen 1 should be your working screen, and screen 2 should be your presentation screen.

Task 9. Check your presentation screen.

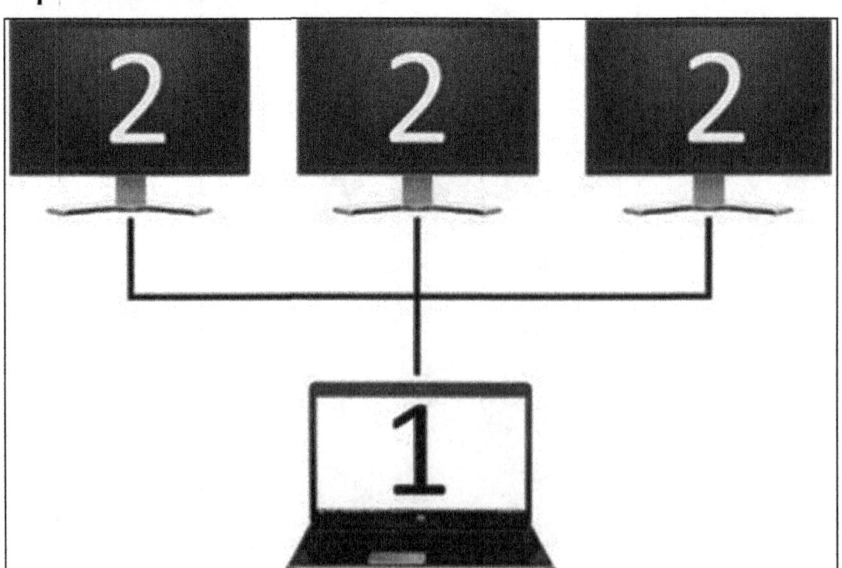

If in extended desktop mode, check that screen 2 is displaying on all courtroom monitors.

Task 10. Check the switch.

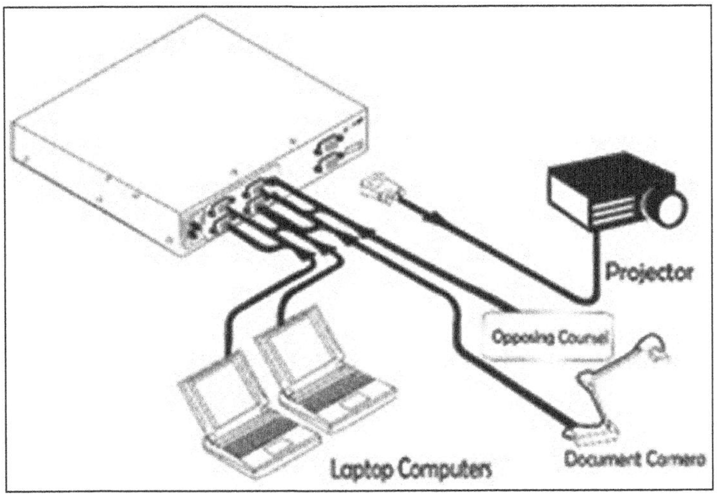

Once monitors are extended and displays are show on screens 1 and 2, check the switch. Cycle through each switch number to ensure it connects and displays correctly. Signs of trouble are if the switch has a noticeable delay or must be reconfigured each time. I keep a sticky note on the switch that correlates the equipment being used and the switch number, and I always place opposing counsel on the last number of the switch to put some distance between my equipment and theirs in case of "fat-finger" (i.e., mistaken button pushing).

Task 11. Check screen corners.

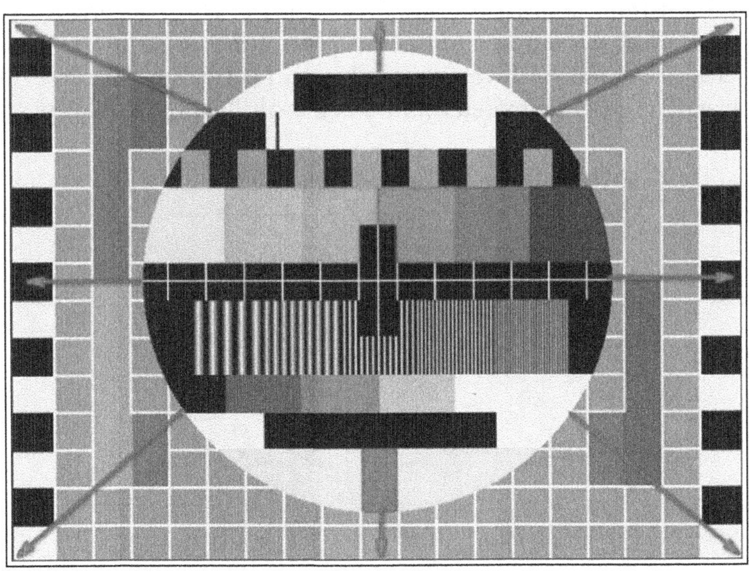

On *every monitor and screen* in the courtroom, ensure that the four corners, top, bottom, and sides fit on the screen. This tests the alignment of the screen to ensure that external monitors match your own. It's not unusual for them to be configured incorrectly. If they are off-center, individually configure each monitor and screen in the courtroom using the screen controls on the monitor. Sometimes, however, you just have to deal with bad equipment and adjust your presentation strategy accordingly. For example, we changed our opening statement at trial once because upon testing it was apparent that the court equipment was configured wrong and there was nothing we could do about it.

Task 12. Check colors.

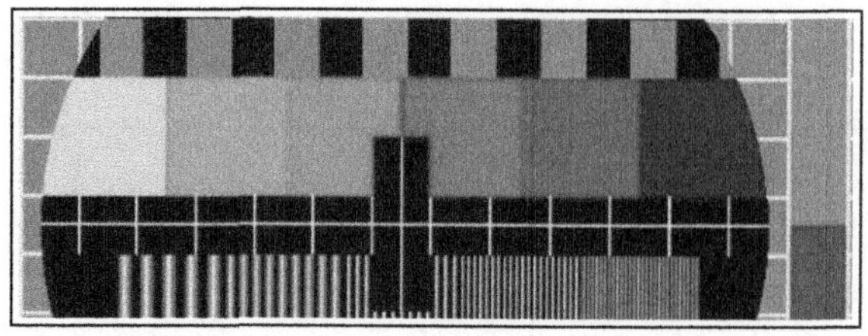

The next item is to check to see on *every screen and monitor* in the courtroom that the color is accurate. Some kinds of DLP projectors project yellow as brown on screen. Unless the court is willing to let you replace the projector, you may want to look at alternative colors for highlighting, like green or orange. (P.S. It also differentiates your presentation from opposing counsel's.)

Task 13. QC a trial presentation exhibit on courtroom displays.

Place on screen a test exhibit from the trial presentation database. Use a generic image. *Do not* use an exhibit that has not been admitted, and *do not* test in front of the jury. If the judge and/or jury are present, have a test image you can flash on screen that's uncontroversial—perhaps a DMV form, the test images depicted above, or some other public document. The goals are to determine whether the exhibits will display and are linked correctly.

Task 14. QC a trial presentation video on courtroom displays.

Place on screen a test video from the trial presentation database. Use a generic video. *Do not* use a video that has not been admitted, and *do not* test in front of the jury. If the judge and/or jury are present, have a test video you can flash on screen (nothing controversial). The goals are to ensure your video plays correctly and looks and sounds as expected.

Task 15. QC the trial presentation sound on the courtroom speakers.

Play a test sound from the trial presentation database. Use a generic sound or .wav file. The goals are to play a brief sound to determine if the sound levels are OK and make necessary adjustments.

Task 16. If there is a problem . . .

Restart your laptop and go through the process again. Check to see if file path or folder names have been changed which would result in breaking the link between exhibit image and database. For example, if a folder named "exhibit" was changed to "exhibit(s)" it would break the file path link from exhibits to trial presentation database (*Note*: Some trial presentation software does not operate via a link and instead converts your exhibits internally.) If both laptops are bad due to, say, a virus or some problematic update, then it's time to look at your backup media or perhaps an older, backed-up version of your trial database. Worst-case scenario: take a backup set of PDF files and use Acrobat to present on a working laptop. (Of course, the document camera would work as well.)

Task 17. Check peripheral equipment.

Check all attached peripheral equipment, like the document camera, soundboard, microphones, VCR, or DVD player.

Task 18. Is opposing counsel ready?

Ask the opposing counsel tech if the team is ready.

Task 19. Ready!

Once you and your setup are ready to go, let the court and your team know. Remember, getting your system up and ready to go is your highest priority. Plan to arrive in the courtroom earlier than the rest of the legal team so you can get started. Being five minutes earlier than the rest of the legal team might be just the amount of time you need to troubleshoot and fix a problem.

Chapter Twelve

A Primer on Exhibits

12.1 Adobe Acrobat Pro Basics

12.1.1 Find and Add Tools

Task 1. Find the right tool for the job

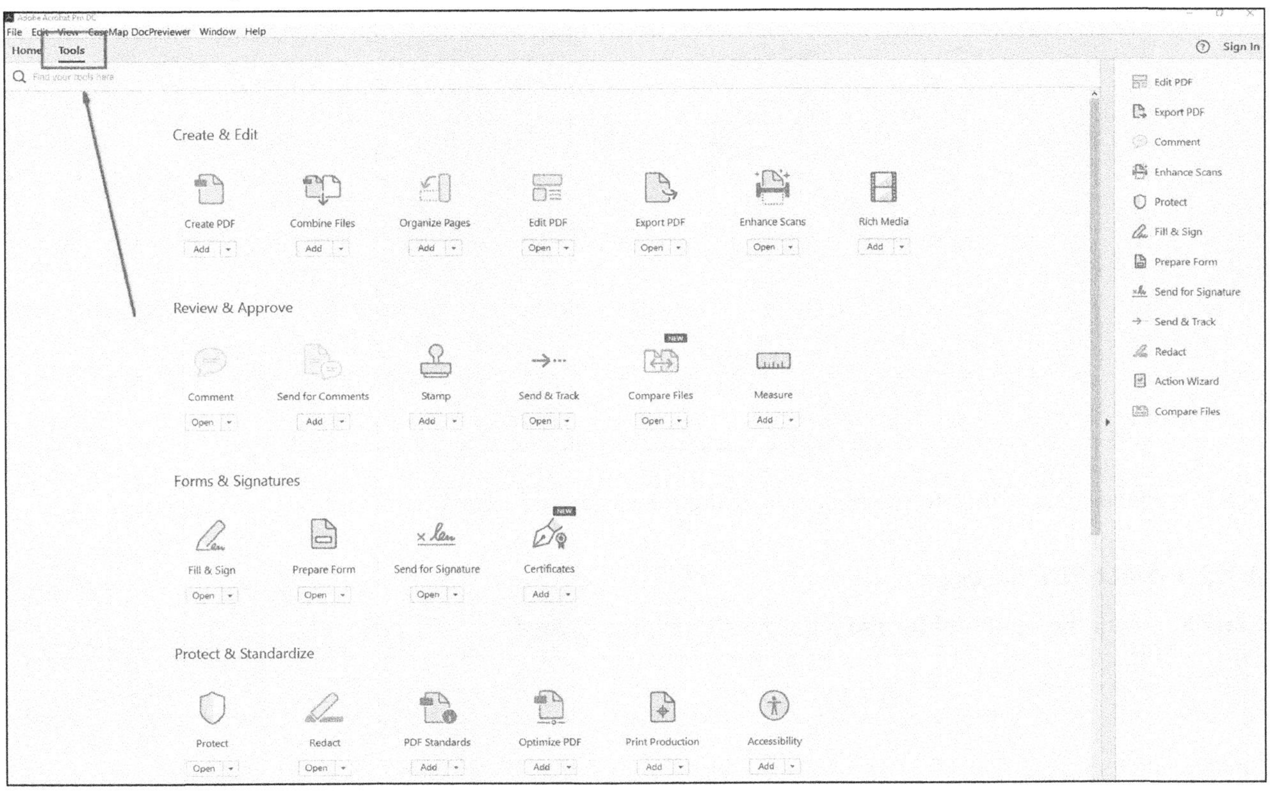

There are many tools available to do a wide variety of tasks in Adobe Acrobat. Start by going to the **Tools** tab.

Task 2. Search for tools.

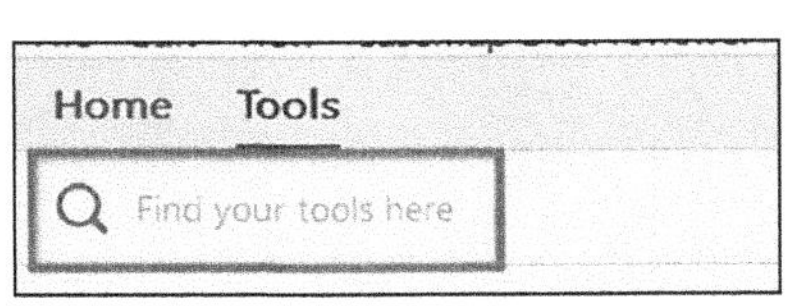

You can either search here for tools you want to use or look through individual tools on the **Tools** tab.

For example, type "redact" or "ocr" to find the tool related to that function.

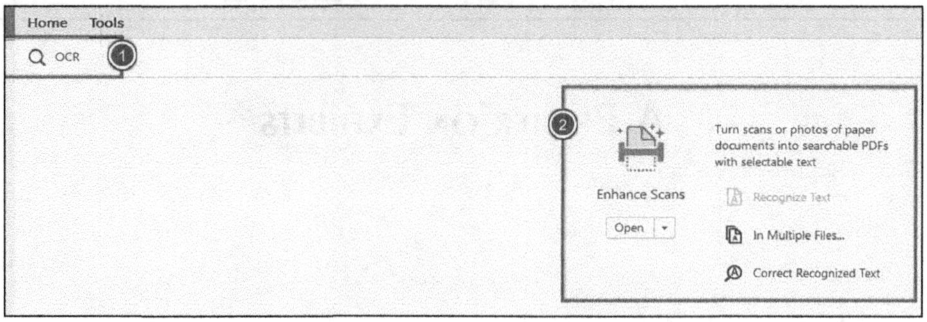

(1) Searching for "ocr" brings up (2) the **Enhance Scans** tool.

Task 3. Create quick access to frequently used tools.

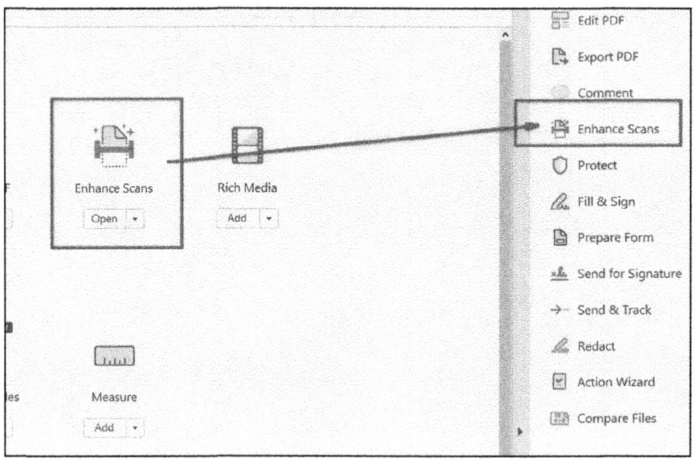

Drag frequently used tools to the right side of the screen for easy access.

12.1.2 Extract PDF Pages

Task 1. Select the right tool for the job using "Organize Pages."

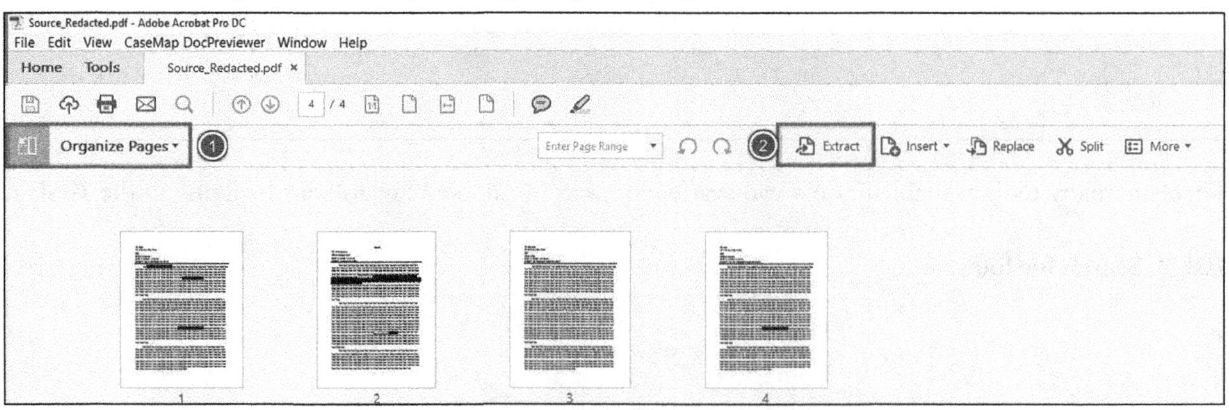

For this function, you need Adobe Acrobat Pro DC so you can use its advanced features. Before modifying a document, save an unaltered copy in case you make a mistake and need to redo it (it happens a lot). In the unitization process, you will be adding and removing pages and reordering pages to create exhibits (which will result in new documents/exhibits).

Open your document in Adobe Acrobat Pro DC to unitize. (1) Select **Organize Pages** tool (if you have an older version, it might be on the right side of the page under the toolbar). (2) Choose **Extract**.

Note: When you create new exhibits by adding or removing pages, the unitization and page numbering of the document will change. For example, a twenty-page document may now be a two-page document. In the exhibit context, this is now a two-page exhibit and the former page numbering is irrelevant. It's important to apply trial exhibit numbers to the new exhibit so that the correct page is called up in court. Legal teams often confuse leftover page and production numbers *to their detriment*. Always use the trial exhibit number to refer to exhibits.

Task 2. Use the Ctrl key to select files to extract.

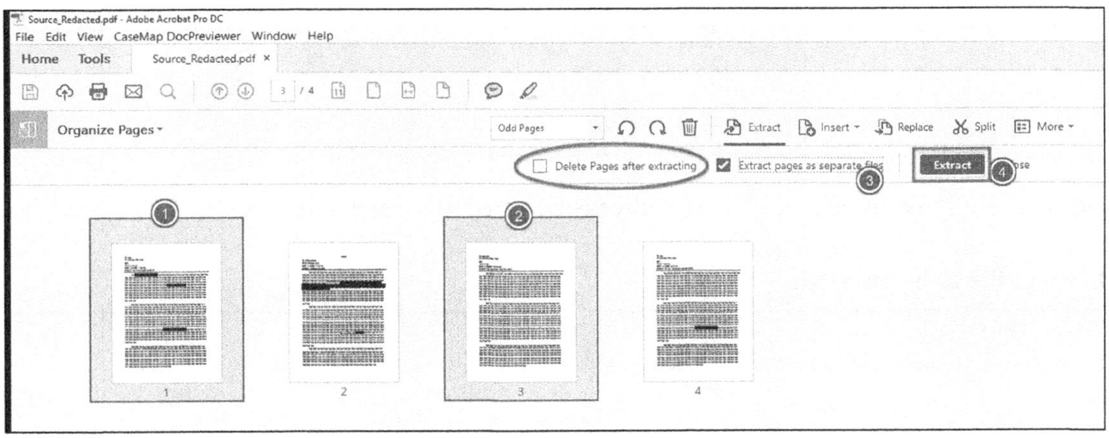

(1), (2) Hold down the **Ctrl** key on your keyboard to select files to extract. (3) Select **Extract pages as separate files**. (4) Choose **Extract**, which moves the selected pages into a folder of your choosing.

Note: You have the option to **Delete Pages after extracting** if you are trying to unitize the open document and want to save the files for later use to build a separate exhibit. Otherwise, you would simply delete the pages.

12.1.3 Insert PDF Pages

Task 1. Choose the right tool for the job using "Organize Pages."

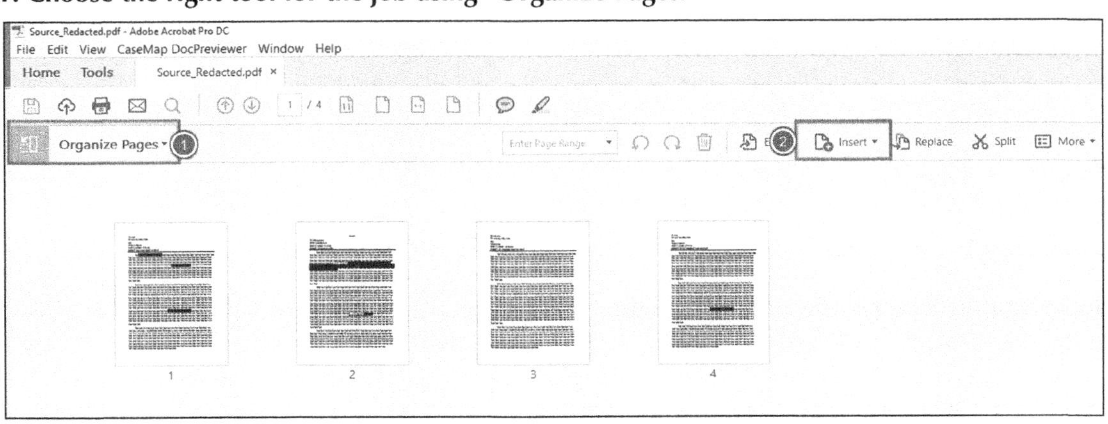

For this function, you need Adobe Acrobat Pro DC so you can use its advanced features. Before modifying a document, save an unaltered copy in case you make a mistake and need to redo it (it happens a lot). In the unitization process, you will be adding and removing pages and reordering pages to create exhibits (which will result in new documents).

Open your document In Adobe Acrobat Pro DC, open the document you wish to insert pages into. (1) Select **Organize Pages** tool (if you have an older version, it might be on the right side of the page under the toolbar). (2) Choose **Insert**.

Task 2. Navigate to the location from which you will be inserting selected file pages.

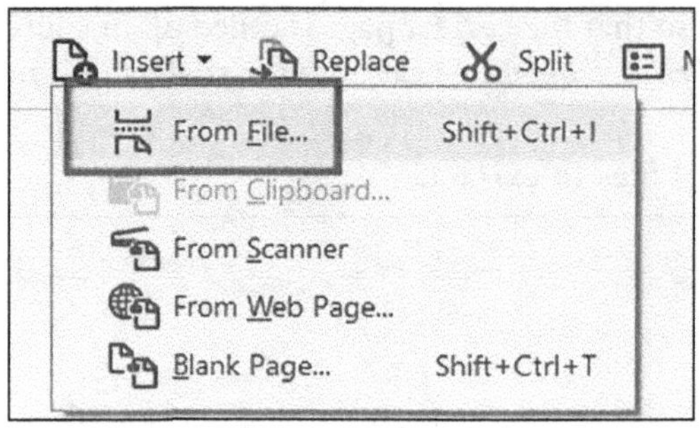

Typically, they are in **From File**, as they have already been redacted, extracted, etc.

Task 3. Select file to be inserted.

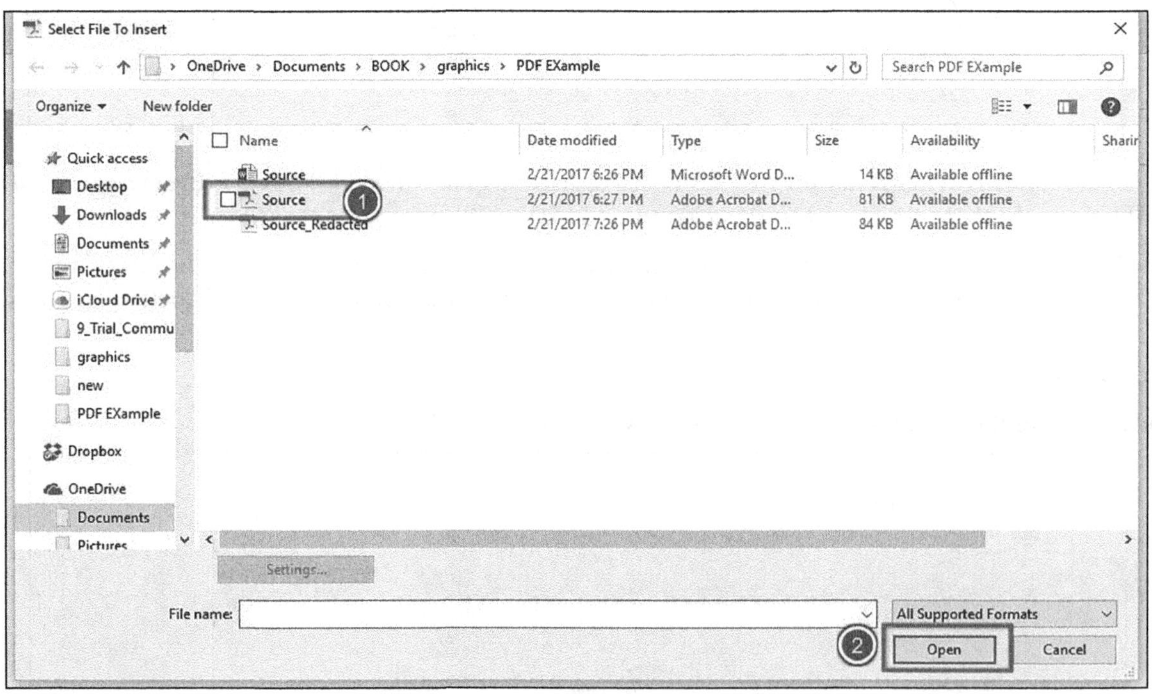

(1) Select file or file(s) to be inserted, then choose (2) **Open**.

Task 4. Choose where to place the new files.

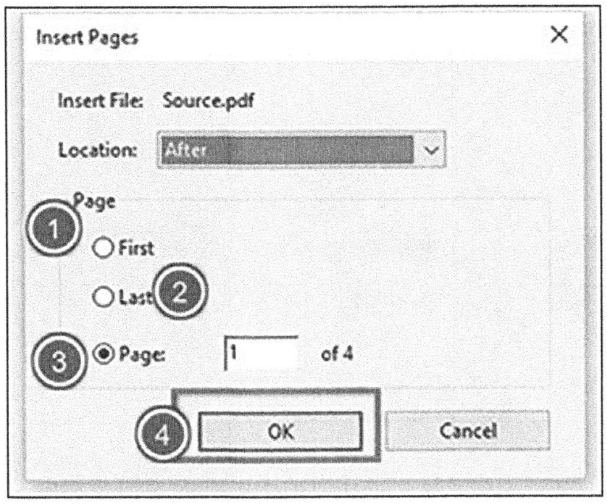

Files can go at the beginning of the document, which is (1) **First**; at the end with (2) **End**; or at a place of your choosing denoted by (3) **Page**. (4) Click **OK** to confirm.

Task 5. QC the file insertion.

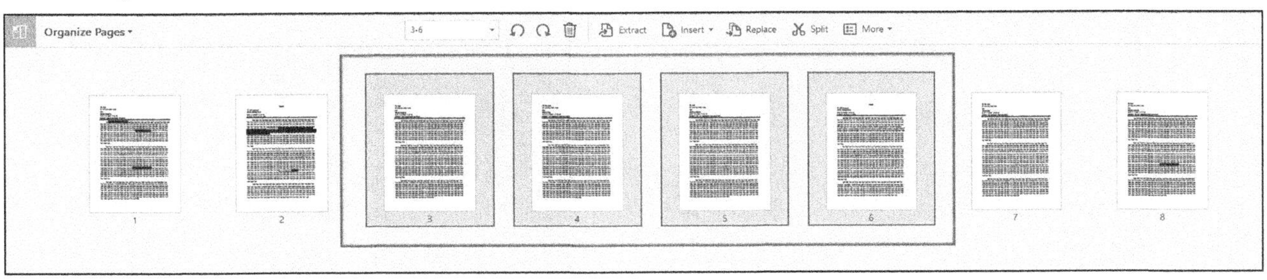

Make sure the files have been inserted into the document at the correct location.

Task 6. Save the file.

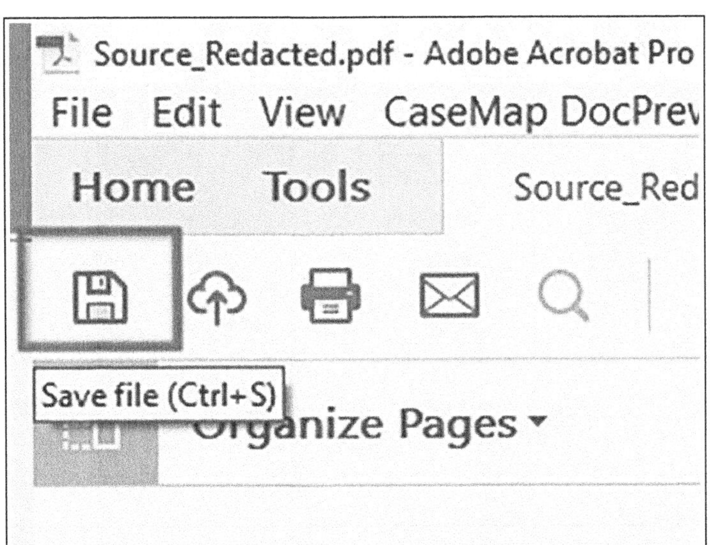

Select **Save file**.

12.1.4 Change Page Order

Task 1. Select the page to be moved.

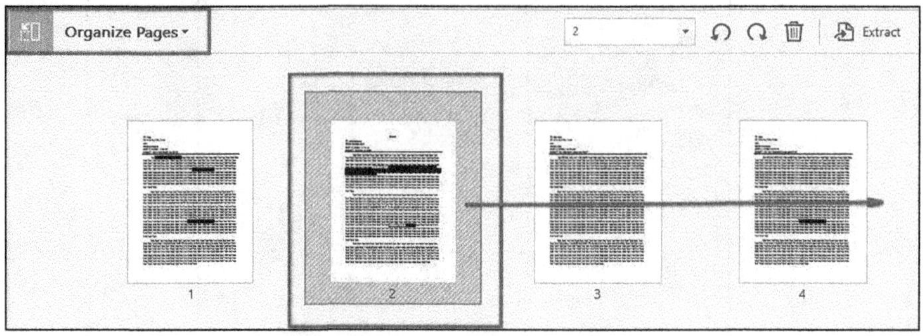

After clicking **Organize Pages**, select the page that you want to move someplace else by left-clicking on it. In the above example, I've chosen page 2.

Task 2. Move the page by dragging and dropping.

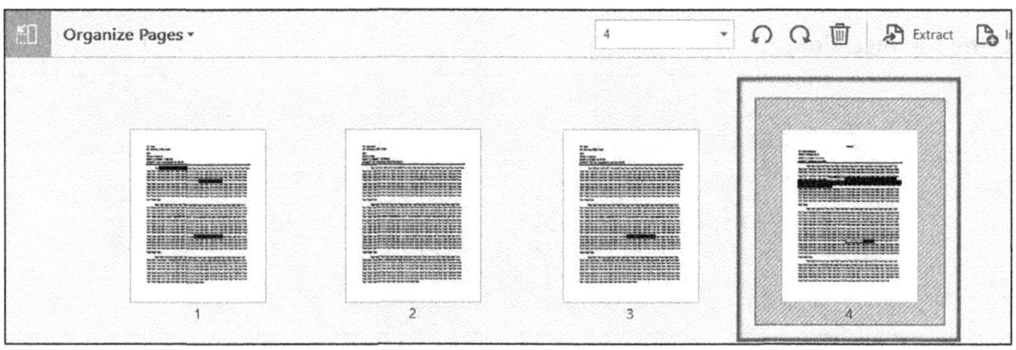

Drag the page by left-clicking, holding, and dragging it to its new location. Note that page 2 is now at page 4.

12.1.5 Delete Pages

Task 1. Select a page to be deleted.

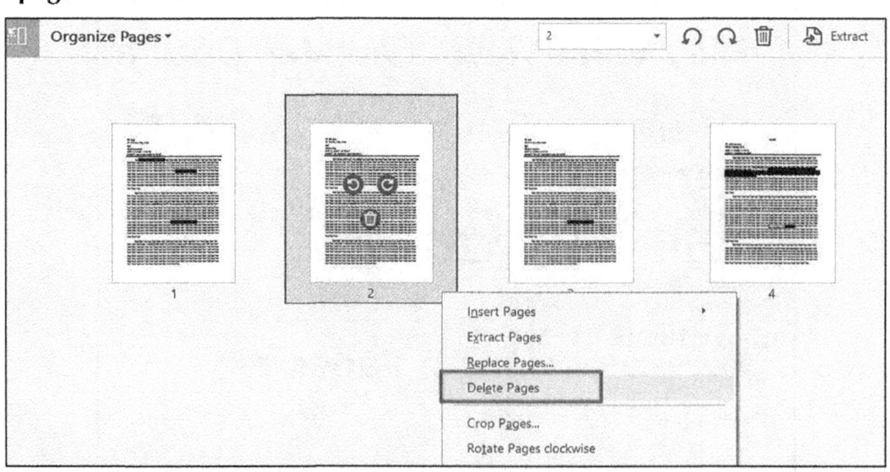

In **Organize Pages**, right-click on page to be deleted. Note that for multiple pages, you can expedite this function by selecting **Extract Pages**.

Task 2. Confirm the deletion.

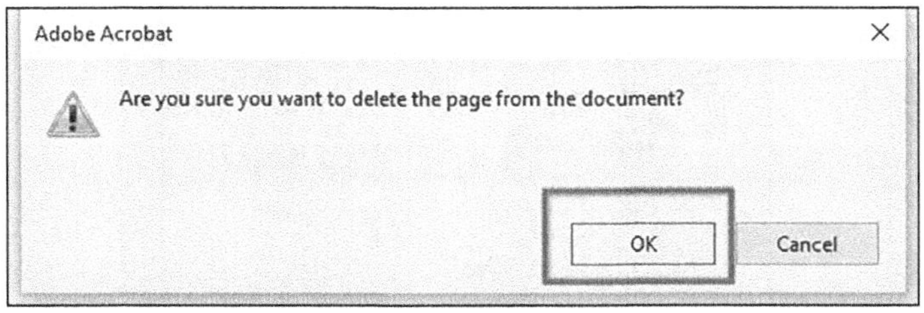

In the **Are you sure you want to delete the page from the document?** window, click **OK**.

Task 3. QC that the correct files were removed.

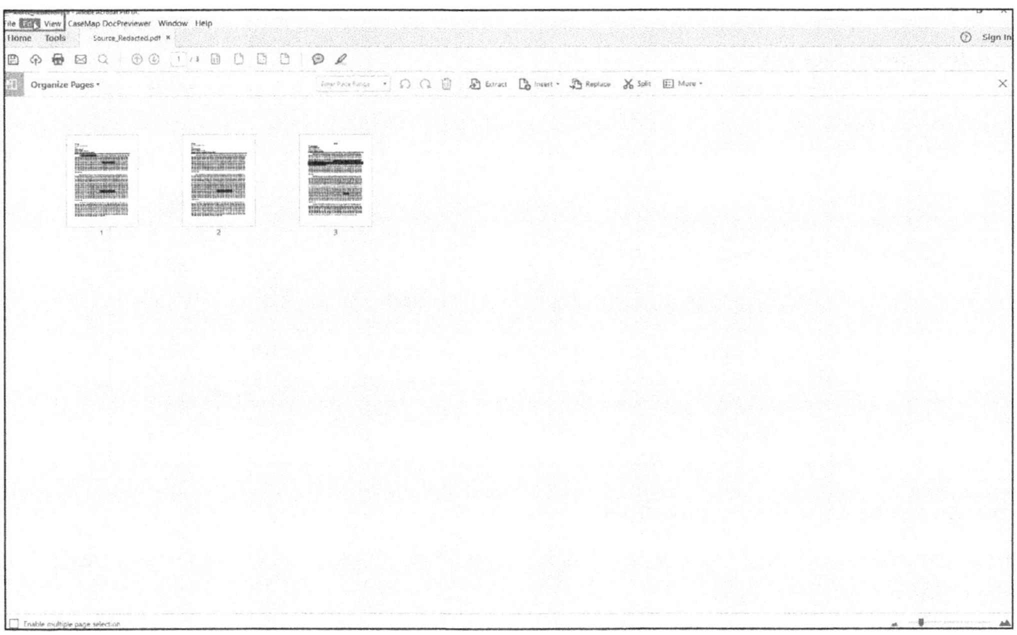

Check the document to ensure the correct page was deleted. Above, 4 minus 1 equals 3 pages, so it is correct.

12.1.6 Redact PDF Documents

Task 1. Select the right tool for the job using the Redact button.

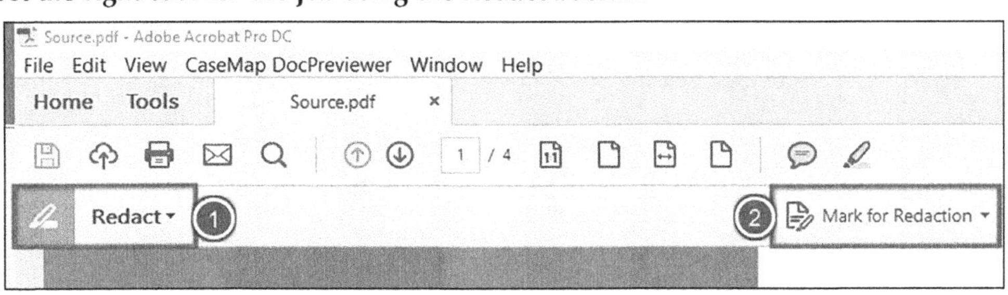

Before redacting or modifying a document, save an unaltered copy in case you make a mistake and need to redo it (it happens a lot).

Open your document to redact. (1) Select **Redact** (if you have an older version, it might be on the right side of the page under the toolbar). (2) Click **Mark for Redaction**.

Task 2. Select "Text & Images."

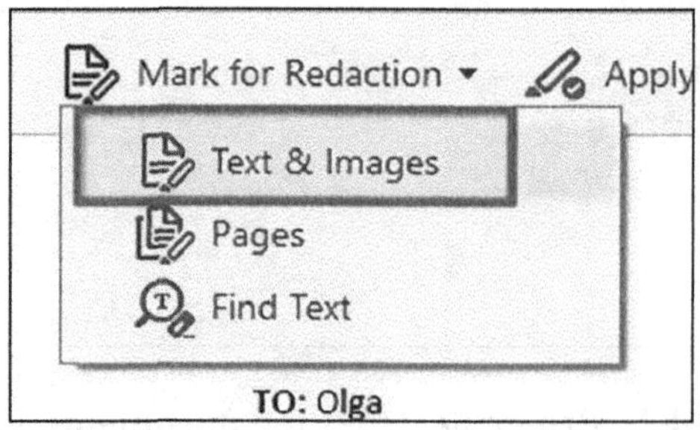

Select **Text & Images** to redact individual words and sentences. Choosing **Pages** marks the entire page for redaction.

Task 3. Mark text for redaction.

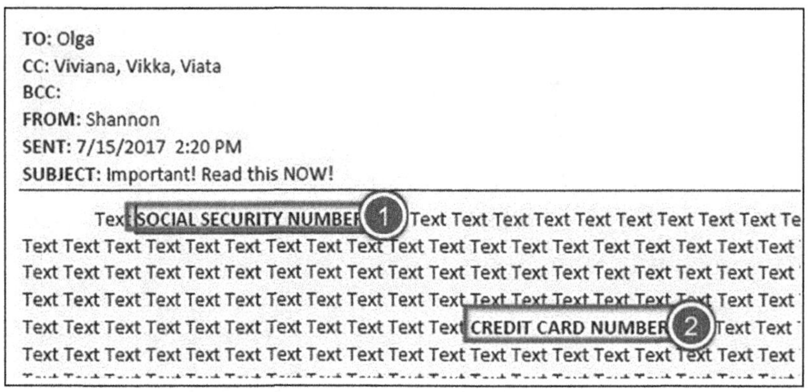

Select the text to be redacted in your document:

(1) "Social Security Number" and (2) "Credit Card Number" to mark them for redaction. A red box will appear around the selected text until it is finalized.

Task 4. Apply redactions.

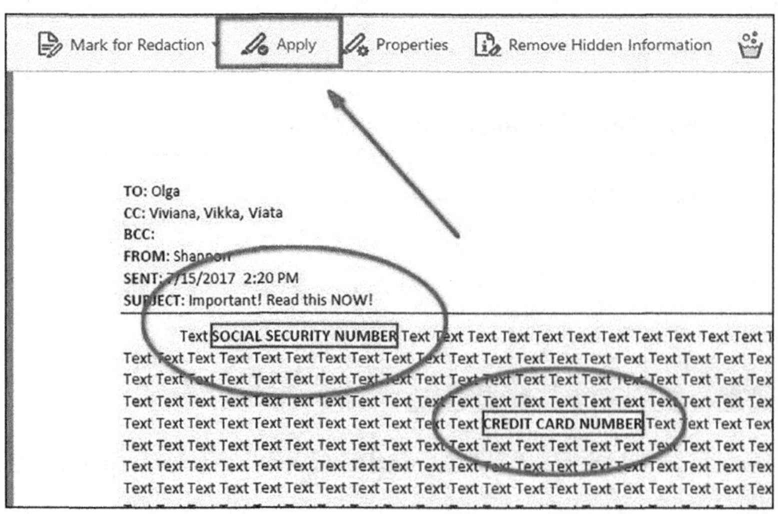

Once the document is redacted and you are sure your redactions are accurate, select **Apply** to apply the black text boxes that will cover the redacted text.

Task 5. For custom redaction text.

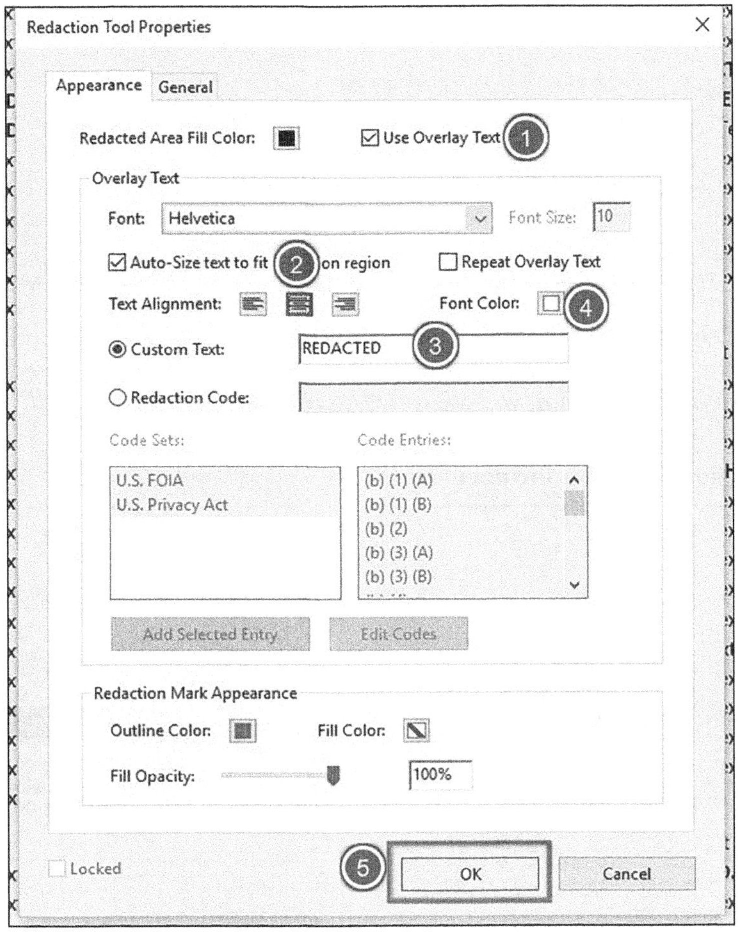

If you need specific text within the redaction, select **Properties** from the **Redact** tool. Then select (1) **Use Overlay Text**, (2) choose **Auto-Size text to fit** and **Text Alignment** "center." Next, (3) Insert the **Custom Text** (here, we typed "REDACTED"), (4) choose the font color, and (5) click **OK** to save.

Tip: Never choose white as a **Redacted Area Fill Color** (i.e., the color of the redaction) without inserting some kind of text to show it is redacted. It will look like you are trying to hide, rather than redact, information.

Task 6. Permanently apply redactions.

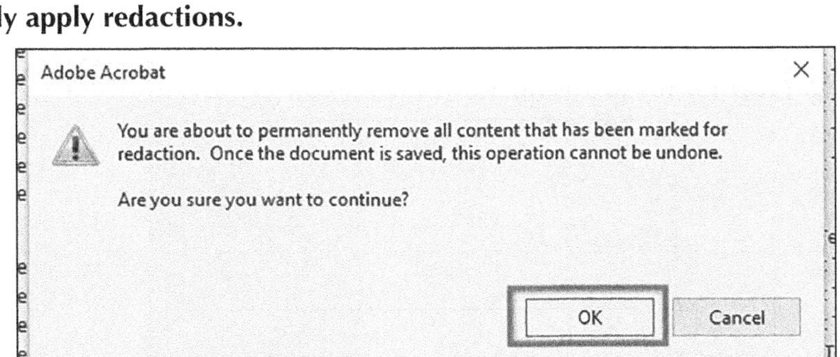

Click **OK** to permanently remove all content that has been marked for redaction. Once the document is saved, this operation cannot be undone.

Task 7. Find hidden information.

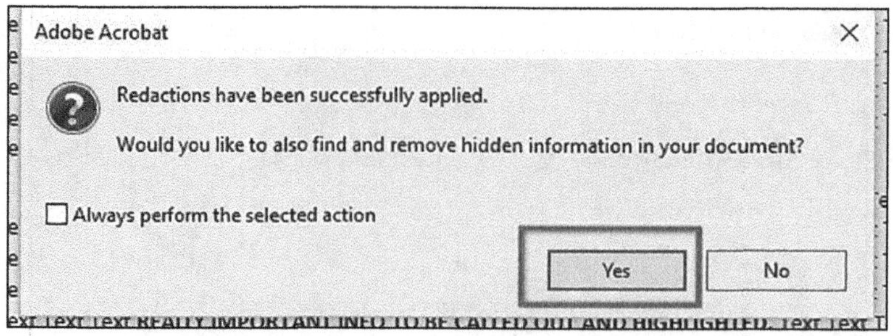

You may want to search for hidden information in your document. Choosing **Yes** finds all hidden information and allows you to remove it. You should always know what you are sending to someone. For example, hidden information could contain the information you are trying to redact.

Task 8. QC your redactions and save the document.

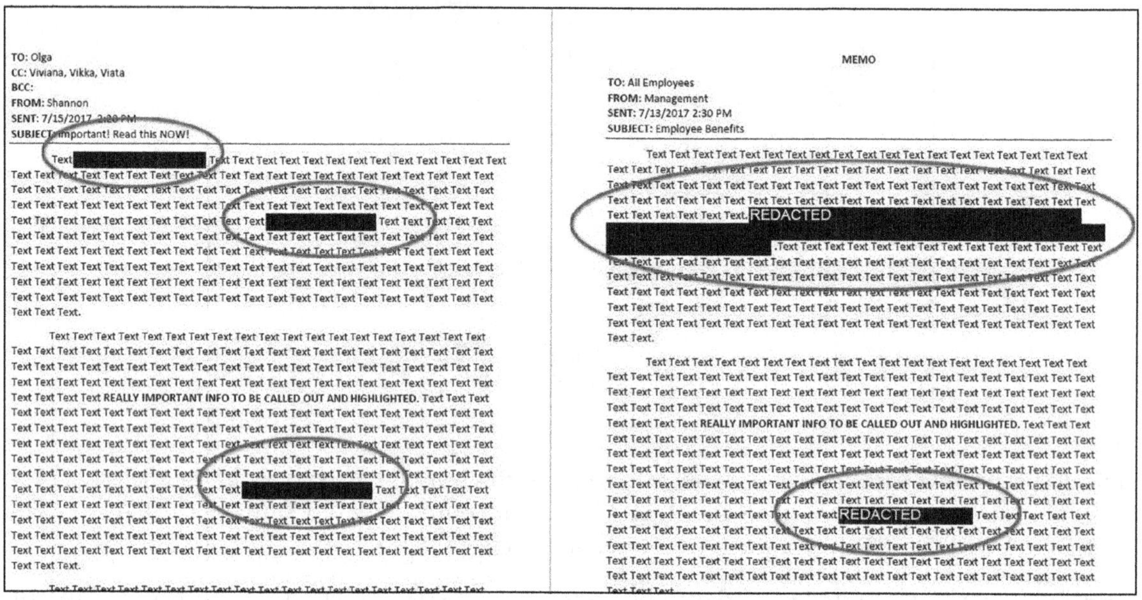

Double-check your redactions and save the document.

12.1.7 Apply Bates Stamps to PDF Files

Task 1. Choose the right tool for the job using the "Stamp" tool.

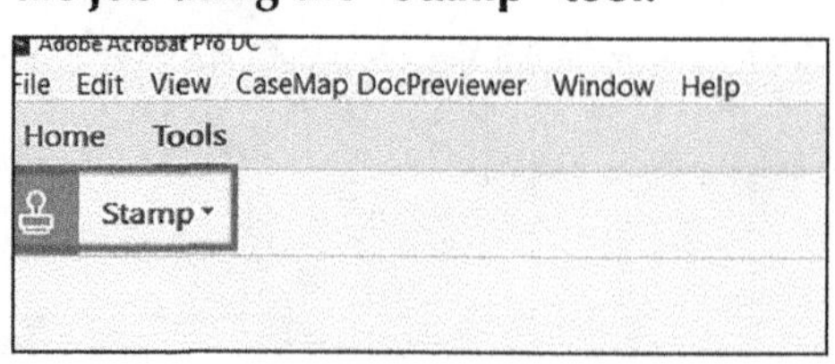

Before Bates stamping or modifying a document, save an unaltered copy in case you make a mistake and need to redo it.

Open your document to apply the Bates stamp. (1) Select **Stamp** (if you have an older version it might be on the right side of the page under the toolbar).

Note: Branding is a good area for you to involve your vendor. Vendors have many software options for branding, and it takes a considerable burden off the shoulders of the person doing the branding. Typically, I would do the unitization and redaction of documents first, and then give the documents to a vendor to apply Bates numbering.

Task 2. Select Bates Numbering.

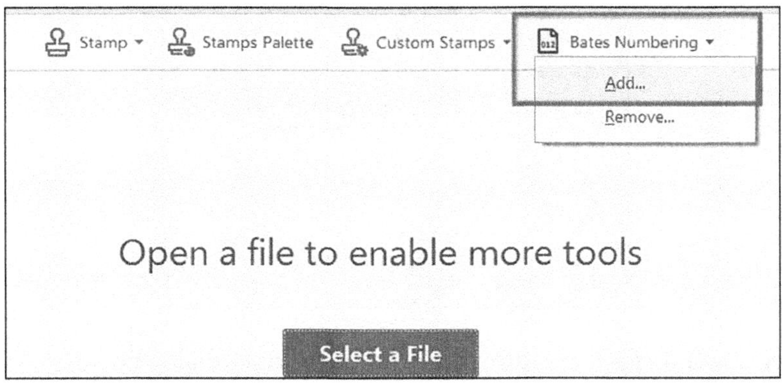

Select **Add** from the **Bates Numbering** dropdown menu.

Task 3. Add files to be Bates numbered.

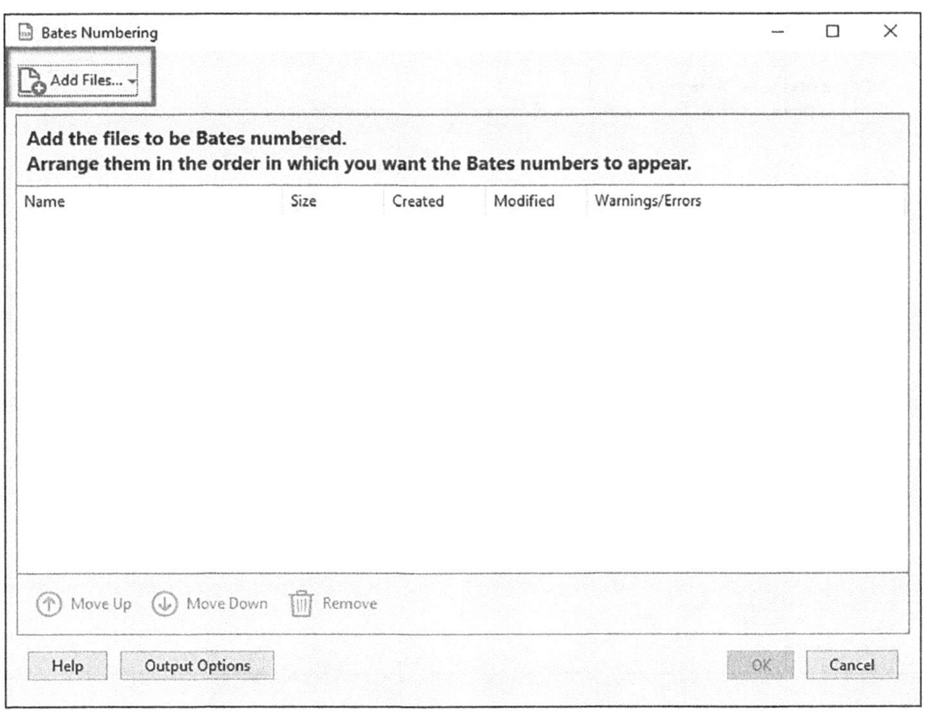

The **Add Files** dialog box appears. You can either select **Add Files** and navigate to a folder location or just drag and drop files into this location.

Task 4. Drag and drop files.

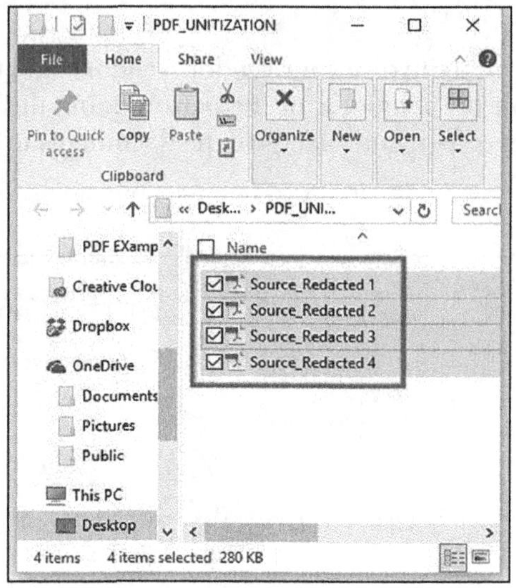

Files can also be selected and dragged and dropped into the previous dialog box.

Task 5. Start the numbering process for the files selected in the dialog box.

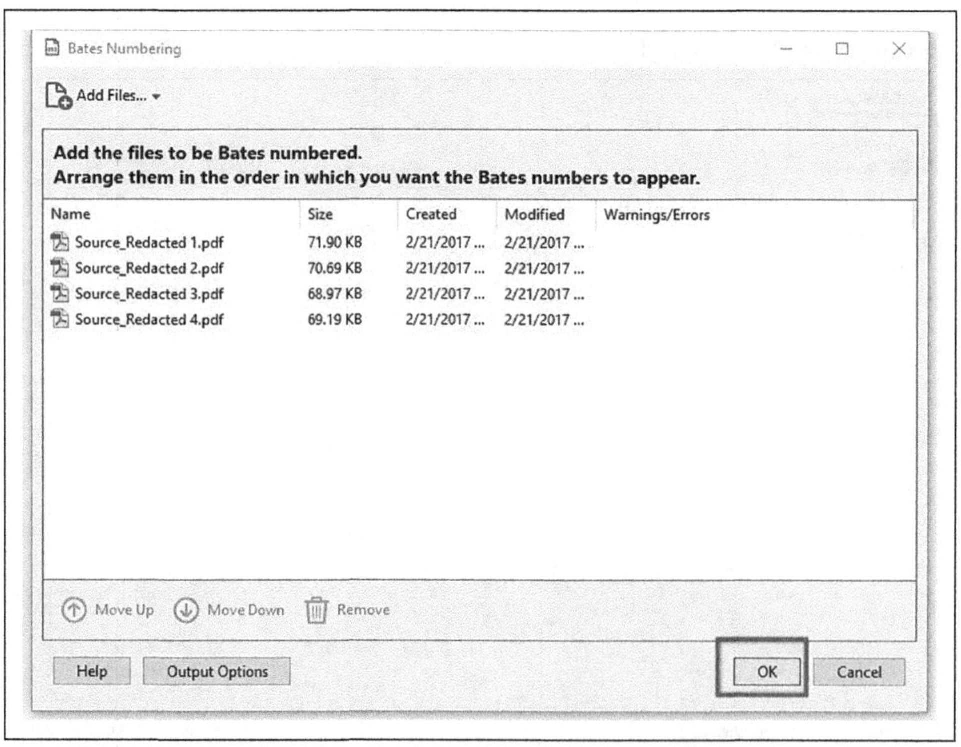

Click **OK** in the **Bates Numbering** dialog box.

Task 6. Select your Bates numbering options for font, point size, and margins.

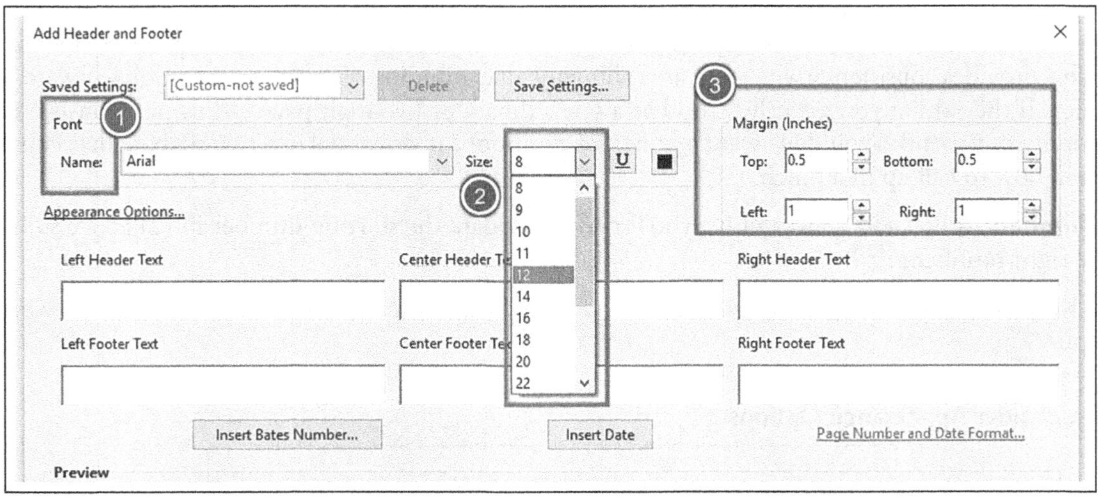

In the **Add Header and Footer** dialog box, choose the options for Bates Numbering for (1) **Font**, (2) **Size**, and (3) **Margins**.

Task 7. Select your options for location and numbering options.

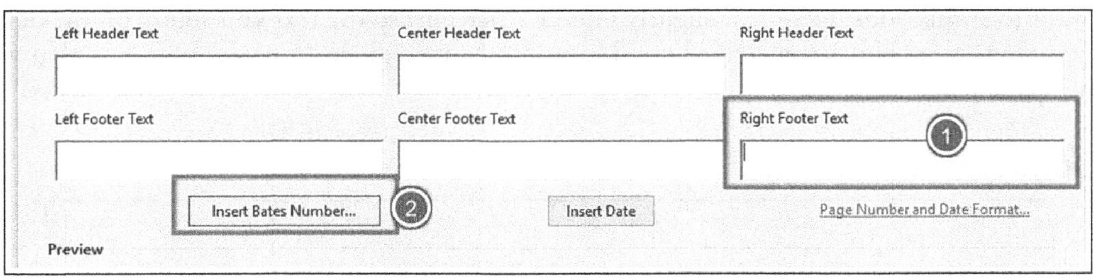

(1) Place the cursor in the section where you want the Bates number to appear. There are six options, but Bates numbers are typically placed in the **Right Footer Text** box. (2) Click **Insert Bates Number...** to select the numbering options.

Note: At this time, you can add additional text, like "CONFIDENTIAL," to the other boxes to brand on each page as well.

Task 8. Customize your Bates numbering options.

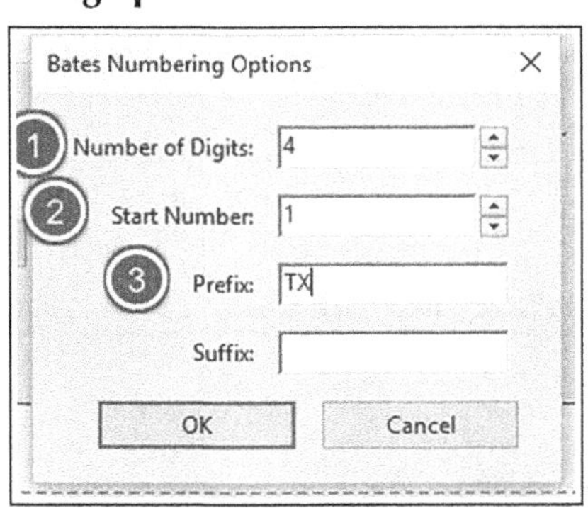

Choose the (1) **Number of Digits**, (2) **Start Number**, and (3) **Prefix** for the exhibit numbers.

Number of Digits: Always pad the number of digits by the maximum number of pages in your exhibit population because you don't want to call up exhibits using numbers that are of different lengths. Therefore, if your biggest exhibit is 2,000 pages, use four digits for your exhibit page number padding across the board for all exhibits. This provides consistency when you are calling up an exhibit in your trial presentation software. You don't want to guess if the exhibit you are calling up has a one-, three-, or five-digit page extension. Consistency in trial presentation is your friend—you don't want a bunch of exceptions in your trial exhibit database that you then have to remember how to call up in a pinch.

Start Number: As you add new exhibits, you'll need to update the starting number in (2) above so it correctly reflects the right number.

Prefix: Keep the prefix simple. Overly complex naming conventions necessitate overly complex workflows to create them.

Task 9. Consider Appearance Options.

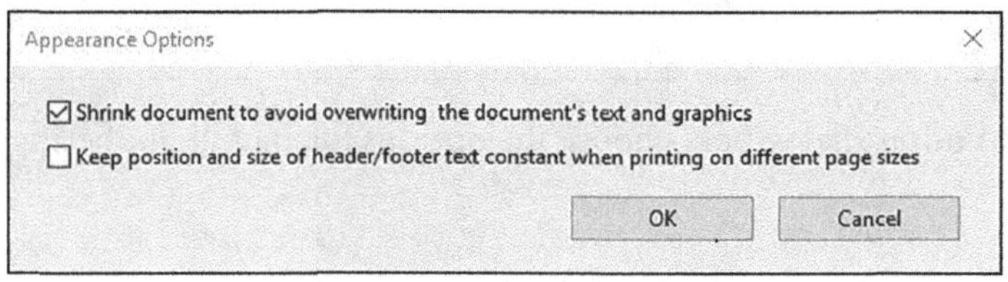

You may want to shrink your document slightly (about 2 percent) so the text you stamp on the document does not cover any existing text. This is generally a good idea, but be careful about repeat branding that would shrink the document too much.

Task 10. QC your Bates numbering.

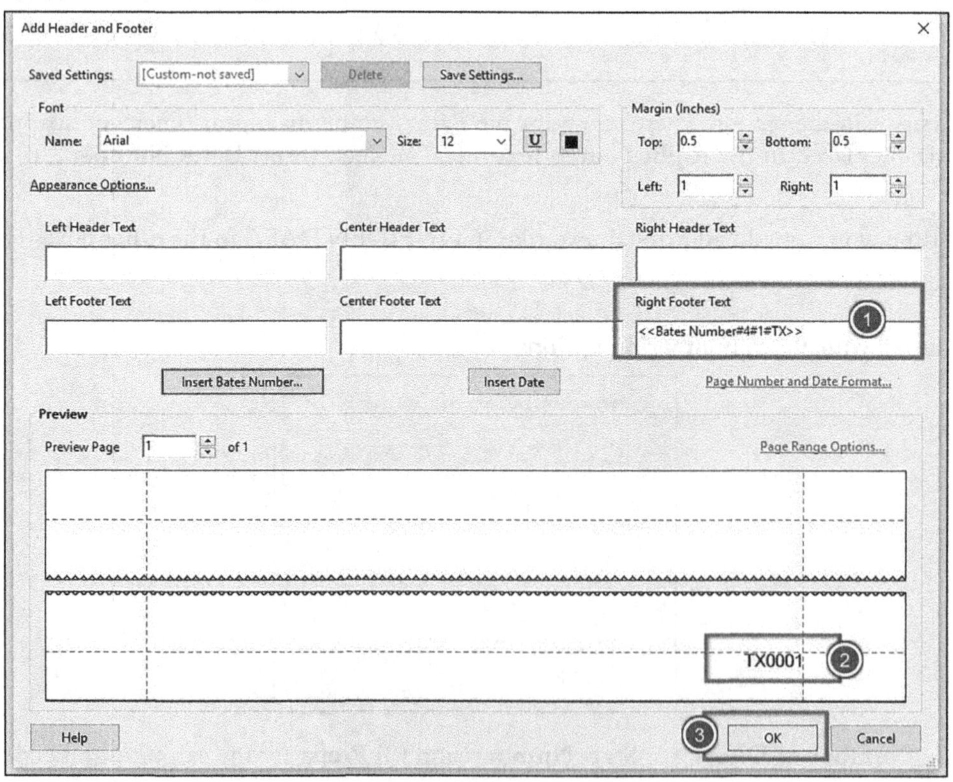

Adobe will place the information it needs to Bates number in the (1) **Right Footer Text** box and you should see a (2) preview of the text below.

(3) If everything looks good, click **OK**.

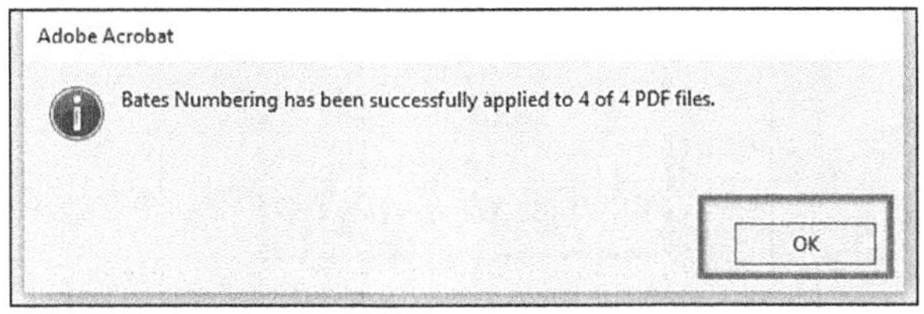

Click **OK** again. Check the exhibit to ensure the exhibit has been placed properly.

12.1.8 Run an OCR Scan on PDFs

Task 1. Select the right tool for the job using "Enhance Scans."

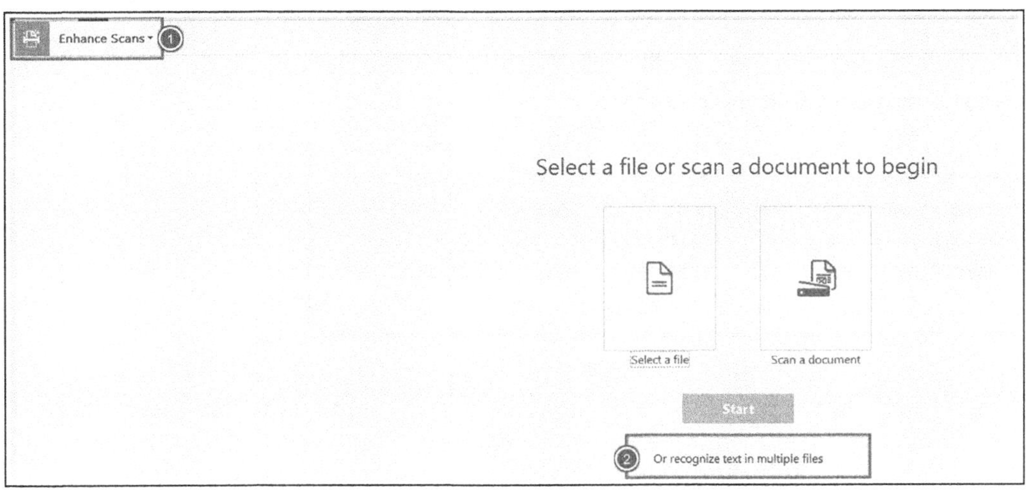

Before modifying a document, save an unaltered copy in case you make a mistake and need to redo it (it happens a lot). In the unitization process, you will be adding and removing pages and reordering pages to create exhibits (which will result in new documents).

Note: OCR adds file size to exhibits and that will not aid performance. Only OCR files that are for legal team and database use—not for trial presentation.

Task 2. Open your document to OCR.

(1) Select the **Enhance Scans tool** (if you have an older version, it might be on the right side of the page under the toolbar). (2) Choose **Or recognize text in multiple files**.

Task 3. Select files to be OCR'd.

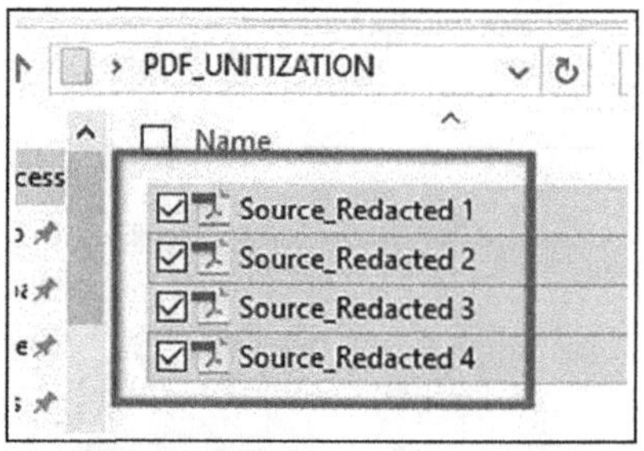

Select files to be OCR'd, and drag and drop into the dialog box on the next screen.

Task 4. Review the "Recognize Text" dialog box.

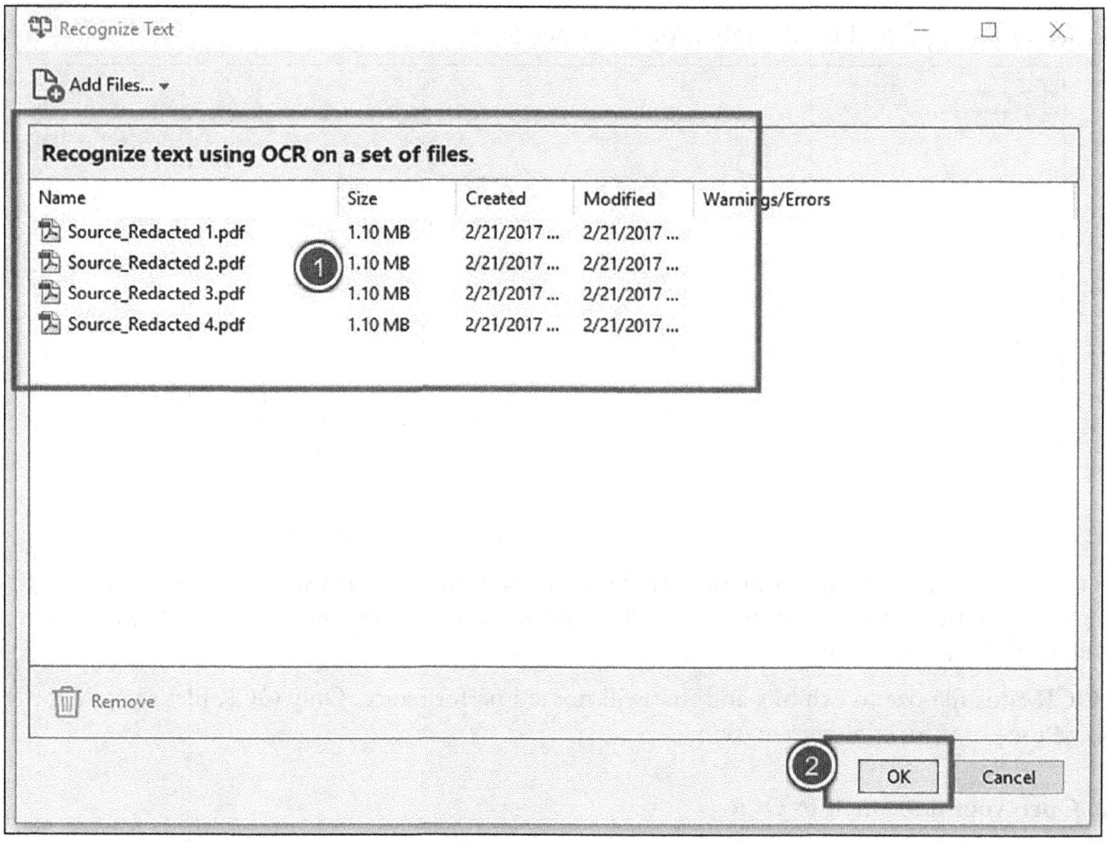

(1) Check that the correct files are in the **Recognize text using OCR on a set of files** dialog box. They can be dragged and dropped or you can use the **Add Files** dropdown menu. (2) Select **OK** to start the OCR process.

Task 5. Select "Output Options."

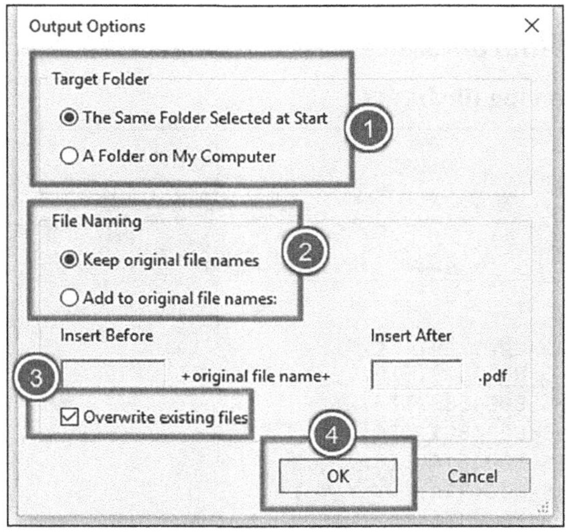

(1) Select where files will be saved. (2) Choose **File Naming options**. (3) Select whether to **Overwrite existing files**. (4) Click **OK** to OCR files.

Note: If selecting to overwrite existing files, be sure to have an original copy in case something goes awry.

Task 6. Kick off the OCR process.

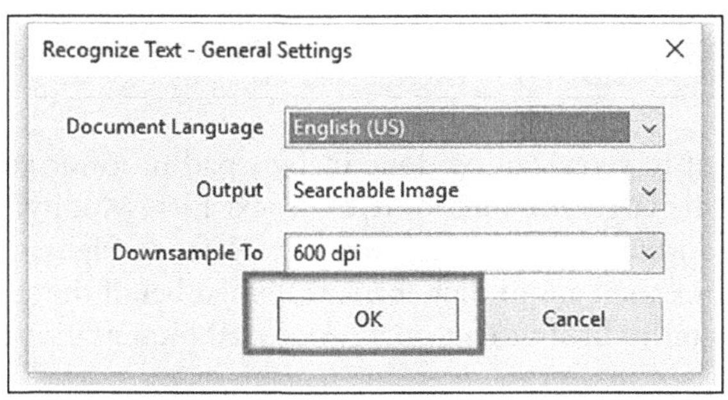

Click **OK** in **Recognize Text - General Settings**.

12.2 UltraEdit (File Path Change)

12.2.1 Review Log Files and UltraEdit Basics

Task 1. Refresh your memory on log file basics.

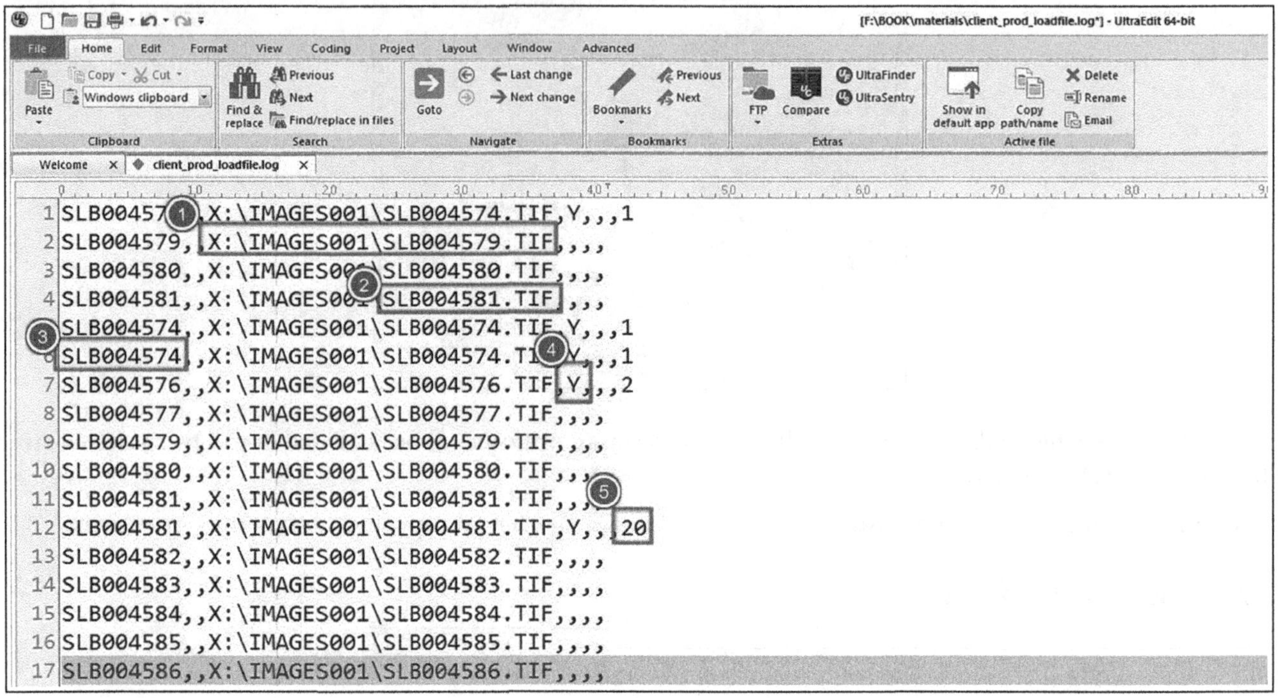

Many of the tasks we are about to show can be done in Notepad in lower volumes. UltraEdit is much more robust in that it can quickly handle larger volumes of data in text files. Modifying text files is typically an intermediate or advanced skill, but it's worth gaining exposure to it. Refer to Figure 3, the TIFF versus PDF chart in section 3.3, where I present the pros and cons of each format. Remember, if there are exhibits of an extremely large file size in a database, you may want to break them up so your trial presentation software has an easier time with them. Big files make big problems.

A quick refresh on the log file:

(1) The **path**—the location of the image. (2) **Image**—the image name. (3) The **image key or alias**—the database reference to the image. (*Note*: (2) and (3) should usually be the same). (4) **Y flag**—the Y flag shows where the document starts. (5) **Page count**—this is the page count of the record, and here, it tells the viewer that the next twenty images are with SLB04581.

Task 2. Review log file basics and QC.

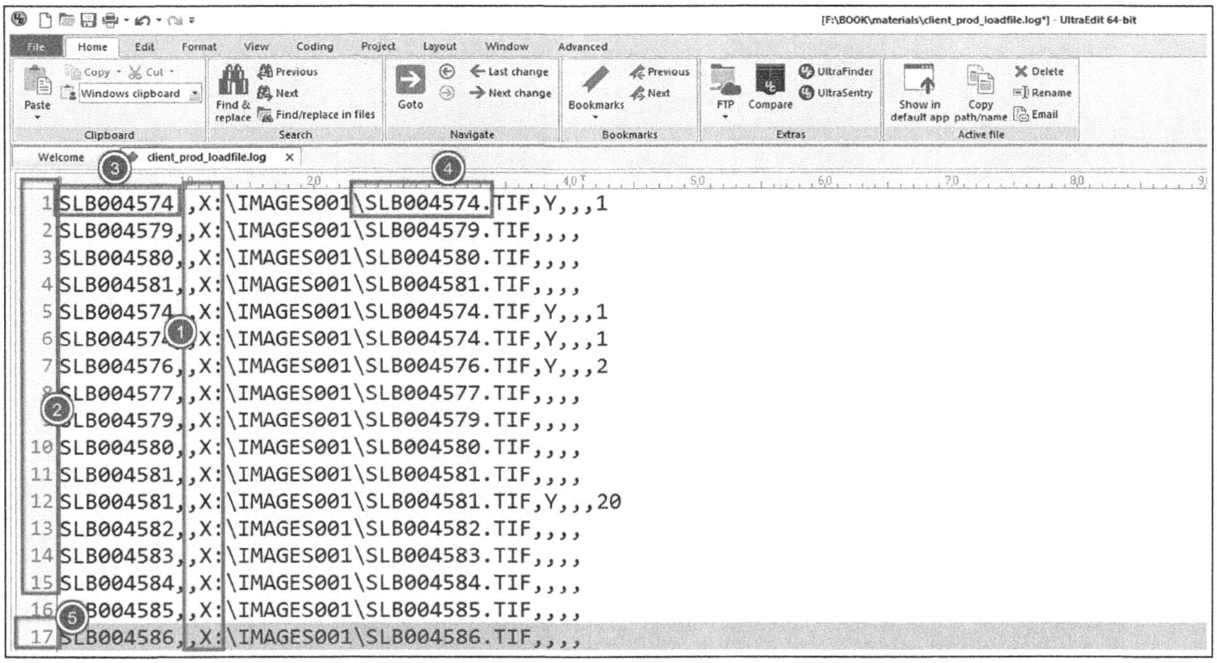

In this example, we are (1) replacing the **X** in the path with the file path where the images will be placed. Vendors usually provide a letter like **X**, **Y**, and **Z** or two \\ to show the portion of the path to be replaced.

There is much we can learn from a log file and use for QC.

QC Step 1: UltraEdit provides a line number (2) for each image in the log file. Look at the last number in this column and compare it against the number of images delivered to you. To determine the number of images delivered, right-click the folder that contains the images and select **Properties** to see how many images there are. Loglines to number of images should be equal.

QC Step 2: The image key/alias (3) should match the image name (4).

Note: Correct log file and exhibit naming conventions should be spelled out in your Trial Management Order (or evidence exchange agreement). This is a prime area for burden shifting when people don't take the time to do it right.

12.2.2 Change Path

Task 1. Copy data received to your trial laptop.

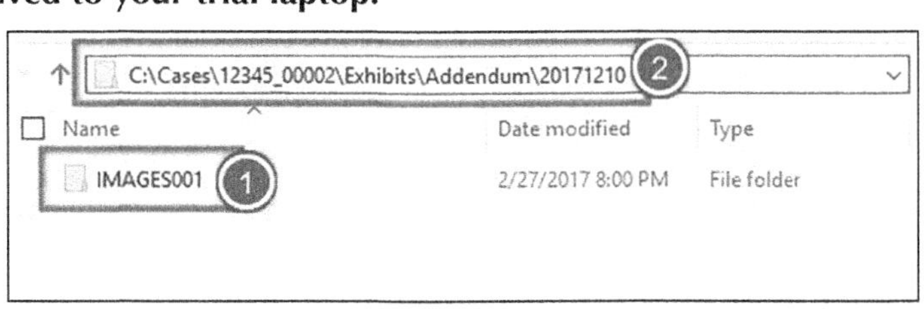

Copy the data received (1) to your case organization structure (2). Note the path in your case structure (2). You may want copy the path by right-clicking on it and selecting **Copy**.

Task 2. Choose "Find & Replace."

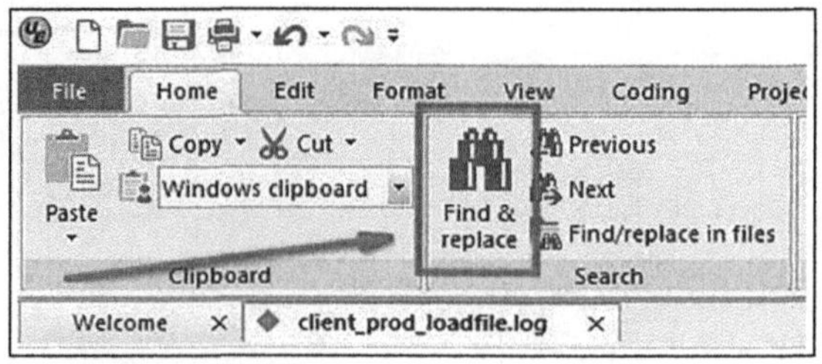

Select **Find & Replace** from the **Home** tab.

Task 3. Fill in your options in the "Find & Replace" dialog box.

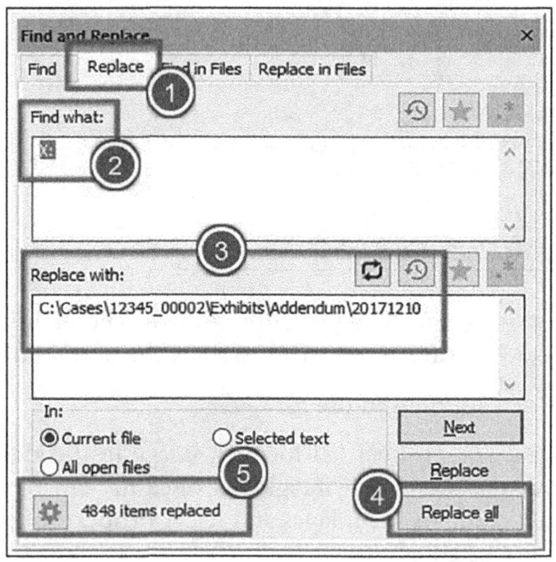

Select the (1) **Replace** tab in the **Find and Replace** dialog box. (2) Enter (or copy) the text to be replaced **X:** in the **Find what** dialog box. (3) Enter (or copy—it's better to copy) the path where the images were placed in the **Replace with** dialog box. (4) Select **Replace all** to replace all the **X:** with C:\Cases\12345_00002\Exhibits\Addendum\20171210. Last, note the number of replacements made (5), which should equal the number of lines in the log file. If it is not equal, there is a problem somewhere (usually meaning a significant problem with the delivery).

Note: We placed the data in our case organizational structure and added it as an addendum (an addition sometime after the first data load).

Task 4. Finish the function and prepare to import.

```
SLB004574,,C:\Cases\12345_00002\Exhibits\Addendum\20171210\IMAGES001\SLB004574.TIF,Y,,,1
SLB004579,,C:\Cases\12345_00002\Exhibits\Addendum\20171210\IMAGES001\SLB004579.TIF,,,,
SLB004580,,C:\Cases\12345_00002\Exhibits\Addendum\20171210\IMAGES001\SLB004580.TIF,,,,
SLB004581,,C:\Cases\12345_00002\Exhibits\Addendum\20171210\IMAGES001\SLB004581.TIF,,,,
SLB004574,,C:\Cases\12345_00002\Exhibits\Addendum\20171210\IMAGES001\SLB004574.TIF,Y,,,1
SLB004574,,C:\Cases\12345 00002\Exhibits\Addendum\20171210\IMAGES001\SLB004574.TIF,Y,,,1
```

The log file can now be imported into your trial presentation or other software.

Chapter Thirteen

A Primer on Companion Software

13.1 Snagit

13.1.1 Capture a Region in Snagit

Task 1. Position the document, webpage, video, etc. to be captured

Region capture allows you to choose the area to be captured rather than the entire screen. It is useful for capturing a section of document, highlighting, and then putting into PowerPoint or an annotated exhibit for trial presentation. Tto obtain fine detail of a document or image, zoom in as close as possible on the document and perform the capture. Capturing a full-page image, then cropping it or expanding it, will produce a low-quality presentation (that's why it's so important to zoom in on what you are capturing). Position the document onscreen so that you can capture it. Too close and the capture will be pixelated; too far away and it will be fuzzy. Experiment with what works and gives the highest quality work product.

Note: Use time-delay to capture something you must click on first, like a menu item.

Task 2. Configure Snagit for a "Region" capture.

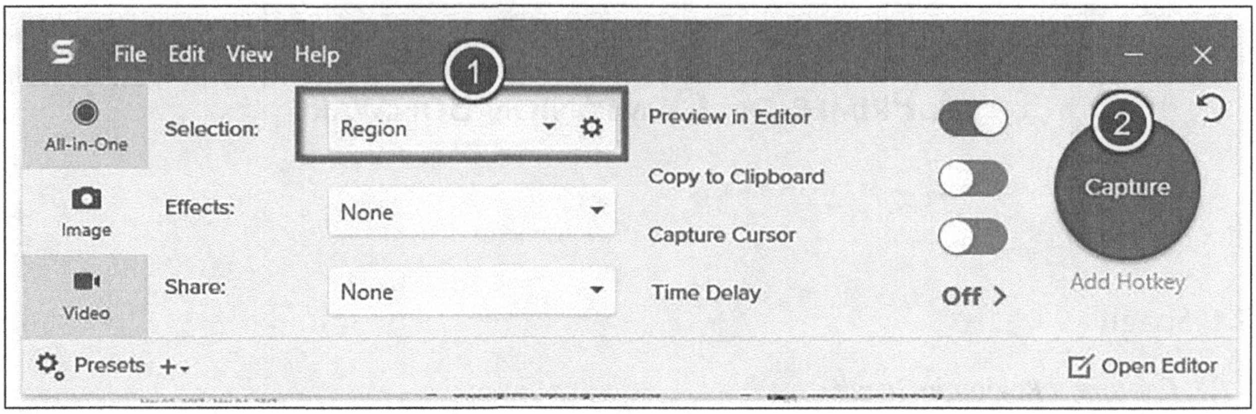

(1) Under **Selection**, choose **Region**. (2) Click **Capture** in **Snagit Capture**.

Task 3. Capture!

Drag your cursor across the screen to capture the section of text or image. It is often helpful to grab a line or two above for context, but in other situations you'll want just the text you intend to enlarge and highlight.

13.1.2 *Use the Snagit Editor*

Task 1. Review the Snagit Editor.

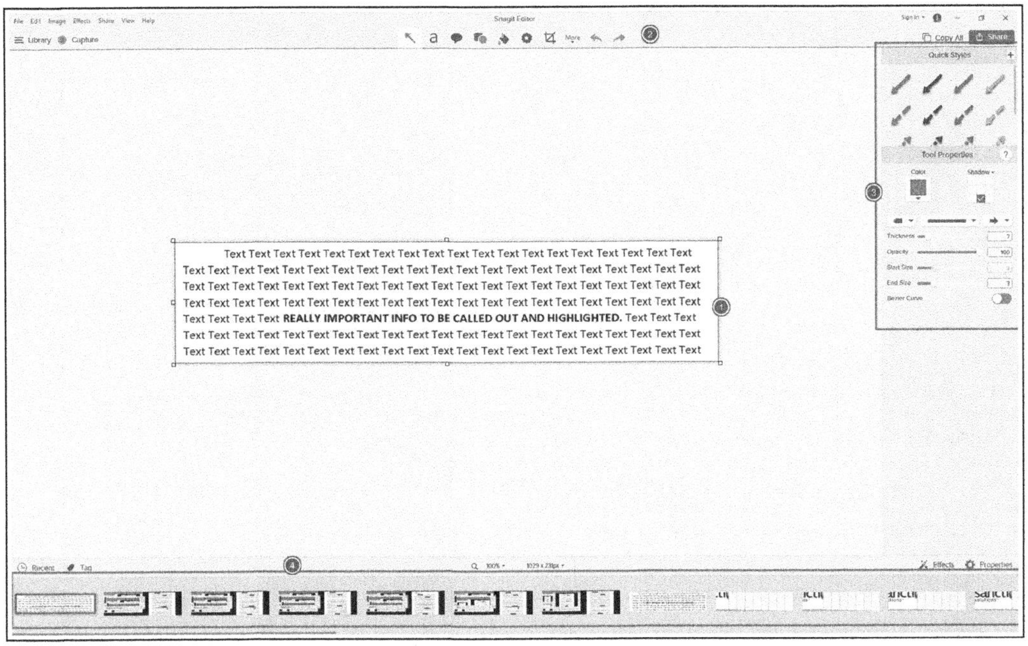

Your captured image will then be placed into the Snagit editor. (1) The captured image. (2) **Toolbar**. (3) **Options** for the tool you select. (4) Previously captured images (very useful).

Note: You can configure the captured image to go straight to the clipboard so it can be pasted directly into PowerPoint.

Task 2. Insert highlights.

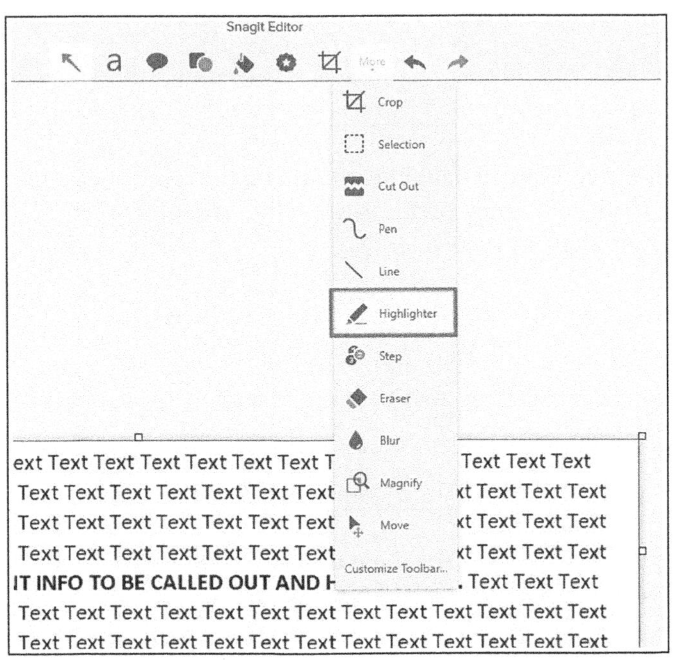

Select the **Highlighter** tool from the toolbar.

Task 3. Begin to highlight.

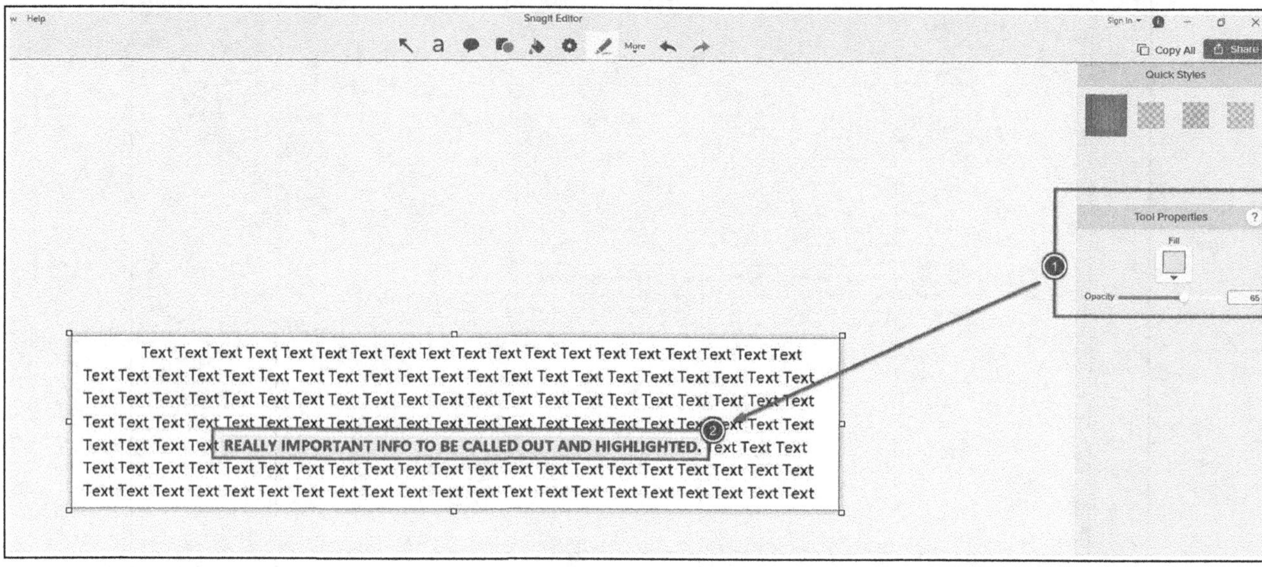

(1) Choose the highlight color. (2) Select the text you want to highlight.

Note: Lots of people are sloppy about highlighting. Be precise.

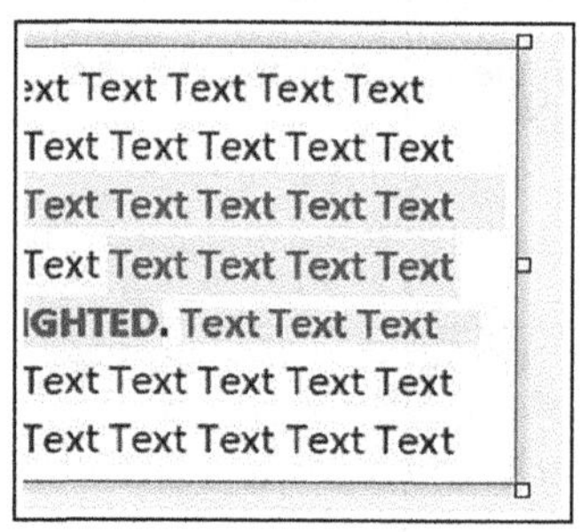

Make your highlights accurate and neat. Highlights should be the same width and height, as well as begin and end in alignment if the text is aligned. Some prefer to see white space between highlight lines rather than have highlighted text appear as a solid block of yellow.

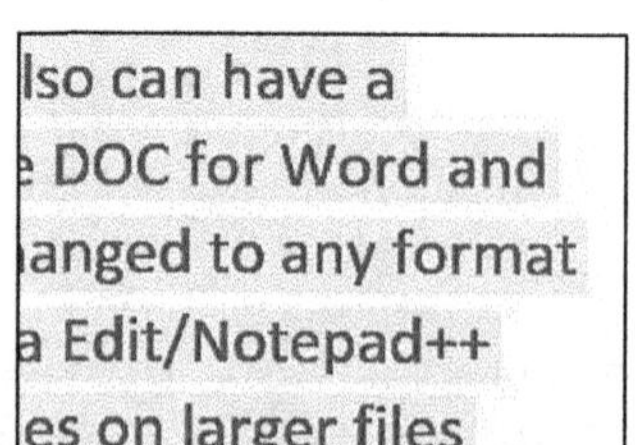

If the text is not aligned, then end roughly the same distance after each line. Be careful not to create a yellow "wall"—*if everything is highlighted, then nothing is.* (I know: deep.)

13.1.3 Apply a Torn Edge Effect

Task 1. Choose the Edge tool.

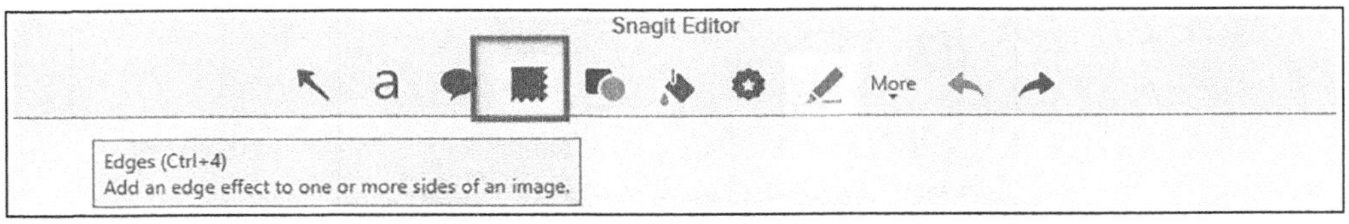

Choose the **Edge** icon from your toolbar. If it is not there, choose **More** to reveal it.

Task 2. Consider your "Effect" options.

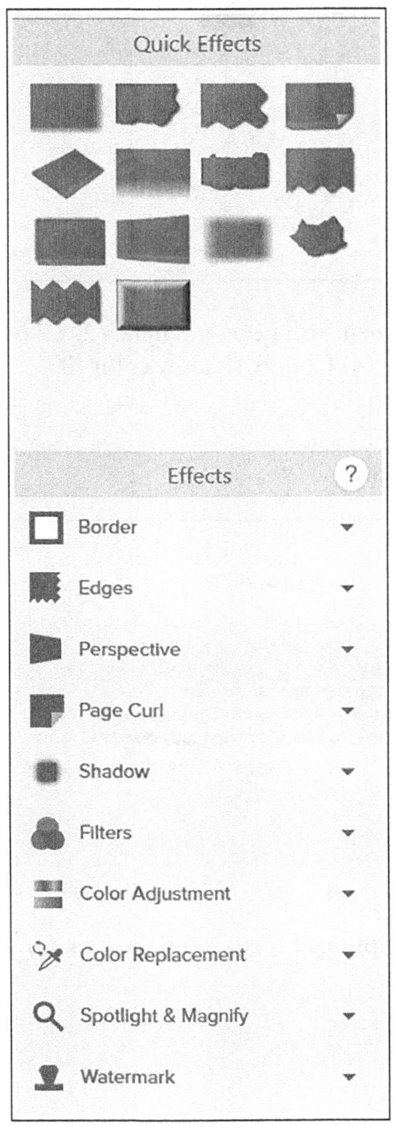

There are many effect options to explore. Choose **Edges** to bring them up.

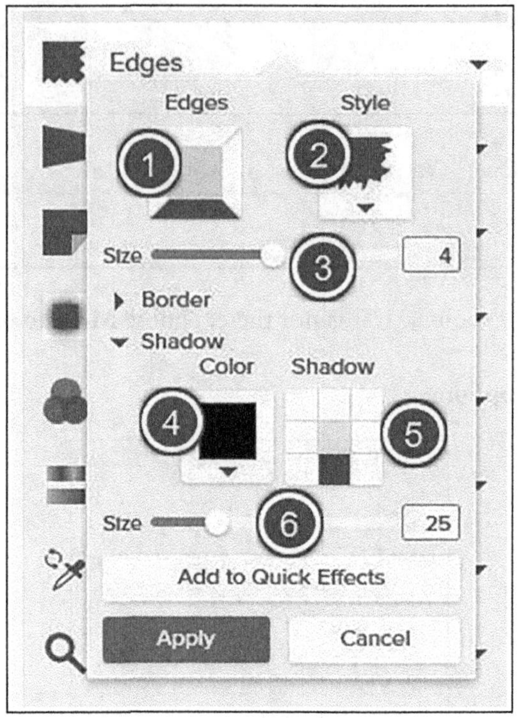

(1) Choose which border of the document will get edges here. (2) Choose the style of the edge. (3) Choose how deep the edge will go into the document. (4) Choose shadow color (if you are using shadows). (5) The angle of the shadow. (6) How deep the shadow will go.

Task 3. Create a torn edge with shadow.

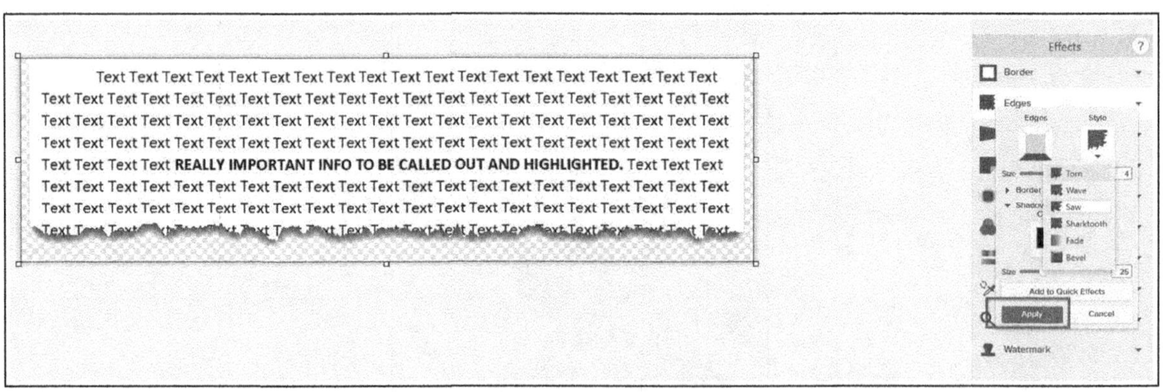

Click **Apply** after going through the options for edge and shadow for your image.

13.1.4 Use an Edited Image

Task 1. Copy the image to the clipboard.

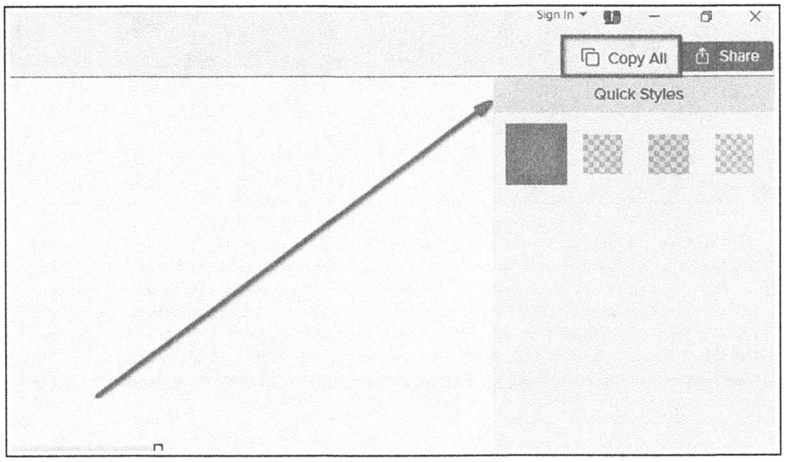

When you are satisfied with your image, select **Copy All** to place the image on the clipboard. Now you can paste it into any program by right-clicking and selecting **Paste**.

Task 2. Go to the PowerPoint slide you want to annotate.

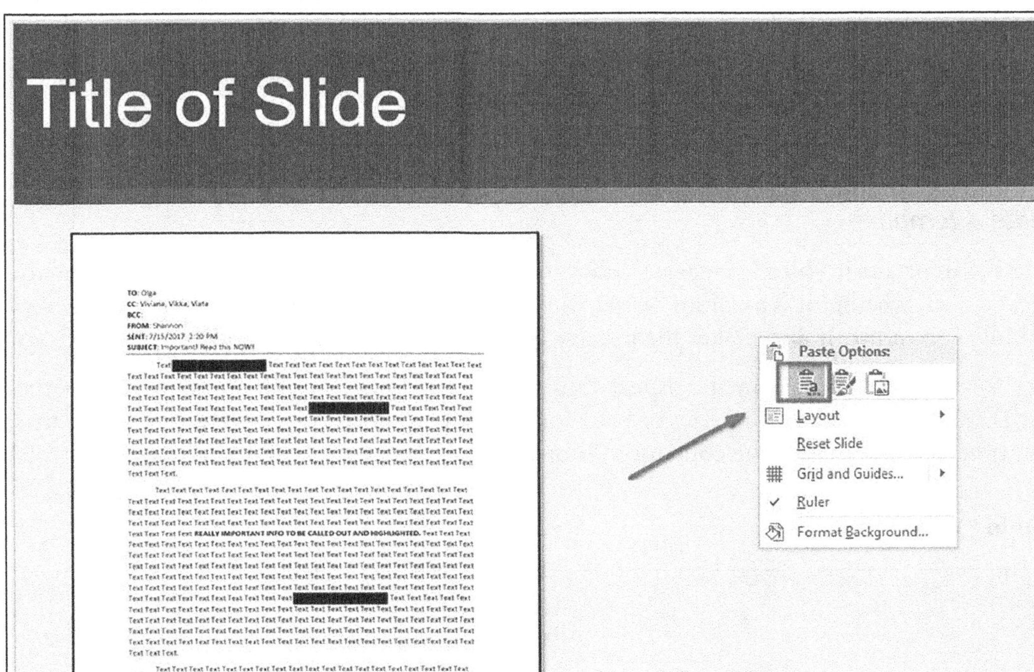

Right-click and paste the image into the slide.

Note: You may need to capture images twice. First, you'll want a full-size insertion of the *page* of the document. If imaged, you could (and probably should) from PowerPoint use **Insert** and insert a picture of the full page from the file. Then, as described above, use Snagit take a screenshot of a zoomed-in version of the image for quality.

Task 3. Position the image.

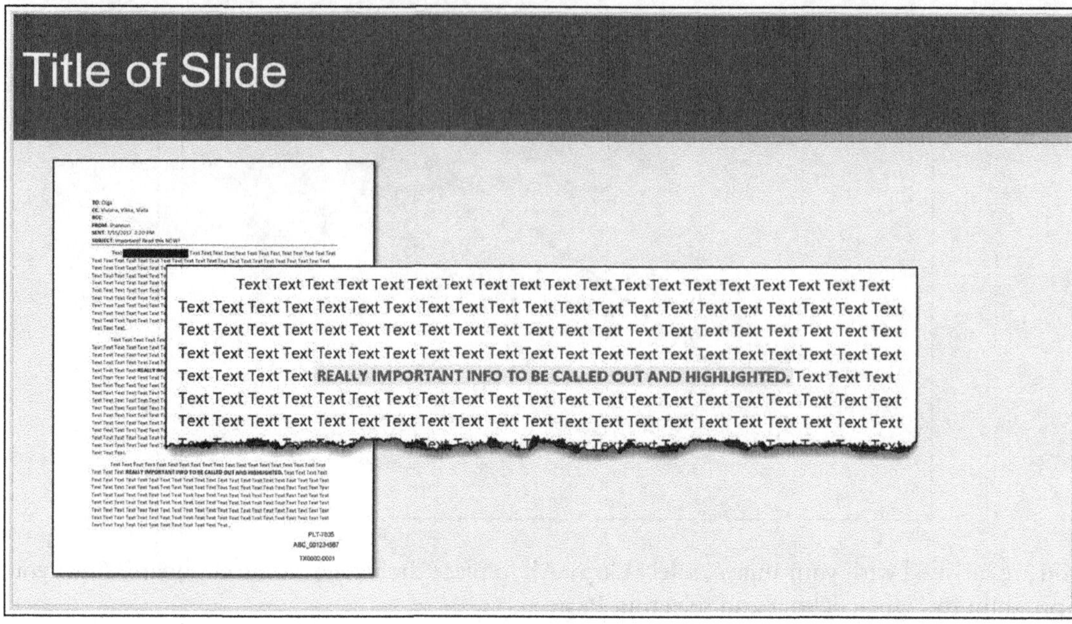

Place the callout on slide and position to your preference. You may want to consider either animating the callout so decision-makers can see the background document first (even if it is a quick flash) or making a slide that shows only the document without the callout.

Don't forget visibility; size your callout (and fonts) appropriately for the courtroom so everyone can see it.

13.2 PowerPoint

13.2.1 Create a template

A template is important if you are creating slides in bulk. You can create custom slides styles to be used for different types of data, whether it is a callout of an exhibit, testimony from a witness (with a spot reserved for their photo), or a bullet-point list. It also makes the process quicker, more organized, and consistent.

Remember to create a template in the aspect ratio of the presentation you want to give in the courtroom (either 4:3 or 16:9), to adjust the point sizes of your fonts for the room you will present in so the text is readable, and the resolution matches that of the courtroom monitors to your presentation will display correctly.

Task 1. Go to "View."

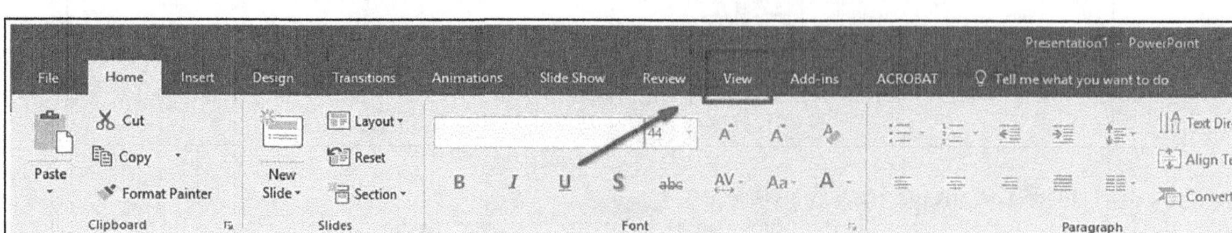

Click on the **View** tab.

Task 2. Choose "Slide Master."

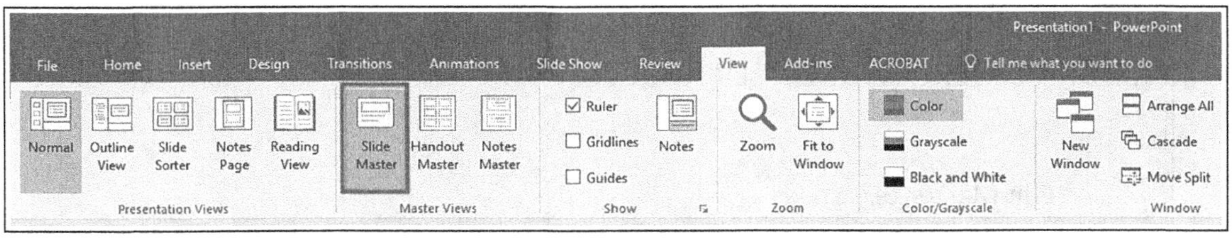

Click **Slide Master** in your presentation.

Task 3. Go the top level master slide.

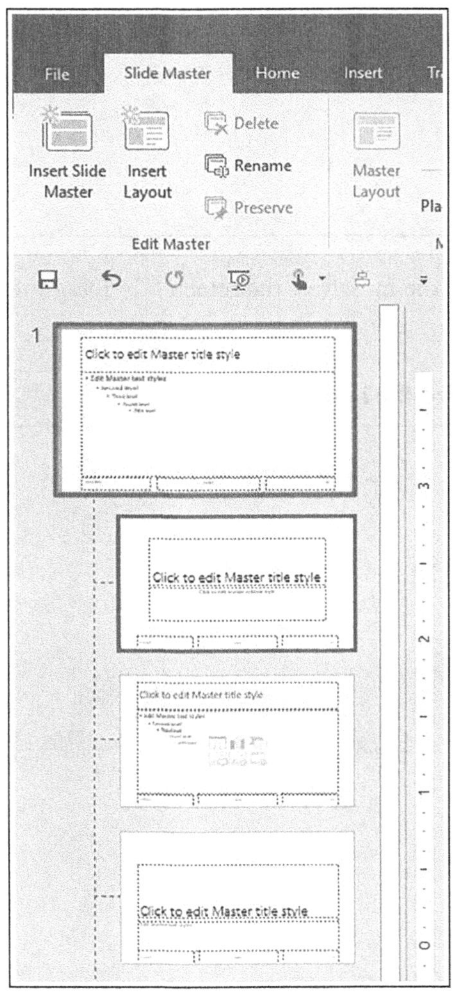

Select the top **Master slide**.

Task 4. Adjust the title to maximize its space.

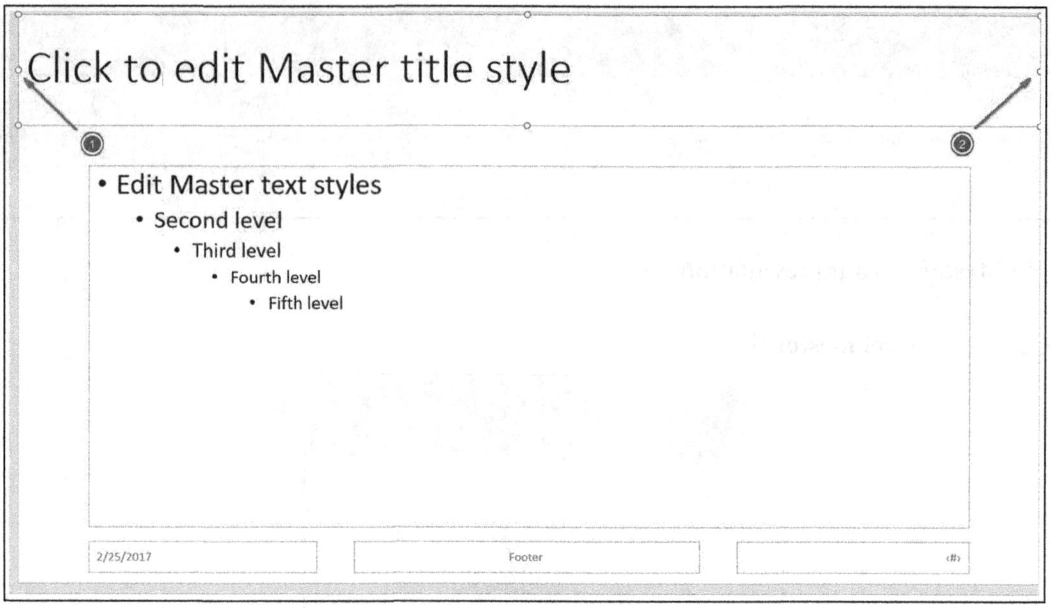

(1) Drag the left side of the title to the far left of the screen. (2) Drag the right side of the title box to the right side of the screen.

Task 5. Adjust the body to maximize the body text space.

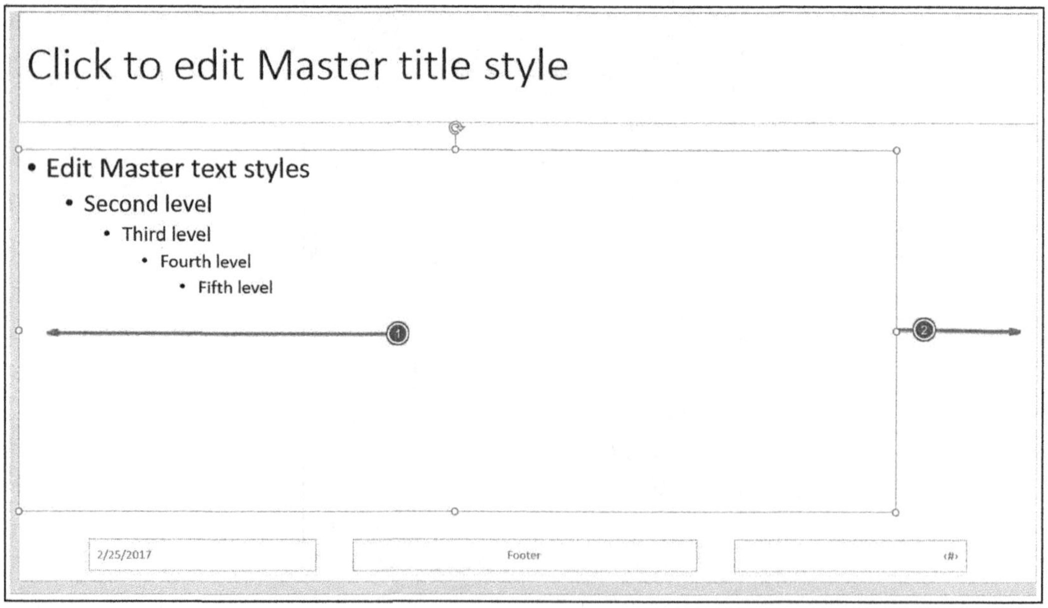

(1) Drag the left side of the body to the far left of the screen. (2) Drag the right side of the body to the right side of the screen.

Task 6. Add some optional razzle-dazzle.

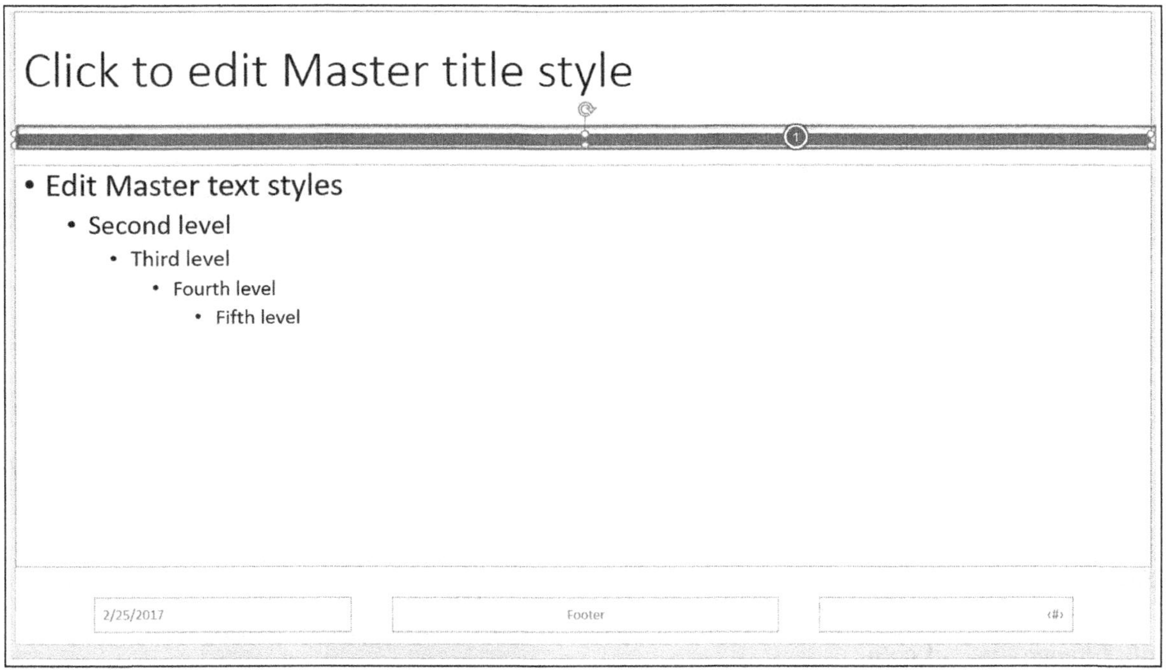

(1) Insert a thin rectangle at the base of the title box.

Task 7. Change the title bar (adding razzle-dazzle) background color.

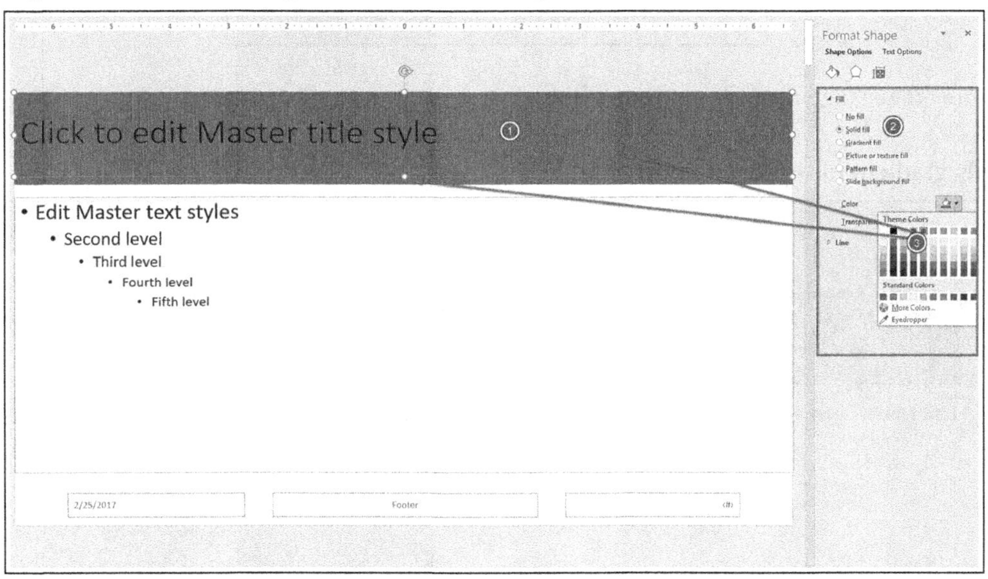

(1) Right-click on the title bar and select **Format Shape**. (2) Go to **Fill** and then choose **Solid Fill**. (3) Choose the background colors to be used. I typically go with a dark color and change the font color to white for contrast.

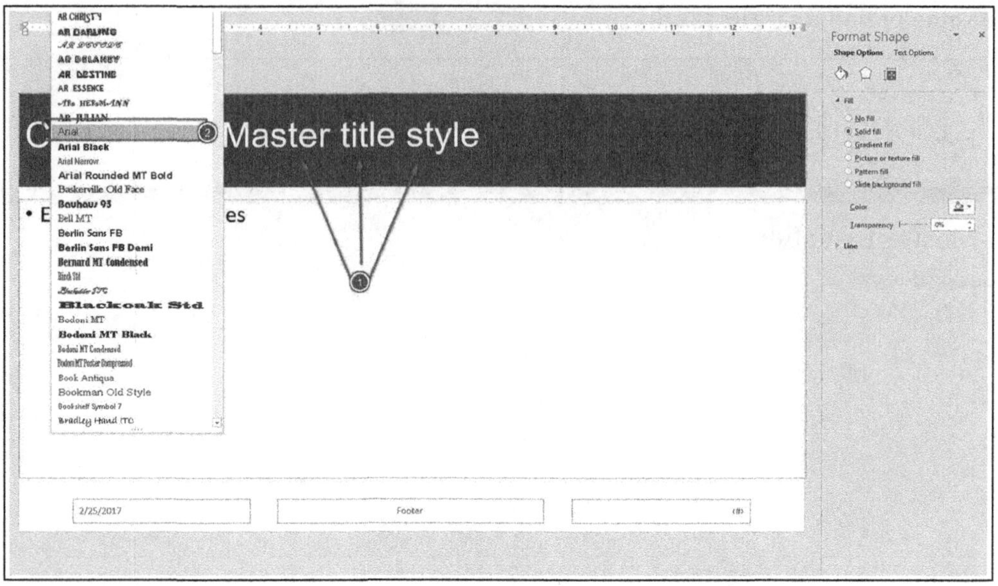

(1) Select the text to change the font style. (2) Change the font to a sans serif font (Arial, Calibri, etc.).

Task 8. Change the font color.

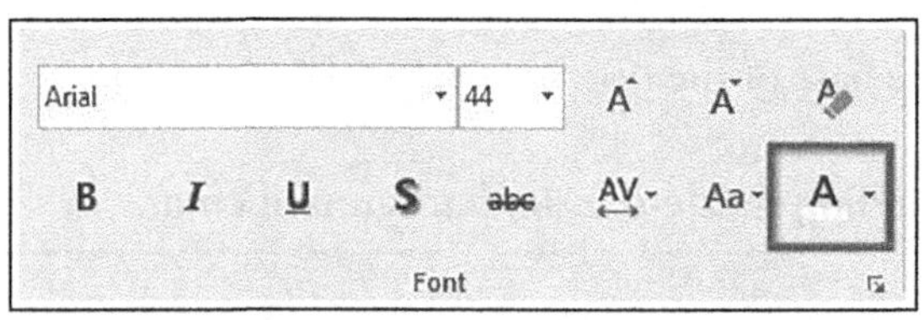

On the **Home** tab, change the font color to white.

Task 9. Apply gradient for optional razzle-dazzle.

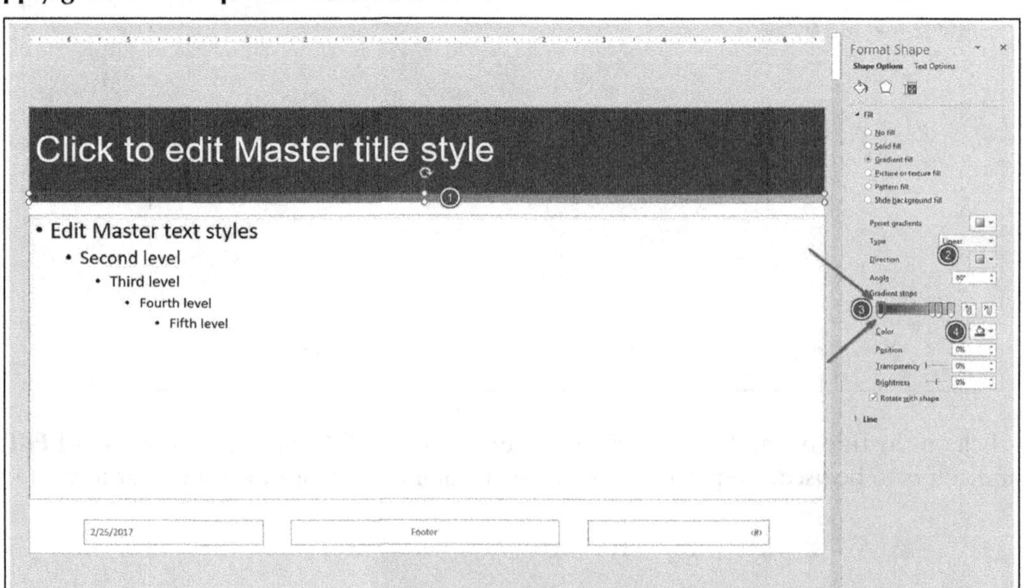

Getting back to our optional thin rectangle, let's apply a gradient that uses dark and light colors to provide a stronger and more interesting delineation between the title bar and body text. (1) Select the long thin rectangle under the title bar. (2) Choose the direction the gradient will flow—usually linear right. (3) Select the far left arrow and change its color. (4) Choose the same color as the background for your title bar.

Task 10. Close the "Master View."

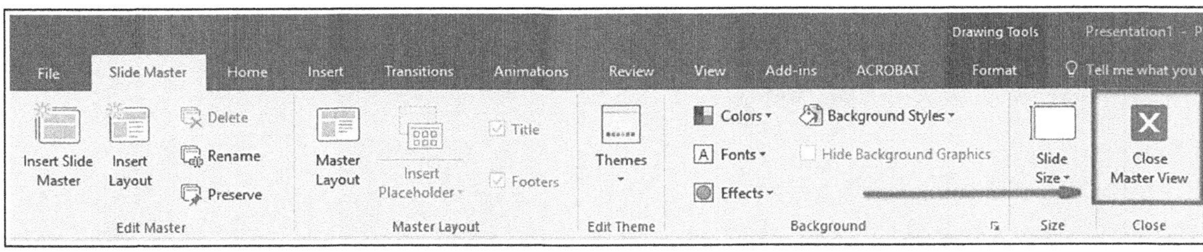

Go to the **Slide Master** tab and select **Close Master View**. You are ready to begin creating slides.

13.2.2 Insert an image

Task 1. Go to the "Insert" tab.

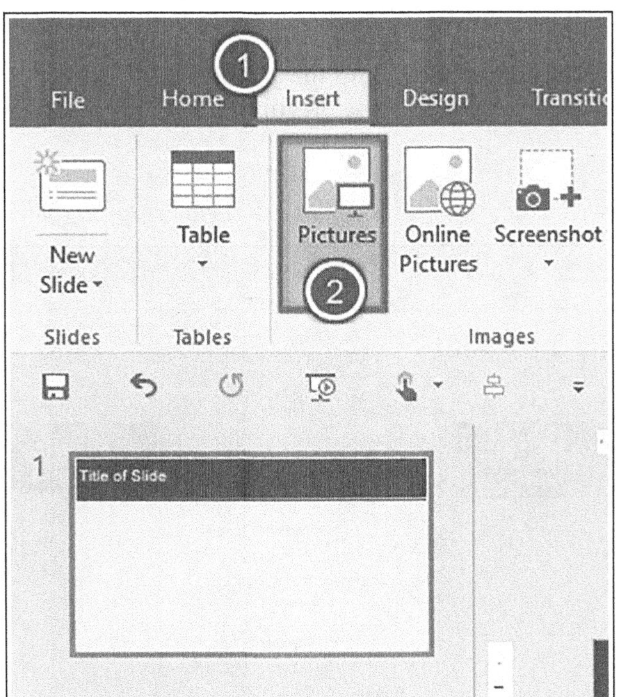

(1) Go to **Insert** and (2) select **Pictures**.

Task 2. Select the picture to insert.

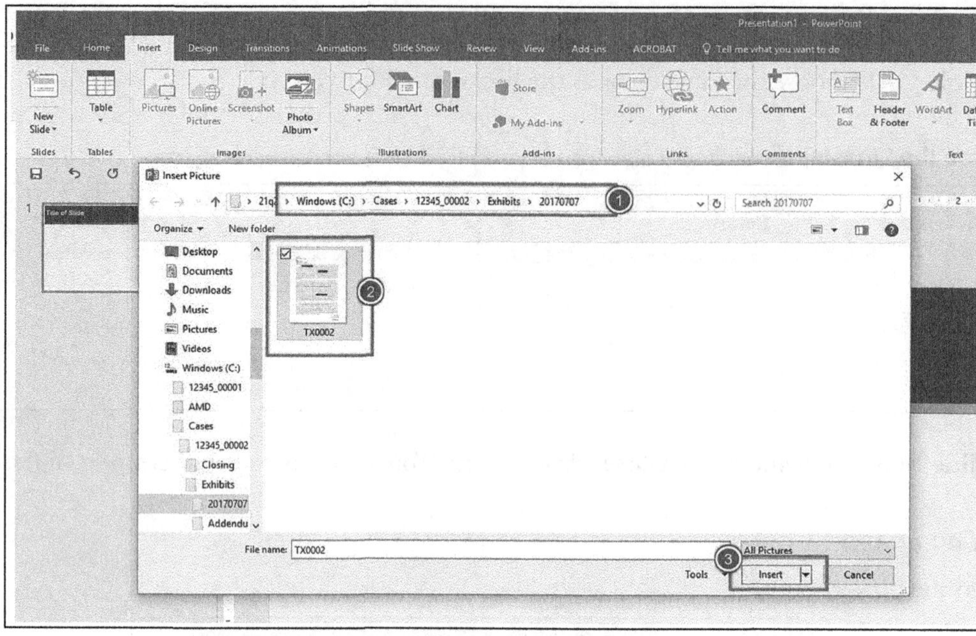

(1) Navigate to the case folder location that contains the exhibits to be added. (2) Select the exhibit to be added. (3) **Select** Insert to place the image in the slide. Case organization is very helpful in creating an efficient process for creating slides.

Task 3. Resize the image.

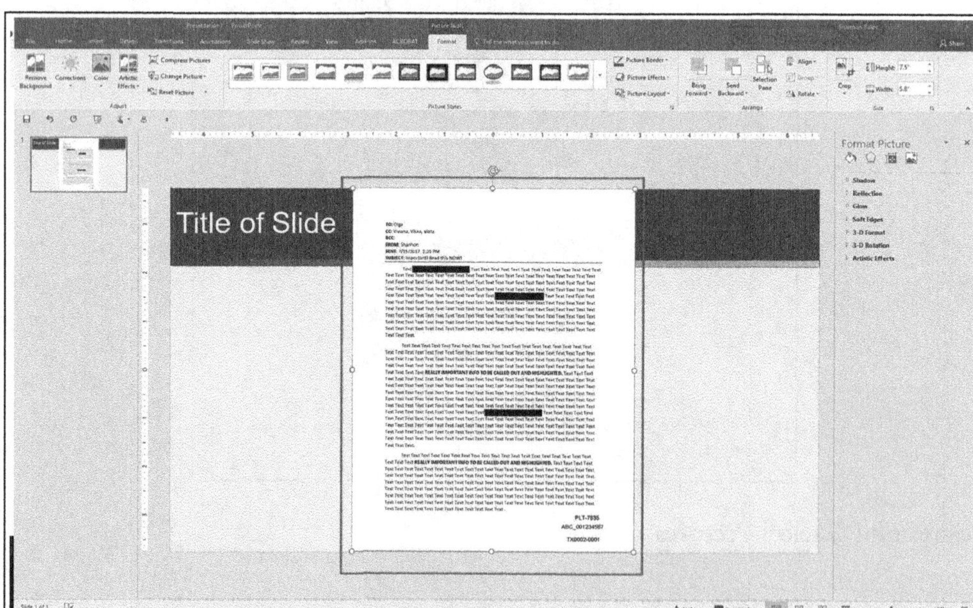

The image will need to be resized. Click the lower right corner and drag until you reach the desired size between the bottom of the slide and the title bar. Being consistent from slide to slide on image size can be tricky.

Task 4. Place the image.

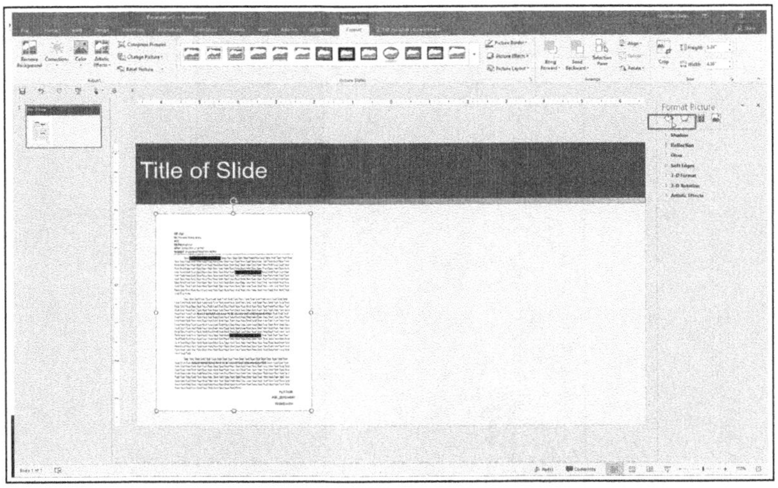

Place the image to your preference—typically, on the left side or center of the slide.

Task 5. Make the image stand out—*pop*!

By placing a hairline frame around the exhibit images in your presentation, the images will stand out more on the page.

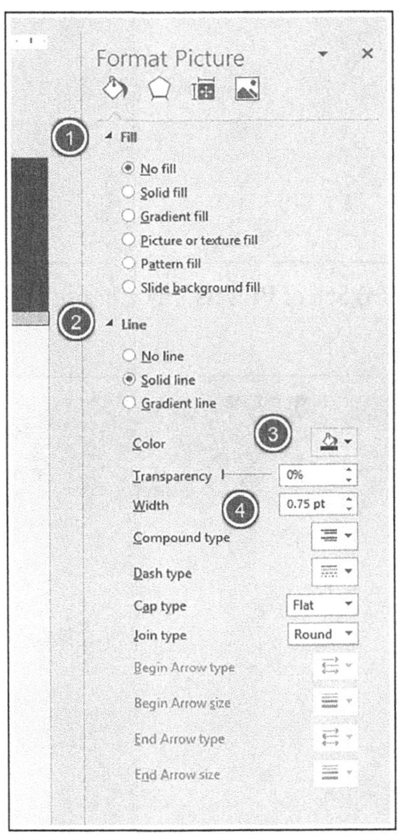

(1) Go to **Fill**. (2) Choose **Line**. (3) Select the **Color** of the line (usually black). (4) Select line **Width** (usually 1.25 point).

Task 6. Apply a shadow.

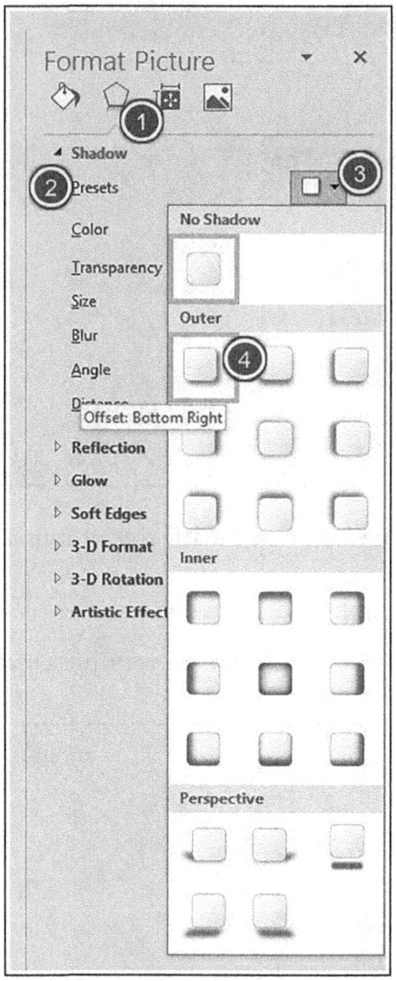

(1) Go to **Effects**. (2) Select **Shadow**. (3) Select **Presets**. (4) Choose **Offset: Bottom Right** (or your preference).

The slide is now ready for annotation.

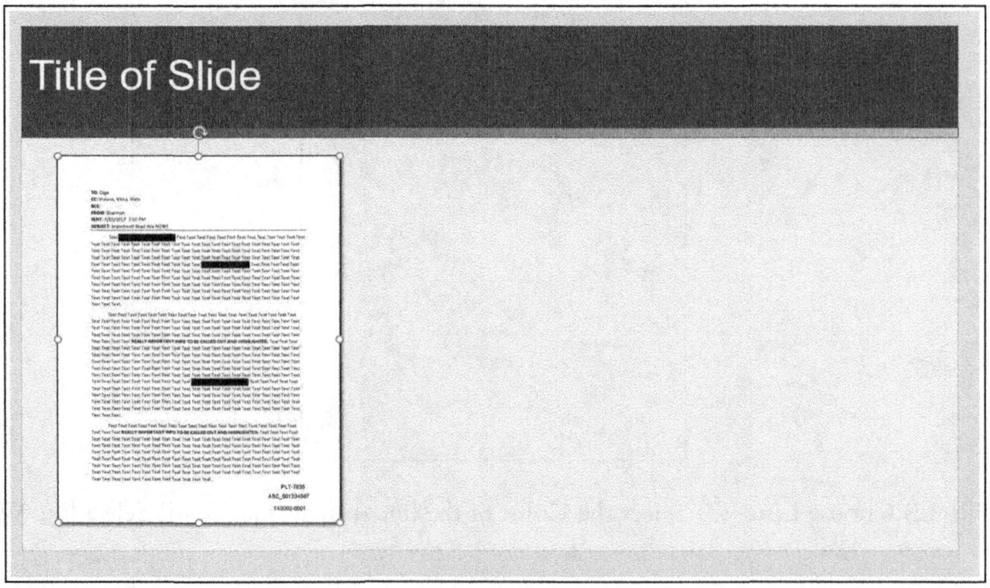

13.2.3 Create Callouts and Enlargements

Task 1. Choose the image to be annotated.

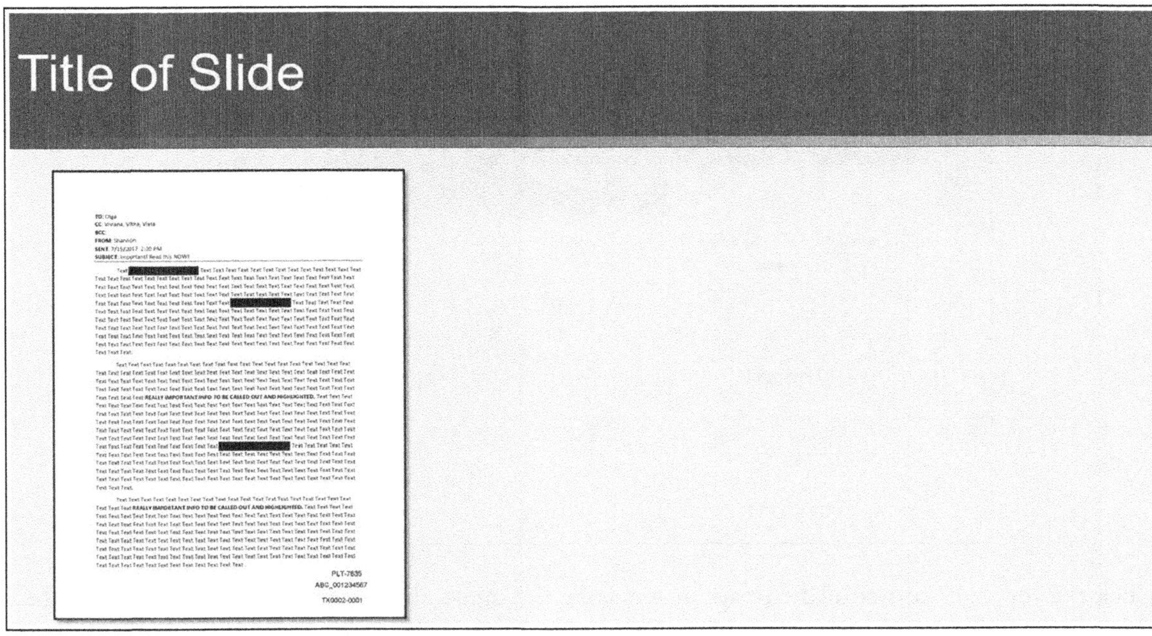

Right-click the image and choose **Copy**.

Task 2. Copy the image.

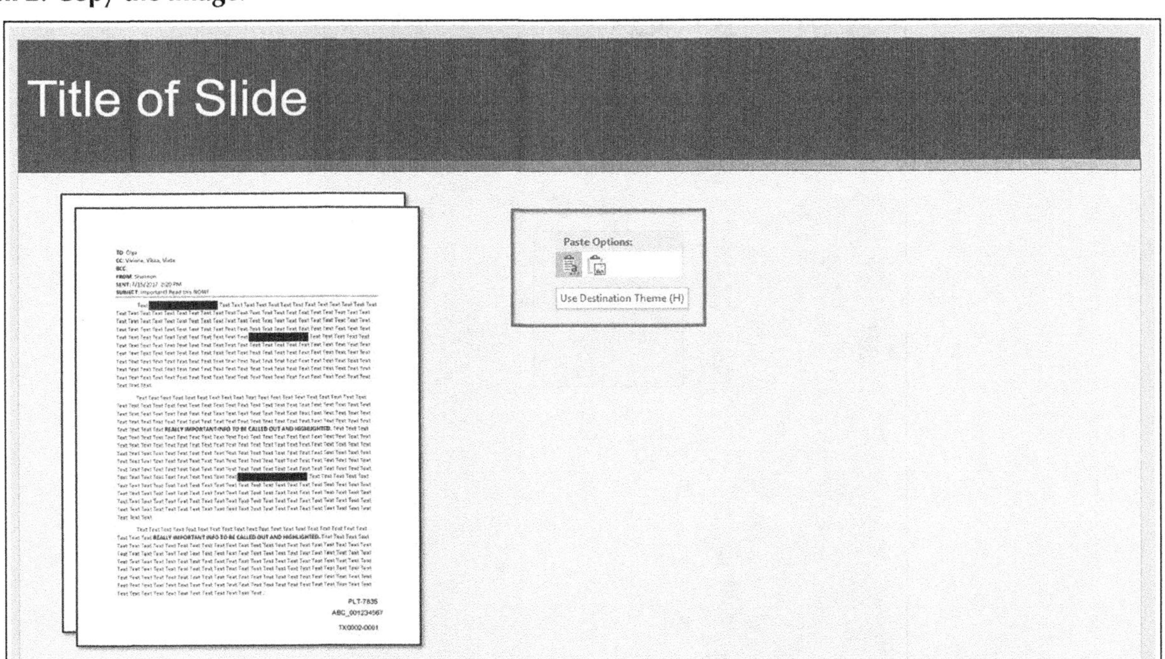

We will be creating two annotations. Both will be enlargements and one with a highlight. Paste two copies of the image on the page. It doesn't matter where . . . yet.

Task 3. Enlarge the image and go to "Picture Tools."

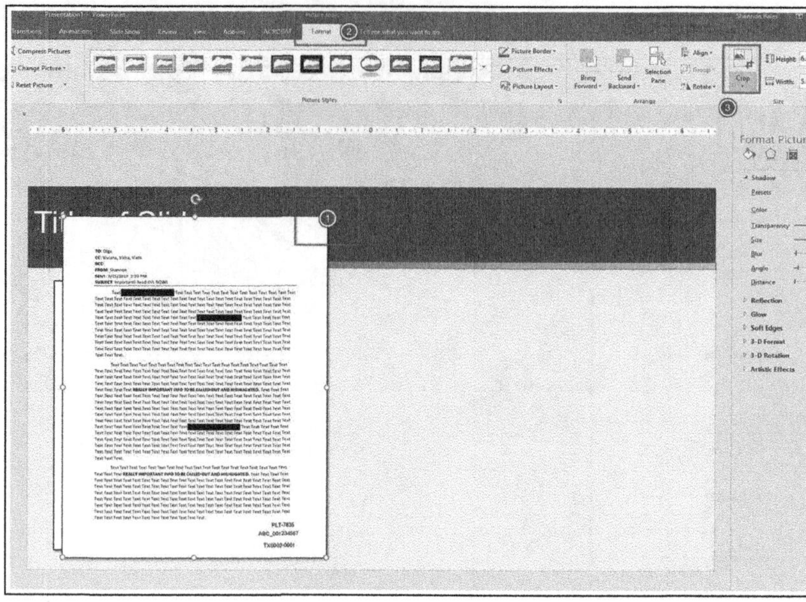

(1) Click the top right corner of the image and enlarge the image slightly by dragging away from the image. Make sure you don't distort the aspect ratio of the image. (2) Go to the **Picture Tools** tab. (3) Select **Crop**.

Task 4. Crop the header information.

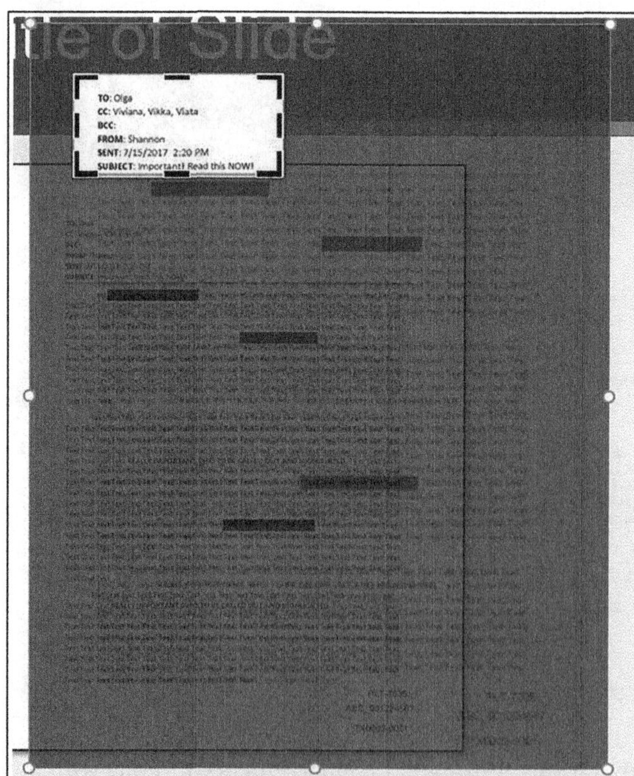

Crop the image using the bold black guides to only show the header info from the email.

Task 5. Place the callout of the header information on the page.

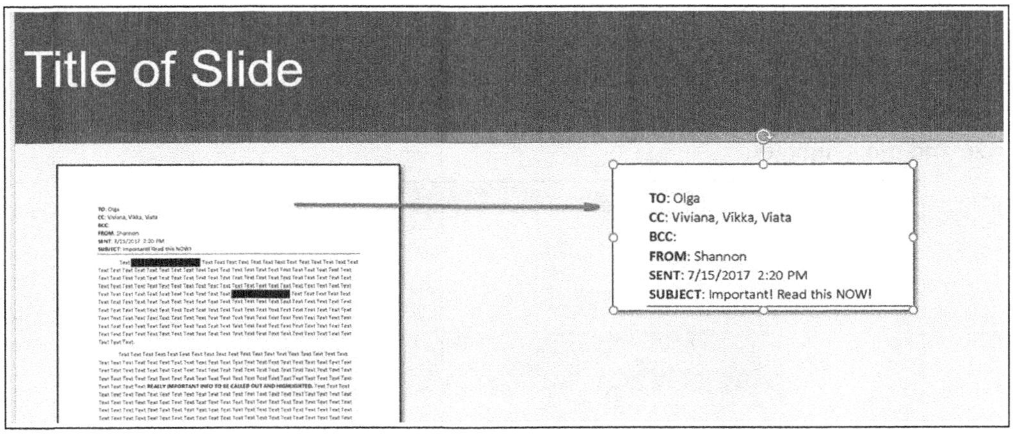

Move the header callout to the right side of the screen. If the line and shadow are not with the document, then reapply, as explained above.

Task 6. Repeat the cropping process.

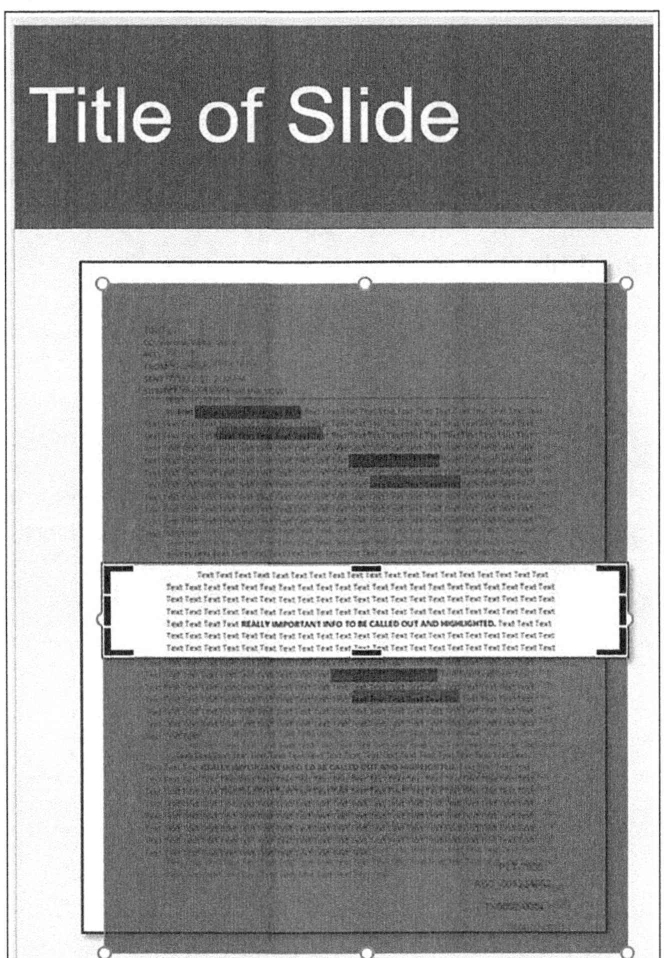

On the second copy of the image, crop the image as previously directed to only show the sentence that you want as a callout. Consider using Snagit to get a better-quality callout image if the current process produces a low-quality result. Keep a few lines above and below the text. By the way, having the document behind the annotated callouts is to show that you aren't hiding the ball as well (Remember "document authenticity" in Part One?)

Task 7. Resize and move images.

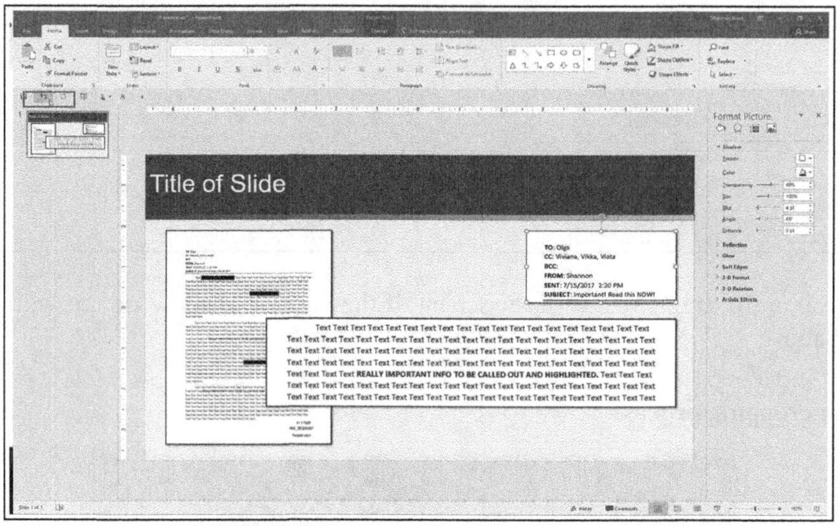

Resize and move the images until they look right on screen. Typically, there is some overlap.

13.2.4 Create Highlights

Task 1. Select an image to be highlighted.

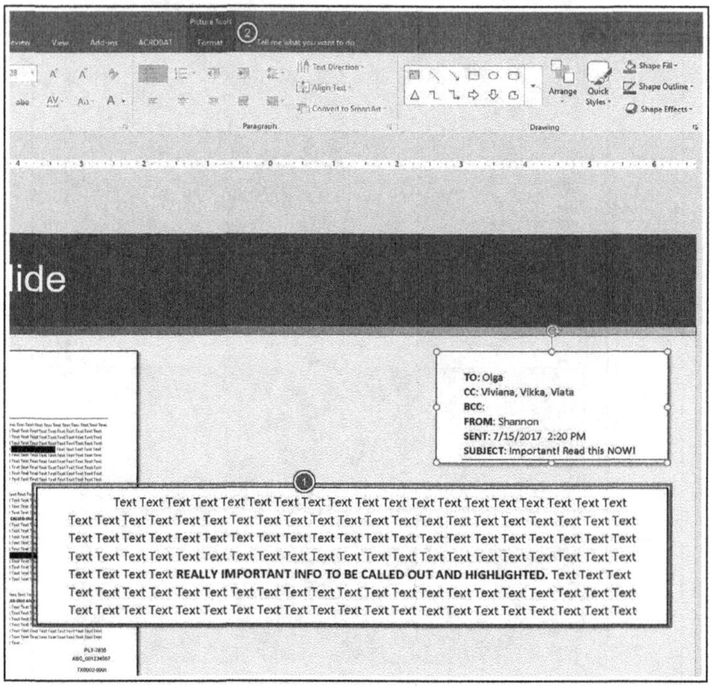

There is *not* a good highlight feature within PowerPoint. The method I describe here is time-consuming, but can produce a higher quality result. Which method you choose will likely depend on the amount of available time you have. In addition to this method where we will place several layers of images behind the text (you'll see soon), you could place a rectangle over the text and adjust the transparency—but this method is horrible and produces a bad result.

I highly recommend you use Snagit or another screen capture utility to do your screen captures and highlighting in three or four steps.

(1) Selected the image to be highlighted. (2) Select **Picture Tools** from the menu.

Task 2. Select "Color."

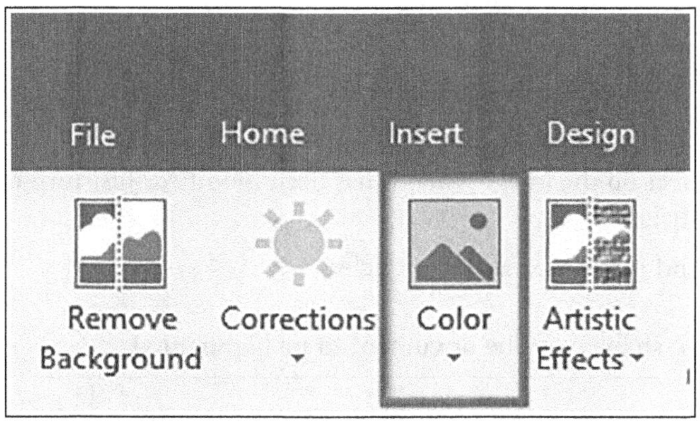

On the **Picture Tools** menu, select **Color**.

Task 3. Set "Transparent Color."

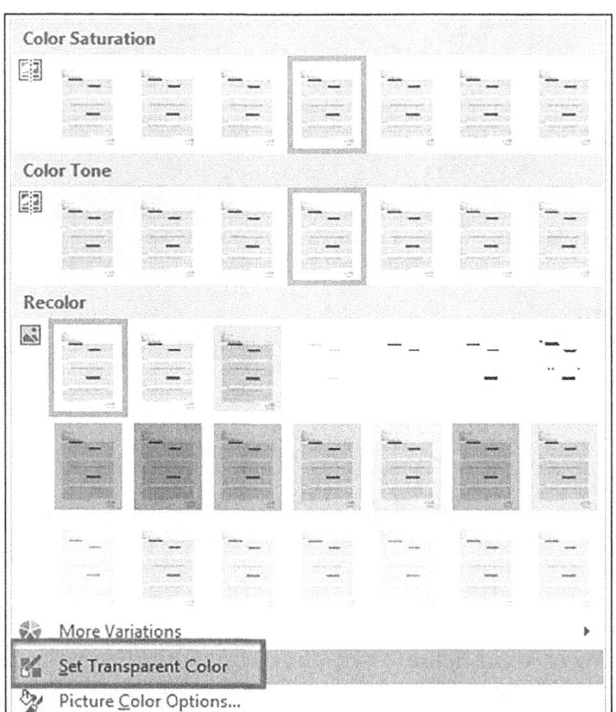

Under **Corrections**, select **Set Transparent Color**. This will make clear a single color from the image. This tool does not work well on low-quality images or images with multiple interwoven colors.

Task 4. Choose color to be transparent.

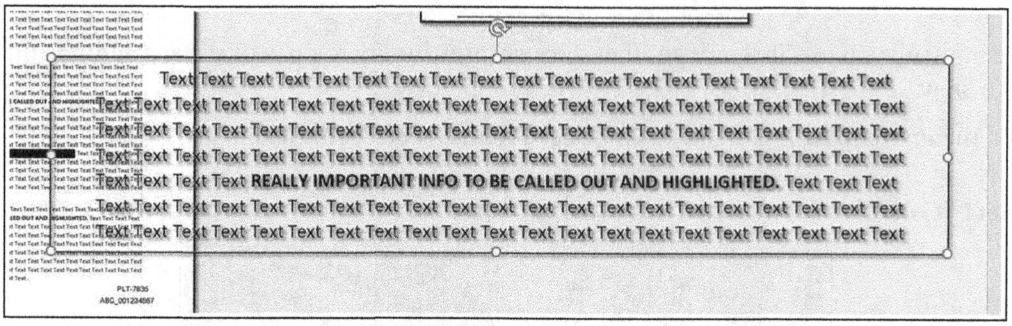

Click in the white area of the image you are annotating. It should become clear. Sometimes the shadow feature will produce an unwanted effect on the image when it has been modified. Just turn off the shadow on the callout if this is the case with your image.

Note: The white background is removed and is now clear.

Task 5. Draw a similar size shape over the document to be highlighted.

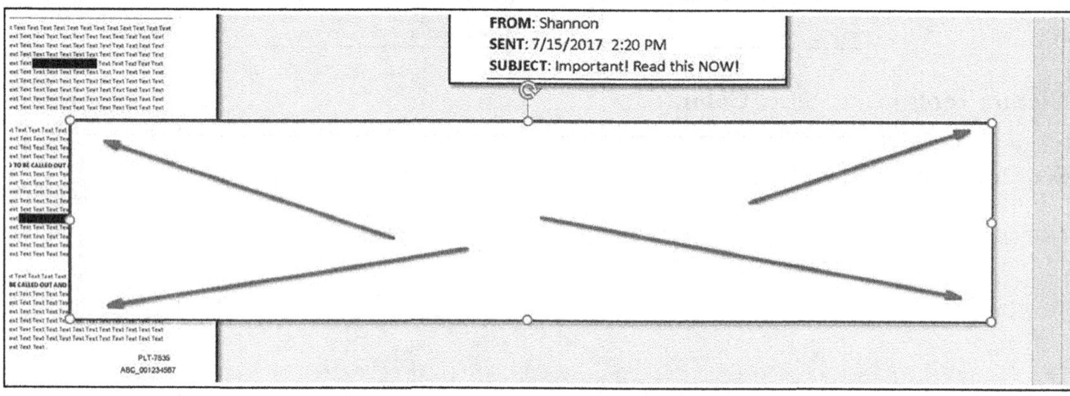

The shape should be white in color.

Task 6. Bring the text forward.

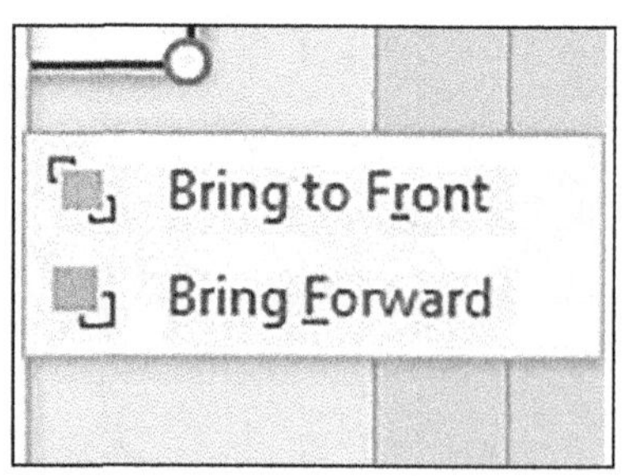

This could be tricky, but bring forward the text by right-clicking on the text and selecting **Bring Forward**.

Task 7. Ensure the background has been removed.

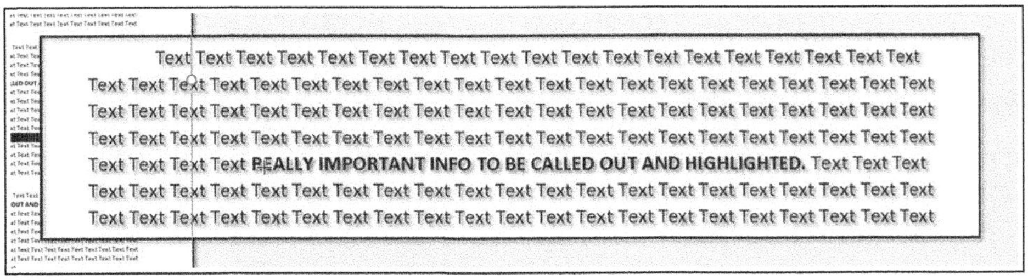

The background is no longer transparent. Sometimes there are multiple layers and you'll have to cycle through the layers until you get your desired result.

Task 8. Apply highlight shape.

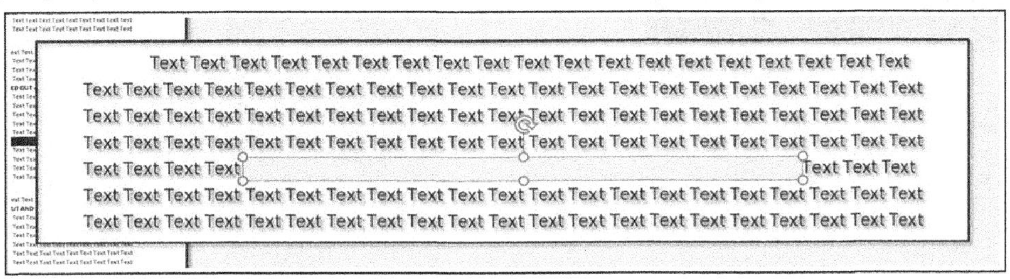

Apply a shape using bright yellow fill to create your highlight (remove shadow).

Task 9. Bring text forward.

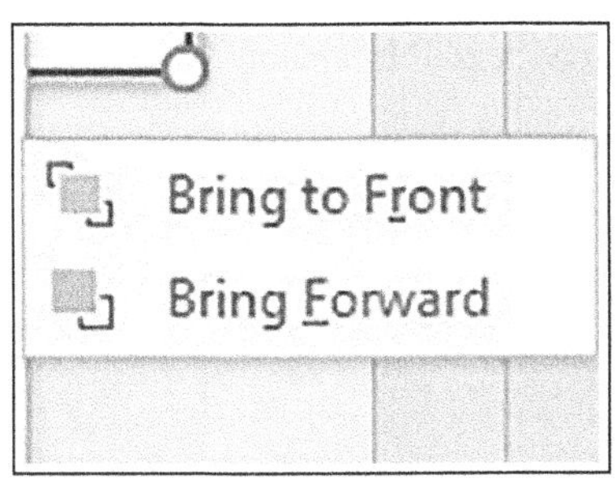

This could be tricky, but bring rorward (second time) the text by right-clicking on the text and selecting **Bring Forward**.

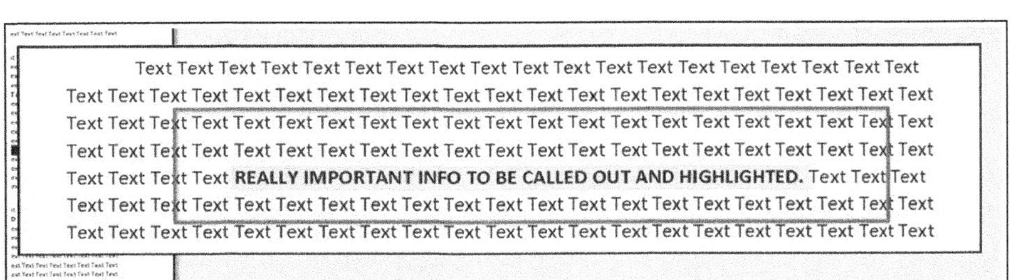

The text has now been highlighted. Be careful, as any resizing or changes to image position will ruin the highlight.

13.3 Movie Maker

13.3.1 Set Up a Default Section

Task 1. Create stand-alone video clips.

Keeping in mind that you can also create clips in your trial software of choice, it is often a good idea to clip them separately. Primarily, you will not waste hard drive space on your presentation laptop and you can enlist other people to help. Do not use this method if you have synchronized transcript video; you will be giving up a lot of technical capability in addition to the synced text. Note that video is the most time-consuming part of trial prep.

Start by dragging the video file into Movie Maker.

Task 2. Set the start point of the video.

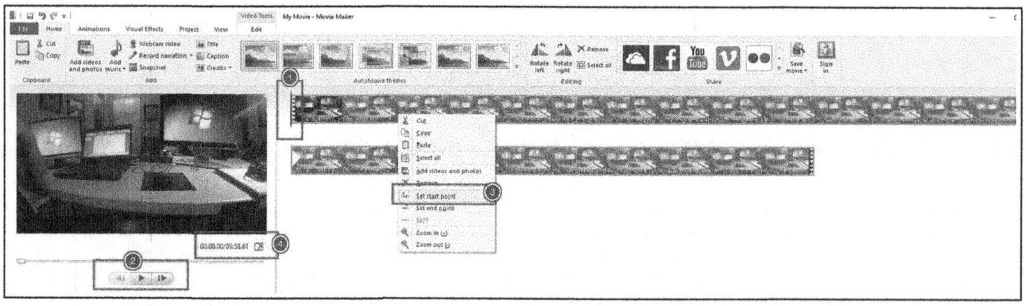

(1) Use the slider to find the time point that the video should start. (2) Play the video when you reach your proposed start time to make sure that the video starts and stops at the right place. (3) Right-click and select **Set Start Point**. (4) You should see a reduction in the total time of the video.

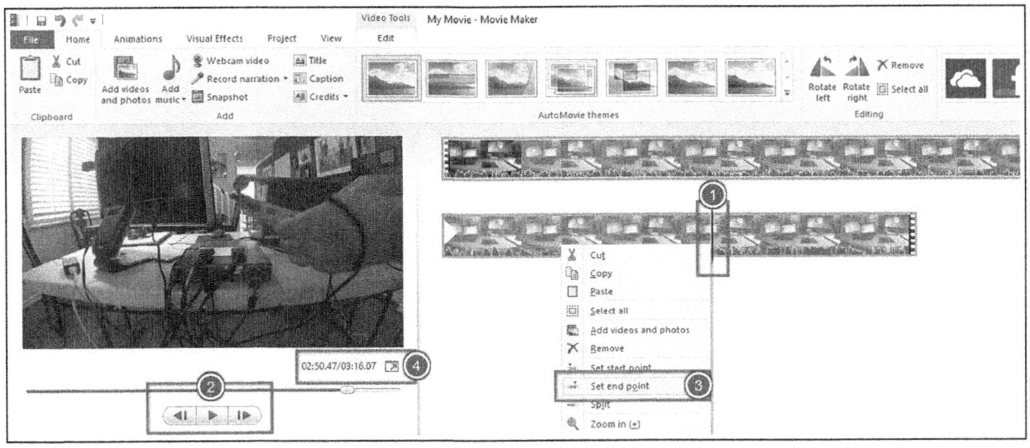

(1) Use the slider to find the time point that the video should end. (2) Play the video when you reach your proposed end time to make sure that the video starts and stops at the right place. (3) Right-click and select **Set End Point**. (4) You should see a reduction in the total time of the video.

Task 3. Save the movie.

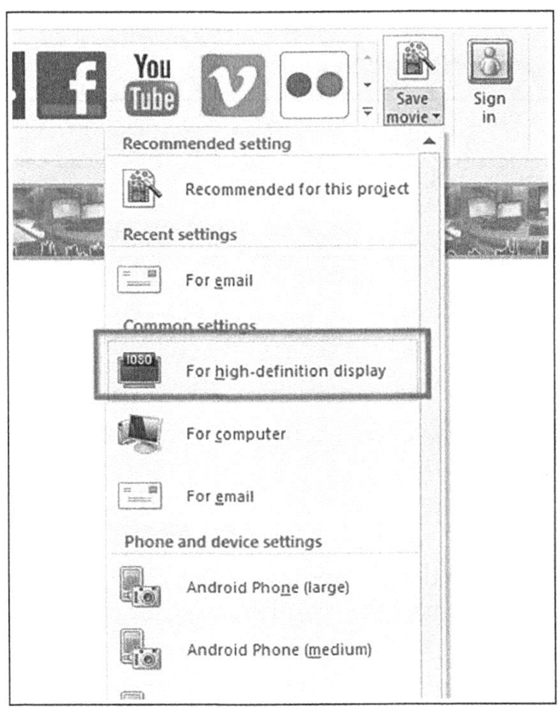

As a beginner or intermediate, use the recommended settings for export. Typically, I choose **For high-definition display**. Each option produces a different file size result, so find the combination of file size and quality that works for you. Also, test on your trial laptop to make sure it works.

Note: If it didn't work and you thought adding a video codec would be a good idea—don't. The new codec can mess with trial presentation software. Always install trial presentation software last.

Task 4. Save the movie.

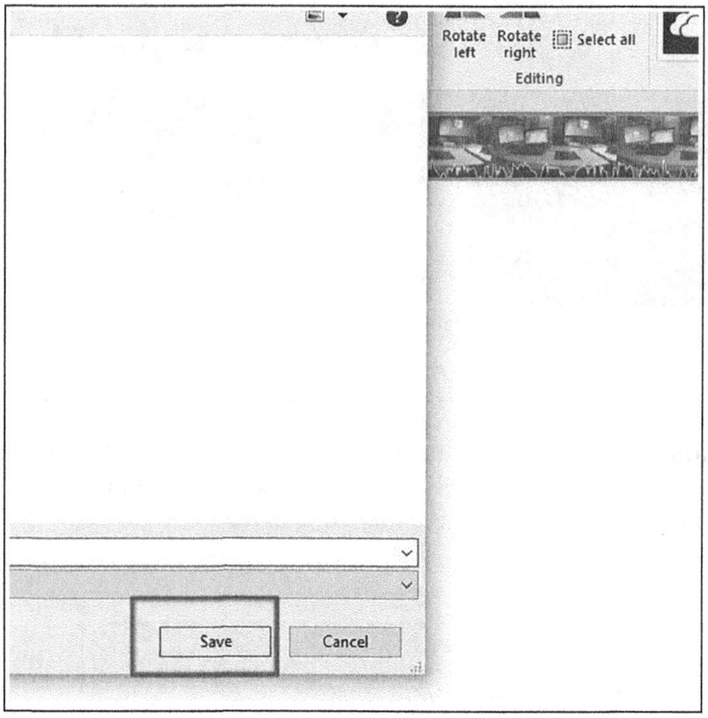

Click **Save** in **Save Movie**.

Task 5. Be patient and test the export.

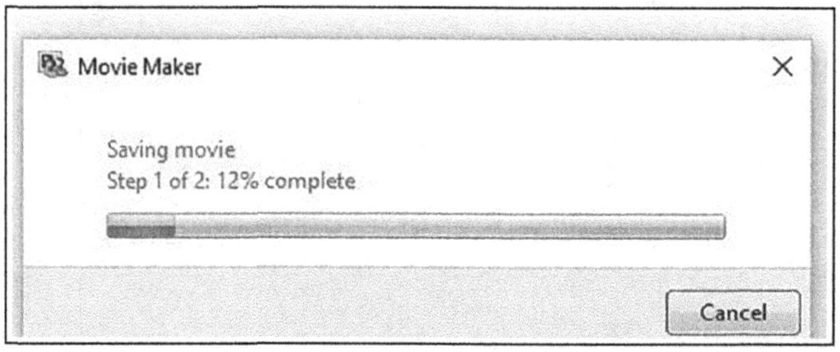

The video can take quite a while to render, depending on size of the video and the choices made for export. Always test your video after export on the machine you plan to use it on.

13.4 Total Commander

13.4.1 Total Commander

Task 1. Take a tour.

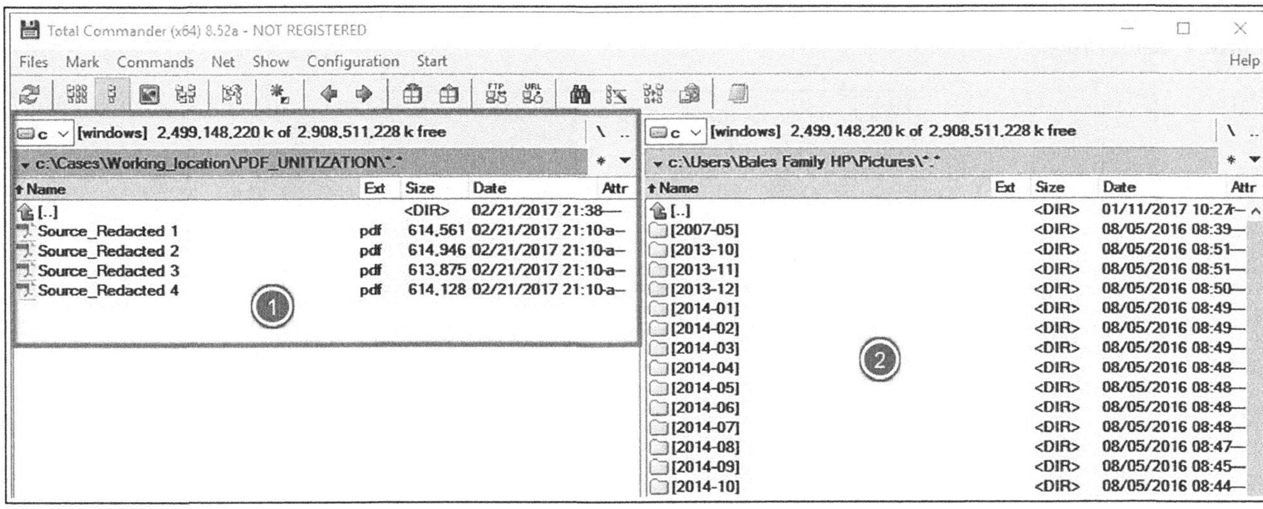

Total commander is a useful utility for a wide variety of tasks. I will go over the basics of file compare and renaming and capturing file names, which is useful for creating lists. The left side of the screen (1) is the working side, for renaming, capturing file names, and many other useful tasks. The right side of the screen (2) is used for file comparisons, which are useful in trying to copy files from laptops, network locations, and backup drives to where they need to go. Think of how this might be used to create a redundant system. Before files are renamed, be sure you have a backup copy that can replace them.

Task 2. Navigate to the location of your files.

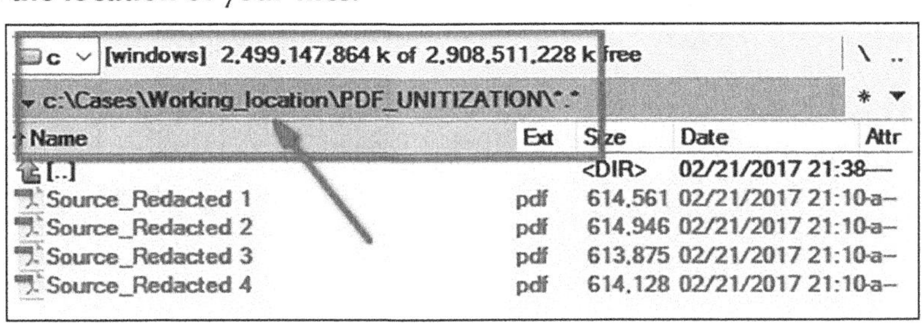

Always start with the files and folders you want to modify in the left side of the screen. Navigate to the files you want to modify.

Task 3. Select your files.

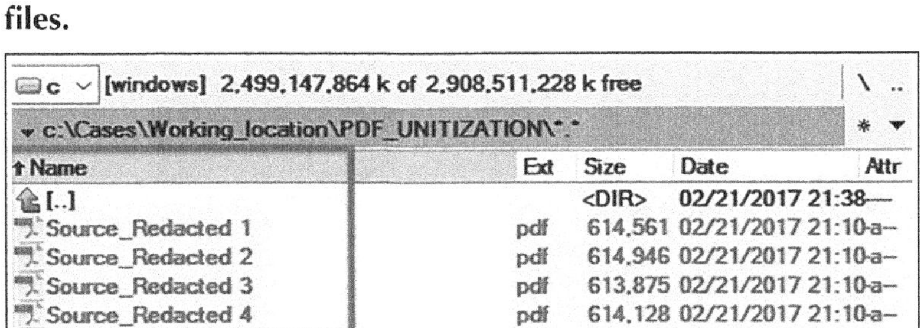

Select the files you want to modify or copy by right-clicking on them. (The same works for folders as well.) Multiple files and folders can be selected by running the mouse over the files while holding down the right mouse button. (You may not be able to see it, but the selected files turn red.)

13.4.2 Rename Files in Bulk

Task 1. Select files.

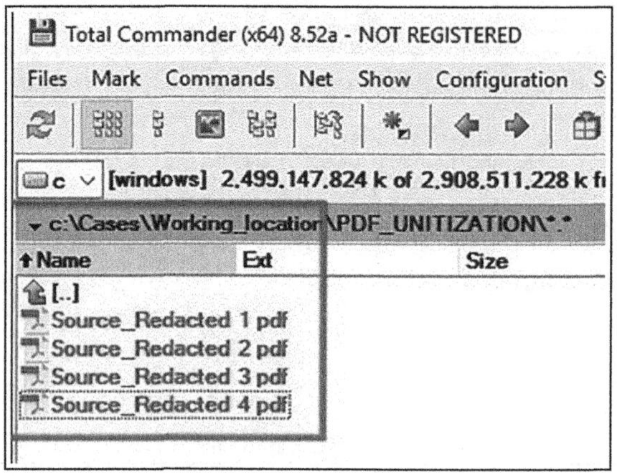

Navigate to the file location and select the files to be renamed by right-clicking on them.

Task 2. Choose the "Multi-Rename Tool...".

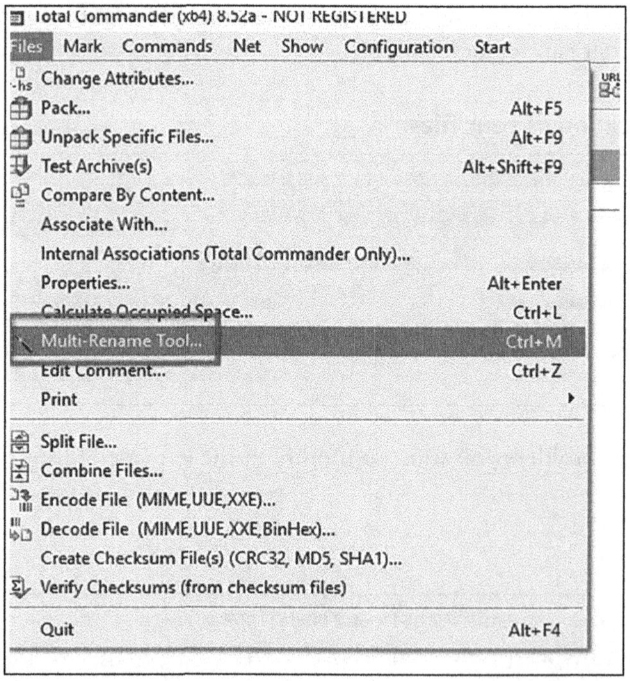

Go to **Files** and select **Multi-Rename Tool...**.

Task 3. Consider the options in the "Multi-Rename Tool...".

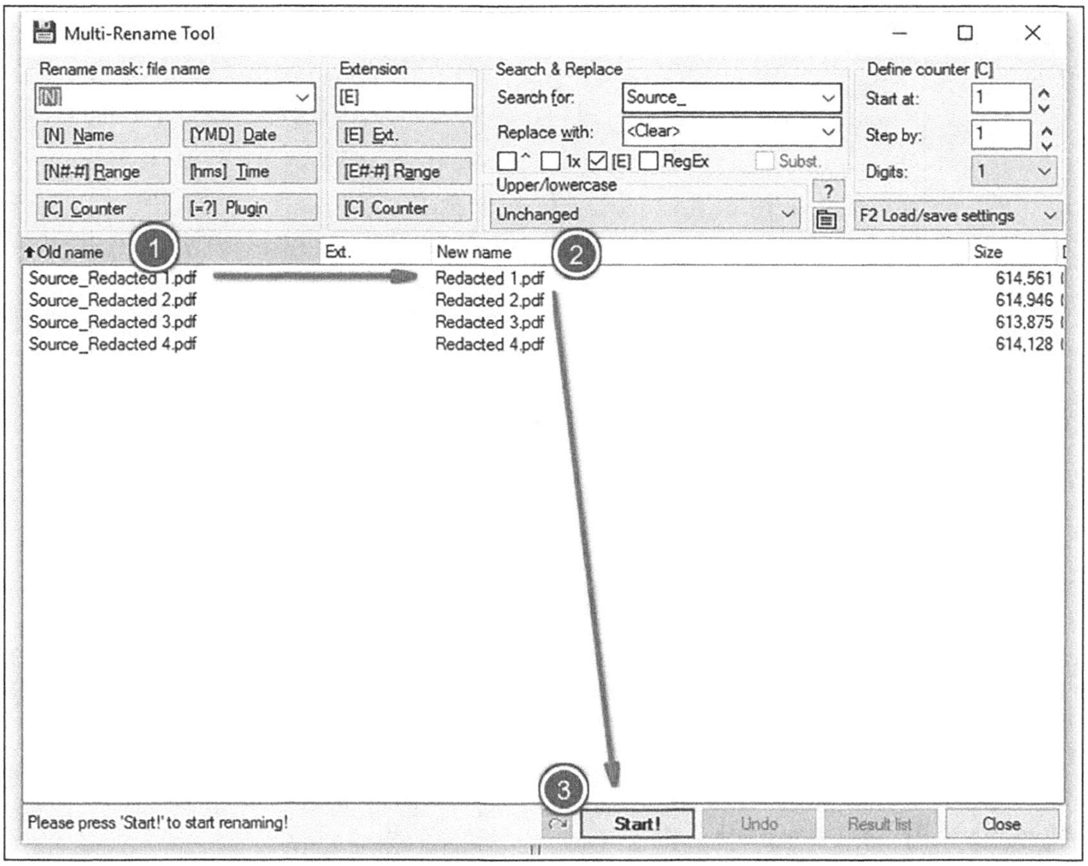

There are numerous options with the multi-rename tool. I'll go over a few for renaming files. You can preview the effect of your file rename by looking at the (1) **Old name** column and comparing against the (2) **New name** column. Changes are permanent until you select (3) **Start**.

Task 4. Learn about "Search & Replace."

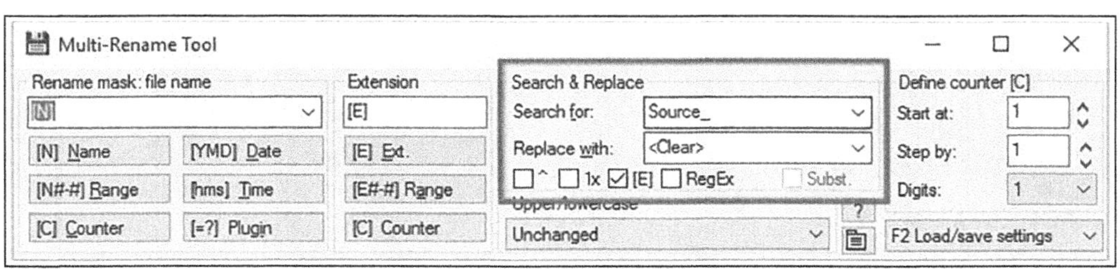

Search & Replace allows you to search for text that is in the file names and replace or remove the text. This might occur because of the way you received the documents from opposing counsel. Perhaps they used an overly long naming convention (like Smith vs. Jones in the Superior Court of Orange County Case No 1234 - Exhibit 123. pdf) or how they were scanned (Xerox_Scanner_Doc_1). In each of the examples, the long file information can be partially or fully replaced. (You might want to keep just the exhibit number in the first example and rename and number everything in the second.)

Task 5. How to "Search & Replace."

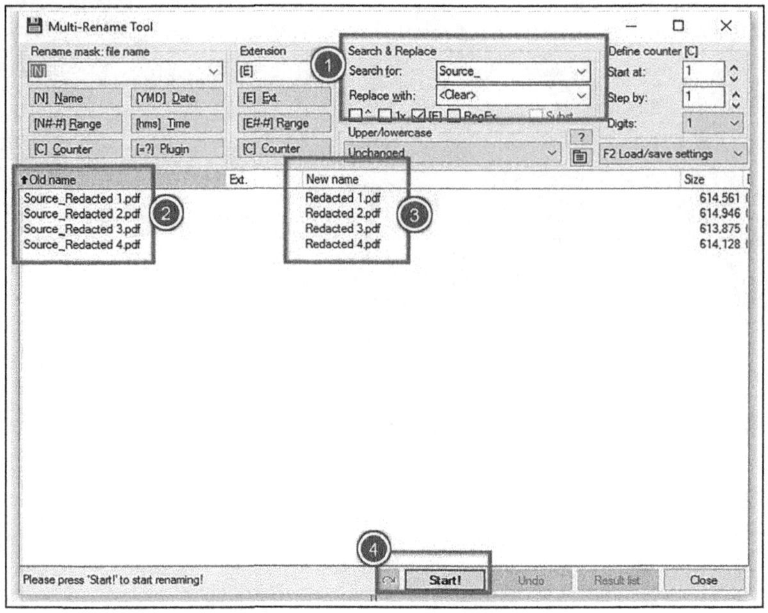

(1) Place the text to be replaced or removed in the **Search for** dialog box. If you want to remove text, enter nothing in the **Replace with** dialog box. (2) Note the original file name: Source_Redacted 1 - Source_Redacted 4.pdf. (3) Note the effect of the replace in the **New name** section, where the files are now named Redacted 1 - Redacted 4.pdf. (4) Choose **Start** to complete the action.

Task 6. How to use the "Rename Mask."

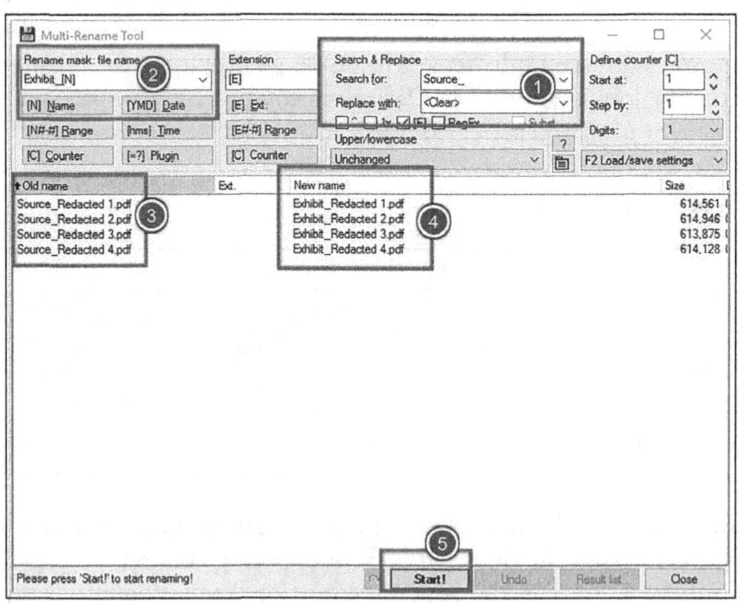

(1) Note I have kept the "search & replace" text from the previous lesson. (2) The **N** in the **Rename mask** dialog box represents the file name and I've added **Exhibit_** in front of it. (3) Note the original file name, Source_Redacted 1 - Source_Redacted 4.pdf. (4) Note the effect of the "search & replace" with the addition of the **Rename mask** text in the **New name** section, Exhibit_Redacted 1 - Exhibit Redacted 4.pdf. (5) Choose **Start** to complete the action.

Task 7. Rename mask to keep existing exhibit numbers, replace text, and add a prefix.

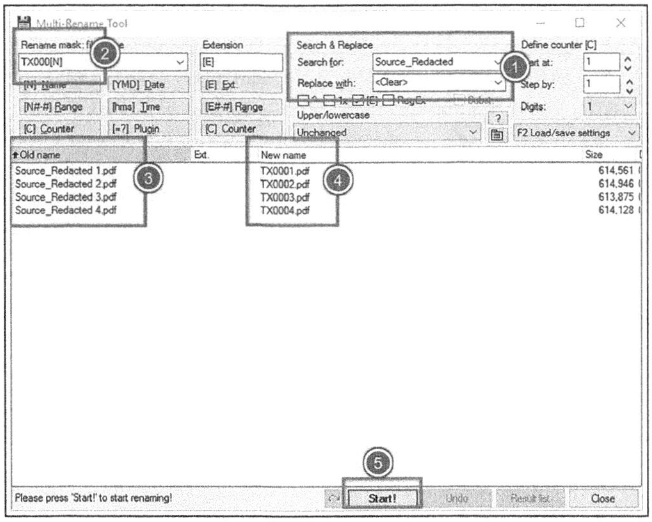

(1) Note we have changed the "search & replace" text from the previous lesson to replace the entire text from the beginning for the file name, Source_Redacted. (2) The **N** in the **Rename mask** dialog box represents the file name, and I've added **TX000** in front of it. (3) Note the original file name, Source_Redacted 1 - Source_Redacted 4.pdf. (4) Note the effect of the "search & replace" with the addition of the **Rename mask** text in the **New name** section, now TX0001 - TX0004.pdf. (5) Choose **Start** to complete the action.

Task 8. Rename mask to create new exhibit numbers, replace text, and add a prefix.

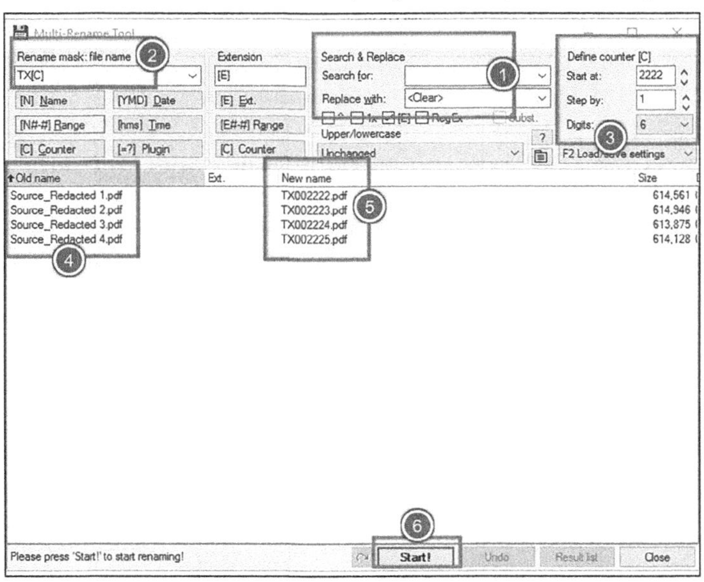

(1) Note that I have removed the "search & replace" text from the previous lessons. I did this because I'm going to completely replace the **N** (**Name**) with the **C** (**Counter**) option. (2) By replacing the file name **N** with a counter **C**, I will renumber the files instead of renaming them. I've also added a **TX** at the beginning of the **C** (**Counter**). (3) The **C** receives its numbering instructions from the **Define Counter** box on the far right where I've defined the starting number **2222** and the number of digits **6**. (4) Note the original file name, Source_Redacted 1 - Source_Redacted 4.pdf. (5) Note the effect of the "search & replace" with the addition of the **Rename mask** counter in the "new name" section, now TX002222 - TX002225.pdf. (6) Choose **Start** to complete the action.

13.4.3 Copy List of File Names

Task 1. Copy a list of file names.

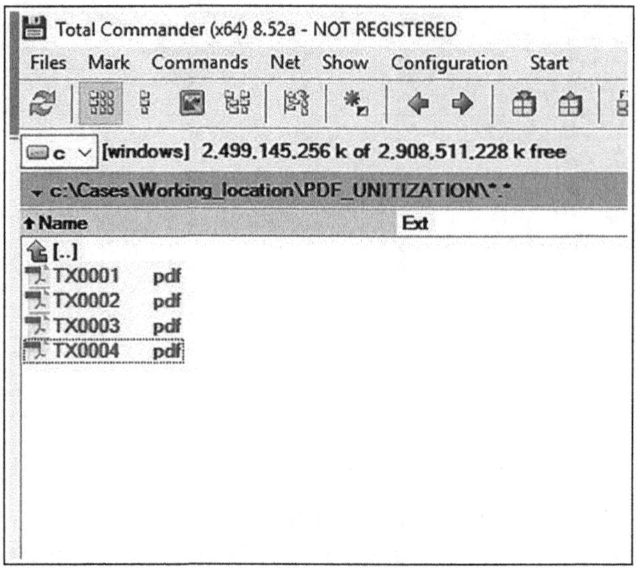

Perhaps you have created multiple folders that contain many exhibits and you need lists of the numbers in each folder. This command will easily do that for you.

First, select your files on the left side of the screen.

Task 2. Select "Mark."

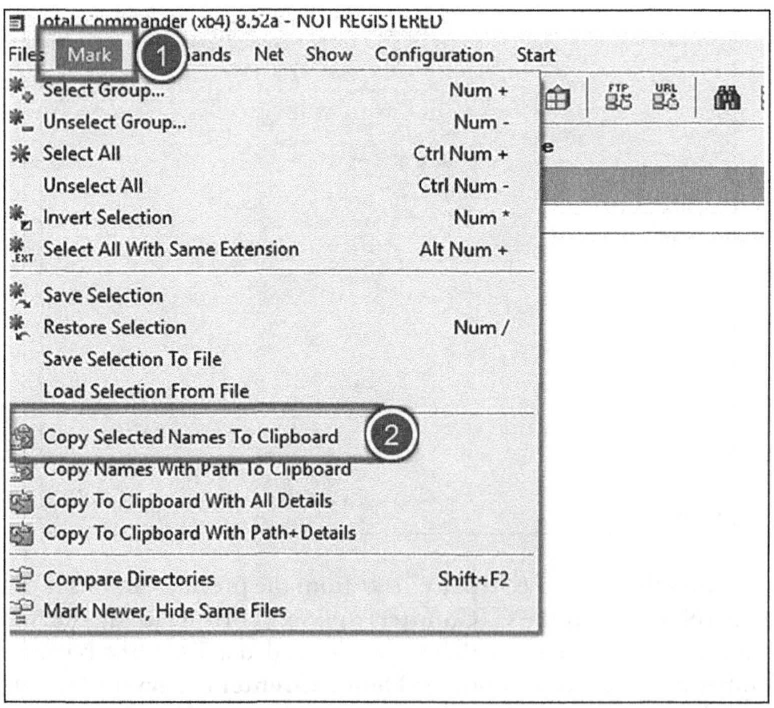

(1) Select **Mark** on the menu bar. (2) Select **Copy Selected Names To Clipboard**. Note there are options here that include path information and other details.

Task 3. Open Notepad (or Excel, Word, or your email).

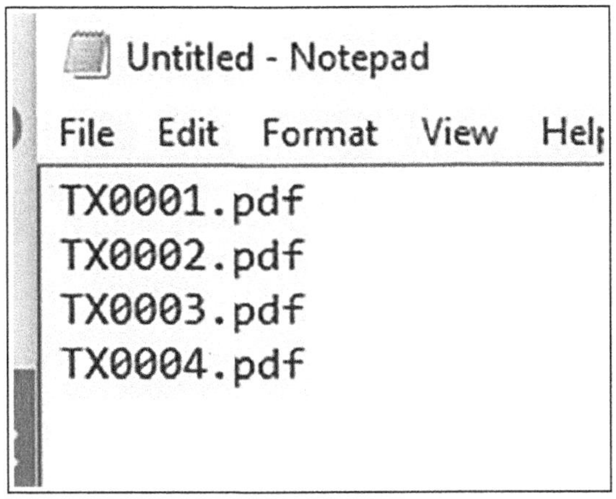

Right-click and select **Paste** to copy the file names to your destination of choice (Word, Excel, your email). This is very helpful in providing people with lists and reports.

13.4.4 Do a File Compare

Task 1. Run a file compare.

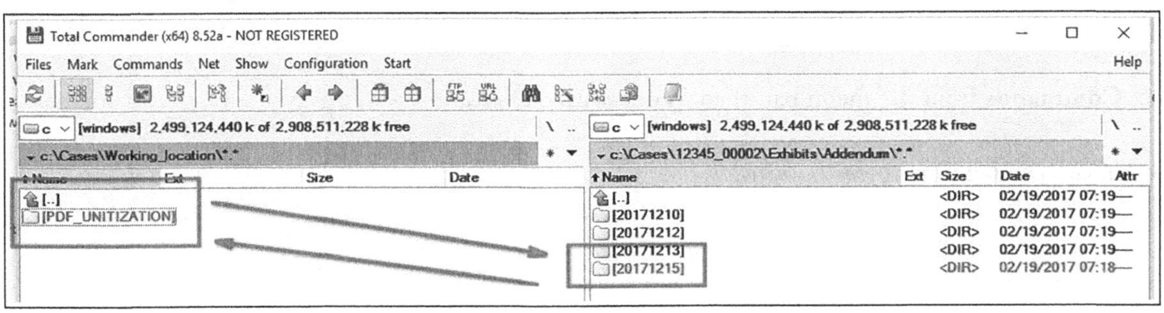

Start by choosing the folders on the left and right sides of the screen you want to synchronize. There are options for coping files a single direction or just to QC to see what is might be missing. This is a great way to create a backup and then copy and QC to a backup computer.

Warning: Use this for exhibits only. Trying to synchronize trial presentation software data files can be problematic.

Task 2. Choose "Synchronize Dirs...".

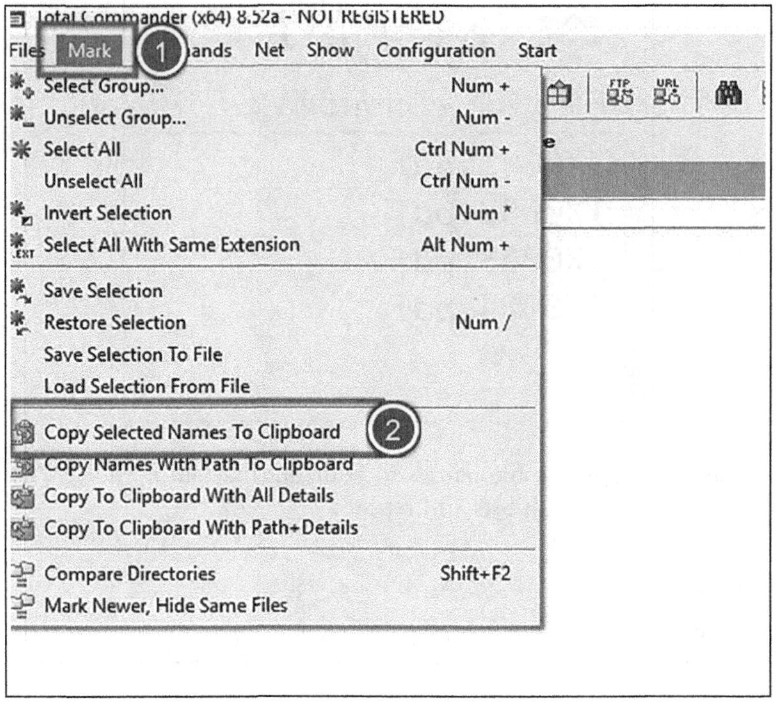

Select **Commands** from the menu bar, then **Synchronize Dirs...**.

Task 3. Synchronize directories options.

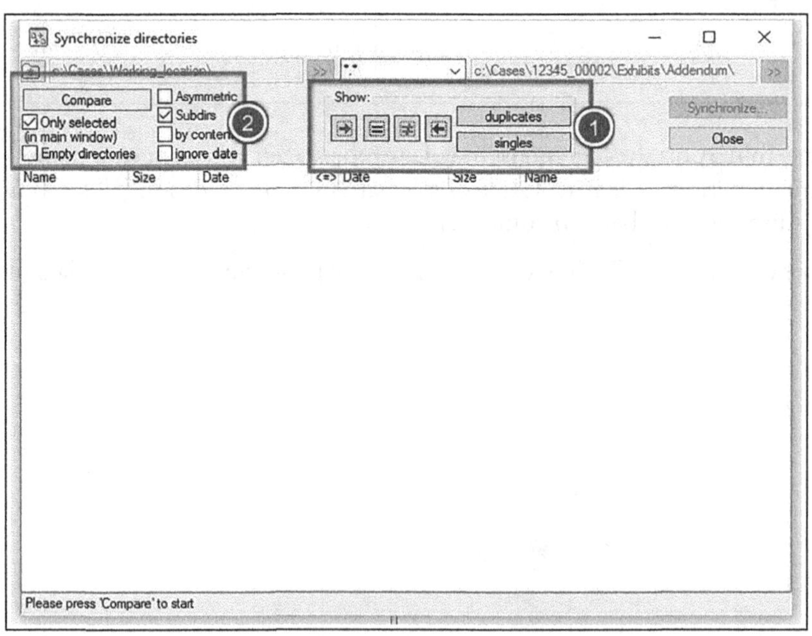

(1) Select the **Show** section options for which direction you want to compare files in. You can choose left to right/right to left, only show equal files or unequal files. (2) Click **Compare** in **Synchronize directories**.

Note: Make sure the option of **Subdirs** (for folder sub directories) is chosen in the compare section when copying multiple levels of files and folders.

Task 4. Synchronize directories report.

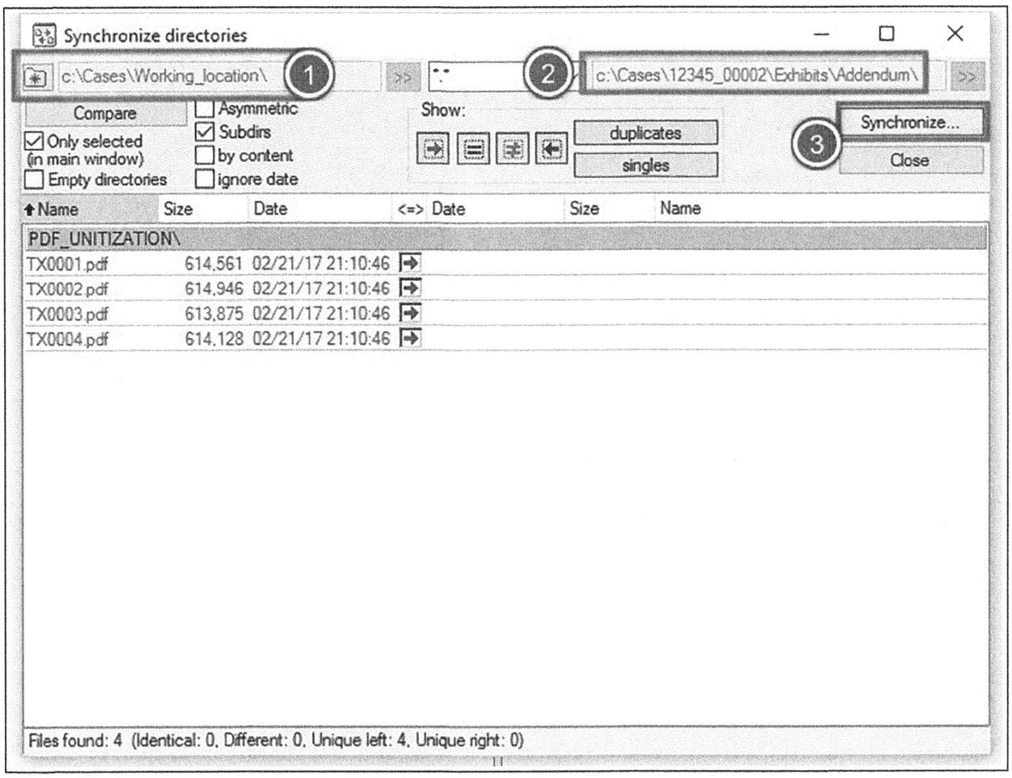

This report shows that four files are on the left screen (1) that are not on the right (2). Choose (3) **Synchronize** to get the process started.

Task 5. Start the process.

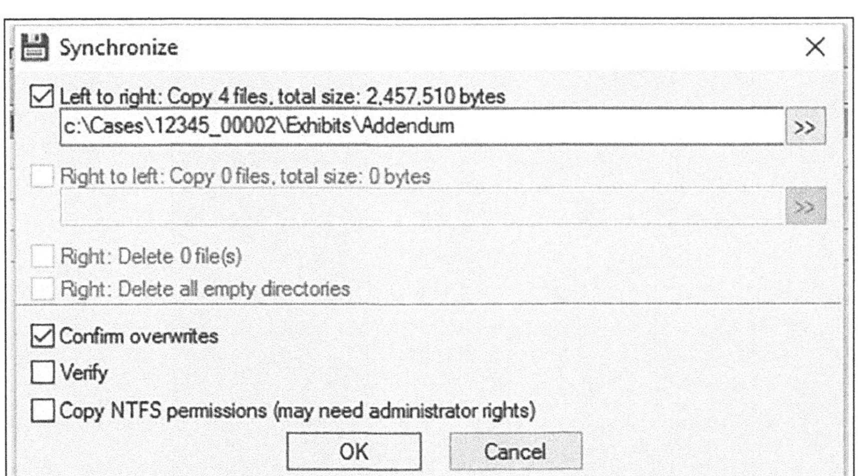

Click **OK** in **Synchronize**. There are options to copy in multiple directions and to confirm overwrites. Typically for backups, we are going one direction and for QC two directions to ensure everything is the same.

Task 6. Do your QC.

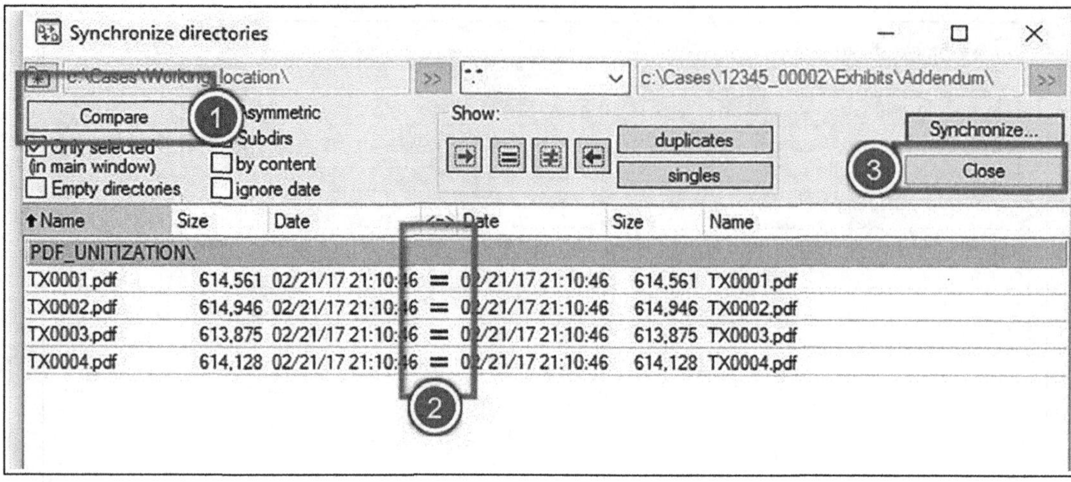

(1) Click **Compare** in **Synchronize directories** to QC and make sure everything is equal (2). (3) **Close** when complete.

Chapter Fourteen

A Primer on TrialDirector

14.1 Create a New Case

Task 1. Create a New Case.

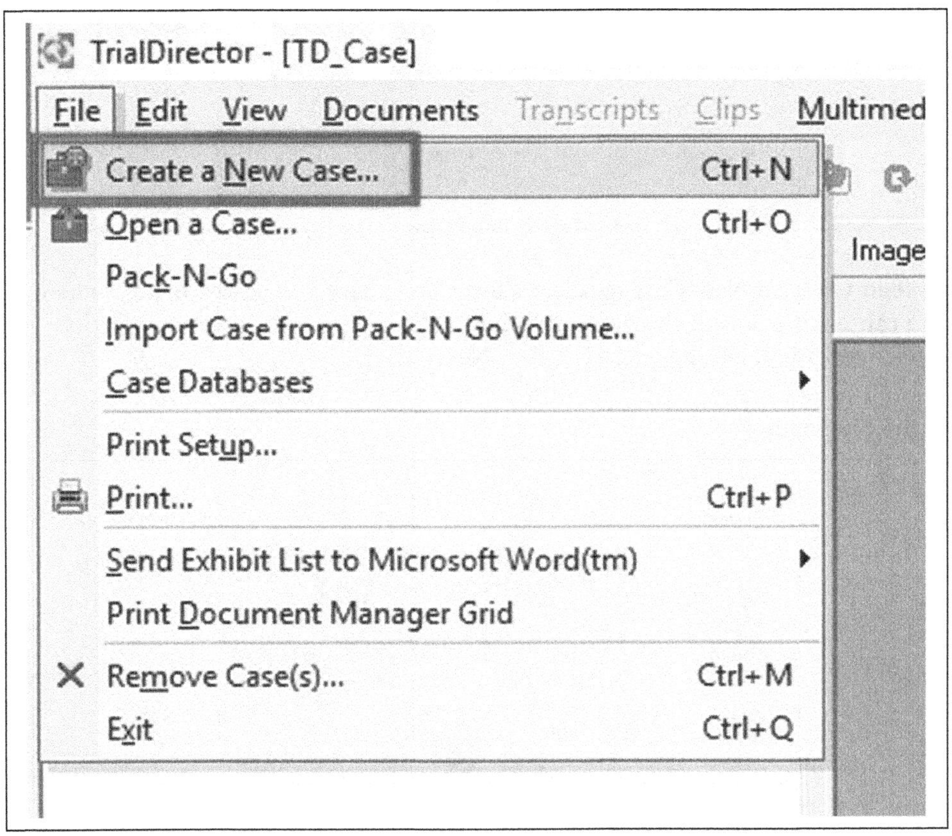

Select **Create a New Case...**.

Task 2. "Create a New Case" wizard.

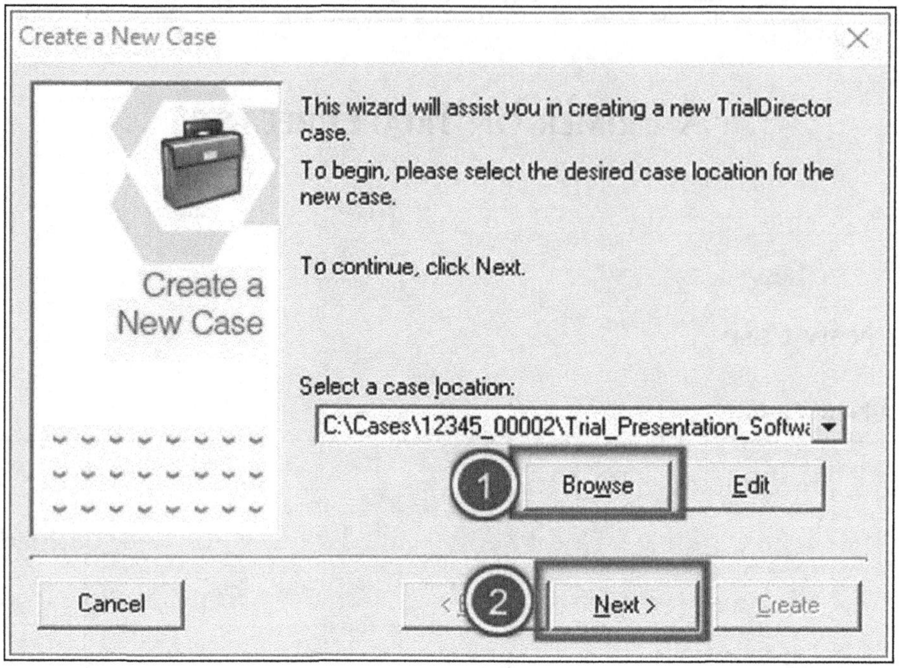

(1) Click **Browse** in **Create a New Case** to select a location to save your case file (i.e., where TrialDirector will store the case). You can use the default (by doing nothing) or place it in the "case organization" location where we put the exhibits, video, opening, closing, etc. (2) Select **Next**.

Task 3. Create the case name.

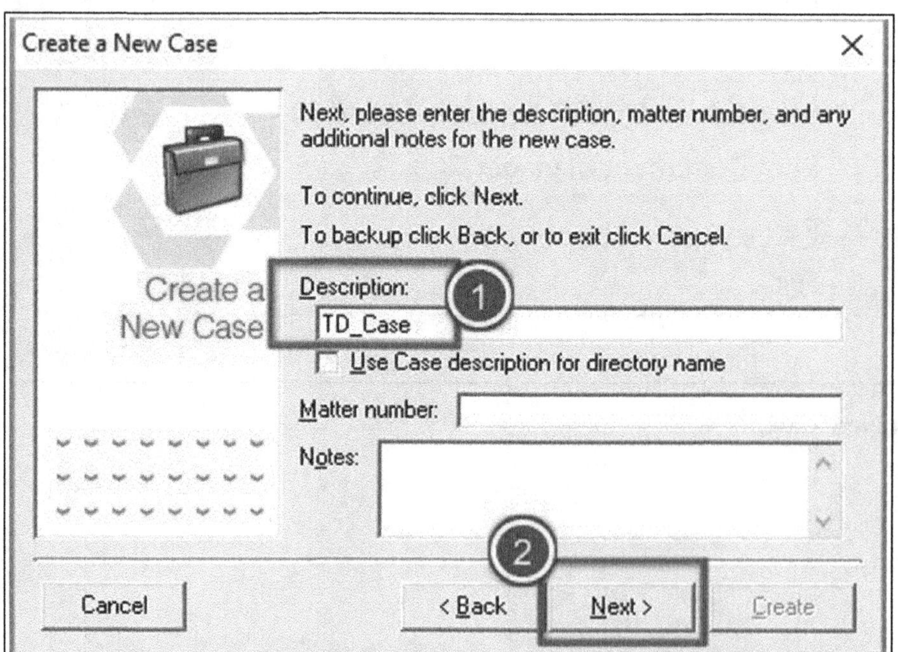

(1) Create the case name in the **Description** field. Here, I have inserted **TD_Case** as the case name. (2) Click on **Next >** in **Create a New Case**.

Task 4. Opt for (or not) case security.

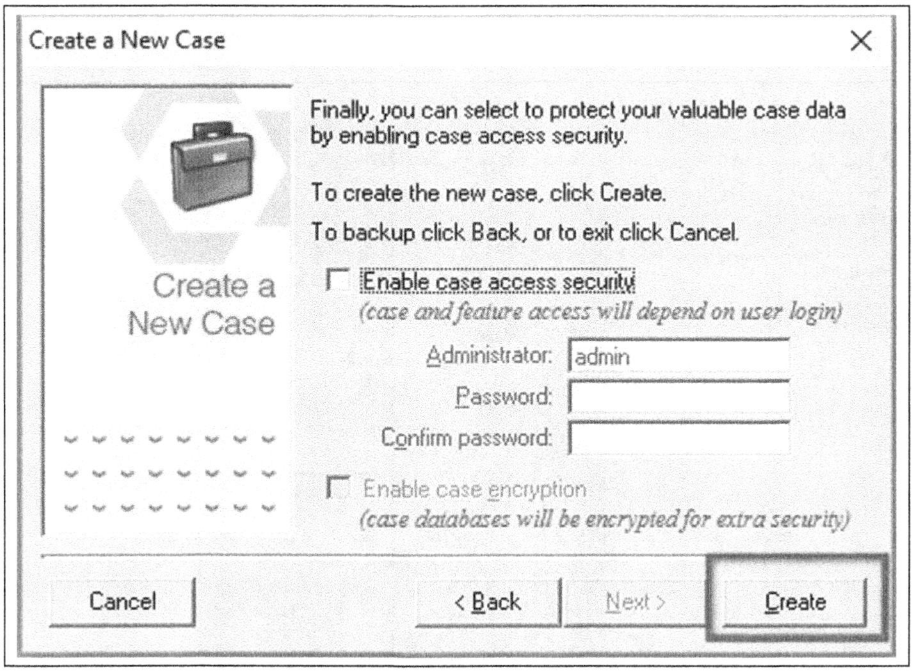

I do not typically enable case security. Click **Create** in **Create a New Case** to complete the case creation.

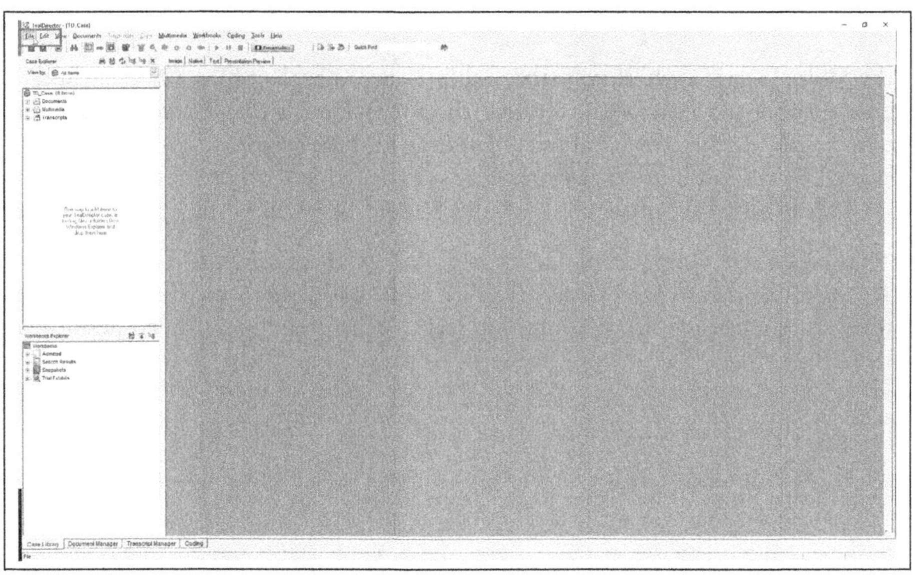

Your case is now ready to import data.

14.2 Import Data

Task 1. Import PDF exhibits.

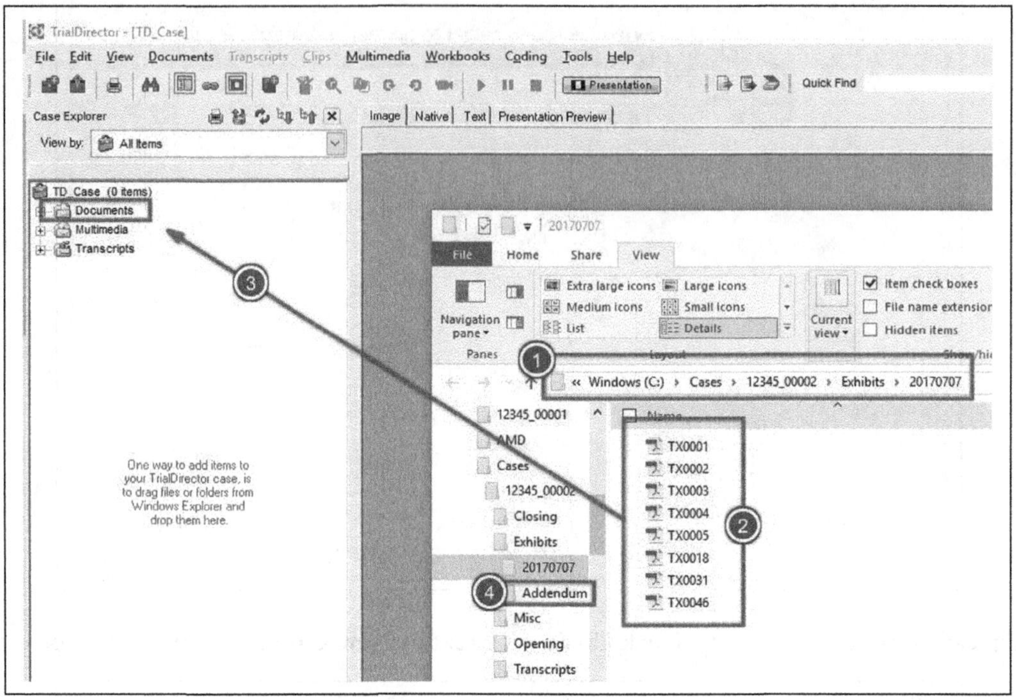

(1) Navigate to the folder location where you store exhibits and (2) select files. (3) Drag and drop them into the **Documents** folder. Remember our case organization structure, which is the source of the exhibits. TrialDirector will build a link to this location from the database when drag and drop (or use a log file with the correct path) is used. Items are organized by the structure that works for you (i.e., video, office files, exhibits; or opening, closing, exhibits, depo video) in **Exhibits**. (4) Subsequent exhibits should be placed into a dated **Addendum** folder.

Note: There are many different kinds of file types (e.g., video, image, MS Office) that can be imported into TrialDirector, but it is a good idea to start out with PDF files, which are easy to brand, unitize and redact. Be careful of performance issues when file size becomes too large. When the file size becomes too large, split the PDF into manageable pieces.

Task 2. Import some "Options."

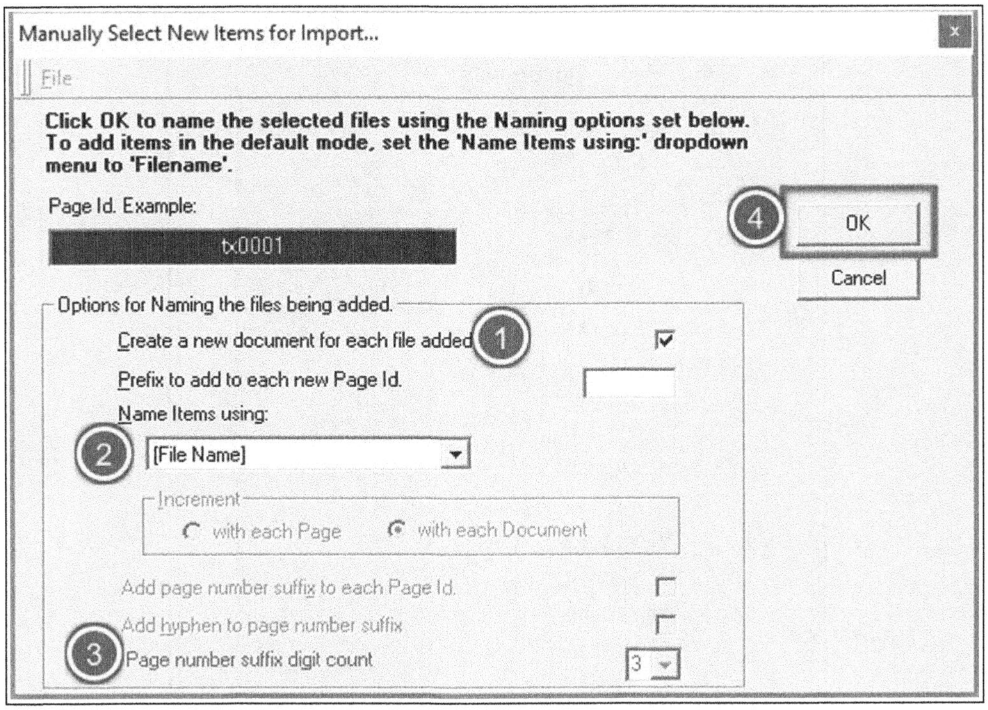

There are many options for the import of PDFs and other files. (1) Typically, you want to **Create a new document for each file added** if you have document PDF files. (2) If you've named your files in advance using the exhibit number as the file name (highly recommended), you can choose to use the file name as the naming convention. TrialDirector can name exhibits on import (and after). It is often a good idea to do the work in advance so the entire team will have access to the complete exhibit. (3) TrialDirector will add a three-digit **page number suffix** to the end of each PDF page so you can call up pages individually. (4) Click **OK** in **Manually Select New Items for Import...**.

Task 3. Check the files you've imported.

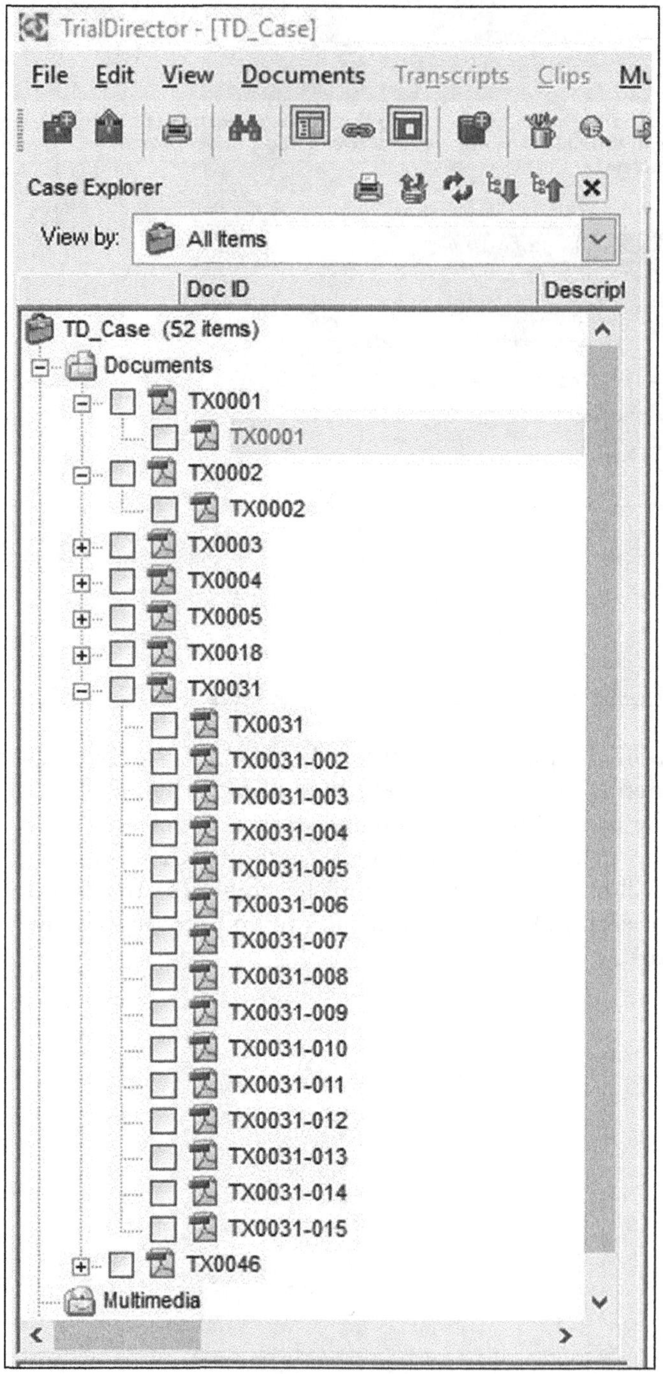

Once the files are imported, they will show up under the **Documents** folder. Click on the exhibits on the left side of the screen and see that the images come up in the center screen and that the branding matches the exhibit number. If not, there is a file path error or corrupt file that needs to be resolved. Click on the files to see that they are imported and go through the QC process (as explained in the next set of directions).

Note: The suffix on the end of each exhibit that was added by TrialDirector. This is to allow you to call up individual pages within the PDF. For example, to call up page 3 of Exhibit 31, you would enter **TX0031-003**.

14.3 Take QC Steps

Task 1. "Reconnect Missing Files...".

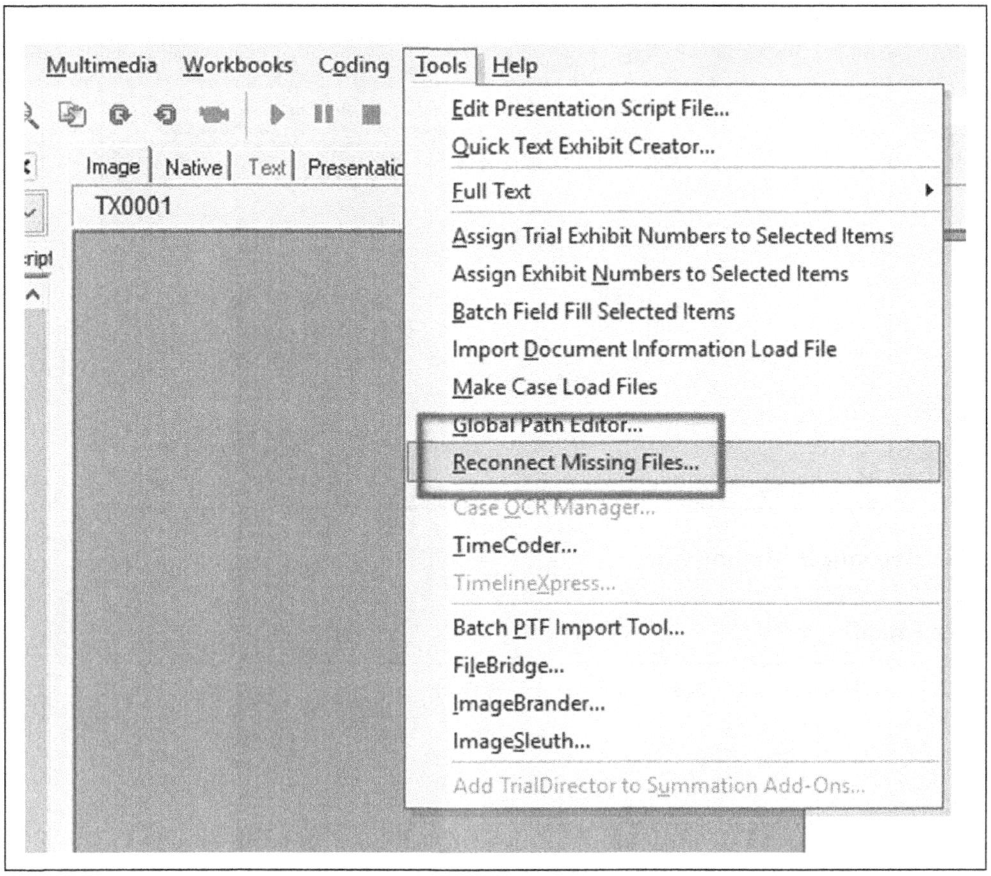

Go to **Tools**, then **Reconnect Missing Files....** This tool cycles through all your exhibits and alerts you to missing files. Files become disconnected for a variety of reasons, so it's important to run this tool regularly. (Time allowing, I do it at beginning of court every day). Examples include external drives that may not be recognized, changed drive letters or file paths, or names that are inadvertently changed.

We'll first run through a working path, then one that does not work with repair.

Task 2. Using the "Reconnect Missing Files" wizard.

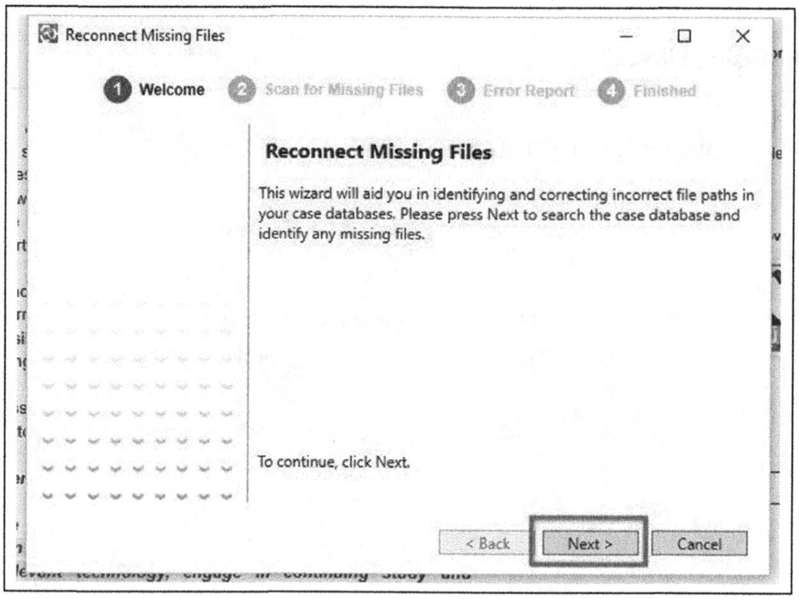

Click **Next >** in **Reconnect Missing Files.**

Task 3. All Files Found!

Congrats! All files are located. Click **Finish** button in **Reconnect Missing Files.**

Two notes:

First, because all files were found, Step 3 **Error Report** was skipped.

Second, this does not check for corruption. To check for corruption, you'll need to cycle through all images, which is a good idea for QC.

14.4 Perform QC with Repair

Task 1. "Reconnect Missing Files...".

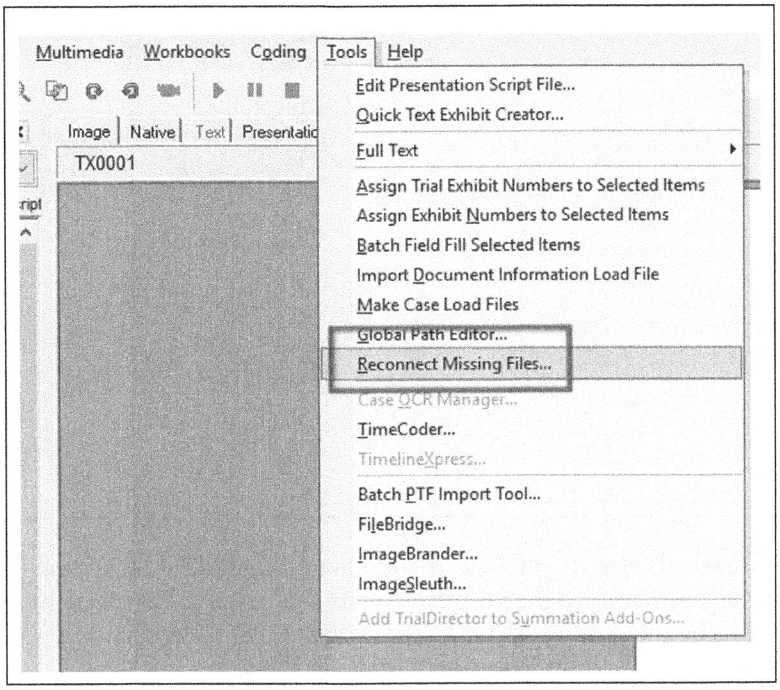

Go to **Tools**, then **Reconnect Missing Files....** This tool cycles through all your exhibits and alerts you to missing files. Files become disconnected for a variety of reasons, so it's important to run this tool regularly (Time allowing, I do it at beginning of court every day). Examples include external drives that may not be recognized, changed drive letters or file paths, or names that are inadvertently changed.

We'll first run through a working path and then one that does not work with repair.

Task 2. "Reconnect Missing Files" wizard.

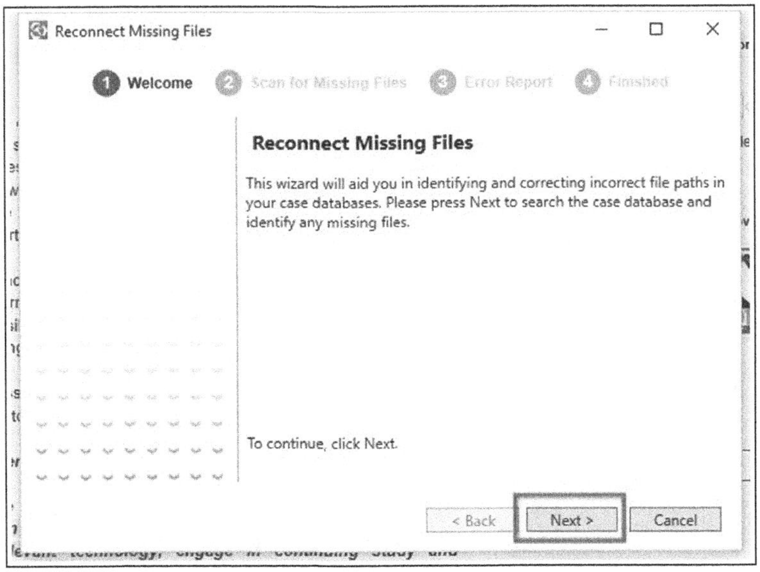

Click **Next >** in **Reconnect Missing Files.**

Task 3. Review the "Error Report."

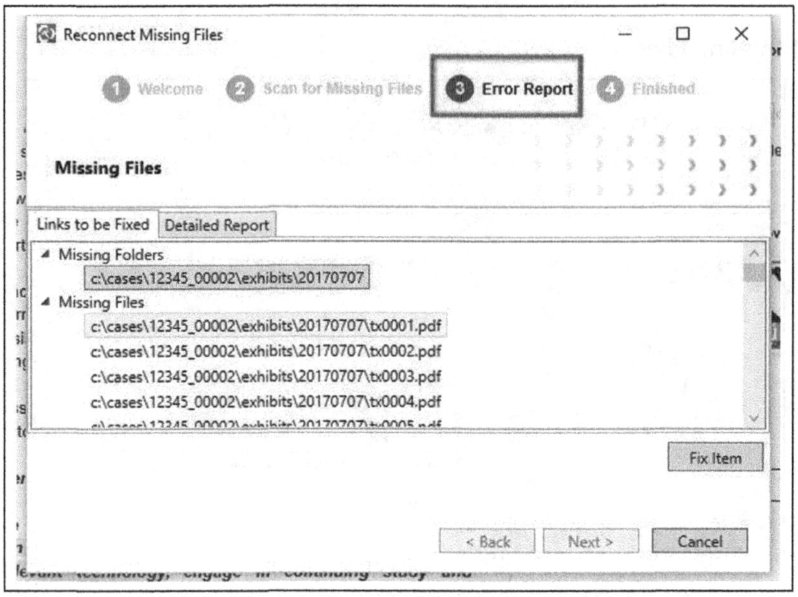

The Error Report shows which files are missing. If you have a standard file structure (file organization), you'll likely have an *a-ha* moment where you see the problem. Typically, files or folders were moved or deleted. Find the missing files, replace exhibits by drag and drop, repair the broken link, or do whatever it takes to fix it. Individual files can be fixed by clicking on **Fix Item** in **Reconnect Missing Files**.

Task 4. Here's the problem!

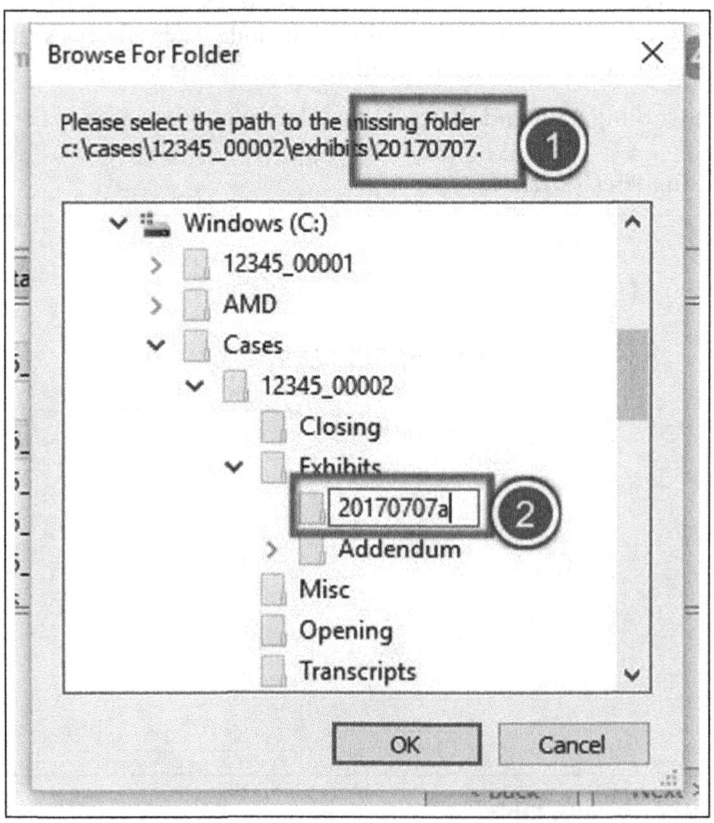

As you can see, the program is looking for (1) a folder named 20170707 and when you look in the folder path info, (2) it has been renamed to 20170707a. By removing the **a**, the folder path the problem is corrected and we rerun the wizard to make sure the problem is solved.

Task 5. Rerun the wizard.

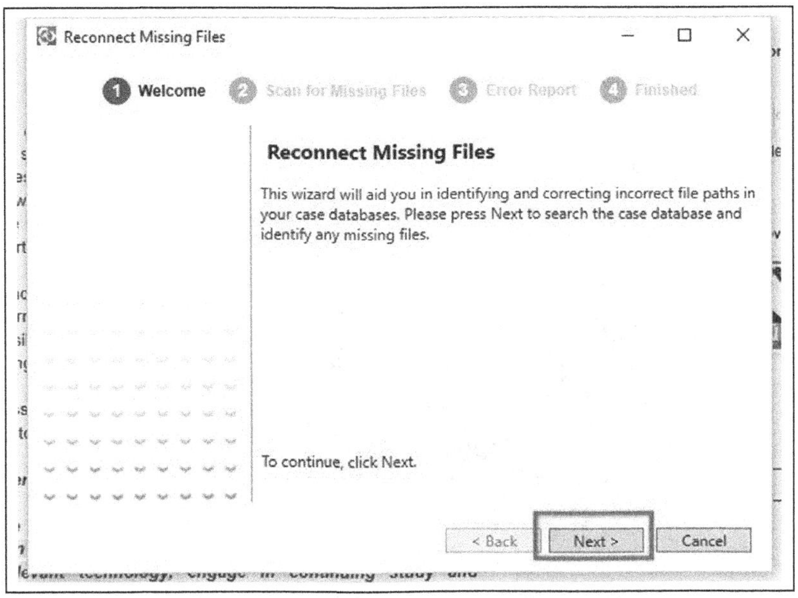

Check to see that the folder name issue was resolved by re-running the wizard.

Task 6. All Files Found!

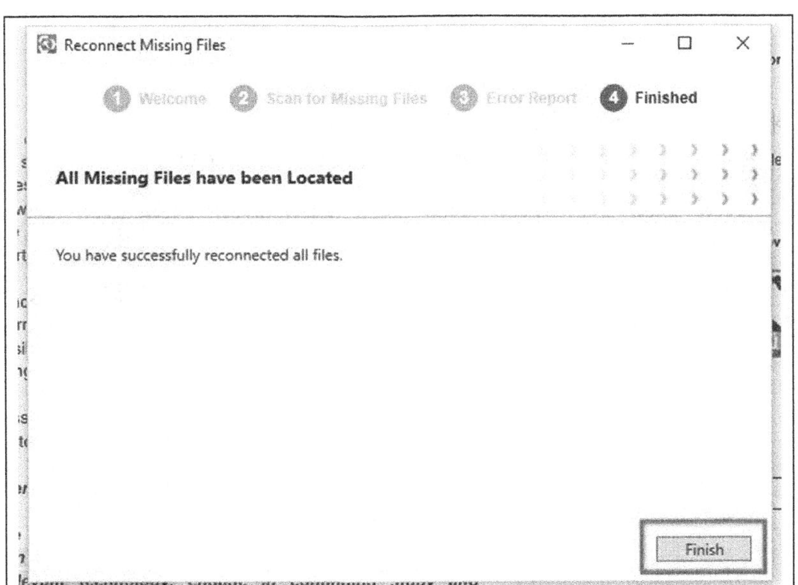

Congrats! All files are located (although this does not check for corruption. To check for corruption, you'll need to cycle through all images.) Click **Finish** in **Reconnect Missing Files**.

14.5 Set Up Mirror Mode

Task 1. Set your presentation in mirror mode.

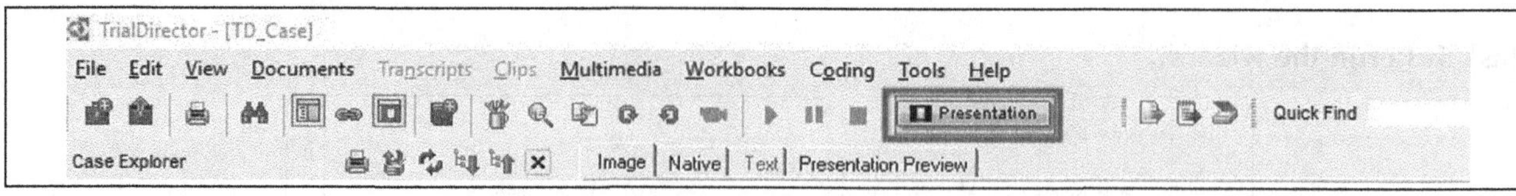

Click on **Presentation** on the toolbar to put TrialDirector in presentation mode. What you see will depend on your display settings (i.e., mirror mode or extended desktop).

Warning: The courtroom should *not* be the first time you perform these operations. Practice makes perfect!

Task 2. View the presentation screen.

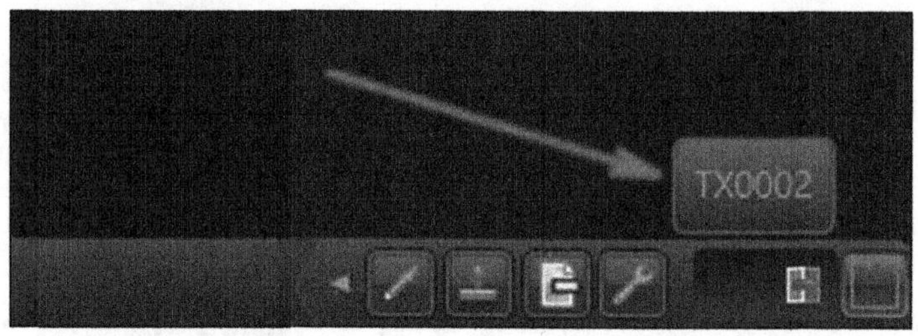

You will see a presentation screen with a toolbar along the bottom. In the bottom left corner, you can type the exhibit number that is associated with the file you want to bring up. Type the exhibit number and click **Enter** to bring up the exhibit.

Remember that if you imported PDF files, page 2 onward will have a suffix at the end consisting of three digits. So, when calling up the first page you would use TX0002, when calling up page 2 it would be **TX0002-002**, and so on.

Task 3. Wait for the exhibit to come up after it's been entered.

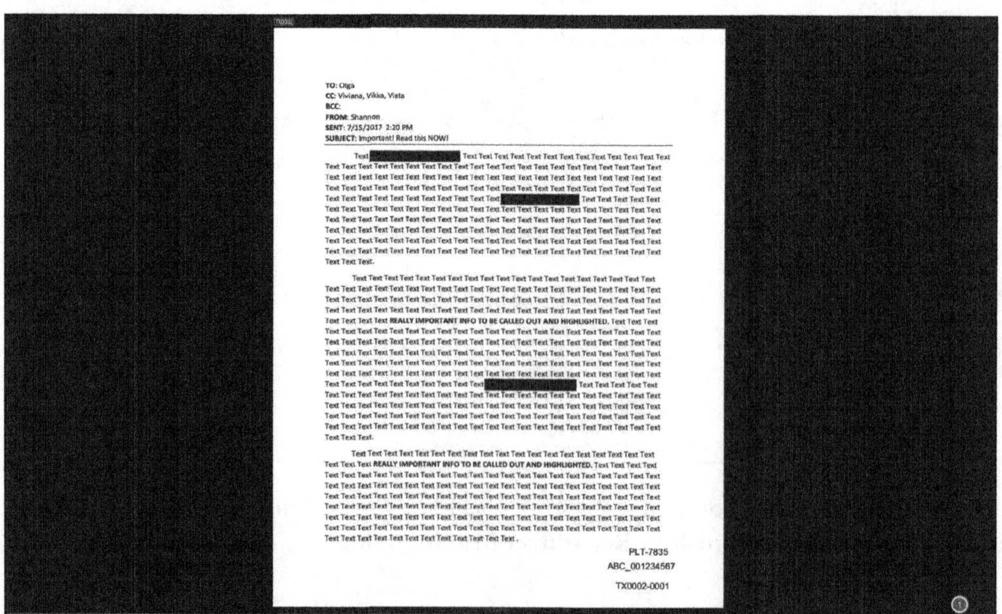

If the exhibit does not come up and there is a red dot here (1), it means that either the wrong number was entered or the exhibit is corrupt or not there. If the exhibit does not come up, try again, making sure you are using the naming convention that you decided upon. This is where a good, consistent naming convention is worth it. If the exhibit does not come up, try again on your backup laptop and quickly, then calmly, let the attorney know it won't be coming up and you'll be switching to the document camera. You might have a rehearsed comment such as, "This might be a better exhibit for the document camera."

Task 4. Annotate the exhibit on the presentation screen.

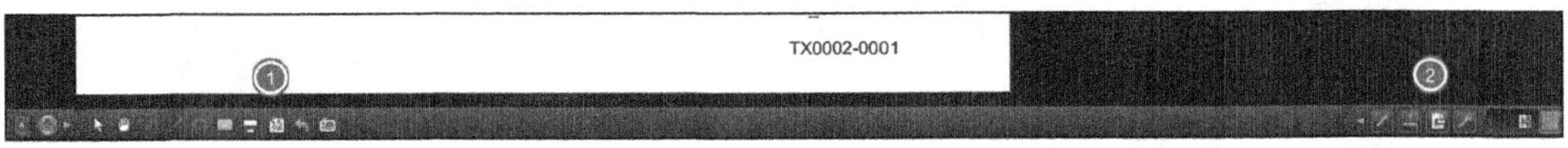

You are now on the presentation screen and can annotate your exhibit. You may use keyboard shortcuts or the mouse to select tools to perform annotations. Commonly used tools are in the bottom center of the screen (1), and additional tools are on the right side (2), which can be added by dragging them to the toolbar.

If you are new to this, just use the mouse and click the tools you want to use rather than attempting keyboard shortcuts.

Task 5. Decide how you prefer to navigate pages.

There are several methods of page navigation. You can enter in a new exhibit/page number, use the page up/ page down keys on your keyboard, or this handy tool to help with docs. You can bring it up by clicking on the **...** at the bottom of the page.

(1) Use the arrows to page up and down through the exhibit.

(2) Use the slider to quickly navigate between pages in longer docs.

(3) Use the arrows to rotate the document if it is the wrong orientation.

Note: This tool is even better in extended desktop because nobody can see what you are doing.

Task 6. Choose projection zoom (aka a callout).

Select the **projection zoom** tool (there are options for the border and line color). Note that the tool is "selected" when you click it.

Task 7. Annotate your exhibit.

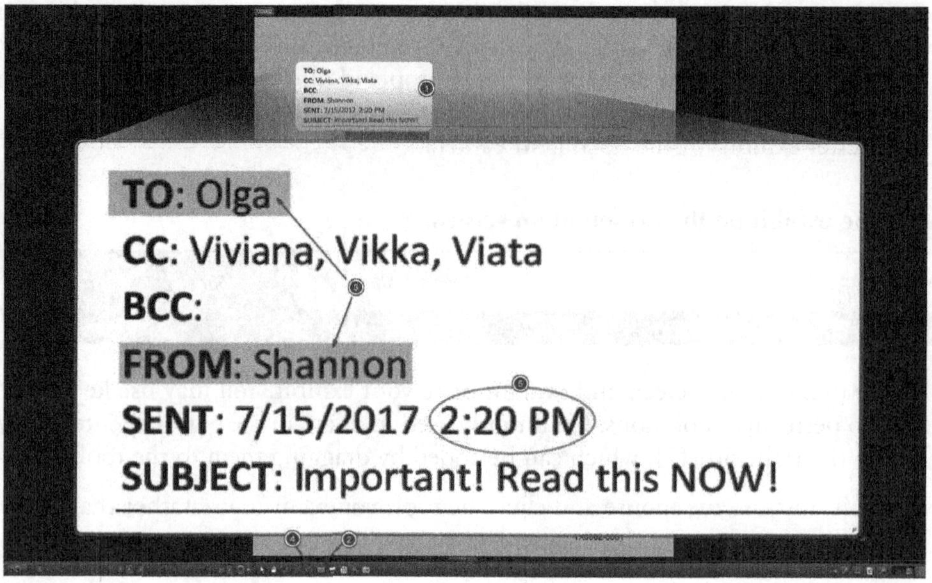

With **projection zoom** selected, navigate to the text you want to annotate and draw a rectangle around it (1). The text will zoom out. If your rectangle isn't accurate, quickly left-double-click on the image to take it down, and draw the rectangle again. (2) Click on the yellow highlight tool in the bottom center and (3) highlight the sections you want to annotate. Select the circle tool (4) and circle additional text you might want to accentuate (5). If this is too complicated, keep it simple and just zoom and highlight.

Task 8. Move onto your next annotation.

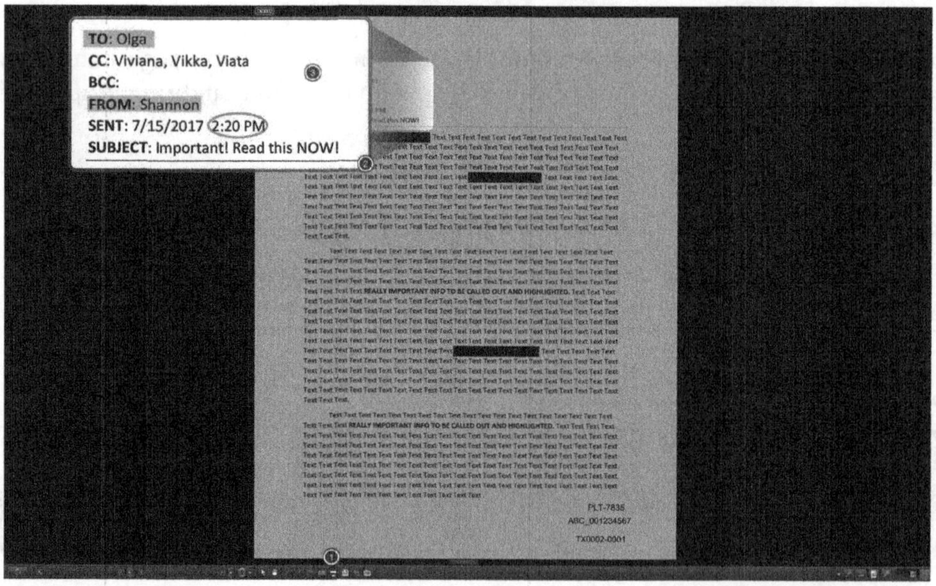

(1) Select the **projection zoom** tool again. (2) Hold down the **Ctrl** key and select the corner of the projection, then drag it to make it smaller (or bigger). (3) Left-click and hold to move it to a new location.

Task 9. Now for a second annotation.

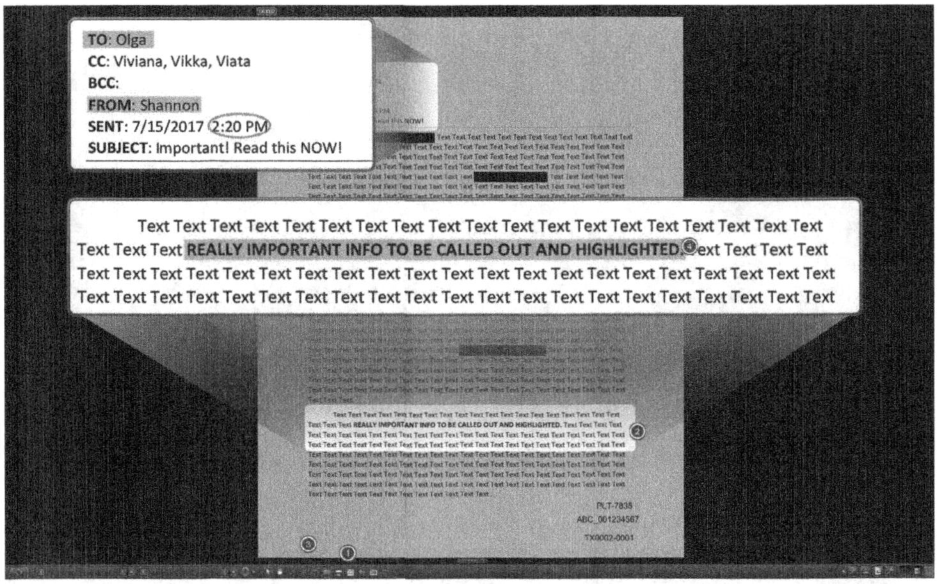

(1) Perform another annotation by selecting the **Projection Zoom** tool. (2) Select text at the bottom of the screen that you want to enlarge. (3) Select the **Highlight** tool. (4) Highlight in the enlarged text the words you want to annotate. Press the **Esc** key to remove everything from the screen (i.e., exhibit and annotations). If you want to keep the exhibit but remove annotations, double-click on each enlarged portion of text. There are also tools that will provide some flexibility in this area as well.

14.6 Set Up Extended Desktop

Task 1. Set up presentation mode with extended desktop/detached toolbar.

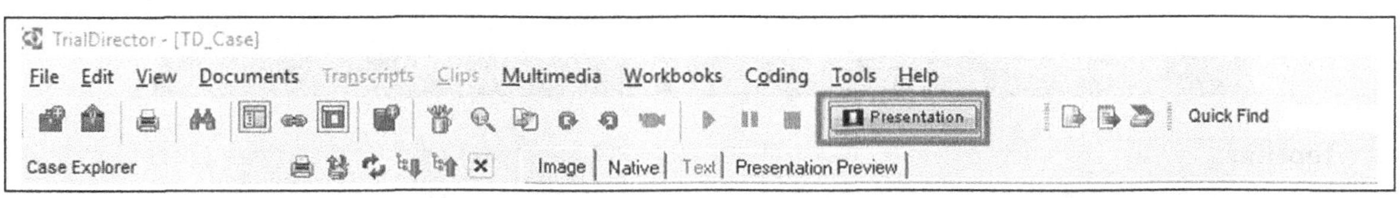

Click on **Presentation** on the toolbar to put TrialDirector in presentation mode. What you see will depend on your display settings (either mirror mode or extended desktop). The detached toolbar is a great way to present exhibits without anyone being able to see what you are doing. It is generally a smoother and slicker way to present exhibits.

Warning: The courtroom should *not* be the first time you perform these operations. Practice makes perfect.

Task 2. Detach the toolbar.

Click on the icon in the lower left corner.

Select **ToolBar**.

Select **Detach ToolBar**.

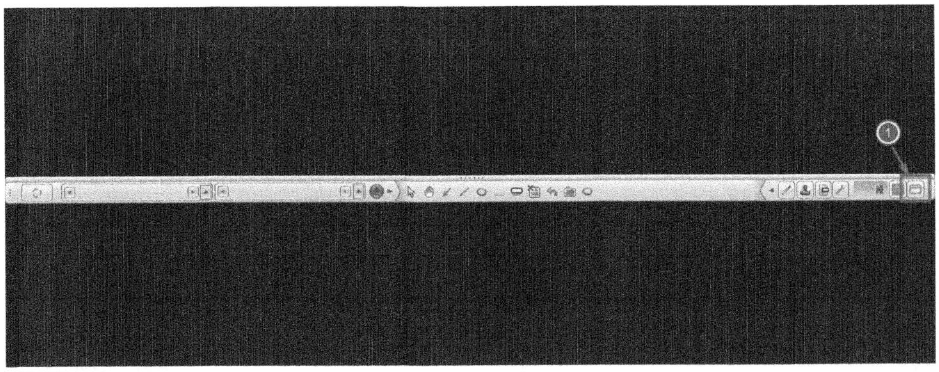

This is the detached toolbar. However, it is more useful if you enlarge it by selecting (1).

Task 3. Review your detached toolbar.

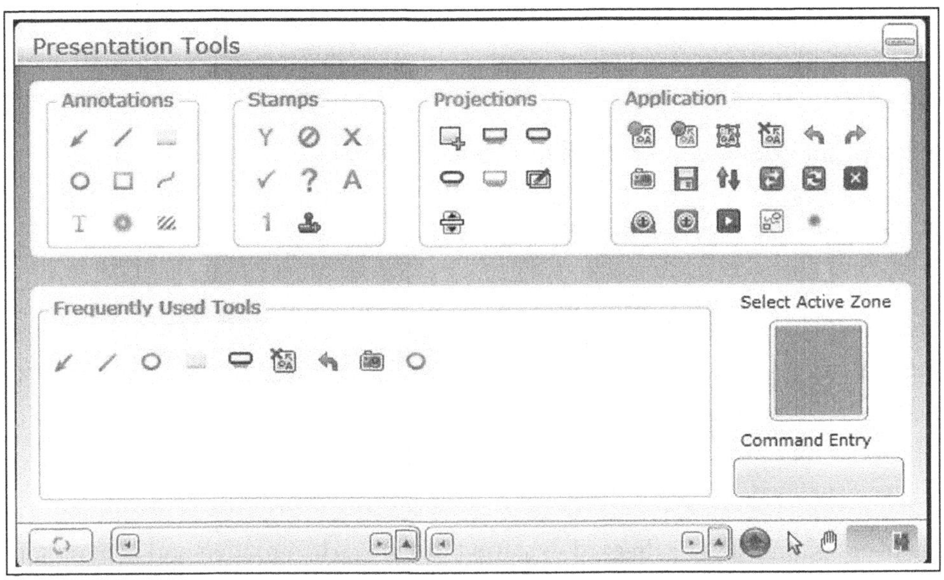

Make sure the detached toolbar is on your working screen and not your presentation screen. Note that many tools are all over the detached toolbar. You can select any of them by clicking on them and can drag them into the **Frequently Used Tools** section.

Task 4. Use Command Entry.

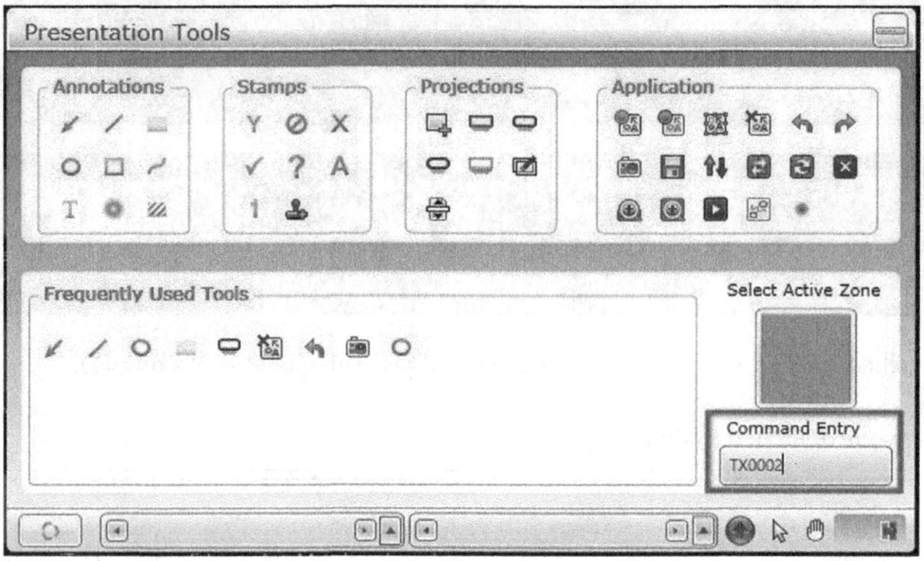

Here, you can enter your exhibit numbers and text commands (a more advanced topic).

Task 5. Get familiar with the page navigation tool.

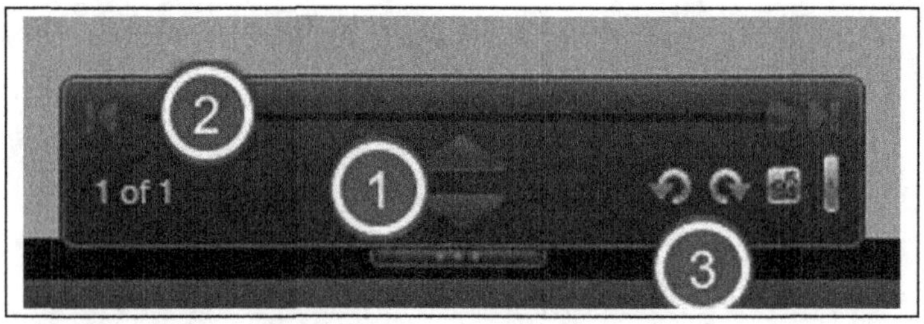

The **page navigation** tool can also be dragged or started from detached toolbar and kept on the working screen. There are several methods of page navigation. You can enter a new exhibit/page number, use the page up/page down keys on your keyboard, or use this handy tool to help with documents. You can bring it up by clicking on the **...** at the bottom of the page.

(1) Use the arrows to page up and down through the exhibit.

(2) Use the slider to quickly navigate between pages in longer documents.

(3) Use the arrows to rotate the document if it is the wrong orientation.

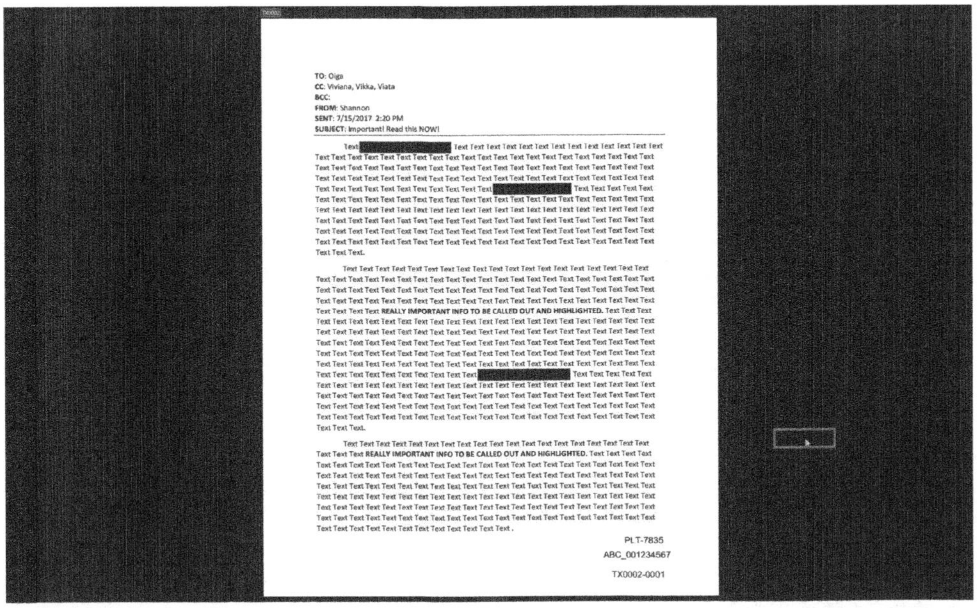

Task 6. Annotate from the detached toolbar.

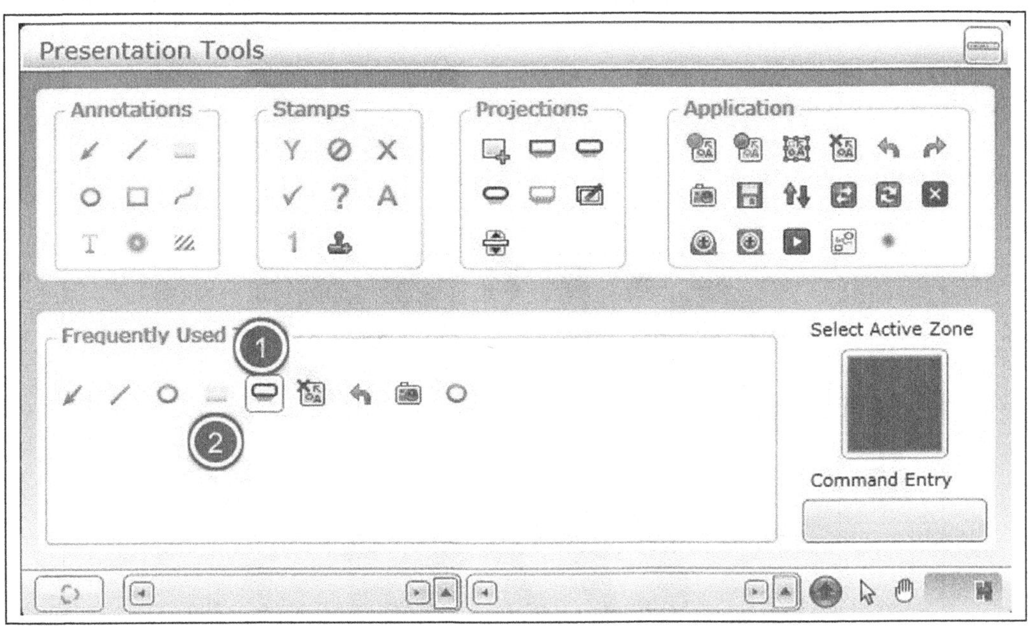

As in previous annotations, select the tool you want to use and apply the annotations to your exhibit. (1) **Projection Zoom**. (2) **Highlight**.

Task 7. Annotate an exhibit.

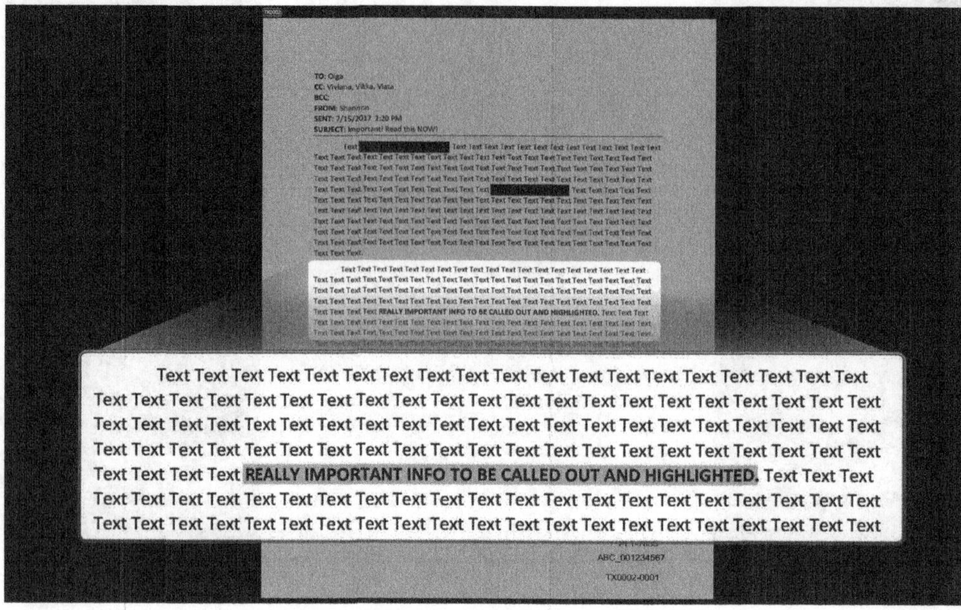

This is an annotated exhibit example. Note there are no visible tools, which keeps your audience focused on the documents.

14.7 Use Additional Tools

Task 1. Tools and options you need to know about and learn.

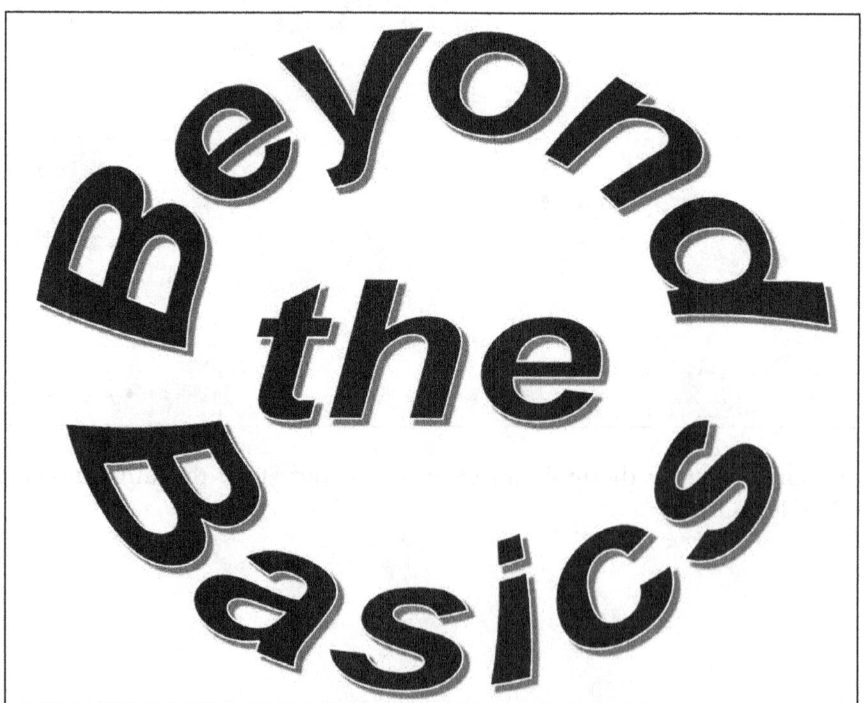

The following are tools and skills that go beyond the basics that you should learn as your skills and comfort level increase.

Task 2. Choose a presentation zone.

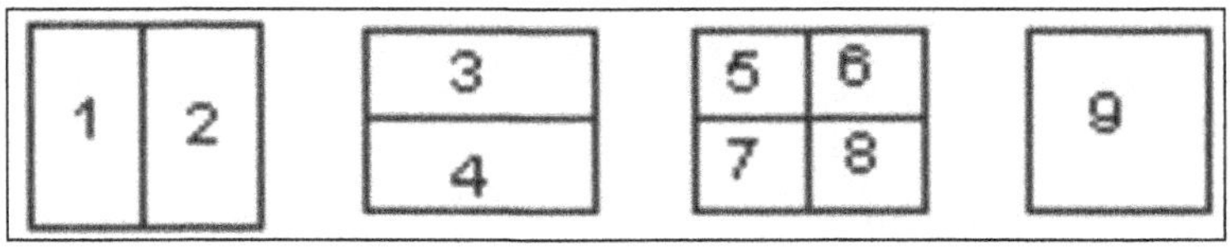

The **Presentation** area is divided into nine zones that you can use to display multiple case items. Zone 9 is the default full screen and how most beginners should start with in TrialDirector (the other tools also use zones but may call them something else and have different commands). It is essential that you practice with zones, and manipulating exhibits within zones, before you go to court. Moreover, even after you understand how to use zones, you should always practice with the files you intend to use in court so you work out any issues in advance.

The zones in TrialDirector correspond to the F1 thru F9 keys on your keyboard, with F10 being used as a command to transfer from one zone to another. It is often helpful to place documents side by side in zones 1 and 2 (F1 and F2, respectively), and that will be the first skill you should learn as you advance your tech skills.

To place exhibits side by side, select the zone you want to place your exhibit or video in by choosing the zone key (F1–F9) that you want to place it in. For example, to place TX001 and TX002 side by side in zone 1 and 2, you would first press **F1**, type the exhibit number TX001, and press **Enter**, and then press **F2**, type the exhibit number TX002, and press **Enter**.

To move from one zone to another, select the zone your exhibit is in, then press **F10** and then the zone you want to put it in. For example, if your exhibit was in zone 9 and you wanted to move it to zone 1, you would press **F9**, then press **F10**, and the destination zone of **F1** (if you wanted the exhibit on the left side of the screen).

Task 3. Choose your presentation preferences.

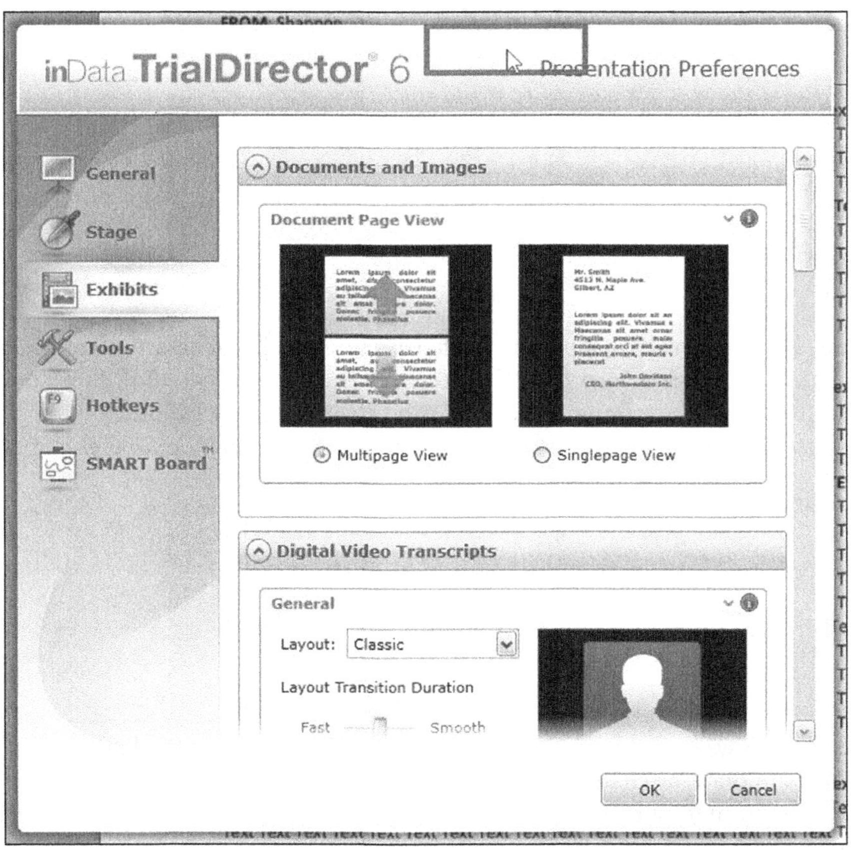

There are many options in setting up TrialDirector. In the beginning, the defaults are typically OK, but you'll want to be able to fine-tune TrialDirector as your skills increase. This is true of any presentation tool you might use, whether it is PowerPoint, OnCue, Sanction, or something else. Again, always test your setup in court to make sure it is properly configured.

Task 4. Check out the Workbooks Explorer.

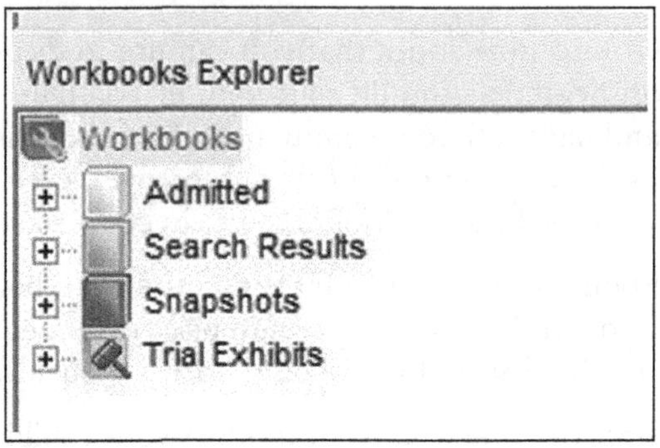

Workbooks allow you to create groupings of the exhibits and clips you want to use so you can simply follow along in your outline and click the "**next**" arrow to advance to the next exhibit, like in PowerPoint. This is a great way of organizing files for opening and closing. Typically, it is a good idea to create a workbook for every witness examination outline as well, but witness cross does not move in a linear fashion the way opening and closing do—it just makes it helpful to have everything in one place.

Task 5. Take some Snapshots.

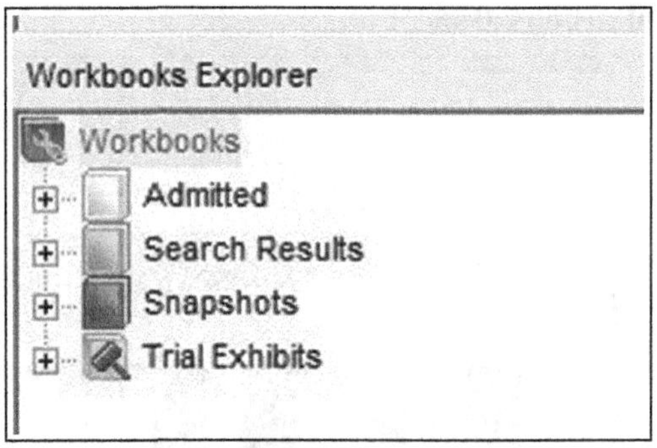

The **Snapshots** tool allows you to take a picture (called a "screenshot") of an annotated exhibit so you can later display it in TrialDirector or import it into PowerPoint or some other graphic tool. Snapshots are a great way of putting annotated exhibits into PowerPoint because it allows you to easily callout, highlight, underline, etc. an exhibit in your trial presentation software and then save as an image that can be used elsewhere.

Task 6. Use Save Stage.

The **Save Stage** feature allows you to save an exhibit with its annotations intact. Later, you can call up the staged exhibit and continue to annotate or change the existing annotations. In other words, you can pre-annotate the exhibit and then continue to manipulate the callouts and highlighting in court (tasks you can't do with a static screenshot or snapshot).

Chapter Fifteen

A Primer on Sanction

15.1 Create a New Case in Sanction

Task 1. Start a "New Case."

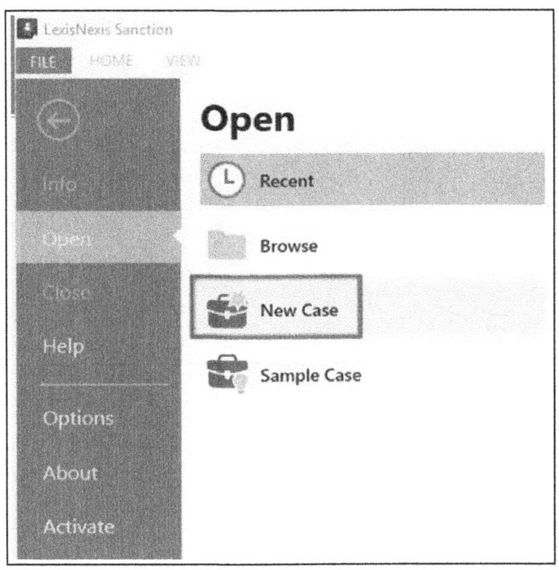

Select **New Case**.

Task 2. Name your case.

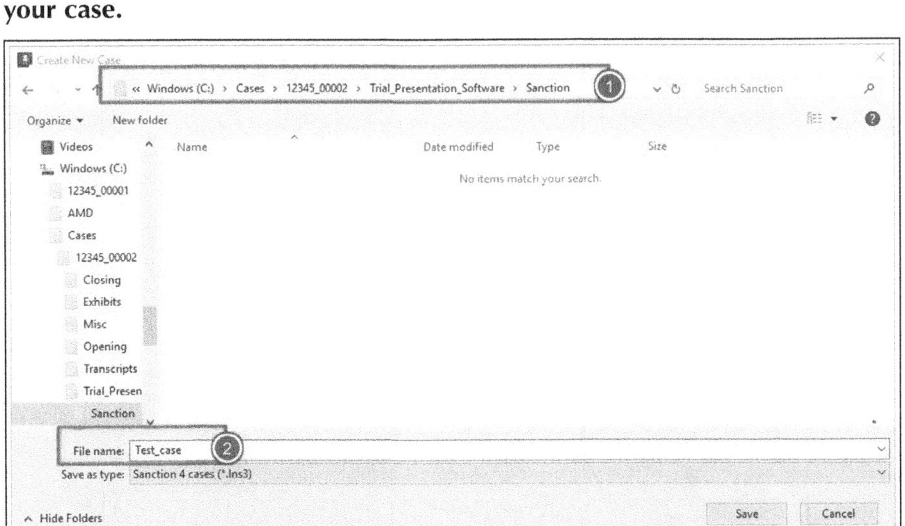

(1) Navigate to the case folders created to organize data and create a Sanction case database by entering the case name in (2) the **File name** dialog box.

15.2 Import Data into Sanction

Task 1. Select exhibits to be imported.

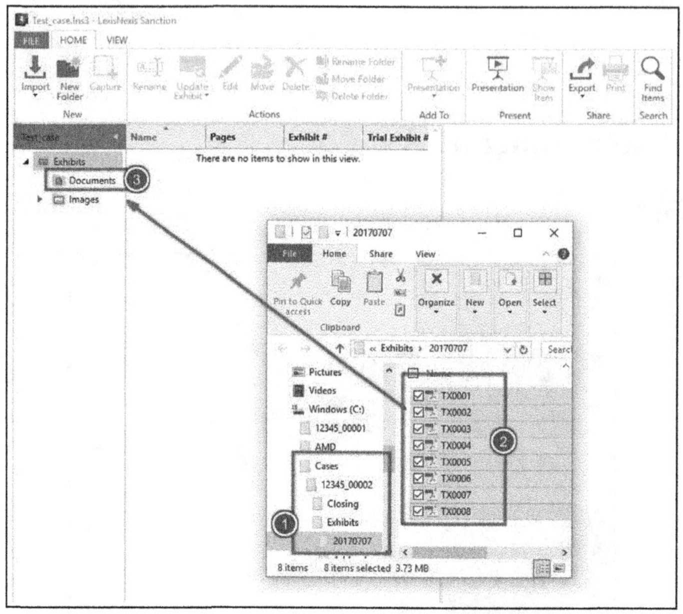

(1) Navigate to the folder location where the exhibits are kept, and (2) select the exhibits to be imported into Sanction. (3) Drag the exhibits into the **Documents** folder. Sanction imports the files into an internally managed location, so make sure you have enough room on your local disk or else configure it for an external drive if you are working with large volumes of data.

Note: You can select multiple individual exhibits by holding down the **Ctrl** key or multiple exhibits by holding down the **Shift** key.

Task 2. Check the "File Import Confirmation."

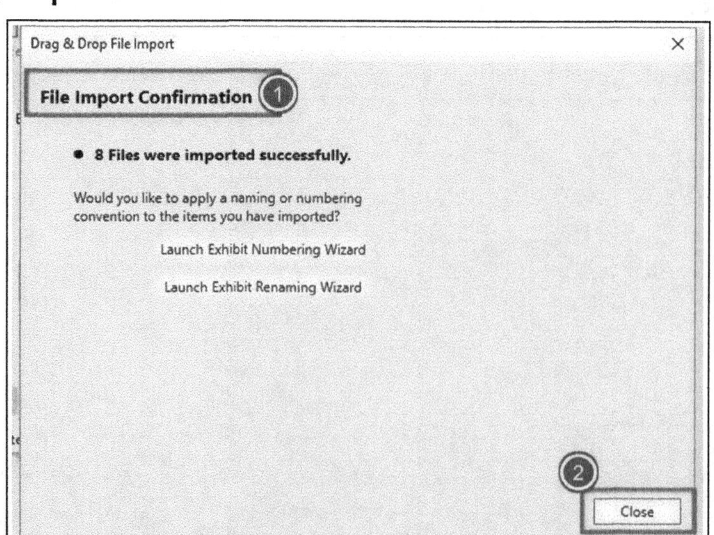

(1) You will receive a **File Import Confirmation** that will also allow you to renumber or rename your files.

Note: For team use, we typically name and number files before import so that everyone can use them.

(2) **Close** when complete.

Task 3. QC the import.

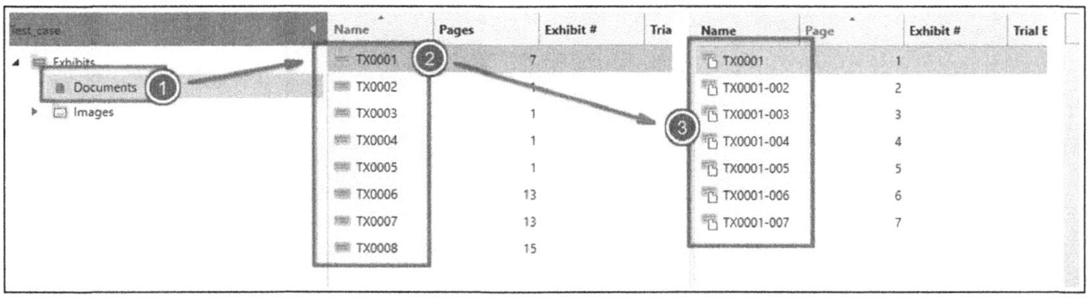

Take a look at the main screen to see that the documents imported correctly. (1) Select documents to see your list of exhibits (2). Click on individual exhibits to see detail about that exhibits. (3) Note that Sanction has suffixed each record with three digits so that individual pages can be called up. Click on a few documents to ensure the pagination is correct and that they come up on the working screen. For example, in section (2), you can see that TX0001 has seven pages; are there actually seven pages in section (3)?

Task 4. QC Import

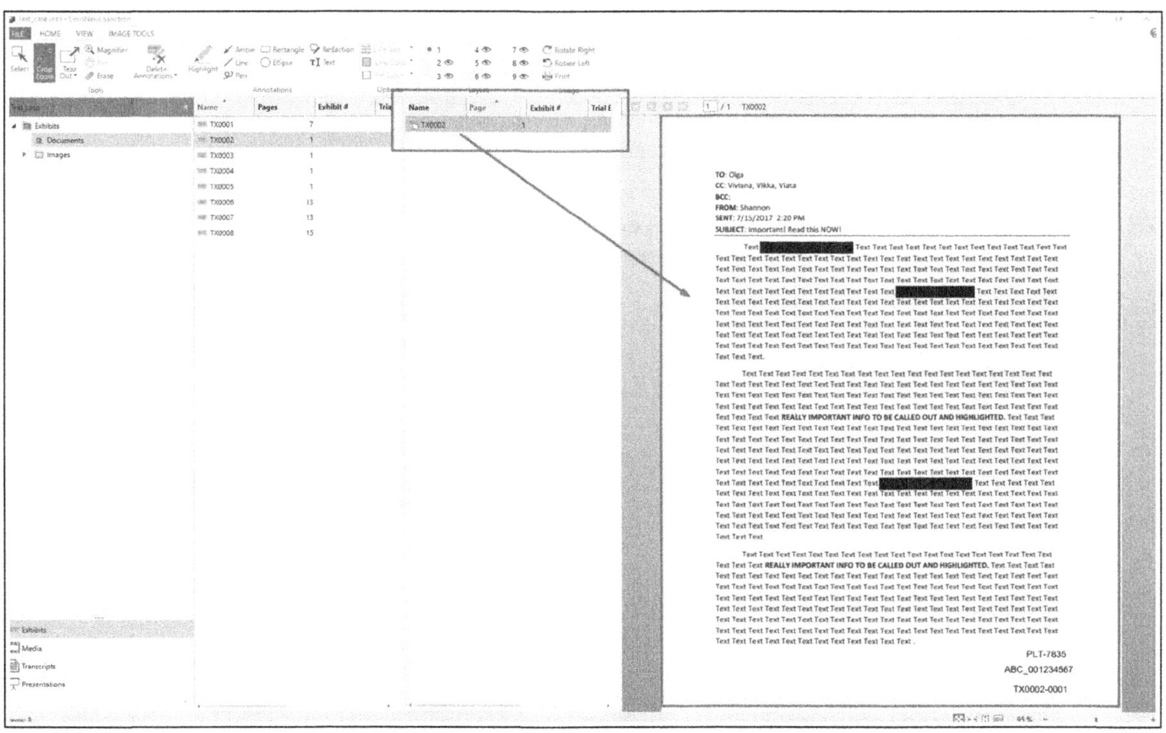

When selected, do the images come up? Sanction copies all files to an internal media location as it imports them. QC by clicking on individual pages and images.

15.3 Sanction Presentation Basics

Task 1. Place laptop in extended desktop or mirror mode.

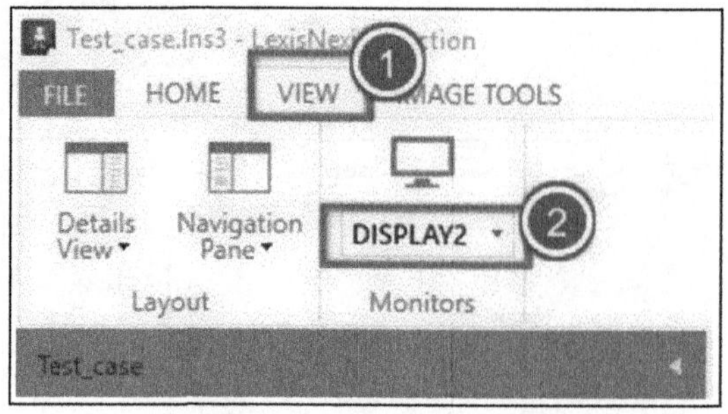

(1) Go to the **View** tab. (2) Choose which display the presentation should be presented on. This will also depend on how you have configured your laptop as either mirror mode or extended desktop.

Task 2. Start presentation mode.

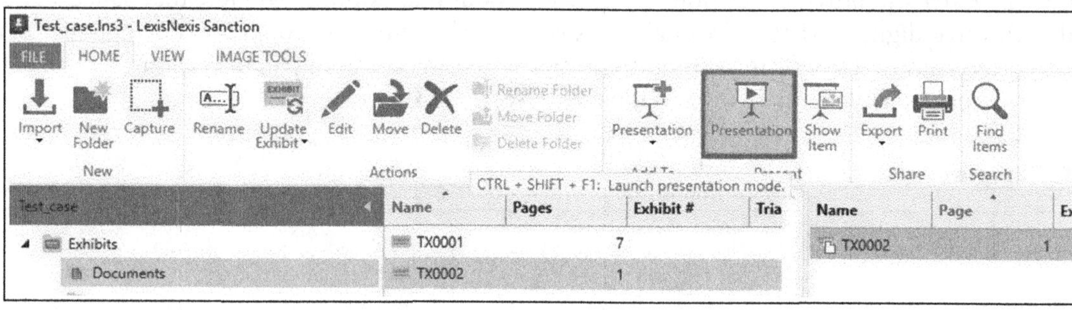

Select **Presentation** to start the presentation screen.

Task 3. Option 1: Present from the working screen.

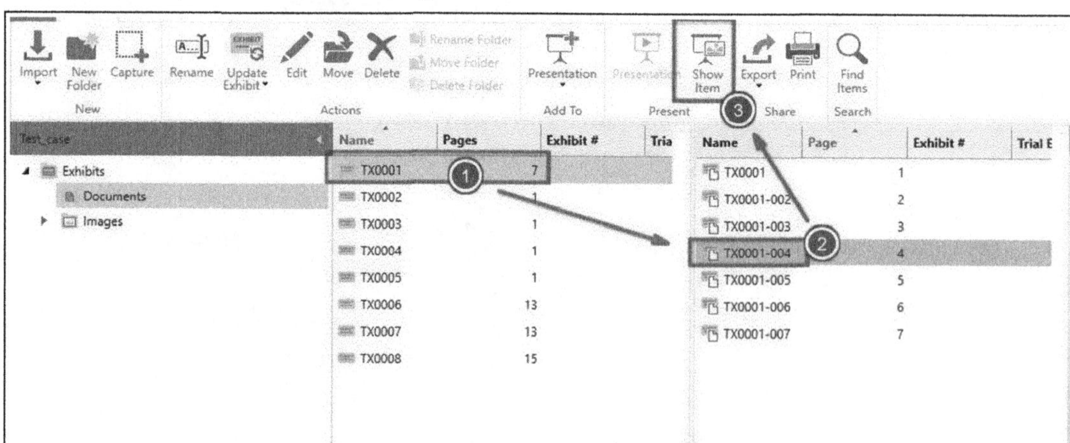

(1) Select the exhibit you want to present. Next, (2) select the page to be displayed, then (3) select **Show Item** to show it on the presentation screen.

Task 4. Option 2: Enter exhibit number on presentation screen.

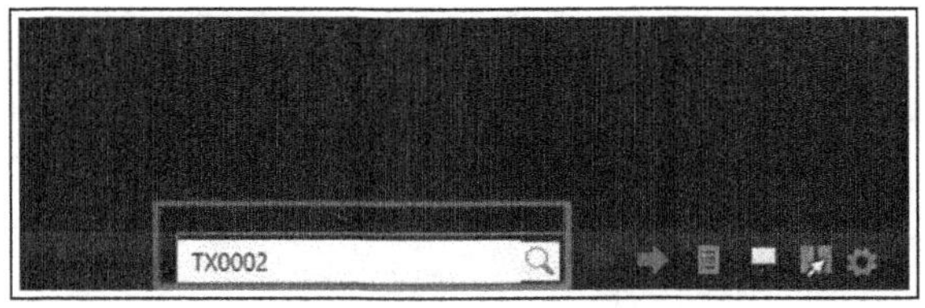

Enter your exhibit number in the input screen. Keep in mind that Sanction may have suffixed PDF records on import.

Note: If you've entered the wrong number . . .

(1) Instead of **TX0001**, an incorrect number was entered. (2) Note the red icon that signifies that the exhibit is not in the system.

Task 5. Choose a zone before presenting an exhibit.

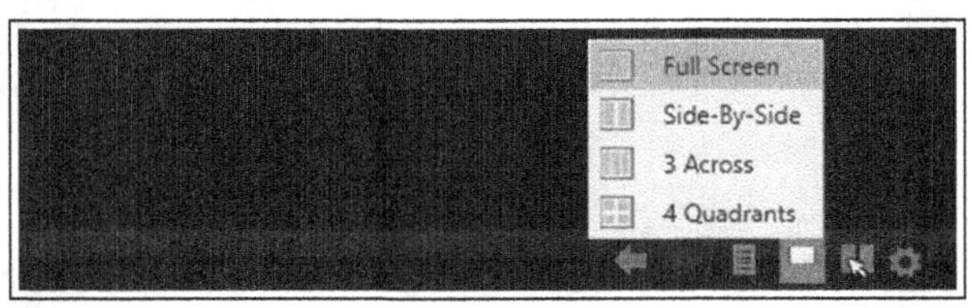

If you want to present exhibits in an area other than **Full Screen**, choose it in the lower right corner of the presentation screen. Beginners should try to use only full screen, highlight, and tear out (projection zoom).

Task 6. Option 1: Annotate exhibit using tools in lower right hand corner.

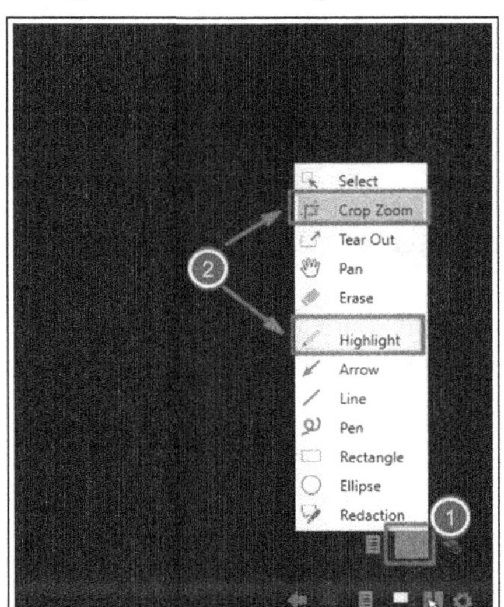

(1) Select the tools menu in the lower right hand corner. (2) Choose the tools using the mouse you want to use to annotate the document. If you want to make multiple annotations or change the existing annotations see the next step.

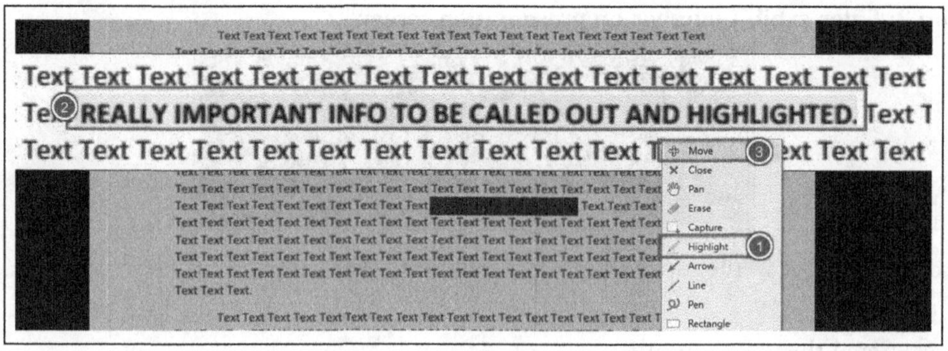

(1) Right-click on the call out you want to further annotate. The **Tools** menu will come up. Choose the tool you want to use, and (2) perform the annotation.

Note: (3) This is where to find the **Move** tool so annotations can be moved around the screen.

Task 7. Create your annotated exhibit.

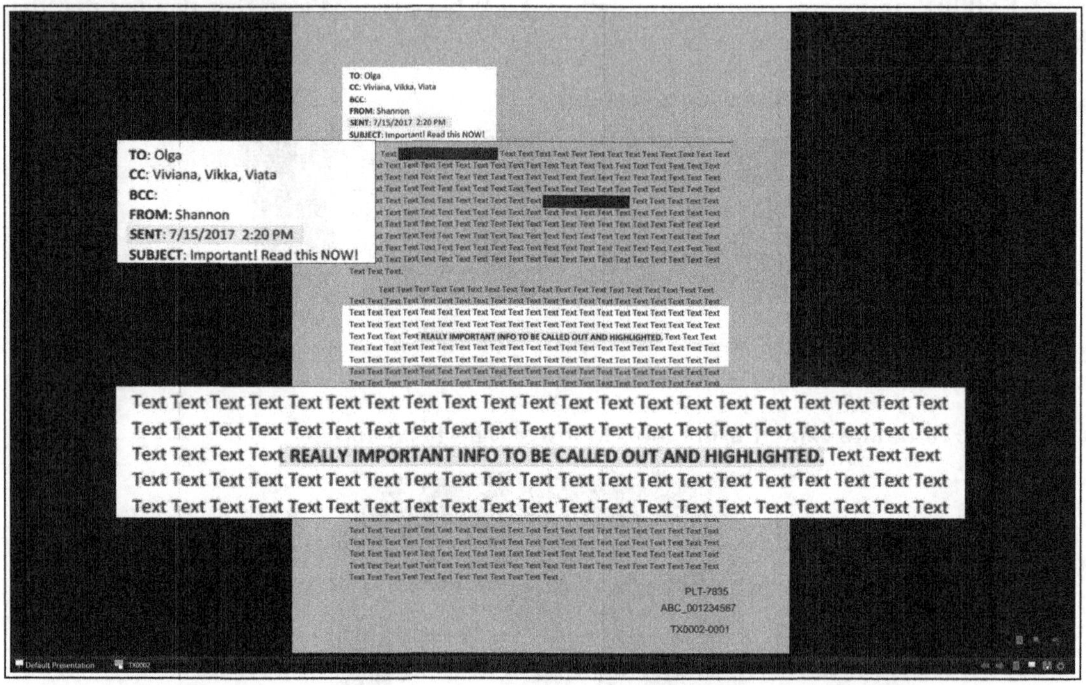

The tools will allow you to build an exhibit that can be created right in front of them or created in advance for quick display. Again, I can't stress enough how important it is to practice with the tools before using them. It will be a complete catastrophe otherwise.

15.4 Create a Presentation in Sanction

Task 1. Create a "New Presentation."

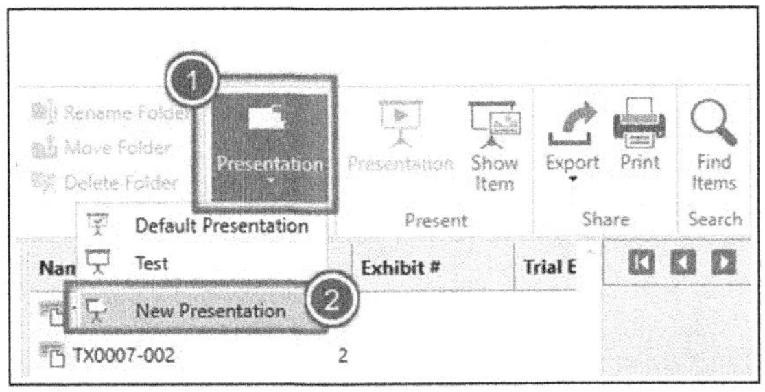

Presentations are planned collections of exhibits that can be played by clicking through using arrows. This is a great way of prebuilding your opening statement/closing argument/witness outlines so you can quickly show them in court and plan the presentation to follow along with the outlines. You might think the difference in time between manually entering an exhibit number and clicking on an arrow is insubstantial, but they are—and manual entery is prone to mis-keying errors. Also, a planned presentation can always be supplemented with on-the-fly callups.

Task 2. Name the presentation.

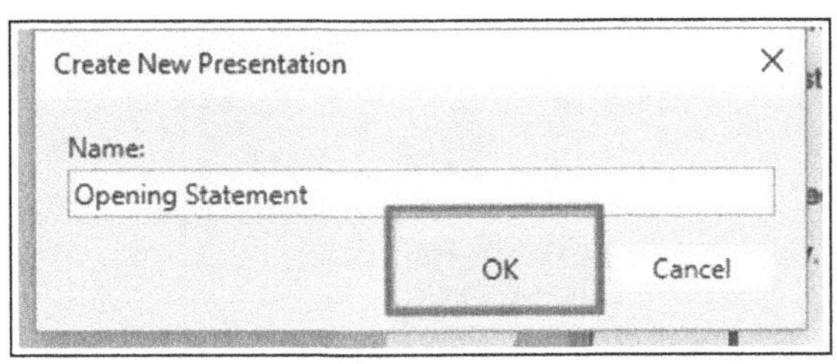

Enter a name for the presentation in the dialog box. Click **OK** in **Create New Presentation**.

Task 3. Add exhibit pages to the presentation created.

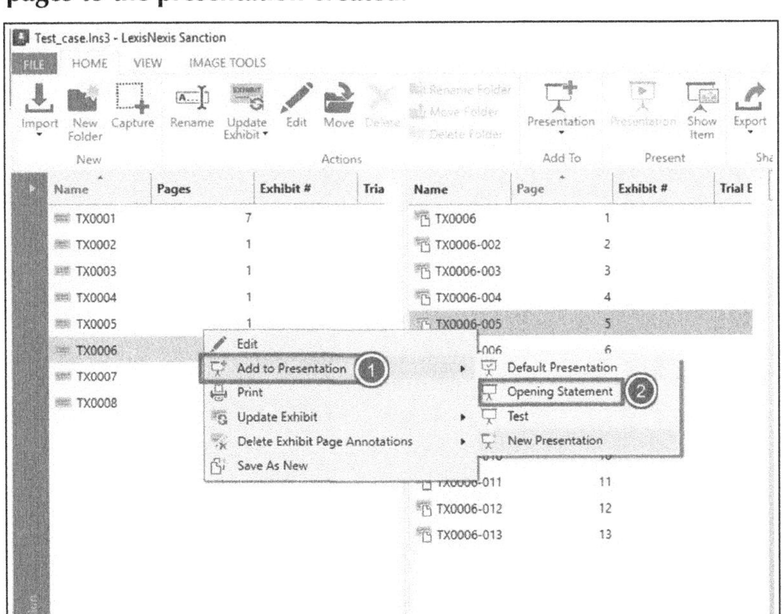

(1) Right-click and select **Add to Presentation**. (2) Choose the presentation you want to add the exhibit to. You can have multiple presentations prepped in advance for different topics or subtopics, opening/closing, and witnesses. It can be difficult to find the balance on how much to plan and what to do on the fly.

15.5 Use Additional Tools in Sanction

Task 1. Create layers.

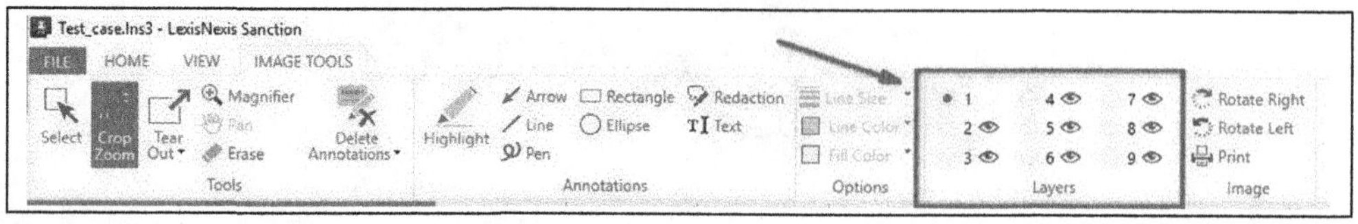

Build annotations so that they can be displayed layer by layer. Creating layers allows you to speed the annotation process in court where time might be limited.

Task 2. Use Capture to take screenshots for annotation.

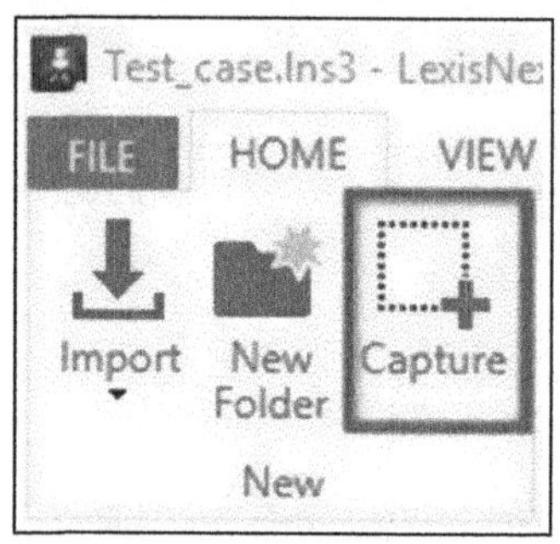

Found on the **Home** tab, Capture can be used to take screenshots of annotated exhibits so they can later be called up quickly or exported to other programs.

CHAPTER SIXTEEN

A PRIMER ON ONCUE

16.1 Create a New Case in OnCue

Task 1. Create a new case.

Select **New**.

Task 2. Set a location for the case.

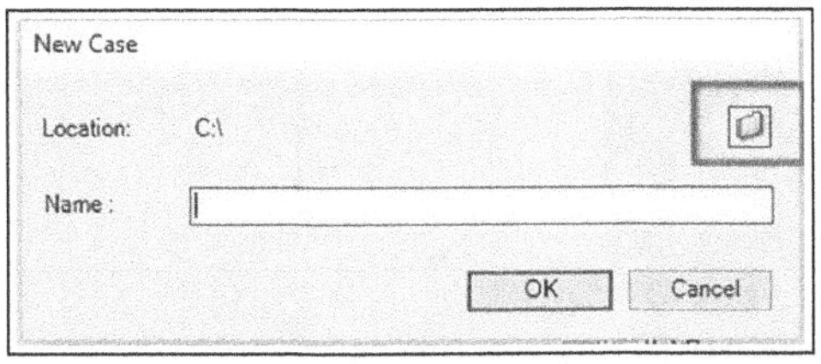

Place the OnCue trial exhibit database into your organizational structure.

Task 3. Choose a folder.

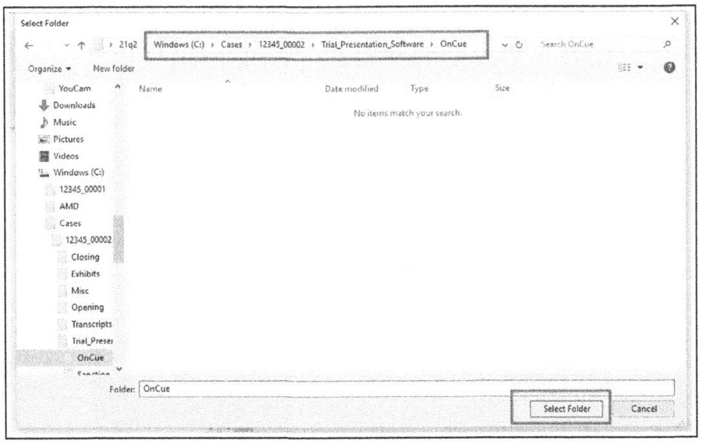

Click **Select Folder** in **Select Folder** on the trial laptop.

Task 4. Name your case.

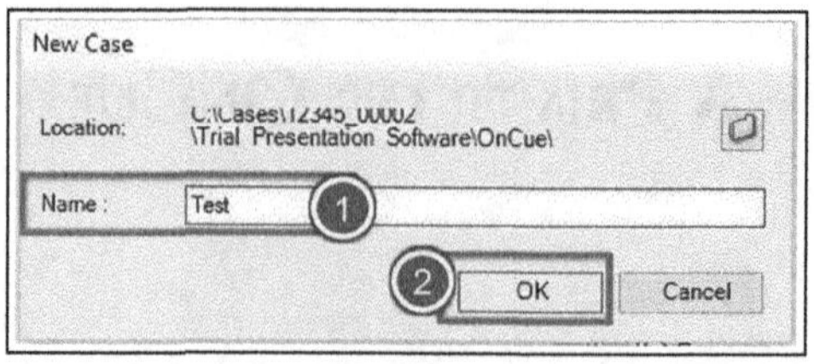

In the **Name** box, (1) type the name of your case and (2) select **OK**.

16.2 Import PDF Documents into OnCue

Task 1. "Add Media."

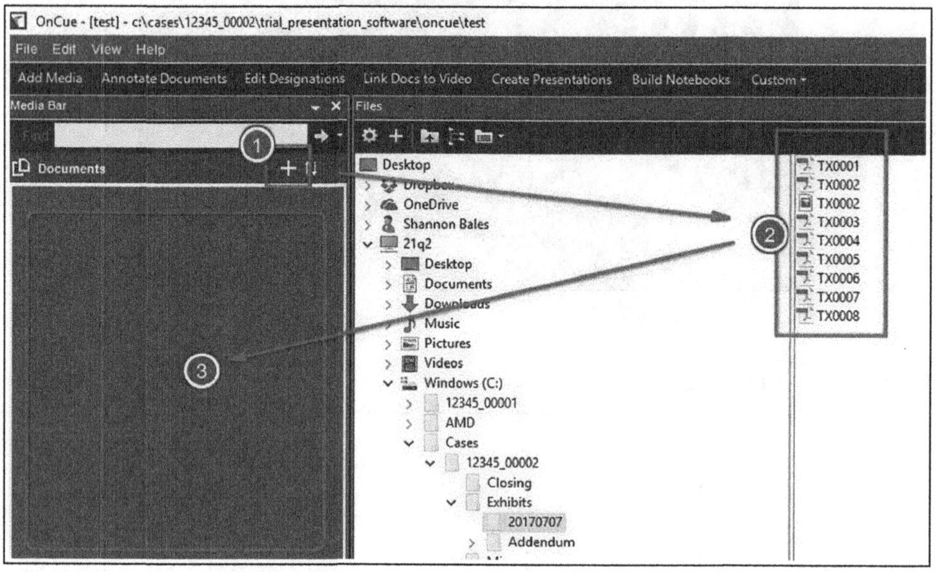

(1) Click the + sign next to **Documents** below the media bar. (2) Navigate to the PDF files to be added. Select and drag them into the media bar for documents (3). Note the media bar is the section on the far left and contains sections for documents (exhibits), videos, transcripts, etc.

Note: OnCue imports and converts documents into the program, where it performs a conversion of the PDF files into individual TIFF and JPG files. Also, OnCue contains its own organizational structure, so you may consider using their organizational structure to import documents from, but I would simply incorporate it into the case organization folder structure, as discussed earlier.

Task 2. "Add File Options."

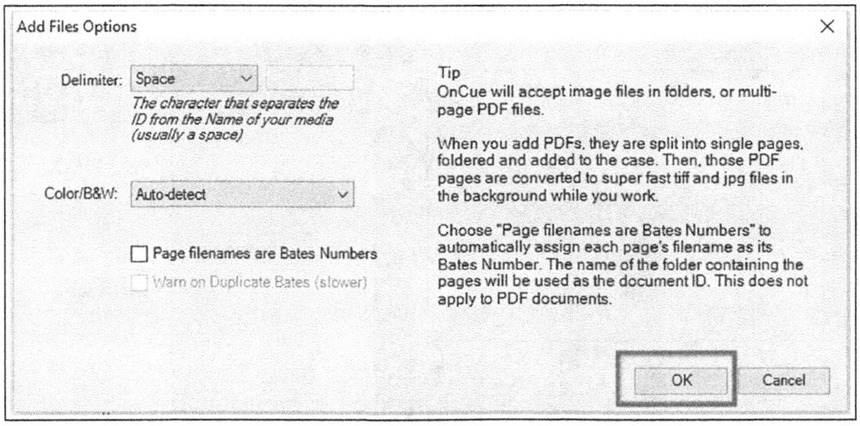

Click **OK** in **Add Files Options** to start the import and conversion process. The default options are usually sufficient for most imports.

Task 3. QC the exhibit load.

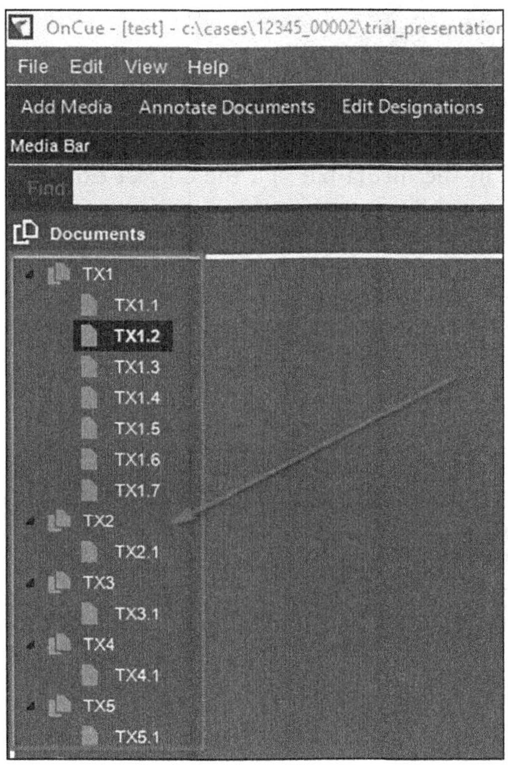

Note that exhibits have been imported and their names changed (for example, **TX0001** is now **TX1**, and each page suffixed using a period and the page number .2, .3, .4, . . .).

Task 4. QC your linking.

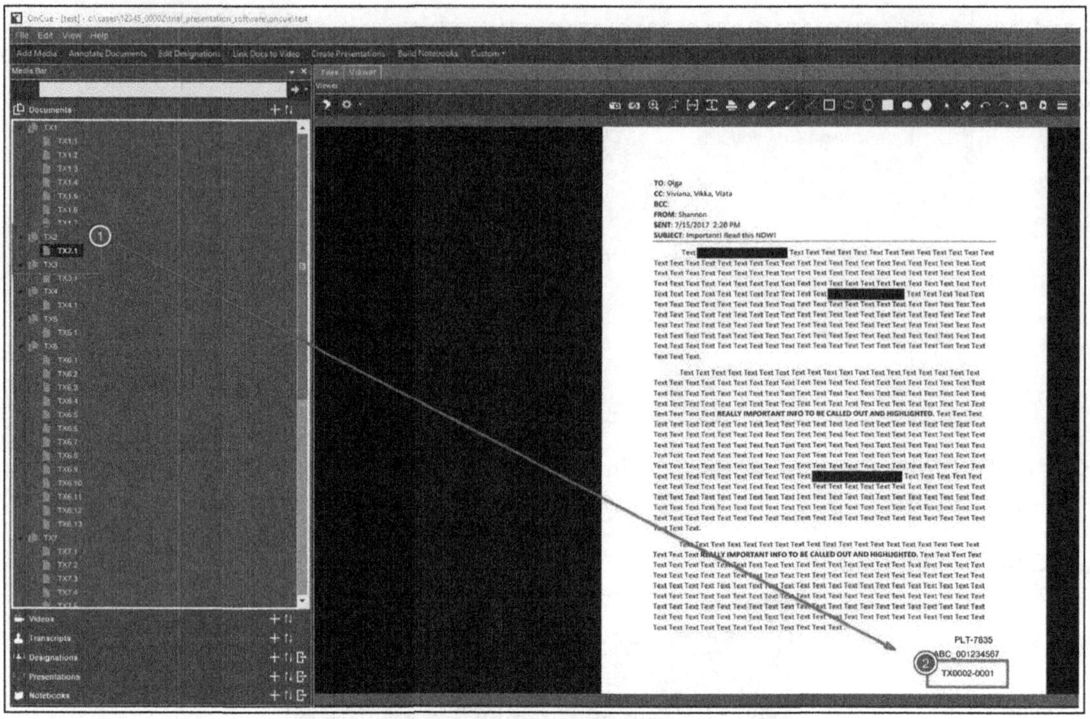

Note when an exhibit is clicked in the media bar (1), the correct exhibit comes up in the viewer (2). QC by comparing the exhibit number to the exhibit brand on the face of the exhibit (here, it is in the lower right corner of the exhibit).

Note: OnCue calls this the production screen. I'll refer to it along with the other presentation programs as the working screen, which is used by the tech to preview and annotate documents prior to displaying them.

16.3 OnCue Presentation Basics

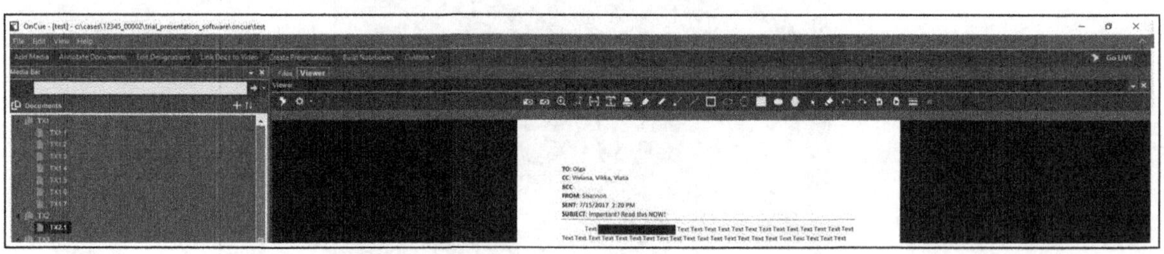

Task 1. Go Live!

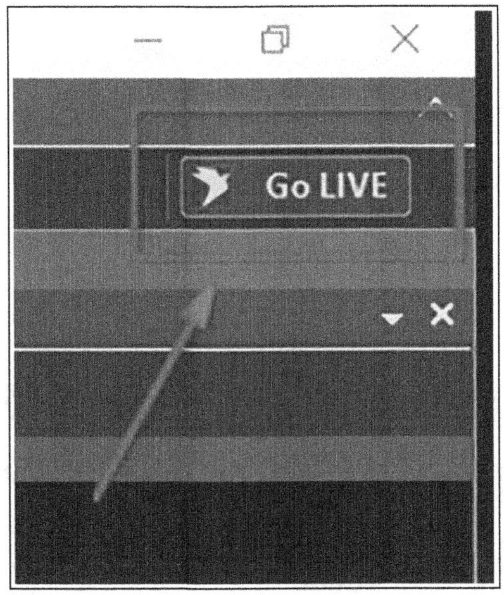

Select **Go Live** in the top right portion of the screen, which opens the presentation screen (hopefully on an extended desktop and not mirror mode). To call up an exhibit, type **X** and the exhibit name shown in the media bar. For example, type **X** and **TX2** calls up trial Exhibit 2. To call up a specific page, type **X** and **TX.2**, which would call up page 2 of Exhibit 2.

Task 2. Decide whether to display the exhibit from the working screen or a black screen.

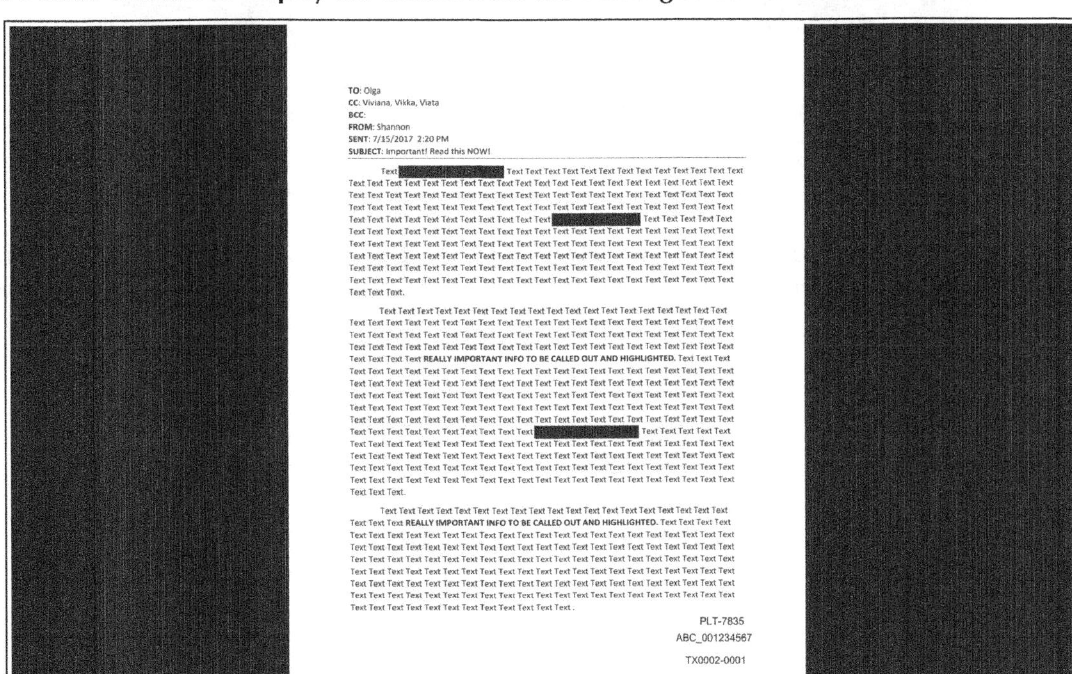

Typically, we start presenting with a blank, black screen. To start with a black screen, use the keyboard command **Ctrl-F5**. However, there may be situations where you want to "Go Live" (present the exhibit) with what is being displayed on the working screen (i.e., the OnCue production screen). To display to your audience the exhibit that is on the working screen, select **Go Live**. Use the right and left arrow keys to move page by page through your document.

Task 3. Bring up the tools.

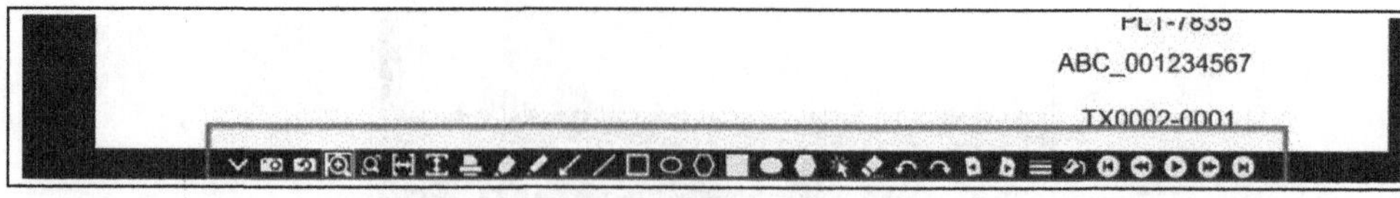

Bring up the tools at the bottom of the screen by selecting **Ctrl-T**.

Task 4. Select the callout tool.

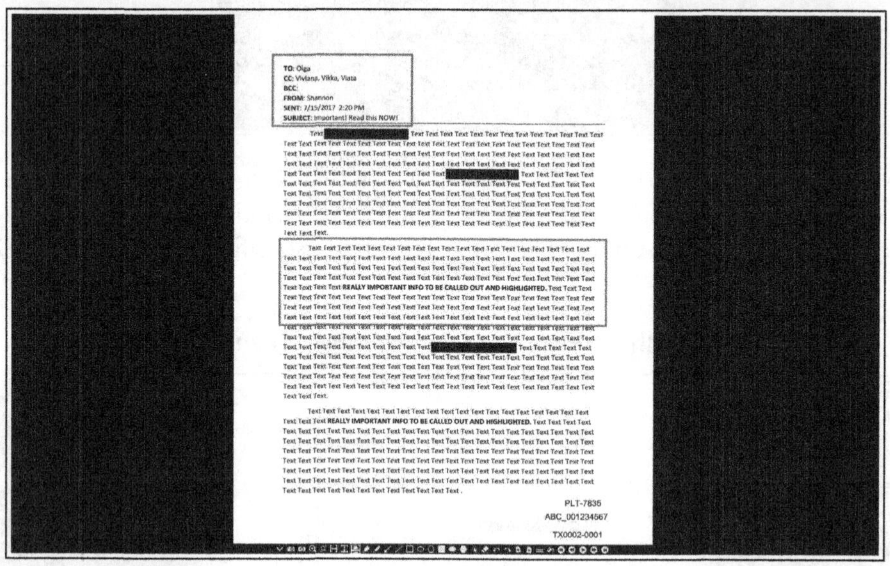

After you have selected the **callout** tool, select the regions of text that you want to callout one at a time. Think about how you want the document to be displayed to decision makers in the courtroom and use a consistent approach to presentation.

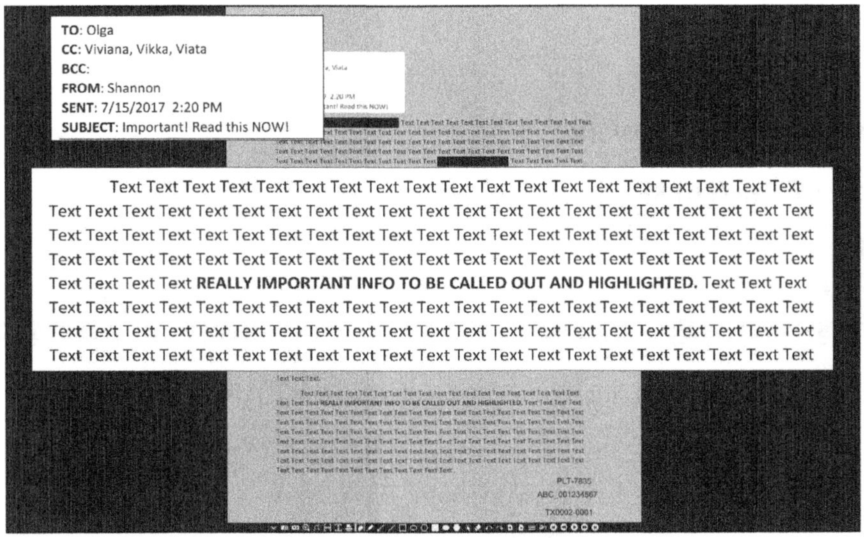

Callout the text that you have selected. You may need to resize the text. If so, left-click and hold the lower right corner of the exhibit and drag the text box to the size you would like it to be. You can also move the callout text boxes by clicking and holding the box with a left-click and hold.

Task 5. Select highlight and arrow annotations.

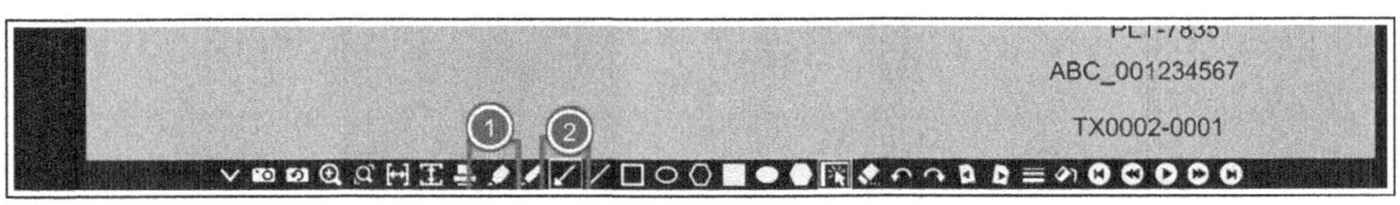

(1) Select the highlighter and annotate the text to your preference. (2) Next, select the arrow and draw an arrow to point out the date and time on the record.

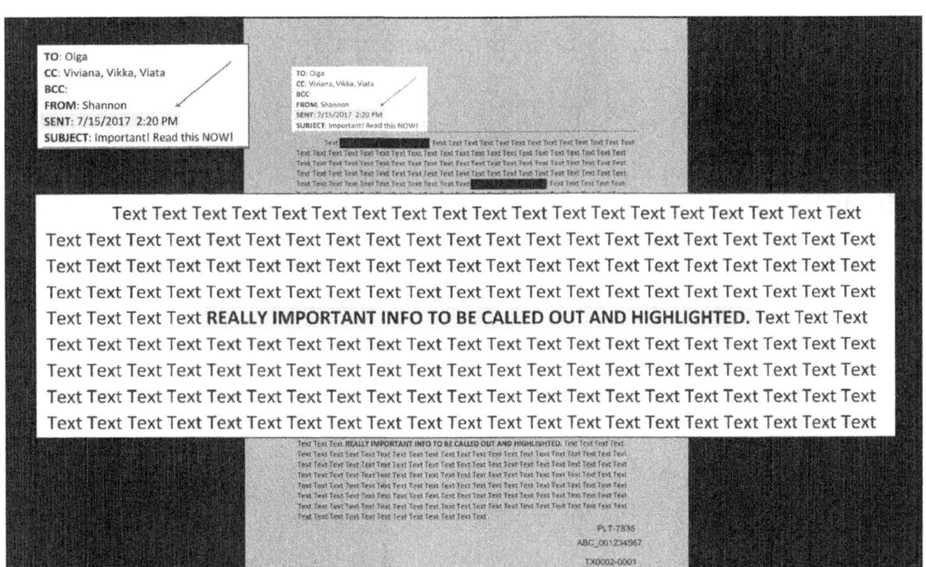

Task 6. Exit GO Live.

To exit **Go live**, hit the **Esc** key.

16.4 Save Annotations in OnCue

Task 1. Choose the camera (Ctrl-S).

Select the camera (**Ctrl-S**) to save an image that has been annotated.

Task 2. Screen capture the location.

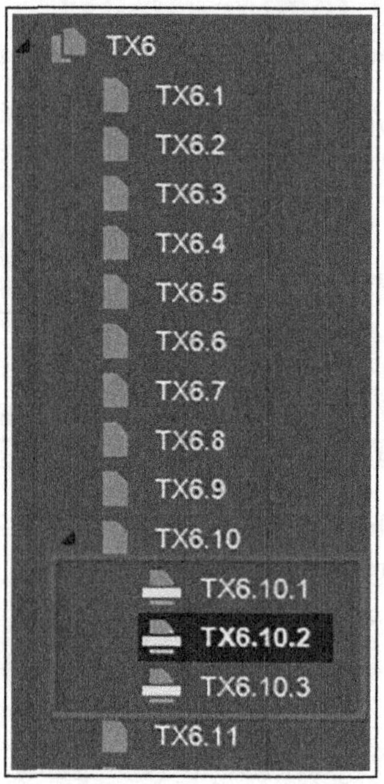

The screen capture will be located under the exhibit number of the document they came from and suffixed with an additional decimal. TX6.10 (Trial Exhibit 6, page 10) becomes TX6.10.2 (Trial Exhibit 6, page 10, capture number 2).

CHAPTER SEVENTEEN

A PRIMER ON ADOBE

17.1 Adobe Presentation Basic Skills

Task 1. Using alternatives to trial presentation software.

This is a technique to use if you do *not* have trial presentation software. I'm demonstrating how to use Adobe in this role, but you could easily add video clips or other applications by embedding them in Acrobat or using your computer's default applications, like media players, photo viewers, or Microsoft Office. This approach works well with low volumes of data, and while it's not as slick as using a trial presentation program, it is OK in a pinch (not to mention a good backup plan in the unlikely event your trial presentation program becomes corrupt).

Task 2. Create a folder.

Right-click and select **New**, then **Folder** to create an easy to access folder on your desktop.

Task 3. Add files.

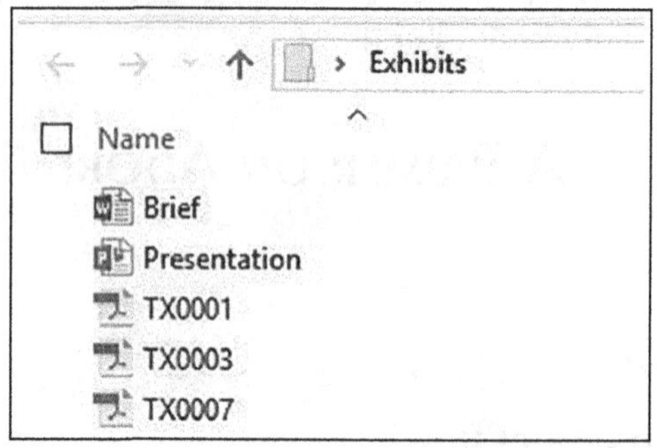

Copy files to the folder so they are easy to access. This also wards off potentially wandering eyes if you kept the files in a more general location where people might inadvertently see other files you wouldn't want them to see while connecting to the court system. Remember that you can put video clips and other file types in here and use the same technique.

Task 4. Set up extended screen.

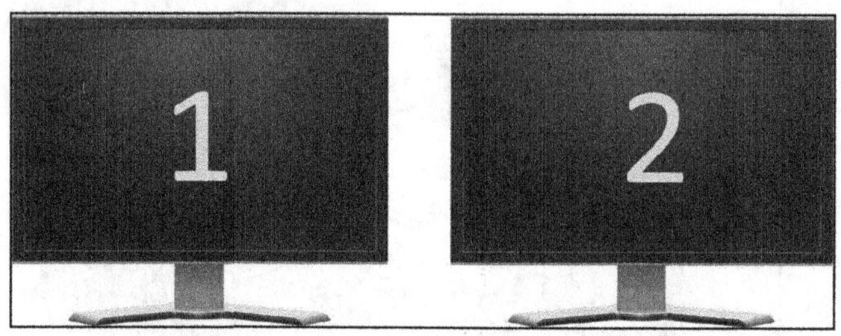

Per the earlier instruction setup on the extended screen, only one screen should be visible to you and the other to the courtroom. I often refer to them as (1) the working screen and (2) the presentation screen.

Task 5. Drag and drop files from the working screen to the presentation screen

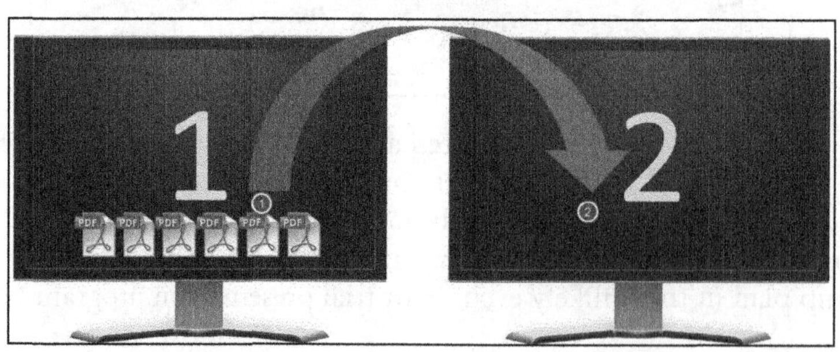

(1) Open files from the folder created on your desktop (the working screen) and (2) drag them to the presentation screen.

Task 6. Get to know some important tools.

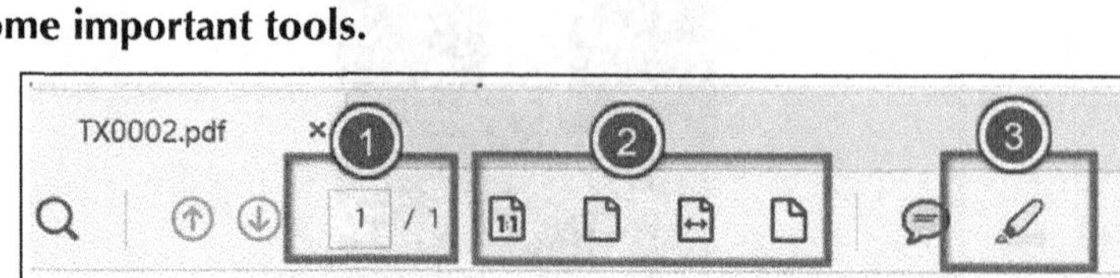

By understanding how to (1) quickly navigate to a page, (2) choose a page view option, and (3) perform highlights, a legal team member without trial presentation software can do a pretty good job of impersonation. Also, it uses skills you already have.

Note: You should still test your equipment, know how to connect it, and practice maneuvers before going to the courtroom.

Task 7. Using the "hand" and zoom tools.

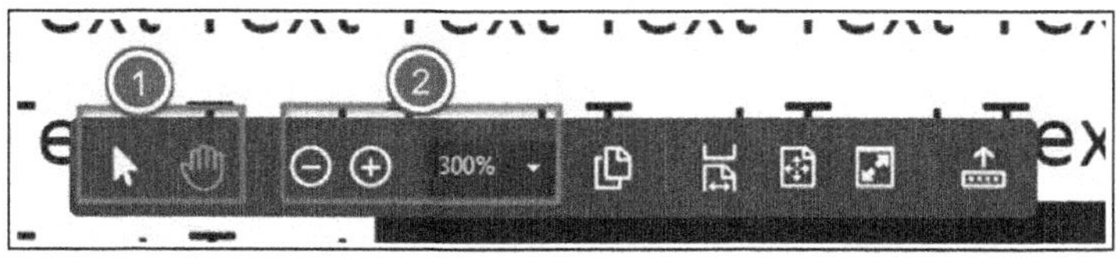

(1) The **hand** tool is used to help browse the document. By left-clicking and holding, you can drag the document around to where you need it. (Practice makes perfect.) (2) The **zoom** tools give more refinement to zoom in and out from the tools on the previous page. These tools are either in your toolbar at the top of the page or will appear when you hover the mouse at the bottom of the page.

Task 8. Get really fancy with Adobe's Pan & Zoom.

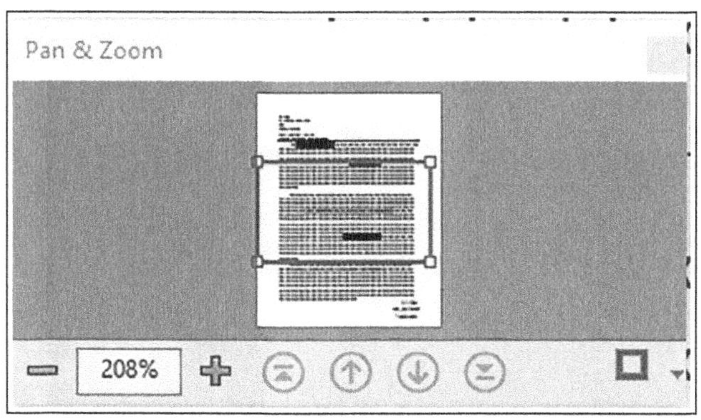

The **Pan & Zoom** tool allows you to navigate the face of the document and zoom in and out without letting others see you control the action (much like a trial presentation tool "light").

Task 9. Put it all together.

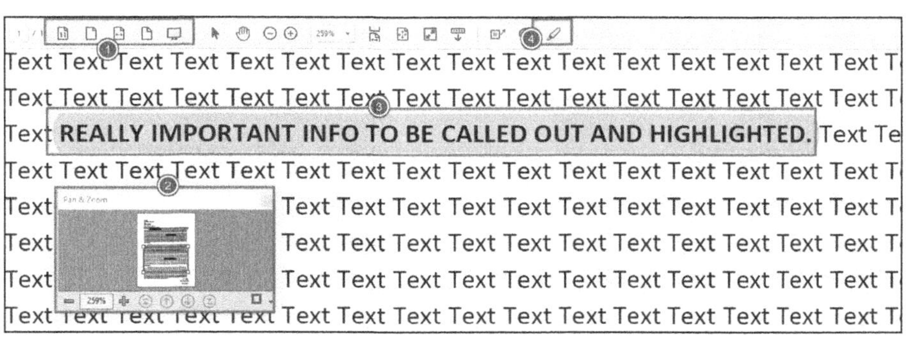

Open your document or exhibit and drag it to the presentation screen. Start by showing the entire page of the document using the controls in either the (1) **Page View** options or (2) the **Pan & Zoom** feature. Then, using those same features, zoom in on the region (3) you want to highlight. Select the (4) **Highlight** tool and select the text to be highlighted.

Chapter Eighteen

A Primer on Video

18.1 Video Basics

Task 1. Copy deliverables to a folder.

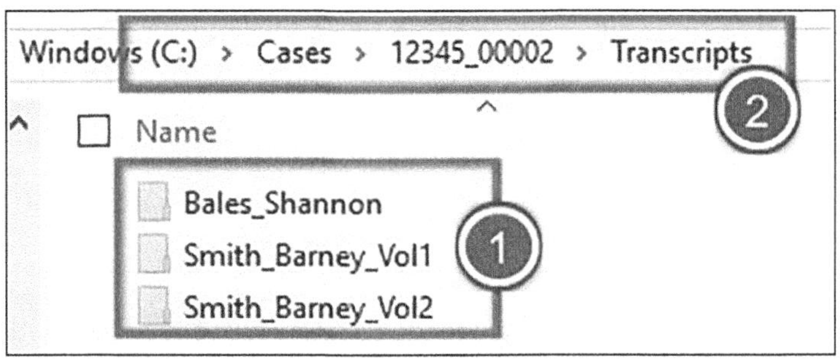

(1) Create a folder that uses the last name of the deponent and any other identifying that you prefer (some like to use date or volume as well). Try not to use any spaces or punctuation in the file path (the_underscore_is_OK). (2) Transfer all of the data received from the vendor to our case organizational structure C:\Cases\12345_00002\Transcripts.

Task 2. Check Deliverables, Part 1.

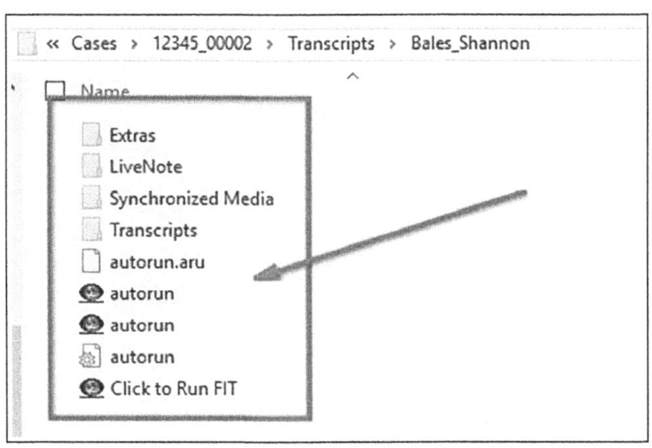

The deliverables are fairly consistent from vendor to vendor and should include a **Transcripts** folder and **Synchronized Media** or **Video** folder. Sometimes they include proprietary players (Yeslaw comes to mind), which can be a great option if you don't have Case Notebook or TextMap (or other transcript tool).

Task 3. Check Deliverables, Part 2.

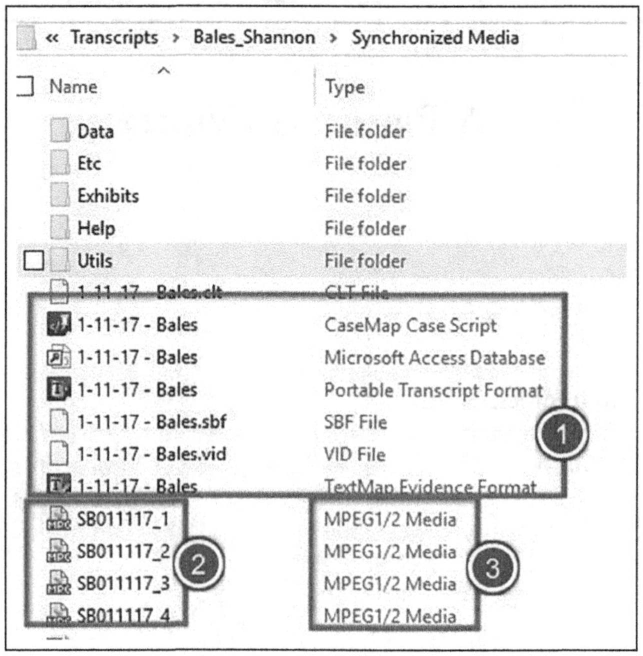

(1) Typically, vendors deliver in a variety of formats for a single charge. This is good because the files sometimes don't work very well and a different format may work better with your trial software. (2) Note video files—there are four full-length videos here, which can take a considerable amount of space on your hard drive and time to edit and QC. (3) Note the format is MPEG. Most trial software works best with MPEG1 or MPEG2.

18.2 Video in TrialDirector

18.2.1 Import Video into TrialDirector

Task 1. Select "Transcript Manager."

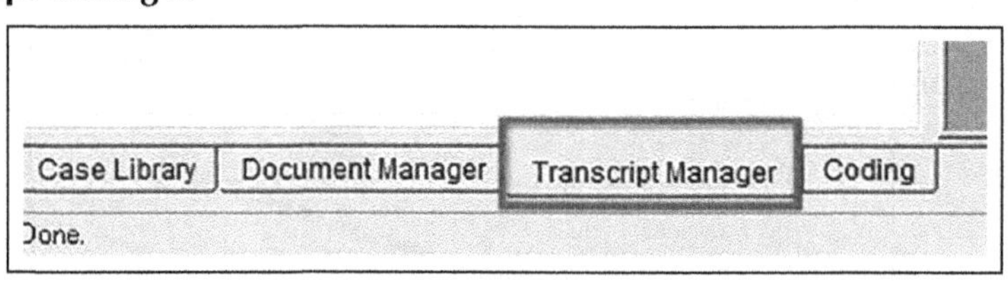

Select the **Transcript Manager** tab in TrialDirector.

Task 2. Select "Transcripts."

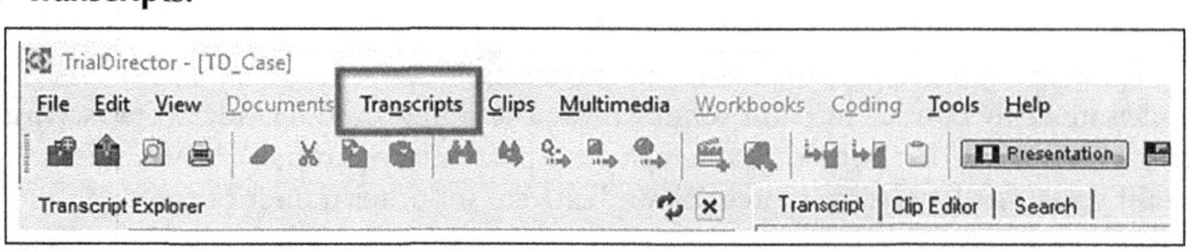

Select **Transcripts** from the menu bar.

Task 3. Import Wizard.

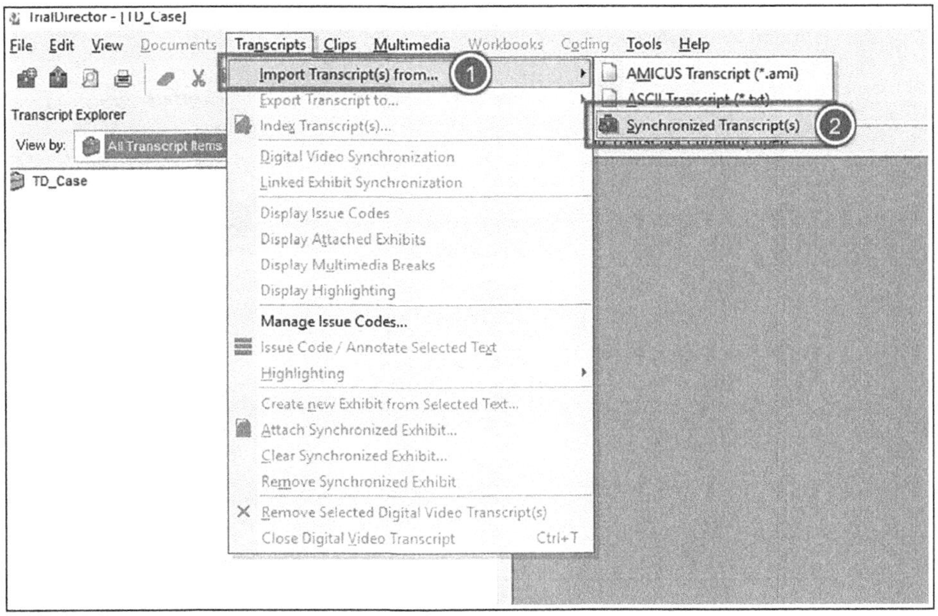

(1) Select **Import Transcript(s) from...**, then (2) **Synchronized Transcript(s)**.

Task 4. Import the CMS file.

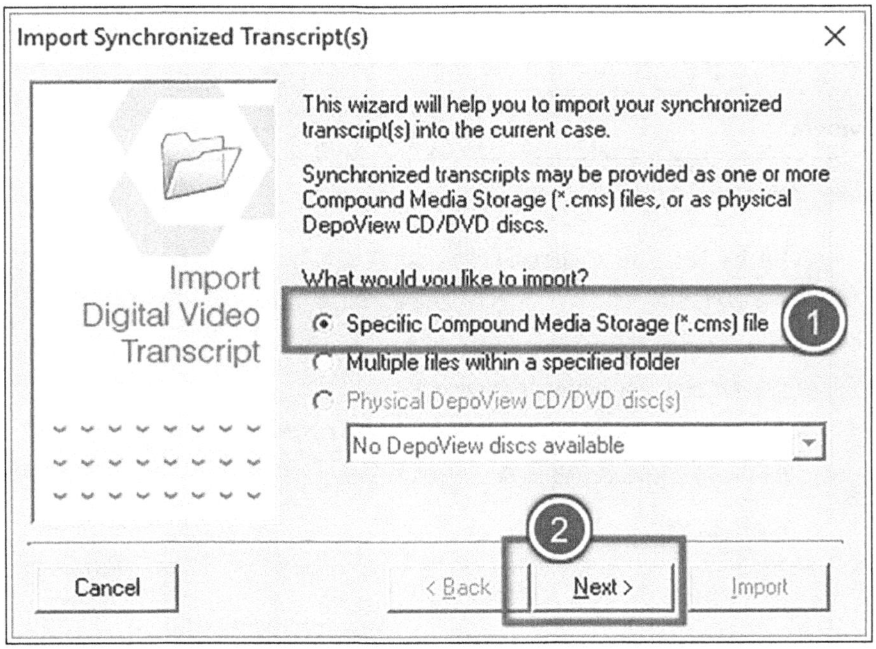

(1) CMS is the preferred format for deliverables with TrialDirector. You could also import stand-alone video clips directly into the **Multimedia** folder on the **Case Library** tab.

Task 5. Browse to the multimedia location and import.

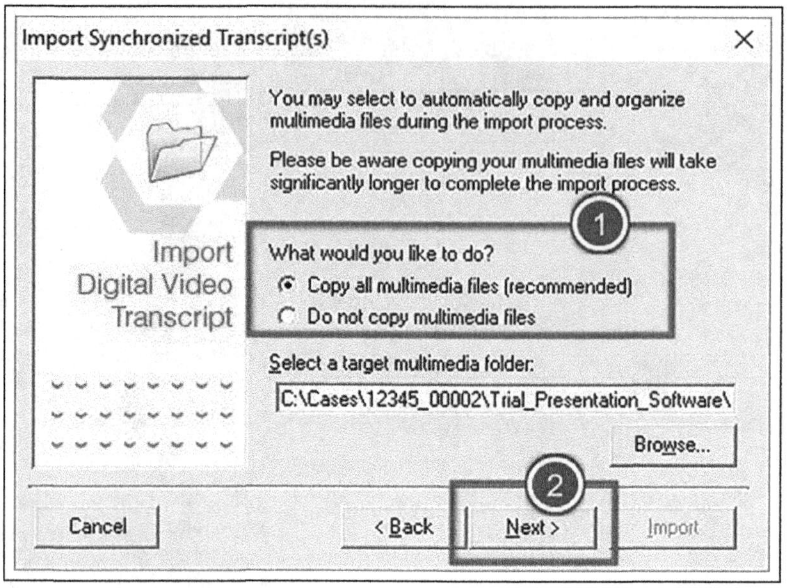

(1) You will be given the option to import all video into TrialDirector or leave it in the location that it is in. This depends on how much hard drive space you can devote to video. If you have more video than space, use an external drive and link to video there (by choosing **Do not copy multimedia files**). (2) Select **Next**.

Note: If you use an external drive, be sure your start up routine is bulletproof (plug in and start up the same every day) and that you check the drive letter that the video is in on the external drive *every time you start*. There is a risk of it assigning a different drive letter and breaking the path.

Task 6. Import video.

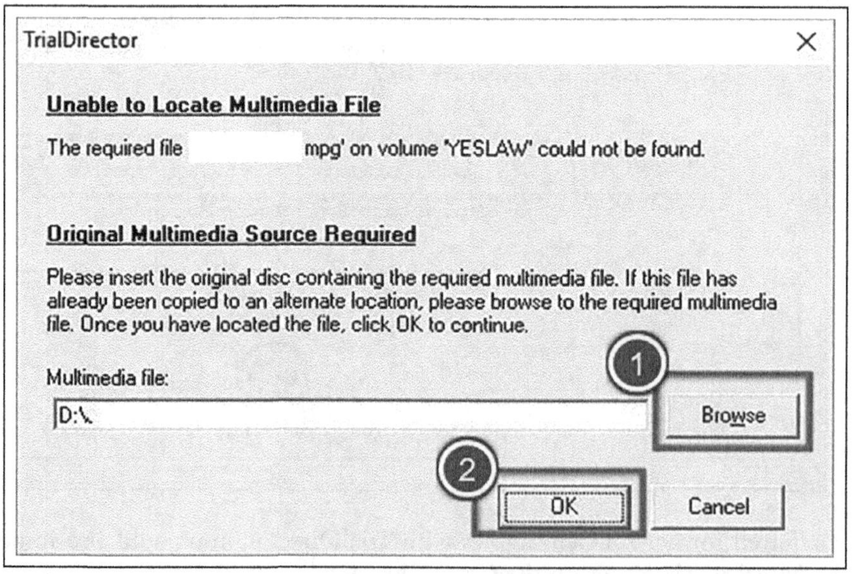

(1) Import video by selecting **Browse** and navigating to your organizational structure under **Transcripts** and selecting each video for import. (The process will repeat for each linked video). (2) Select **OK** to import.

Task 7. Select OK.

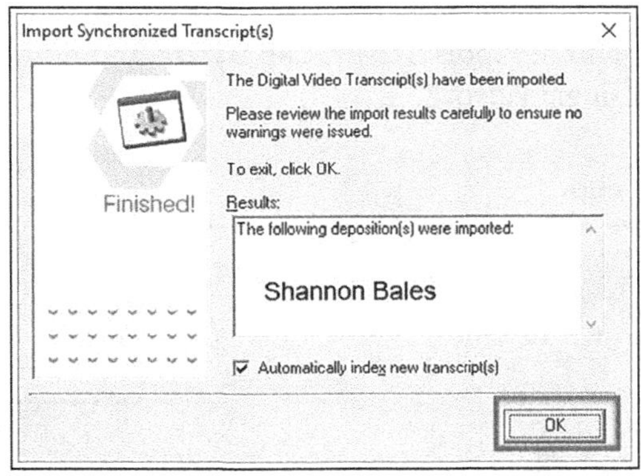

Select **OK** and the transcripts will be imported and indexed in TrialDirector.

Task 8. Look for video that's been imported and transcript added.

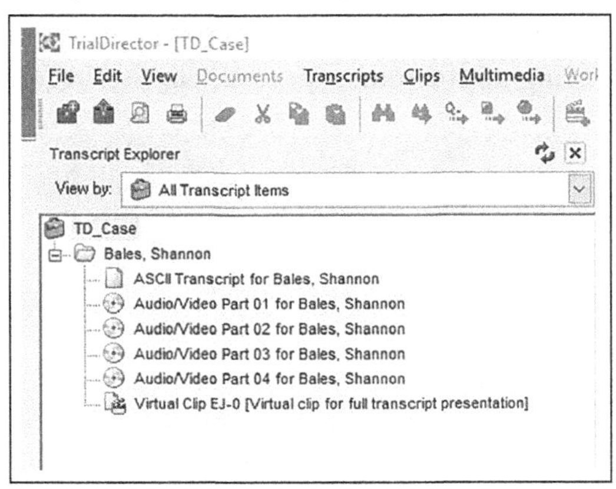

The video and transcript should appear on the left side of the screen, along with the transcript.

18.2.2 Create and Play a Clip in TrialDirector

Task 1. Clip notes.

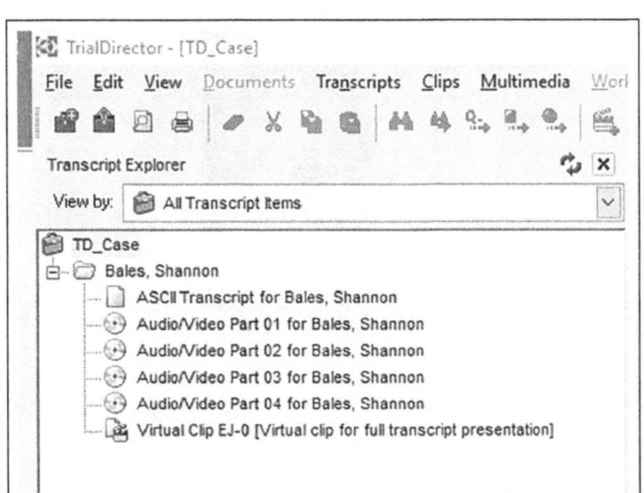

There are many correct ways to create a clip in TrialDirector. I'm going to cover the basics, but I did briefly mention clip formats in Chapter Seven, Trial Software. As you progress, you'll want to learn how to create scripts called Clip Creation Script (CCS) and use tools like the clip wizard and others to more efficiently create clips and connect many together to create a single video.

Task 2. Select the transcript to clip.

On the **Transcript Manager** tab, select (1) the transcript to be clipped on the left side of the screen. Then select the tab (2) **Transcript**, which will bring up the transcript to be clipped in front of you.

Task 3. Be accurate.

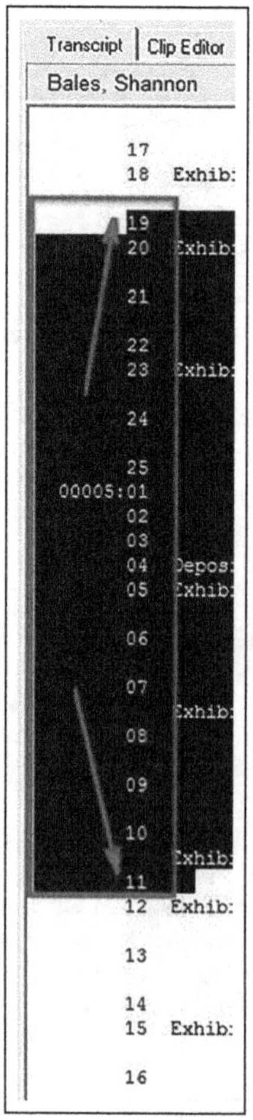

Select the lines of text to be clipped. Accuracy counts here; if you select a line above or below, that text and video will be shown and heard.

Task 4. "Create New Clip from Selected Text…".

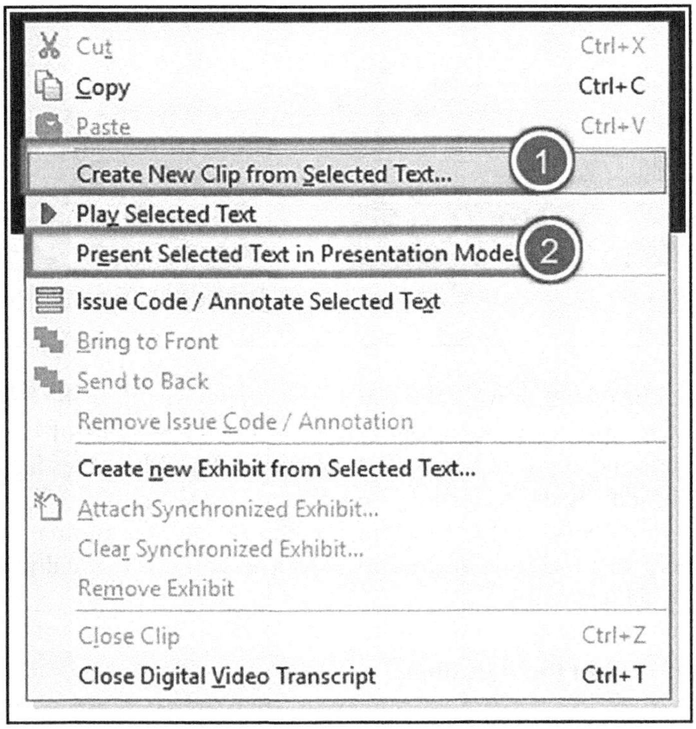

(1) Right-click and select **Create New Clip from Selected Text…**. This will clip the text so it can be edited and adjusted.

Note: You could also play the video on the fly in court by selecting (2) **Present Selected Text in Presentation Mode**, which will play the video and text on the presentation screen. There is always a balance between choosing to clip in advance or not because of the time it takes to do. Last, when you play video on the fly, you never know if somewhere in the middle is where the court takes a break, so always QC your clips and be ready for anything!

Task 5. Select the clip to edit.

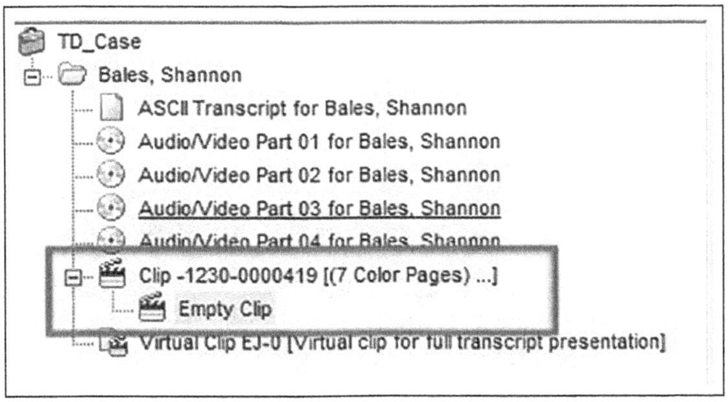

From the left side of the screen, select the clip you just created to adjust the begin and end times.

Task 6. Review the edit screen.

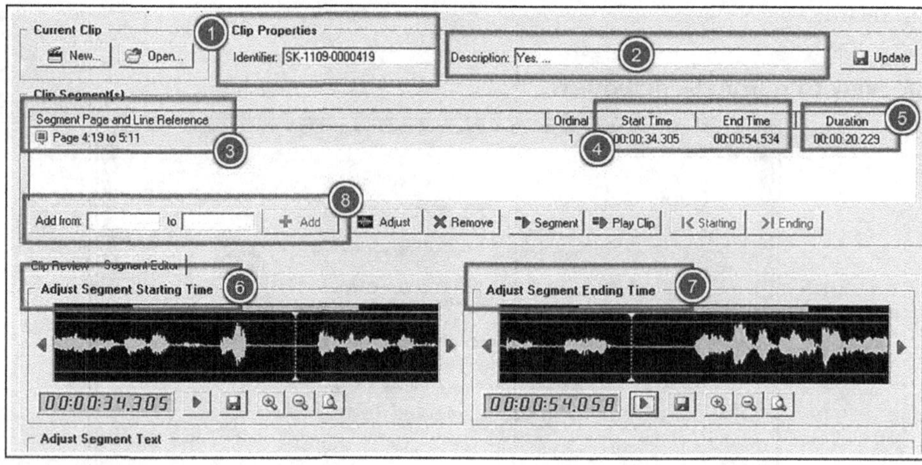

When you select a clip to be edited, it will take you to this screen to adjust the beginning and ending times as well as name it and add a description. A quick tour: (1) Identifier—the name of the clip. I typically change this to the initials of the deponent and clip number, so, e.g., **Shannon Bales** becomes **SBclip1**. (2) Description—add the page/line range here. (3) This is the page and line reference for the clip. (4) The start and end times on the video (not the time stamp on the video). (5) How long the clip is (look for anomalies here, such as too long). (6) The start time of the clip. (7) The end time of the clip. (8) Here, you can manually add additional clips to create a single clip that plays multiple segments.

Task 7. "Segment Editor": Adjust the start time.

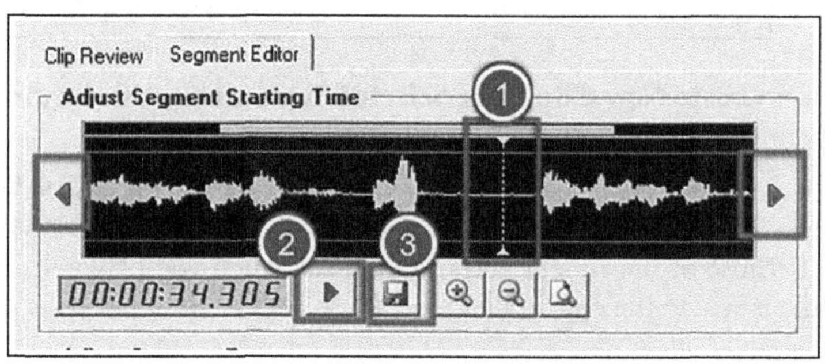

(1) Use the slider bar to find the beginning of the clip and adjust it so that there is not too much time or that it does not start in the middle of a word. Generally, it should be very close to the start/end time. (You may need to use the arrows on the left and right to find the start time.) (2) Play the clip once you think you have it adjusted and listen for the beginning. (3) When you are satisfied with your start time, click **Save**.

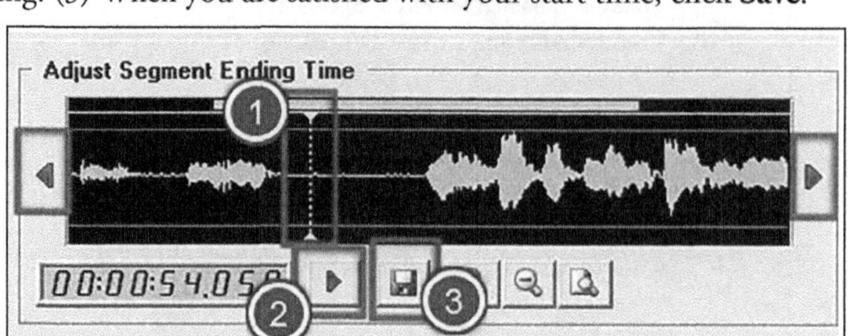

(1) Use the slider bar to find the end of the clip and adjust it so that there is not too much time or that it does not start in the middle of a word. Generally, it should be very close to the start/end time. (You may need to use the arrows on the left and right to find the start time.) (2) Play the clip once you think you have it adjusted and listen for the end. (3) When you are satisfied with your end time, click **Save**.

Task 8. Name and update the clip.

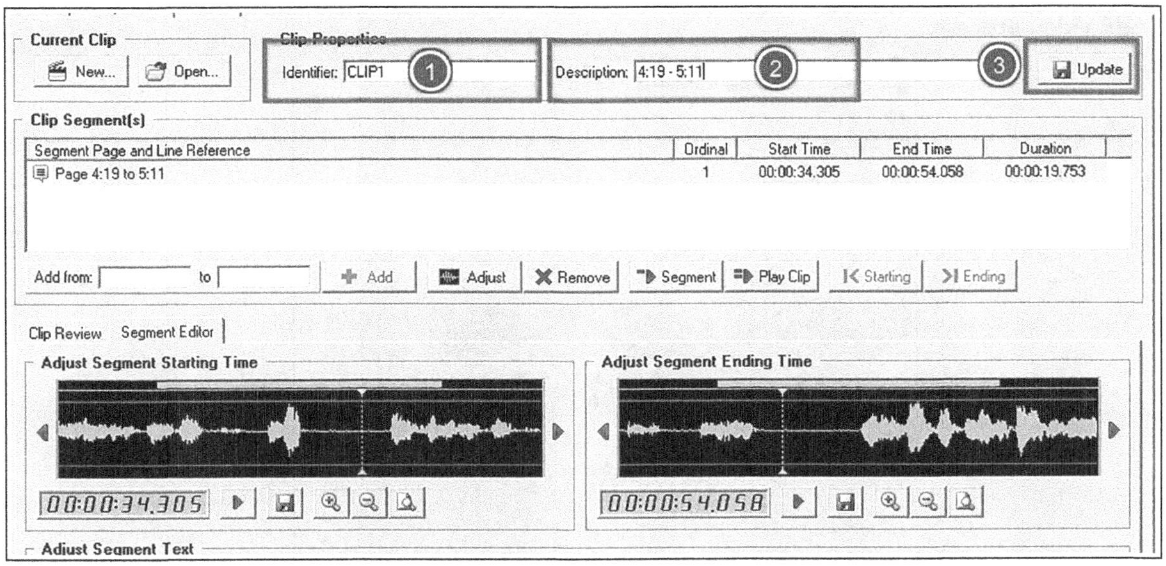

(1) Name your clip, and (2) provide a **Description** (typically the page/line number). (3) Select **Update** when done.

Task 9. Play the video, just like loading an exhibit.

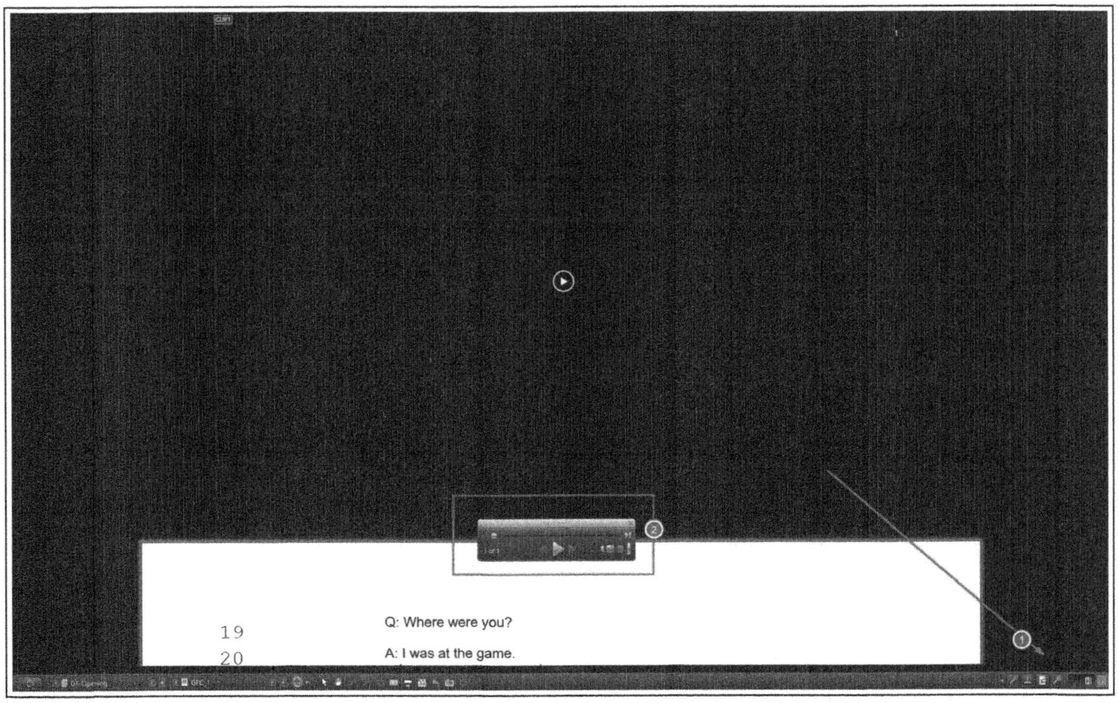

Enter the clip name in either the (1) presentation screen or detached toobar. You can play the video by using the **Detached tool box** (media player controls), which can be dragged to your working screen.

18.3 Video in Sanction

18.3.1 Import Video into Sanction

Task 1. Add video process.

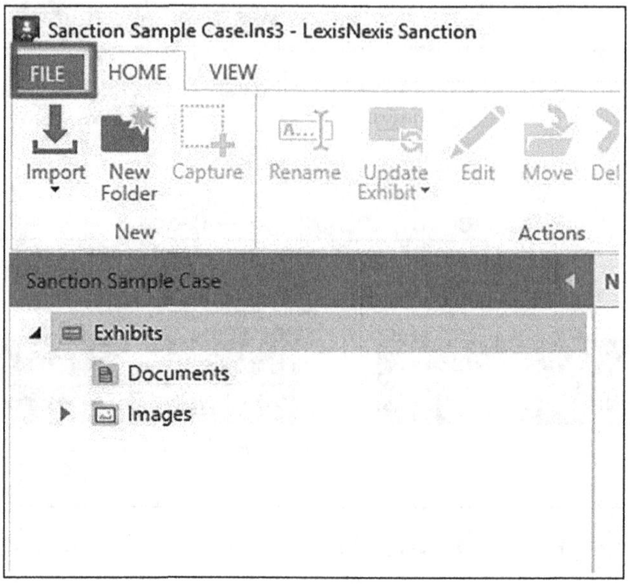

Go to the **File** tab.

Task 2. "Add Items."

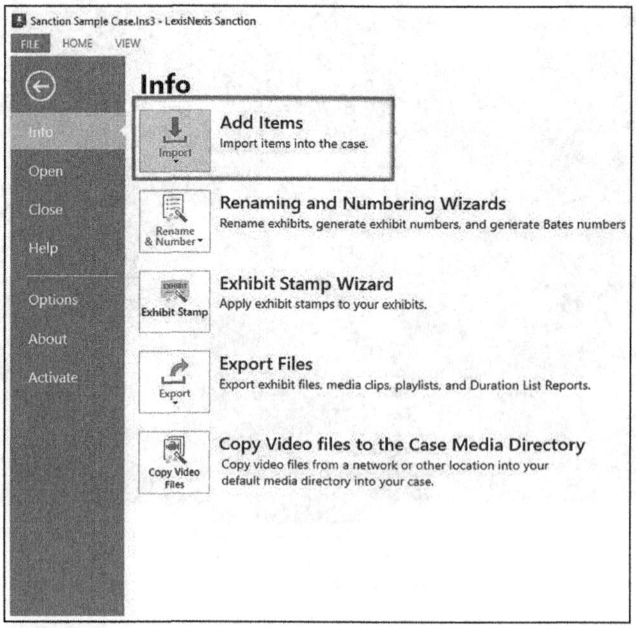

Select **Import** under the **Add Items** section of the **File** tab.

Task 3. Choose "Transcripts."

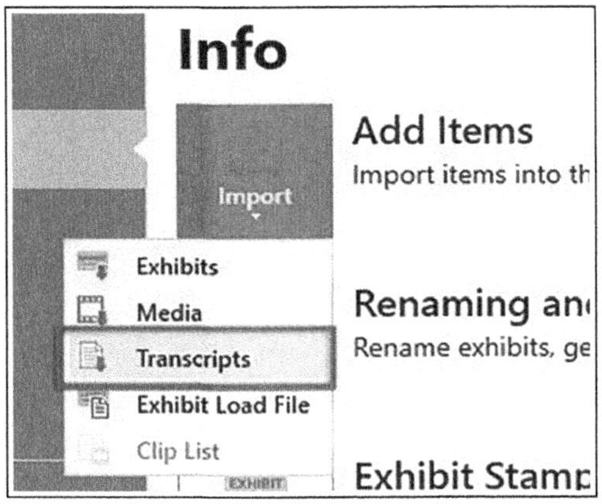

Choose **Transcripts** from the dropdown menu.

Task 4. Launch the "Transcript File Import Wizard."

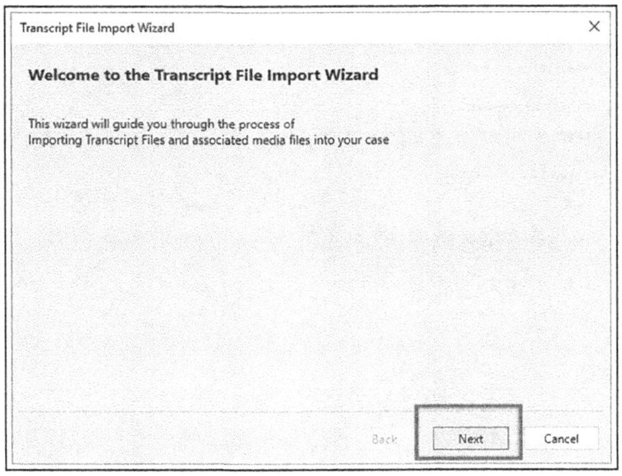

This is the wizard used to import transcripts and video. (*Note*: Transcripts can be without video as well.) Select **Next**.

Task 5. "Select Transcript Files to Import."

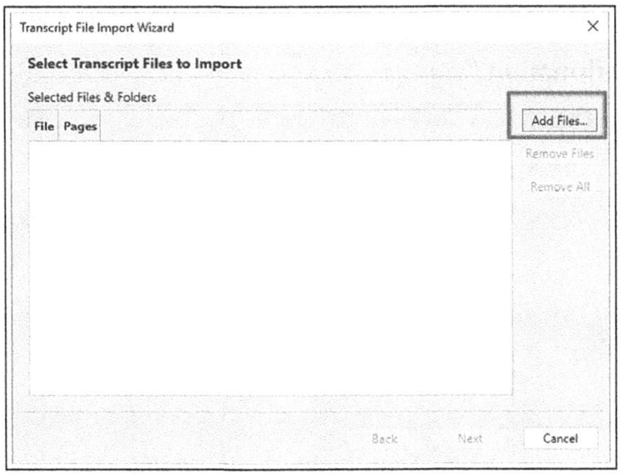

Select **Add Files**.

Task 6. Add a transcript.

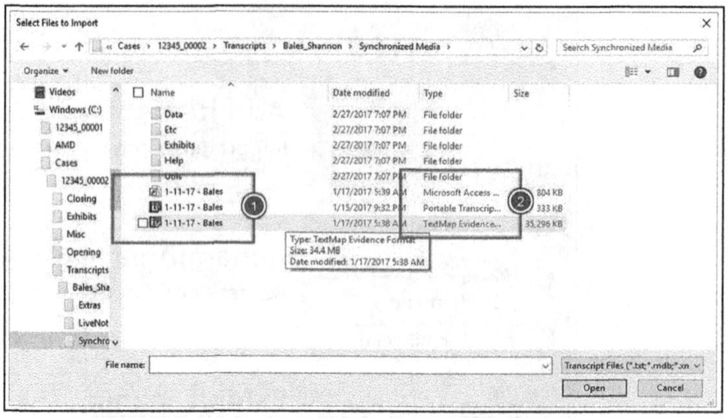

(1) Select the transcript or synchronized transcript to added. (2) Note that Sanction will import a variety of transcript formats (e.g., TextMap, Access, and PTF).

Task 7. Get "Ready to Import."

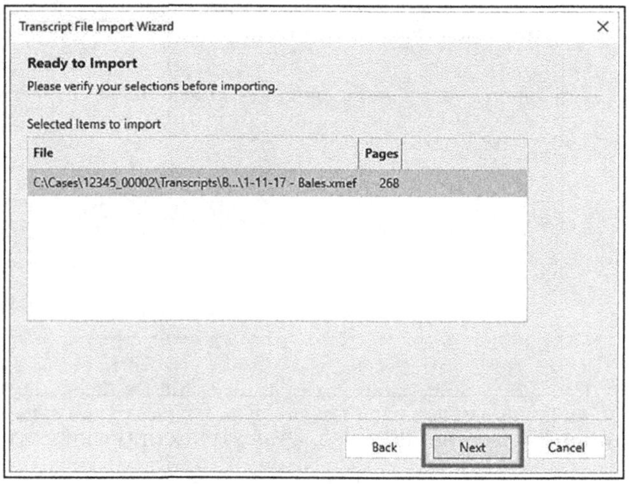

Confirm transcript import by selecting **Next**.

Task 8. Review "Import Confirmation."

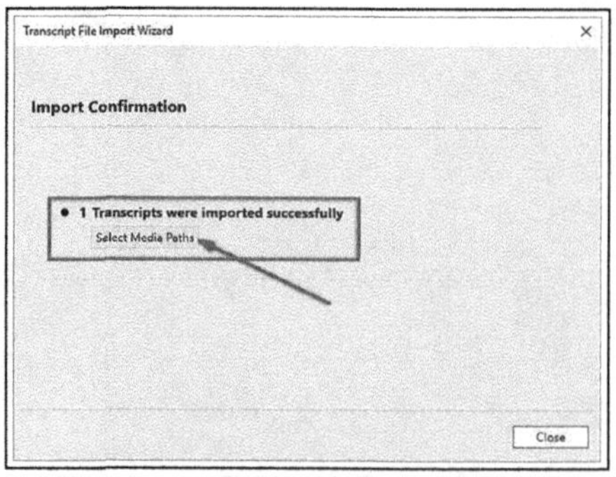

Note import confirmation. Choose **Select Media Paths** to add the video location (from our case structure) to the case. If you don't add the location, Sanction won't know where to find the video.

Task 9. Add "Case Media Path."

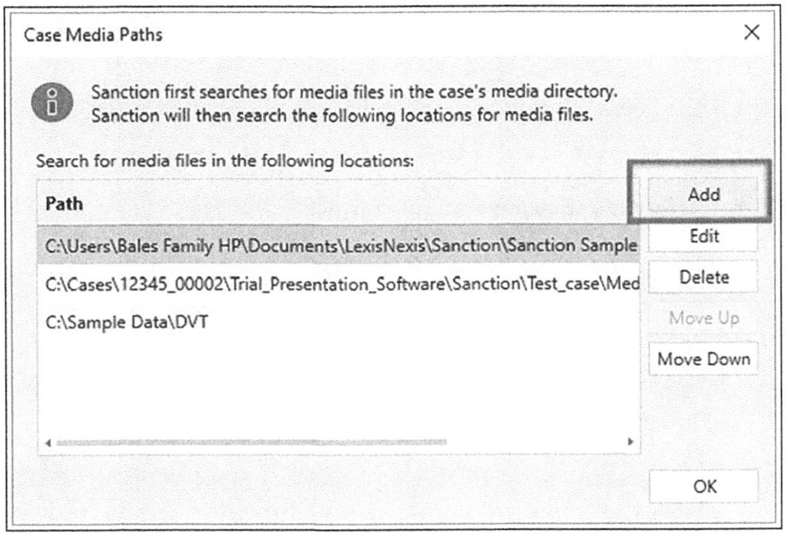

Select **Add** to add a new media path to the case. Some teams like to place all case video in a single folder. However, I recommend individual folders for each deponent.

(1) Browse to the media location and add. (2) Select **OK**.

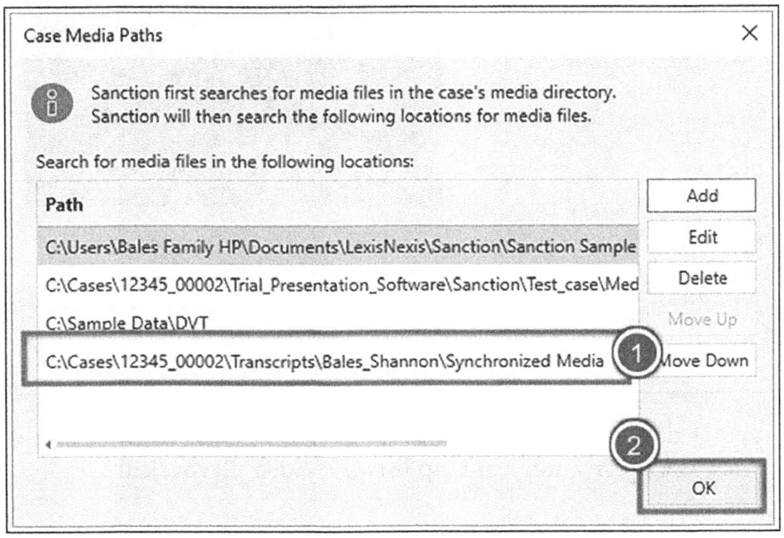

(1) Confirm that the location was added, then (2) select **OK**.

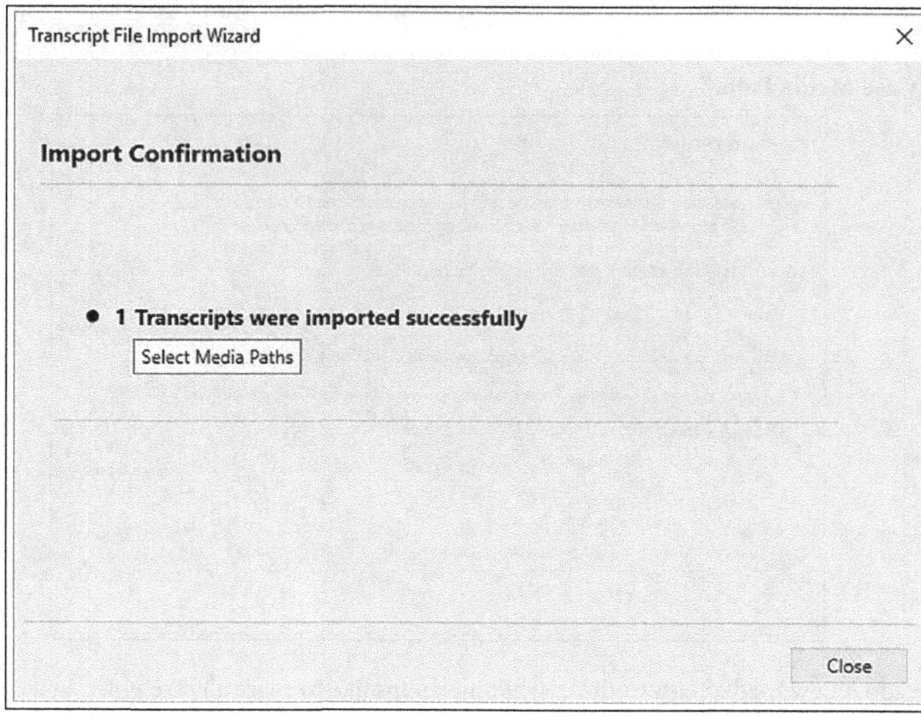

18.3.2 Create a Clip in Sanction

Task 1. Review transcript screen.

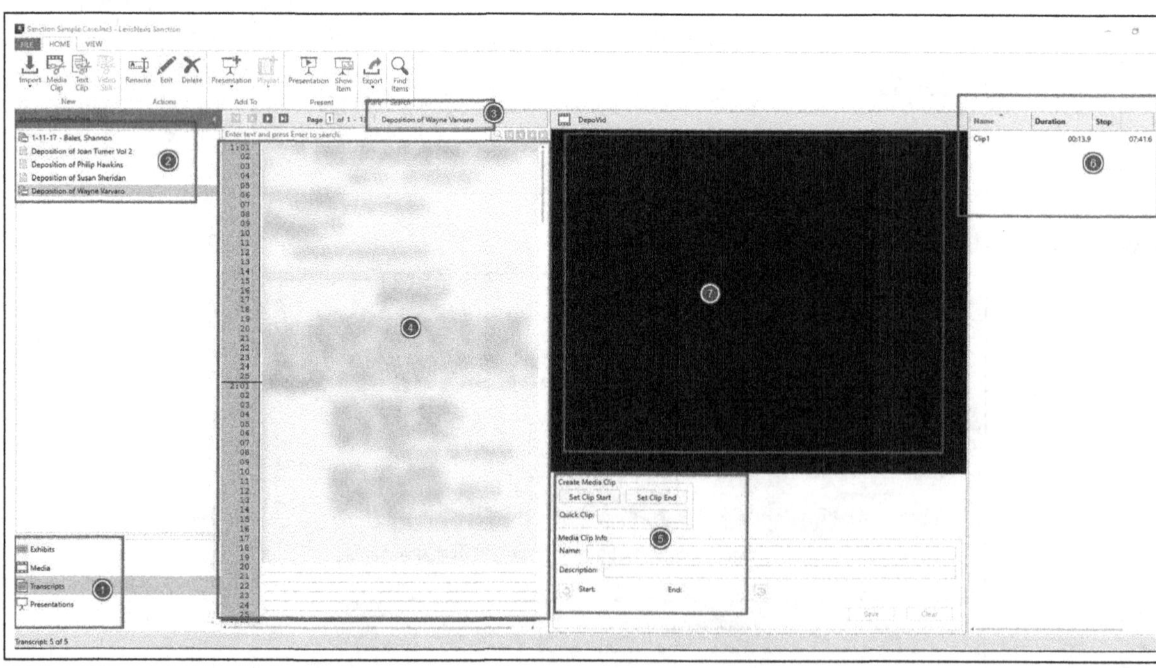

(1) Choose which type of data to view. (2) Transcript list. (3) Name of deponent whose transcript is being shown. (4) Transcript area. (5) Clip creation. (6) Clip list. (7) Video playback area.

Task 2. Clip screen.

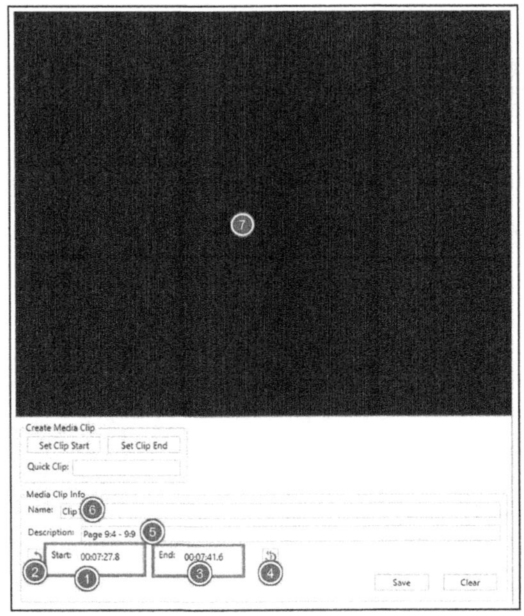

(1) Set clip start time. (2) Go back to start of clip. (3) End time. (4) Go back three seconds. (5) Description of clip (usually page/line range). (6) Clip name—give your clip a unique name. (7) Playback screen.

Note: Left-click on the (1) **Start** or (3) **End** to move the time back one second. Right-click to move the time forward one second.

Task 3. Choose the transcript to be clipped.

(1) Select **Transcripts** and then (2) the deponent.

Task 4. Check that you have the right transcript.

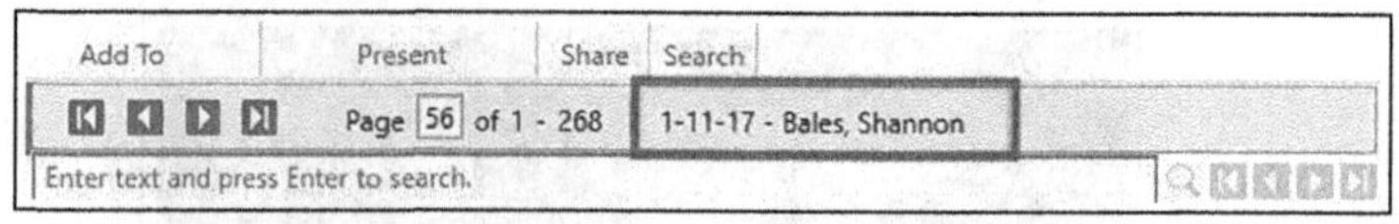

Task 5. Accurately select the transcript text.

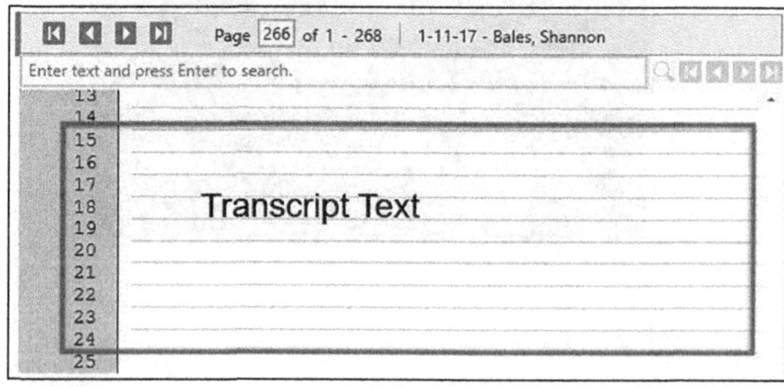

Select the transcript text that you want to clip.

Task 6. Create a "New Media Clip."

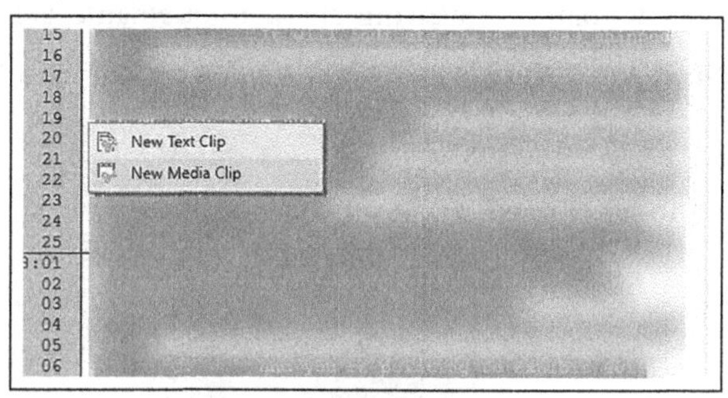

Right-click and select **New Media Clip**.

Task 7. Edit the start and end time.

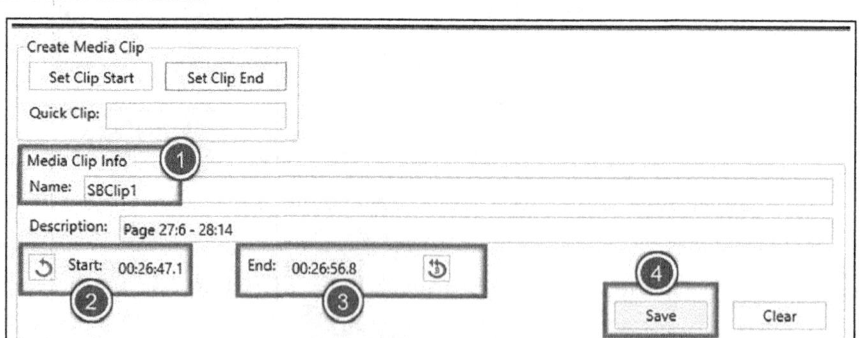

(1) Enter a unique clip name; I typically use deponent initials and a number like **SBClip1**. Adjust the (2) **Start** and (3) **End** times by using the video controls, and select (4) **Save**.

Note: Left-click on the (1) **Start** or (3) **End** to move the time back one second. Right-click to move the time forward one second.

Task 8. Check and test clip.

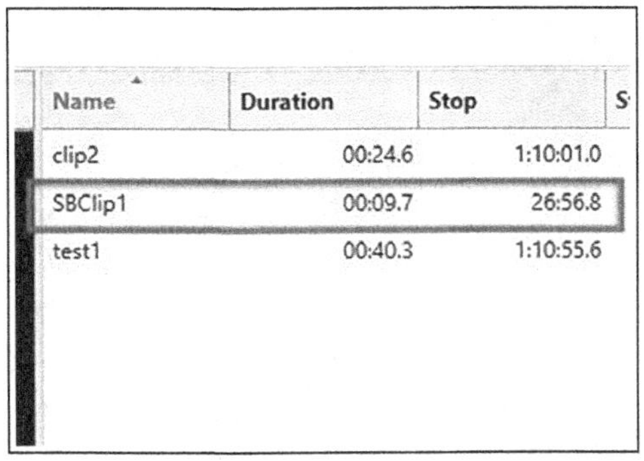

Make sure your clip shows up on the right side of the screen in the clip list. Click on the clip to play it back for testing. Play the clip as you would any other clip by entering the clip name on the presentation screen.

18.4 Video in OnCue

18.4.1 Import Video into OnCue

Task 1. Select Transcripts in the bottom left of the screen.

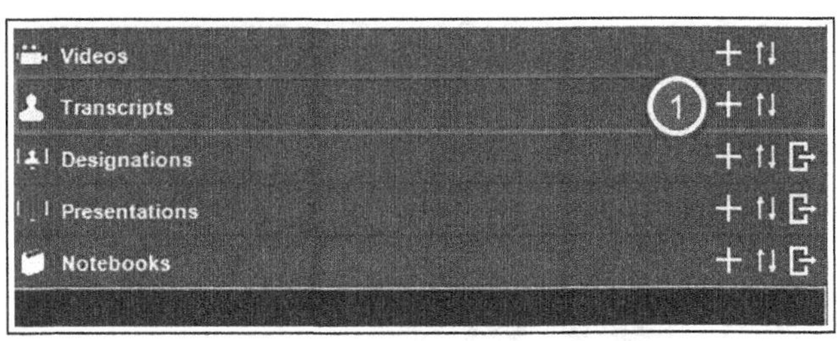

(1) Click on the **+** sign in the bottom left portion of the screen.

Task 2. Select sync file.

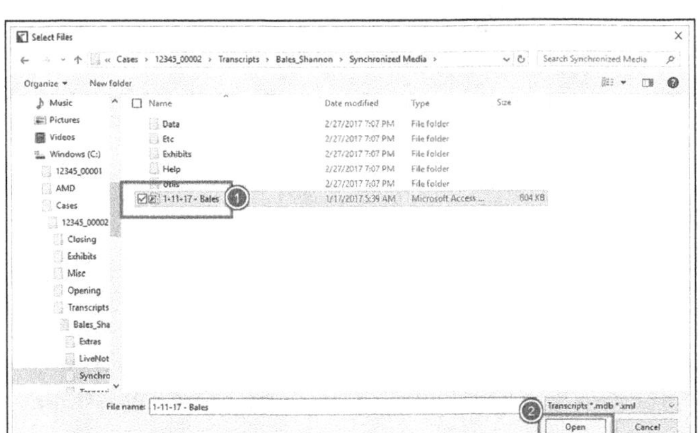

(1) Select the sync file under your organized case data folder structure. (2) Select **Open**.

Task 3. Import.

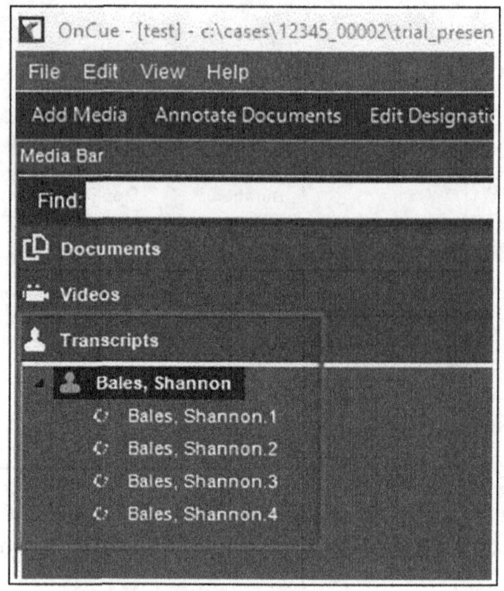

The transcript will import and you will see a list of the videos.

18.4.2 Create a Clip in OnCue

Task 1. Take a screen tour.

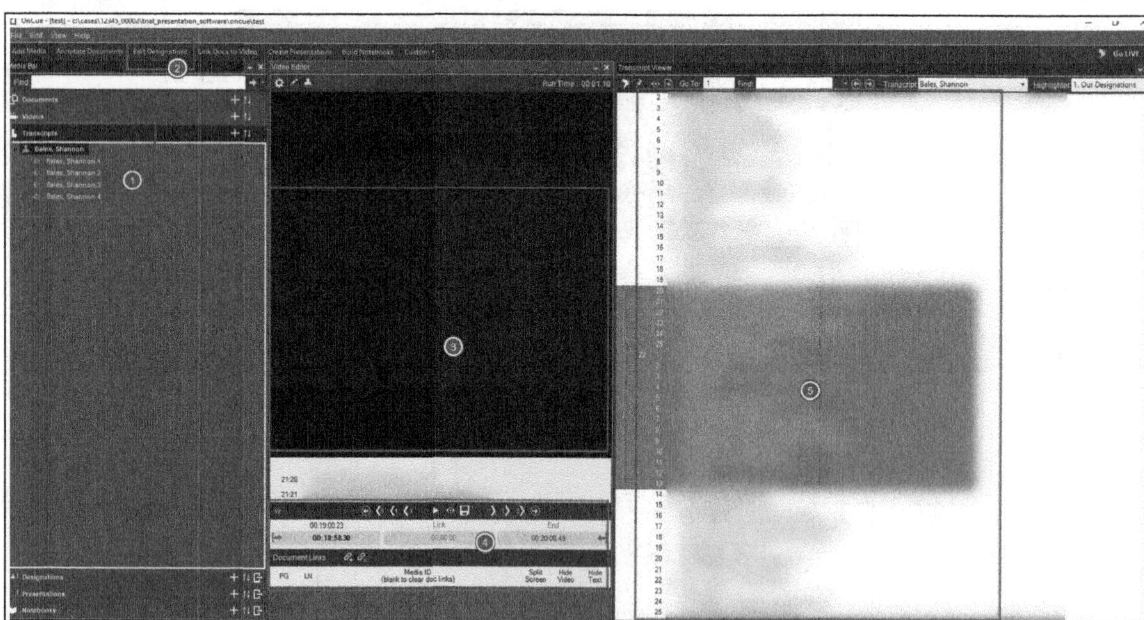

(1) Transcripts section of the screen - select transcript to be edited here. (2) Select **Edit Designations** to bring up the video editing tools. (3) Video playback window. (4) Video editing controls. (5) Transcript (the blue area is selected text; it's always important to be accurate with your page/line designations).

Task 2. Video edit screen.

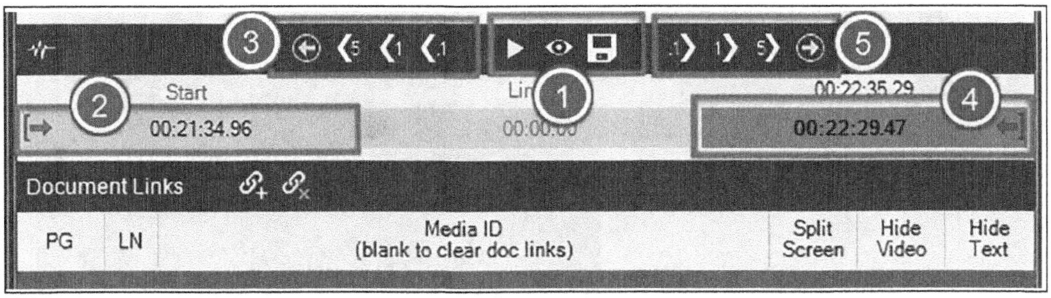

(1) Play a three-second preview and save. The three-second preview is the control that allows a small preview to find out if the start or end times are accurate. Use the three-second preview at the **End** of the clip to hear and see what was said directly before the clip ends. When you are satisfied with your clip adjustments, select **Save** at the end. (2) Clip start time—this is the clip start time; if you make a few adjustments and want to start over, just click on this area to start over. (3) Reverse clip adjustments—this adjust the clip backwards in five-second, one-second and .1-second increments. (4) End time—this is the clip end time; click here to start over if you are unhappy with your edits. (5) Forward clip adjustments—this adjusts the clip forward in five-second, one-second and .1-second increments.

Task 3. Review "Designations."

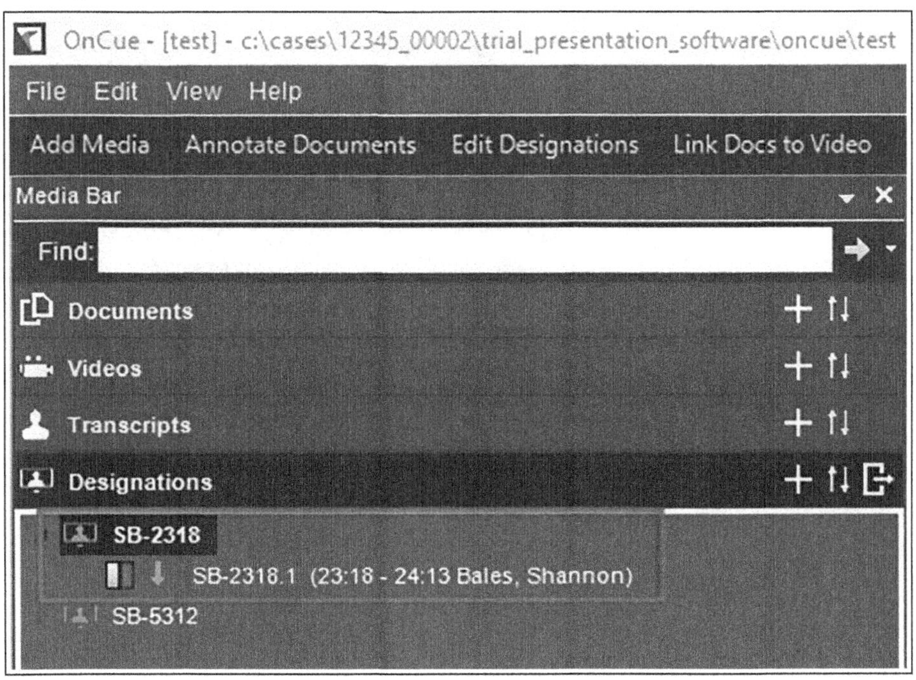

Your clips will be added under the **Designations** tab on the left side of the screen.

Play your clips by using the clip name on the presentation screen (with an **X**, per the OnCue exhibit callup process) or selecting the clip on the working screen and selecting **Go Live**.

Task 4. Choose from multiple methods of importing designations.

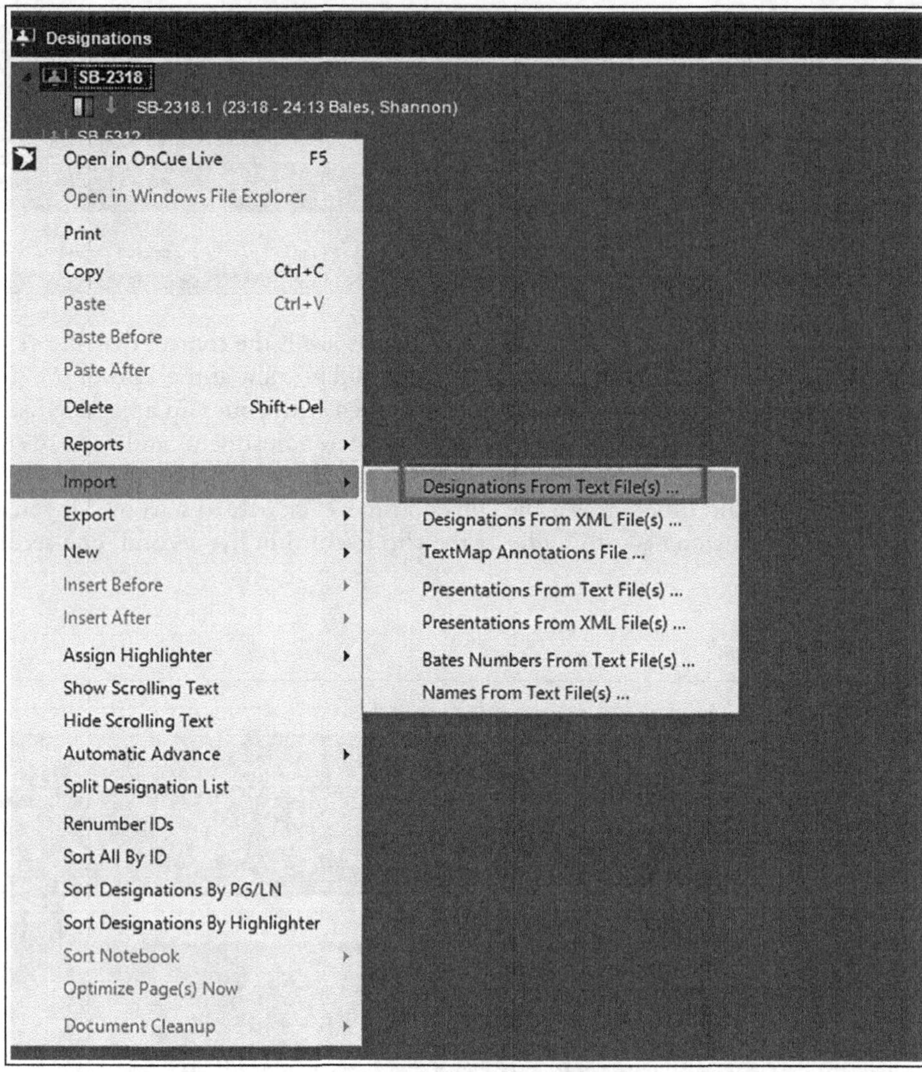

Per the discussion in Chapter Five, Companion Software, recall there are multiple methods of creating clips and clip lists that can be imported into OnCue.

About the Author

Shannon Lex Bales is a Managing Director at FTI Consulting and is based in Los Angeles. As a member of the Trial Services group in the Forensic & Litigation Consulting segment, he is responsible for building a technical environment for legal teams to present their case in that maximizes decision-maker understanding and minimizes downtime and security risk.

Prior to joining FTI Consulting in 2017, Shannon led a diverse eDiscovery team at Munger, Tolles and Olson for fourteen years, specializing in complex trial needs. Shannon has worked on some of the largest and most technically difficult cases in the country, like the BP oil spill and mortgage-backed securities litigation, and has built the technical environment for two war crimes tribunals for the United Nations in Rwanda and Cambodia. He has worked with legal teams from Munger, Tolles & Olson; Gibson Dunn & Crutcher; Latham & Watkins; Sidley Austin; Shook Hardy & Bacon; and Zelle Hoffman. His representations have included work on behalf of Rambus, Transocean, Wells Fargo, Johnson & Johnson, NBC Universal, and Motion Picture Association of America, just to name a few.

Shannon also gives back to the legal community: he teaches legal technology at UCLA and is a frequent speaker at his alma mater, the University of Oklahoma, where he often presents on legal technology topics to the law school. Shannon was awarded the LegalTech Award for "Best Use of Technology at a Trial" for his work in Cambodia and was a finalist for his technology work at the BP oil spill trial. In addition to writing *The Trial Presentation Companion*, published by the National Institute for Trial Advocacy (NITA), he is a frequent contributor to NITA's blog, *The Legal Advocate*, for which he has authored a number of articles on legal technology topics. His YouTube channel is a wealth of instructional videos that demonstrate concepts from his book and other related material.

You may reach Shannon Bales at shannonlexbales@gmail.com.

ABOUT THE AUTHOR

Index